FROM MY OLD BOAT SHOP

WESTON FARMER'S

FROM MY OLD BOAT SHOP

One-Lung Engines, Fantail Launches, & Other Marine Delights

ELLIOTT BAY CLASSICS VOLUME 2

BOAT HOUSE

FORMERLY ELLIOTT BAY PRESS
PORTLAND, OREGON

The Elliott Bay Classics

Vol.	Title & Author	Year
1	*The Steam Launch* by Richard Mitchell	1994
2	*From My Old Boat Shop* by Weston Farmer	1996

Published by **Boat House**
6744 S. E. 36th Avenue, Portland, Oregon 97202

Library of Congress Cataloging-in-Publication Data
    Farmer, Weston 1903-1981
    From My Old Boat Shop; One-Lung Engines, Fantail Launches, & Other Marine Delights.
    (Previously published by International Marine Publishing Company in 1979)
    Present edition has new foreword and introduction and is Volume II of the series,
    Elliott Bay Classics)
    ISBN 0-9641204-2-9
    1. Boatbuilding.   2. Naval Architecture—History.
VM321.F28 1996

Plans by Weston Farmer can be obtained by first sending $10.00 for a drawings list to: Weston Farmer & Associates, 18970 Azure Road, Wayzata, Minnesota 55391

Plans of Picaroon, page 71, from *Boatbuilding in You Own Backyard* by Sam Rabl. Copyright © 1947, 1958 by Cornell Maritime Press, Inc. Information on complete sets of these and other Rabl boat plans are available from Cornell Maritime Press, P.O. Box 456, Centerville, MD 21617

Plans for the Steam Launch (page vii and back dust jacket), and for a list of steam engines, boilers, propellers, and fiberglass fantail hulls, can be obtained by first sending $10.00 for a study drawings packet to Boat House, 6744 SE 36th Avenue, Portland, Oregon 97202

Contents

Weston Farmer
and the Era of the
Owner-Built Boat

Weston Farmer in the editor chair of Modern
Mechanics Magazine, 1938

rom My Old Boatshop is about the era before noisy power and mass marketing corrupted boat design. It reminds us of the variety that once existed, and leads us down the gangway to the old boat dock, behind the old boat shop.

Weston Farmer, boatbuilder and naval architect, unrolls for us no fewer than fifty small boat designs from the 1920s to 1960s. Farmer's designs are from the era when boats were still individualistic and the majority of designs were originals. He began his career when motors and modern materials first made new opportunities in boat design. These years were full of promise, the future looked wonderful, and the past was a resource from which to glean elements for evermore exciting design.

From My Old Boat Shop is a compilation of articles originally published in *National Fisherman,* and later published under its present title by International Marine Publishing Co. in 1979, just two years before "Westy" died.

Farmer's tenure as writer was remarkable; his by-line first appears in May, 1919, *Everyday Engineering,* and last appears in *National Fisherman* more than sixty years later!

Rudder, Motor Boating, Sports Afield, Motor Boat, How to build 20 Boats, Yachting, National Fisherman, Model Craftsman, Everyday Engineering all published Farmer's seductively drawn boats. According to Bob Pickett, of Flounder Bay Boat Lumber service, who devoured these articles as a child, "He knew how to make an amateur feel like he had ten extra years experience,"

His promotions were not limited to boats however. He also influenced that genre of magazine from the 1930s known for its fantastic cover art. He edited *Mechanical Package Magazine,* 1931-1932, and the general circulation giant, *Modern Mechanics and Invention* (Later *Mechanix Illustrated,* Fawcett Publications 1938-1984). "The amateur's science magazine should tell more than, say, 'why lions roar,'" complained Farmer.

From *Mechanical Package Magazine's* "Experiment Station" Westy wrote in 1931, "We'll build and test seaplanes, boats, airplanes, new photoelectric applications such as television and sound electronics, race cars, gas engines—most anything that has a real lesson to teach an which is frought with opportunity and which is at the same time glorious fun to build."

Westy delivered dreams that his subscribers could build themselves in the family garage. First a naval architect, second an editor to a depression-era audience, he thought the boat was "the universal escape machine." He believed a boat should be easy to build, by

THE MECHANICAL PACKAGE MAGAZINE

Here is "Lady Mary" as she will appear in the water alongside of a wharf, steamed up ready for adventure. What boy of 8 to 80 couldn't have a circus running this little ship, complete as she is in boiler, engine and bunkers? Just like a big tug, but midget in size.

PLANS FOR A MAN-CARRYING MODEL TUG

by WESTON FARMER

WHILE the making of magazines happens to be this writer's business, naval architecture has for many years been my hobby. Of late years the study of small boats—the tabloid kind—has intrigued me, and way back behind all of the small boats it has been my pleasure to study out and plan, the matter of cooking up a small steam model tug has been looking for an outlet. Here she is, and her name is "Lady Mary."

A long time ago, as all boys do, I planned a lot of things which some day I would reduce to practice just to have fun with. Finally along came the Packmag and the Experiment Station, and I'm running plans of "Lady Mary" for those of you who may have had similar dreams.

She is a little fellow, and built in accordance with launch practice. Her keel is white oak sided 2", and her frames are ⅞" white oak, square, and on 9" centers. She'll displace about 1000 lbs

without crew, and she carries the little Howard boiler of ½ h.p. and the Howard engine of ½ h.p.

This may not sound like much power, but as with all forms of steam, the power curve is very flat and constant, and no amount of horn work seems to cut down the turning effort which you can get with a steam engine. For the fun of the thing, I have shown the engine hooked up with a 3-1 reduction gear which will allow of high piston speed, and hence good steam consumption, at the same time a large, slow turning wheel is being used.

The hull is 13½ ft. by 4½ ft. by 26" draft. The aft grating is used for a seat for the engineer, and he has the steam throttle and pressure gauge in front of him at all times.

To divide up the work among the crew who will man this little hooker, I've seen to it the helmsman must keep up steam. "Lady

MODEL BOATS   19

THE MECHANICAL PACKAGE MAGAZINE

The outboard profile and the lines as well as the inboard construction plan are shown in this drawing. The small steam engine of ⅛ h.p. has been shown linked to a 3-1 reduction gear so that a large wheel might be used, but it can be a direct line drive if need be.

18   MODEL BOATS

Farmer's Mechanical Package Magazine *of 1932, which evolved into the long-lived* Mechanix Illustrated *is crowded with imaginative, even visionary mechanical projects. It epitomized the American notion that your average magazine-reading citizen could invent or construct any mechanical or electrical device his dreams suggested. Bill Durham remembers the "Pack-Mag" #3 that he wheedled his mother into buying—in Bountiful, Utah in 1932—as a seminal force that colored his whole life. WF's miniature steam boat design steered Durham toward a career in steamship enginerooms ten years later, and to editing his own journal,* Steamboats & Modern Steam Launches, *that launched a hobby among small boat builders.*

the professional or the backyard builder. He simplified designs and showed his readers that naval architecture is not "black magic," as he called it, but an age-old methodology accessible to anyone. Farmer's pageheads shouted the credo: "Anyone can build this!"

Westy definitely had an "angle." He assumed his audience could use the basic tool kit—handsaw, brace, level, plumb-bob, plane, marking gauge, scribe and square. After all, every school child of Farmer's day was taught the skills needed for the Industrial Age. His designs were fantastic, practical, and alluring, and they were pitched as if the younger generation continued to have skills equaling those of their fathers. The basic tool kit could accomplish dreams. Its applications were limited only by the skills of the user.

An affluent generation began to emerge, however, who had money to buy dreams, and who were not getting instruction in Manual Arts. By the end of his career, this new breed looked upon Farmer's early work as naive; "Who would expect to build that in their garage?...Impossible!" Boating magazines that had published his plans fifty years before no longer published plans, just pictures of what could be bought from someone else. The "build-it-yourself boat" was "that still-healthy area of marine publishing," Westy recalled about the 1920's and 1930's in his *Nautical Quarterly* article in 1978.

"Even the 'classic revival' boat magazines degenerated," in Westy's words, "to promoting certain boats as 'correct.'" To build a perfect Whitehall skiff was to become a real boatbuilder. In the 1970's boatbuilding became as precious as auto restoration, a slavish adherence to how the car had come off the assembly line, at a specific factory, at a certain date.

Even among traditional boatbuilders, Farmer squared off with statements like, "The zen experience is not important—a boat is to keep your feet dry." Or, "I don't like the cross-planked skiff because I can do the whole thing with plywood." Westy the Midwesterner stood on the side of the pragmatist, not the purist: "When good enough is adequate, perfection is not demanded."

Farmer was a complex mix of the idealist and the practicalist. He always had a nose for mass-market schemes, but his personal energies always fell back on products that were antithetical to mass production. He began a "standardized hamburger" restaurant chain but dropped it (a decade before Krock began McDonald's). His private energies were always focused on the individual and personal dreams.

Farmer makes us realize there has been a vast decrease in the number of people capable of building something with their hands and basic tools. When he edited *Modern Mechanics*, the population possessed the manual skills needed for industrial society, but later, as the "information society" emerged, fewer workers with manual skills were required in the work force. The personal computer has become the tool kit. Today, the modest number of individuals capable of building a boat can be viewed as a measure of what we now call the "de-skilling" of America. The tide began to flow the wrong way for the old editor and designer.

Dwindling subscriptions told Farmer that readers with skill were dying off, and he also sensed the skill shift. He feared that his old formula—his magic of selling dreams to the backyard builder—would not sell without a sufficiently skilled, self-reliant readership. His last publishing scheme was to be like *Woodenboat* or the original *Small Boat Journal* a half decade before these appeared.

Farmer struggled to resolve how to sell to a readership that wanted their dreams built by someone else. He placed his hope in kits because they can be gauged to the skill level of the target audience. "The future lies with the amateur, and I want to be very encouraging on the idea of kit boats." He was an optimist even in retreat.

Farmer's designs will continue to resonate in our grandfathers within us. He saw the clouds of the post-industrial age, so gathered this text as a small Ark, filled with enthusiasm for skills, self-reliance, building, and dreaming.

The first Elliott Bay steam launch was built for a tour-boat company owner on Seattle's Elliott Bay waterfront. Hulls, engines and boilers for boats like this have been supplied, to date, to backyard boatbuilders in seven foreign countries and in all parts of Canada and the United States.

When I first began to read Farmer I realized he was different from proprietors of boatshops around Portland and Seattle where I grew up. Farmer was forward-thinking about skills of the past. Proprietors of shops that I knew feared that shared information would go to the competition; Farmer did not want information lost to the ages.

I built my first boat, a steam launch, in the backyard—just off the kitchen. "Kitchen-built" boat projects were still tolerated in Seattle neighborhoods in the late 1970s. Because my property was without a garage, I first had to construct a shed; materials came from a discarded "Black Velvet Whiskey" billboard. As a boat project quickly includes the whole family, the children soon had a hammock over the lofting floor; they had their own bench and made boats of cedar in the vise with their tiny plane. They began to measure and drive plugs and learn from their old man that "Paint comes from the end of the bristles, not the sides!"

Out of this project came the beginning of Elliott Bay Steam Launch Co. Also I came to believe, like Westy, that anyone with a fundamental skillset and basic tools can build a boat as magnificent as any ever built. We began to supply to other backyard builders those components they preferred not to make themselves, such as steam or electric propulsion machinery and our fiberglass replica of a fantail launch hull.

Elliott Bay hull customers embrace Westy's philosophy; they are building their dream. They are using their skills learned in public school shop, and some are using their grandfathers' tools (the lucky ones whose Grandpa's tools were not sold at the garage sale to raise money for a computer). They include men and women, and their day jobs were as diverse as architects, musicians, plumbers, physicians, dentists, artists, machinists, locomotive engineers, and even a gunsmith-stockbroker. Only three had built a boat before.

Inevitably we hear: "I don't have the tools; I need to get a lathe first..., or a milling machine..., or a bandsaw..., or etc." We reiterate that only the *basic tool kit* is needed, and we add that we built our first two steam launches without bandsaw or lathe. How to build a boiler? I built one on the tailgate of my car, taking it around from shell roller, to machine shop, to tube supplier, to welder, to heat-treater, starting Monday and finishing Thursday.

Anyone with the basics can do it. Rediscover your native skills and how to use Grandpa's tool kit. Pick one of Westy's designs, or use his instructions to design your own, and build your dream.

Pat Spurlock
Portland, Oregon
Christmas, 1996

N. b.: The editor invites readers to submit additional citations to complete the Farmer's bibliography so that a more complete list might be added to a second printing of this edition. Also, a future volume of the Elliott Bay Classics series will be a history of the pioneering motor boat era 1900-1920, now in process by Bill Durham. We will be grateful for the loan of any primary materials or boating magazines from this era for use in this project. Our purpose in this series is to make available original source materials for the dedicated builder or historian.

Letter from a Naval Architect to a Son at College

Dear Son Mike:

I have your letter written in the engineering library at Ann Arbor. You say you have no money and no friends. You also say you are switching from your present major study into naval architecture, and want my advice.

As to the first two conditions, I advise you to make friends in a hurry.

As to the switch to naval architecture I can advise you as one who has, for fifty years, been an obstetrician attending the birth of new boats. These words of wisdom come from one who has stayed very healthy in this occult calling when it comes to avoiding the ills attendant upon superfluous wealth.

You will have to make up your own mind, but be dead honest with yourself.

If you want money, go into the junk business, or become a doctor, or a labor "leader". You will not find it in doping out lovely floating objects that go forward when the power of gases is applied. At some moment of great dawning in the career of being a midwife and dealsmith in bringing boats and owners together, you will learn one sublime truth: the money for such efforts is relatively hard to come by, and never seems to be in sufficient quantities to justify the amount of <u>time</u> you'll have to put in to satisfy the inner man and the client.

It takes a lot of <u>time</u> to create a craft that acts with docility, competence and grace under the turbulent and wild conditions the sea pitches up. Designing is knowing what to draw.

Only by living on the sea, with wind and wave and water, can a man know the extended limits of this world his craft will face. It cannot be found in books. More, you will have to be able to know materials and manipulation in order to put them together in a structure that is worthy. You can get this knowledge only by apprenticeship with tools in your own hands. Books can show you how, only experience can show you why.

This probably is why the best designers today are the unsung naval architects in the various yards about the country. You never hear who they are, but they, because they have feedback from actual doing, know more—a very little more, from the doing of each next design. Some of these men are clods, and will never be anything else, but to those with the gift of great perception, which is needed to become a true virtuoso, the experience in a yard brings to the top those with the great gift.

I speak of course of yacht and motor yacht design. That is the course you will take if you want variety. You will find big ship work is pretty cut and dry—once you have done one, the others are more the same. Insurance ratings, bureau numerals and such foo-foo pretty well standardize what you can do. Some shipyards have a standard bow, and a standard stern, and your variety comes when an order comes in telling you how many feet are wanted between. There is little fun in that. To get the joy of creation you must go to smaller, more frequently built vessels. I learned this the hard way, and pass along ten years in one chapter worth fifty thousand dollars to you.

If you are going to take the veil and decide, willy-nilly, to be an artichoke, as long as you are in engineering school, I tell you emphatically: get your math <u>cold</u>. Your other tools,— physics, strength of materials, mechanics, heat, chemistry will be tools you can climb on. They're wonderful tools, teach you to think logically from cause and effect; the most useful of these is math. Don't think you can compete against others without it. You'll find this discipline the Great Separator.

You have also to ask yourself some honest questions about your own make-up. The great designers I have known, say, the likes of J. Murray Watts, Ralph Winslow, Wm H. Hand, Jr., Sam Rabl, to name a few, were lonely introverts standing in the need of mother love. They sought recognition from the world through their designs. They became famous in their day, making the discovery that there is little nourishment in fame, because you can't put it in a breadbox.

When you reach the plateau of recognized ability, you will discover two things; you had better do your own work, not hiring others. If you do, you will soon find yourself digging up payrolls, and that is not the work of a designer. Also, the men who come to you for special designs are usually men of wealth, and are in every case hounds for detail.

You will also find little gratitude. They've paid you, haven't they? If the boat is a winner, it will be felt by the owner that he has been the genius who selected the winning combination,— never was there such a great crew of sailors. If the boat doesn't win everything in sight, the Corinthians have been out-designed, and go at it again. You will find every variation of this syndrome. Nobody is so deep an expert as the man back from his third boat ride.

These are a few of the flavors you will find in the daily fare. If you are not to be denied, and want a go at it, I bless you with these words: the law of averages will always take care of a man who works. The building of a reputation resembles the slow growth of an oak tree. It takes years to produce strength and size. But inasmuch as you have paid the freight on your corpus to the campus, stay there and expose yourself to the knowledge of the place. The basic object of your tenure there is to learn to use your mind, disciplining it to think. Once you've got that, it little matters whether you follow naval architecture or not, because you may find, as John Alden once told me, "There isn't the price of a turkey sandwich in plans. You've got to build the stuff and convert it to property before you'll see money."

In closing, I can give you some sunlight to be found in the words of John C. Hanna, the Dunedin genius who stated, "There are a million kinds of work in the world, each and all returning some money, but only one kind for any certain man that pays the richer gold of fulfilled desire, of captivated interest, of contentment that obliterates weariness. Why shouldn't he choose that kind?"

If you feel that call, go to it. I enclose check for fifty to ease pain. When you come home this spring, shave the beard. Mother has a deadly fear of woodticks.

Love,
Dad

Written by Weston Farmer from Annapolis, Maryland, 1944 to his son, then a sophomore at University of Michigan.

Remembering Westy
by David R. Getchell, Sr.

Weston Farmer at age 70.

Unique is a word I use very sparingly, because it is overworked and almost always misused, because few things or persons are ever so unusual as to qualify as the one and only. But I feel comfortable in saying that E. Weston Farmer, N.A., was unique. ☐ What follows is a somewhat disjointed account of the last ten years of his life by one who worked closely with him through that time. It is disjointed because that was the nature of his relationship with everyone, including his sweet and forbearing wife, Bylo, his four sons, his friends and this beleaguered editor. Westy was not easy to get along with; but his lovable traits outweighed the unlovable, and most who knew this remarkable man admired the wealth and variety of his talents and basked in the warmth of his personality. To some of us, he meant much more.

He was best known as a naval architect. Many of his boat and yacht designs were classic, and though his output was not great, his skills at the drawing board and his knowledge of boatbuilding and engineering were large indeed. "Westy was a beautiful draftsman," says William Garden, a long-time friend of Farmer and himself a legend in his own time. "His work was beautifully done...He was thoroughly competent. But I'll bet if you were hiring him, the work would come slower than the Second Coming!"

"Like all N.A.s, he was tough to build from," says Martin C. (Mike) Kelsey, president of Palmer Johnson, Inc. of Sturgeon Bay, Wisconsin, whose respected yard built some of the largest Farmer yachts. "It's a manhour-intensive business, and his boats were ten times overbuilt. They will last indefinitely, and every time his *All-*

Ten-B has been sold, it has brought a higher price than it cost to build it. Same holds true for *Misty*. It proves two things: we build 'em too cheaply and Westy knew what he was doing.

"Westy was a kind of Thomas Edison, a gentleman scholar, a renaissance artist. He would have loved to have been with Darwin on the *Beagle*. You don't often meet people like him; I've never met another like him. He was one of life's great experiences. He could be cranky and ornery to anyone. And he had a heart of gold."

I knew none of this at the beginning of 1971. In fact, I had never heard of Weston Farmer, despite the fact that I had been editing National Fisherman and the old Maine Coast Fisherman since 1959 and had dealt regularly with Howard I. Chapelle, Sam Rabl, John Atkin, Bill Garden, Pete Culler and other well-known naval architects. The "old" National Fisherman was in its heyday then, an odd halfbreed, part commercial fishing trade publication and part boating magazine printed in tabloid form on newsprint. In its pages, long-time NF Technical Editor John Gardner, unbeknownst to his unpretentious self, was in the process of becoming the guru of the traditional-boat set; real and imagined naval architects debated the merits of everything from hull shapes to cedar buckets both in the letters column and in the thick boat section; pleasure dories and tabloid cruisers vied for attention with lobsterboats and steel trawlers; and everyone seemed to be having a good time—or at least their say. National Fisherman, we soon discovered, was a perfect platform for E. Weston Farmer, N.A., erudite nautical philosopher, outspoken critic, humorist, historian and boat noodler par excellence.

Typically, Westy introduced himself over the telephone in the first of approximately 757,000 phone conversations I was to have with him over the next decade. He lived by the phone, and his listeners died by it. Call this morning and write this afternoon was the Farmer motto. Ma Bell was one of his principal mourners. As Bill Garden stated in the opening line of a recent letter to me: "Since Westy's death, the phone company must have suffered a real loss of revenue."

In a follow-up letter on January 13, 1971, Westy elaborated on his phone call:

Dear Mr. Getchell:

It was rewarding to make your acquaintance by phone yesterday afternoon. It was a "fishing" call, looking for a glimmer of action anent this problem of semi-retirement forced by annual numbers that exceed my actual situation. I am in robust health, don't need money, but want something worthwhile to do in fields in which I have heavy experience. These areas are in magazine publishing and in naval architecture.

These were outlined in broad brush in my spiel to you: I founded the magazine Mechanix Illustrated for Fawcett Publications when they were a-borning out here in Robbinsdale, Minn., and built their mechanical department, publishing also one-shots such as The Flying Manuals, and How to Build Twenty Boats. This effort came along during a drought in naval architecture, which has been my main life effort and in which I have been active fifty years.

In the six years interim just past I have been active in the designing and construction of large luxury yachts in aluminum, having done five or six of them to the tune of about three million dollars. That kind of money has evaporated, which is fine with me, because I closed my office last launching at Sturgeon Bay. Too much grief, and too much work for the rewards. Thus, I am on the beach.

Having no idea what your basic editorial gambit might be—that is, the general line of editorial approach aside from the desire to make money—I can't come up with anything brilliant in the way of suggestions. I have no idea whether I write well, but if I put the mental needle on a spinning platter and just let it run, things seem to have come out well.

I enclose a few leads that sample my lingo. You can judge from these. They're all from stories done for other publications. If you sense a slot for me, wire me collect every fifteen minutes until I can get there.

Regards,
W.F.

The next month I received more calls, some of them taxing my patience even while adding to my knowledge of the caller. The samples of his writing had been interesting but smacked of the style of the 1920s and '30s. I listened, but was not overly impressed. On February 12, Westy sent an advance billing:

Dear Dave:

Yesterday I airmailed a noodling piece on Jack Hanna's *Foam*. I neglected to say I would be glad to give it to you—no charge.

Only favor I want in return (assuming the piece is interesting and not too long) is to run the picture of *Misty*—the 80 ft. aluminum Palmer Johnson yacht I designed for Borwell—with the story exposure, or near it. I need a little "name" build-up.

I think one of the charms of Nat'l Fisherman is the diversity of opinion exhibited by your contributors. You let 'em run, and that is interesting and hurts no one.

It is also evident that some contribs can write, and others can't.

You seem to have a firm sense of what to cut and what to let ride. Damned good noodling for all segments.

Thine,
Westy

Upon first perusal of the article, I *was* impressed, and a second reading told me we'd tapped a gusher. I attached a brief inter-office memo to the manuscript and sent it down to Roger Taylor, president of our sister company, International Marine Publishing Co. A publisher of marine books, Roger was a skilled sailor whose opinion I frequently sought with regard to sailing articles. My memo read: "Lookit this! It shows that if you listen to a guy's gab long enough, it may pay off!" I was to regret that memo.

Roger shared my enthusiasm for the *Foam* article, and when Westy called the next day, I was saved the need to write my acceptance and offer to buy the article at our usual rates. He followed up his call with another letter which not only showed he was not averse to money but also opened the gates on a long-running commentary on NF and boat publishing in general:

Dear Dave:

In my last phone call made earlier this week I was pleased to learn you liked the Hanna *Foam* piece. Of course, if you want to pay space rates, I won't object...

I like the freedom of each contributor to say what he feels: he likes wooden boats, he likes 'em built of gunk or rock and chicken wire. This spectrum of opinion lends real authority to your paper, because the contents are believable. For years and years all boating rags have talked in code, fearing to step on some dainty advertiser's toes. You've got to get circulation to sell advertising in this economic day and age, and God knows there's enough bullshine in boat ads themselves to enable you to refute any objection to real truth, which becomes believable only in forums of wide opinion. One of John Hanna's charms was that he took a position, reasoned out the sanity of his statement, and then fired away. Reading him today is convincing. So let the charm of diversified opinion shine through. The reader will have his own opinions, and may differ, but there is no game under the roof of Heaven in which you'll find so many conflicting opinions by "experts" and almost all of them right. Yea, man!

I've often thought that if boat design and construction were a matter of life and death, as in airplane design, all naval architects would have a cinch. They'd be believed, and the demands of the trade would separate the skilled from the mountebanks in a hurry.

Thassall at these rates.

Yrs,
Westy

During the next week, three more Farmer tomes crossed my deeply papered desk, and I began to realize I was dealing with someone other than your average freelance correspondent. If Westy's calls were irritating, his letters were irresistible:

Dear Dave:

It may help you to understand my swordsmanship when it comes to voicing opinion about anything I detect as phony: I'll tilt windmills with a hairpin or charge hell with a half bucket of water

if by doing so I can save others from happily flapping into what I know to be the road of grave mistakes. The reason I let out an occasional warwhoop and go on the warpath is found in a condition peculiar to the boat game: real art and knowledge is awfully hard to come by, yet it is a game in which everybody is an instant expert. Or they think they are, and start pontificating....

Zevver,
Westy

Dear Dave:

...Even more rewarding has been my brief phoned contacts with Dave Getchell, who seems to be very quick on the uptake, who possesses a nice personality and is visibly a damned good editor.

This has heartened me, because I am a confirmed noodler with a long career as a pro, and knew all of the editors of the above rags (Yachting, Motor Boating, Rudder). From Tom Day on I knew all of Rudder's editors: Aldrich briefly, Jerry White (all speed and no direction), and recommended Bill Crosby to Andy Patterson for the job when I founded Mechanix Illustrated. Also knew Leonardi, Chas. Chapman, Herb Stone and sold an ocean of stuff to them years ago. Now that I'm a "snoring citizen" I can probably be of use to you, because if each piece of noodling material I own was a cornflake, my home would look like W.K. Kellogg's factory.

Last week, I sent you the electric launch yarn, neglecting to tell you to edit it any way you wish. I'm not a bit sensitive when it comes to the slash—nothing of mine is a priceless, polished gem.

Thine,
Westy

Dear Dave:

I have been pacing the floor unable to sleep this 1:30 a.m. because there is a violent blizzard pelting the house with white pellets of snow...So I have decided to make the pacing amount to something, and have gone to work for you as Chairman of the Board. Our business: "What makes the National Fisherman tick?"

Boat noodling, of course. Hunger with a marine flavor. Hunger for knowledge of who's catching what, what the dollars are. Hunger for picture news of new boats. Hunger to answer the ever-elusive "Why?" about craft from other sections. Or just hunger to play, vicariously, Captain Hornblower to the hilt.

It's all as broad as the sea spectrum, and should remain that way because therein lies its charm. It is perfectly delightful to realize that there are readers with enough winter leisure to call down the cove and find the neighbors frying doughnuts and that Uncle Willie hasn't mailed his Christmas cards yet! Right neighborly sort of paper in this boob tube world. And that new tuna clipper *Apollo!* Wonder if the boys who promoted her realize that this fish killer will slave-drive the hell out of them paying back the financing? I've designed tuna clippers; did the first West Coast one built in steel for Harbor Boat and Van Camp, so fishing economics aren't new. They'll have to work their pants off for years to pay her off. Reminds me of the little mackerel purser I financed, so successful an idea that the first school podded up sunk her, Glub! Great mackerel swindle of Balboa. And so it goes along: you start out march, march, march to drink the paper in, and before long you are—NOODLING.

Now I noodle in my own peculiar way, within my referential experience framework. So does everyone else, from the busy shipbuilder sitting at his Friday afternoon desk, to Ma Webber over at Lobster Harbor. The down-to-earth commercial character of the paper is sheer packaged charm in print. It is small wonder that you do have a following.

What is more surprising to me is that you have a gold mine here and aren't exactly aware of it. You expressed surprise, Dave, when I told you old-time readers of the yachting press were sloughing off their interest in the standard sheets. Nothing in them. And what is in them is the hack work of dull, dull, dull wordsmiths. Jevver try to read one of these standard rags these days? Words, words, words, without a succinct glimmer bespeaking intelligence. No reader hook, no glue, no substance. Thus, readers come to you with cheers for your solid substance. What does amaze me is that more yachtsmen don't know about National Fisherman. If they did you could pick up substantial readership, and keep it, as long as you stayed away from the crap the standards are carrying: showroom boats, stereotyped "cruise stories." Club news. Who needs any? Yuck.

So I will remain, dear David: overqualified, over-energized, under-occupied—as usual,

Yrs,
Westy

Meanwhile, back at my desk the phone was ringing. It got to be a joke with the receptionist. "Guess who?" she would ask sweetly. "Jeesus!" was my usual reply, knowing what was coming. "No, it's not, it's Westeeee!"

He knew his calls were not always welcome, and noted as much in the following note of March 7:

Dave:

Bylo, my wife, who answered the phone, sez to let the other guy talk when he phones. She also sez if I don't buy a business, or get out of the house, quit marking up the wallpaper with tit-tat-toe, she's going to establish quick lines of communication between cause and effect, and bring one up from the floor that will put me in a pine box. For which the world will be the loser, for all the dashing energy, bubbling creativeness, bucolic analytics, and heavy post office traffic I contribute to the world scene.

It's gotta be the snow: the breakfast food of the angels, she calls it. Huh! 'Tis vitriol to the eyeball!

Yrs,
Westy

In April, when his thoughts always began to turn to the family summer home on Isle Royale, in the middle of Lake Superior, he wrote:

Sir Writesalot:

...On Isle Royale, you see, there are no roads, no cars, no horses, no telephones, no telegraph, no TV—nuthin' but water-washed fresh air and Seattle-Norway scenery. So no telephone bills!

I've got those down from about $250 a month to $90 now, and I can cut them out altogether and feed my face with groceries on what I spend here for the wind coming out of it.

Been nice working with you, Dave, and I am most apologetic for the poosh'em-up phoning.

Thine,
Pesty

Isle Royale was very special to Westy, a place of escape, of fond memories, and of people closest to him. The land at Rock Harbor had been "homesteaded" about 1901 by his canny grandfather and, for all intents and purposes, had been developed by Westy's mother, Bee Farmer, a strong, beautiful woman known as the "iron hand in the velvet glove." She built the family holdings into a successful resort and eventually came to an agreement with the National Park Service that assured that the family would enjoy its retreat for many years to come. Father Matt, from a small-town farm family, played a lesser role. Westy adored his mother and basked in her permissiveness. He had his own boat at 12, a gift from his Norwegian-born grandfather, and had the whole of Lake Superior as his playground. "No one ever had a boyhood like mine," he liked to say.

His mother was the force that sent him to the

University of Michigan for two years, but he couldn't keep up with his wealthy fraternity brothers and returned to his home town of Minneapolis where he attended the University of Minnesota. At the age of twenty (October 1923), he eloped with Bylo Murray, his 18-year-old sweetheart of four years, and moved to Alexandria, Minnesota, where he began selling insurance.

In the years that followed, he worked in New York, Florida, California and points in between. Sometimes Bylo went with him, sometimes she stayed home in Minnesota. At different times he was an idea man for a hardware company, an important editor for Fawcett, an itinerant draftsman, the head of a propeller development program for PT boats during World War II, the host of an inventors' show on television, an assistant in developing a color system for Snow White and the Seven Dwarfs at Disney Studios, a restaurateur who was ahead of his time with fast food, the creator of a successful but short-lived challenger to the Erector Set called Buildo, and an inventor of machines for Toro, including a power mower that bagged grass, and a snowblower. And all the time, back and forth, he was a naval architect.

I knew none of this as our relationship grew, except from snatches of phone conversations that had a tendency to become fragmented, if not ethereal. For the first several years of our association, Westy contributed six or seven well-researched and highly entertaining articles a year, happily accepting the pittance we paid for his work and thrilled with the strong response he drew from NF readers. Within a year, he was back in the 1930s again, influencing thousands with his incisive commentary on boat design, winning a new generation of followers, sniping with uncanny accuracy at those he considered fakers or ignoramuses at the boat-design game. He was a shining apple in my editorial basket, but I was getting most of the bruises.

To understate the case, Westy was a demanding contributor. When he wasn't phoning about this, that and everything, he was jamming my In basket with letters of advice, praise, wrath and belly-shaking humor. At times, I couldn't stand him, at others I loved him, but never could I ignore him.

I was happy with the way things were going when I opened his regular letter one morning—and my heart jammed into my socks. There, as big as life, was my memo to Roger Taylor: "...if you listen to a guy's gab long enough, it may pay off!" Westy's terse note said something like: "You looking for this, by chance? Signed:

Gabby." For some impossible reason, the memo had been included with some material being returned to him. He won a friend for life, however, in his casual reaction to the gaffe. I immediately dashed off this memo:

Dear Gabby:

There's nothing like getting caught in the act to keep a man honest. Reminds me of some famous typos that have got into print from time to time. Or the famous blooper of Unca Don, the famous children's story-teller on the radio who, upon completion of a program—believing his mike was switched off—muttered "That will take care of the little bastards." Two million kiddies learned a new word and Unca Don took an unpaid vacation.

The attached famous memo, which you are welcome to pin on your favorite dartboard, was writ early in the game when you were known only by a half-dozen phone calls. It accompanied your first manuscript and followed along a private joke between Roger Taylor and me, both of us listening to a lot of phone calls from writers with ideas. Fortunately, we both have a rule—never judge a man until you see the color of his writing—which should be posted on the wall of every editorial office. I won't tell you what Rog's return memo said because its compliments might make you think we were getting soft.

Needless to say, your stock has been on a continuous rise with us almost from the outset, and your returning this memo has pushed the curve a little higher. Many people would have taken it as a personal affront and simply said, "To hell with them," and cut us off. You preferred the needle. Oddly enough, Rog walked into my office just as I opened your letter, and both of us had to sit down we were laughing so hard.
                    Warmest regards,
                    Dave "Foo-Foo" Getchell

A few days later he was still chuckling, and continued to needle me about it over the remaining years of our relationship:

Ahoy, Dave!

Still getting a belly laugh out of our mutual pratfall on "Gabby." You come out ahead on this!

Always most glad for criticism, real or implied. How else do we learn the gift of seeing oursel's as ithers see us? As far as getting acerbic on responses, I like Abe Lincoln's premise: "Never wrestle with a hog. When you come up out of the mud, no one can tell you apart. The hog loves it." Unfair attacks I'm willing to battle forensically, but isn't the best way of winning a tug of war just to let go of the rope? Dumps the other guy on his arse and you can walk away on two legs. Send the stuff along, and, if it warrants, I'll make a snappy comeback. It'll be brief, I promise you.

Love, but no kizziz,
Westy

At times, Westy's sense of humor was as hard on the ribs as his phone calls were on the ears. In that first year, we ran one of his articles on aluminum boatbuilding, which drew this response from Henning Nielsen of Roy Duffus Associates:

Dear Mr. Farmer:

Your article on marine aluminum in the August issue of National Fisherman is a beautiful piece of work.

If we, as public relations counselors to the Aluminum Association, wanted to give the fiberglass folks a case of the flying fantods (and we might) we never could do better in the way of good, solid, and very pleasantly convincing information.

Just wanted to add a few words to the many compliments that by now must be floating in. Very best wishes.

Cordially,
Henning Nielsen
Vice President

A few months later, in the wake of another story on the metal, Westy reported the following:

Dave, old friend:

My attempt to isolate and interview Mr. M., the alleged naval artichoke for the Aluminum Association, was like looking for the janitor on the movie set of Gone With the Wind. We finally zeroed in on his lair, a tumble-down white-fenced shanty in Pascagoula, over-run with Spanish moss and weeds. I knocked on the door of his "office," and could hear someone scurrying to the back of the house. Shortly, from the back door, there emerged a slattern in a screaming yellow wrapper, hair just-out-of-bed style, shrieking, "What chall want?" I told her. "He doan see no one 'ceptn by ahhpointment." Then, "Where ya from?" I told her, and also my name, and she immediately belched forth, "This is Sattiday, Man! You can git them plans from the Loominum 'ssociation." My diagnosis is the guy was drunk; Lawson's was that he was afraid of me. His stuff is well done, and Clary's analysis was that some of Ingalls' drafting room help had moonlighted the work. SOME representative for the Loominum peepul!

Thine—
Westy

Westy visited us in Camden for a couple of days in October of 1971. It was the only time I ever met him in person, and I must admit that I was completely taken in by his charm: a face full of smile wrinkles, an unthinned thatch of handsome gray hair and a twinkle in his eyes that reflected both humor and intelligence. The two of us formed a warm personal relationship in that brief period that was to stand the stresses of work and strained tempers in the years to come. The long, fatherly letters he would send me, letters laced with marvelous insight and common sense, helped immensely with my work and with my Midlife Crisis, the latter a similar period of trauma for Westy and his family, I learned much later.

He was on the West Coast soon after Maine, and his comments about the trip reflected those of a person who was always willing to work hard, who had pulled on his own bootstraps time after time, and who loved young people but despised young know-it-alls:

Hey Dave—yoo hoo—peekaboo!

Am back from a week's swing along the California and Oregon and Washington coasts, radiating from Berkeley and Astoria...

I couldn't help reflecting on the decline in youth morality and derring-do; looking at the vaulting grace and beauty of buildings on the Berkeley campus built by the taxpayers, and contrasting it with girls 14 to 16 running about in sandals, naked to the skin in nightgowns worn as day dress, pregnant, and squatting openly on the lawn, urinating like dogs. And they used to burn witches in Salem! Four letter words like s-o-a-p and w-o-r-k and c-a-s-h they'd never heard of...

Thassal at these rates, luv—
Westy

But like many of us who had difficulty understanding that traumatic period in our history, he later mellowed, as revealed in this letter of October 5, 1978:

Dear Dave:

I have just returned from Port Townsend out in Washington, where the Wooden Boat Symposium, followed by a week-long festival of wassail and jubilee, turned out to be a huge success...I was elected to lecture for openers in the Fort Worden Little Theater, and faced a packed house of demanding questioners. It was an eye opener, I tell you!

Immediately I was struck by the demographic phenomenon before me: the bearded flower children of a decade ago have turned in droves toward trade skills, finding that trying to sink battleships with flowers ainta gonna work, but if they want coin of the realm and security, they themselves will have to. Boatbuilding, and designing, and the escape it affords is a natural outlet. I saw the Wooden Boat side of it. But there is a lot more to it—

Best wishes,
Westy

A willing scrapper when the battle seemed worthwhile, he was quick to avoid mudfights where arguments would confuse readers unless long-winded explanations were given—and where he might look bad otherwise:

Dave, old chick,

In the letter from S. which you Xeroxed and sent me—and which whence is none of my goddamn business—he, in his last paragraph, makes weisenheimer with the statement that if we plot all kinds of boats on a speed/length ratio dimension against weight per horsepower, all boats will fall in line, and that "the older boats were not faster."

Taint so—the fallacy in the good P'fessor's landslide math is that there is no account taken for the matter of slimness: i.e., B/L, the well known factor of beam-to-length ratio.

I do not question that a sort of buckshot pattern will derive from such a plot, but having done about 400 boats, I know that EXACT weight, EXACT hosspower and EXACT speed are NEVER known. Not with sufficient accuracy to differentiate on such a graph the fact that the difference between a fast boat and a slow one is merely a matter of one or two knots. The information fed into such a plot will not cover these variables, or take into account other factors, B/L among them, wave-making, etc.

I dinna wanna get into a garbage fight, so don't print this. But you'd better not print his poop either, because it is highly fallacious.

Kizziz,
Westy

Early in 1972, I received his semi-annual evaluation of the American boat publishing scene, and as usual it showed where his immediate love lay. However, I was all too aware that the difference between a cooked and uncooked potato depended on which one was in the oven. My day might come:

Dear Daffodil:

I let out my clutch last night and settled down for some marine reading. I had your May B Section, thoughtfully sent by you, also a current copy of Yachting for which I invested one buck on the suspicion it might teach me something ...and a spare Rudder for Dec. 1971 (three months old).

I read the whole batch cover to cover, and came up with the cast iron conviction that National Fisherman, edited by Dave Getchell, carries the best writing on the marine scene today. Malcolm MacDuffie's work is literature of enduring quality, readable for content, rewarding for philosophical truths that give understanding. Easily the best scribe on the marine scene today.

Also I commend you as an editor. You do wring the juices out of subjects—briefly and to the point...I am glad to have you working on my efforts to instruct and at the same time entertain.

My cold-turkey reaction to the wares of other publishers is that the stuff is junk—sheer N.Y. office c-r-a-p! See Rudder's cover enclosed. Tom Day would whirl in his grave if he could see it.

Lookit the silly blurbs: "The Sea Knife—Will it Revolutionize Hull Design?" Any experienced boat man could say "no" at a glance, and dismiss the notion—and the man who perpetrated the scheme—to the limbo of the novices who arrive on the marine scene and proceed to invent their way of how a boat ride should be handled. The damned thing is nothing but an Albert Hickman Viper with a looney deck scheme. Then take the next blurb: "Exclusive Report on Lyman's First Glass Runabout." Exclusive? Jeesus, what a find! Belongs to the school of publishing that thinks in the vein, "Exclusive Report on Who Flushed the Toilet on the Third Floor."

Then I see how I can convert my Sailfish for sailing on ice. Do I own a Sailfish? Remind me to check. Glare ice is only found on ponds and lakes for one-week times above the latitude of Illinois. And it says right there where I can learn to sail this winter. I might suggest water would be a good place to start.

No wonder these books are in trouble.

Yachting ain't no exception, neither (heh) because it takes Bill Robinson three hundred words to say "Scat." Reading the thing is like a dry land sail through a barn full of chaff. You come off with a musty feeling, wishing to hell some of the people who go boating and who do have the money and leisure to experience and tell, could write. Most of them have their egos showing and you can tell that They Sat Down To Write. Everybody hush!

I come off the reading spree with cold detachment and some clearly banged-home reactions. One is that you have the only format that can carry a cargo adequately. You have space enough to do your subjects justice. I suppose you feel "tight" on this space problem perpetually. But you have the format, and your readership presumes boat knowledge and feel, so in contrast to the other rags you have a better menu and cuisine to present boat-hungry palates.

Back to the hay for snoozing—
Lonesome Luke

I was finding that Westy's ego was sizable and that his search for fair and proper recognition was a lifelong quest. I suppose a psychologist would trace this to his back-country boyhood and his failure to graduate from an engineering school. My own view is that it was deeper than that. If people thought Westy was hard on them, few realized that he was doubly critical of himself. He knew his weaknesses—intolerance, arrogance, pettiness—and as fast as they were exhibited in his daily life, he fought them back with kindness, humility, and regret.

Recognition came to him in many ways from his articles and letters in National Fisherman, but none pleased him more than the following:

Dear Dave:

I have just come from the telephone absolutely stunned at one fellow's reaction to the stuff I'm doing for National Fisherman.

Material from John Winslow at Merrimack, N.H., hadn't shown, so I was chasing it down. He'd delayed mailing it to spend Friday with Walter McInnis, who lives in Newton. John's father, Ralph E. Winslow, worked with and for Walter, who is now 80. McInnis, reports John Winslow said, "Mr. Farmer must be a very old man to have accumulated the wisdom he has in naval architecture. I've been reading his stuff for years and years."

Odds Bodkins! And here I think of myself as an aery faery Ariel, tripping down life's path strewing rose petals in the way of life's arid march!

The reference to age wouldn't have thrown me so much if it hadn't been an echo of what Malcolm MacDuffie wrote me last week. He'd been talking to L. Francis Herreshoff. I quote, verbatim, MacDuffie's report on what Herreshoff told him: "Mr. Farmer must be somewhat older than I, and I am going on 83, because I seem to remember reading his work as a child (!) I certainly enjoyed his piece about the old engines in National Fisherman—so much more agreeable than the flip talk one finds in modern yachting magazines."

And that from The Beard, in THE CASTLE, at Marblehead!

So, sweetie pie, WE must be doing things correctly—you and I—if the AUTHORITIES approve. But this reference to age simply floored me—and here I'm buying psychedelic pants and my wife is getting me hippie shirts, and I see at least 25 more active years if I stay off pot and don't let my hair get too long.

Sizzons grittings,
Westy

There was never any doubt that his first love was boat designing, but it was a love he hated as often as not:

Dear Dave:

The day is coming when I'm going to have to kick the boat designing habit. Too goddam tough on the old carcass for the rewards therein.

But let anybody yell "New Boat!" to a N.A., and no matter how old he is he'll come flying out of the barn like a fire horse flapping down the alley, harness on but no fire wagon. I've chased guys up an alley for a ton of coal in exchange for a cruiser design, in my day, and the NEW BOAT call appeals to the motivating machinery that gets its creative kicks from pre-determining an outcome, then purring at a launching with an indefinable inner glow.

The bagging patent on rotary mowers runs out this fall, and that income will die. Hence: PREPARATION!

Westy

Later in that summer of 1972 he wrote from Isle Royale:

Dave, old Posey—

This fall I'm going to retire from the drawing board stint if at all possible. I've logged 60,000 hours in front of one, and the legs are giving out. I was pooped to exhaustion when I got here two months ago, but have restored muscle to a great extent. If at all possible, I'd like to do my book this winter—one on the Farmer System of Elemental Naval Architecture, using flotational models to check the work as it is carried along. Then I'd like to do a few stories for you packed with goodies of a new and novel nature calculated to titillate the risibilities of purists, and then chase the sun for a few months...

More anon—
Westy

He was a craftsman as well as a superb draftsman, and was lavish in his praise when he thought he was being well treated. I was frequently the recipient of his accolades, but to the very end I always flinched when one of his letters dropped into my In box—with Westy one never knew what was coming:

March 24, 1973

Sweet pee—

Dismissing the Davis interest as nostalgia is too simple. You're too goddam busy to give it any thought; writing you is like dropping love letters down a forty-foot length of stovepipe. ...I'm still steaming about the handling of the Atkin story, and in a good-natured way I'm composing a letter calculated to blister your paint. The headings, pic treatment, and cutlines are very good, bordering on the great. But I can hardly believe that Dave Getchell edited the story: full of miss-spelled words, hacked-off paragraphs, suppression of color, continuity of thought dropped—the works. As one old editor to another young editor, I'm going to mark my copy and point out a few thoughts for you to contemplate while shaving. My agreement with you was that YOU would edit my stuff—not hand it to the kids in your back boiler room. If teacher wants to correct Johnny's paper, Johnny has a right to ask teacher to be RIGHT, too...

Love, but no kizziz,
Doghouse Dick

My fuse reached the powder on that one:

Hi Luke:

Here's a word from 40′ down the well... which is just about where I am. This past week was something out of Dante, or wherever, and went by the board with a lot of talk but damn little work accomplished. Just tried to call you, but you were away, so this is faster.

The Johansen piece is fine, but a little heavy on aluminum promotion; I'll edit it in a day or two and send it back to you, as from now on there won't be *any* changes made in your copy without your approval...even if it means we don't make deadlines. When I get to the office tomorrow, I'll send you the Atkin backup—and then let's let that sleeping hound snooze. If it was screwed up, I'll take all the blame, but I don't want to kick it around any longer. I get enough fresh challenges each day without dwelling on those already by the board.

As for writing you, I'd like to do so every day, but I simply cannot. Some guys have talking jobs, some writing jobs and some mechanical jobs. Unfortunately, I have all three; I'm not complaining, but it does limit my time on any one thing...

So, I'm thinking of you, Luke, even when I'm not saying it on paper or over the phone, for I value your friendship as much as your competence.

See you,
Daff

His volume in NF tailed off by the mid-1970s mainly for the reason I had worried about in the beginning: the high-paying boating magazines had rediscovered Farmer's gold. Noodling in NF was fun, but it didn't pay much; noodling in the big-circulation magazines might not be so much fun but it paid more, a lot more. Here is an excerpt from a memo I wrote on August 29, 1974:

Dear Luke:

I just re-read your last letter and am happy to know you've struck paydirt with your writing: $400-$1500 a piece. But those figures are a little rich for NF's blood. As I've said before, I think you're worth the higher figures, but it's like the little guy with two bucks in his pocket looking at the gorgeous lady of the street—"I know I can't afford her, so I'll have to win her on love alone." Now I'm not comparing you to a sexy hooker, but the reasoning has its parallels. And, no, you have not worn out your welcome. Even a sweetie gets sour at times.

One thing...if you can make a living writing, why do you hassle with designing? Or are you like the sailor going to sea "for the last time, this time, for sure"?

Be good,
Daffy

As the number of his articles in NF climbed year after year, I fully appreciated Westy's contributions to the field of naval architecture: dozens of drool-producing small boats, including the first outboard cruiser; magnificent aluminum yachts that would bring out the peacock in a king; reworkings of other N.A.s work such as his fabulously successful adaptation of Hanna's *Tahiti* into the slightly larger steel ketch *Tahitiana*. Good as these were, it was his writings that fleshed out his work and made it so much more important than that of equally famous contemporaries. As he thrashed about in his mind still looking for a "direction," I broached my thoughts on the subject in this December 1974 memo:

Dear Luke:

Why not consider a book? You've said so many times that all the greats of the first half of this century should have recorded their lives, but so few really did. You ARE among the N.A. greats, you know, and you also have a long memory, a wealth of experience and a gist for writing. You might also bear in mind, that as with other IM books, we would like to use a few chapters in NF for which we would pay you directly. This might help a bit in considering any financial arrangement you would make with IM. No, I was not asked to encourage you, but I want to anyway. As is so often the case with artists, you CAN take it with you, and once you are gone (as all of us go eventually, I believe), the world is the poorer.

With kizzus,
Daffy

I continued to bang away on this theme for the next several years with reactions from Westy ranging from total disinterest to thoughtful acceptance. Meanwhile, his articles continued to mount in number, and Roger Taylor, ever mindful of book possibilities, wrote Westy that there was enough material on hand from NF alone to make a fine volume. Flabbergasted, Westy asked my opinion; I responded wholeheartedly in the affirmative. Westy replied in his fashion:

Dear Dave:

I thank you for your kind observations about the impending book. I seem to be a nervous Nellie about the thing. My reaction is about what a housewife would feel if she'd been told she was nine months pregnant. Roger phoned one morning and told me I'd written a book, had done 28 pieces for you in NF. I was so amazed I simply said "Sure, go ahead." No work, you see. About an hour afterward I thought I'd better call and find out what the deal was. . .

I do know that when I have assessed an idea for salability I have been quite successful. Witness *Tahitiana*, now pushing 600 sets sold in 15 months. And it all started when Malcolm Mac-Duffie—God rest his sweet soul—kicked me in the pants and said, "You owe it to others to tell what you know. Quit grousing and go to work." And so here I and my shadow are now aged 75, with one leg in a coffin and my head under the lid, wondering whether to pull in the other leg and call it quits. Beats hell what you can do with a cast iron, fifty-year-old Underwood if "we" try.

One joy dispels a
hundred cares—luv,
Westy

Westy's only book, entitled "From My Old Boat Shop," appeared in 1979 and was an immediate hit as far as books of that genre can be called hits. I recently reread it, and the chapters—each a former NF article—brought back memories, and laughter, and tears. Once again I realized just how good he was, and how luckily it had been National Fisherman that caught his fancy. At least some of this man's genius has been recorded

for posterity.

Through the late 'seventies and into the early 1980s, Westy's health began to suffer. I was bogged down with work on NF, the founding and sale of the Small Boat Journal, and a massive change of direction for the National Fisherman from a general marine newspaper to an out-and-out fisheries trade publication. Contact with Westy was correspondingly lean, his missives more plaintive, mine more terse. It is always difficult for younger people to fully appreciate the loneliness of age until it is too late. One heart attack followed another, but the scrapper kept coming back. In December 1980 he wrote to me:

Dear Daffo—

The congestive heart failure route to an enforced idleness is to be avoided at all costs. I came to that conclusion sometime between the night of Oct. 29, and Sept. 14 (sic) when I begged my way out of Methodist Hospital to return home. Most of that time I spent writing imaginary, complimentary obituaries to various nurses, cooks, druggists, and to myself. Heart Failures just aint worth it. . .

One obit seems permanent: no more forums anywhere for boat noodlings. Tragic loss of lore.

Luv—
Westy

Then a small miscue in NF triggered the most vitriolic letter he ever penned to me:

Dave, dearie—

I am sick enough to puke! On page 66 of your April issue there appears a special section entitled, "The Hows and Whys of BUILDING ROUND-CHINED STEEL FISHING VESSELS."

The headline writer and the author do not know the meaning of the word chine. What they are describing are *round-bilged* boats vs. boats that have chines.

A chine is a structural member in a V-bottom or deadrise boat. It is installed to bring together the bottom and topsides of a boat in a manner that will tie them securely. Thus, a boat with a chine becomes a chine boat. That is enough for any old salt or experienced boatbuilder to call it. If you see a number of chines installed to effect a general turn of the bilge, you have a multi-chine boat. . .

The tragedy of your damfool headline is that once printed, the print becomes law—we've been taught since kindergarten to believe it if printed.

I have been designing steel and aluminum vessels since my first one in 1931. I have worked in 25 shops as designer and layout-loftsman. I never yet have heard any man of experience call a round-bilged hull a "round-chined steel fishing vessel" or anything but round-bottomed.

I will send you a few pertinent illustrations to correct your bad marine lingo.

Meanwhile, dear sir, I remain,

Nauseated,
Weston Farmer

There was little contact after that: a couple of phone calls sufficed to restore our personal relationship if not our professional one. In mid-May, the tough old naval "artichoke" finally agreed to bypass surgery, but it was more than his battered system could take. He died on May 14, 1981, at the age of 77.

My feeling of loss at the time was tempered by many other things more closely weighing on my mind and my personal life. It was not until I began work on this story—he is deserving of a book—that the importance of the man to the world of boating, to his relatives and friends, and especially to me, was fully recognized. Reading today the scores of letters he wrote to me, I sense he was telling me more than words could say, but in my daily rush I failed to read the message that lay between the lines.

Weston Farmer was a great naval architect and a great man. How could I say otherwise after reading once again this eleven-year-old letter?

Tuesday, Jan. 16, 1973

Ahoy, dear boy—

You are really a ver' nice guy, Dave. Just now received your puff about the Davis piece and with it the nice compliments from Jay Hanna of Rockport, taking the chill off'n my cockles, as you put it, and making my day completely happy. Nobody likes to die of cold cockles.

Candidly, I've been so meeserable I've alternated between wondering whether I was going to die, and the next minute wishing I had. This downside up, bass ackward bug has blasted me both sides of the diaphragm, chastened my ego, chased my path to the podie, and had me enquiring of Lakewood Cemetery to see if the family plot was diggable in this weather. Not in living memory have I been decked so seriously for so long. So, if you have a touch of the stuff, don't fool with it. Die in advance—stay home, be good to yourself, and dinna go oot.

I've had abundant time to assess the current values of life, and don't like what I've paid on the N.A. doormat one bit. If the average engineer paid as much attention to balancing his checkbook and budgeting his time in his own interests as he does wrestling with the math and imponderables of artichoking, he'd die rich. At 70 it's

too late to change, I guess, but one can continue to interpret the human condition with respect to man's universal escape machine—the boat.

I can see I'm going to have to change me letterhead, too. The general idea behind it was serenity in a wild retreat, from which clouds of romantic vessels sailed off on paper dreams. A truer picture right now would be to have a white-haired old guy coming to the front of a snow-pillowed porch and flinging the contents of a night jug at the whole name and scene.

But this too will pass.

Meantime, all paper, printer's ink and publishing poop aside, and eliminated from the equation, thanks for being so thoughtful, and for being such a good guy.

"I hear the blessed angels calling,

Old Black Joe."

Joe

Weston Farmer at age 30.

Preface

This volume is largely a compilation of stories I have written for *National Fisherman*; stories about the lore and techniques of boat design that, over many years, I had encountered in many shops and yards and drafting rooms while engineering new boats. These yarns had been written for fun, to share at random an appreciation for forgotten old ideas or to recall the men whose methods and work built the values basic in boating art today. To write a preface for such a book is a humbling experience.

It is especially humbling because the articles became a book without my knowing it. There has been no chance to contrive any semblance of progression toward a central theme. No heavy message was freighted into these shop-talk yarns. Usually I sent them to editor David Getchell with the implied message, "Here's some inside scoop. I lived it and stick by it. Yours, 'Lonesome Luke.'" Eventually over a period of seven or eight years the articles totaled a respectable number. They were merely chips tossed into the stream, floating along here and there on tributaries to the main river of experience that someday floods toward full understanding, which is the basis of Art. As I re-read the galleys now, these are my stories and I am stuck with them. How do you get a "handle" on an enveloping title? As I said, it is a humbling experience.

The hobby of boat noodling becomes a quest for knowledge. This is a noodler's book, a peek over the shoulder of a man at work who has been there and who is willing to impart guidance. This is the essence of all shop talk, so why not encompass all this revelation, advice, opinion, experience, and candidly irreverent jocular pokes in narrative vein with the title, FROM MY OLD BOAT SHOP?

In assessing whatever contribution I may be making, I feel I can claim the Big Picture View. My lifetime has spanned the entire development of the internal-combustion engine as applied to boats. The biggest portion of my lifetime has been as a design engineer on the drawing board. When the Grim Reaper packs me into my coffin, I'd like people to say I have supplied a Big Picture perspective to boat and yacht design as a calling, and that my drafting has been professional and elegant. That will be enough. It is little, but enough.

Now to the main carcass of this book as we critical wolves growl for a sinking of the teeth. Three hundred years ago, the Bard of Avon, William Shakespeare, while putting pen to tongue when writing *Hamlet* caused that dour Dane to admonish a friend, "And therefore as a stranger give it welcome. There are more things in heaven and earth, Horatio, than are dreamt of in your philosophy."

These are just about the wisest words old Bill turned out—unless, of course, he has written something better lately.

I have mentioned that this became a book before I knew I had written it. Here is the story behind that story.

The sun was only an hour high that morning in frigid February when Roger Taylor, the skipper of International Marine Publishing, phoned to tell me I had written a book. Would it be okay if they published it? This was news to me as, having been called from waking slumber, I stood at the phone in a frost-glazed shiver trying to rev up my gyroscope and steady my understanding.

I was dumbfounded when Roger told me that my writings that had appeared in *National Fisherman* totaled around 30 articles, and that he and his staff would collect them and edit them. I wouldn't have a bit of work to do. The book, Roger said, would appeal to lots of people who had been asking for it. An inner fright seized me in a sort of call-off-your-dog-off-before-I-kick-off-his-head-off panic. I had been trapped, and by my own mousetrap.

Boat buffs *wanted* it? Thus does the butter of flattery grease the skids of many a launching—even of books. I didn't think to ask Roger what the deal was; I just said, "Sure, go ahead." No work, you see. The little man within me said, "About time! All the other shellbacks with horticultural names have written books—Culler, Garden, Gardner, so why not Farmer?"

Roger Taylor sent a big, thick bundle of *National Fisherman* columns for me to update, to square with present fact. Without pictures this was cold-turkey reading to me, as though written by a stranger. I found myself agreeing with everything written. I chuckled here and there as some pertinent poke let hot air out of a few stuffed shirts. An unsuspected value popped prominently into sharp focus: here were some root values about the building and designing business, written by a man who had been part of the entire three-quarters of a century in boat and related engineering development.

The old pelican had been around.

Roger Taylor has asked me to shed some light on this old bird: why I write, something about the track record, to show a few of the boats I have designed that have proved popular, and to include a few new philosophies about those angles of the game that time will never give again. I'll make it brief, the better to submerge the boring perpendicular pronoun I prefer over the passive editorial "we." Why share credit with one's shadow?

My great grandfather on my mother's side of the family was one Kneut Kneutson who owned a shipyard at Grimstad, Norway. It seems rather logical that boatbuilding was in my genes. This Kneut and one son lost their lives in a fire that destroyed the yard in 1858. My grandfather, also a Kneut Kneutson, was brought to the United States via sailing ship on a 90-day voyage from Grimstad by his mother, accompanied by a sister and a baby brother. Gamps Kneutson, as I knew him, became General Agent for the Connecticut General Life Insurance Company of Hartford, operating in Minnesota, and at the time I came along, Gamps had organized several prospering mutual insurance companies from which he derived abundant income until his death at 99 years of age.

My father, Matthew Farmer, was what was known as a "traveling man" in my childhood. He was a sweet, humorous, hard-working Irishman who, by what was the only method at the time, would embark on a steam train for three or four weeks at a time, making overnight stops in different small towns to work his territory. "That Mattie," my grandfather used to say, "could sell icicles to Eskimos!" I saw a lot more of my grandfather than I did of my dad during my childhood. I knew that Matt owned three farms in addition to the icicle business, so the Farmer family lived well, albeit as pretty much of a matriarchy. My mother, Bertha Kneutson Farmer, was beautiful, and strong of character, will, and mind. Always a superb administrator, she meted out warmth on a maternal basis and discipline on a strictly legal basis: If you were wrong, you "got it"; if you were right you were praised. If you wanted anything like a bike or a telegraph key, you earned it. No handouts in this house, kid.

We lived in Minneapolis in the winter and on Isle Royale in Lake Superior in the summer. There were 10 boatbuilding shops or works in the Twin Cities area in those days, reachable by streetcar. A 35-cent ticket on the Great Northern Railroad would take you west to Wayzata from Minneapolis on a steam train that ran four times a day. There, Lake Minnetonka became my Mecca. I was fascinated by the motorboats and the two engine works and four boat shops out there, and haunted them. Our summers were spent at Snug Harbor on Isle Royale, where Gamps Kneutson had his summer home—a haven for hay-fever sufferers—and where I played about in the family steam launch *Atalanta,* and watched a stream of guests come and go. Eventually Snug Harbor became Rock Harbor Lodge, a gem now part of the National Park System.

I doubt that any kid has had as lovely a boyhood as I had. I was given a 16-foot lapstrake launch with a 2-hp one-cylinder Caille engine. When the family work ethic had been satisfied by my daily chores, I was free to become the Crown Prince of Rock Harbor, haunting the fisheries, cruising, and exploring, with only one admonition, "You be home by supper!" Great life for an only son who was heckled by kid sisters Theresa and Edith!

It seems little wonder I became hooked on boats and big water and the romance of it all. I have never ceased wondering at the miracle of water—the weight of it, the many states of it, the ferocity wind brings to it, the fact of its being an almost universal solvent and part of nearly everything on earth.

Following these early stars, I got school credits for working in Shepherd's Boat Works in winter, then earned an apprenticeship at the Ramaley Works in Wayzata, and, being a resident of Minnesota in the winter and Michigan in the summer, it logically followed that I studied naval architecture for two years at the University of Michigan under Professors Sadler and Bragg. I finished up in mechanical engineering at the University of Minnesota.

Why do I write? My first story was sold in 1919 to Raymond Francis Yates, editor of *Everyday Engineering.* Quietly I had researched the subject of propellers; quietly I had submitted the story. It had fascinated me and I wanted to pass along what I had learned. Not so quietly, I let out a war whoop when a letter from *Everyday Engineering* disgorged a check for $35 just as my mother was needling me to get busy and earn a bit of pocket money by selling off the last few dozen of that last case of eggs Matt had brought in from the territory. This check beat selling eggs all hollow at a dollar a case profit. My mother let out a cackle that didn't die down for years. Thus, I became hooked on engineering writing. I am sure that all my aunts and grandmothers and relatives and neighbors eased up on their diet of eggs, and told Bertha Farmer to keep that insatiable boy busy writing.

From time to time I have continued to bug editors with ideas I from Minneapolis on a steam train that ran four times a day. There, Lake Minnetonka became my Mecca. I was fascinated by the motorboats and the two engine works and four boat shops out there, and haunted them. Our summers were spent at Snug Harbor on Isle Royale, where Gamps Kneutson had his summer home—a haven for hay-fever sufferers—and where I played about in the family steam launch *Atalanta,* and watched a stream of guests come and go. Eventually Snug Harbor became Rock Harbor Lodge, a gem now part of the National Park System.

I doubt that any kid has had as lovely a boyhood as I had. I was given a 16-foot lapstrake launch with a 2-hp one-cylinder Caille engine. When the family work ethic had been satisfied by my daily chores, I was free to become the Crown Prince of Rock Harbor, haunting the fisheries, cruising, and exploring, with only one admonition, "You be home by supper!" Great life for an only son who was heckled by kid sisters Theresa and Edith!

It seems little wonder I became hooked on boats and big water and the romance of it all. I have never ceased wondering at the miracle of water—the weight of it, the many states of it, the ferocity wind brings to it, the fact of its being an almost universal solvent and part of nearly everything on earth.

Following these early stars, I got school credits for working in Shepherd's Boat Works in winter, then earned an apprenticeship at the Ramaley Works in Wayzata, and, being a resident of Minnesota in the winter and Michigan in the summer, it logically followed that I studied naval architecture for two years at the University of Michigan under Professors Sadler and Bragg. I finished up in mechanical engineering at the University of Minnesota.

Why do I write? My first story was sold in 1919 to Raymond Francis Yates, editor of *Everyday Engineering.* Quietly I had researched the subject of propellers; quietly I had submitted the story. It had fascinated me and I wanted to pass along what I had learned. Not so quietly, I let out a war whoop when a letter from *Everyday Engineering* disgorged a check for $35 just as my mother was needling me to get busy and earn a bit of pocket money by selling off the last few dozen of that last case of eggs Matt had brought in from the territory. This check beat selling eggs all hollow at a dollar a case profit. My mother let out a cackle that didn't die down for years. Thus, I became hooked on engineering writing. I am sure that all my aunts and grandmothers and relatives and neighbors eased up on their diet of eggs, and told Bertha Farmer to keep that insatiable boy busy writing.

From time to time I have continued to bug editors with ideas I the summer time you can, as in my case, knock off for four months and enjoy an extroverted, carefree summer. I go back to Isle Royale, to my summer home, Coffee Pot Landing, where as I gaze seaward over my Coffee Grounds, ships from all parts of the world sail past in lanes two miles from my picture windows.

For the nonce, this must serve as a view from within and without at Coffee Pot Landing.

Weston Farmer
18970 Azure Road
Wayzata, MN 55391

1

Getting a Blast Out of Boatbuilding

Lemon extract as an aid to increased boat shop production was discovered in Wayzata, Minnesota, about 1918. For a long time I believed it helped one to tie knots in steamed oak frames—but, I get ahead of my story.

Go sometime to Wayzata on Lake Minnetonka. You'll find yourself on the northern shore of a large lake the shoreline of which resembles the Chesapeake. The lake's hundred miles of shore has welcoming arms that shelter nine or ten little cities such as Deephaven, Excelsior, Tonka Bay, Navarre, Spring Park, Crystal Bay, Mound, and points west in the meandering geology.

Once, a scant generation ago, Wayzata was a town where many were called and everybody got up to work in one of the four boatshops that made the town the boatbuilding capital of the great 10,000 Lakes state. Today, many are called, but few get up. There is not much need to now in Wayzata. The main hum of industry is the noise of scissors clipping bond coupons for mailing to Merrill Lynch.

But the water is still lovely and challenging on Wayzata Bay; the Burlington Northern railroad from Chicago to Seattle still pre-empts the space between shore and town; the "depot" is still there, and across the tracks down the west shore a different boat merchandising operation occupies what once was the site of the old Ramaley Boat Company, once the Middle West's largest.

It was at Ramaley's—pronounced R'mAY-li—that I went to work in 1918 as a boatbuilder's apprentice. It was at Ramaley's that I learned that lemon extract is a great adjunct to boatbuilding productivity.

1

The Ramaley Boat Co. was the Midwest's largest boatbuilder when the author went to work there back in 1918. The main building shed was also the scene of the Lemon Extract Incident described here. Old Nellie, the boiler, spluttered in a lean-to building just beneath the tall stack at the corner of the wing.

No longer is there any need to keep this astounding R & D secret from the world. The technical premises are as follows: at one time in these now guzzling United States there was a tipple considered by many to be the best cocktail of Bacchus—lemon extract. That this was drinking nectar came about in a strange way, impossible to believe in this day and age. But there are men just above forty who can attest to the fact that this country once was as dry as a sun-baked sponge in Arizona. They will chuckle as they tell you liquor was illegal in 1918 if above 3.2 percent alcoholic content. The country's laws rendered the near-beer of that day unfit for washing windows.

The drought was due to a fanatic teetotaler named Andrew Volstead who, as a member of Congress, politicked that confused body into outlawing John Barleycorn. Aimed at Stopping Sin, laws were written with dour devotion and dedicated incompetence that succeeded only in parching the nation. Prohibition had arrived. No workman could buy his Saturday pay-envelope schnapps. No sailor could have his tot of grog. And no boatbuilder could celebrate the shutter, or whisky plank.

The hell they couldn't, as we shall presently see!

The sun didn't completely disappear from over the nation's yardarm, but Old Sol did get mighty dim.

At the beginning of the drought, the solar orb was saved from total eclipse by grocery stores, which enjoyed a run on flavoring extracts. These flavors, because they were of high-proof alky, were way above legality in alcoholic content, but because they were foodstuffs, weren't illegal, either. Washington's solons had just overlooked them in their traditional ignorance of economics. Until the legal dikes were eventually plugged, such snorts as vanilla extract became vintage drinks.

2

While market pipelines were being primed with nourishing new flavors, the more enterprising of the cocktail set filled their Martini shakers from the taps of auto radiators, until this type of research proved by subsequent development that embalming fluid had the same terminal effect.

Eventually, of course, fine whisky was offered, or so the labels said. In general, this Balm of Gilead was spooned out of the bathtub mash at three o'clock in the afternoon, passed over charcoal, and well aged an hour before being served to the supper trade.

In their dilemma of suddenly enforced thirst, the twenty boatbuilders at the Ramaley Boat Works (glass cabin cruisers, airplane-engined speedboats, sailboats, rowboats, and canoes) made the monumental discovery that lemon extract was the ideal wetting agent to use on oilstones while sharpening chisels and plane blades. Being an aid to production, and because of an office oversight on the part of management, it was purchasable to company account. The men sharpened tools right merrily, laying in lemon extract copiously on company requisition with cupidity and cunning.

The bottler's formula for this Swig of Vulcan called for a mere three drops of citric acid in little glass bottles much like the ones in which Three-in-One oil was sold, the remaining volume being filled entirely with potable high-proof grain alcohol yellowed by a pinch of harmless vegetable dye, the better to con in a suggestion of lemon. This juice was great on oilstones.

There isn't a mechanic around who can't find new uses for a shop standby. Ramaley's men found it was also good at milling new keyways in gullets, and it was considered a cozy swig by those who could get the upper hand of it. It sizzled in a man's bilges like a length of hot chain. The Ramaley men termed it "Boat Builder's Pop."

Now, I go to some length about this stuff, because you can't be too careful when you're writing specifications. Lemon extract had pop, all right. Raw alcohol, without citric acid or dye, but laced with a dash of nitro-methane and a dollop of benzol, is the hydrocarbon that today drives little old ladies at 600 mph in cars over the Bonneville salt flats. It has, as the French murmur at Le Mans, "Beaucoup bang."

Boatbuilders at Ramaley's were getting a bang out of sharpening tools. Because tools aided production, because oilstones sharpened tools and needed "oil," lemon extract as a substitute at 25 cents a bottle was innocently deemed by Rachel, the works bookkeeper, to be a legitimate company expense. This old gray pudding of a female, with a heart as big as an ox, and a rump and brain to match, wrote 24 purchase orders for this aid to production in the month before J.E. Ramaley, owner of the plant, on the fateful morning, which is the focus of this yarn, made the discovery that each requisition was for a *case* of lemon extract, not just one bottle.

We will get to that stark drama, but we must now juice up our conversational cocktail by introducing the innocent boy rumrunner. Coming up: a budding naval architect; squeeze well, and hang as a twist on the glass.

As a brand-new boatbuilder's apprentice in that borning day of a lifetime romance with boats, I saw nothing menial nor anything to tarnish my dignity in being the lemon extract messenger between the Ramaley Boat Works and the grocery store three blocks up the tracks. In fact, I welcomed the walking time to conjure dreams of a glorious future life as one of those men at the top of the whole boatbuilding heap—those glamorous naval architects! The moonbeams of high ambition glancing about in my young skull told me it was going to be easy for me to join these selected few.

Easy, the way I dreamed it, because my first name is Earl and was not used, so as E. Weston Farmer I would naturally berth alongside J. Murray Watts, E. Lockwood Haggas, A. Loring Swasey, C. Padgett Hodson, and A. Cary Smith, whose elliptical names proved their nobility as aristocrats of spline and slide rule.

That was where I belonged, right up there with the bong-tong elite. That image was pretty well polished by the time I had written to William H. Hand, Jr., suggesting he'd make more money as H. William Hand. And "Captain Nat" was an outrage! He'd do better as N. Greene Herreshoff. Anybody'd know that!

I could tell I had a lot going for me.

Thus for my first 30 days in this new job, earning money and high-school shop credits, these orienting self-improvement walks to the grocery for lemon extract were of great benefit. They released me from gnawing shop worries such as where to sweep the next basket of cedar shavings, and gave me time to buy a railroad or two, or merge Cramp's Shipyard with Bethlehem Steel and the Yellow Cab Company.

I doubted that these trips for lemon extract were justified by the amount of tool sharpening going on, but to have questioned the shenanigan was beneath my dignity. This dignity was a quality I had managed to elevate to a point where a few boatbuilders no longer treated me as a pretty trellis of sweet peas.

So, hey hey and heigho for youth! It little mattered to me, as daily I delivered the juice to Dean Leaman, head boatbuilder and town drunk, that it was January, that the ice in the lake was four feet thick, the wind blowing white rime, or that the old boiler in the pit to the south side of the shop was straining every rivet to deliver steam. Didn't I have the world by the tail for a downhill haul? I'd landed this job with the best darn ol' boat works anywhere!

You must have the stage setting for any drama: at that time the largest boatbuilder between Chicago and Seattle, the Ramaley Boat Works was housed in a big but ancient two-story clapboard building perhaps 150 feet in length, east and west, by 70 or 80 feet south to north. It stood on the west shore of Wayzata Bay, about a block south of the Burlington Northern depot, which, I have noted, is still there.

A launchway ran to the water, and all around the shop were piled molds for boats that someday again would never be built. This clutter was dotted here and there by that certain rusting marine engine awaiting the same hopeless fate.

The shop was approached across the railroad track from the main road at the railroad station, down along shore on a meandering dirt road through a meadow. At the end of this two-rutter hard to the right was the Campbell Marine Engine Company—"Buy a Campbell and Keep Going." To the left was Ramaley's.

You entered from the west end door, passing an office cluttered with old Harthan and Hyde propellers, sawdust, old magazines of boating falling from the shelves, past a time clock to your right, after which you were in a veritable palace of romance. Two long lines of boats were always in frame or being planked beside wall workbenches on the north and south sides; steamboxes were bubbling, planing mills were howling, craftsmen were hammering away and cutting wood, and were happy at it.

You must remember the scene: boats used to be built that way before plumbers learned to wrestle eels of slippery cloth in tubs of slime, barely managing to stay out of jail for fraud by calling the resulting pot a Mark III Bangeroo.

The musical accompaniment to the aura of romance at Ramaley's was the hissing of the boiler, sunk in an earthen excavation or pit hard by the south wall, and covered by a corrugated iron lean-to which sported a 60-foot sheetmetal stack.

This turned out to be a very important boiler.

The Old Nellie of a kettle had started life out on the Dakota prairies as a big J.I. Case steam threshing tractor, with locomotive-type boiler, pulling a gang of 16 plows across oceans of grain fields clear to Montana. She had eventually waddled her way from harvest to harvest toward Lake Minnetonka, where her engine was removed and her wheels taken from her axles. She was next bedded down in Ramaley's pit to spend the rest of her life huffing, puffing, and clucking like an old Orpington hen on the nest.

She hatched out heat for the shop and steamed delicious smells from steam boxes where good white oak was cooked to frame-forming tenderness. She pinged and panged and supplied with gusto the Muzak of the shop.

Ramaley's bustling boatbuilding plant produced more boats in this boat capital town than the other three boat companies combined, but could never manufacture a dividend. Despite this hidden fact, Ramaley chugged along, seemingly prosperous, for years.

Such management takes genius, and when in the presence of that rare quality, 'twere well to examine these managers whose heads are screwed on with left-hand threads, for they are not like the rest of us. Let us examine that rare bird, J.E. Ramaley, more closely.

Mister Ramaley, or Father, as we used to call him, was born Jean, not Gene, and bore the feminine name because his mother had prepared for a girl.

When her baby arrived with an outboard bilge bailer attached instead of a centerboard trunk as ordered, Mrs. Ma Ramaley raised Jean as a girl until he was old enough to fight his way out of it.

This had happened before to Mrs. Ma Ramaley, and Jean's brother Florence went through the same drill. This may be why both men were good scrappers and had clawed their way to prominence in their fields. Florence became owner of a large bakery. Jean became stuck with a large boat works.

To the eye, Father Ramaley looked more believable as a comic burlesque tramp than as a dynamic boatbuilder. He was fuzzy-bald except for a few long upright hairs on his upper deck. These raked aft stiffly, encrusted with sawdust and dandruff. Winter and summer, indoors and out, he wore the same full-length, heavy Ulster overcoat, set flying. Generally, you could play cards on his coat tails. In his mouth were some teeth. These were in evidence Sundays, when he scrubbed and became a pillar of the local church, passing the collection plate with the spare smile frequently employed by foreclosing mortgage fanciers. His deep-set eyes of electric blue got across the command, "Cough up, you."

This broad-brushed image of a vaudeville clown is a contradictory one, externally, for the man whose undeniable energy and selling skill kept the old works a-humming. He was respected, liked, and as are all front runners, he was jeered at behind his back.

Notoriously preoccupied, at times he wore an expression of distant and pondering vacuity. He had been known to stroll off the end of a dock when making fast a boat. On occasion he had driven his car into the Boat Works Garage without first opening the garage door. When in these trances he always made a good job of it, and the reality when the external world caved in on him always triggered a bit of a temper. His profanity was sublime and would blister the bus bars of Hell, as is always the case when God-fearing men blow a fuse.

One frigid Saturday morning a few hours before the envelopes con-

Key figures in the Lemon Extract Incident are shown in later years in the Farmer-designed, Ramaley-built 30-footer *Hillcrest*, which could do 40 mph with her 200 hp motor. In the bow seat is Rachel, the bookkeeper; the helmsman, in white hat, is J. E. Ramaley himself.

taining our cash wages were due to be distributed at the noon time clock, Father Ramaley was discovered to have been missing for two days.

No one, not even worried Rachel, knew where he was.

At seven thirty in the dark of morning as work started, his whereabouts was a rumored question. By nine it was a puzzle. At ten it became an alarm. Would we get our money at noon?

Father Ramaley was missing, and it was colder than Charity this payday morning. Fourteen below, outdoors, and diving. Along the sunlit windows above the benches on each side of the shop, melancholy white vapors escaped from steam joints. Winds whistled through chinks making fans of frost, and the old boiler in the pit struggled to hump enough warmth to heat the shop and steam the frames.

Oak costs money! If it starts to cook, it must be worked and finished, or all effort is wasted. Every man knew it. Pipes banged and spanged, steam hissed everywhere, and though the grates of the old boiler were bedded with red-hot anthracite coals at full draft, the polar leakage overcame British Thermal output. Cooled frames broke as they went into boats.

Production prospects were miserable. Pay prospects were dim, too. The time in the week had clearly come for all hands to cut out the monkey business and sharpen things up.

Thus, in all workshops of the world do knights of the workbench lay down tools to preserve the guild heritage by casting aspersion's asparagus at things alien, such as employers suffering from payroll scratch.

7

There should have been no worry. Had I been older or wiser, I would have known that Father Ramaley was out hunting among bankers with kneeling pad and tin cup, or stalking wealthy customers with cold chisel and mallet, hopeful of sculpting chips of cash from the stony bank accounts of the delinquent rich. As always is true of any up-to-date boatyard (I later learned), there is a Mrs. Cadwalader O'Shucks or a Doctor G. Suffern Katz who feel that the boats they buy in June do not need to be paid for until New Year's.

Their noble names guarantee their involuted notion of credit—the longer things run the better it therefore is—and they always pay, which may be some day or doomsday. But not today.

Father Ramaley was missing. So was steam, so was heat, so was hope. The mice were at play. Discipline relaxed until the whole shop was speculative babble. Lemon extract was in evidence and becoming shorter in supply. Our future naval architect had by now become uncomfortable at all the roistering.

Two heaping five-bushel baskets of shavings had been swept up as my Saturday morning's duty, and were placed as always per shop routine at each side of the stairway to the boiler pit, the better to kindle Monday morning's fire. So I was relaxing by leaning on the janitor's broom handle when a roar was aimed at me from the bench of the head boatbuilder, Dean Leaman.

"Hey, kid!" he yelled, "Go in to Rachel and get an order for some oilstone juice!" Then, turning away toward the others, he half said, "If we pour it down the steam boxes it'll soften the ribs." He chuckled.

This was a new one on me. Might be a boatbuilding trick I hadn't picked up yet. I complied. So did Rachel, who by this time was looking at secretarial life as being immoral and shortly to become unnecessary, as she issued the requisition and I was off up the tracks to the grocery.

It does a man good to take these frequent trips away from business—gives him the long, detached view of his affairs. As I breathed the cool bracing air, this thought swung over into larger matters concerning a merger I was cooking up between U.S. Steel and the Ford Motor Company. You could sure save money on stenographers in a deal like that. The thought of stenographers swung over to a certain high school girl I had encountered in the hall at school. She had swept past me with a challenging glance and with the pace and swing of a destroyer in a following sea, exuding unattainable hauteur.

She was a stunning flower; I had vowed I'd bring her to heel. She'd probably accompany me to Tahiti on those four trips a year I'd take as head of my Big Combine so as to get my detached view. Tahiti and Papeete were the logical destination because people out there wore hardly any clothes, and I wanted a surreptitious estimator's peek at the pistil of this orchid. Tahiti would be ideal.

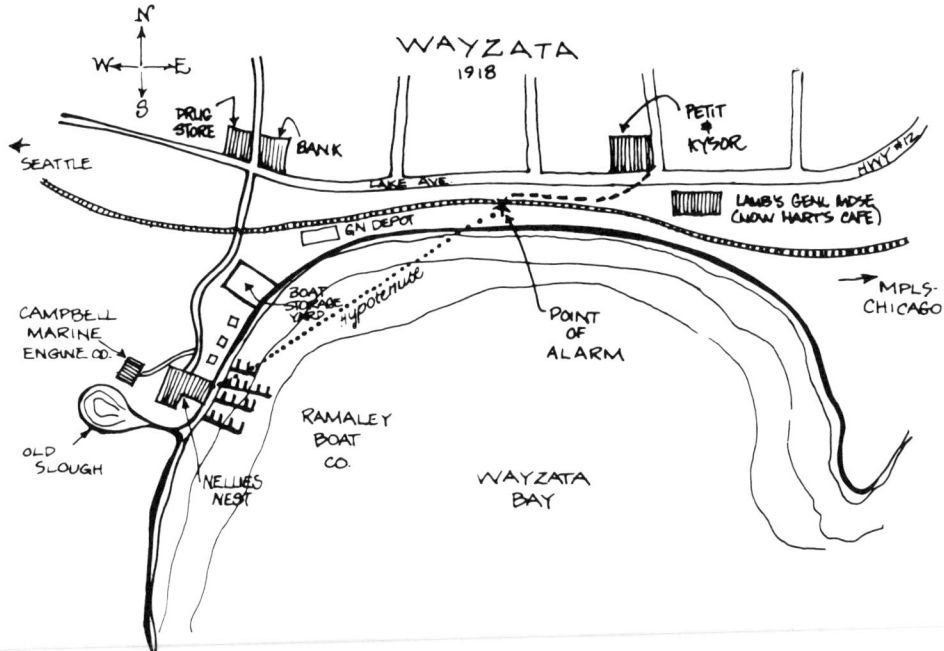

The scene of the Lemon Extract Incident is shown in this map of the Wayzata waterfront. The author, returning along the tracks from Lamb's store with a case of extract, spotted Mr. Ramaley headed for the plant in his Model T along Lake Avenue. Wanting to get back before his boss, the youth ran down the bank and across the frozen bay, arriving minutes before Mr. Ramaley and the explosive climax that followed.

The travelogue was interrupted by the door of the Petit and Kysor grocery closing behind me as I presented the Ramaley purchase order to Mrs. Kysor. I scarcely heard her yammer about how many lemon pies a boatyard could make, and would I have Mister Ramaley call her in time so she could get to the bank and pay her delivery boys. Yep, Tahiti would be the place, all right.

I picked up the case and headed across the street. I gained the tracks and ambled toward the boatshop.

As I walked along the track westward at the lake's edge, despite the frozen scene, the orchid and I were about to step into our boat, leaving beautiful Tahiti as the sun sank slowly in the west, where it generally does. A vulgar blast from a familiar Klaxon horn, a "Goo-ga—Goo-ga!" jerked me back from Tahiti to the snowy railroad right-of-way in the space of three ties and a temperature drop of 94 degrees.

Father Ramaley and his model-T Ford touring car with top down were flying down the main drag paralleling the track with spark and throttle levers kissing each other at full bore. A black bag was in the seat and no hat was on his head at fourteen below. The whole lash-up headed for the rail crossing a block west toward the left hand turn into

9

the meadow and the front door of the Ramaley Boat Works. Oh my gosh. . . .

Guilt dropped anchor in my stomach.

This provoked traction, celerity, and a sublime grasp of geometry. If Father Ramaley had seen me, gone would be the lemon extract racket, innocent though it was, at least on my part. But gone would be my detached view, my great empires.

Ramaley had two blocks to go; one west to the railroad crossing, one south to the plant and the shop front door. I opted for the hypotenuse, and let the sum of the squares of the other two sides take care of themselves. Tumbling off the track to the lake ice, I sprinted for the shop along the lakeshore under the willows.

I made it through the lakeside door of the plant to the end of Dean Leaman's work bench while Father Ramaley was making an awful racket up behind the office corner in the other end of the shop. Sounded like—falling lumber? The shop was cooling.

On Dean Leaman's bench I deposited the case (about the size of a storage battery and now twice as heavy) and, denying myself breath, I sauntered past the telephone which was hung on the center post of the shop just across from the boiler pit opening, picked up my broom, and leaned on it. Panting does sometimes come from an overworked broom.

"Father's done it," tittered Leaman, in glee. "Drove through the doors again."

The head boatbuilder was now so far along this early Saturday as to be well into his Sunday role as town souse. Some others of the crew were half as smashed as a sack of ripe grapes.

Into this scene around the office corner, slowly, like Hamlet's ghost, stalked Father Ramaley. The triumph on his face faded to consternation as comprehension dawned. He stopped frozen by the scene. A few twitters left him like birds fluttering from a nest, then these were followed by a bellowing roar.

"What the hell's going on here?" It was not the voice of a meadowlark.

He strode to Dean Leaman's bench and picked up an empty bottle of the great citric rib softener. He smelled the tipple. Then he knew what was going on.

"Devils! You get back to work!" He lowered his voice, then, so it could be heard only a scant eighth of a mile. "Your money's here and you'll be paid!"

Next, he turned his fury on Dean Leaman, whose face wore a hooligan smile.

"Where'd you get this stuff, Leaman?"

"Groshery store," said the best wood cutter in the shop. "Sharpens toolth." His head wobbled, unpenitent.

"Did Rachel buy this stuff for you?"

"Yup."

"You're fired!"

"Okay. It's Satterdy anyway. Wan' me come a' work Monday?"

"Of course!" Ramaley couldn't have got along without the weekday efficiency of the old soak.

The re-hired foreman's Irish mental machinery was in the condition of a pen of turkeys. Ideational birds might tumble out gobbling in a huddle, and might get together afterward, or might not. Threaded through it and underneath, steam clearly had to be his apologia.

"Nobody bends oak widdout shteam!" This was a triumphal idea that would set Father back on his heels.

"Steam? I'll give you steam." Ramaley jumped into the pit to the front end of the boiler. In a couple of fluid moves he donned asbestos gloves, unlatched the fire door, grabbed the slice bar, and raked out the entire fire of glowing coals on to the earthen apron at each side of the boiler's red-hot maw. The fact that you cannot get draft through a bed of clinkers hadn't occurred to Leaman. He had neglected his charge.

One beautiful turkey of an idea had hit him while Ramaley was employing corrective thermal techniques below. He was doing away with the evidence by pouring lemon extract over each of the five-bushel heaps of shavings near the boiler room companionway—nearly pure alcohol on cedar.

Father Ramaley leaped out of the pit, raked the piles toward the lip of the companionway with his feet, jumped back into the pit, and began stoking the stuff into the boiler with hands in an unsweeping motion. I was reminded of Toscanini whooping it up with the William Tell Overture. Only, Ramaley used his feet, too, stuffing the fire box full.

A faint alarm overtook me at the thought of this nascent gunpowder being crammed into Old Nellie. Evidently I was about to see how an old, experienced boilerman cleaned flues! I was learning something new around here every day.

So far—only blue smoke.

Just then, the telephone rang.

Ramaley jumped out to answer, slamming the fire door shut. He'd taken on the whole world this morning—a payroll, a bunch of drunks, a balky boiler—and Ma Bell's imperious summons could not throw him. It was Mrs. Kysor, demanding some payroll money of her own.

"Money? How much, Mrs. Kysor?" He was gargling the gravel of anger, dredging for the gold of diplomatic sweet-talk. If there was blue smoke around the phone, there was now very blue smoke leaking from the fire door of the boiler. There was a ping, and then a pang.

Over the phone came an explanatory squeak, sounding like a muffled mouse, but obviously the noise made by an irate female, rising to a stream of screeches. To my alarmed eavesdropping it sounded suspiciously like "Your shop boy. . . ."

"The kid?" Father leaned away from the phone as his eye swept me in.

A mighty metallic *bloink*—followed by a straining sound, as of box car wheels screeching—signaled that the old Orphington hen in the boiler pit might lay an egg.

Ramaley wheeled and dove into the pit just in time to open the firebox door. That was just what Old Nellie did not need—a breath of fresh air. When the oxygen in the air hit the hot hydrocarbon gases, there was a roaring blast of flame up the stack.

Then the old tea kettle quit fooling and sneezed—k—ka—KA ZOOMPH! In a mighty blast of thunder and soot, Old Nellie blew up. Out of the airborn maelstrom of slats wafted the odor of springtime in a lemon grove. Mingled with it was a faint odor of hot fish, emanating from lake water steam.

Over the threshold level of the boiler pit sill presently peeked the Ramaley face. He was blackened by soot that was made darker by the pale underlay of fright.

His eyes fixed me in a blaze bluer than Yule Tree lights; there was that instant of dire confrontation and exact mutual understanding.

"You *bas*——"

I didn't wait to hear. In no much of a mean panic of a hurry much I gained the shop door and went into orbit toward the North Pole. Tracks in the snow leading north at 10-foot intervals later were said to have been made by my shoes. If that is true, and I was in them, my take-off run was longer than I thought. There is such a thing as dropping your undercarriage, you know. The shoes could have run on by themselves!

Time's mantle of charity mercifully erases subsequent details. We did get paid. I continued to work for Ramaley, planking and framing rowboats.

It was not many weeks before Jean Ramaley took me up to the designery in one corner of the second floor loft, put me in front of a drawing board, and said, "You're *it*. You may be ready. Draw me up a 22-footer for Win Wood. He's got an OX5 Curtiss engine he wants in her. He's Gar's brother, y'know."

I then stood in the exact ghostly footprints of Charles D. Mower and George F. Crouch, right at the very board in the same shop that once for a brief time had been each man's personal fief.

"As the twig is bent, so grows the tree" is an oldie. I guess I'll have to thank lemon extract for having put another kink in my then already bent twig.

You can't beat the stuff for getting action around a boat shop!

2

19th-Century Naval Architect's Philosophy

Eighty-seven years ago, in 1891, there was published in New York City a magnificent book on yacht construction and design. Its title: *Small Yachts: Their Design and Construction*. The fly leaf added, "Exemplified by the Ruling Types of Modern Practice with Numerous Plates and Illustrations." The publisher was the Forest and Stream Publishing Co. Text and drawings were by C.P. Kunhardt, who was the yachting editor of *Forest and Stream,* at that date the bible of American yachting. Kunhardt, moreover, as all oldtimers know, was the most highly articulate and respected yacht designer of his time. I have this fact at first hand from an oldtimer.

A copy of *Small Yachts* by Kunhardt has become my property by the eructation of 40 bucks, said eructation being a $40 word for "coughing up." And being in the $40-word area, let me "elucidate the circumstances of my acquisition."

For 40 years—a dollar a year—I had searched for a copy. Making my wants known to Richard I. Robb, who runs The Wizard's Bookshelf at Savage, Minnesota, I found myself facing Dick in my study, with Kunhardt on my lap, talking to a world traveler, a sailor, an adventurer with a yen for boats. I bought the book.

In it was adventure, nostalgia, and magnificent drafting. The royal-sized volume, 12 inches by 15 inches by 2 inches, weighing about 6 pounds, reeked with Edwardian adequacy and crisp ink illustrations done with ruling pen and India ink. I have excerpted Exhibit 1 to show you the tenor of Kunhardt's drafting.

Exhibit 1 calls to mind drafting "as she wuz did" when I started out years ago, wrestling with starched, bluish, linen cloth called tracing vellum, which was held to the drawing board by thumbtacks that had a

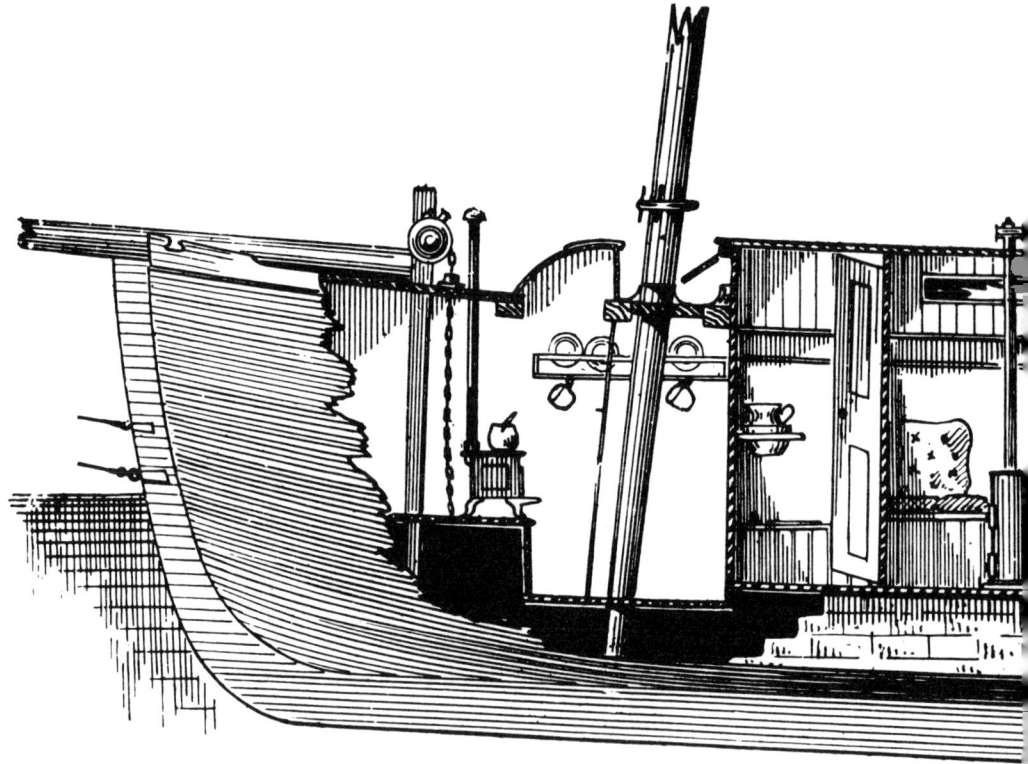

An example of the drawing skill of 19th century naval architect C.P. Kunhardt is seen in this little schooner. Given the inks and tools of the time, it was necessary to wait after drawing each line until the ink had dried. A blot virtually assured that the entire subject had to be redrawn.

perverse propensity for popping out as you were applying "pounce" powder to the surface to give it tooth. This was in a day when butter was sliced nine to a stick instead of 90, and how well you drew was the criterion, not how fast.

To the uninitiated, Exhibit 1 will appear as a mere picture. To any-one who ever worked with Mr. Higgin's India lamp black juice, which is compounded of carbon, graphite, gutta-percha, and camphor in solu-tion, it will be apparent that Exhibit 1 must have taken Mr. Kunhardt a month to draw. As everyone knows who has prayed over a ruling pen as he struck a line, each line of Kunhardt's was laid in and then allowed to dry before he moved to the next. 'Twas the only way to avoid blots. There isn't a detectable blemish on this plate. It is a testament to patience, not a mere picture.

Note also, if you are a student of such things, that Mr. Kunhardt clearly has constructed his drawing from a set of lines with the bow facing to the left. There is absolutely no valid convention that dictates that the bow must face to the right. I have seen it stated that loftsmen get the fantods if the lines are not stemmed to the right. This is pure hogwash. William H. Hand, Jr., and John Hacker and many not so well

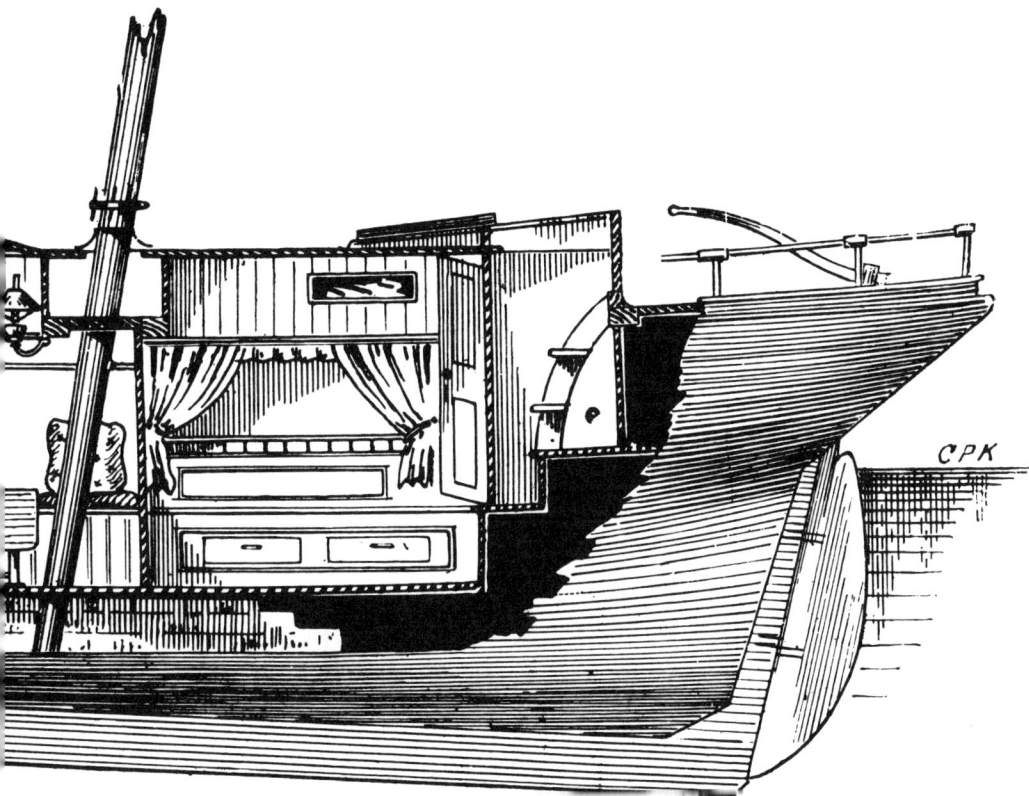

known men have consistently drawn to the left. I believe it is a matter of the designer being either "left eyed" or "right eyed."

Now take a look at Kunhardt's Plate LXXVII, Exhibit 2. And tie your hat on, for the preliminaries of introduction are over and Mr. Kunhardt is about to take you on a fast ride. His dissertation on whether naval architecture is a science or an art, or what proportions of each, will be like tossing a match into a hayloft, or discovering the man who shot Santa Claus, or, not to mix similes, like driving down a dead-end alley with your steering wheel in the hands of a maniac. You will be subjected to shock.

Remember, this is Mr. Kunhardt writing about his method of applying science to the design of his schooner, Exhibit 2, which obviously has been laid out with a passing swipe at curve of trochoid and curve of versed sines, as well as an area curve, all gussied up to scare hell out of poor boatbuilders. He says—and I merely quote him:

. . . At best, the customary calculations are meager and paltry. To dignify them as "science" and proclaim a great gulf between the "rule of thumb" man, who designs just as our schooner has been designed and the "scientific" designer who supplements the work with a few trifling calculations is an unwarranted exaggeration.

The so-called "scientific" designer has no material advantage over his rival, as results fully attest throughout the history of yachting. Both schools meet with

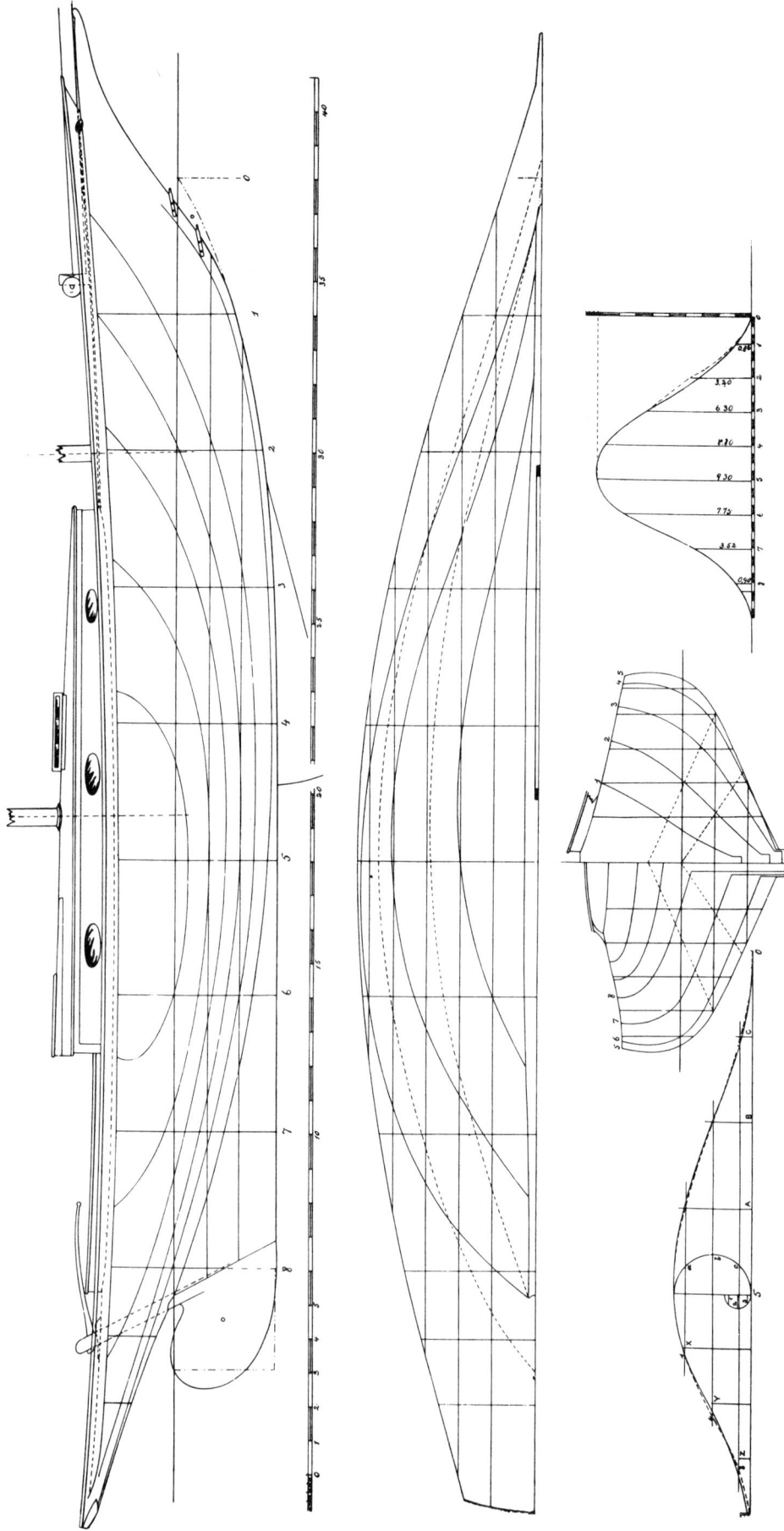

PLATE LXXVII.

LIGHT DRAFT CENTRE-BOARD SCHOONER.

This schooner shows Kunhardt's touch of both art and mathematics.

success or reverse, just as they bring experience to bear and stick to standards already tested or display intuitive gift in making wide departures.

The student is therefore counselled to educate his eye through observation and store his memory with "lines" to which he has access as the most likely road to his goal. To carry out the calculations will be a pleasant diversion obtained at the loss of little time.

Theory is estimated by results. Successful design is the outcome of compromise between antagonistic features. The worth of theoretical naval architecture is to be gauged by the extent to which it supplies information upon the best compromise as a final result.

Fully aware of the degree to which *individual* elements of design may be present, the originator casts about for some means of estimating the effect of *combination*.

Where elements are in antagonism to one another, knowledge of the elements in their individuality leads up to nothing in predicting their behavior in the aggregate.

If the pursuit of theoretical naval architecture affords only an appraisement of separate elements, without submitting directions for their combination or summing them up in joint action, naval architecture may be thrown aside so far as we expect from the science definite instructions through which to insure predetermined performance. (Wow! Now isn't *that* a lungful?—W.F.)

A science which is confessedly scarcely equal to measuring elements one by one, after all transfers the responsibility for their successful combination upon judgement.

Naval architecture encompasses only some of the factors contributing to performance, leaving others untouched.

The estimates undertaken cover specific conditions and positions, leaving others untouched.

The estimates undertaken cover specific conditions (which are) generally the exception instead of the rule.

Some are computed upon approximate base and others upon assumption. There is besides a vast range of phenomena *totally beyond* the scope of mathematical expression, and in such phenomena the performance of a sailing yacht may undergo more crucial ordeal than in the narrow belt within the manipulation of figures.

Upon reviewing the exigencies to which a successful yacht must be adapted, the inability of theoretical naval architecture to cope with the science is sufficiently apparent.

The progress won in the shipping world is to be reckoned by the profit gathered from periodical advances in *practice.*

Theoretical investigation may sometimes translate an existing state of affairs. The conclusions to which it then points are only broad in their nature, and not to be prized more highly than the dictates of good judgement.

It has been said that the science covers only a fraction of the factors influencing performance. Resistance, for example, one of the most vital considerations, refuses to be quoted by exact expression. The manner in which different forms negotiate the seas, the telling swing of weight, the division of rig and other primary practical considerations so completely outrank the few specialties dealt with by science, that it cannot rank with the techniques devised from practical exploitation.

In face of these facts, the science can only be viewed as a third expression of form.

The model is one, the plans comprise the second. Either taken off and manipulated by the formulae of naval architecture make up the third. This is a picture of the vessel in figures, as the block is in relief and the plans in projection.

To a limited extent the third representation may convey supplemental information upon points not immediately disclosed by the model or the draft. More than this it is futile to expect. (Oh, yeah? I was about to mentally jump on Mr. Kunhardt when he ended up with the following paragraph.—W.F.)

Experiments upon models, however, are of a different nature. To them we may turn for results obtained from the elements in joint action. They are competitive tests on a small scale, just as yacht racing is in a larger way, with the advantage of multiplied opportunities for observation and varying upon conditions. Confidence in experimental deductions is well founded if the circumstances surrounding large vessels are carefully produced in miniature.

There, laid out 87 years ago, is an evaluation of how much Kunhardt felt may be assigned to art, and how much to science. When I finished reading it, nodding my head in agreement with parts, and shaking it negatively at others, I found myself realizing that here was a carefully reasoned, logically stated philosophy on naval architecture that commanded deep respect for its penetration and honesty. For awhile I was suspended in a vacuum. Kunhardt seemed to have shot down Mother Love and apple pie.

Then, the perspective of time takes charge of reason. One knows instinctively that Kunhardt has to be placed in the bracket of his historical time frame.

As to Art, Kunhardt is right. As to Science, he is, in light of today's engineering knowledge, naive and wrong. Kunhardt could not foresee flight in machines, nor fire moved from a boiler to directly inside an internal combustion engine, nor color pictures and voices transmitted without wires, let alone carriages without horses or shooting men to the moon.

How then can we assign values to what he says? When confronted by complex decisions, I fall back on the words of Ralph Waldo Emerson, who pointed out that as to methods, there are a million and then some, but principles are few. He went on to say that the man who knew how would always have work, but the man who knew principles would know *why*, and would always be the other fellow's boss. Mr. Kunhardt was discussing methods, not principles. It has been the work of science to establish principles—a vast body of information to assist the judgement factor Kunhardt continually refers to.

Older men, engaged in serious design work of their own, or working in drafting rooms, will know the plus and minus values of Kunhardt's analysis. They can apply his thinking to their own knowledge. But for the gifted young noodler who aspires to become a naval architect or yacht designer, to swallow Kunhardt whole would be what today's vernacular terms a cop-out. Kunhardt's position swings more heavily to the "dump-her-in-the-drink" kind of designing that paints waterlines after harbor scum has formed. His is the rationalization frequently heard from those with minimal mathematical skills. Aligning one's self with this thinking is, today, just blind stupidity.

I would advise young men to get all the schooling they can get in the designing game. Books are one source of knowledge in the art and science of boat design, but even better are the courses offered by mail by the Institute of Yacht Design of Brooklin, Maine, or the Westlawn School of Yacht Design of Greenwich, Conn. These schools have several thousand students in all parts of the world. Westlawn carries study far enough so that college credits can be offered should a young man want to get into the heavy industrial end of the game, designing big ships, by going to college at MIT, the University of Michigan, Webb, or several other fine schools.

So much for advice. The argument as to how much of yacht and boat design is art, and how much is science will rage on the Hot Stove Circuit as long as boats are built.

My F.B.I. (Farmer's Bump of Inquisitiveness) brought me to Kunhardt's old book. I have felt it better to air Kunhardt's accurate analysis than to quietly fold the volume, and then to consign it to some musty shelf where old age and darkness would turn the book into a mouse's outhouse.

3

C.G. Davis

The name Charles G. Davis has appeared frequently in recent marine articles. All references seem to frame his name as the Original Authority on nostalgic boat matters. Davis is quoted so often on boatbuilding, or is referred to as being the designer of some "first" boat, or is so often mentioned as the arbiter of marine lore in the golden age of sail, that his image shapes up as a Marine Moses chipping The Law from stone tablets.

Who was he? What did he do? When? Where? Why? Pull up a chair—

Charles Gerard Davis was the first of the great tramp naval architects who, during the '90s and the first two or three decades of this century, moved from shop to shop doing layout work and technical calculations that others couldn't. This was in the day before stock boats were built. It was an era of the steam train, of isolated but numerous watering spas, and of many localized boatbuilding concerns. Each hull was a custom creation, and if the vessel amounted to anything, she needed special ministrations. As a result, itinerant naval architects were highly respected journeymen with territory staked out in a romantic calling.

These men generally were seamen and ex-boatbuilders turned designers, then writers, and in some cases, editors. There has been a surprising number of such men: William Atkin, Bill Crosby, Edson B. Schock, Tom Day, Charles D. Mower, William Washburn Nutting, Morris Whitaker, Fred Goeller, Sam Rabl, and John G. Hanna are a few who come to mind as being members of The Old School. All had been tramps of the spline. Each of these men had the rare gift of infusing the printed page with a high quotient of boat yearning.

C.G. Davis at 45 stands on the porch of his Brooklyn home with "all the *Rudders* from the first issue."

The mightiest of these itinerant naval architects was Charles G. Davis, who was the first to knock down much of the sham that creeps into print. He brought a driving wind of reality into early design thinking and was the first to do a thorough job of teaching others "how to build."

The Davis gift of breathing life into drawings with a few slashes of India ink even today stands out to prove that true art is timeless. The sketches shown here attest to this, and the signature "C.G. Davis" stands for great economy of line. No man before his time, and no man I know of since, has exceeded him in the ability to capture the essence of a complicated marine picture in so few strokes.

I can tell you about him with fairly close knowledge, because my drafting room tracks crossed his on occasion. At one time I worked at his drafting table. I had access to sheaves of his early drawings—Davis originals, right in my own hands! I have even heard his voice, but I never met the man.

Davis was born in Poughkeepsie in 1870. In 1884, when only 14 years of age, he and his older brother Bill Davis bought a 15-foot centerboarder on which he erected a cabin and to which he attached

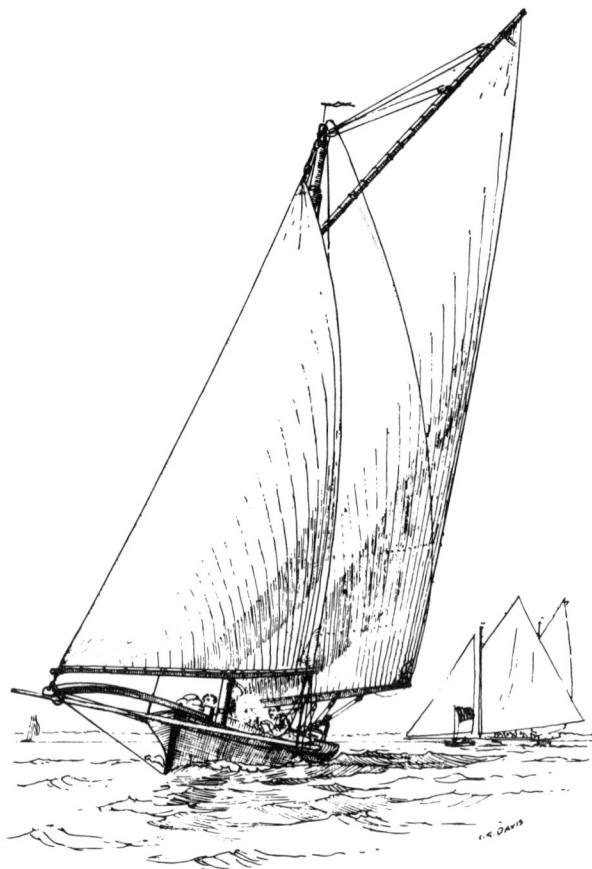

The sandbagger *Rambler.*

the name *Porgie.* The two brothers cruised the Hudson and the western end of Long Island Sound for a couple of years, and then bought a famous old sandbagger, formerly the *Addie M* but re-named *Rambler,* and extensively raced in the gung-ho fashion reported as being competitive to the point of bloodshed by men who wrote of the sport in that day.

The lines of *Rambler* were taken off by Davis and appeared authentically in his hand-lettered book, *The A B C of Yacht Design.* The entire format of this book—all of every page of it—was printed on letterpress as engraved from Davis's own hand lettering. The drawings and illuminations were in his own inimitable style. It is from this early book, now treasured in my library, that I can infer some of his history, or lift it from his own statements.

In 1889, at age 19, Charlie Davis went to work in the No. 1 Broadway office of William Gardner, a Clydeside Scotsman who was the leader in designing those big, opulent steam yachts for New York's Four Hundred.

In Gardner's office for three years, Davis had old John Harvey at his elbow. Harvey was an Englishman, a steam yacht designer and a deep hull cutter buff. From Harvey, Davis learned design processes. Davis's sketch of Harvey—all tail and vest and rumpled shirtsleeves held up by garter bands—is a classic in depicting the flavor of early design offices.

Davis about this time had a fill-in job with T.R. Webber, who had a boatshop at 152nd Street and the Hudson River. At that time, 152nd Street was up-country, and the sketches of Webber's shop show a few shacks in the bushes at river's edge. Webber moved to New Rochelle, and Davis began to do some designing for him.

The stint in Gardner's office had affected Charlie's eyesight, and the sea was calling. In 1892 he signed on as an A.B. before the mast in the bark *James A. Wright*, out of Boston, for a voyage around Cape Horn to Chile. Any such voyage is packed with adventure, and Davis was to make good capital of it in stories he wrote years later for *Rudder* and *Yachting* in the 1930s.

Upon his return from Chile, Davis went back to work for William Gardner. After another year in this office, again the call of the sea proved too strong, and he shipped for one more year to the West Indies in the *J. Percy Bartram*. (Davis kept copious notes on the construction and rigging of these last days of commercial sail, and in 1926 he gathered these together and published them in a book put out by the Marine Historical Society of Salem, Mass., as a guide for ship modelers. The drawings are very detailed.)

When he returned from the West Indies voyage, Davis designed two sloops for Tom Webber, the *Dragoon* and the *Hussar*, which he raced for their owners on the western end of Long Island Sound. Some time around 1898 he joined Thomas Fleming Day's staff on *Rudder*, and was for several years that magazine's design editor. Here he got out the skimming dish Lark, which could trim the socks off anything floating. She was a simple boat, for home building, and she got her speed from square feet of sail—lots of feet, plus fast feet in the cockpit.

On a length of 16 feet with 6 feet of beam and 1 foot of draft, Lark had a 6-ounce sail 17 feet 6 inches on the foot, 10 feet 6 inches luff, 9 feet 9 inches head, and 23 feet leech, with 19 feet 10 inches on the diagonal. This figures at 202 square feet! Thousands of Larks were built, and you saw them on every lake and protected waterway and sound. Not until Snipe came along in 1928 was any class to eclipse Lark in numbers built. Lark was designed in approximately the year 1900.

I owned one once. I am here to say that if the crew of any marine museum who wants to recreate the past by building a Lark will build her, they'll get a sailboat ride for which they will have to tie their hats on! They'll have some respect for the hair on Grandpa's chest, I tell you.

PLANS OF SMALL RACING CAT-BOAT LARK

66 FOOT LAUNCH DESIGNED BY THE HUNTINGTON MFG Co.
NEW ROCHELLE N.Y.

Back in 1905, this Davis-designed launch was considered fine for afternoon sunbathing. All oil is in the engine lubricators, and the throttle is set to "start." On 36 hp she'd do 12 knots. The engine was air starting.

Davis's work tenure from early *Rudder* designing days onward can only be guessed at. He appears as doing designing for Elco over in Bayonne, N.J., around 1901, and it was in the Elco design office that I discovered his initials carved into the drafting table at which I sat and worked, and it was in that office where I discovered a sheaf of Davis tracings at the very bottom of an old tracing file. They had been buried there nearly 40 years! Among them was the tracing for his *Alcatorda,* of mention in his *A B C* book, and which along with others I promptly sent to the blueprint shop.

That he was a resident of Bayonne and a member of the Bayonne Yacht Club is mentioned in an anecdote he recalls of the burning of that yacht club, and with it his favorite catboat *Harbinger.* In about five well-chosen ink lines Davis shows the bones of the smoldering *Harbinger.*

In an attempt to pin down this Electric Launch tour of Davis, a few years ago I phoned Elco's dear old Skipper Irwin Chase at Deep River, Connecticut. Chase remembered Davis.

"Old Charlie?" he chuckled. "Sure, I remember him well. He was a writer, you know. Wrote and designed for the magazines." This, I allowed, I did know.

"He used to run our Boston showroom," the Skipper went on. "We had an Elco showroom in Boston selling electric boats." This was news, indeed.

"His widow is still living down in Fort Lauderdale," Chase stated, and if that was true, and she was Charles Davis's age, she must have then been 102 years old. I couldn't believe this, but, through a cooperative man in Fort Lauderdale, I did discover there was a Davis family living at the northeast arm of the town. No one could be raised by phone. This seems to have been an authentic lead, but the matter was not then pursued further.

From about 1903 to 1906, Charles G. Davis's work appears as coming from the shops of the Huntington Manufacturing Company of New Rochelle. I asked Bill Crosby, past editor of *Rudder,* about this at one time, and Bill told me he understood that Webber had been bought out by Larry Huntington and, with Davis doing the designing, quite a trade had been worked up. Huntington had a reputation as a great designer, but all of the drawings I ever saw that were credited to Huntington were either signed "C.G. Davis" or were patently done in his unique hand.

To judge from published work attributed to the Huntington Manufacturing Company that appears in print dated from 1904 to 1907, Charlie Davis was then 36 years of age or thereabouts—fully mature and in his prime of creativity. I show here the plans for a 66-foot "launch" designed by him for Huntington in 1905. Long, lean, and slinky, with what was then termed a "compromise" stern, such a boat would drive easily without fuss and would be very comfortable.

I know it to be true that the original and famous little *Tamerlane,* sailed by Huntington to win an early Bermuda Race, was not Huntington's work, but was drawn by Davis. *Tamerlane* appears in Davis's *A B C of Yacht Design.*

One rare Davis creation, which is an honest-to-gosh canoe yawl, is the double-ender entered by the Huntington Manufacturing Company in a 1906 design contest. In the next chapter, I show the whole plan as being an ultimate consensus of sea-faring, sea-keeping men who were designing at a time when sail was used to *move* boats and not run up to please photographers.

There is no doubt about this boat being a yawl. There is no doubt about her being a canoe-sterned type. And any boatbuilder familiar with wooden construction can see that she was planned as to frame and scantling by boatbuilders who knew wood and where to place it, scarph it, and fasten it. The plan is top study. For sheer sailing versatility, I would place this boat ahead of any canoe yawl I know of, including Herreshoff's Rozinante, because this little doll has rags to move her and a bottom to hold her up. Moreover, she represents the summation of development in a day when sail was sail.

The first big bang on the powerboat horizon was produced by Davis in his *Pop Gun,* a dory-type bottom designed for *Motor Boat* sometime prior to 1909. The plans of this launch appear in *Nine Motorboats and How to Build Them,* published by *Motor Boat* about 1910. For 15 years thereafter this book was the bible of backyarders.

Along about this time Davis was working for *Motor Boat,* and in the June 10, 1910, issue he published a design for a little catboat-hulled raised-deck cruiser called *Beaver.* Another of his *Motor Boat* designs was for a 28-foot cruiser called *Mollyhawk,* which had an unusual steamship-type stern. When John G. Hanna first broke into print in *Motor Boat* in 1919 with his *Pelican,* a similar but improved idea, Hanna wrote:

Altogether, I have bedevilled poor *Molly* until Charley Davis would scarcely recognize the child of his brain if he should meet her. In truth (my) *Pelican* is altogether a new boat. Nevertheless, acknowledgement is due the man whose plan furnished the germ of her growth. And I might as well say right now for the benefit of new hands—the old ones already know it—that Davis is one of the greatest influences for good in the history of American yachting.

A hundred years after he is dead we will build him a monument and pass resolutions—at present we are too busy criticizing his designs and calling him a bit behind the times. 'Twas ever thus with the real benefactors of the race.

Popgun, Beaver, and *Mollyhawk,* designed by C.G. Davis for *Nine Motorboats.*

FROM MY OLD BOAT SHOP

The 10 years from 1935 to 1945 register a blank for the Davis output. At that time I was conscious of his absence and had a back-of-the-noggin resolve to learn about it because the man had been The Oracle in my boyhood.

In March of 1947 I was on business in New York, president of a flourishing manufacturing company that had happily made a handsome bundle, and I was able to afford a gift for Davis, which, out of gratitude for his having helped me in earlier apprentice years, I was anxious to deliver to him. From an editor friend on one of the yachting magazines, I got his address. I was motivated by the noblest emotions: behind all art there stands a man, and great artists in any line always have lives that excite interest. They are great salesmen as well as great creators, and to most men the study of how their talents were formed makes one's own insight richer.

I had hoped to elicit from Mr. Davis some dates that would authentically throw his life and work into correct perspective. I located Mr. Davis at his home over on Long Island. This was by telephone in an effort to effect a meeting. I told him I had some blueprints of his early work and wanted to deliver them, and that I had another surprise for him. I did not tell him it was a respectable gift of cash.

Davis's voice was resigned, almost grumpy, deep timbered and very negative. He was approaching 80, hated the way the world was going, wasn't well, and did not want to see me. This fact I was forced to respect. After being rebuffed, I felt reservations about pressing anything on him. Prudently, I put the contents of a fat envelope back in my wallet and tried to let the matter slide.

But hell hath no hurt like loyalty spurned!

I was too old to nurse notions of going out to a garden to eat worms. So spitefully I cooked up a spectacular idea by which His Eminence could be guaranteed expenses for a splendid burial. He could sell tickets to his funeral, by Golly, and his leap from a high building would put the show on the road. Conclusively!

The mood soon passed. Sober reflection assessed that it was not the grumpy, aging man for whom I bore the real affection. It was for the images that had been conjured forth in my own mind by his work! Thus reconciled to reality, I began reflecting on the Sunset Slope that carries all great talent away. Somehow, the boat business is more callous than other callings about giving credit to living men. The game's great professionals have to die before they are lauded.

I like what Hanna wrote of the game's rewards. From it Charles G. Davis—wherever he is—might take comfort:

The boat game can't be better summed up than in the one sentence, "We might have made more money in some other game, but think of the fun we'd have missed." Conditions in that respect have not changed much today.

I know several young men who are struggling and starving to get a foothold in various lines of boating right now. I have given them much sound advice, telling them that the same amount of work or less would have made them rich in many other lines.

But it didn't do any good. They all applied the thumb of scorn to the nose of contempt and wiggled the fingers of derision at me, saying, "Why didn't you take your own advice, Wise Guy?"

To that I could make no answer. After all, they may be right. There are a million kinds of work in the world, each and all returning some money, but only one kind for any certain man that pays the richer gold of fulfilled desire, of captivated interest, of contentment that obliterates weariness. Why shouldn't he choose that one kind?

We'll stay dead a long time after we die, and no amount of money will do us any good in that long time, but maybe happy memories will. They certainly help a lot in this life, and can't be lost or stolen.

These words of great wisdom were written 50 years ago. They seem to me to have applied to the life of Charles G. Davis. I do not know when he passed from this earth, shedding designing's parsimonious coils, but I trust he rests well. There is gratitude in the hearts of many men now living who know of the work he did. The truth of his great art lives on in print.

4

Jenny Wren, *C.G. Davis* 22-Foot Yawl

Sailors who are born with a natural sense of the sea are hungry these days for the sweet boat, the graceful boat, the kind of boat that once was understood by everybody as belonging to her own national watery locale. That kind of indigenous boat is so rarely seen nowadays in the ad-oriented popular press that the young pamphleteers of the boat-publishing world term any type that is strange to them a "character boat." They apply this asinine term to almost anything that is not a stylized Clorox bottle with an engine in it.

The correct word is "traditional."

All traditional boats have character. A good one is *always* good. Such boats are timeless.

A prize-winning example of timeless hull sweetness in traditional form is the little 21-foot 8-inch overall canoe-sterned yawl shown here, designed by that revered old master, Charles Gerard Davis.

She has been resurrected, dimensioned, and preserved for boat-building posterity by Yours Truly, weston farmer. You'll notice I keep the caps off my name when in the same company with C.G. Davis. The resurrection has been a labor of love.

In 1905 or thereabout—a lifetime ago—Davis entered this little two-sticker in one of *Rudder's* design competitions conducted by editor Thomas Fleming Day. She was originally designed by Davis for Larry Huntington of the Huntington Manufacturing Company, boatbuilders at New Rochelle, N.Y., when Davis was working in Huntington's employ. Charlie Davis thought that this design of his might win honorable mention if entered in the *Rudder* contest. She won handily, and the Davis drawings were presented in *Rudder*.

Chas. G. Davis' 21'-8" OA Canoe-sterned Yawl -1905
Scaled & redrawn 1976 by Weston Farmer

In writing about the work of Charles G. Davis for the *National Fisherman* article reprinted in the preceding chapter, I had remembered this fetching design, so I dug through an archeological collection of clippings and came up with the old magazine page. I rearranged the drawings, which were originally only 4 or 5 inches long in printed form, into a montage and I included them with the article.

The yawl looked awfully sweet to me; she gave me the kind of restored faith one might get from seeing a beautiful young girl among a clutch of hard-bitten streetwalkers.

She must have looked as sweet to Dave Getchell, editor of the *National Fisherman,* because when Dave saw the drawings he relaxed the frugal Yankee eye he keeps cocked at his publisher's budget nickel. He let go two of the four hobbles he keeps on the legs of the U.S. Buffalo by giving this little yawl some paper and ink—that is to say, he gave her generous space.

The response to that story about Davis was electrifying. Within two weeks my mail was up to flood stage. Among all the letters were offers from exactly 15 different men who separately demanded building plans for this singlehander at almost any price.

But I had no plans. The Davis drawings had been reproduced with no dimensions except one: a measurement scale below the tiny sail plan. Her original lines were drawn to show hull shape; the buttock lines were useless on a loft floor. It was a pictorial exposition, probably planned that way by C.G. Davis, because never published were any offsets from which the boat could be recreated.

Too bad! So many men wanted to build and own her.

Now comes a turn in the story. A Californian, Kenneth McMahon, who lives in Anaheim, not too far north from the one-time Alhambra location of Clarence ("Newporter") Ackerman's old Hi-n-Dri Cooperative boatshop, wrote to me again about this boat last winter.

I gave Mr. McMahon my standard answer. I said again I had no "plans"; that is, no offsets or vital construction measurements. Since he said he could work from embryonic sketches and a table of offsets, and because I was and am loaded with design work with my time sold out for a full year, I wanted to discourage the request.

But, thinking that only an afternoon's work would be involved—in fact, not thinking it through at all—I named Mr. McMahon a figure for an offset table calculated to send him screaming to the top of the green Verdugo Hills. He called my bluff and sent me a bank draft for the price of a good outboard motor. He not only did that, but he said, "Take your time." He also said that I could make building prints available to others after I had done the work for him.

I was caught in an irreversible situation, facing reality. To get an offset table, I would have to do a proper set of lines suitable for lofting. One darned thing started leading to another. I would also have to produce a sail plan to go with the work. I would have to weigh the boat as Davis originally drew her in order to subtract the 1,500 pounds of iron keel he specified, so as to get the scantling weights and check the waterline. This would be needed to see whether C.G. Davis had recommended or had needed inboard ballast. (Note the correct word is inboard, and not "interior," which is a pamphleteer's word.) In short, I had unwittingly swallowed a complete re-design assignment.

With a large gulp, I sez to meself, I says, says I, "Here we go again, old kid. Running up Charity Alley, a lane known to all old delineators. Tie your hat on and get to work."

The result is that I have produced a set of lines supplied with as accurate a table of offsets as can be scaled, but which needs lofting to fair out. I have also drawn a scaled sail plan, which is readable, along with spar sizes shown, and the dimensions of foot, luff, and leech for each sail. Mr. McMahon felt he could do his building from these drawings if I sent these full-scale 3/4-inch to one-foot prints, and an enlarged repro of Davis's original scantling plan, brought up to the same scale.

Designed by C.G. Davis

This hull has a balanced metacentric shelf!

Offset dimensions are to outside of ⅞" planking. Believed accurate. Not guaranteed.

HALF-BREADTHS from ₵ — Ft, Ins ¿ 8THS										
Station	1	2	3	4	5	6	7	8	9	10
Sheer	1:5·4	2·5·3	3·1·5	3·6·3	3·8·5	3·8·5	3·6·2	3·1·2	2·4·3	1·1·4
Keel	0·1·4	Taper	to	0·2·4	0·2·4	0·2·4	0·2·4	0·2·4	0·2·4	0·1·4
W.L.A	1·1·0	2·1·6	3·5·7	3·8·4	3·8·4	3·6·2	3·1·2	2·4·0	0·10·4
W.L.B	0·9·0	1·10·3	2·9·0	3·4·2	3·4·0	3·8·4	3·6·2	3·1·2	2·2·0	0·4·4
L.W.L	0·3·6	1·4·6	2·4·0	2·11·6	3·4·0	3·6·0	3·4·6	2·11·2	1·7·0	—
L.W.C	—	0·8·6	1·7·4	2·4·1	2·9·6	2·11·5	2·9·0	1·10·6	0·4·0	—
W.L.D	—	—	0·9·0	1·4·4	1·10·0	1·11·6	1·7·5	0·7·4	—	—
W.L.E	—	—	—	0·4·2	0·9·2	0·10·0	0·7·0	—	—	—

HEIGHTS ABOVE BASE, FT, INS, ¿ 8THS										
Station	1	2	3	4	5	6	7	8	9	10
Sheer	6·5·2	6·2·2	5·11·2	5·9·6	5·8·0	5·8·1	5·8·2	5·9·2	5·11·3	6·2·2
Keel	3·8·6	2·9·2	1·10·7	1·2·1	0·8·2	0·5·6	0·5·0	0·6·0	1·3·6	4·5·0
Rabbet	3·10·6	3·1·3	2·7·2	2·3·3	2·1·2	2·1·1	2·3·6	2·9·0	3·5·4	4·4·0
Butt.I	4·4·4	3·5·3	2·11·4	2·7·4	2·4·6	2·4·1	2·6·3	3·0·2	3·7·4	4·8·4
Butt.II	5·8·6	3·11·3	3·4·0	2·11·2	2·8·4	2·8·1	2·10·2	3·3·3	3·10·6	
Butt.III		4·8·4	4·5·0	3·3·3	3·0·6	3·0·2	3·2·0	3·6·2	4·4·0	
Butt.IV		4·5·1	3·8·2	3·4·4	3·4·3	3·5·5	3·10·4			
Butt.V		—	4·6·0	3·11·4	3·10·0	3·1·7				

All waterlines 6" spacing

All buttocks 8" spacing

Scale ¾" = 1 Ft

Keel, 1500 lbs. Iron

Siding of Keel, 2½

This hull has a balanced metacentric shelf!

I can now tell the fellows who wanted plans earlier that, in all fairness to them, and to all concerned, I'll mail them this bundle if they care to reimburse me for my costs, my time, and my trouble. I put the matter this way to discourage mail that is merely curious, which is time-consuming and hence costly to me.

I never know what price to put on this kind of share-the-fun service. You buy mailing tubes and prints, and shag eight miles to the post office for weighing, because different men live in different postal zones. You can't stockpile prints, because you do not know whether one set or 20 will be sold. So each share-the-fun service is a custom proposition.

It seems to me that the information ought to be worth the price of a weekend bag of groceries, so with that target I set here a price of $30 on the theory that a magnet will collect more iron from filings, in the aggregate, than if it were aimed at a 50-pound anchor.

My address: 18970 Azure Road, Wayzata, Minn. 55391. Allow 10 days.

Davis did not contemplate inboard power. At the time this boat was drawn, nobody had heard of an outboard "kicker." Probably one should be hung on a bracket. Five to seven horses will get you home when the wind goes pixie on you, dying just as you make for port on an ebb tide. One thing I can tell you about her is that she may not need a kicker. She will be a terrific ghoster.

This little yawl was designed in a day when men used sail, and sail alone, to slop about on the ocean and to make port. I have been struck with a number of hidden qualities in swimming about in this boat's innards with planimeter and cubed ordinates. One is that C.G. Davis, being a famous skipper himself, knew how much canvas to spread to the wind, because in his writings he always made much ado about the proposition that *weight* of wind, caught by square feet of sail, was the best prescription for forward motion in a sailing yacht.

Davis lived before anyone had heard the term "aspect ratio." It has been my experience that you sail with sail, not aspect ratio, which is a term borrowed from later aerodynamical research. I think this little yawl will sail the britches off some of these raked-forward bottles of today that seem to have knife-blade "aspect ratio" rigs that look like they were pulling at a hull of reluctant Jell-O being dragged through a sea of glue.

Another quality that was hidden is the fact that this boat has a nearly perfect metacentric shelf. I went into this out of an instinct for peering at the backside of the moon to assay the quality of green cheese said to be there. Years ago I had corresponded much with Dr. T. Harrison Butler, noted British designer of tabloid yachts, about the Turner Theory of balanced metacentric planes in achieving self-steering, docile boats. Admiral Turner also gave much to work with, because at that time I was working on the West Coast designing much in sail. Edson B. Schock had put me on to the development.

Thus, I had the curiosity to carry along with Davis's work, and a cursory check, which isn't difficult if you understand it, proved that Davis had achieved in this boat a nearly perfect, balanced metacentric shelf, working by his intuition. I believe this boat will be self-steering. Her symmetry should provide it.

About the only sop to modernization that I feel might be acceptable even to Charlie Davis, were he living today, would be the addition of one more strake of topside planking, say 4 to 6 inches—no more. In C.G. Davis's day, hull windage was a sin. Sailors who depended completely on sail were sensitive to the amount of time they'd have to spend in making leeway. Thus, they kept their hull profiles low.

Today's 18-foot sailing condominiums do not seem to worry about leeway—the jolly afternoon crews in these craft term leeway "going sideways" and think it normal. So, maybe we can cope with a little sin, boys, and add one topside strake.

Another thing I think Charlie would not object to would be to knock off the coaming at deck level on his little bathtub cockpit, making a squateroo of all that nice aft quarterdeck. Something other than the old-fashioned bathtub might be in order. It looks penitential.

But there we go, Mates! 'Tis the devil in every man, wanting to lay hands on perfection.

The secret of this boat's grace is to be found in the natural sweep of good boatbuilding wood. This has been bent to God's own natural curves and formed into balanced shape by one of those old-time men who learned his design art in the old-time way—by an apprenticeship of four years in a shop, years at sailing and journeyman boatbuilding, then on to the design board at big league designing. That was Charlie Davis's route.

The Davis brand of skill is perceived at a glance. Men who went his route always turned out lovely hulls because they understood materials, knew what could be done with them, and what the sea wanted of the stuff from which boats are built.

The above observations are a prelude to cranking up my right leg for a well-aimed kick: This boat's art is in wood, so please don't succumb to plasterer's pyorrhea and dream of building her in some pet fad you've embraced such as foam sandwich, fairy-seement, sawdust in aspic, or hard boiled hen eggs. Weights in such cookery seldom agree with wooden construction and are murder for an amateur to control. If you want home cooking, stay home. Wood is the right thing.

Here is a bill of scantlings as lettered on Davis's sectional plan:

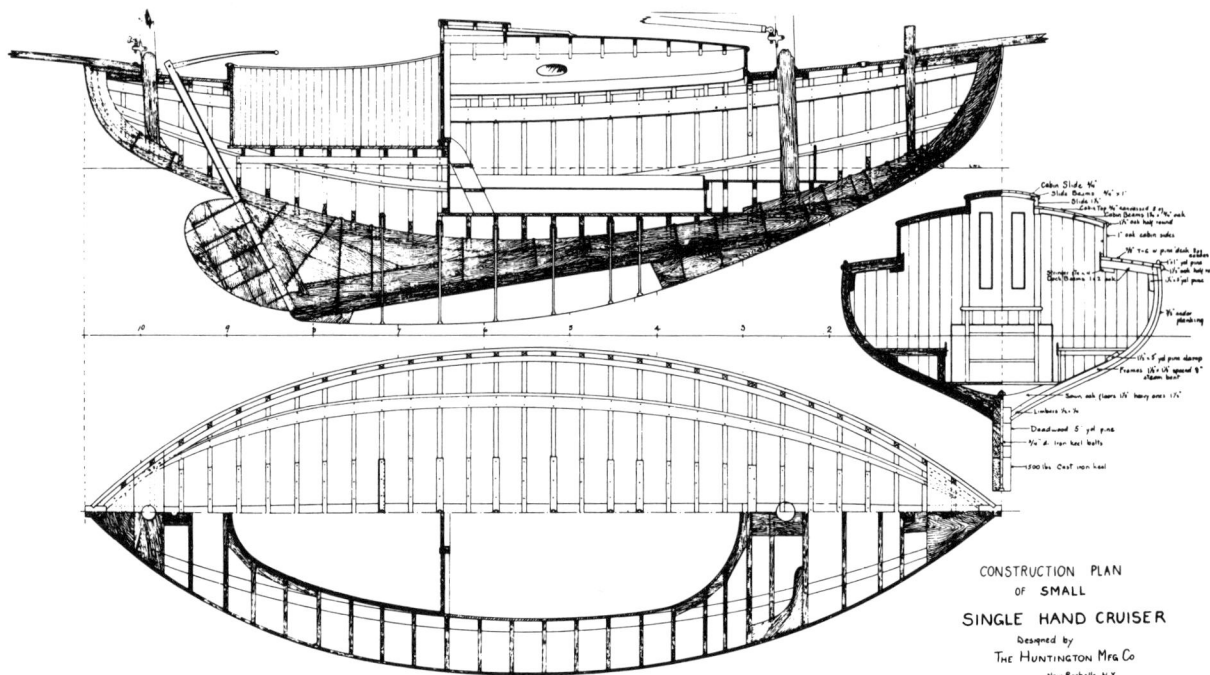

CONSTRUCTION PLAN
OF SMALL
SINGLE HAND CRUISER
Designed by
The Huntington Mfg Co
New Rochelle N.Y.

Starting at the top, and going around clockwise, we read that the sliding hatch is decked 3/4 inch. Slide beams, 3/4 inch by 1 inch; slide, 1-1/2 inches. Cabin top decked 3/4 inch, canvas 8 ounces. Cabin beams, oak, sided 3/4 inch, molded 1-1/2 inches. Trim, 1-1/2 inches half-round oak. Cabin sides, 1 inch oak. Decking 7/8 inch by 3 inches T & G white pine, 8-ounce canvas. Toe rail, 1 inch by 1 inch oak. Cockpit harpin, 1-1/4 inches by 4 inches yellow pine. Deck beams, 1 inch by 2 inches oak. Sheer molding, 1-1/2 inches half-round oak. Planking, 7/8 inch cedar. Bilge clamp, 1-1/2 inches by 5 inches yellow pine. Frames steam bent 1-1/2 inches by 1-1/2 inches white oak. Sawn oak floors, 1-1/8 inches, heavy ones 1-1/2 inches white oak. Limbers 1/2 inch by 1/4 inch. Deadwood, 5 inches yellow pine. Keel, 5 inches oak. Stem and horn timbers, 3-1/2 inches white oak. Keel bolts, 3/4 inch galvanized iron over burrs. Keel casting, 1,500 pounds iron.

This boat was termed a canoe yawl in her original exposure. I think a more correct description would be "canoe-sterned yawl." But we can't go on calling her "Charles G. Davis's 21-foot 8-inch canoe-sterned yawl" in every reference. What to name her?

As I write these lines, it is noon of a Saturday in early June, lovely with the promise of spring—a day when birds sing music to the burgeoning of the green. Outside my window, perking about on the wren house, is the summer's newly arrived tenant. This wren is a feisty little cuss, about the size of my thumb, warbling like Caruso for his soon-to-arrive bride. If a human could produce such melody in direct proportion to weight, he could be heard from Seattle to the coast of Maine. What do you say we name this canoe-sterned little yawl *Jenny Wren*?

She sings of Davis's great art. I think Charlie would like that.

36

5

John Hanna's Foam

Escape to the romantic reaches of the sea has never seemed more alluring than in these troubled times. Out on the briny, snouting through the blue just south of Cancer, clouds there sail serenely white before the wind, and a man need not worry about the human rat-race as reported by the boob tube.

With his own vessel around him, a man can scud before the trade winds, coast down the face of combers where dolphins leap in golden flashes, where skittering squadrons of flying fish plop into patches of Sargasso weed lying yellow in the sun, fallow as wheat ripening for harvest. New ports, new lands, new scenes are ahead.

Though this ancient call never seemed so strong as now to the land-stranded sailor, there is another side to the picture that some dreamers do not know.

It rains out there, often blows to beat hell, and there is fog and there are shoals and dangers. A man needs a vessel designed for the work—one that will take care of herself and of him on a dark night. Hence that incessant search for a hull and rig that has been tried by time and by the experience of others.

I believe I have found just such a vessel. She is *Foam,* developed out of Slocum's *Spray* by the Sage of Dunedin, old John G. Hanna, who led an introspective life and made his way as a loner, living by the sea and designing boats just for the sea.

Foam is a husky ketch of medium-to-heavy scantling, rigged for deep sea work and all oceans, carrying a squaresail on her foremast for running before the wind in the Trades. She is 41 feet 9 inches overall, by 32 feet 3 inches waterline, beam of 12 feet 10 inches, a draft of 5

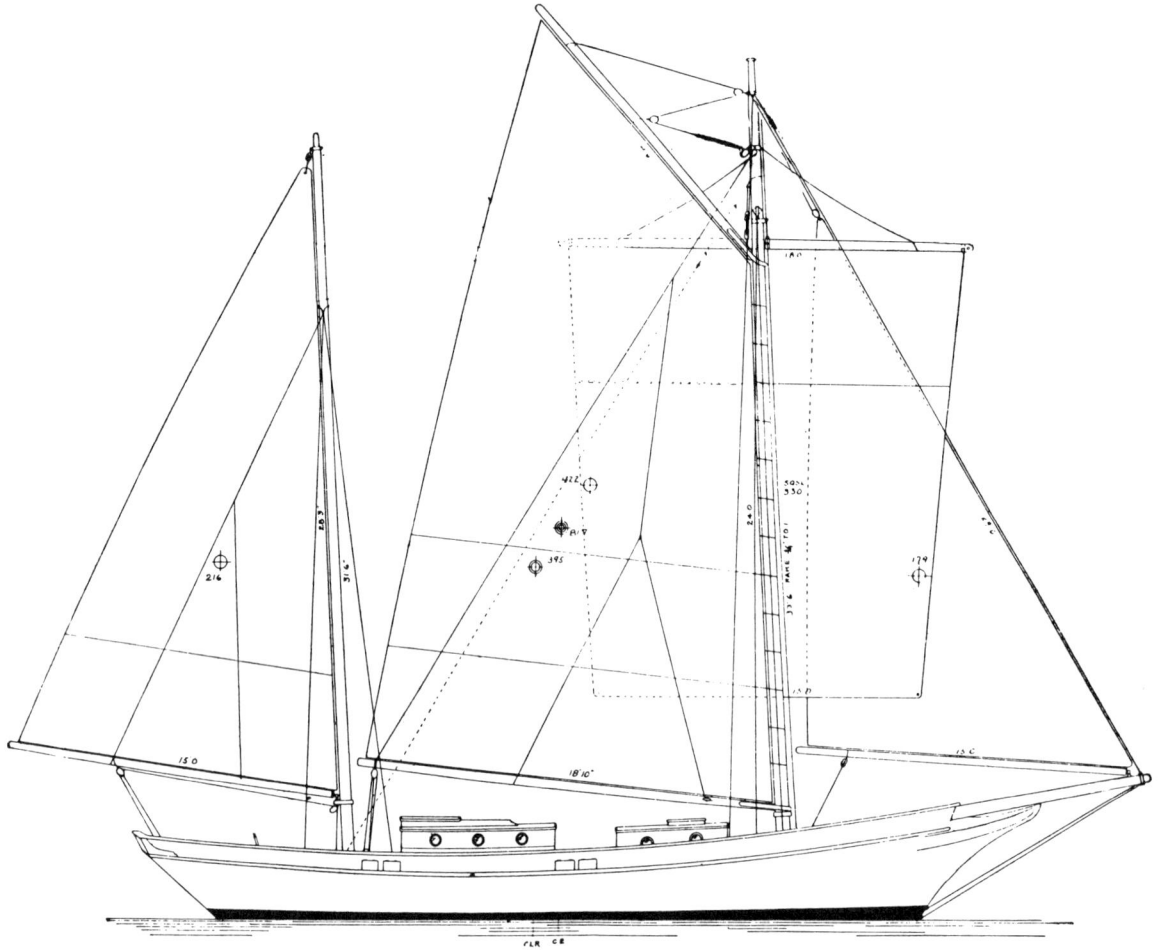

With the *Spray* as a starting point, Hanna evolved the *Foam*.

feet, on a displacement of 35,658 pounds. Hanna designed her to eliminate some of *Spray*'s known faults, pointing up the good qualities of Slocum's craft, and, all in all, to provide a vessel that could go anywhere safely. To attest that he succeeded well, be it known that many *Foam*s have been built the world around. One that I know of is owned by the Smothers Brothers, Tom and Dick, based at Balboa harbor, California.

To refresh the memory of those who dimly know the history of world navigation in small vessels, it was Captain Joshua Slocum, a retired windjammer skipper, who was given an old oyster sloop after he had retired from the sea, and who rebuilt her piece by piece when she was about 75 years old, then fitted her out and made a circumnavigation of the world at the turn of the century. His successful exploit can be picked up in these words written by Thomas Fleming Day, founding editor of *The Rudder*:

38

Captain Slocum was what we may call an uncommon man. He was extremely intelligent, and in his love of roaming and adventure reminded me of the celebrated Moorish traveler, Ibn Batuta, who wandered from Cape Spartel to the Yellow Sea, making friends with white, black and yellow. . . . Slocum, like Batuta, was a friend-maker, and everywhere he went the best of the land welcomed him, bid him to the board, and gave attention, while in his inimitable way he spun yarns of his voyages. . . It was not until he reached this country and anchored in the Port of New York that a welcome was refused and his efforts belittled and ridiculed. The American newspapers, when they deigned to notice his voyage, made fun of his boat and of himself and several more than intimated the story of his single-handed world-circling voyage was a lie.

The Rudder was a small struggling affair, but I at once saw the worth of the Captain's story and came out in strong support of it.

One day he came into the office with the story of his voyage and asked me if we could publish it. I saw at once that the story was worth more than we could afford to pay, and suggested that he take it to one of the large general magazines. He did, and *The Century* bought and published it. Afterwards he brought in the model of *Spray* and Mr. Mower took the lines off as they appear in his book.

Thus occurred the coagulation of effort, persistence, and perception of three men to produce *Sailing Alone Around the World,* the classic first, and still best, literary account of such a voyage. It was Captain Slocum's enterprise, understood by Tom Day, and, technically, preserved in the lines taken off by Charles D. Mower, which resulted in the world learning about it. It was from the lines of the *Spray* that another man sparked continuing analysis of how and why the *Spray* was such an easy ship to sail singlehandedly.

Cipriano Andrade, a well-to-do engineer, patent lawyer, and developer, hired Sam Rabl, a then-struggling young Baltimore ship draftsman, to reduce *Spray* in direct geometric proportion to a length of 25 feet, a length Andrade felt he could afford in producing an all-around small cruiser for Long Island and Chesapeake gunkholing. During the analysis of the *Spray*'s lines as done by C.D. Mower, Andrade and Rabl discovered that all of the *Spray*'s centers fell in one spot: center of buoyancy, lateral plane, and sail effort. Andrade's analysis was published in *The Rudder*.

John G. Hanna became a student of the *Spray* and, knowing that while the old oyster sloop had a most competent hull form, attributed the disappearance of the *Spray* and Slocum in a subsequent voyage to certain faults. About 10 years after Andrade's publication, Hanna was mulling the validity of Andrade's criticism and became seized with the fever to provide rectification. He had felt that the *Spray*'s exorbitant beam and shallow draft had resulted in a flip-over, pumpkinseed capsize, and set about to analyze the *Spray*'s terminal stability.

Hanna found the *Spray* extremely stable up to a point, then found she had almost none. He then was in a dedicated, creative mood, and worked for 22 hours, backing and filling *Spray*'s lines until he had rectified her faults, had added adequacy to her form and to her "yawl sloop" rig, and came up with the ketch *Foam*. The drawings of this effort are shown here. Hanna made out a good case for the result, and I here exhume and excerpt from his presentation in *Motor Boat*, the "old green sheet," now long since discontinued and abandoned to tearful memory. Hanna wrote:

Considering *Spray*'s 46,000 miles of proved performance, she ought to make a pretty good yacht type, what?

For many years I have stood second only to Mr. Cipriano Andrade Jr. as a student and admirer of *Spray*. I immediately dug up my file of *Spray* data and started thinking in high gear, not of *Spray* as herself, but as the basic form of a yacht—an alteration to bring her within limits a yachtsman would consider, and yet keep strictly to her characteristic form and preserve as far as possible her marvelously perfect balance, as proved by Andrade's analysis of all her centers. This question was so alluring that I dusted off the old drawing board at once, grabbed a pencil, and was unable to let go for 22 hours. The results are presented here, simply because the comparison is so striking that I believe anyone interested in sea cruising will find it fascinating.

To begin with, the outstanding drawback of *Spray* for our purpose is her great beam. A beam one-third the overall length is the very most a yachtsman of today can contemplate without fright.

Exclusive of figurehead, *Spray* was 38-1/2 feet overall, and one-third of this is 12 feet 10 inches. So, taking Mr. Andrade's offsets for his one-third reduced *Spray* model, I laid down the lines to 3/4-inch scale, shrinking all half-breadths one-tenth. Thereafter, measuring this drawing with the 1/2-inch scale, I obtained the effect of expansion back to the full length of *Spray* herself, but with 15 inches less beam, preserving the same hull form.

The new lines looked mighty good to me. Still a full-bowed hull according to racing yacht notions, but far less blunt than *Spray*. She still had one drawback from the standpoint of today's notions—light draft. Now deep draft is not necessary for running before the wind. All long distance ocean sailing must be practically all off the wind, since the idea that small boats can get across the ocean by fighting the wind, beating against it instead of seeking and following favorable breezes, is. . . merely an idea in the heads of smooth-water yachtsmen.

Spray had sufficient draft to sail well enough to windward to meet every emergency of 46,000 miles, and at that she had no engine for use in entering harbors, as *Foam* has. Her weakness to windward was not so much a matter of draft as of driving power for her heavy and blunt hull. Give her wind enough to drive her . . . and she was stiff enough to stand up and carry all the sail she needed when other boats were reefed—and she could step out to windward well enough to beat some crack racing boats. There is no use saying she could not do this because there are plenty of men living who saw her when she did do it. . . .

Hanna makes out a pretty good case for *Foam*, does he not? He added a foot of draft, to bring up *Foam*'s lateral plane to 140 square

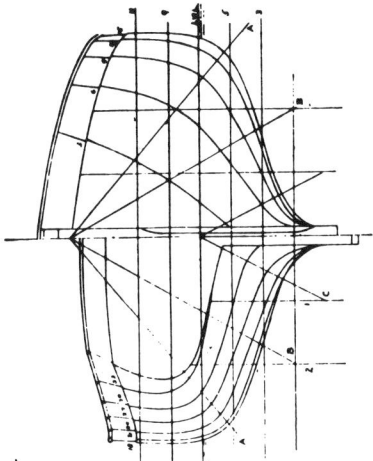

— FOAM —

A MODIFICATION OF CAPT JOSHUA SLOCUM'S SPRAY

LENGTH OA	41'4" W L 37'3"
BEAM	12'10 12'8
DRAFT EX	5'0 DISP 35,658

FREEBOARD INCLUDING RAIL
BOW 5'1' - LEAST 3'6"- STERN 3'8'
AREA LATERAL PLANE 134 76 SQ FT

JOHN G HANNA
DUNEDIN, FLA
MAY 5, 1953.

CENTER OF BUOYANCY
35,658 LBS.
17 AL SHORT TONS
15.94 LONG TONS

CURVE SECTIONAL AREAS

RIGHTING MOMENT
IN FOOT POUNDS

70,000
60,000
50,000
40,000
30,000
20,000
10,000

10 20 30 40 50 60 70 80

DEGREES OF HEEL

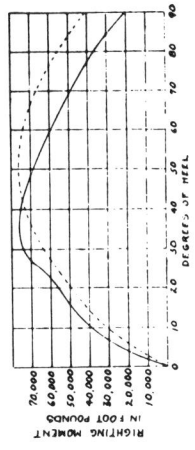

—— ANDRADE'S STABILITY CURVE FOR SLOCUM'S SPRAY
·········· PROBABLE APPROXIMATE FORM OF CURVE FOR FOAM

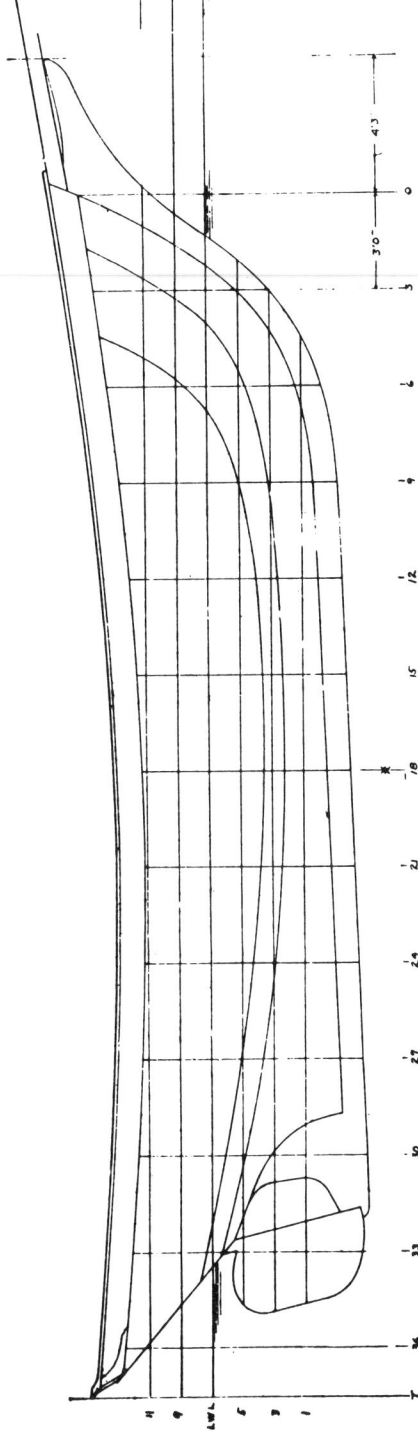

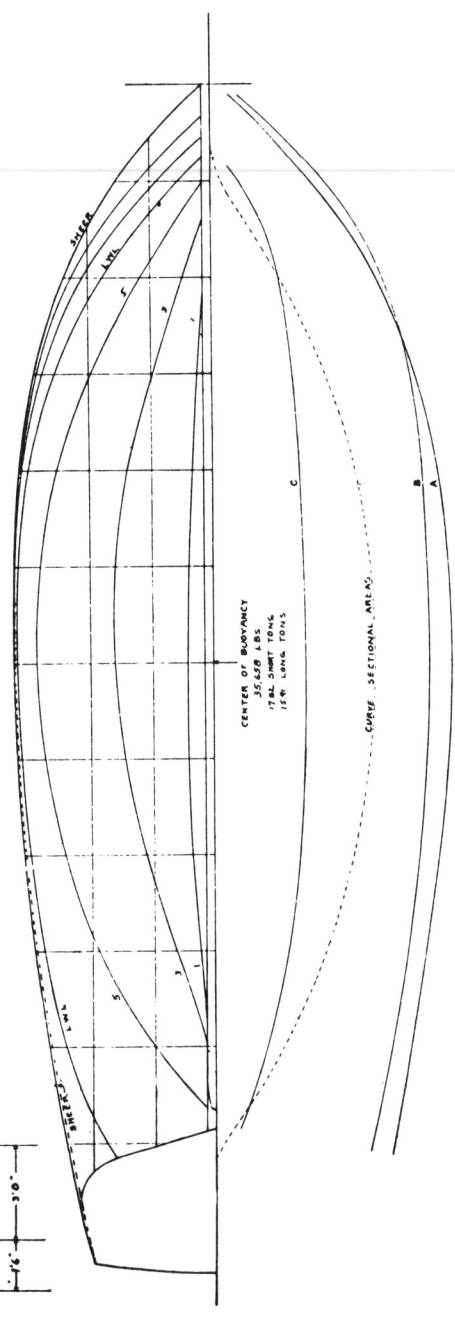

3'0"

3'0"

1'6"

43 0 3 6 9 12 15 18 21 24 27 30 33 36

feet against which he balanced 817 square feet of sail, exclusive of the squaresail.

In the exposition just quoted, Hanna presented no construction or accommodation plan. He went on to finish it, and a few years ago his widow, Dorothy Hanna, showed me the original ink tracings.

There is an interesting chain of "passing the torch" in the transmission of this knowledge about *Spray* and *Foam* to your eyes. I knew Tom Day in his sundown years after he had left *The Rudder* and had a small marine hardware store on Day Street in New York. I had my naval architect's office at that time at 85 Chambers Street with the E. J. Willis Co., the marine hardware outfit. When business got slack, which was chronic, I'd drop in and gam with Skipper Day. Among the clouds of nicotinic smoke he emitted from a gurgling pipe that had charitably been saved from dumping at sea (perchance otherwise to poison a shark), he would hold forth at length about Slocum and *Spray*. I drank it up.

Later, in peregrinations from one yacht yard to another yacht yard as a tramp naval artichoke, I came to know Jack Hanna. It surprised me to learn that this Dunedin genius was introspective because he was stone deaf, and undoubtedly this fact accounted for his seeking recognition through his designs and the boating press. He was born in Galveston, Texas, in 1891, of prominent parents, gravitated to New York after graduating as an electrical engineer from the University of Texas, worked for a while for Glenn Curtiss as an aeronautical engineer, then settled in Florida, where as a loner living by the sea he designed boats for the sea. All of this Sage's work has stood the test of time.

I think *Foam* just about fits the optimum consensus as to size and form needed for long, small-boat voyaging. This consensus I gathered through the 50 years in which I was accumulating over 50,000 "cockpit hours" in front of a drawing board designing yachts of all kinds, always with an eye on someday designing my own escape machine. Naturally, in such a calling, I came to know in person nearly all the greats of the era: Murray Watts, Ralph Winslow, Bill Atkin, William H. Hand, Jr., John Alden, Phil Rhodes, Sam Rabl, Thomas Fleming Day, C. G. Davis, and others. Most of these were all personal friends with whom you could always get a gab-fest going by talking world voyaging. Their consensus as to length was 40 feet. *Foam* fits this. As to rig, all liked the ketch rig. Moderate draft and running sails, such as a ballooner, a raffee, or squaresail, were always indicated. *Foam* has these.

I may build her; I'm debating aluminum for construction, as I've done six large luxury yachts in this material over the past five years. Done by good shipwrights, aluminum is hands down the modern material. I will eschew cement—ferro, alumina, or chicken wire. I've not had good luck with it because it will not stand freezing. And I'll not side with gunk, because the good Lord never intended boats to be built on the inside of a big bathtub by plumbers wrestling eels of slippery cloth into what they term an apollo or a barracuda. That's just to keep out of jail for misrepresenting them as boats.

So I think I'll opt for *Foam*. If I overcome a natural laziness brought on by too much serenity, I may just fire up the sliderule, get out the planimeter, and convert *Foam* to an aluminum hull, with modern stainless-steel rigging, a few electronic pieces, such as radar, depthfinder, ship-to-shore phone, and VHF stuff, and let old salts like Captain Slocum and Jack Hanna roll over in their graves with a beatific change in their snoring. They won't have to worry about this boat!

6

William Atkin, Part I

We were snouting along through the blue just south of Capricorn, William Atkin and I, in one of his double-enders—*Eric,* I think, was the boat—and it was balmy going. Purple seas marched southward in majestic phalanxes, cresting like mountains sawing away at the horizon. The white wispy puffs of cloud sailed serenely past and flying fishes broke from the faces of combers to flash golden in the sun.

This was the scene between us in our mind's eyes Thanksgiving Day, 1926, as we sat in a restaurant in Huntington, Long Island, telling each other what wonderful fellows we were. William Atkin could always invest any marine dream with the euphoria of reality and glamour! Before us were opulent helpings of Vermont turkey, Wisconsin cranberry, Maine potatoes—viands such as Sultans crave what time the bulbul sings. We forked at the feast with a will.

We were snug in a rustic tavern, the kind George Washington was much taken with whenever he needed a night's sleep, but outdoors the November day blustered gray and cold as charity.

Having presented the bill, which totalled $4.68, the strong, silent waiter stood by. If this tab seems high, remember it was for two, and this was Thanksgiving. This is a restaurateur's traditional day to fatten people for the kill. Billy pushed back his chair and looked at me. I pushed back my chair and looked at him. Neither of us had a cent, each thinking the other was standing treat.

As the blood rose red in our facial thermometers, the waiter grew stronger and more silent. I had no fear. After all, I had supposed I was an invited guest of William Atkin. He was 20 years my senior and I was sure that he, being well known locally, was equal to the emergency.

But not that well known, or was he?

44

Which may be why we left our overcoats as security with George Washington's butler, repaired some distance down a raw Huntington street, and climbed a second-floor office stairway beside the street door of which hung a guild-like outboard rudder bearing the sign *"Fore An' Aft* Magazine." We got down on our knees before the corporate safe that housed the liquid assets of Billy's new yachting monthly. Larceny—grim larceny—was in our hearts.

Billy's cane was laid aside and his slight, 140-pound body, somewhat the loser in a boyhood bout with polio, was propped on one elbow as he struggled with the dial combination only vaguely remembered. At last, a clicking of the dial produced bail—just barely. Although Bill's magazine was going great guns with the public, *Fore An' Aft*'s coffers, as I was shortly to be made aware, were thinner than a pancake stepped on.

In my pocket was a letter from Bill inviting me to come to work for him, bearing the enticing words: "—draftsman and assistant editor of *Fore An' Aft.*" I still have that letter.

This was to have been our day. Bill's wife Dorcas and their little boys William and John had gone back to Montclair, N.J., to be with the old folks. This was the men's day to eat a dinner together and to settle my job terms and duties.

My role in this anecdote will be brief. Nothing daunted at that youthful age, I'd driven a Model T flivver from Ramaley's busy boat factory in the Minnesota big lake country, heading east for the Big Time. The route was one mile here, another mile there along the farm section fences of that day to get to Huntington to honor my job commitment. At Erie, Pennsylvania, Uncle Henry's collection of automotive defects expired. I drove the car and bandaged tires into an Erie garage determined to sell the heap. I found it would sell for just barely enough to cover two scanty meals and an all-day and overnight railroad ticket to Huntington. The sum was $15. Into Huntington on a camel-back steam train I arrived Thanksgiving morning. Yes, I was ready to eat.

This adventure and the Thanksgiving dinner were my introduction to the persona and the then modus operandi of that gentle genius of small boat design, William Atkin.

To shorten a very short matter, my tenure lasted a week. Bill, apparently, had seen me as a possible financial angel as well as assistant editor, a hope soon grounded on the reef of reality. So the disenchantment was abrupt and practical. A firm in New York needed a man with V-bottom speedboat design experience. I qualified and accepted with singular alacrity. Bill dismissed me with $30 for my trip and trouble. By this adventure I also learned of Billy's lack of worldly instinct for the financial jugular vein.

We remained firm friends. You couldn't help it with this man. His open, eager smile, his gentle face, his limp with his cane (without which he could not walk)—his large, almost doe-like brown eyes, his mezzo-tenor speaking voice, and his well-bred gentility were captivating. He sold you by being just Billy. A man without guile.

I grew to know him well through the years, bought designs from him, commissioned several boats in later time, building two of them. As have thousands of boatmen down through the years, I have taken much from the gentle copy and charming boat plans into which William Atkin poured so much noodling romance.

Bill is gone now. He died August 20, 1962—a natural death, tired out, less than two months before his 80th birthday. Yet he seems ever to be living; I miss him mightily, mightily.

Of all the numerous Bills who wrote design history during early marine engine days—Bill Nutting, Bill Rogers, Bill Deed, Bill Hand, Bill Fleming, Bill Crosby, to recall a few—no one of them had the Peter Pan touch that William Atkin had. He could write about nothing at all and make it fascinating. If he wrote about Swiss cheese, he would fill the holes so full of moon dust you'd swear you were Sailing Along on Moonlight Bay, listening to the windswept Harps of Memnon humming from the heavens black above. The cheese itself would glow.

Atkin's gift for Strauss-like, Vienna-like, marine schmalz is even today a wonder as one reads again his *Of Yachts and Men.* This is a must book of treasurably complete boat designs, and the kind of building philosophy needed by every man interested in traditional designing. Get it for your shelf—don't miss it!

Billy Atkin's writing contains Art that defies analysis. He was a product of the times even before radio when the printed page was every man's instructor and entertainer. In that era, writers of stature were in demand, drawing prices that exceeded those paid to star entertainers of present boob-tube days.

Bill Atkin was apprenticed to both the design and writing trades of his time. And he learned well. Yet for all of his life he had the soul of a little boy. He was victimized by his sense of fun, his lack of financial acumen, his love for his unique trade. It is tragic that Billy did not share in all the wealth he created, as we shall see.

Bill Nutting, inscribing the flyleaf of his *Track of the Typhoon,* wrote: "To old Billy Atkin (if he hadn't done so many things for fun, he'd be a millionaire)—Bill Nutting, Jan. 24, '22." (The "old" was a term of affection.) Bill realized all of this, but his rationale was, "I am happy in the knowledge that my forebears left upon me not the urgency of making money, but rather the urge to create for the joy of making something."

And yet, innocently unaware of his fame, or maybe because of an overflow from it, he provided for a family of soft-spoken, affectionate, and sensitive people—a wife, Dorcas, and two sons, William and John. He made a final haven of call at Anchordown, his fine home and workshop on the Boston Post Road in Darien, Connecticut. There, his son John, who inherited Bill's sensitiveness and designing ability combined with a sharper draftsman's hand and a better business sense, carries on the Atkin tradition.

William Atkin left a legacy of work that staggers the mind for its requirement of energy. Here is where the overworked word "fantastic" is too weak: How do you become the most prolific designer in *Lloyd's Register,* answer over 4,000 letters a year from fans, turn out (on the side) one design a month that is the featured centerfold blueprint of a national boating magazine—one published new design every month for 30 years!—turn out over 854 separate designs of boats for all types of people all over the world, write a dozen or more books, make thousands of friends, and still get time to breathe?

The record is substantiated by statistics and averages 20 designs a year. Much of this was done by Billy at night when people couldn't bother him.

It was Billy's nature that from this agony and ecstasy of creating he kept the agony and projected the ecstasy.

William Atkin's life story begins in Harlem, New York City, where he was born October 14, 1882, the son of William P. Atkin and Gertrude Davenport Atkin. Harlem was then spelled Haarlem (Dutch) and was a bailiwick of substantial homes. Bill's father, an Englishman, owned a good-sized printing plant in New York City where *Leslie's Weekly Magazine* and the *North American Review* and other national magazines were printed.

After Bill's birth, the family moved to a new home in Montclair, N.J. At about the time he could toddle, he suffered the scourge of babyhood: infantile paralysis, which affected his left leg. All his life he was lame and could not walk without a cane. To so free a spirit this was no handicap; one scarcely noticed it.

Bill Atkin's boyhood among brothers and sisters was a happy one. Billy saw the flowers, the brook that ran past his fine, new home, and the spreading elms, and heard the peaceful clop of horses—he listened with the sensitivity of a poet. Montclair was pastoral then.

He built his first boat before he was 12, marshalling the pennies and energies of his playmates. A pair of 12-foot boards was purchased at the local lumberyard, and an 11-foot boat resulted, staked out on the Atkin lawn near the too-shallow creek.

"She's a belle!" a chum remarked, so Billy Atkin's first boat was named *Isabelle.*

Adolescence and dawning manhood were spent along the Jersey

beaches. Seabright, Red Bank, Monmouth, and other spots had boat-shops that he later stated had claimed his affection and study.

A lad four years Bill's junior, Cottrell C. Wheeler (no relation to the Brooklyn boatbuilding Wheelers), became Bill's alter ego and lifetime friend. Together, when Cot was 19 and Bill was 23, financed by heaven-knows-whom, the boys built William Atkin's first motorboat, *Buddie II*. *Buddie II* was so successful she fired interest in Bill's designing talents.

Seeing a spark here, as boys will in such cases, Cot and Bill thought it would be the right thing to fan all the fires of hell and have a boatshop. It would be great fun! They browsed around, nearly buying a shop at Bayville, on Long Island's Oyster Bay, but gravitated to Huntington because of the pastoral charm of the town, the good water in Huntington Bay, and the availability of a shop owned by Charles Sammis, veteran boatbuilder.

Wheeler's family was wealthy and Bill's folks were well off. The deal took a year to gell. Billy wrote of a trip by livery horse and wagon made by Cot Wheeler and himself over the Mill Dam Road with a tired nag, enroute to Sammis's shop, to make the deal or break it. Wheeler rode reins and whip, Bill sat with legs dangling aft, dragging a pole leisurely in the dust. It was on this journey they decided to close the purchase.

They were aided in this by August Heckscher, owner of the Huntington bank, a tiny wisp of a man who wore a tall derby hat that might have belonged to a Keystone cop, the better to extend his height. Or it may have been worn to accommodate the vapors arising from a hot financial mind that was capable of producing 45-percent dividends every six months on the Heckscher bank's stock. Those were the days, my friends—Oh, yes! Those were the days! Bill once told me that Heckscher loomed large in the background of the new shop's life, both as banker and customer.

By these agencies the Atkin-Wheeler Co. was formed, doing business under that banner in the Red Boat Shop. The year was 1906. Cot Wheeler was 20 and Billy was 24. The Sammises, father Charles and son Percy, continued to work as hired hands and were the journeymen boatbuilders, with Bill and Cot working alongside them. It was a happy place, the fishing was good from the shop windows, and notable boats began coming forth. Bill's picture at this time is shown in an accompanying photo.

Does he look worried? The joy of living sparkles in his eyes and smile; veritable kilowatts of charm pour forth from this guileless face. This is Billy Atkin at his drawing board in the Red Boat Shop days. As against that bane of all small places, "friends of the shop," who drop around and goggle and waste a man's time, Billy seemed to welcome them. An innocent fraternity of nicknames sprang up, by which Cot

Billy Atkin, age 24, in the Red Boat Shop of Atkin-Wheeler in Huntington, Long Island—boy boss of a new venture.

Wheeler was known as Tatter Shirt, George Fairfield as Tatter Finger, Roswell Davis as Tatter Hat, and Bill Atkin as Tatter (Pa) Jama. The Order of the Tatter.

Most of the boats produced by the Red Boat Shop were of good size. The first was *Rosetta V,* a bridge-deck cruiser 40 feet by 10 feet by 3 feet, built for Dr. Ferdinand C. Valentine, gynecologist, who had 16 children, all adopted.

The emphasis of the shop, being in the hands of young men, was all on speed and performance. The Atkin-Wheeler shop became famed for the long, lean speedboats of the day, and eventually, through the influence of prominent customers, was selected as the base for Harmsworth Trophy races.

Among the yard's customers, aside from Heckscher, who owned the big steam yacht *Anahama,* were Arthur T. Vance, editor of *The*

Vic IV, a husky 30-footer, was the first boat built in Atkin-Wheeler's New Boat Shop. She was a double-ender of heavy displacement. A 4-cylinder Wisconsin automobile engine provided power and drove her along at a comfortable 10 mph. She was designed and built for Carleton L. Negley of Centerport, Long Island.

Pictorial Review, and Andre Bustanoby, who with his brothers Louis and Jacques, owned the Cafe des Beaux Arts at 6th Avenue and 40th Street, New York City. The Bustanobys catered to the Wall Street crowd and the theatrical trade, and had influential customers, such as Diamond Jim Brady, who often dined at Bustanobys' with Lillian Russell, the enchanting actress, in open defiance of the laws of Avoirdupois. The Bustanobys lived in Huntington, and conducted also the famous Chateau des Beaux Arts on the shore of Huntington Bay. They also owned an Atkin-Wheeler boat, *Yvonne,* which they drove like Mad Hatters over reefs and logs. *Yvonne* was always in the shop "for feex," as Andre Bustanoby termed it.

Society gravitated to the Bustanobys, and the Bustanobys gravitated to Atkin-Wheeler. The Harmsworth gravitated with Society. It was important business.

The original Red Boat Shop was only 30 feet by 50 feet. Machine tools, boats, and the usual clutter of a boatshop soon dictated the need for more adequate facilities. One can be sure that August Heckscher, with an eye on an upcoming semiannual dividend, had much to do with the New Boat Shop. This was a two-story affair, 50 feet by 80 feet, with a machine shop in the basement. Billy, in writing about it, is vague about the real reason for expanding, seeming to think that the original shop was so far up the creek that the vagaries of tide caused much

50

distress to Cot and Bill's landlady, who never knew when to expect them for meals. This is a typical Atkin viewpoint; one may be sure there were entrepreneurial reasons.

In the years from 1906 to 1912, the Red Boat Shop had turned out many boats that caught the eye of the public and were widely publicized in the yachting press: *Nameless, Vim, Ketewomoke, Wolf's Head, Sara, Gray-AW, Gobang II,* all high-performance, fast cruisers and runabouts. There were few sailboats.

In 1912, when the New Shop was built, Sir Edgar Mackay's big *Maple Leaf IV* lifted the Harmsworth Trophy. The deed of gift stipulated that the winner's parent yacht club had the right to determine the place, course, and date of the next race to meet a challenger. The Harmsworth went to Cowes, and Society and the attendant hoopla and bustle and trade went to England.

The year 1912 had further special significance for Bill Atkin. On April 6, 1912, he married Dorcas Wilson at the old parental Atkin home in Montclair. Dorcas had been born in Brooklyn on January 1, 1893, and was 11 years younger than Billy. To this marriage came two sons, William W(ilson) Atkin, born January 21, 1913, and John D(avenport) Atkin, born August 19, 1918.

Two years after marrying Dorcas, William Atkin pulled off his biggest designing coup. He and Cot Wheeler, in the new shop, built *Cabrilla,* a gasoline express yacht 115 feet by 13 feet by 3 feet 6 inches; she ran 30 mph. To get this speed, special engines larger than anything the market afforded were needed. Each had to produce 750 hp. Billy designed both the boat and the engines.

Each of these motors had 8 cylinders of 8-inch bore by 14-inch stroke in a V configuration, with overhead valves driven by "silent chain," having intermediate reduction from the camshaft to the crankshaft so as to give proper half-speed for the four-stroke cycle. The carburetion was down-draft, the valves were sodium cooled, the rotation was opposite hand: true twin screw. Cottrell Wheeler designed the clutches and built the engines; Billy designed the motor itself. The gasoline feed lines were 1 inch in diameter. Each engine weighed 5,500 pounds, or about 7.3 pounds per horsepower.

Cabrilla was built complete in nine months by Atkin-Wheeler, which dispels any fiction about their actual work pace being sluggish. That building speed would be remarkable by today's over-staffed, undermanned standards.

In some way not known to the Atkin family today, the Atkin-Wheeler combination dissolved. One suspects it was World War I conditions; Mr. Heckscher was aging, not to live long; Cot Wheeler went to California. (He died there in the 1950s.)

Cabrilla, built by Atkin-Wheeler in 1914 for August Heckscher, emerges for launching from an extension of the New Boat Shop. She was 115' x 13' x 3'6", with 1¼" yellow pine planking, and did 30 mph on 1500 hp. Note the then ultra-fashionable corset stern. Her main decks (and bulkheads) were two thicknesses of ¼-inch plywood—glued together with scattered butts—and covered with canvas. The plywood was imported from Russia and sold under the name of Venesta board.

Billy had been contributing literary work to the marine press, and in 1916 took over the editing of *Yachting* when Herb Stone was called to war in naval service. When this three-year stint was over, in 1919, Bill Atkin became Technical Editor on *Motor Boat,* then under the editorship of a competent yachtsman and professional engineer, William Washburn Nutting. This became a world-famous team, responsible for the trans-Atlantic adventures of Nutting, Uffa Fox, Jim Dorsett, and Casey Baldwin, who made the voyage in Billy Atkin's *Typhoon,* a design that brought him full-flower back into wholesome sailing yachts.

Of Bill Nutting, whose aunt left him an income, of the design story of *Typhoon,* of Bill's return to Huntington in the Mizzen Top home, I shall write in the next chapter. This will include tales of palmy days in the stock market boom times, of disaster by being caught by a client's bankruptcy during the 1929 crash, of *Fore An' Aft,* of Florida wanderings, of a wipe-out by the 1938 hurricane at Norwalk, of a courageous fight to become re-established, of his success at Anchordown, in Darien, Connecticut, especially of his fabulous output there with the aid of two stalwart sons. All of which makes Bill Atkin kin to every man who has wrestled with the same challenges.

The second half of Bill Atkin's life is more dramatic than the first, if such a thing seems possible. From buoyant boyhood, through mature

52

manhood, William Atkin underneath it all was a scrapper who never gave up. He projected the ecstasy of creating wholesome little ships; to read him you would have thought life was a lark. This is why I think that in his ode, "To a Skylark," Percy Bysshe Shelley's immortal words summed up the essence of William Atkin:

> Hail to thee, blithe spirit!
> Bird thou never wert,
> That from Heaven, or near it
> Pourest thy full heart
> In profuse strains of unpremeditated art.

Atkin's wholesome little yachts, as attested to by the drawings here shown of some of them, became the Gold Standard of desirability, buildability, and cruisability in the years just past.

'Twas Gold Standard stuff you were, Bill. Your story is continued on the next page.

7

William Atkin, Part II

The cablegram that arrived at the *Motor Boat* editorial offices in New York on August 9, 1920, read:

REMARKABLE PASSAGE BADDECK COWES TWENTY-ONE DAYS. CAPE RACE BISHOPS ROCK FIFTEEN DAYS. CONGRATULATE ATKIN.

—NUTTING

William Atkin had designed Nutting's *Typhoon* after signing aboard *Motor Boat* as Technical Editor in 1919. It must have gladdened Bill's heart in more ways than one, for the *Typhoon* enterprise seemed at the time an improbable bit of lunacy: the editor of *Motor Boat*, William Washburn Nutting, conceived the bright idea of building an ocean-going ketch, which he would sail eastward across the Atlantic to cover motor boating's Big Casino: the Harmsworth Trophy race to be held at Cowes in August to determine the fastest motorboat in the world. On the surface this sounds like a flash of Nutting genius—broad, simple strokes, with Ma's Boy taking the bows.

Nutting did pull it off, but back of the doing is a story concerning other men who ran tangent to William Atkin's life at the time, and whose participation gave Billy a boost.

William Washburn Nutting was the scion of two prominent families. An aunt, one of the Washburn milling family, had, before her widowed death, set up a fund for Nutting that provided him with $10,000 a year endowed income. Nutting was a capable man. He was a professional engineer, a competent yachtsman, and possessed that rarest of all human gifts: a deft editing touch that hooked readers in enthusiastic droves. His magazine sold like mad, until he was later lost at sea.

Nutting's guidance and patronage and the power of *Motor Boat*'s

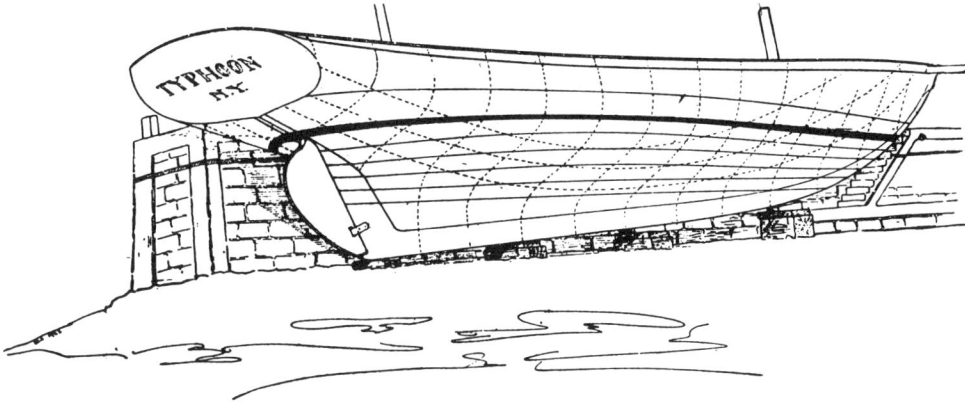

Typhoon's fat stern and lean bow are clearly pictured in this clam's-eye perspective drawn by William Atkin to show her form.

press presented Bill Atkin in strong light. But William Atkin would not have become Technical Editor of *Motor Boat* had it not been for the competence of George F. Crouch, who had started *Motor Boat*'s Forum Department and had made a big thing of it. Crouch ran The Forum as a nuts-and-bolts, pitch-my-propeller, fix-my-engine column that was a great teacher.

George F. Crouch and his brother, Albert (Ab) Crouch, had come to New York from Stillwater, Minnesota, where, as young men, they had operated The Bluff City Boat Works. This venture had gone belly up, possibly due to an inherent fallacy: the shop was built on a bluff and operated on the same principle.

Both Crouches were crackerjack designers. Ab went to Tams, Lemoine and Crane, naval architects of New York, and George, running The Forum, became professor of math at Webb Institute of Naval Architecture, then later, dean of the school, and even later, chief naval architect for Horace E. Dodge Watercar Co. I knew both men as fine gentlemen and the incarnation of competence.

When George Crouch moved from *Motor Boat* and the conducting of The Forum, Nutting chose William Atkin, a seventh-grade drop-out, to replace him. It is to Atkin's credit that his talent and savvy made The Forum department of *Motor Boat* even bigger and livelier.

When Nutting conceived the *Typhoon* venture, he had the means with which to build her. Naturally, he chose William Atkin to design her. The story of her designing, the discussion of pros and cons, all of it inviting readers to kibitz and sound off, provided exciting reading. It was a good circulation-building uproar for *Motor Boat*.

Typhoon is here shown in William Atkin's own perspective of her from a clam's-eye view against a stone wall, showing the ham-sterned, hog-nosed lines that were much criticized at the time of conception and eventually did—almost—prove to be her undoing as she was rolled over to 120 degrees by a following sea on her return voyage from Cowes.

Famous names ran tangent to the venture all the way, and all connected with *The Track of the Typhoon* later made their mark. She was crewed on the eastward voyage by Bill Nutting, F.W. (Casey) Baldwin, and a local lad picked up for a third hand, Jim Dorsett. She was built in the Baddeck, Nova Scotia, shops of Dr. Alexander Graham Bell. Jim Dorsett won the Trans-Atlantic Blue Ribbon for seasickness both ways, east and west. Casey Baldwin became the Rt. Hon. F.W. Baldwin, Premier of Nova Scotia. Uffa Fox, then a bubbly 22-year-old Sea Scout master who was signed on for the return voyage, left a heavy record in naval architecture.

Nutting, after covering the Harmsworth by arriving at Cowes in time to record Gar Wood's recapture of the trophy with *Miss Detroit V,* wrote *The Track of the Typhoon,* then a bestseller and still a classic of the sea.

The cablegram that had announced *Typhoon*'s arrival at Cowes after a very fast passage, ending with "CONGRATULATE ATKIN," seemed to vindicate Billy's fine-lined entrance on her hull. He later thought otherwise. *Typhoon*'s passage of 2,158 nautical miles in just 15 days, 9 hours, and 25 minutes—averaging better than 5.8 knots—from Cape Race to Bishop's Rock was due in great part to strong sou'westerlies for the first 1,038 nautical miles.

Atkin's designing talent, so long under a bushel as far as his light with the public was concerned, now was to become luminous. *Typhoon*'s fast time across the Atlantic, and her sea-ravaged return, kept his name before the public.

Somehow, every man who sails seems to have a fetish for speed. *Typhoon* had the reputation of being fast. One nautical reporter waxed wildly poetic in writing, "*Typhoon* flew across the Atlantic like a goose in a mill race sluice." Try as I will, I have never discovered in any handbook the speed/length ratio of a sluiced goose.

But no matter. Bill Atkin, who had been around for 15 years as a pro, now became nationally known. Work flooded in, and though he continued to commute to New York from Montclair, New Jersey, whence he had moved his family in with Dorcas's mother, Mrs. Wilson, the press of that time shows him advertising in a professional card with the address as being Montclair. Bill's designing for the magazines became widely known, because his boats were as wholesome as home-made bread.

After the success of the *Typhoon* venture, Nutting and a friend of his, Arthur Hildebrand, discovered in a book by E. Keble Chatterton the lines of Colin Archer's typical North Sea rescue boat, the redning-

Freya, a sistership to *Eric,* is shown on trial runs at Huntington. Atkin sold 175 sets of plans for this boat, possibly his most popular design.

skoite. She was a whale of a ship, something like 47 feet overall, with lines like a pregnant whale. The sea-keeping qualities of the Norwegian rescue boats were legendary.

Nutting and Hildebrand thought that by pulling the lines down to 32 feet, a Colin Archer type small cruising yacht could be built that was above reproach as a sea-keeper. They entrusted the design work to William Atkin, and the result was his *Eric,* the first of a long line of double-enders he designed.

Eric, as I understand it, was not built by Nutting, who found it more economical to buy a redningskoite in Norway and sail her across. This decision cost him his life. He and Hildebrand were spoken at sea near Greenland, but were never heard from thereafter. Billy Atkin, in his poetic way, shed barrels of tears over the fact. Here is one of dozens of passages he later wrote concerning the tragedy of Nutting's loss:

—I have reasons to believe that, had *Leiv Eiriksson* [Nutting's boat] alone been plowing her way into the west, she would have arrived ahead of time, and with all well aboard. Old Neptune and his handmaidens splashing about in Davis Strait must have remarked upon the multiplicity of those modern white-hulled Norse craft splashing through his sea. How long a time, he must have mused, had bandled by since the Dragon and the Long Serpent pressed on to make the land? Aye, a full thousand years for sure!

Perhaps he smiled—or swore.

At any rate his handmaidens hit their stride; and somewhere there in the Northern Sea the *Leiv Eiriksson* lies silently, while her crew sleeps on forever.

Mr. Henry D. Bixby, of the same family that grew wealthy on Bixby's Black Shoe polish (remember the black wax in little pry cans?), bankrolled Huntington boatbuilder Dick Chute, and three *Eric*s were built by Chute & Bixby of Huntington. They were *Freya,* owned by Henry Bixby, *Valgerda,* owned by Langley Isom of Garden City, and *Eric,* still owned by Herman Hollerith and going strong in Chesapeake waters today. These were ketch-rigged craft, 32 feet overall, 27 feet 6 inches waterline, with 11-foot beam and 5-foot draft. Displacement was 19,000 pounds, and the sail area was 650 square feet. So popular were these boats that Atkin sold 175 sets of plans for *Eric*. Bill thought $25 to $35 a set was about right, which may have had something to do with the number sold. Always, always, Atkin under-priced himself.

With Nutting no longer at the helm of *Motor Boat,* Atkin stated that "there were still too many Bills around," and he returned to Huntington in 1923, buying a home he called the Mizzen Top and from which address he kept very busy, specializing more in wholesome sailing auxiliaries than in other types, although he could, and did, design fetching little powerboats and motor cruisers.

In 1924 he signed on as the featured writer-designer for a nationally known boating magazine that cleaved more to power than to sail, and for over 30 years contributed one complete design a month, missing only two issues, one lapse being due to being overwhelmed by a hurricane at Norwalk. These were complete designs—lines, offsets, construction profile, sections and text—the works! The magazine for a long, long time featured the plans as the main selling feature: a blueprint section that folded out.

His initial fold-out design was published about 1924, with considerable fanfare acknowledging Atkin as the foremost American designer of small yachts. The year before, in *Lloyd's Register,* he'd had listed to his credit more boats than any other American naval architect.

Bill's work was a goldmine for the magazine, and, for that matter, a source of wealth to the entire marine industry, because hundreds of his

These Atkin drawings of *Njord* are a complete lesson in Atkin's method of designing and are worth complete study. She was a later double-ender and had room for four to cruise in comfort in any waters.

UNDERSIDE RAIL CAP

GILT COVE

SHEER

L L 4

L L 2

B 2

PAINTED W.L.

L.W.L

L.W.L

B 1

B 2

B 1

RABBET

RABBET

TOP OF LEAD

BASE

BASE

5·3

13½

13

5·3

5   12   11   10   9   8   7   6   5   4   3   2   1   0   0

C.C.L.   C.B

28"   31"

31"   35"

SHEER

L L 2

L.W.L

L L 2

L L 1

SHEER

W L 1

B 2

W.L 2

B 1

L.W.L

W.L 3

D 0

D 1

D 2

D 3

D 4

D 5

D 5

FRAMES: ON STATIONS. SAWN FROM 2" W.OAK: DOUBLED AND THRU BOLTED WITH ¼" D. GALV. BOLTS - TO FINISHED 2" X 4".

INTERCOSTAL FRAMES 2" X 2" W.OAK: TWO BETWEEN EACH STATION.

BOTTOM FRAME

HATCH

COCK PIT SAME CONS. AS DECK

THREE DOUBLE HACK KNEES

TWO ¾" X 2" BR. STRAPS

FOR'D HOUSE

DECK FRAME

2" KNEES.

STERN POST W.OAK MOULDED AND SIDED IN PLANS. FASTEN-INGS ⅝" D. CALV. DRIFT BOLTS STERN BREAST HOOK 2½" HACK. KNEE. BR. STUFFING BOX OUT SIDE. 1¼" D. SHAFT.

EIGHT ⅝" GALV. TIE RODS EA. SIDE.

⅛" X 6" TOBIN BR. STRAP. LET INTO DECK BEAMS FLUSH WITH TO'PS BR SCREW FASTENED

TWO OAK KNEES THRU BOLTED TO DECK 2½" OAK

BOOM FRAME: 1¼" D. PIPE STANCHIONS: 2" TEAK HD. PIECE

DECK HOUSE: HATCH AND SLIDE. TEAK 1¼"

FOR'D HOUSE TEAK

1" D

COMING.

CHEEK PCS 1⅝" W.OAK TAPER TO ⅞" AT BOTTOM

SEAT FRONT ⅞ TEAK

SCUPPER

4" D BOLTS

¾" D DOOR HD PANEL

DUMMY DOORS

SHELF

BIN

OPEN LOCKER

L.W.L

L.W.L

EXHAUST

STEM W.OAK. MOULD-ED AND SIDED AS SHOWN FASTEN WITH ⅜" THRU GALV BOLTS

RUDDER 2" THICK W.OAK. DOWEL WITH ½" DIA. CALV. ROD. HANGERS-CAST BRONZE. TAPER AFT EDGE OF BLADE TO ½"

STRAP

BR MAST STEP.

LEAD KEEL 3600#. EIGHT 1¼" D. GALV. IRON BOLTS ON BALANCE STAGGERED 6"- LEAD AND GALV. WASHES INSIDE.

CEMENT TO TOP OF FLOOR TIMBERS.

BASE

BASE

5   12   11   10   9   8   7   6   5   4   3   2   1   0   A

28"   31"

31"   35"

GALLEY SINK: 20" COPPER 2" DEEP WITH 6" X 6" X 17" SUMP: PUMP TO DRAIN SINK: PUMP FOR SUPPLY.

2'-0"   2'-1"

KEEP EXHAUST OUT LET WELL ABOVE W.L.

COAL

DISH SHELVES

LID   LID

BOX BERTH

LOCKERS

LID

COPPER SINK

HANGING LOCKER

LOCKER

CHEST OF DRAWERS

WATER TANK 20 CCE TINNED COPPER. 2 SPLASH PLATES 4 IN. DIA FILLER CAPACITY 50 GAL

GASOLINE TANKS UNDER COCKPIT SEATS

HATCH OVER FLOOR

SUMP

SOFA TANK UNDER

BERTH

FLOORING

PORT GASOLINE TANK 3' LONG LEAVING ROOM FOR 1'X1'X1' KEROSENE TANK IN FORE END OF SEAT: STAR'D TANK FULL LENGTH SEAT TOTAL GASOLINE CAP'Y 45 GALS

ASPLAM. MAST STEP

EXHAUST

MUFFLER OF SPHERICAL FORM

OPEN FRONT LOCKER

LID

ICE CHEST OPENS AT TOP

EXT. LEAF TABLE

EXTENSION BERTH

TANK UNDER

SHELVES

BERTH

LOCKERS

LOCKERS UNDER

18 CCE COPPER 2 SPLASH PLATES

CLOSE VALVE 3" SCREW PLATE WITH COPPER TUBING SUPPLY PIPE LEAD TWO TANKS TO STRAINER BELOW COCK PIT FLOOR: THENCE TO CARBURETTER

2'-6"   4'-1"   6'-6"   3'-6"   16"   6'-2"   15"

21"   21"

boats were built. Motors, propellers, paint, lumber—the dollar wealth created was enormous.

I have stated it is tragic that William Atkin did not share in the wealth he created. How much would you think he should have garnered from all this work? Let us indulge in some tablecloth dealsmithing. This is a sport excelled in by American luncheoneers—the zeros roll off the tablecloth on their way to the bank, but the game is to affix a significant integer in front of those goose eggs.

Let us suppose a reasonable magazine circulation of 48,000 copies. Let us also suppose the magazine is one-quarter-inch thick. Four of them stack an inch high. Twelve inches, or one foot, would contain 48 copies. If you divide 48,000 units by this 48, you get a stack of magazines 1,000 feet high. About equal to the Empire State Building.

Would you think a penny a copy too much to pay for a nationally touted circulation builder? Say $480 per design? About half of their true worth, and far from the standard 10 to 12 percent of the building cost of the boat needed for a designer to stay in business?

William Atkin for years was paid $100 per design story, about two-tenths of a cent per copy. The figure was increased slightly in later years.

When John Atkin, Bill's son, returned from duty in the South Seas in World War II, he put an end to Billy's gullibility. If William Atkin had had a few dollars from each sale of the blueprints of his published designs, he would not have had to work in his declining years. The request was made to the publisher.

Motion denied! Billy had signed each check to an endorsement form that conveyed all rights. Commerce does have its martyrs.

For a while, William Atkin thought this was lush pay. Even later, in his palmy days after becoming well known as a result of the *Motor Boat* stint and the other connection, Bill would ask only $600 to $800 for a full-fledged design such as a *Typhoon*, a *Fore An' Aft*, a *Njord*, or similar work.

But I get ahead of my story: when Bill returned to the Mizzen Top, the United States economy was beginning to heat up. Work flowed to him in plenty. In 1926, he and Henry Bixby teamed up on a publishing venture. They would put out a magazine named *Fore An' Aft*.

Printed on cream stock, enamel finished, with a crinkled stock cover on which some section of a chart always appeared, *Fore An' Aft* at first had immense charm. The circulation never went over 5,000 or so; there was little organization, and when Bixby put in an accountant and general business head, Billy defected out of distaste for being curbed.

61

The cutter *Fore An' Aft* struck yachtsmen's fancy when she was designed in 1927.

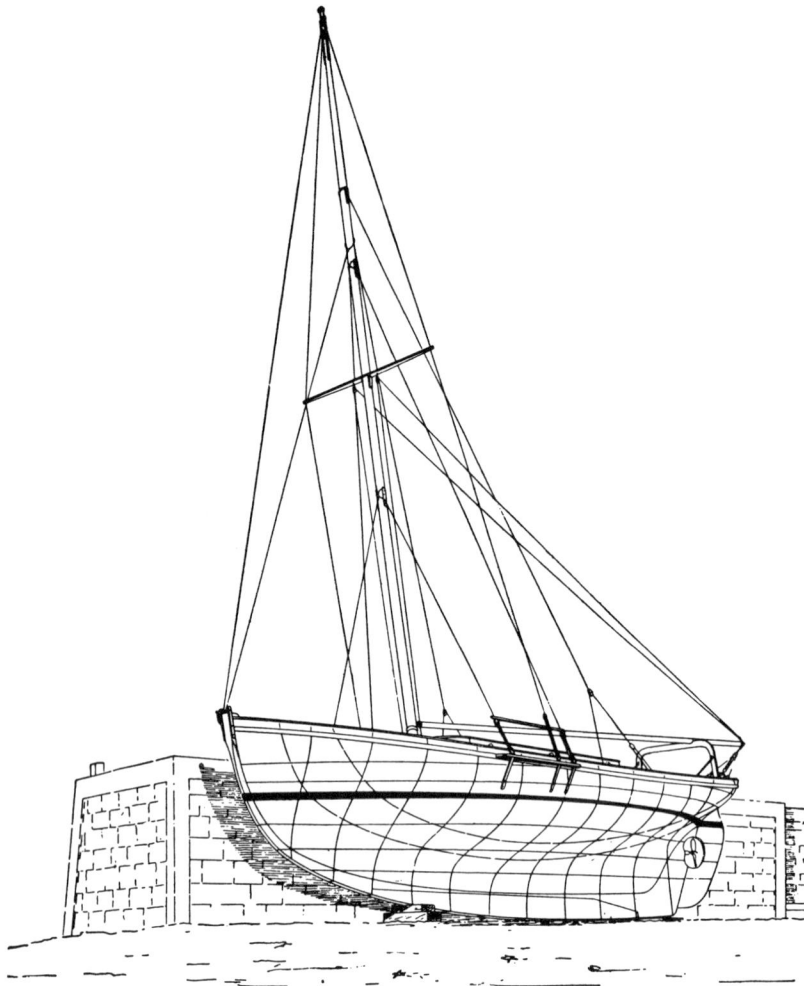

Ben Bow was built by Chute and Bixby for Atkin's personal use. On a 28-foot length, she carried a 50-foot mast. She was based on his *Fore An' Aft*.

During these years, Bill rode high again. He designed the cutter *Fore An' Aft* for Newt Wigton, and *Ben Bow* for himself, and a line of little ships too numerous to mention here—each and all of them being someone's favorite boat.

The increasingly over-heated American economy was zooming along on bigger and better prospects each day. Bigger and better boats were ordered from William Atkin; he never stinted on work.

For those too young to remember the Great Depression, it must be explained so as to give focus to the thin and precarious ice all men were treading then. It was an ingenuous span of years. From 1926 through 1928 and part way into 1929, nearly every boot-black, waitress, and coal heaver had a stock "portfolio" bought at five cent margin on the dollar. Each day, in every way, their fortunes grew bigger and better— on paper.

To reach the Nirvana of golden wealth, all you had to do was watch the market, keep your ear to the ground, keep your eye on the ball, put your shoulder to the wheel. How is anybody going to get a day's work done in that position?

Shifting from its great pioneer work homilies, the American motto became, "Let George do it!" George soon had more than he could handle, and so did William Atkin. The bubble burst. Smoke ceased pouring from the chimneys of American industry. Cities grew silent and bankruptcies were rife.

It is no discredit to William Atkin that the crash of others tumbled debris on his own fortunes. He had designed *Alone* for William P. Boyce of Boyce MotoMeter fame and went thence to the production of a 70-footer for the Mr. Veeder of the Veeder-Roth Corp., then riding high on bicycle odometers, tally counters, and speedometers.

The Veeder stock plummeted. Atkin had bought, as design agent, about $4,000 worth of marine equipment for Veeder's boat. WW&J Tiebout were the main suppliers. Veeder went bankrupt. Bill Atkin was one of the sackholders. Tiebout had no choice but to press for payment.

At this time, on top of that catastrophe, the Mizzen Top home, carrying a second mortgage by this time (as did many homes) slid into delinquency, entitling the mortgagor to threaten and to initiate foreclosure. The sum, John Atkin recalls, was $3,000 or less. It may as well have been three million dollars.

Piled into two Chevrolets, one a roadster and the other a touring car of around 1931 vintage, Bill, Dorcas, and the boys drove away from Mizzen Top, from Huntington, from the rosy past. It was the only out. In Florida, at a "proposed development" that looked lush in prospectus but was mostly sand "streets" and palmetto bushes overrun with vines, Bill found a shack to rent, but production of his monthly design became difficult. One cannot draw fine little ships when seated in despair on the edge of a dingy bed, while palmetto bugs (Florida's Mack Truck cockroaches) are hauling your shoes around the room!

Cliff Hadley, hydroplane builder, once of Halesite, Long Island, had moved to Florida and was established. From this friendly aid in Gulfport, Bill and his family re-grouped, and Bill started to pay back the Tiebout account. Eventually every penny went back to Tiebout.

There is a lesson here for budding young designers: never put yourself into an agency position as a supplier or middleman for any owner on any boat!

After a year seeking Florida roots, the Atkin family returned north to the familiar shores of Long Island Sound. Locating at Norwalk, in a home on Pratt's Island rented from another friend, A. William Pratt, William Atkin fought back. But Fate's big, fat finger was to hand William Atkin another stab. On Wednesday, September 21, 1938, a

William Atkin, age 76, near the end of his illustrious
creative life, which ended in 1962. Pictured at the helm of
We're Here, he still thought it great fun to get wet.

vagrant Florida hurricane hit Long Island Sound. Bill and his two sons,
William and John, managed in a frantic half hour or so to scoop out
portions of his office, tools, and records, carrying them to higher
ground. Bill was the last baggage carried across wild waters on the back
of his oldest son William. Little was saved. An immense, unusual jugger-
naut of a tide floated some boats as far as two miles inland before a
raging gale.

This, any way you dump it, is a large bucket of tragedy. And still Bill
Atkin and his family fought back.

In a home provided by Bill Pratt, one of the owners of the deluged
island, Bill and his family lived awhile. On newly acquired land in
Darien on the Boston Post Road, Bill and the boys built Anchordown,
the final Atkin home. It is a delightful place, all shipshape. There, the
walls are bulkheads and the doors are shaped like bulkhead doors, with
round corners and a high step over from the "decks." From this new
place, with adequate accommodations, a fine workshop, and a well-

64

placed drafting room, William Atkin, pere, and John Atkin, fils, sailed into a new cargo of work. Bill was by then about 57 years of age.

Young William Atkin went into book publishing work. John Atkin, senior president of his high school class, apprenticed at Consolidated Shipbuilding in the Bronx, then—of all the coincidences!—understudied Ab Crouch at Luders before joining his father in producing a long line of fine boats. It is John Atkin to whom I am indebted for much clarification in this story.

I have attempted to acquaint today's reading public with William Atkin as a man. A very human man, with tremendous ability and artistic sense both in designing, and Heaven knows, in writing. Most treatments on him show him as a sort of cherubic angel flitting through sunlit puffs of ecclesiastical mist. I knew him for a likeable, generally gentle man, who ate, growled, slept, worked, planned, dreamed, and ventilated even as you and I do. He had a temper, and at times it seemed as though the rabbit was spitting in the bulldog's face. At such times, he would usually conclude the rise in temperature with, "I'd like to punch him in the nose." Ah, yes! He could chortle over what he liked, but he could snort at what he didn't!

William died a natural death, tired out, August 20, 1962. Toward the end he fretted a bit, asking his younger son, "Why does a man have to live so g.d. long?"

Once he wrote, "I joke about the day when for the last time I shall lay down my drawing pen, and some other hands than mine cover my typewriter. I hope then that someone will set my ashes adrift in the tide stream that flows across the sand off Eaton's Neck. Can you think of a sweeter place to rest?"

Ten years after his death, John and William Atkin, his sons, carried out his wish from an Atkin boat built with loving hands by John Addicott.

Thus William Atkin returned to the sea.

8

A Tribute to Sam Rabl

In Sam Rabl's day, a scant half-generation ago, every red-blooded American boy dreamed of building his own light airplane, or ham radio, or salty tabloid cruiser. Today, some of this has changed. The air is full of planes and laws; the radio ham is strictured by licenses and more laws; a young man's whole world seems like a lawyer's hayride. Escape leads down paths to the ocean.

There, things never change: the heave and the hurl and the crash of wind-hounded seas, or the golden ripple on a sun-danced inlet where water-kissed breezes gently call, "Come hither."

A fellow can answer this call with the right boat.

No man of the past 50 years knew this better than Sam Rabl, the Baltimore naval architect whose genius lay in designing tabloid cruisers simple enough to build for very few dollars—a lot of boat for a buck.

No one can dip far into annals of boat development without encountering some of Sam Rabl's work. He was a naval architect who worked on big ship design; a major domo in the design department of the Sparrows Point Yard of the Bethlehem Shipbuilding Co. in Baltimore. But Rabl's inner soul lay nearer the babbling brook of boyhood than to the turbid river of age. One first discerns this in his design of the famous little sloop *Picaroon,* which burst Sam into national attention and print in the June 25, 1925, issue of *Motor Boat* magazine.

The stir this little $1,000 cruiser kicked up in the boating sky made even the rainbow look like a hunk of old lead pipe. Every kid with a pair of pliers, a crescent wrench, hammer, and nails wanted to build her. She made Sam Rabl famous, and though he could and did design

Picaroon.

ships of all sizes and other yachts of many hues, it will have to be *Picaroon* and her sequels about which a Sam Rabl story must swing to moorings.

Before bobbing to and fro about the central theme of his life, let me say that Sam is gone now. He died at the age of 66 in St. Agnes Hospital in Baltimore on January 16, 1962. A rare blood diaphasia had wasted the cartilage in his joints; his illness was lingering and long.

He is buried in the Catholic Cemetery of the Holy Redeemer on Belair Road in Baltimore, survived by his wife, Margaret, to whom he was devoted. He had no children, but all men's children were his, for he loved to teach, and his workshop was frequently cluttered with kids. The great talent that marked his genius was accompanied by simplicity and self-effacement. "He was a perfectly marvelous man," is an accolade of most who knew him.

There is so much of Rabl in boat noodling literature, and there has been for so long a time that organizing him chronologically seems impossible—just dip into his life with a sponge: each dip is good for a full-bailing squeeze. It will eventually bring us back to *Picaroon.*

Sam's father, Frank Rabl, I am told by one of Sam's sisters-in-law, "migrated from Austria-Hungary as a young adult male." This is a pretty good thing to be if you're a man. Franz Rabl (Frank) married Susanna Hendricks, a woman of Dutch or German derivation from Phoenixville, Pennsylvania, and their son Samuel Supplee Rabl was born in Hoosick, New York, February 11, 1895.

Frank Rabl, the father, was a trained mechanico-electrical engineer of great ability. Four years after Sam's birth he moved his family to Baltimore where, for the U.S. Army Engineers, he had charge of all marine activities concerning fortifications on Chesapeake Bay, quartered from the Fort Howard base. Sam Rabl grew up in this environment, and it is little wonder he should take up shipbuilding and graduate to naval architecture.

During World War I, Sam was a shipfitter at the Union Yards, and became a bosom friend of a young M.I.T. graduate, Philip L. Rhodes, considered by most professionals to have been among the greatest artists in naval architecture in America. Phil once told me he lived near Sam's home in the confusing conformity of the Dutch Burgher's style of housing then prevailing, and could only tell where his own house was in relation to Sam's by counting paces from a certain tree. Rhodes had many a meal at Sam's home, prepared by Sam's mother, Susanna. He recalled Sam's designery. This drafting room consisted of a clothes closet: open the door and there were the board, the files, the tools. It was from this place at 6 N. East Avenue in Baltimore that Sam in 1925 sent *Picaroon* into the world.

Sam Rabl went to grade school in East Baltimore—the Highlandtown area. He graduated from the Polytechnic Institute and took further work in engineering at Maryland Institute Annex. He married Margaret L. Napfel on May 12, 1920, taking over the home at 6 N. East Avenue. Sam and Margaret had bought it the year before. It was a matriarchal home. Sam was surrounded by wife, sisters-in-law, and many nieces. He was fond of saying, "Blessed am I among women."

Sam seems to have held several jobs at this stage of life, as do most young men, and these were with a machine shop outfit, then a dry dock, then a full-fledged shipyard, where for 24 years he held forth as head of the shipfitting drafting effort. This fact was generally known to his public, and hence his image in the press was that of a two-fisted Erection Boss spitting hot rivets and cuss words. His voice on the phone was rather deep timbered, which did nothing to dispel an image of the buccaneer.

Perhaps this image was supported by Sam's crisp masculine writing. He had reduced written communication to that succinct use of word which is Art, giving 24-carat yield. I have been surprised to learn that Sam wrote novel after novel in the hope of a bestseller, but only succeeded in getting published his *Mobtown Clipper,* which wasn't a very big bag as a book. This hobby obviously disciplined his writing, which may be why his technical stuff had smash impact. Today, two of his books are high on the list of demand in every bookstore.

The hottest of these is *Boatbuilding in Your Own Backyard,* and next is *Practical Principles of Naval Architecture,* which is simple, lucid, and clear. I consider each the best in its field, because they are written in one-cylinder words by a man who thoroughly understood his subject and does not need to grandstand in the use of "Fo'c's'l Spoken Here." His publishers, Cornell Maritime Press of Centreville, Maryland, must have appreciated this.

The public did, and Sam had a nice income on the side from his incessant spare-time output. He wrote books on navigation, he painted maritime pictures, and he modeled everything from airplanes to ships in bottles; this seems dilettante in retrospect, for in his motor boating design stories, the converse image came through. In these he was the doughty buccaneer.

Which is why his friendly face unlined by warrior's woes may come as a surprise to the thousands who today, as newcomers to the boat noodling sport, are re-discovering Rabl. His fine blond hair, blue eyes, and five-foot-nine frame at 165 pounds were hardly the armament of a black-bearded pirate.

I believe it was Sam's appeal to the escapist that is in all of us that accounts for the public's generally held image of him. Sam Rabl fired up the "Dammit, I'll DO it!" streak in Rover Boy hearts beyond counting. Take the case of young Hank Hemingway as an illustration of the Rabl phenomenon.

Hank was Ernest Hemingway's kid brother. Hemingway the elder had written *For Whom the Bell Tolls* and had repaired to life in Cuba. Young Les (Hank) Hemingway had his own formula for stealing brotherly thunder in the Caribbean; he would build *Picaroon* to Sam Rabl's plans—build her in Mobile, which he did, and with a compatriot pirate he would set sail to roam the Spanish Main. This, too, he and his friend did. Up to a point.

Setting out in *Hawkshaw*—imaginative name for a poking adventurer!—the boys sailed from Mobile for Key West. They were abundantly armored for a cruise to the Orinoco with a pail of ham sandwiches, some water, and a lot of scruffy radiance.

On a slant for Key West, "running their southing down," they got belted in the butt by a howling Norther, a wind which frequently waxes wroth in the Gulf. *Hawkshaw* and her crew were knocked galley west in two days of scudding to near the coast of Yucatan. As the wind abated, the kids and little *Hawkshaw* fought their way north through a secondary storm to the latitude of Florida.

Reaching the Florida parallel, they began to "run their easting down," and 20 days after leaving Mobile, a housefly came aboard. Land was near! Two more days and they fetched up at Fort Myers, Florida. They were completely out of food and water.

Dauntlessly, *Hawkshaw* next threaded the Florida Straits. By this time, Cuba's most renowned immigrant had his end of the island in an uproar and the Cuban Navy in another looking for his kid brother. With boundless dash and fervor, the Cuban Navy searched the Florida Straits, ostensibly in target practice, immolating as many as six of the enemy at a time until all innocent yachts were proven guiltless. Eventually *Hawkshaw* was discovered moored off the beach at Nuevitas, where Ernest found the adventurers digging their bare toes lusciously in the sand, washed by the luculent lapping of a limpid sea. He chased the kids home.

This was Sam Rabl's fire at work under the boiler of Romance!

How did he do it? Perhaps it was Sam's flamboyant drafting. Much of his early work looked broad-brush, if not smeared on with a putty knife, or lettered boldly with a trowel. He used to tell Phil Rhodes, "It's the Bolshevik boats that get 'em." Meaning "rebellious," for which the Bolshi word was a synonym. At any rate, Sam's boats "got 'em." Hank Hemingway's adventure was repeated with variations by hundreds of others, unsung.

What manner of boats were these? Take a look at *Picaroon*. Her name is Spanish for "Petty Pirate." The pictorial aspect of her is worth ten thousand of any words I could write, so I'll merely say she appeared in sketch form in a short, three-page article in *Motor Boat*. She was 18 feet long, 7 feet 6 inches beam, drew 2 feet 9 inches of water, and carried 180 square feet of sail in a simple jibheaded-sloop rig. At the time of first exposure in *Motor Boat*, *Pic*'s plans were in pencil on brown wrapping paper. Wherefore they were not then published. Sam did do a good set of drawings later, and they are carried in his backyard boatbuilding book.

A follow-up on *Picaroon* appeared in the September 25, 1925, issue of *Motor Boat* giving the "now it can be told" outcome. Sam wrote, "She's the slickest handling little piece of wood I ever got my hands on. Given equal loading in a decent breeze, she can lick a Star."

Sam tried to improve her, but the more sequels he did, the more he came back close to the original *Picaroon*. *Pic*'s first sequel was *Peggy*, which ran in William Atkin's *Fore An' Aft* magazine, issue of June 15,

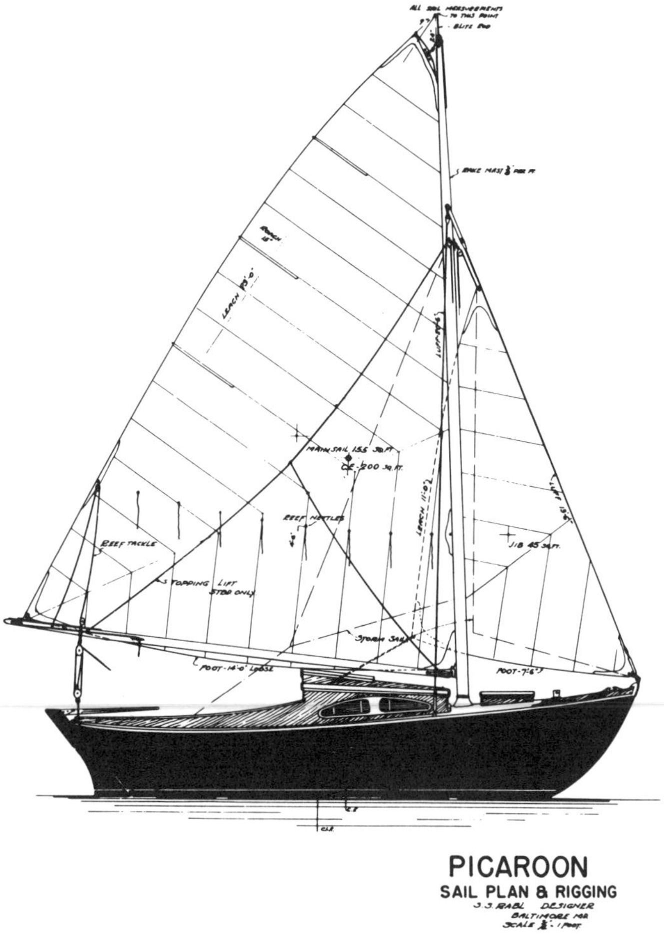

PICAROON
SAIL PLAN & RIGGING
S.S. RABL   DESIGNER
BALTIMORE MD
SCALE 3/8" = 1 FOOT

Sail and accommodation plans for a plywood *Picaroon* as they appear in Rabl's *Boatbuilding in Your Own Backyard*.

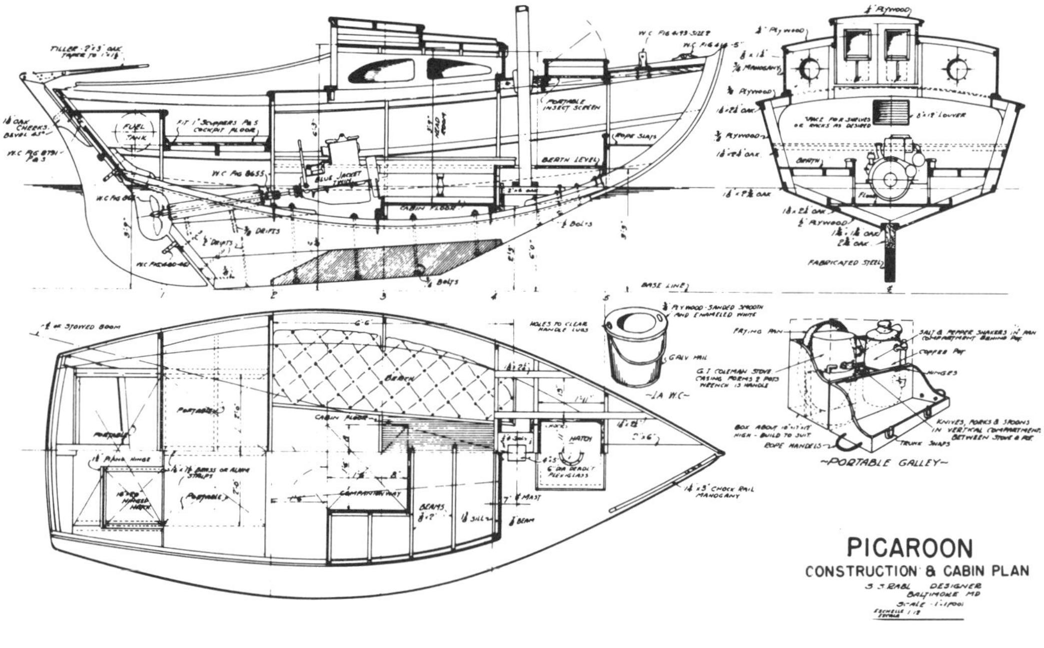

PICAROON
CONSTRUCTION & CABIN PLAN
S.S. RABL   DESIGNER
BALTIMORE MD
SCALE 1" = 1 FOOT

~PORTABLE GALLEY~

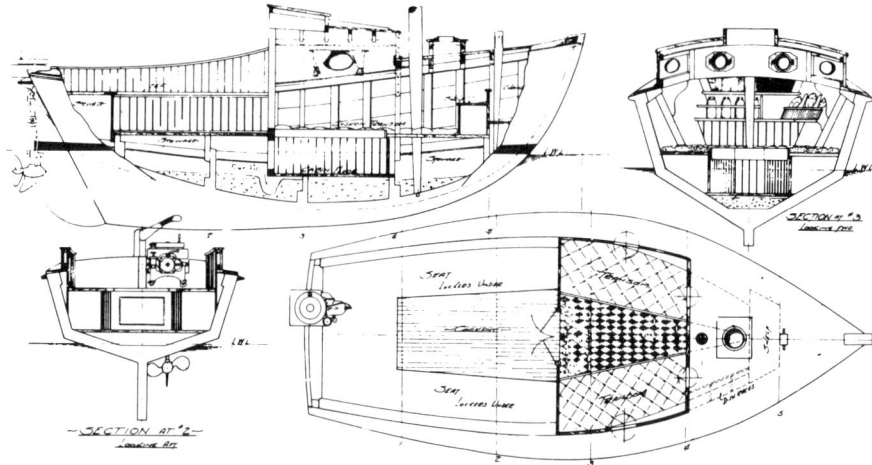

Above: Peggy was *Pic* with too much deadrise. *Below: Buddy* was *Pic* with raised deck.

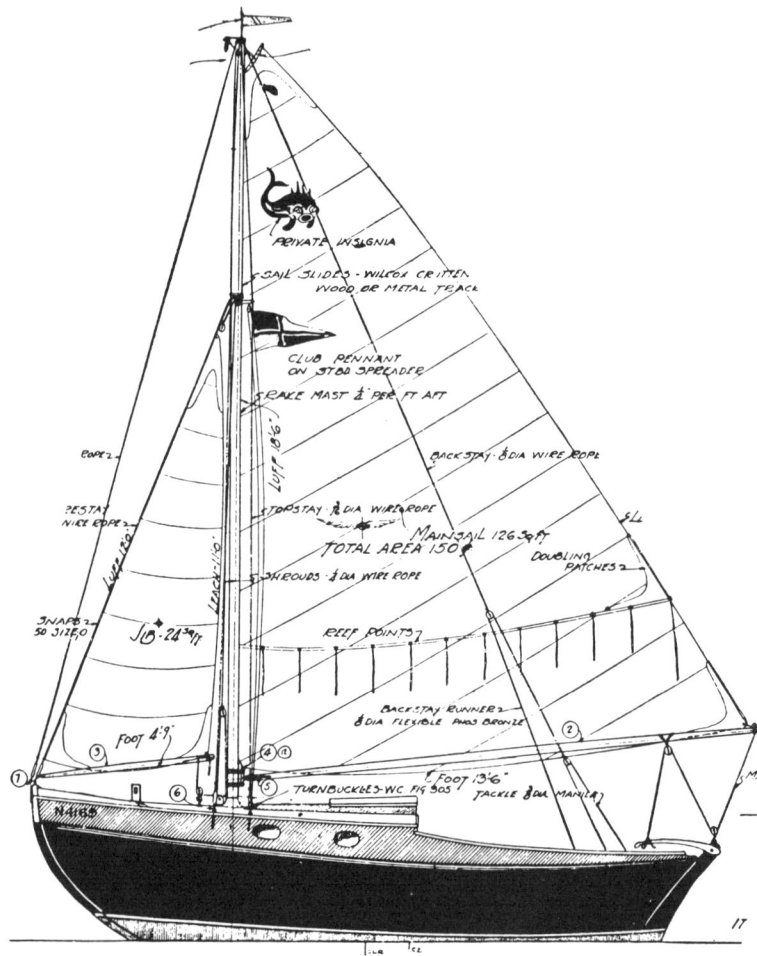

1927. *Peggy* was not as good a boat as *Picaroon*. She was the same size, with 3 inches less draft, 178 square feet of sail area, but used a long-shaft outboard and had much greater deadrise. The latter was her undoing. As any experienced designer knows, the V-bottom hull is very sensitive to the amount of deadrise in the resulting boat feel—so much so that men like William H. Hand, Jr., never departed from the amount of V he put in a bottom. Sam found this out, and designed *Buddy,* the third sequel, to follow *Peggy.*

Sam Rabl designed *Buddy* for me—that is, for the magazine I was editing then, *The Mechanical Package Magazine.* By way of explanation, in 1928 I had stepped out of naval architecture in New York in a laudable desire to eat, and the finger of Fortune had succored me from the feast-and-famine trade by a meeting I'd had with Captain Billy Fawcett, of the then-struggling Fawcett Publications in Robbinsdale, Minnesota. The result was *Modern Mechanics* (now *Mechanix Illustrated*) and subsequently *How to Build Twenty Boats* and *The Flying Manuals.* These I edited on the generous budget (for those days) of $1,800 a month.

I had fine luck with publishing "roast beef" material on boats and light airplanes, and sailed the stormy Depression years unaware of grief. I was able to keep Jack Hanna and Sam Rabl and others of the boat noodling fraternity eating well.

Knowing of *Picaroon,* I had Sam design *Buddy*—same hull as *Picaroon* except for a cabin, sides brought right up from the hull, Dutch fashion. *Buddy* appeared in the October 1932 issue of *The Mechanical Package Magazine,* and in a subsequent issue of *How to Build Twenty Boats.* This started my intimate business and professional relationship with Sam, even if at considerable distance.

Buddy was just about as good as *Picaroon,* but of course had more leeway and windage. She was extremely popular, and Sam, with *Buddy,* got down on his hunkers and really showed what a slick drafting job he could do.

Picaroon II was done in plywood, for a later editor, and of what was called Harborform shape. She didn't do well, Sam told me, and so we can let her image waft away without mourning, or exposure here.

Sam's last sequel, *Picaroon III,* was printed in the 1959 *Sports Afield Boatbuilding Annual.* She is *Picaroon* grown from a boy's boat to a young man's boat, expanded from 18 feet to 23 feet in proportion. She is a masterpiece, both as a development with much experience behind her, and as a marvelous piece of drafting. Beautifully done, she is Sam Rabl's last boat.

Before I returned to naval architectural work, Sam and I had quite an adventure. I talked with him frequently by phone. This is faster and

~ DATA ~

LENGTH O.A. 23'-0"
" W.L. 18'-6"
BEAM 8'-0" MOLDED
DRAFT 4'-0"
DISPLACEMENT 5175 LBS
LBS PER 1" AT DWL 480.0
CB LOCATED 13.6' AFT FP
AREA LATERAL PLANE 43.6 SQ FT SANS RUDDER
CLR LOCATED 12.1' AFT FP
AREA DESIGNED WL 90.3 SQ FT

~ OUTSIDE BALLAST ~

TOTAL VOLUME 3.00 CU FT
50% LEAD 960 lbs
47% CONCRETE 125
3% STEEL 45
WEIGHT OF SHOE 1170
TOTAL WEIGHT 1300 POUNDS

No 582
PICAROON III
~ WORKING LINES ~
S S RABL DESIGNER
BALTIMORE MD

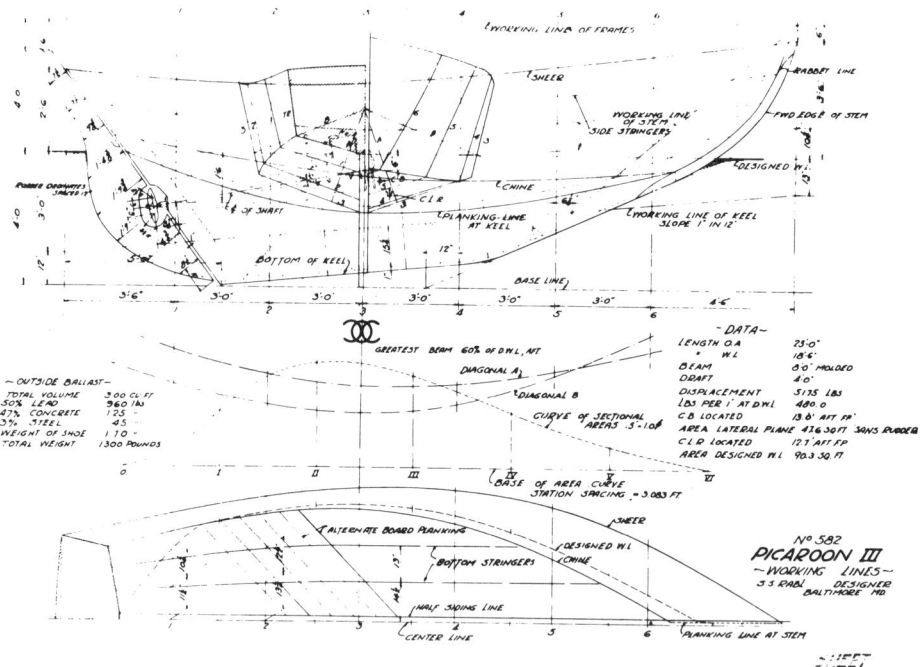

Picaroon III was Sam Rabl's last piece of work, based on his accumulated knowledge from having designed several sequels to his original *Picaroon*. She has the same bottom form as the original, but is 5 feet longer at 23 feet. An interesting design note is that her greatest beam is at 60 percent waterline of the DWL. This accommodates cockpit loads.

cheaper than letter writing. In discussing the Rabl sequels, Sam always came back to *Picaroon* as being his favorite. He also said he'd gone to work for Glenn L. Martin on the design of the Martin Flying Clipper.

If Sam had imbued me with the Romance Isles theme in his boats, our light airplanes fired his urge to hop serenely from fleecy white cloud to fleecy white cloud in a little plane of his own. He asked me if I'd publish his design for a small, single-seat seaplane.

I knew he was a good engineer, knew basics and reasoned that with Martin design talent looking over his shoulder, he could probably pull it off. Thus came about the only real Rabl design failure I know of. The plane was designed for a 23 hp Heath Henderson engine. She had large areas of paper in her construction, of a new phenolic-bonded type, and had light aluminum floats. Orville Hickman of the Swallow Aircraft Co. built her in our Robbinsdale experimental shop. All the time she was a-building, untried, the presses were running off a hundred thousand bids to birdland with complete plans for the glorious Rabl Seaplane.

The Rabl Seaplane Just Would Not Fly.

She was "flight" tested on Medicine Lake, Hennepin County, Minnesota. This was a wild, uninhabited spot four miles west of our shop. The motor functioned perfectly. Came roars of prop and thunder of motor, with a premier pilot of the air, Gene Shank, at the test try. Just No Dice! She just would not plane.

Finally a gust of wind got under the tail of the Rabl Seaplane and somersaulted her. We then learned that the holder of the world's loop-the-loop record could not swim. Gene was thrown out, and paddled around on instinct, batting water with clenched fists, his terrified eyes popping like a Boston bull pup with a goiter.

We rowed around the nearly drowning man, photographer Bruce Sifford and I, taking pictures, because I knew that without them Sam would never believe me. Until we fished Gene in, the photographic evidence was dramatic.

That night I phoned Sam. He was on the edge of his chair waiting to see his child in print. To learn his bird was a kiwi would be crushing. I tempered the news in the realization that the arrows of anguish stab deeper than we think. The news left Sam incredulous. I expected thunder, cuss words, and brimstone. Instead, in his voice was an expression of sorrow, deepened with regret and gently tempered by the patient forgiveness of a connoisseur of design who cannot be understood.

Rabl's *Sea Gull* proved to be a Kiwi. Despite the high hopes of her designer, the little single-seater not only failed to get off the water but dunked her test pilot in the process. This is part of Rabl's original drawing for the author, then editor of *The Mechanical Package Magazine.*

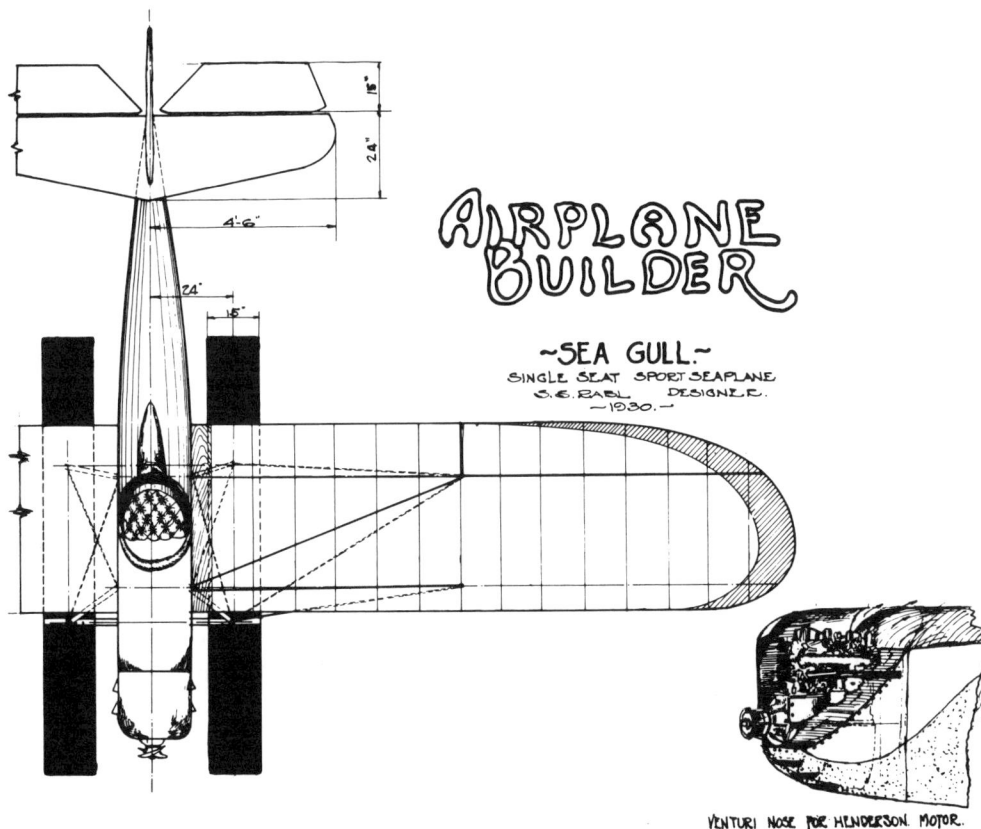

AIRPLANE
BUILDER

~SEA GULL.~
SINGLE SEAT SPORT SEAPLANE
S.S. RABL   DESIGNER.
~1930.~

VENTURI NOSE FOR HENDERSON. MOTOR.

Sam finally got the idea his dream child would not fly. The paper in her had soaked up weight from moisture in building; she now was soaked apart. But the resilience of youth had been a habit of Sam Rabl's for so long he could not shake it; he showed it with this response: "Okay, old son. I'm sorry as hell. We're at the wrong end of the car line. Can't we ring up two fares and both ride back on the same car?"

We surely could, and did, the best of friends.

At another time, when I asked Sam what he called something he had designed, he said, "You don't call—just go on betting." This pixie humor flashes from Sam's work. His "copy" dances along in lucid simplicity, freighted with stimulating observation. In all his writing there is whimsy, tolerant of human foible, that sometimes explodes one to aching laughter. His was the perception of genius.

The following anecdote about Sam will show his boyishness: About 10 years after the seaplane debacle I had returned to my profession and found myself in charge of the drafting room at Annapolis Yacht Yard, which later became Trumpy's, riding herd on the Vosper PT boat design for Herreshoff, Robert Jacob, Harbor Boat, and the Annapolis Yard. Sam was about 18 miles north in his drafting room at Sparrows Point. I thought it would be a good idea for us to get together, so I phoned him. We set up a date for a later meal, which, in the event, was never to happen. Over the phone Sam told me the following yarn in a rather lengthy, old buddy-to-buddy gab fest.

The past summer he'd been up on the upper East Coast where they use "R's" at the beginning of words, but "ahs" at the end. Cruising with a pal, they'd made a small fishing port at dusk. They secured ship and went up town to make wassail and jubilee, thus to save the village from stagnation. The hope was forlorn, for it was a Friday night, and the townsmen had bugged off in their gas buggies for whoopee in the Big City. There was no proper stimulus or food to be found.

Sam and his friend repaired to a fish house about to be closed for the weekend, determined to partake of the viands of the environment. They bought a fine four-pound fish. Back aboard in their galley, this denizen of the deep proved to have been out of water since before its granddad had died. The sea's bounty was putrefied to the brink of botulism.

Next morning, before casting off, Sam and his pal rammed a dowel rod down the fish to put some spine in him, wrapped him up in brown paper, and, the time being Saturday forenoon, took him to the post office. They affixed five-cent stamps in profusion from head clear down to tail, bought a Special Handling stamp, and returned the cod by mail.

From this, Sam got much tee-hee.

I never met Sam Rabl personally. Our date for a meal in Baltimore was interrupted by a summons to me at Annapolis from the Coast Guard. A fire extinguisher aboard my cruiser was missing at a routine inspection, and by the time it was found, the electric car to Baltimore had rattled off, and I'd missed my chance. Our meeting became, "Some other time," between us. There was to be no other time. It has been one of my life's deepest regrets, for I knew him so very well—his spirit and mind. They are alive today, and after you discover him, you'll say, "Isn't he a daisy?" Present tense!

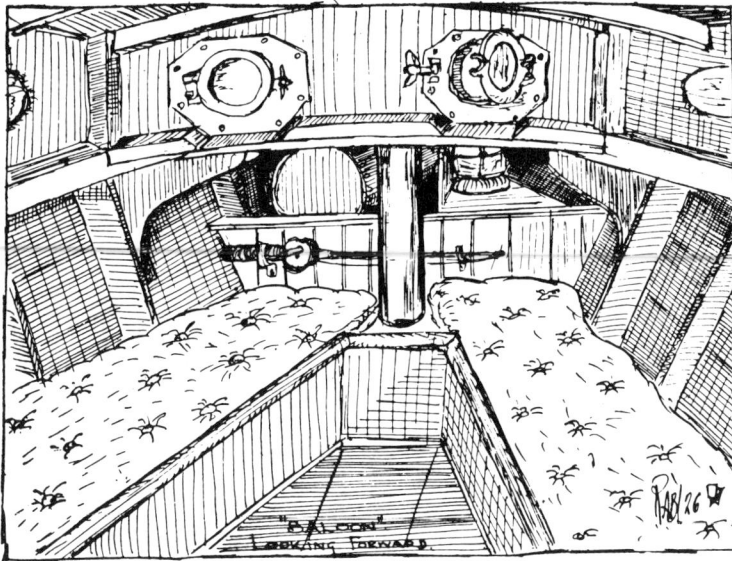

Sam Rabl's enormous output will live a long time. As long as men read and dream about boats, Sam will be with us. He keeps on enriching us all. No one better had his knack of showing how boats are built à la Maryland and Chesapeake Bay.

With *Picaroon,* Sam hit the nail on the head by turning out a little masterpiece. Every once in a while a guy does it: without knowing exactly why, his bean hits on all six, his guessometry of ruling factors is sharp, and his happy craft becomes an inimitable, unimprovable classic.

Such a craft was balanced, saucy, able *Picaroon,* now proven on all seas, designed by Samuel Supplee Rabl, the great master of simplicity.

9

Ralph Winslow, Powerboat Designer

In 1904 the Boston office of Small Brothers, naval architects, was situated in a loft at 112 Water Street, at that time a region of grimy marine chandleries, bakeries, and cobblers' shops. From the dusty windows of the Smalls' boat drafting emporium, above neighboring chimney pots, could be seen tall masts and the pall of smoke funnelling from big ships sliding silently out to sea.

Small Brothers were pioneering something called "gasoline motor boats," which had "compromise" sterns. Their cruisers were in high vogue, and Small Brothers were very big in compromise sterns.

Into this establishment one morning in 1904 there entered a smallish young man of 19 seeking employment as a marine draftsman. His name was Ralph E. Winslow, and he was destined to become more famous as a naval architect than the prominent men from whom he sought a job.

In the manner of employers at that time, the senior brother, John F. Small, probably told Winslow that he could come to work the following Monday; that he would be expected to cut his own goose quill pens and supply his own India ink, and that he would be expected to arrive half an hour before work began each morning to mop the floors. After two years, if he had kept shaved and neat, had bathed each week, did not smoke tobacco, had attended church punctually each Sunday, and had made no drafting errors in that time, he would be given a raise of 5 cents an hour if business conditions warranted it.

Winslow got the job. Wonder-struck by the romance of it all, he left the office, then re-opened the door, reminded of an interviewing oversight.

Ralph E. Winslow, world-famed naval architect noted for his versatility in both sail and power boats, is shown at age 66 in 1951 working happily at his board in Quincy, Massachusetts.

"Don't you want to know my name?" he called to John Small.

"It'll be the same Monday as it is today," was that Yankee's laconic rejoinder.

That is how Ralph Eldridge Winslow moved a rung up the ladder from a young apprentice boatbuilder in a Quincy, Massachusetts, boatshop (Baker Boat Basin), to become an initiate into the art of designing boats in the engineering manner on a drawing board.

For the next 53 years, until his death from Parkinson's disease on March 29, 1957, Ralph Winslow's name stood for yacht design excellence and drafting of the highest order. Few have equalled him and no one, in my estimation, has topped him in the thoroughness of his art.

I knew him personally but briefly. I knew him professionally for a very long time. The publication of any of his designs I greeted with purring satisfaction, retiring cozily to study each one. Consequently, I know his work well, recognizing his drafting "hand" and techniques from a long association going back to my apprentice days circa 1918 when Ralph graciously sold me sets of plans for the mere cost of blueprinting them. I have many.

Nearly all dyed-in-the-wool boatmen of seasoned maturity know the Winslow name. Generally he is thought of as a past master of the solid seagoing long-range yacht—ketches, schooners, cutters, yawls, and here and there a dainty tabloid sloop. His line of "Tamars" is well known throughout the yachting world, some 80 or 90 of them having been built the wide world over. To catalog just the profiles and arrangement plans of these yachts would occupy an entire chapter in this book. A few examples are shown here on the Winslow artistry in sail.

But it is a surprising thing to most men that Ralph Winslow's main body of work was in powerboats during his early years up to 1920. As draftsman for Small Brothers, then with William H. Hand when Hand was developing his famous Piute string of V-bottom boats, and next as chief draftsman for Swasey, Raymond & Page (high-grade Boston naval architects), it was largely Ralph Winslow's work on the board that was responsible for the product that made these enterprises go.

It is high time that due credit be given to Winslow for his heavy contribution to the world integer. A modest, unassuming man, doubtless his personality did not bomb the yachting press of the immediate past, because in my library of long continuum with major marine and yachting journals, I found only mere mention of his death. On fairness alone, editors should have documented Ralph Winslow's work with due praise.

To properly give this great designer credit for his early and little-known—let us say, "less well known"—contribution to the art of motorboat design, let us start where I did in this survey of his work. In threading such a series of needles we can throw Winslow's work into understandable perspective. This requires the reader's indulgence for a minute or two of inserting the perpendicular pronoun, for which I beg forgiveness. My tale can be told no other way.

One day, about 20 years ago, I was sitting comfortably on my shoulder blades against an elm tree on my lawn, gazing over my toes at the deep blue seascape and contemplating the vicissitudes that beset naval architects in the 70 or 80 years immediately preceding their funerals. In this reverie I began to think about Winslow and of how much of my own powerboat work had been built upon his generosity to me. It struck me that I hadn't seen any of his work published for quite a while.

Gazing at wide waters, I recalled he had come to Annapolis about a matter in naval design at one time, and we had had a rich hour or two of comparing notes. He had said, "I was just getting my sailboats to a point where they'd pay me a living, and then this darned war came along." After that, silence.

The sea breezes stirred strongly, I got off my shoulder blades, went into the house wondering, and wrote to him at his home, 39 Ridgway, Quincy, Massachusetts. From his wife, Jennie Winslow, I received a note stating Ralph was mortally ill and that she'd be glad to sell me all of his work for $5,000. I didn't have that much, but found a man who had built one of my boats who offered to put up the money. He sailed to the South Seas before I could nail him. The matter died.

A few years ago, in the autumn of 1971, I ran across Jennie Winslow's letter again. Able then to muster the funds, I made the offer by mail, again to the old Winslow home address. The letter was returned marked "Unknown." I then vowed, in a true antiquer's snit, to locate, and if possible, buy the Winslow plans. They would be a designer's treasure!

No trace of the family could be found via gumshoe at 39 Ridgway. I felt strongly that someone in that locality must know the whereabouts of the Winslow heirs.

I put the matter up to talented Pete Culler, well known to traditional boat noodlers. Culler eventually wrote, after some sleuthing, stating that Mr. William A. Baker, designer of the *Mayflower II*, had informed him that George D. Follet, long an engineering draftsman for Electric Boat at Groton, Connecticut, had secured the tracings. A letter was sent hot-foot to George Follet, wanting to buy the plans.

George responded promptly with the news that in December 1971, while Pete Culler was trying to find a home for my money, the plans had been donated by him (Follet) to the Marine Museum at Mystic Seaport. Mrs. Winslow had given the plans to George Follet, an old friend of the family, feeling that the Winslow sons, John E. Winslow and Charles B. Winslow, were not interested in them. Also from Follet I learned that John Eldridge Winslow, Ralph's oldest son, was alive and well in Merrimack, New Hampshire, in charge of some government property nearby. Ralph's younger son, Charles Boutillier Winslow, also hale and hearty, is a regional sales manager for National Lead Co. (Dutch Boy Paints) and is living in Wheaton, Illinois. I have been in touch with both men.

It is from John E. Winslow, who responded generously, that I learned of the Small Brothers anecdote with which I opened this story. To John Winslow it came as a great surprise that I knew his father's main body of design work was more in motor craft than in sail.

The earliest record known to me of Winslow's design work was published in *Motor Boat* (the Old Green Sheet) in 1906, when Ralph was

21 years old. She is shown here: a 33-foot by 8-foot double-cabin job, compromise stern, in reflection of the then Small Brothers vogue. Ralph's natural gift for proportion and sweetness is evident. You see in this drawing two permanent Winslow drafting characteristics: his method of inclined lettering, all in capitals, and his style of drawing flags. This Winslow chirography never changed and easily identifies his work, no matter in what design office he may have been working. In this 1906 drawing are evidences of unknowing blunders in design—the oversize propeller without sufficient tip clearance and the weak plate rudder with stock and pintle attached to the blade edges—all to be expected of so young a man.

In 1914, when he was chief draftsman, office manager, and general factotum for Swasey, Raymond & Page, Ralph was in his salad days. He had joined this prestigious firm in 1909, taking the place of J. Murray Watts, a graduate of Yale's Sheffield Scientific School who had departed the firm some time previously to set up his own board in Philadelphia.

In 1914, the year World War I erupted and Ralph designed a blockbuster of a double-cabin cruiser which, for sheer originality in getting away from the then-fashionable sharp stern on cruisers, stood the motor boating world on its ear. Ralph was 29 at the time. Fortunately, I have a print of this boat that Winslow sold me 10 years later. This is reproduced in arrangement plan here. This boat was his "straight sheer" model, with engine far aft in the stern cuddy. She is 30 feet by 8 feet, powered by a two-cylinder, 4-cycle, 12-hp Sterling engine.

From its inception and for about 10 years, this was the most imitated motor cruiser on the marine scene. Elco, John G. Hanna, Allan O. Gould, and Arthur P. Homer designed boats inspired by this general model of Winslow's.

Swasey, Raymond & Page as a design firm produced many notable powercraft. Under Ralph's guidance, they turned out *Aramis*, the first large diesel yacht to be built in this country. She was 165 feet l.o.a. and was built at City Island by Robert Jacob. She was powered by Craig diesels. Her owner was Arthur H. Marks, Akron rubber magnate.

The exquisite mini-destroyer-type yacht *Paragon* was Ralph's work. The company also turned out later the large steel diesel-electric yacht *Guinivere,* a 190-foot schooner. S., R. & P. got the credit, and Ralph did the drawings. In all such firms, the chief draftsman is the fellow who does the design work, the nitty-gritty, digging the boss out of work while the boss himself is out digging up the scratch to meet the payroll instead of staying on the job in the office and doing what he made his reputation at—designing.

A. Loring Swasey, head of the firm, was a first-class naval architect,

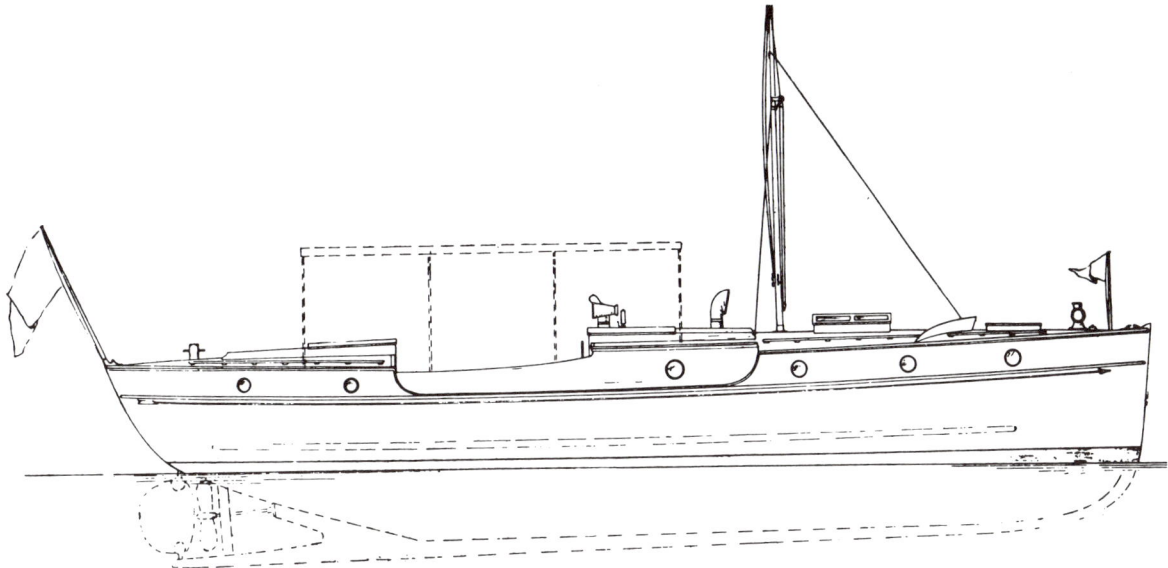

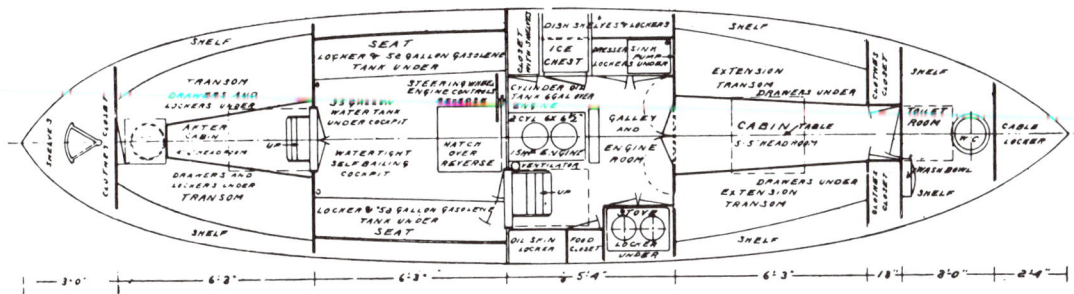

Above: In 1906, Winslow, then 21 and working for Small Brothers of Boston, designed this typical Small Brothers compromise-stern power cruiser. *Below:* This 30' x 8' straight-sheer, double-cabin cruiser was designed by Winslow as a "home venture" when he was chief draftsman for Swasey, Raymond, and Page, and was novel for its engine placement. Date: circa 1914. This boat sparked much imitation.

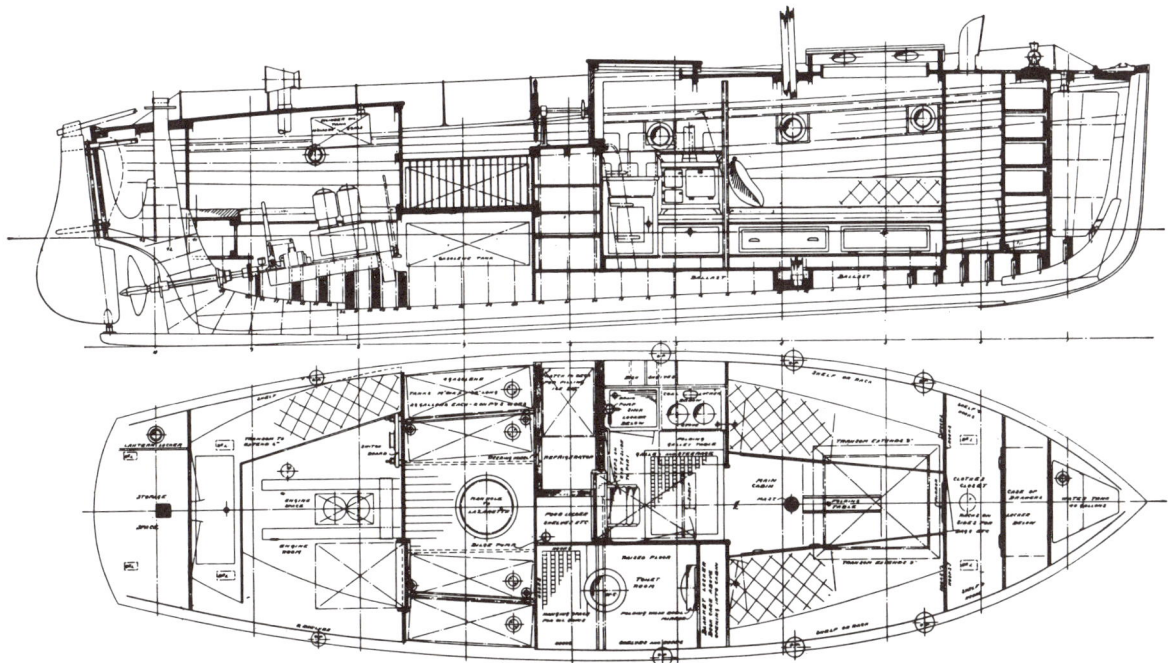

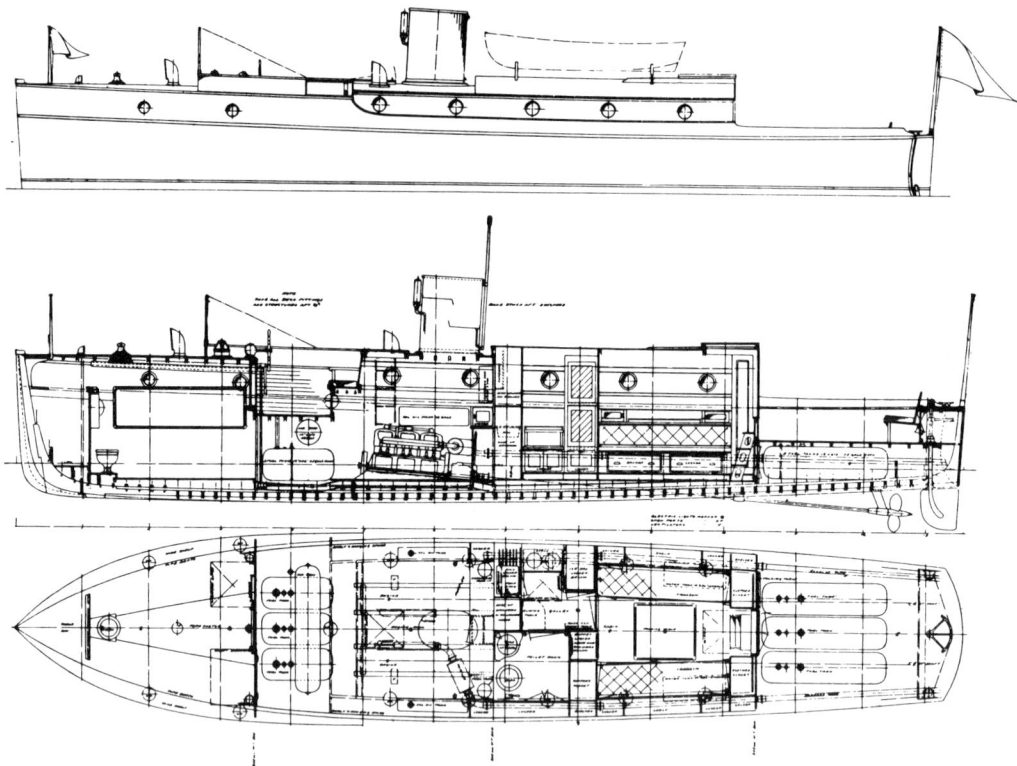

Above: In "preparedness" days before WW I, wealthy men were commissioning military-type express cruisers for Power Squadron donation to the U.S. Navy. Here is one designed by Ralph Winslow when he was chief draftsman for Swasey, Raymond, and Page, naval architects of Boston. These would be fine, fast boats today. *Below:* After a Herreshoff Manufacturing Co. interlude, Ralph struck out for himself, designing all types of vessels. This harbor police boat shows his forthright understanding of construction. Put a ruler along her waterline to see how pretty this boat is.

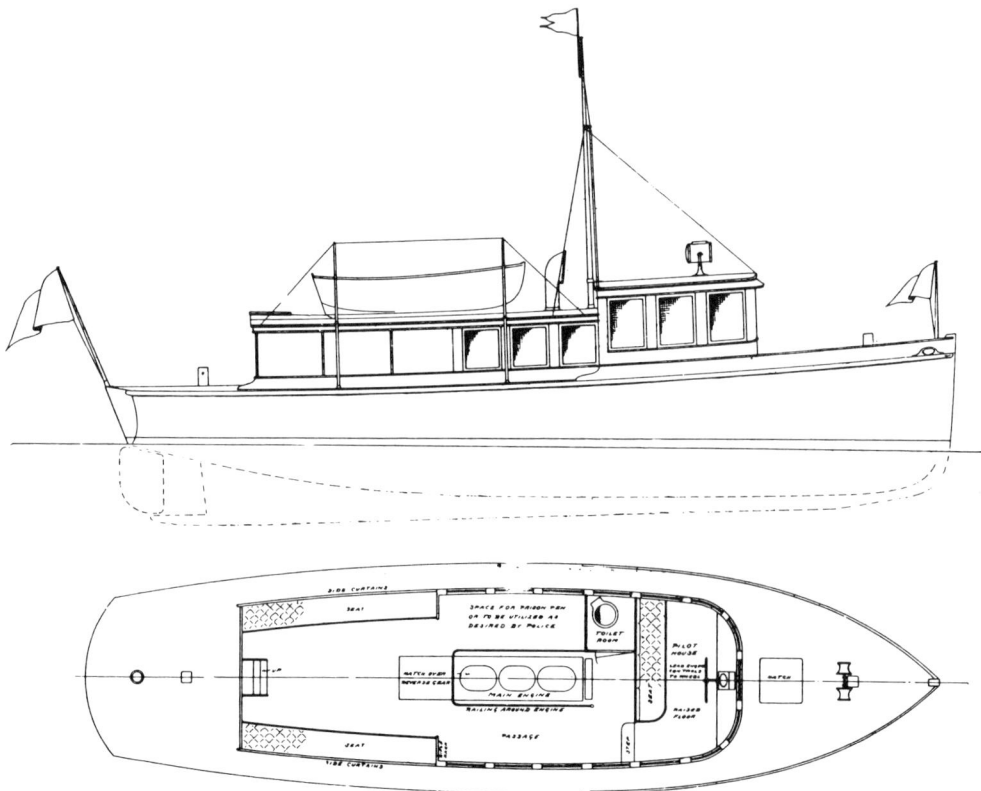

one of the well-known Swasey family, long a big name in the New England machine tool industry. This is the same Captain Swasey who was chief of the small-craft design bureau of the Navy during World War II. He was a most imposing man with great personal presence. Winslow and Swasey had a long association, of which more later. Having known both men, the working relationship was well known to me. It persisted for years, as will be shown from Ralph's personal work resume. At the time Winslow joined S., R. & P., there was beginning a great ferment in what was called Military Type Express Cruisers. The Great World War I saw the neutrality of the United States persist from 1914 until 1917, yet all this time the German Navy was sinking much neutral and U.S. shipping off our coast. This was the era before reliable planes were suitable for submarine patrol work, so the U.S. Navy was forced to enlist all available and suitable yachts for offshore patrol spotting of the Kaiser's "Unterseemotorbootes"—U boats.

Patriotic men started building the specially designed, tough, speedy, military-type offshore express cruiser. They then turned them over to the Navy. The leader in this design work was the Swasey firm. The engineering was Winslow's. Plans are shown here from his hand. Ralph was 32 years of age when these were drawn. Under his masterful touch, these were smashingly beautiful boats. The lessons of long, lean lines and the advantages of length had not then been forgotten as they are today. These patrol craft were powered by 6- or 8-cylinder Sterling engines, with cylinders the size of nail kegs. When these engines rotated, things moved—25 honest knots or better, with great endurance.

To round out the pictorial chronology of Ralph Winslow's work in powerboats, I have selected a launch he designed for the Boston Harbor Police in 1924. From the stark, utilitarian requirements of such service he produced an extremely pretty boat.

Because a man's working resumé is more brief than any writer's exposition can be, I insert here the history prepared by Winslow himself when he was living. Transcribed word for word by John Winslow, his son, it gives us a unique and authoritative record of Ralph's working history during his formative and most prolific years:

1904 to 1909—Draftsman with Small Brothers, B.B. Crowninshield, Fore River Yard, Wm. H. Hand, Jr.—naval architects, principally yachts.

1909 to 1917—Chief draftsman, office manager, salesman, construction supervisor, Swasey, Raymond & Page, naval architects and engineers.

1917 to 1920—Chief draftsman, hull supervisor, salesman & customer's man, Herreshoff Mfg. Co., Bristol, R.I. Loaned by them to U.S. Navy in charge of designing U.S. 110-foot submarine chasers. Navy Dept. offered me charge of their construction, but returned to Herreshoff as wished back by them. Offered charge of converting *Massachusetts* and *Bunker Hill* into mine layers, also inspection of destroyers at Fore River during that period by Navy, but always asked to stay at Herreshoff. Salary, $3600.

1920 to 1928–In business for myself at Atlantic, Mass., as naval architect and marine engineer. Income varied from $5,000 to $10,000 per year.

1928 to Nov. 1931–Member of firm of Eldredge-McInnis, Inc. (Vice president), Naval Architects, Marine Engineers and Yacht Brokers. Same work as when at Herreshoff's and Swasey, Raymond & Page. Salary $6,000 per year plus 5% of gross income of firm.

1931, November–Naval Architect in business for myself.

Here the resumé ends. Bear in mind, when assessing this income pattern, that the price of a loaf of bread was then 5 cents. Food prices are an accurate index of money's purchasing power. One may deduce that Winslow's income was high in his day and time.

During the Depression of the 1930s, Ralph engaged in his natural love, sailing yacht design. During the World War II years immediately following, he was in Washington in charge of U.S. Army design work. There was also a stint in John Alden's Boston office, where his health broke down, as reported by Al Mason, who worked in Alden's office at the same time. Thereafter, Ralph retired to his home and worked again on sailing yacht design until his death.

Though the main thrust of this story is to bring to light the knowledge of Ralph Winslow's work in powercraft, which greatly outnumbered his output in sailing yachts, I show here a couple of examples illustrative of the wide range of Winslow's work in sail alone. These seem unusually illustrative of his artistry in sail.

One is of a pretty little tabloid cutter of 21 feet waterline designed in 1924; the other is an 87-foot topsail schooner of exquisite proportions designed in the mid-1930s for round-the-world capability. No finer vessel for the work could be designed or built today. It is presumed her plans are now at Mystic in original form.

Ralph traced his New England genealogy back to the Plymouth Colony. His father, John H. Winslow, coal dealer of Quincy, was a direct descendant of the John Winslow who was the ship's master of the original *Mayflower*. This forefather was born in England in 1597, coming in the famed ship to Plymouth in 1621. His brother was Edward Winslow, the third governor of the colony.

To the first marriage of John H. Winslow was born a son, Harold L. Winslow, Ralph's half brother, who was for many years the Chief Officer of the S.S. *Leviathan* of the United States Lines. Harold Winslow was famed for a daring sea rescue in 1929, succoring a Grand Banks fishing schooner in a raging North Atlantic storm. For this he won a Navy citation and a gratuity and medal from Sir Thomas Lipton.

John H. Winslow married Alice B. Cross, daughter of Eldridge Cross, and to this marriage on October 26, 1886, Ralph Eldridge Winslow was

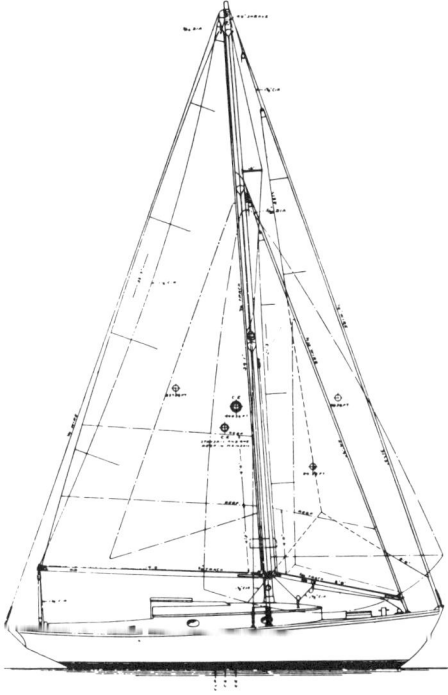

Winslow's deftness with yacht types is shown in this sail plan of a tabloid 21-foot-waterline cutter, designed in the mid-20s.

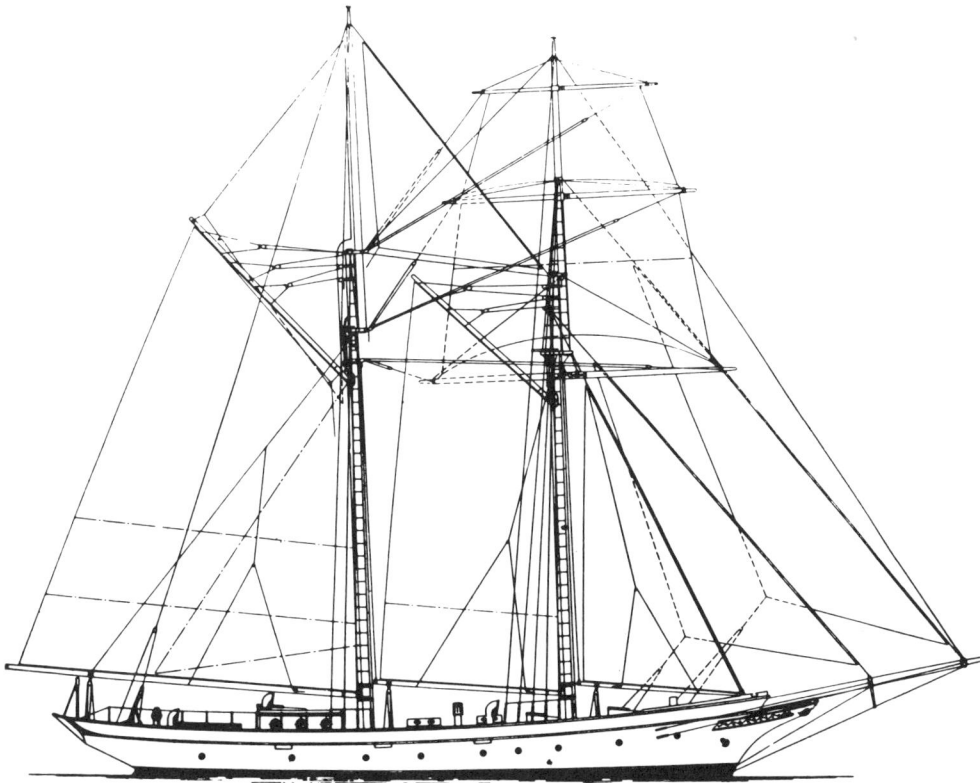

Winslow's work in sail had the master's touch, as may be seen in this profile of an 87-foot topsail schooner, designed in the mid-'30s for round-the-world voyaging.

born. This event was followed shortly by the birth of another brother, Wadsworth Winslow.

At Quincy, on June 17, 1918, Ralph E. Winslow married Jennie Alice Boutillier, daughter of Alexander and Jennie (Wood) Boutillier.

Ralph died at Merrymount, Quincy, on March 29, 1957. He is buried in the Mount Wollaston Cemetery, Quincy, Massachusetts. His wife, Jennie, died October 22, 1965. Both were of the Unitarian Christian faith.

On my scale of genealogical Brownie Points, all of the Winslow clan are entitled to cock-a-snoot at any Boston blue-blood. It is beyond challenging that Ralph E. Winslow, all 5 feet 4 inches and 145 pounds of him, was a giant at his trade.

10

Tips from an NA's Notebook

Every editor knows more about what transpires in his trade than he can possibly pack into any one issue of his paper or magazine. A lot of information slops over that is never retrieved. In the same way, every boat designer goes through a similar drill on every boat he designs. Much of the research backing his engineering decisions develops side-lights of artful recall that cannot be passed along in drawings.

Eventually these tidbits of information, minor in themselves but useful study nonetheless, pile up to interesting proportions. Some-where, at some time, to someone, a particular fragment of information could be of extremely high value. In that spirit I pass along some retrieved design lore right from my own School of Rapped Knuckles.

Some examples:

What is it that makes some boats good to ride in, while others are dogs that engender seasickness? Comfort can be measured.

Why do round-bilged boats always tend to heel outward on turns? Why do fast V-bottom boats heel inward? Ever stop to ponder the reason for this?

How can you pick the right rudder area? Usually, a blade area equal to one-fourth the immersed midsection area is right for a powerboat. If she's twin screw, divide the area between two rudders.

Such questions, and their short and snappy answers, are the gist of this writing.

Propeller Size

Before I answer more of the above posers, let's dispose of a perennial question: what size propeller should you use on a one-cylinder, 2-cycle, old-timer inboard engine, the kind that run between 600 rpm and 1,000 rpm? Here's the rule-of-thumb on that one:

These engines ranged in size from 2 hp to 10 hp in the one-cylinder size. I presume more 4 hp to 6 hp sizes were built than any other. If a manufacturer wanted to sell more horsepower, he added cylinders. But early on, I noticed that the one-cylinder engines were supplied with 2-bladed wheels of exactly the same diameter as the engine flywheel. (See Figure 1.) Usually, these propellers were "square," meaning they had the same pitch as diameter. They came in a variety of patterns, from the broad-tipped blade down to narrow-bladed S-snakes that were touted as weedless. Generally, the elliptical blade with a blade width of 30 percent of the diameter was standard.

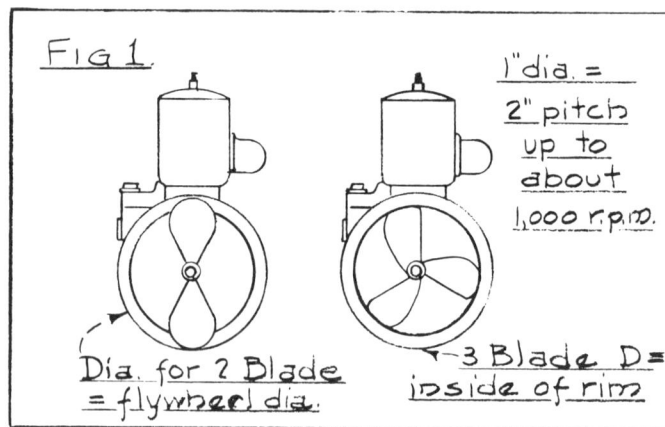

If a 3-bladed wheel was required, usually because of skeg or draft limitations, the diameter of the propeller then became about equal to the diameter of the flywheel inside the flywheel rim. In most cases, the two-bladed was the more authoritative on "push." This is because disc area is larger. Everyone who has fooled much with propellers eventually learns that the middle third, or boss portion, of the disc area swept by a wheel is worthless. In fact, if it could be eliminated, as eventually was done by some outboard engine makers in later decades when the exhaust was led through the central propeller boss, the wheel was more efficient. The high blade angle in the central third of a wheel doesn't contribute much thrust—only torque resistance.

It is interesting in this connection that all old engine builders used to state that "one inch of diameter is the equivalent of 2 inches of pitch" in holding revolutions down. (Then, as now, no boatowner ever felt he had just the right wheel for the engine he'd bought for his boat, and propeller problems and servicing were a significant proportion of factory overhead.)

The one-cylinder, 2-cycle engine is a notorious "lugger," and it is hard to whittle a propeller problem down to much finer points than the rule-of-thumb. These mills will run well with anything they'll turn, and the boat speed never seems to change much, no matter how much prop experiment goes on.

What is Comfort?

What makes for a comfortable boat to ride aboard? Some boats act like floating potato chips, and others heave and scend like floating lead mines. Too much action is nerve wracking; but the sluggish unresponsiveness of a boat that is a slow but deep plunger frequently finds the unseasoned stomach fighting to stay inboard of its owner's teeth.

If you study the problem at first hand, out on the heaving briny, and have been recently wrestling with such design "factors" as metacentric height and rolling periods, you'll conclude that these are fine drawing-board targets, but that there is another design dimension you do not perceive and which cannot be resolved entirely by drafting: it is the lift and lilt, and the gyrating and corkscrewing motion imparted by a sea-way. I suppose these motions are susceptible to computer analysis, but who has time or savvy enough to properly program and solve them? There must be some rule-of-thumb target, or ruling factor, that will provide a boat which will be comfortable at sea and which Mr. Joe Average can apply. I believe I have discovered one.

I think you'll find the answer in the pounds-per-square-foot loading of the waterplane area. This means the plane intersected by the boat's waterline. I think you'll find that anything less than 64 pounds displacement per square foot of waterplane will give you a light and corky boat motion. This estimate is based on the knowledge that the old Elco 34 Standardized Cruisette was right on that 64-pound figure. Highly developed and carefully evolved, this motorboat was the finest power-craft I ever had my hands on. Her "feel" was just right. (See Figure 2.)

In a fast V-bottom cruiser, a lighter figure than this may be what you need. In a cruising boat for long vacation cruising, the 64-pound figure seems about right. In a boat that is to be a workboat, about 80 pounds of displacement per square foot of waterplane seems to produce a solid, "with it" feel. (See Figure 3.)

I have not amassed a wad of figures on this; the perception and propositional discovery are a new hunch.

In the early days of my love affair with engineering, I designed and flew a number of light airplanes. Then, and even today, wing loading per square foot was the chief determining characteristic of forgiving performance. I believe that if a few experienced designers got together and compared figures on pounds-per-square-foot of waterplane area, a pattern would emerge, and that their best medium-size boats would be near the 64-pound rule-of-thumb.

My theory is based on a simple fact which I may be able to get across with a few simple sketches. Look at Figure 4. If you want to figure the average waterplane of a transom-sterned motor cruiser, you will find that a rectangle equal to the waterline length times the waterline beam multiplied by a fineness coefficient of .70 will just about equal the actual waterplane area (Figure 4-a). If you were to saw a solid block of wood to this outline, one foot deep, and load it to 64 pounds to the square foot, it would have zero buoyancy with its upper face just level with the boat's waterline (Figure 4-b). The tendency of any surface disturbance would be to move the block gently with the same feel and

Figure 2 (top). The inboard profile of the famed Elco 34 Cruisette, showing her waterplane line. On 11,000 pounds of displacement and a waterplane area of 170 square feet, her loading was at the ideal 64 pounds per square foot of waterplane area. *Figure 3 (bottom).* This sturdily constructed 42' x 13½' x 4½' aluminum gillnetter has 362 square feet of waterplane area, with a loading starting at 80 pounds per square foot when light to 118 pounds when fully loaded.

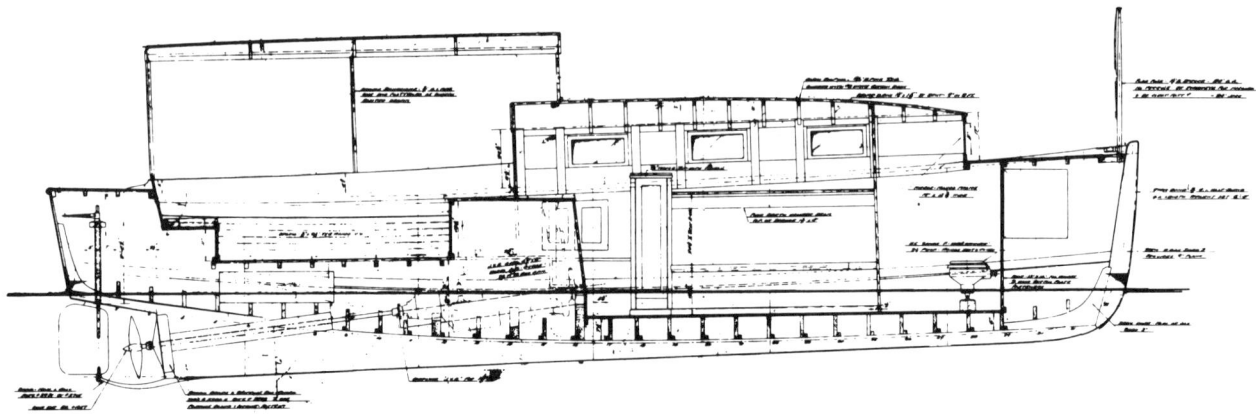

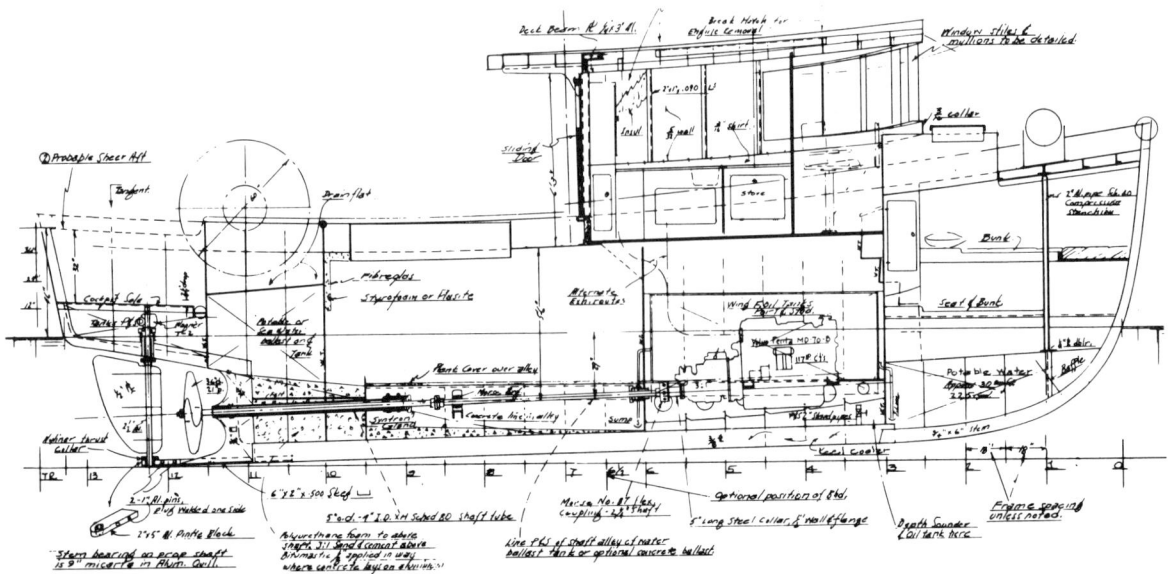

speed as the surface disturbance, because each cubic foot of seawater weighs 64 pounds. Thus, in boat action, you would get the "feel of the water."

Now suppose you cut this same waterplane block 4 feet deep, and loaded it to a square-foot figure of 4 times 64, or 256 pounds per square foot. Instead of the waterplane block being in kinetic equilibrium inertially, it would take a fulsome heave of a sea to start this mass upward. Once in motion, it would tend to keep going upward long after the sea had passed. Then, support being lacking, it would inertially plunge down below the water level. In plain language, the craft with this loading would be "out of synch" with the sea. Figure 4-c shows this. Boats that have this characteristic are highly uncomfortable. It does not matter what the metacentric height may be, the boat is uncomfortable.

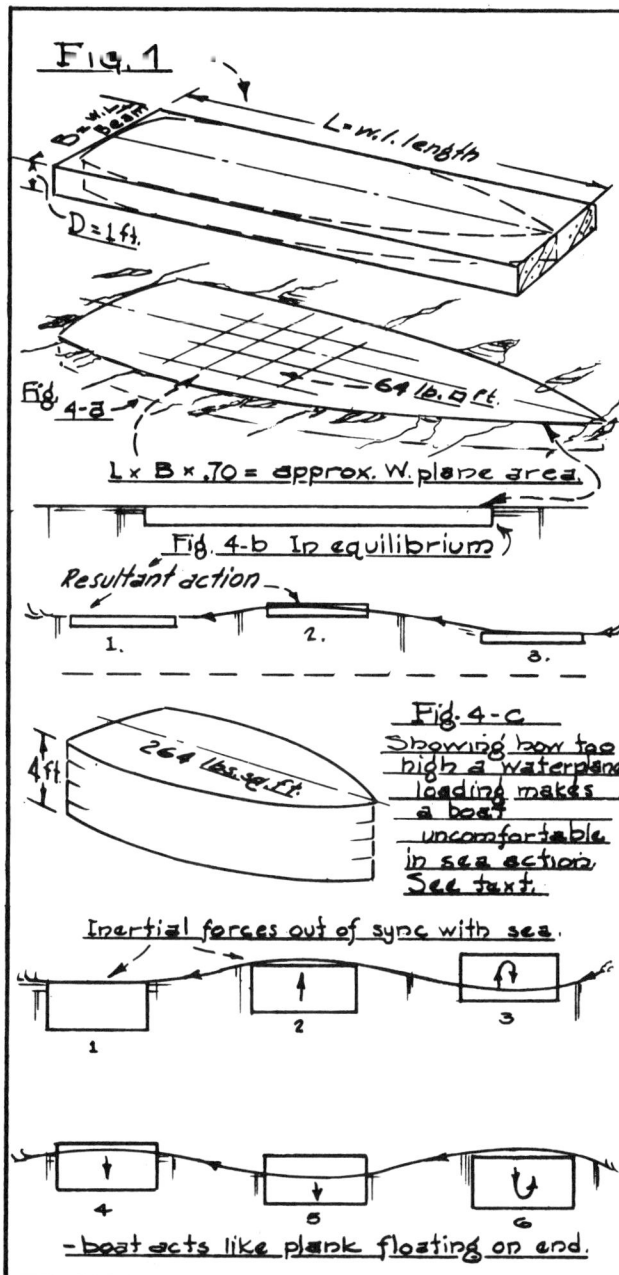

Light boats, loaded at less than the weight of sea water, may require a light loading to achieve speed, but the reverse of the above action takes place, and considerable tossing and slapping results. Speed always costs *something*.

Now, I am talking to the design tribe as a designer, just as a doctor might talk to a medical student. The innocent bystander may not tune in, and to him all this is garbage. He may be of the school that says, "Waterline? Hell, toss her in and we'll paint to the scum line next fall."

'S all right with me, chum. But without feedback, no designer can amass figures that serve him in cuffing-in, in predetermining his design. I think the waterplane loading idea will yield more good boats than all the metacentric studies around. See the sketches for a visual grip on the idea.

The Waterline

In professional yards staffed with competent naval architects, the motor yachts are always designed with half-tank fuel and water loads. Then, upon launching, first the draft marks are established for the bow and stern without fuel, then with half fuel. This is done by bringing the craft alongside a pier and dropping a 3/4 inch by 3/4 inch staff from the stemhead until it kisses the water, and then marking the stemhead point. The same is done aft at the centerline of the vessel at the crown of the transom, and the point is marked on the staff. Then half water and half fuel is stowed, and another set of marks is taken.

With the two staffs, the naval architect then goes to the loft and, by means of the staffs, produces the actual line as launched and the line with half fuel load. Then he strikes the new line on the floor with a chalkline and finds out where his immersed sections are actually topped transversely.

If this is too finicky, he may content himself with striking a pair of actual waterlines on a print of his lines, and, projecting the new sections, run up a displacement calculation based on Simpson's Rule. (All boat delineators will know the Simpson method, so I'll not go into it for general consumption.) With his new waterlines—the actual ones "as built"—he can then come up with the actual launched displacement (weight) figures, and see what his "miss" factor amounts to.

Only once in over 50 years of designing have I ever designed a boat that hit the designed line right smack on the nose. This was the hogged-sheer Elco 32 à la PT Boat outline, which Hank Uhle and I worked up together at Elco. I have never seen one designed by anyone else that was exactly right, either. Eli Gunnell of Burger once told me he'd never seen one that hit the mark on the nose. But bear this fact in mind: *The boat is always right.* It is the designer's estimate that falls amiss. Usually it is slight.

Generally, the bow will be low by an inch or two, and the rump will be high ditto. And, dear friends, the reason for this is *not* that calculations go amiss—although they sometimes do—but it is due to an inherent five percent or so error in jolly old Mr. Simpson's rule that favors the fat end of any curve.

We will not belabor the point. An entire article could be written on the subject. Suffice it to inform the general reader that all designers use Simpson's Rule when calculating displacement from revised sectional areas such as "as-launched" waterlines.

The way this is done in design offices is with a polar planimeter, which traces over the known vessel section and comes up with a measurement answer on a little wheel. (See Figure 5.) Possibly the general reader will not concern himself with the how of Simpson, or worry about how Amsler's polar planimeter works. But any odds and-ends story like this that doesn't pass along some scoop about both Mr. Simpson and Mr. Amsler isn't worth its salt. I have gone to great length to unearth a bit of biography about these two patron saints of naval architecture.

Thomas Simpson was an Englishman born at Market Bosworth,

Figure 5. Yacht designers use the polar planimeter to measure sectional areas. From known immersed areas they can "weigh" a boat and find her designed displacement.

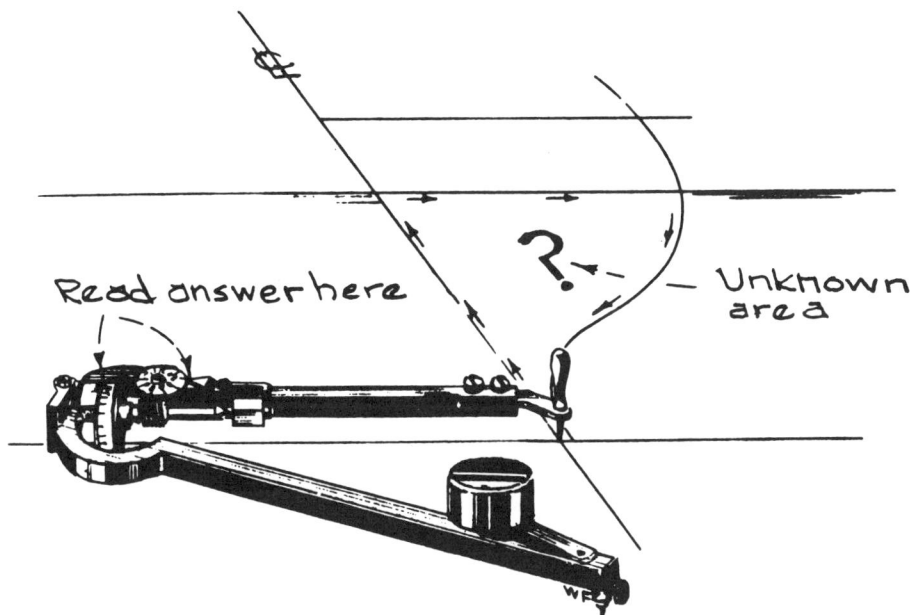

Leicestershire, on August 20, 1710. As a boy, according to the custom of the times, he was indentured to the textile trade, and while at the looms at Spitalfield he amused himself by learning mathematics with such self-taught proficiency that he was appointed Professor of Mathematics at prestigious Woolwich College in 1743. He was then 33 years of age.

The mathematical philosophies at this pre-dawn of the Industrial Revolution had been given a great injection of vigor and ferment by the *Principia* of Isaac Newton (1642-1727), written after Newton had been bonked on the head by a falling apple and had come up with his theory of gravity and the invention of calculus.

There must have been some powerful apples falling in those days. Thomas Simpson, born 17 years prior to Newton's death, was also a contemporary of the Scottish inventor James Watt (1736-1819), whose invention of the double-acting steam engine and condensing power plant was about to harness the energy of coal, and thus to usher a new way of life into the world. It was Watt, you'll remember, who defined the unit of power that we use today. It is based on the work done by a horse: the lifting of 33,000 pounds one foot in one minute. One horsepower. (It is presumed the horse was full of oats and willing to grunt.)

Simpson, the young weaver, while still at his looms, came up with a theory for solving fluxions, and on the way to this intellectual triumph, still in his twenties, he evolved his famous series of rules for getting areas and volumes from linear plans and linear measurements.

Simpson is reported to have lived a turbulent life, passing from mortal coils on May 4, 1761, not yet 51 years old. It will certainly come as a relief to naval architects to learn that Simpson was not a sheep herder. The subject of naval architecture is wooly enough. Simpson is the patron saint of today's naval architects.

Now we come to Amsler's polar planimeter. For about a hundred years after Simpson's death, engineers had to face the mechanical task of determining areas of irregular outlines, such as the shape of a ship's sections below water, by either triangulation or by ghosting scale square feet over the section and counting manually. The method can still be used, but, because of the inherent guessometry, is not very accurate. The polar planimeter will get the area five times as fast, accurately limning the nuances of all curves. It was the invention of this device by Amsler in 1854 that made yacht designing a lot easier.

Jakob Amsler was born November 16, 1823, at Staden bei Brugge, Switzerland. His first interest was theology, which he studied under Franz Neumann at Koenigsburg, but in 1848 he moved to Geneva, then to Zurich as Professor of Mathematics and Physical Science when only

25 years of age. In 1851 he married the daughter of a prosperous Zurich druggist, M. Laffon, who was himself a scientist and had the means to be a patron of scientific discovery.

Amsler's genius at mathematics perceived that the radians of polar co-ordinates, which is a discipline of analytical geometry, were susceptible to mensuration by a rolling wheel of definite relation in circumference to a fixed polar point. Amsler's invention was simple and accurate, and could be manufactured and sold profitably for a price engineering people were willing to pay. It was a tremendous labor saver.

Jakob Amsler started producing his polar planimeter in 1856, in a works known as "System Amsler." He had sold 50,000 machines by the time of his death, prospering hardily. He made Simpson easy to work with.

Heeling in the Turn

Why does a round-bilged hull list outward on a turn, while a V-bottom leans inboard on a turn? Here, you have to define the kind of round-bilge hull, and her speed, and the kind of V-hull, and her speed. But above factors being equal, the phenomenon of the difference in handling usually persists.

Let us take the case of a fast, narrow boat of each type. In such an illustration we get the greatest demonstrable difference. Both boats are 25-milers. Both are 25 feet long, 6-foot beam. Engines are identical—same propellers, no skegs.

Throw the wheel hard to port on the V-bottom, and she heels inboard on the turn and doesn't slow down very quickly. Eventually, as the turn tightens, she'll slow down, and, if the throttle is closed, she then will heel outboard, assuming at very low speed the same turning attitude of the round-bilger.

Take the round-bilged, flat hull and throw her into a tight portside turn. For a short space she'll try to bank, but all of a sudden she'll list heavily to the outboard side with such vehemence that a prudent skipper will pull the throttle back, slowing her more, and accentuating the heeling tendency.

The reason is found in this fact: As each boat is thrown into a turn, the momentum force tends to keep them going in a straight line, but the rudder produces a turn, the centrifugal resultant of which is a skid. When skidding, the V plane on the starboard side of the V-bottom presents a lifting force, lifting the starboard side up as the skid and turn progress. At the same time the skid leaves a hollow under the port side, or at least enough water in motion to have no buoyant resultant, and the boat banks.

There is no banking force inherent in the shape of the round-bilge hull. On the outboard side of the turn the water rolls up the topside a bit, but there is no uplifting force. Centrifugal force alone, acting through the relatively high center of gravity, produces a rolling moment in the hull to the outside of the turn.

Of course, once down off any planing action, both boats behave alike. Ornery!

Low-Tension Spark

This past winter, while pondering the marvels of solid-state ignition, and the Piezo crystals that spark out a lightning bolt when merely tickled by a cam, I inadvertently put my hand on an old 1908 copy of *Power Boating,* which was going strong in that era. In this old magazine I perceived the working drawings, or rather the drawings of the workings, of a 1908 4-cylinder, 4-cycle Buffalo marine engine. Modern, ultra, up-to-date job for 1908!

The singular thing about this 4-cylinder marvel was the low-tension

Figure 6. This longitudinal section of a 4-cylinder Buffalo marine engine of 1908 shows the interior construction. K1 and K2 show the spring-loaded make-and-break ignition system.

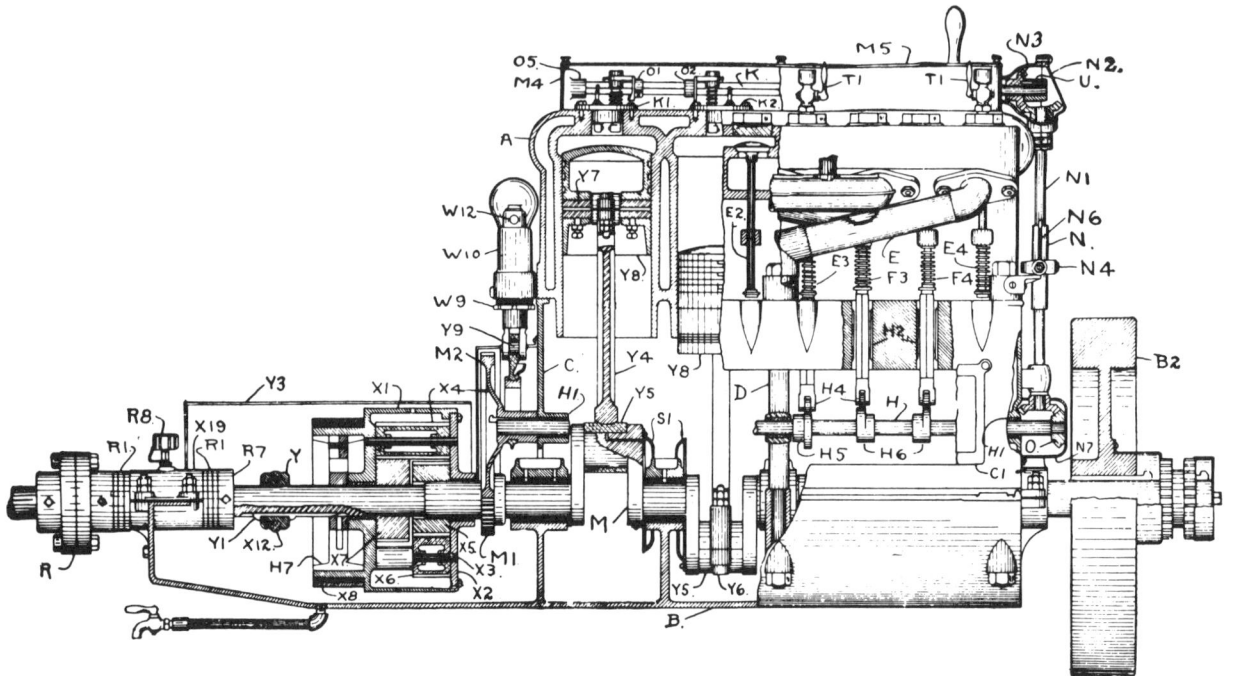

ignition system: igniters in each cylinder head—make-and-break—operated by an overhead cam shaft!

All buffs of old engines, gather ye and marvel! Obviously, the highest speed at which this engine could roll was set by the speed with which the igniter springs could close the points. At that, there was probably time for the necessary two strokes of each piston. Wasn't this engine a daisy?

11

El Cheapo Planimeter

This yarn is about a 50-cent knife-blade planimeter you can build yourself to use in accurately measuring hull sectional areas. I've put one through R & D and am here to tell you it works.

Usually, if I mention the word "planimeter" in an editorial office, everybody runs screaming up the wallpaper for a fingernail grip on the coping, yelling for mother. How, then, do you get a story like this printed?

Why not "tell it like it is"? It has taken 60 years to write this tale, and maybe the human juices of the story would so dilute the horrible word that it would be allowed to filter through. Most especially so when, today, all design offices own a planimeter and find it indispensable. It's a case of different pokes for different folks, and learning by peeking over another man's shoulder.

Along about 1918, when I was learning the boatbuilding trade, one of the best boating magazines was the now-long-dead *Power Boating*. This rag had a sort of Gee-Whiz column for trivia that, in one issue, showed how to measure areas with something called a planimeter. I learned that it was pronounced pl'-NIM-eter. There was a simple drawing of a hand holding one end of an upright 45-degree triangle, to the other end of which was bolted a safety razor blade.

I remember the picture vividly because I filed it as a clipping in my scrapbook. I even remember the name of the contributor. His name was Schaphorst, a man who evidently was picking up a dollar here, a dollar there by peppering editorial offices with nifty ways of doing hard things. All editors know the breed.

The clipping got lost before I could learn how the device worked. Now, unfinished business bothers me. I kept asking fellows in the engineering trade if they'd ever seen the razor blade planimeter. For 50 years I drew blank stares. Then one day I got to talking with a man who had seen the same triangle and razor blade in the same magazine.

He was Nelson Zimmer, the Detroit naval architect whose eye for a sweet line and whose long tenure at the board have made him highly respected. Yep, Nels told me he'd seen the piece. Way back when.

When he was going to high school, Nels was nuts about boats. He found in the back room of his Detroit library a mammoth collection of old *Rudder, Power Boating,* and *Motor Boat* magazines. This stuff was something like it! And so, to heck with school.

From Thanksgiving of that year until New Year's Day, Nels went dutifully from home each morning and put in the school day in the library. By the time New Year's semester rolled around, the principal of Nels's high school began to wonder where Nelson had gone, and he sent a minion of the school system around to the Zimmer home to inquire.

By that time, Nelson Zimmer was hooked on naval architecture. He was forgiven, finished school, and apprenticed in the office of John L. Hacker, later becoming one of the best on his own.

Last summer, at the 13th Annual Antique Boat Show at Clayton, N.Y., Nelson asked me if I had ever found the answer to the way that darned razor-blade planimeter worked. No, I had not.

Procrastination that extends for 50 to 60 years ripens curiosity! Always willing to putter around on the back side of the moon for the answers to the basic philosophies of designing, I resolved to root into the theories of mathematical instruments and dig out the reason why a razor blade, attached to a pointer arm, would give the correct value for an irregular area.

Areas, you see, are of terrific importance to the designer of boats. I'd say, offhand, that the measurement of areas and volumes is 85 percent of the mathematical end of designing, the rest being given over to proportions, lever moments, and the solution of triangles. At least, I have found it so.

To cut to the heart of why a planimeter works, there's an explanation due for the man who uses one.

There are two types: polar and planar. The polar planimeter—the one with the wheel—was invented by Jakob Amsler of Switzerland in 1854. The planar planimeter was invented by Capt. Andreas Prytz in 1887—the hatchet or knife blade planimeter.

See Figure 5 of the preceding chapter for a look at one form of Amsler's polar planimeter. A diagrammatic sketch of one form of the

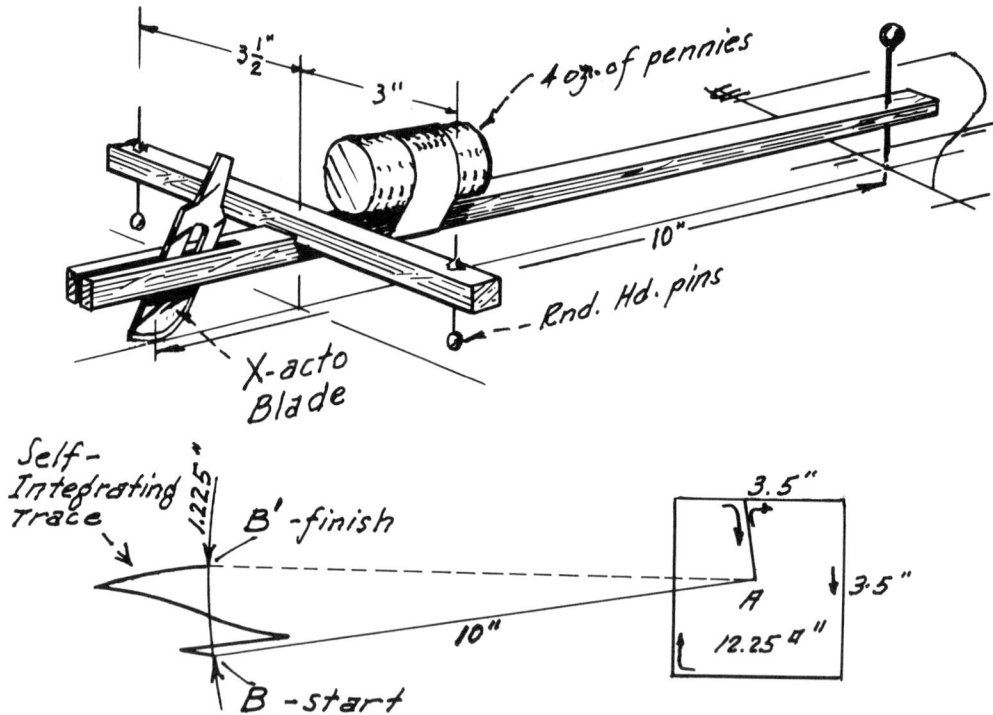

This is a Prytz type of planimeter that you can build easily from the diagram above. The length of the arc BB' multiplied by the length of the arm AB is equal to the area traced by point A, starting near the center of an area.

Prytz planimeter appears above. Both instruments are based on a simple principle of analytical geometry. This can best be explained in lay terms by understanding the Prytz, or planar form first:

In its initial form the Prytz planimeter was merely a bent rod, one end of which formed a pointer and the other end a rounded, hefty knife, resembling a hatchet. Hence the name, hatchet planimeter.

To make it function, a point is chosen within the area to be measured, somewhere near the center of the area. A radial line is run from this point to the boundary line of the area.

Then the knife blade is pressed into the paper to make a dent or kerf, and the pointer is run up the radial line, around the periphery of the area, and back down the radial line to the starting position. Again the knife edge is pressed into the paper to mark a terminal point, or dent.

If A-B is the initial position of the arm and A-B' the final position, the area circumscribed is equal to the length of the arm multiplied by the length of the *arc* B-B'. Note that the key word is arc, not chord. (Around the circumference, not across it.)

No muss, no fuss, no mathematical moonshine. Just a simple scale measurement. The problem is laid out visually in two-dimensional form, hence the word planar.

The polar planimeter of Amsler goes one better and picks up the integrated trace of the planar form on a rolling wheel from which B-B' can be read directly. Because Amsler's instrument is based on the polar coordinates of analytical geometry, rather than on plane geometry, it has an arm that swings about an externally fixed point. Hence, polar. Amsler has greater range.

All of these facts were made known to me by the grace of a neighbor and friend, Rufus Jefferson, who dug up some photocopied pages from an ancient mathematical encyclopedia his father had owned. Rufus has a big grapefruit ranch in Texas and in his spare time, which is most of the time between harvests, he builds boats like mad. He's a demon for philosophical details.

When I saw the Prytz reference I recalled the 45-cent triangle and razor blade of the 60-year-old *Power Boating* clipping. And I can tell you now, Nels, that the shape of the triangle had nothing to do with the matter. It was merely used as an arm. This triangle had puzzled me. Immediately, when light dawned, I resolved to "put the matter in train," as our English cousins say; that is, to give 'er the usual American Research and Development, better known as "R & D."

I reached for a Gillette thin blade, a 1/4-inch-square balsa stick, a tube of model airplane cement, and, repairing to my wife's Calico Engineering Dept., I found in her pin box some round-headed pins to use as a pointer and upside-down stabilizers. In a trice I had a working version, but with an eight-inch arm and a razor blade "cutter." The trice consisted of the amount of time needed for Mr. Testor's glue to dry.

Now, let's fire her up. Comes the big moment for all R & D boys. How did she work?

Well, as I swallow pride, to tell you the truth, she wasn't worth a handful of sour owl feathers.

The razor blade made paper dolls of my drawing, and was so wobbly that a good trace couldn't be had. This Model A outfit needed a good knife and a longer arm, because the shorter arm gives a longer, harder-to-measure arc. So, back to the drawing board for Model B.

What to use for a rounded end knife? Aha! An X-acto blade knife from my set of X-acto model carving tools. The very thing! Just as shown opposite.

I extended the arm length to 10 inches because 10 times B-B' was easier on mental math. Then, approaching the firing up of Model B with care and reverence, I made a trace of a 3-1/2 inch by 3-1/2 inch square, measuring 12.25 inches in area. Arc B-B' should measure 1.225 inches on my engineer's scale, which is divided into tenths. How now, Brown Cow?

Well—(no gargling this time)—right on the money! Simply SUPOIB!

In Model B the X-acto knife blade had been underlaid by cardboard, so that the edge would not cut the parent drawing, and the stiffness of the knife blade gave a rigid trace. This trace was made even more positive by adding about 4 ounces of pennies taped up in a roll, causing better operation and a cost over-run of 36 cents.

With the 8-inch arm on Model A, the reading on a 3-1/2 inches by 3-1/2 inches square of 12.25 square inches should have been around an arc 1.53 inches long. Instead, due to a wobbly thin blade, it read 1.82—unacceptable. But Model B checked out very closely. On an area of 12.25 inches (known), the arc of a 10-inch arm would have to be 1.225 inches, measured on an engineering tenths scale. This it was. Eureka! Much closer and faster than counting squares.

Bill of materials

1 X-acto knife blade
3 pins
1 tube Testor's airplane glue
1 pc. 1/4 x 1/4 balsa wood, 18″ long

And as they say in bayou country, that's all they is to it. Between Captain Andreas Prytz, whose name suggests either Polish or Czech background, and Nelson Zimmer, Rufus Jefferson, and Weston Farmer, the secret of the hatchet planimeter need no longer be as obscure in the next 60 years as it has been in the past 60.

You can't beat Research and Development.

12

Flotational Models, Part I

If there are 9,000 graduate naval architects in this country, with possibly 900 at work in the profession, nine of whom are eating well, there must be 90,000 doodlers at boat delineation who are gripped by the wonderful hobby of noodling their dream boats with paper and pencil. These 90,000 aspirants to designing skill will range in age and calling from school boys sketching profiles of proposed yachts, through a spectrum of young men possessed of fair drafting skill with equipment perhaps kept in a closet, to well-heeled executives who have equipped themselves adequately in dens or special rooms where, armed with books, they titillate the Muse of Marine Design.

Each of these men's personally held opinion of his own boat expertise and engineering infallibility usually is in inverse proportion to his experience. Each man is an expert in his own eyes. This truth must be why there is no game on earth so full of self-anointed experts as is the boat business.

The schoolboy just naturally knows that his drawn waterline is right. The man back from his third boat ride has ideas that will revolutionize boat shapes because he just found out what water is—he thinks he has invented it. The executive-type man has been used to issuing orders. Therefore the boat he pictures will do what he dreams she will do because he has ordered it.

Oh, yair? The Old Pro is not so sure about all of this. He knows from bitter experience that Father Neptune is full of dirty tricks and astounding surprises, many of which can be traced back to the drawing board and its optical illusions. Two-dimensional drawings are a poor way to represent three-dimensional boats.

Models are better. The half model is time-tried in this respect. I have found that flotational models are even better. You will be stunned and amazed by the things these little boats will teach you—about your own insight into the design process, about hydrostatics, about building itself.

I have built barrels of them. From time to time through the years, as I have sought to pass on to younger men some of the dearly bought wisdom of experience, I have presented in the marine press and popular magazines some of the methods I have evolved for building these paper and balsa models. It's time I pulled all the bits and pieces together and told the whole tale. Once the mechanics are disposed of, I'll point out some of the things they'll teach you, so that your tropical delusions do not become victims of optical illusions inherent in drawing board designing.

As to supplies, you'll need a few sheets of photo mounting board. This is the stiff 1/16-inch-thick gray-fronted, blue-backed kind available in all art supply stores. Anything thicker won't scissor, and anything thinner, such as laundry cardboard, is too floppy. One sheet of 30 inches by 48 inches size will be about right for supplying the requirements of one model.

You also will need a supply of 3 inches by 36 inches by 1/8-inch-thick half-hard balsa flats. These are standard in any model airplane supply shop and are around 20 cents apiece. For a normal model you will need about 10 sheets, say $2 worth.

About four tubes of the 25-cent-size Testor's Extra Fast Drying Model Airplane Cement will be needed. Also a kit of ladies' fingernail filing sanding boards will be wanted, and some double-O fine sandpaper. A few little sacks of T-head modelling pins are very useful in holding spiled balsa planks in place until the glue dries.

Less than $5 will "warehouse" your miniature shipyard stockroom. Get *all* the stuff together before you start anything.

As to the tools: a package of Gem razor blades—the stiff backed, single-edged kind is needed for perforation of the cardboard, for trimming balsa, and so forth. You will need a sharp, tough, man-size pair of shears—dressmaker's scissors or very sharp, easy-working tinsnips are ideal. Don't use the kitchen shears Mother cuts up meat with; you must mark your work accurately, then cut cleanly, saving the marking line. Shears that shred will discourage you.

A pint of real spar varnish and a small brush will complete the workshop. Make it real, genuine *marine* spar varnish—not the synthetic cigarette package cellophane stuff now being palmed off as being spar varnish. It just won't work.

Material in hand, the next step is to get a blueprint of your lines tracing. Lay the blueprint over the gray side of a suitably sized piece of cardboard, and insert a piece of carbon paper. Tape the sandwich together with drafting tape so the assemblage won't slip.

With a stylus or pin, using French or ship's curves, make an outline of the keel-to-sheer profile, and the deck outline as shown in the flat, or plan view. Cut these out carefully with scissors or razor blade as need be, saving the line.

At this stage of the game you have the two elements shown in Figure 1. I have illustrated a V-bottom model, because the boxiness of this type of boat lends itself to illustration. If you are building a slab-sider, these illustrations apply fully. If you are building a round-bilger, you can eliminate the chine plane flats and spacers, or substitute a waterline plane piece instead.

Before gluing together, run a razor cut around both faces of both pieces to partially perforate the board. The idea is to get a piece of cardboard stiff enough to hold shape while cementing, but which will part company at the right place when we gut the falsework out of the model. A little practice with the blade on a side fragment of board will show you how deep to go.

Cutting the profile will give you no trouble, but if you find it hard to sketch both sides of the boat symmetrically about the centerline in plan view, draw one side, then flip the pattern over about the centerline and draw the mating other side. Any small jogs in any curve usually are smoothed up by cutting when you use scissors. Reference to this process is covered in the steps in Figure 2.

To stabilize the chine plane or the waterplane (if used), spacers dead square across must be used as shown at Figure 3.

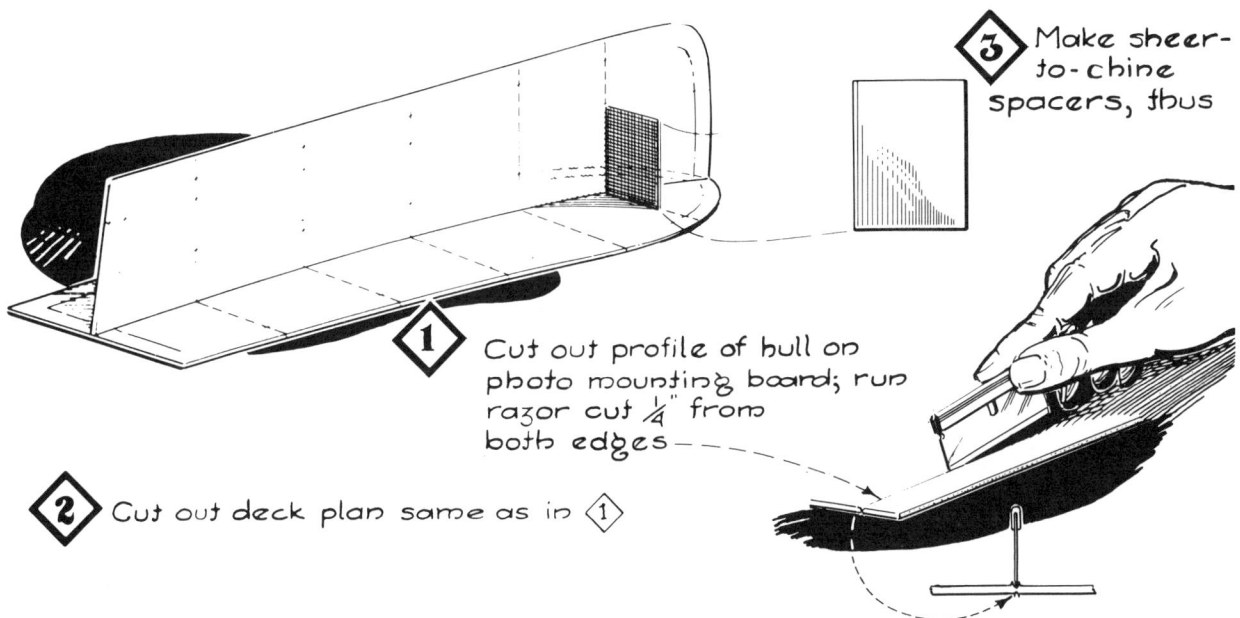

3 Make sheer-to-chine spacers, thus

1 Cut out profile of hull on photo mounting board; run razor cut ¼" from both edges ----

2 Cut out deck plan same as in **1**

In gluing the profile and the deck plan together, and when setting in the chine-to-sheer spacers, the technique to use is to hold the piece to be glued in the left hand, and with the tube of cement held in the right, to apply a bead of cement through the tube nozzle to the edge to be glued. It is like putting a ribbon of toothpaste on a brush.

Using the flip-flop method, the chine planes or waterplanes can be got out, Figure 4.

When assembled, your outfit will begin to appear much as shown in Figure 5. If you are contemplating a slab-sider, in which straight frames are used, you can install pieces of 1/8-inch by 1/4-inch balsa between chine and sheer and between keel and chine. The "drift" of this can be learned from Figure 5 and the photo showing the bottom frames glued across the chine plane.

If you are building a round-bilged hull, the respective mold stations can be substituted for the chine spacers. Just remember to subtract planking thickness! By this is meant the thickness of the balsa itself. The way to get this line is as follows:

If you use 1/8-inch balsa for planking, draw your mold section to the body plan of your draft or blueprint, then run a pencil line 1/16 inch inboard of this on the cardboard section. Cut to this line. When planked, the model will be 1/16 inch too fat on each side. I have found that the sanding required to smooth up a hull takes off this 1/16 inch, leaving the skin of the model coinciding with the body plan. It is important to preserve this dimension, because if you don't, your displacement check-out later will not be exact.

On certain slab-sided models, the topside can be planked in one sheet with 1/16-inch or 1/32-inch balsa, as the drawing indicates. I would

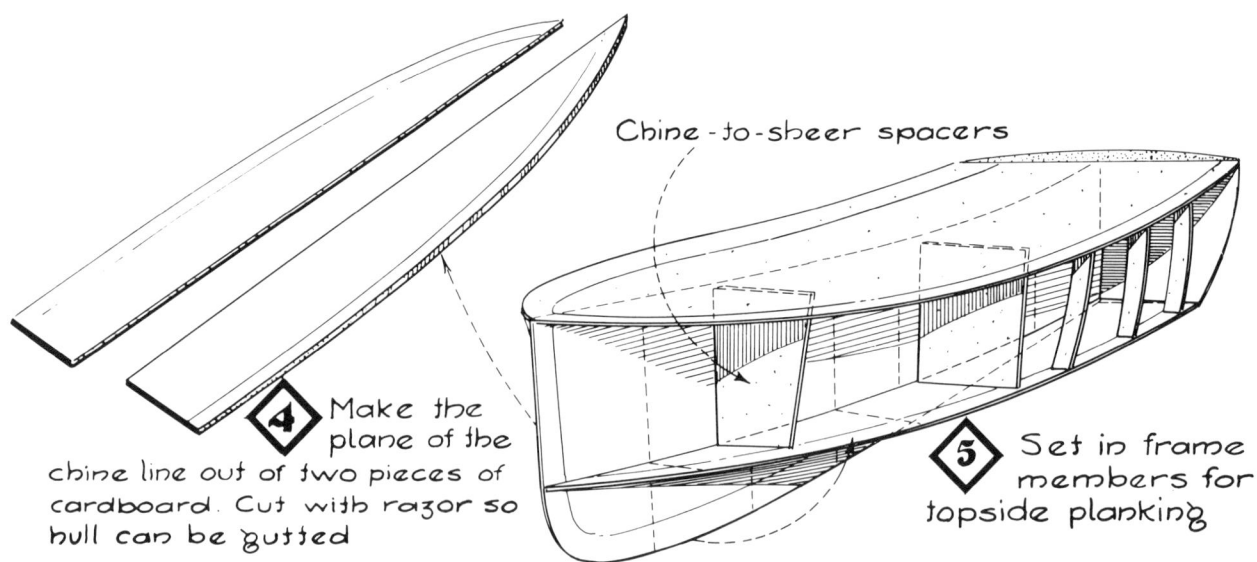

Chine-to-sheer spacers

4 Make the plane of the chine line out of two pieces of cardboard. Cut with razor so hull can be gutted

5 Set in frame members for topside planking

After framing, the model is ready for planking. Note razor cut clearly shown at stem.

choose the half-hard balsa and sand it, as I have found that sanding does remove just about the right amount of wood. (Balsa comes in three grades—soft, half hard, and hard. The hard stuff doesn't sand or shave well, and the soft stuff crushes at the frame points, leaving gentle bumps that cannot be faired.)

The topsides are best planked first. If you use strakes, put on one strake and its equivalent on the opposite side to avoid the pulling occasioned by the drying of the glue. If you work in a dry room at about 70-degree temperature, the glue will set up hard in about one minute, and you can get on to the next piece. It does, however, keep pulling until bone dry, and it is wise to avoid excessive deposits of the stuff. Avoid getting splats of glue across the razor cuts, as this will make it hard to rip out the cardboard framework.

You will find the T-head pins most useful for holding strakes in place to the cardboard formers. The T-shape facilitates pulling. Ordinary dressmaking common pins will do, of course, but they are murder to push in through the wood and cardboard, and hard to get out again, short of using pliers.

As the strakes run past the transom, trim off each one, one at a time, as you build up, using a razor blade. See Figure 6. Put a dollop of glue on the end grain and smear it thin across the transom face. This will form a glue gusset helping to hold the plank to the transom side. Also, in gluing the strakes, use a fingernail to slice off the bead of glue that squeezes out. If you don't and it settles into a dried extrusion ridge, you cannot sand it easily when dry. A cloth can be used to keep the face of the seam free of glue, but do it while it is wet, not when it becomes rubbery, or set up.

When the hull is completely closed in, sand it to flowing lines, using some care not to let daylight in. Brush it off well and apply four coats of spar varnish, all over—the balsa as well as the cardboard deck.

Figures 6 and 7 cover the steps leading up to this condition. Now take a look at Figure 8. Here, a razor blade first having been used to pry up one end of the falsework, pliers or scissors are used to pull out the inboard frame, which now is not wanted. You snip a little here, shave a little there, bend a shade more on the refractory pieces you haven't quite got perforated, and in this fashion the entire inboard portion of the model is freed of the hull. It can be cast away.

What is left will be very close in scale weight, that is, model vs. prototype, to the full-sized boat if built either of wood or aluminum in prototype. This is for bare-hull comparisons.

Varnish the inboard areas with two to four coats of spar, letting each coat dry well. This protects the cardboard against wetting, which will disintegrate it if it is not covered.

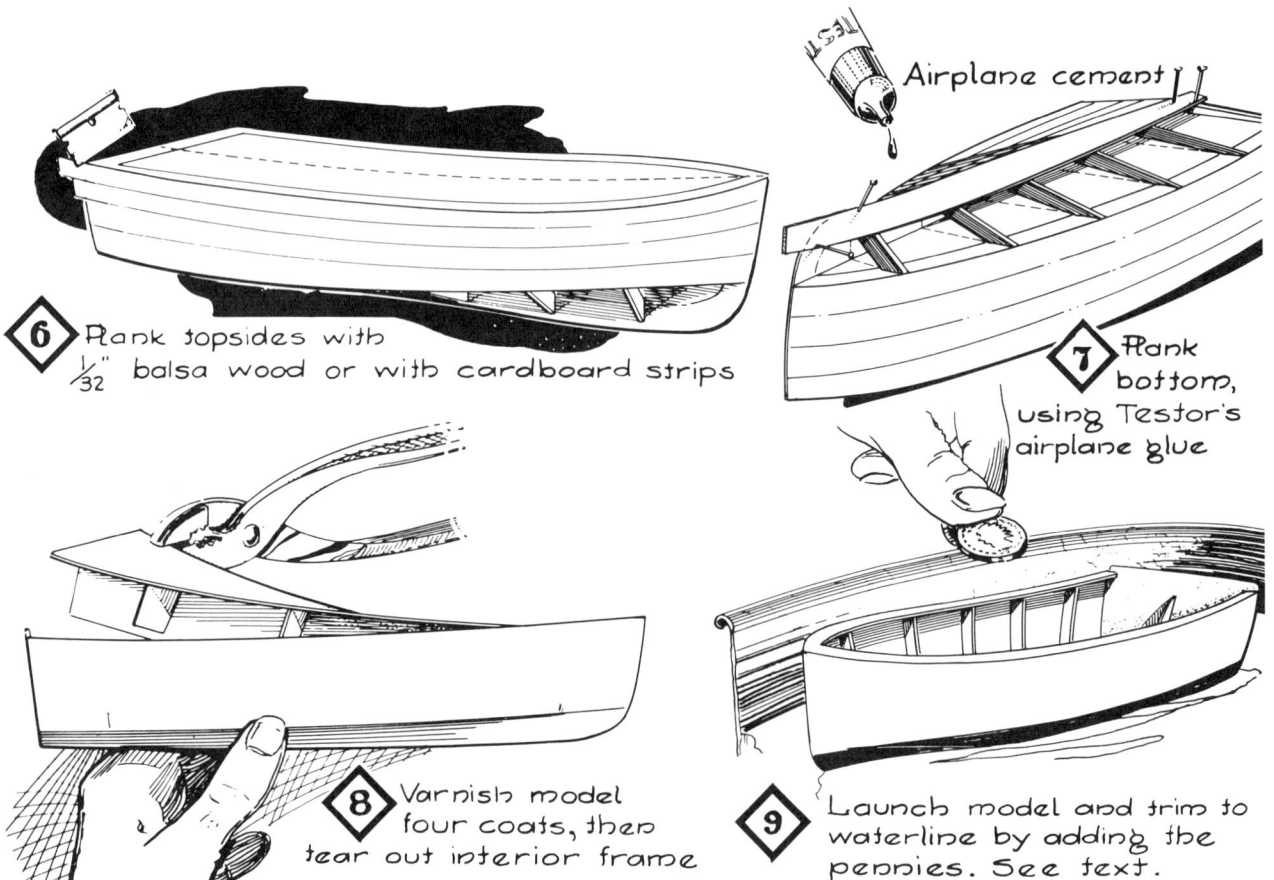

6 Plank topsides with 1/32" balsa wood or with cardboard strips

7 Plank bottom, using Testor's airplane glue

Airplane cement

8 Varnish model four coats, then tear out interior frame

9 Launch model and trim to waterline by adding the pennies. See text.

Now comes the launching! This, and the testing for trim and wake pattern, is where the real fun comes. Here I must get in a word or two about the simple mathematics of similitude.

There is a law in naval architecture which states that as to speed, the model of any vessel varies to that of the prototype nearly as the square root of their linear ratios. (The actual exponent is 1.83 not 2—i.e., the square, but this involves logarithms.) As to weights, the variation is as the cube of the linear ratios.

Let us take an example to show you what is meant. Suppose you have worked in the scale of 3/4 inch equals 1 foot. This is 1/16th full size. The linear ratio then becomes 16. If you use 1/2 inch to the foot scale, you are working at 1/24th full size. The linear ratio then is 24. If you work at 1 inch to the foot, this is 1/12th full size, and the linear ratio is 12.

It is fortunate that 3/4 inch scale—the layout generally used in boats under 50 feet—being 1/16th full size, is easy to square, extract square roots from, and to cube. In this, as in any other scale, the speed in scale proportion will be to the prototype as the square root of the linear ratio. The linear ratio is 16. The square root of 16 is 4. Therefore the model when towed will exhibit the wake and behavior of the prototype at one fourth the speed of the larger vessel. If your prototype is to be powered for a speed of 16 mph, tow the model at 4 mph. This is a brisk walking pace at water's edge, and the behaviors will be similar. For a 40-mile prototype speed, one fourth of 40 being 10, a moderate running gait will give you 10 mph and similarity. Because these towing speeds so readily lend themselves to a gait a man can achieve on his own legs, the 3/4-inch scale to 1 foot becomes doubly useful.

As to displacement, or weight, the scale varies as the cube of the linear ratio, or, on 3/4-inch scale as 16 times 16 times 16. This is 4,096. If your model, after trimming to the waterline, weighs 1 pound, the prototype will weigh 4,096 times 1 pound, or 4,096 pounds.

After launching your model, a most convenient form of ballast is multiples of the Lincoln penny, which scales out at almost exactly 25 pounds scale weight in 3/4-inch scale. By adding pennies until you reach the waterline trim, and gunking these pennies into permanent place with glue, the model, after being removed from the water and dried, can be both weighed and balanced along a 1/4-inch-diameter dowel rolled on your drawing board until it maintains balanced equilibrium. This is the CG and CB point—actual, not theoretical—and you can check back to your drawing to put a proper placement on it.

After ballasting, weigh your model on a photo scale or on a druggist's balance. There are 16 ounces in a pound, and 480 grains in an ounce, Troy weight. Thus the total weight of the model in pounds, ounces, and

10 Weigh model on photo or druggist's scale, then multiply by 4096 for disp.

11 Scram Pram with 3 pennies & hairpin for 80 lbs motor weight

Pennies
Corks
Balsa

12 Each new Lincoln penny weighs 25 lbs scale weight on 1/6 scale (3/4" = 1 foot).

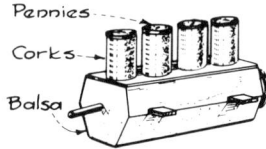

14 On 1/6 scale, model is towed at 1/4 speed of prototype for comparative behavior

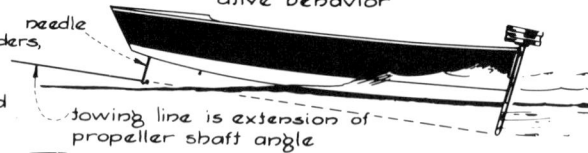

13 Using corks for cylinders, pennies for weight, and balsa for a base, you can simulate inboard motors of any weight.

needle

towing line is extension of propeller shaft angle

grains can be converted to pounds and decimals of a pound, multiplied by 4,096, and presto!—you have the displacement of the prototype. The method is very accurate, and a thousand times better than "expert" guessometry.

When weighing, use a gravity balance scale only. Spring scales are worthless. I have two scales in my drafting kit—one is a photo scale on which I can get up to a couple of pounds very accurately by adding 8-ounce plastic sandwich bags of sand tied with drafting tape. The other is a 12-pound capacity gravity beam postal scale. Both are made by the Pelouze Manufacturing Co., on Chicago Avenue in Evanston, Illinois.

The small photo scale was ordered with ounce weights, not metric, and cost $4.50 when purchased. The larger scale cost 50 bucks and is the same type used in post offices in extracting the last penny of blood permissible on short-stamped mail. Both have earned their keep.

Up to this point in your modelling, you have been able to check the total weight of your bigger ship, the exact center of buoyancy fore and aft, and the ditto CG fore and aft. You doubtless wish to check the wake pattern under simulated speed. Figure 9, 10, and so on show the launching and weighing and give suggestions whereby engines of different weights may be simulated with balsa, corks, pennies, and pins.

As to towing methods, it is important in order to simulate the proper thrust vectors to extend the towing thread along the same line as the propeller shaft. In tank work, the towing force is usually applied at the thrust block, but this is not practicable for our simple experiments.

I call these models "flotational" instead of "floating" to signify that they are functional. A wooden half-model will float, solid or not. But it will not tell you a single fact about engineering factors.

Let no one downgrade these little boats with a snort and the exclamation, "Foolish fleet!" I built my first one many years ago as an exercise in that extra two percent of grunt that I feel separates artists and achievers from hacks. I was baffled by a stability problem and so, believing in the serious importance of doing something for the hell of it, I cobbled up a model using cardboard for planking and paraffin wax to waterproof it.

The model immediately showed up a blind spot in design, sparing an embarrassing launching and probable lawsuit, turning a drawing-doomed failure into a happy ship.

I was amazed at what I'd learned. From still other models I've learned why profiles in the hands of the unknowing always produce a shallow-bowed boat. I learned why most boats are down slightly by the head at launching, and how to allow for it. I learned that Simpson's multipliers—this "1, 4, 2, 4, who ya gonna yell for" stuff—is not always accurate. I learned why the "We never have any trouble" boys are usually in hot water at launching time.

I learned that calculations for moment of inertia can go as sour as week-old milk, throwing out metacentric heights from the safe column into the red light *no go* column. But all these are another story. This model subject could be pursued to great artistic depths.

It is my claim that, as a designing tool, flotational models are *les pyjamas du chat sauté*—what you'd murmur in France to describe the fried cats' pajamas.

It is beyond contesting that the flotational model is self-integrating. The little vessel will instantly proclaim any glaring design oversight. As you pick up skill, it is the best method of arriving at the ultimate boat. Calculations and design go along together, and if you've pulled a boo-boo, trim adjustments can be made in minutes without resort to having to recalculate weights, curves of loading, and all the tedium of basic design.

Using the flotational model, a designer takes his answers from the water and the boat itself. In concert, these two elements make the method of design infallible.

13

Flotational Models, Part II

Recently I found myself in old West Coast haunts, happily engaged in helping to establish a small shipyard. During my stay, I ran into an old-timer, a fellow naval architect who long has been designing boats in the Pacific Northwest. During the course of our conversation, we swapped tales of how we used to work together for Walton Hubbard, Jr., who had a naval architect's office on Wilshire Boulevard in Los Angeles, and who founded the South Coast Company at Newport Beach. This was 40 years ago!

Talk got around to a philosophy on which we both agree: the older that men become in this boat game, especially the design end of it, the more they agree on everything, and the clearer it becomes that the "wisest" men in the game are the kids who just about know everything when they set up their first boards.

Now, I'm going to have to give my old pal a name, or nom de plume, because I am going to have to quote him about some of his observations about flotational models, a subject which he and I believe to be worthwhile for probing the mysteries of design. So we'll call him J. Eddywake Taylrace, because he is reticent about himself, and because that explains the branch of design at which he is a master: propulsion.

He runs an office with a couple of associates in the back room and, knowing that I had in my travelling kit a couple of flotational models I had constructed to show the prospective owners and the builder just what the boats looked like, he invited me to bring them over to his office and explain their uses to his young men.

"I wish I'd known about these flotational models 30 years ago,

Naval architect Robert P. Beebe of Carmel, California, is another designer who believes in flotational models. Here he and a friend record the wake of a small model being towed at scale speed.

boys," J. Eddy told them. "They look like toy crutches to design, but we're going to use them in everything we do from this date on. Mr. Farmer, take over!"

There was little need to interest these students of design. J. Eddy-wake Taylrace had just defended a lawsuit by a builder who had launched a 63-foot V-bottom boat that was 14 inches down by the stern and had a built-in list to port that took 800 pounds of balancing weight to put into trim. The lawyers had taken the cockiness out of the associate who had calculated the weights.

As I went into the subject, all three professionals—one old-timer and two beginners—flapped their ears. I give you here, without the usual quotation marks, the seminar as I presented it, taking the associates over the basics of designing boats in the engineering manner on the drawing board, all with a view to showing some of the pitfalls.

To understand the extreme value of a flotational model, you have to take a cold look at what the word "designing" means. First, let it be known that drawing a boat is *not* designing. Designing is the process of pre-determining the outcome of various inter-related forces, prices, materials, water characteristics, and aesthetics that make an accurate conclusion to all of the compromises that are confronted in each and every boat afloat.

I have watched cocky young men "draw" boats, go through the school motions, and then seen dismay set in when the boat was laid down. The body plan looked so small, there on the loft floor. Then, when the frames were erected, they started biting fingernails. Wow, she looks big in the shop! By the time launching takes place, all fingernails are bitten off up to the elbows, because—at the bottom of it all—they realize, in some consternation, that they are not sure of what they are doing.

J. Eddywake's associates agreed with this. J. Eddy himself was chuckling in agreement.

In the second place (I went on) no drawing tells the truth about what you will see when your boat is finally launched. If you think you know what she will look like, take your outboard profile to a mirror. That alone should shock you into believing what I am telling you.

A drawing is two-dimensional. One might illustrate this by saying that if the boat were pressed down through the drafting paper, the profile would leave a line—anything with an edge to it would leave a line. All bulks become flats. Contoured surfaces are nonexistent.

Lines must be used on a drawing that are not in the boat but which show up hard, and weight the visual impact of a drawing. A case in point is the line depicting the profile of a transom. This is merely a shadow line, and does not exist in the boat.

The process of shaping a boat in two dimensions leaves much to be desired. It is a process that engenders great optical illusions. One of these illusions becomes apparent when the supporting perpendiculars of a drawing, the waterplanes and dimension lines, the arrowheads and spots of lettering are peeled away and disappear as in the finally erected hull. The things that were illusory visual supports fall away. Your boat looks different.

Stems tend to look more plumb. Sheer lines frequently look unrecognizable, their studied delicacy completely missing. Subtle sectional modelling disappears altogether. All too frequently, particularly with a beginner's boats, the bow depth forward looks much too shallow, and is. You have seen many a boat idling along with a rump-high look, as though her bow was about to step down cellar into Davy Jones' locker.

Another sometimes fatal illusory aberration, due to the two-dimensional deficiencies in proportioning, is the question of heights—deckhouse heights, mast heights, freeboard height. As the eye of the draftsman looks toward the top of his board, his sense of perspective foreshortens everything. Dimensional erections receding from his eye, which really are heights on the drawing, are most difficult to judge. You can prove this vividly by laying a section of ladder on a lawn. Flat, and receding from your eye, it seems dimensionless and small in relation to its surroundings. Stand it up, and see how it has grown!

(At this point, J. Eddywake interjected an observation.)

"That's why I hang every profile and sectional drawing up on the shop wall," he explained. "Much easier to proportion things when you stand them up."

Another manifestation of the drawing-board foreshortening effect is frequently seen in perspective drawings of boats that, when reduced for publication, are grotesquely out of whack. On the board of the man who drew it, and from the point of view of his eye, the perspective execution looked perfect. It was the drawing board that was to blame: a physicist would explain the optical phenomenon as being two-dimensional parallax.

There are certain other illusions connected with flat two-dimensional drawings that become pure delusions to an untrained, unskilled eye. Take the sections of a body plan, for instance. Gentlemen with a modicum of expertise (say, a tweezerful) will look at a set of body lines or a midsection alone and declare that that hard turn of the bilge will ".... make her stiff and able to give a good account of herself." This is self-deluding bull (bleep), a large and copious crock of it. Just think it out:

In the first place, the mid-section is generally the only section being looked at. One has to include *all* the sections to get the whole boat, but it wouldn't affect the false foible anyway, because hardness of the bilge hasn't anything to do with the matter. That portion under water is already in loaded equilibrium, having done its work in flotation. It is only in the in-and-out wedges as the whole hull heels that stability lies.

These in-and-out wedges of immersion and emersion run the entire waterline length of the boat. It is their general bulk in relationship to the center of buoyancy, and these two factors in relation to the center of weight, that determine stability. In technicalese, it's the metacentric height, and the weight of the boat in relation to that.

"Nobody looking at a piece of paper can make an offhand judgment on that!" J. Eddywake chortled. "They won't know the displacement, and can't 'feel' that with an eye!"

(His associates looked stunned. Their confirmed, eye-oriented beliefs had been proven to have been misleading.)

As simple proof of this, it was pointed out that you will find boats with sections as round as a barrel that are stiff as a church, and boats with a hard V-chine that are tender as pimples. The human eye seems to put a man's shoulder and back under the turn of a bilge section, especially at amidship, and equate this "hoistability" to stability. It is illusion: water has no shoulders.

In summation of this point, it should be evident that as the in-and-out wedge is constantly changing in a seaway, and the center of buoyancy is flitting about like a spot from a flashlight, and the center of gravity is gyrating, it should therefore be obvious that the important question of stability is not one of turn of the bilge of one section so much as it is on the triple relationship of wedges, volumes, and spread of centers.

There are other aesthetic and physical points about flotational modelling that are worthwhile.

In a design office, the tabulation of weights and the calculations for all conditions of trim are most tedious and time-consuming. Frequently, after these are done, some change comes along, and the whole bundle must be re-worked, or old figures plucked out and new ones plugged in. Here is where grievous error is apt to set in.

To circumvent the tedium of next calculating all the shifts in centers of weight, flotation, and metacenters, the engineering profession has invented the use of curves, generally plotted on one sheet.

These curves look scientific, but are nothing but fallible crutches, or guides. The points are suppositions, the curve line itself is an average, and the convergence points are problematical. If changes in loading are required, the process requires a digger who would go to the back side of the moon for an answer.

And yet, all the answers are readily available in a small tank containing less than a half cubic yard of water: the flotational model is self-integrating. It will give, within seconds, results of all required changes without tedious hours ploddingly spent reconstructing points on another curve. It has been my experience that at about this time the gnomes in the back room begin to settle for fewer and fewer points, and lots and lots of curve.

Vertical center of gravity can be found to a gnat's fanny by a simple compensating vertical weight on a 10-32 threaded upright, while the model rests on razor blade trunnions.

I have found that a 4-foot tank welded up out of 3/16-inch aluminum, about 1 foot square in section, is manageable at the design office sink. There, it can be filled and dumped, and rests at an elevation where the eye can study waterline planes and the contours of a hull as she nestles down into the drink. A shot is shown of this tank with a model at rest after trimming to proper waterline.

Another picture shows an eyeball model, before planking, that has novel features. The waterplanes were cut, in duplicate, of the DWL. Then the plan view plane was cut in photo mounting board and hung at the proper stem and transom freeboard heights. By dipping the board a bit here, lifting a bit there, a pleasing sheer was easily found that directly related to the deck outline. Rare feat, easily accomplished this way!

Next, the above-water sections were put on top of the waterplane (DWL), as cut out by eye, and glued into proper station spacing. This gives the desired shape above water. Taking an identical waterplane and clipping it to the top half turned bottom up, it was a simple matter to eyeball the bottom sections in place. Then these were marked off on file folder manila, run to a centerline and the waterline, giving quickly an embryonic body plan that merely needed sweetening. By turning the picture upside down, you can see how little bottom is really required on an 80-foot power yacht.

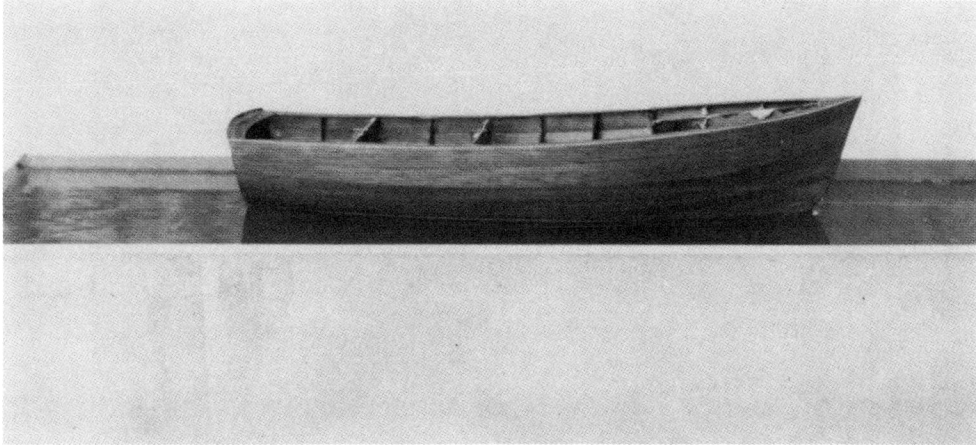

Above: Scale model of Lawson Clary, Jr.'s *Simbie* in the author's 12" x 12" x 48" tank checks out for correct waterline. *Below:* Flotational models tell a lot, such as the unplanked eyeball model at right, which shows how the above-water shape can be joined to the underwater form on identical separable waterline planes to give a full assessment of hull form.

When planking a flotational model with balsa, usually in 1/8-inch thickness, cut the sections out to agree with the outside-of-planking line on the body plan. Then, after cutting these out, run a line 1/16 inch (half the model plank thickness) around the contoured section by using your middle finger as a marking gauge while you hold the pen between thumb and forefinger. An illustration of the method is shown on the next page.

Model shops generally carry model maker's razor blade planes. Into these, Gillette double-edged blades are dropped and secured by a plate seized down by a thumb screw. These great little tools come in a

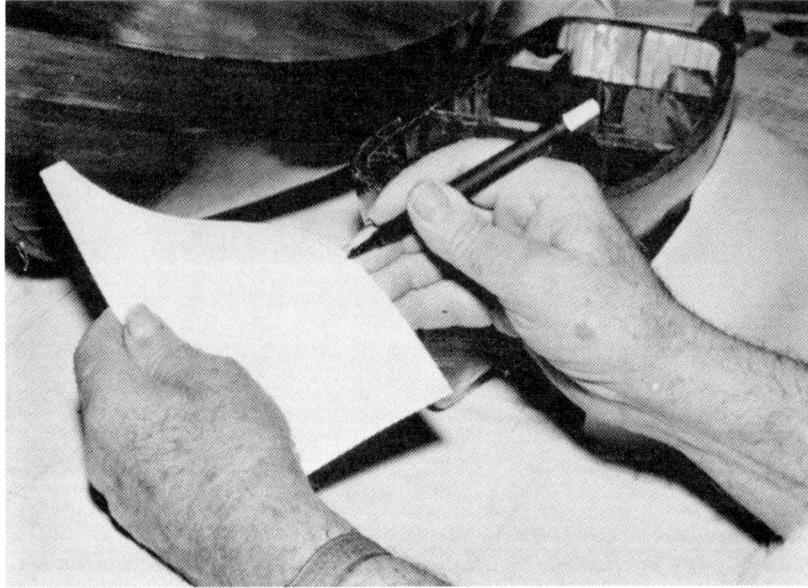

Above: Hull sections are cut to agree with body plan, then one half of planking thickness is marked and removed. *Below:* Razor blade planes with round and flat bottoms are shown here with gouge chisel in relation to size of hand and model. Wheel measuring scale is used to expand plating areas.

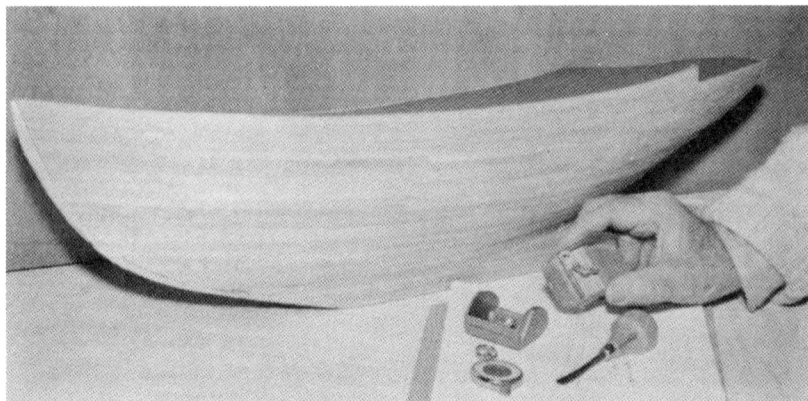

round-bottomed form for getting at garboard and keel tucks, and also in a straight-bottomed form useful for edging strips, or for diagonally scuffing off the outside planking to prepare it for final sandpapering. A small Miller's Falls gouge is useful for removing initial excess wood around keels and rudder posts.

Also shown is a wheel measuring scale which I have found to be great medicine for expanding plating girths when calculating a Bill of Materials for the prototype plating, because, you see, the flotational model can double in brass as a plating model.

Ordinary kitchen parowax has the same weight as diesel fuel oil. Poured and frozen in place, the topped-off tanks can be simulated to exact scale weight as shown in white areas.

At the close of this exposition of the horse-sense of designing with flotational models, one of J. Eddywake's boys, T. Anthony Lefkowitz (which is not his real name), introduced me to the other associate, A. Willem von Hoorn (which is not his real name either), with a most sensible suggestion, which showed his complete conversion to the idea. Why not use ordinary kitchen Parowax, obtainable at all supermarkets, as a fixed substitute for No. 2 diesel fuel oil? Being a petroleum derivative, it has almost identical weight with diesel oil. I thought it such a good suggestion I tried it, and took a photo to prove it, showing you that this method of designing works!

After which, the seminar came to a close as the doomed men— doomed to be boat designers because their names began with an initial— went across the street with J. Eddy and myself to get a dipper of schnapps at Dottie's Mistake and conclude proceedings with a liquid foundation under our tongues.

14

Sam Rabl's Towing Rig for Models

This shows how to build a towing outfit for testing models that was devised by Sam Rabl 45 years ago.

Rabl, in case you don't know it, was head of the hull drafting department at the Bethlehem Shipyard in Baltimore. He knew his trade, loved to design practical boats that delivered a whale of a big bang for a buck, and he had the moral excellence to detail almost everything that went into his work. What Sam designed, he first tested.

One of his tools was a simple towing outfit he had devised from odds and ends of springs, a "scandalized" old alarm clock, some polar graph paper and what some writers of this day would term, wonderingly, "an ingenious arrangement of levers."

The other day I ran across a most complete diagram of this device. From the reproduction shown here, you can see how it was built. The diagram was drawn by Yours Truly and inked by the art department of *Mechanical Package Magazine* when at one period of my Rover Boy professional life, I had invented that magazine and had become its editor.

Later, Sam's alarm clock idea popped into my noggin when I had to prove that a proposed design was beyond the realm of possibility. I built one, have the old snapshots to prove it, and thereby hangs the stark drama of A Shipyard Saved From Death. Here's the tale:

When Austin T. Levy, the New England textile magnate, came to Gibbs Gas Engine and Drydock Co. so long ago, he had just bought the island of Eleuthera. Yes, THE Eleuthera in the Bahamas.

Mr. Levy wanted a 100-foot fast ferry to run from Miami to his new

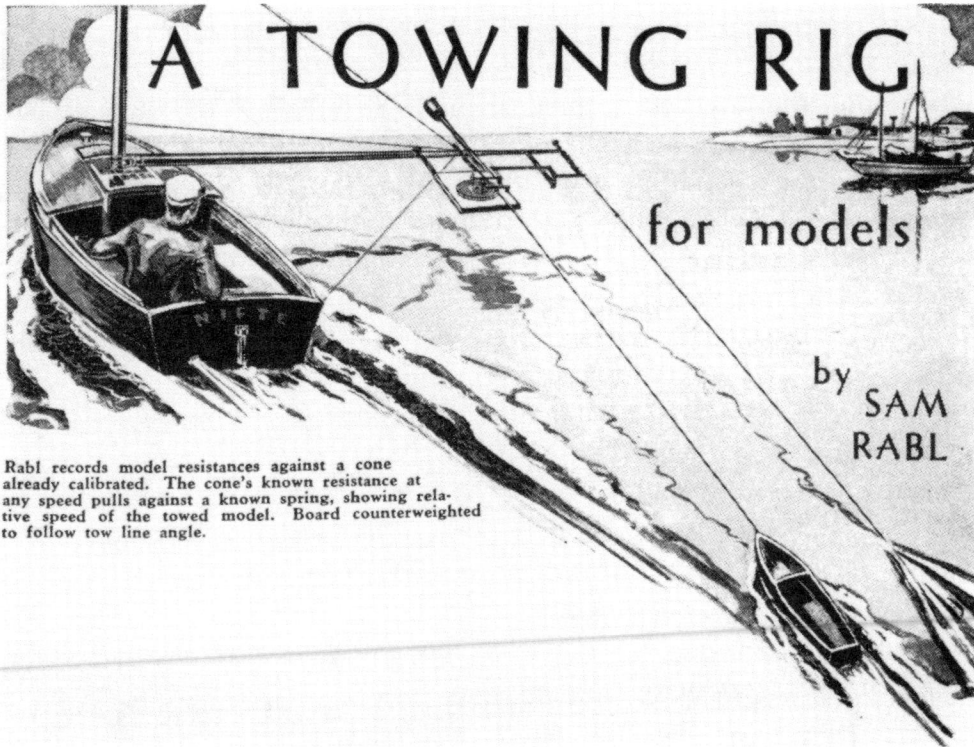

A TOWING RIG
for models
by SAM RABL

Rabl records model resistances against a cone already calibrated. The cone's known resistance at any speed pulls against a known spring, showing relative speed of the towed model. Board counterweighted to follow tow line angle.

Above: This drawing headed Sam Rabl's article on his towing rig that appeared first in *Mechanical Package Magazine* and later in *Twenty Boats. Below:* A 98-cent pawnshop alarm clock provides the "motor" when the escapement is removed and a small flywheel (shown underside) is affixed to a shaft extended from the gear next to the escapement. This slows the rate of turn.

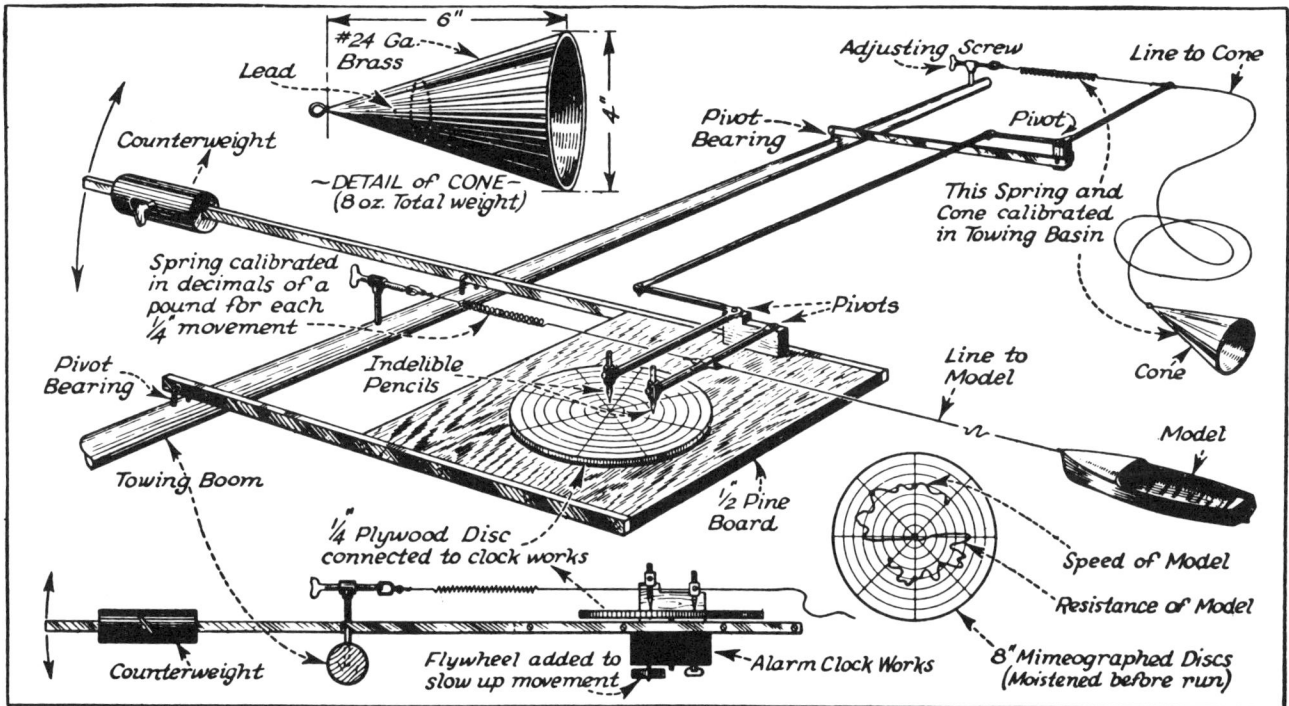

Counterweight

Lead

#24 Ga. Brass
6"
4"
~DETAIL of CONE~
(8 oz. Total weight)

Adjusting Screw
Line to Cone

Pivot Bearing
Pivot

This Spring and Cone calibrated in Towing Basin

Spring calibrated in decimals of a pound for each ¼" movement

Pivots

Line to Model

Cone

Pivot Bearing

Indelible Pencils

Line to Model

Model

Towing Boom

½ Pine Board

Speed of Model

¼ Plywood Disc connected to clock works

Resistance of Model

Counterweight

Flywheel added to slow up movement

Alarm Clock Works

8" Mimeographed Discs (Moistened before run)

empire. This vessel had to carry 300 passengers at 30 knots; she would serve as a shuttle running on a streetcar basis back and forth.

The effect on the Gibbs yard was electric. Things were so tough all over at the time that every man on the payroll was wired dielectrically through his feet to be receptive to any charge of static, ionized, pre-lightning news emanating from the front office. We knew there was a "live one." Mr. Gibbs must have discharged like an electric eel when he heard Levy's request for the yard to design and build a steel vessel capable of the task.

To this day I believe I knew what was coming when Mr. Gibbs sent for me and laid out the proposition in the presence of Mr. Levy. Before I entered the office door I had the premonition, "This one we can't handle."

"What I want," said Mr. Levy, "is a fast, seaworthy commuter for 300 people. John Alden tells me people don't weigh anything, so let's make her commodious. She will have to do 30 knots in all weather to make schedules I am planning."

I gulped, conjuring visions of a Navy destroyer, Parsons turbines backed up by a producing oilfield.

Mr. Gibbs went on, "Mr. Levy has been talking with the Alden office, but John Alden says he is too busy to take on the work. Would we have to furnace the plates?"

Cagey John Alden! He had sent Mr. Levy packing. Hungry Gibbs Drydock! Already furnacing plates! I shook my head negatively.

"You'd need a 300-footer with 180,000 hp, gentlemen—" I said, adding "—I think."

The frozen glare Mr. George Gibbs shot at me preceded the laser beam by years, but it has still left a scar on my spiritual tissue. I will always admire Mr. Gibbs for his willingness to be shown.

I had remembered Sam Rabl's 98-cent alarm clock dynamometer, and I offered to build one, build a model, and verify my position if Mr. Gibbs would foot the bill for the test. Mr. Levy nodded that he would back Mr. Gibbs.

It was a swindle from the start. Gibbs possibly thought that Mr. Levy would carry my chunk of the payroll for a couple of weeks, and I fired off a letter to Westinghouse to see what they had in the line of 180,000-hp turbines on the shelf in the back room, and made noises on the phone to Babcock and Wilcox about the availability of boilers to match.

It was a strange fix: A few days on the board to produce the lines of a 6-foot model, then to build a model towing outfit to prove the impossibility of the wealthy textile merchant's dream; prove it by resistance readings to be taken from a Gibbs dory on the St. John's

These snapshots show the author and his Rabl towing rig proving the impracticality of Levy's proposed ferry. The snazzy motorboat shown is a 1934 Gibbs Power Dory, powered with a 6-hp Wisconsin air-cooled engine.

River above Jacksonville, using a busted alarm clock as the major tool! Never worked so hard to get out of a job!

I still do not recall the upshot of the tests, but I did build the model, and I did get substantive readings, and I did take some snapshots to substantiate here, years later, that the event took place.

For the life of me, I cannot recall whether the answers called for 30, 300, or 3,000 passengers or a 3,000-footer doing 3 knots and taking 3 years to get to Eleuthera.

Mr. Levy evaporated and later ran for the U.S. Senate from Rhode Island. By that time I was eating well, and was in safe surroundings.

To the lay reader, let me explain the basic arithmetic of model testing. Professor William Froude of Great Britain established the fact in 1867 that identical hulls, but in different sizes, vary in speed as the square of their relative scale, and that they vary in weight as the cube of their relative scales.

For instance, a model to 3/4-inch-to-the-foot scale is 1/16th the size of the prototype. The relative scale is 16. Proper speed for the model is the square root of 16, or 4.

Suppose the prototype must do 20 mph. One fourth of 20 is 5. Thus, at 5 mph, the behavior of the model simulates the same wave-making characteristics as the parent vessel. So said Professor Froude.

As to relative weight, or displacement, the cube of 16 is 4,096. Thus, the model, when weighted to the waterline, can be weighed and the reading multiplied by 4,096 to give the displacement of the prototype. Again, Professor Froude.

Any naval architect who wishes to build this dynamometer can grab the idea visually by a look at the diagram. Sam Rabl's own words of description follow:

I'm showing here a way I worked out for towing models from my boat. Better than the sink method, and accurate to within 5 percent. Briefly, the rig consists of a boom guyed out from the chainplates of my boat as shown in the sketch. On this boom is a counterweighted board which will follow the pull of the towline.

Below this board is a set of discarded alarm clock works in which the staff of the gear next to the escapement has been extended and a flywheel added to slow up its motion when the escapement was removed.

On the hour hand shaft there was mounted a disc of 1/4″ plywood 8″ in diameter arranged so that it would turn, and on this disc is pasted a moistened sheet which was mimeographed with circles one-quarter inch apart.

You will note that there are two arms on the rig, each attached to springs. One spring was calibrated to decimals of a pound for .5 of a pound total movement and each division means so many parts of a pound. We found later that the divisions aren't really necessary as we read the resistance of the model off with the scale and compare it with the calibrated cone.

Here, in the original story, a line or two of runover type is missing. But no matter. The runover concerned a few coefficients Sam gave for the resistance of the cone shown in the diagram. I found that the cone did not work. It trolled and was attacked by fish.

So, I substituted a model of a vessel with known performance. This resistance behaved itself. Also, I worked up about 250 feet of heavy trolling line into which knots were tied at fifty-foot intervals. This was placed on a reel. The starting end was anchored near the shore start, and the knots were fed through a pair of brass springs. On the end of one spring arm was attached a pen that would make a tick when the knot passed. This gave an accurate rate of advance for speeds.

The results? As I have said, it proved convincing to Mr. Levy and Mr. Gibbs and vindicated my position of not giving in to anything except convictions of honor and good sense.

It is highly probable that, hence, some young reader who is now between his Ivory Soap bathtub boat and that ocean liner he someday hopes to design, will be stumped by some problem in hunch-and-guess that is beyond his experience. Sam Rabl's outfit, as seen over my shoulder, may save HIS shipyard from a fate worse than death.

15

The Kitchen Rudder

Breathes there the man with hope so dead who never to himself has said, "Boy! With *this* idea I've got the world by the tail for a downhill haul!"? If he gets to talking about patenting some new whiz-bang-hedral bottom, or nailing down for himself a way to make the wind shove a boat two miles to a normal sail's one; if he thinks he has hit a way to design a boat that will roll across the Atlantic on big wheels, or has the idea that his clever contraption will collect the waves and ride on air (a perennial fallacy)—I say to him, "Save your breath and money, Buddy."

The chances are that his idea has been thought of a hundred times during the past hundred years.

Please note right here that we are embracing only that field of invention that relates to controlling water in its behavior under or around a hull. The subject covers water flow and propulsion. A book could be written about the inventing syndrome as it bears on this facet of the marine scene. There have been dozens of nutty novelties invented and patented in good faith that look infallibly clever on paper but that won't work when you ask water to behave as stated in the patent claim. And there have been many "inventions" granted patents by the patent office which are heralded by their inventors and licensees as Great Big Breakthrough Ideas which do work—after a fashion—but which are not new at all. Hence, in a court test, these inventions would be found to have been anticipated by what the trade calls "Prior Art."

Result: the patent is worthless, null and void.

Anybody who has been designing boats a hundred years or so can tick off much of this prior art in the wink of an eyelash. The idea of a planing boat was advanced about 1870 by an English clergyman, Reverend Ramus, who put forth the idea that a boat would go faster over the water than through it. As is so often the case, the idea was ahead of the power technology of the day.

Are you thinking step hydroplane? Alfred E. Luders, in 1907, designed a one-step planing boat. W.H. Fauber, popularly thought of as the father of the hydroplane, came up with the multi-step idea. In 1912, his *Maple Leaf IV* captured the Harmsworth Trophy.

Are you thinking deep-V bottom? Gordon B. Hooton, a resident of Michigan, advocated, in 1928 in numerous writings supported by photographs, the adoption of double and triple the deadrise or di-hedral angle then in vogue—five degrees. He built many 15- to 30-degree boats to prove his point.

Are you thinking peeling strips, or "longitudinal steps"? Heavens to Betsy! George Crouch was using them in 1915 on his Peter Pan series of racing boats. I used them in 1928 by outlapping clinker planking on planing hulls.

Are you thinking diagonal cross slots for ventilating a planing bottom? Elliot Gardner of the Albany Boat Corp. used them on his Tarpon series in the mid-Twenties.

Are you going to invert the V of a planing boat once or twice or more times transversely, cat-hedral as opposed to di-hedral, and take a bow for inventing what the unknowing public will inevitably call a "cathedral" hull? Albert Hickman patented his Sea Sled over 50 years ago. It was the original basic cat-hedral idea: if a V-bottom boat threw out a lot of side spray, the obvious cure was to slice a V-bottom hull along the keel line, and join the two chines together. This would suppress the side wash under the hull. The boat would ride on air!

Theoretically, this would lower resistance. Unfortunately, air is only one-eight-hundredth as dense as water, and the hoped-for air ride aspect was proved by later technology to be false: turbulent water full of air has much more resistance than undisturbed water in laminar flow.

Even in Hickman's day, the wave-collecting idea was not new. Cox & King of London was a firm of naval architects that came out with a boat called a "wave collector," which was a round-bilged hull with down-swept hard corners (chines) that were supposed to slap waves back under the hull and make them behave. Working on the same idea, the highly respected firm of Collings & Bell of Auckland, New Zealand, in 1914 produced a little 21-foot flyer called Fleetwing, which used the so-called wave-collecting principle. Fleetwing used a 20 hp Red Wing motor of about 1,200 rpm and did 20 mph.

Morris Whitaker, naval architect of Nyack, New York, produced his

Morris M. Whitaker, N. A., at the wheel of his wave-collecting runabout off Nyack in 1915, proving that there is nothing new about inverted chines or the cathedral bottom configuration. Speed: about 25 mph.

own version of a wave collector. I tender here a photo postcard mailed to the firm for which I was working. The postmark reads, "Chicago, Ill., 1915."

I could go on—but you see that wave collectors are nothing new. Generally, this is true for everything throughout the whole spectrum of modern-day marine development. And yet, here and there in marine thinking over the past hundred years, there have been men who, well grounded in marine practices at designing or building, have come up with something of real merit. One of these was the Kitchen reversing rudder. Another was the Kort nozzle.

The Kitchen rudder did away with all reverse gears and variable-pitch propellers and enabled control of a boat to reach steamboat flexibility. It seems to have disappeared from the scene; certainly the idea is now in the public domain, because the U.S. Patent No. 1,186,210 was granted to Admiral Kitchen of the British Navy in 1916. Seventeen years later it would have run out. That dates the public domain from 1933.

The Kort nozzle, of course, is economic and viable, and is still being used where an increase in static thrust is required, giving as high as 25 percent more push to tugs and particularly to river towboats. The Kort nozzle does limit top speeds a bit, but it is a fixed, foil-section shroud around the propeller and employs a variation of the Bernoulli principle in aiding the propeller to achieve higher acceleration to the slipstream. The Kort nozzle is a breakthrough idea that "made the grade."

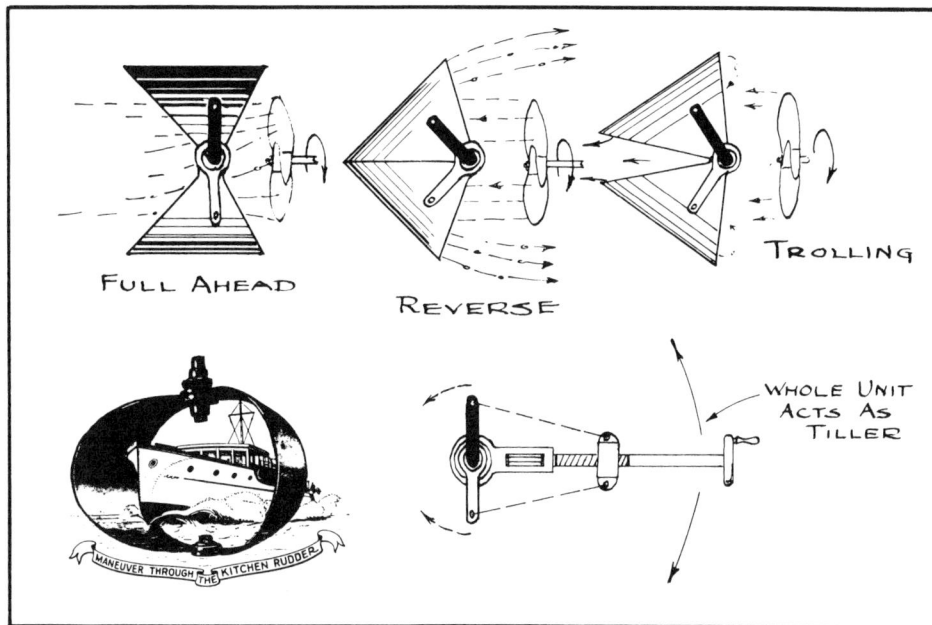

FULL AHEAD

REVERSE

TROLLING

WHOLE UNIT ACTS AS TILLER

MANEUVER THROUGH THE KITCHEN RUDDER

The semicircular rudder blades of the Kitchen rudder are mounted on a common center. The black arm is on a solid center stock. The bright arm is on a tubular stock encasing the solid one. Both short tiller arms are toggled to a screw jack, which is adjusted by the wheel on the end of the main tiller. In ordinary steering the whole unit swings. Speed and reverse are effected by adjustment of the screw, which can be remotely controlled electrically. Reverse efficiency is 37½ percent.

But what of the Kitchen rudder? It was widely accepted in Great Britain, so it certainly must have worked well. It was apparently not so successful in the United States, and thereby hangs a mystery that I can solve only partly, because the marine press of the time is extremely hit-and-miss, and the company image and promotion is and was, by today's standards, extremely sketchy.

The Kitchen rudder was obviously the work of a man who understood propulsion. It consisted of two semi-circular rudders, port and starboard, which partially shrouded the propeller and which could be closed, from partial clamshell folding to complete restriction. Each half was mounted through a common-center solid and tubular rudder stock. From each stock extended an arm which controlled the angularity of that blade. A worm screw with a rotational wheel and handle, resembling the tailstock wheel on a lathe, was mounted on the end of this screw, which served as a tiller. By rotating the tailstock wheel, the clamshells could be opened or closed. By swinging the whole screw assembly from port to starboard, the boat could be steered.

By some freak of fate, or maybe because of a reluctance to validate any part of any patented marine gimmick, I never used a Kitchen rudder. But I have witnessed its operation on several occasions. I saw at one time the visitation of some British naval brass who pulled dockside

This stern view of a Kitchen rudder shows the device in an open position. The little handwheel at the end of the tiller is used to adjust the opening of the rudder.

with what appeared to be a Vosper gig, at the stern of which stood a coxswain who was a virtuoso with the Kitchen rudder. He could slow down, back and fill, swing in the stern, and, with motor never missing a beat, hold his boat dead still while securing to cleats.

At another time I saw an Evinrude one-cylinder outboard approach a dock with the knuckle-buster whirling away merrily, but the boat was slowed, reversed, and held in position while a passenger leaped airily into the craft, after which, without any adjustment to the spark, the boat slowed down to perfect trolling speed and fish lines were streamed for inshore trolling. It was an amazing demonstration, because the old Evinrude 1-1/2-hp, 85-pound iron knuckle-buster with mixing valve carburetion had two speeds only: full blast (if you could get it to start) and stop.

In an unusually complete library of bound volumes of the yachting press of the Kitchen rudder era—from 1916 to its apparent demise economically in 1926—I can trace only sketchily its course on the American marine scene. In *Rudder,* which once was the bible of yacht designers with technical orientation, I can find only one reference. This is on page 15 of the February 1921 issue. Depicted in the illustration is the old compromise-sterned cruiser *Violet,* 38 feet by 10 feet by 3.3 feet in dimension, powered by a 22-hp tractor engine, swinging a 20-inch-diameter by 30-inch-pitch three-blade wheel. The installation was made by the McNab Company of Bridgeport, Connecticut, who supervised the trial and provided the equipment.

Representatives of the U.S. Navy witnessed the trial, and it was stated that at 12 mph the boat could be stopped in her own length. She could be steered more effectively because of the barrel-like funneling of the entire slipstream. The vessel could be rotated about her own centers, in her own length. It was stated that her timed speed in reverse was 4.5 mph.

This indicates a reverse efficiency of 37-1/2 percent. This speed compares to a slight disadvantage over conventional reversed-propeller efficiency as to speed percentages obtainable in reverse, but the action carries with it the advantage of being able to steer accurately in reverse with the Kitchen rudder, whereas such speeds in a normally ruddered vessel would find the lead on the rudder at 80 percent, overpowering the helm, chattering, and backing up every which way, uncontrollable. Thus, the comparison favors the Kitchen rudder.

It would seem inescapable that the Kitchen rudder would, if properly researched again, and developed in light of today's knowledge of fluid flow and in light of today's economic pressures on wages, make an indispensable place for itself in that class of fishing vessel where a man works alone.

A Kitchen rudder would be like having a paid hand aboard that you didn't have to feed or share the catch with. Your speed could be set to troll just so. In hard chances with big seas running, you could lay-to stern first with just enough way on to keep her stern to the gale while you got some sleep. You could snake in and out around reefs you were trolling at your own best speed regardless of where your diesel best idled, and you would have sidethruster maneuverability built into your stern end.

Nevertheless, furthermore, and to the contrary notwithstanding, the Kitchen rudder is not currently on the marine scene in the United States. I have pondered why this might be, or how it came to die. If the back-flushing action is 37-1/2 percent of forward thrust, weeds should easily be washed out. As far as hitting driftwood is considered a hazard, it has been my experience that most of this is surface floating. I see no more liability on this score than one has with the occasional water-logged pulp stick. It would be easier to repair a bronze sheet, or galvanized sheet, than it would be to remove and re-pitch a whacked-up wheel.

It would seem to me, also, that the shroud effect of the Kitchen rudder would be kinder to nets around the propeller itself. But if that objection was borne out by operating fact, a basket of pipes acting as a screen, after the manner of the Nipigon wanigan tugs, would kill that objection once and for all.

Pulp tugs, or wanigans, thrash through, over, around, and on top of 8-inch to 10-inch pulp logs with complete immunity to propellers, using such a provision.

I think the Kitchen rudder went out of business on purely manufacturing economics, a victim of the then state-of-the-art in design, coupled with the "patent" phobia of over-burdened royalties, together with the high cost of sales and inept marketing. I refer in this case to the United States picture. The advertising and promotion seemed to be in the hands of mechanics rather than qualified ad agencies.

The McNab Company was based in Bridgeport, Connecticut, for

McNAB KITCHEN RUDDER

FROM THE OUTBOARD MOTOR TO THE OCEAN MOTOR SHIP
NO BOAT TOO SMALL — NO SHIP TOO LARGE

Steers!
Reverses!
Brakes!
Maneuvers!

Regardless of the size of your craft you will realize better steering and maneuvering through the use of the McNab-Kitchen Rudder.

The McNab-Kitchen Rudder eliminates the necessity of reverse gears and gives full power ahead or reverse without changing propeller speed or engine revolutions. From full speed ahead vessel can be brought to a dead stop in its own length. Furthermore, vessel can be turned on its own center without progressing ahead or astern—impossible with any other rudder.

The "McNab-Kitchen" gives to any outboard or inboat motor a maneuvering ability that is unsurpassed and is most useful to anglers, hunters, yachtsmen, and anyone requiring a delicate speed control.

The McNab-Kitchen Rudder not only assures very fine steering, but also protects the propeller from weeds and snags—and the boatowner from much trouble.

Control your craft this year, with a McNab-Kitchen Rudder. Write for full details.

THE McNAB-KITCHEN RUDDER CORPORATION
BRIDGEPORT, CONN. U.S.A.

This McNab-Kitchen ad in the February 25, 1925, issue of *Motor Boat* magazine covered the main points of the unique rudder. The unit offered special attractions to outboard motor owners of the period, since the early knucklebusters had no reverse gears and generally poor throttle controls.

about 10 years, from 1916 to about 1926. They advertised fairly consistently only in *Motor Boat*. I say "fairly" advisedly; the ad was scheduled in many issues, and the name McNab appeared in the ad index, but many times McNab drew only a blank line for a page number—and no ad. A little problem in credit, maybe? Or late copy arriving post-deadline?

Once in a while the advertisement would be changed, but there was little attempt to jazz up copy or to dramatize results. In the September 1926 issue of *Power Boating,* page 81, the McNab Company was listed with a Yonkers address, and thereafter dropped from the scene. Technology on the Kitchen rudder went down the drain. It was successfully applied to outboards, large ships, and cruisers as well as to launches. Once in a while a McNab ad would appear showing application to several types of power, and I show one here.

One possible key to the demise of the British admiral's rudder might be found in this fact: at the time it appeared on the scene, all boats were custom built. There were building yards at every watering place. Into the hulls went the owner's own selection of engine, the owner's selection of propeller, and often as not, the owner picked out the reversing gear. The sales train was heavily "watered down." This is one probable cause of demise for the McNab-Kitchen Rudder Company.

The latest address I have on the parent British Company is 53 years old! In an issue of *Motor Boat* for July 25, 1920, there is a publicity release which ends, "Full particulars can be obtained from Kitchen's Reversing Rudder Co., Ltd., 7 Royal Liver Bldg., Liverpool, England."—Lotsa luck!

The Kitchen rudder has merit and was original, and a first. In today's market, with today's know-how, the possibilities are tantalizing.

And now, Shipmates, before we tip back our chairs and collect our liquid resources for a last potshot at the shop stove, I have an observation to make:

In a long and merry life as a midwife to the marine and mechanic arts, I've done a passel of inventing myself. My operational philosophy coincides with that of James Ford Bell, a great amateur sailor and the guiding genius behind General Mills. He once told me his criterion for a good idea was, "Keep it simple, make it big."

The History of
The Motor Boat
Part VII

By
William
Harnden
Foster

GASOLINE

The first man to mix his lubricating oil with his gasoline

The first man to mix his lubricating oil
with his gasoline.

Simple? Big? Whaddaya mean? As an example, consider the unsung genius immortalized in William Harnden Foster's cartoon of 1919. Being from Maine, this genius knew how to make a buffalo nickel bellow. With one swoop he put all the lubricator and oil cup people out of business by merely dumping the lube oil into his gas tank. Simple idea, and now very big. Ask any ecologist!

The Kitchen rudder was sublimely simple. I believe someday someone will come along who can make it big.

16

Choosing the Right Propeller

The selection of the proper wheel for an engine or a boat is often an exercise in blind guessometry. Too frequently it is "pin the tail on the donkey" engineering. The result is that more boats are running around with wrong propellers than with right ones.

The chart on page 138 will prove a help in cross checking all the different recommendations you get when you: (a) write to three propeller makers, or (b) riffle through catalogs to get a fix on what's cookin', and (c) cagily write to three engine builders who make engines like yours, asking what their recommendation would be. None of them know any more about it than you do. They haven't seen your boat and if they haven't built your engine, you'll get an off-size prescription.

It is better to go at the problem from elemental engineering principles first. Later, you can refine your judgment according to hull shape, loading, and service. These refinements are variables calling for niceties of discrimination, but they are in the "delicate" or fractional areas of measurement, the main fences of which must be boxed in by sticking to basics at the outset.

The three elemental answers that must be determined for propeller pegging are (1) diameter, then (2) pitch, and (3) slip. It is diameter that holds your engine to rated revolutions more so than does pitch. Diameter adjusts itself more sensitively to engine torque—power—than does pitch, because it is a pretty good rule of thumb that one inch of diameter absorbs the torque required for two or three inches of pitch. And bear in mind that there can be no thrust without slip. A workable norm is 25 percent.

Pitch is easy to arrive at. Diameter is not. Pitch is a function of the boat's speed. This can be fairly judged by any skipper, and quite accurately by a man designing from known speeds in previous hulls. Pitch is the distance a wheel would travel worming its way through a solid. It is pegged in this manner: the number of inches a wheel should travel in one turn (pitch) is first multiplied by the rpm. This gives the inches of advance in one minute. Multiply this by 60 for the inches-per-hour rate, since there are 60 minutes in an hour. Divide this figure by 12 to get the number of feet travelled per hour, since there are 12 inches to the foot. Divide the number of feet per hour by 5,280 for speed in statute miles, since this is the number of feet in a statute mile. Or, divide the number of feet per hour by 6,080 to get knots, because this is the number of feet in a nautical mile. To your basic pitch must be added a prudent percentage for slip. About 25 percent will do the trick.

The word "slip" is an unfortunate term. There can be no thrust without it. In reality, it is the vector in a force parallelogram, where the sideways travel of the angular blade is plotted against the resultant travel of the water in an aft direction. That this force is rotating, delivering a rotary aft travel to the water that resembles a corkscrew pretzel, is often confusing, but there it is: there can be no thrust without the vector unhappily termed "slip." Slip is not waste. It is a necessity.

If pitch is easily understood, the relationship of diameter to power is not. All engines have turning power at the crankshaft end. Horsepower is determined by measuring this torque, or turning power, on a brake. The brake can be a simple arm with clamp screws that brake the rpm to a fixed figure. Then by an arm extending to a scale, the force in foot-pounds is converted to horsepower, since 33,000 foot-pounds per minute equals one horsepower. Generally, electro-dynamometric brakes are employed, which calibrate outputs in terms of horses, directly.

It was to establish the amount of torque propellers would absorb, which in turn would eliminate guessing at diameter, that this chart was prepared in the engineering department of the Elco works in 1941. Before I tell you about the labor of preparation, let me tell you how to use it.

On the chart, pick out the power of your engine, slide down the power line to rpm, then trace this intersection over to the left-hand index, and you will find the diameter required to hold the engine to rated rpm. This presumes the stated horsepower is for an engine in full service regalia, ready to begin work in your boat. Seldom is this the case. It is better to work to about 90 percent of rated top power in pegging your propeller, because the brake test curves are all made in ideal conditions: high water jacket heat, proper fuels, a minimum of power-take-off attachments. There is always an honesty factor involved, too, depending upon the manufacturer. Some curves are supplied on a blood-and-guts basis for a stripped engine that is forced to the ultimate.

Other makers are too conservative, rating their engines at about 75 percent of their capacity, at which point they nominate the power for continuous duty. This, if taken literally, will give you an engine that will slightly overpower your propeller. Experience has taught me to use about 90 percent of top-rated power and apply this to the chart, and the resulting diameter will give satisfaction throughout the whole range of power actually delivered by the engine.

The reason for peeling back your power expectation just a bit can be understood by looking at the three rectilinear performance curves in Figure 1. These are for the Volvo MD3B three-cylinder engine and are shown because they are typical. The top curve is the rate of fuel consumption. One g/hkh equals .002236 lbs/hp/hr. The middle curve is for torque, wherein 1 kpm equals 7.233 lbs/ft. The lower curve is "horsepower," where 1hk is .986 hp. More torque is delivered at the 2,000 to 2,250 range than at terminal rpm. Fuel consumption is better. The power curve above this point is flattening out. Continuous output is

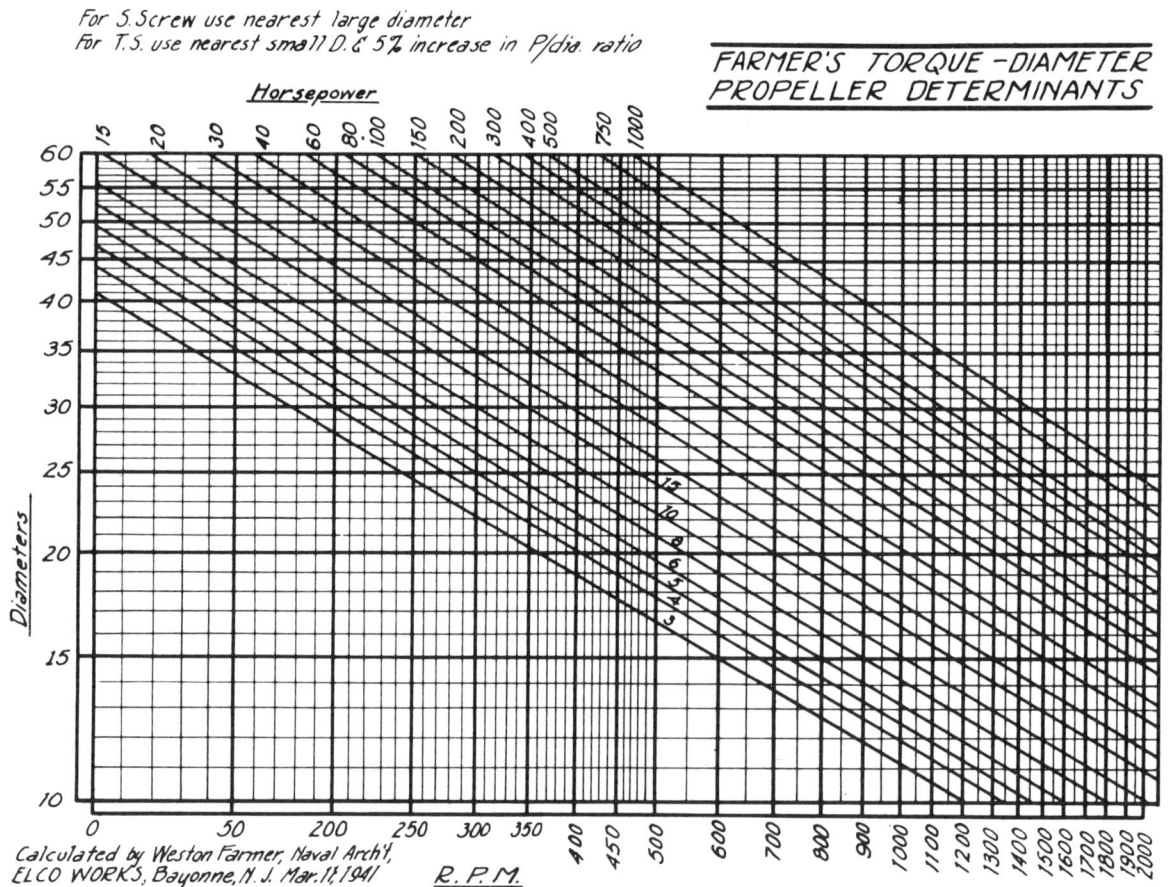

For S. Screw use nearest large diameter
For T.S. use nearest small D. & 5% increase in P/dia. ratio

Horsepower

FARMER'S TORQUE-DIAMETER PROPELLER DETERMINANTS

Diameters

R. P. M.

Calculated by Weston Farmer, Naval Arch't,
ELCO WORKS, Bayonne, N.J. Mar. 11, 1941

138

better at the slightly less demanding rpm. A wheel pegged at 2,250 to 2,300 will best use the whole picture.

The torque-diameter chart is accurate, based on honest torque. The determinant values on the chart are based on pitch-to-diameter ratios of 1:1; that is, a "square" propeller.

The "how-come" of the thing is an interesting story, emanating from conditions at the famed old Elco works 38 years ago. Elco—short for Electric Launch Co.—was at that time the best and the most experienced stock boat builder in the country. The yard stretched two blocks

Volvo MD 3 power and consumption curves can be used with the chart on page 138 to determine propeller diameter.

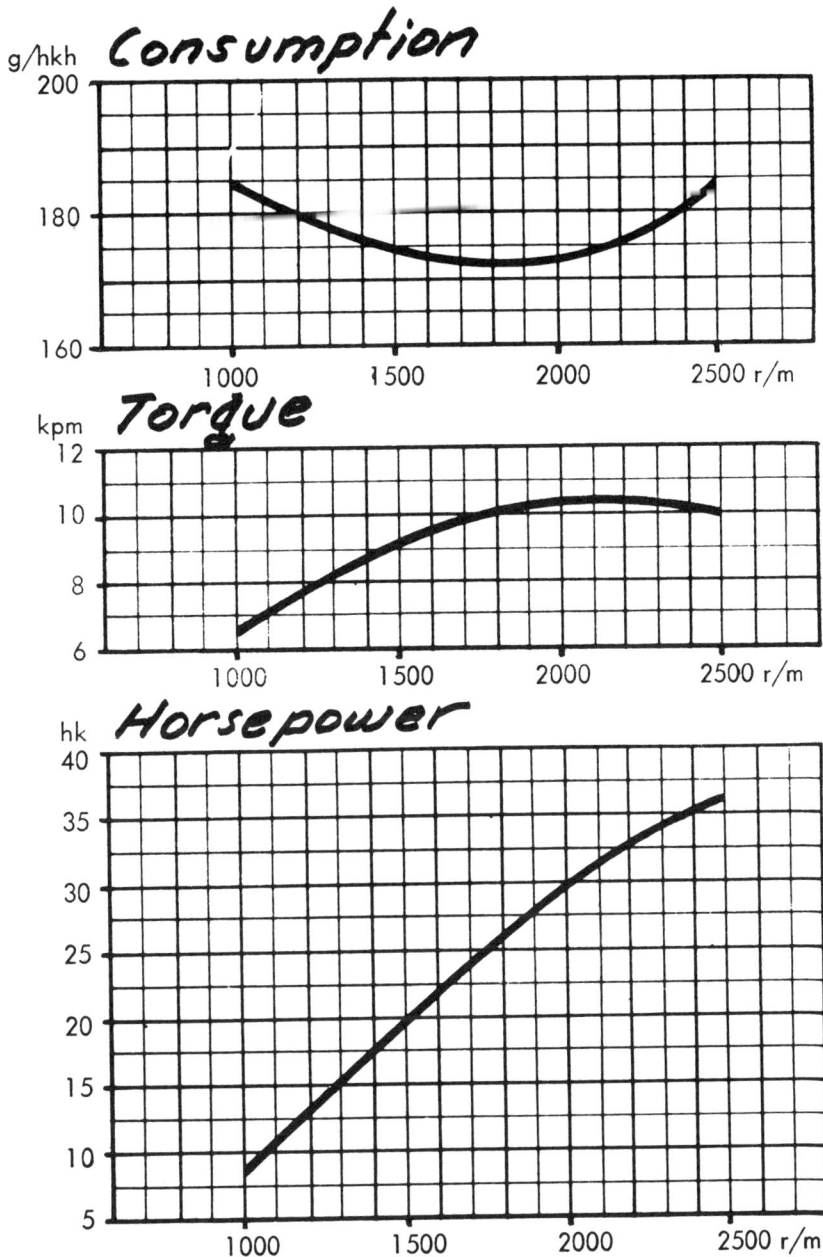

along Newark Bay at Bayonne, New Jersey, and about a block eastward from the water along the Jersey Central railroad track toward Hudson Boulevard off the railroad bridge leading across Newark Bay. Elco was the Cadillac of motor yacht builders, the Metro-Goldwyn-Mayer of volume boatbuilding. Elco's motto was quality: do it right, do it big, go first class.

Elco's plant and organization met these standards. They employed nine fully qualified naval architects at the time I joined the design staff there in 1938. The plant had its own joiner shops, its own pattern works, its own copper, tank, piping, and wheel fettling departments, even a small foundry. In short, the works. I found myself working with the likes of Irwin Chase, Alfred Fleming, Glen Tremaine, and Morris Whitaker.

One day during a lull in drafting room activities, Preston Sutphen, the general manager, suggested that in a new model series, the cost of trying out many suits of twin-screw propellers was burdensome. Why not establish some firm, tested data so that 30 pairs of twin screws wouldn't have to be shelved because of a bum preliminary stab resulting from a "consensus"? The old consensus method of asking everybody and taking an average had proved fairly accurate when determining pitches, but out of whack on diameters. Over the previous 40 years, Elco's stock of shelved wheels had become impressive, and if melted down again, would have resembled a river of molten bronze. Why not make calibrated runs testing known hulls against engines of pre-tested torque, using a wide range of propellers and powers? Hundreds of these runs, collated from hundreds of charted points, ought to give some firm data that would be worth a pile of money.

On a standard hull, say an Elco 57, the initial boat would be tested to a honed edge before the discount-size propeller order would be given. But suppose some buyer wanted a pair of Superior diesels instead of a pair of reduction-drive Chrysler Royals? What size wheel prescription for a customized version?

The wonder of it was that Sutphen's idea hadn't been worked up years before. Agreed—then who would do the work? In conclave assembled, I was elected.

At first I was overjoyed. I'd been designing PT propellers, locked secretly in Irwin Chase's private office, drawing on planished marble to thwart the heat and humidity. To be put afloat in a fleet of Elcos, running tests on Newark Bay, seemed at first to be a plum. In the tedium of the task, I found out why I had been generally considered a good guesser, and why the other designers had had more important work elsewhere, or a vacation coming up, or other evaporative activities. The job was soon boring. I was stuck—but it beat looking for a job elsewhere and was lots better than sleeping in a Jersey Central boxcar.

The result is the chart presented here. When all the measurements were in hand, and plotted, I showed the curves to others, and it was pointed out by a knowledgeable professor that my curves plotted on a rectilinear scale were exponential. He recommended the logarithmic construction of ordinates and abscissae, and that is why I finally plotted the values to go in straight lines across the Elco graph. Each space is a tenth less than the previous space.

If your engine is a reduction-gear job, divide the engine rpm by the large number in the reduction gear ratio to get the prop-shaft rpm. Thus, on a 1.95:1 gear, divide the engine rpm by 1.95 to get the correct rpm to apply to the chart.

I cheerfully admit that no such compilation as this will answer all of the theories held about screw propellers. There are many, and then a few more. I also freely admit that much scientific data improvement has been collected about propellers since the 1941 date, such as the importance of the B or beam factor in speed having so much influence. I also know that every propeller professor has his own barnyard English to apply to his interpretations. I also know this: Wind and wave and the size of horses in horsepower haven't changed. Diameter in relation to engine torque is still the basic stab.

I hope you will find this chart useful.

17

Marine Aluminum

Aluminum as a material for the building of one-of-a-kind hulls hasn't seen much reporting from those who have had experience with it. Feedback from the field of usage has been slight.

Since this scribe has designed and has had built a number of large and expensively equipped yachts in aluminum, I think it might be worthwhile to report how the metal has worked out in service. What follows is nothing deep—just wheelhouse gab as we sag along out to sea.

I think aluminum is tomorrow's material, and it is here today, right now. There'll be some diehards who will raise an eyebrow and install a facial question mark when I say this. For them, I have a parable to relate. It may serve to adjust their thinking.

Up on Mount Ararat when Noah was building the Ark, there was an old sheik hanging over Noah's fence telling the Master Mariner just how to build her. This sheik, whose name was Alotabul, knew all about ships (of the desert, that is), for he'd just sailed his camel through a sandstorm and knew that if Noah wanted to make any speed with his tub he'd better put legs on her, with great big feet, and teach the Ark to trot. But Noah crossed up the sheik. His ark worked just fine, and safely delivered enough of Adam's sons and Eve's daughters to start today's apple stampede. You see, Alotabul didn't know a darned thing about rain.

Noah's descendants, being professionals, are still in argument as to what makes a good boat, but never waver about building them of the best stuff obtainable. Wind and wave and wild skies over are forces for which they have the respect that comes from experience. Where life is at stake, the best is demanded. On the other hand, descendants of

Alotabul—who seem to be getting more numerous—are still telling the sons of Noah just how to do things.

Now, I'm a descendant of Noah. All of Noah's progeny are professionals; they know something about rain, and water, and wood, and fastenings, and know how to work with them. Their big trouble is that good boatbuilding wood is getting scarce and very dear. Decent fastenings cost $10 a gross, and a stout boat, even in nominal sizes, drinks up thousands of fastenings. What is more, boatbuilding as a guild trade is dying out.

Good boatbuilding is slow boatbuilding. Much search has gone into ways to cut costs, knock down building time, make the job amenable to simpler skills. Hence the search for easier ways to close in hulls. For multiple manufactured units, plastics have been adapted. This stuff is a chemical ester, a super-cooled liquid in solid state which is amorphous in character, fracturing like glass or ice unless reinforced with tension strands of some fabric, such as spun glass or other fiber. Plastics are expensive, and are heavy. They do have the advantage of being buildable in female molds by fractionally skilled labor, but to get a one-off hull, two boats must be built: the mold itself, and then the hull lay-up.

The old idea of reinforced concrete is another method of closing in hulls. It has burgeoned at the end of every war during the period of inflation; it appeals to builders who understand plastering; it is time-consuming as to the making of the armature; and is over two-and-a-half times as heavy as wood, only 10 percent less expensive, and greatly penalizes speed.

The ideal closure would be a light material that is at home in salt water, as strong as steel or nearly so, could be worked with the usual woodworking machinery, wouldn't need an ocean of fastenings, and would allow skill to be quickly built up in its use and application.

Such a material is aluminum. It has 10 times the impact-absorbing capacity of steel. It weighs only a third as much. It is as light as wood in boats up to 30 feet in length, and much lighter from that length on up. An aluminum plate 1/4 inch thick has the shock/impact strength of 3-inch fir planking; it is, in this 1/4-inch thickness, abundantly strong enough to plate up to 80 feet in length. It does not corrode or rust as steel does. It is easier to flip around a shop manually because it is light. It is the most weldable of metals. Welds of 90 to 95 percent of plate strength are usual; in steel, 75 to 85 percent of plate strength is more nearly the norm.

Aluminum has had much metallurgical development in recent years, since the days of the old cast-aluminum cook pots you knew. Alloyed without copper, in marine usage, its life is indefinite. A boat built of it usually will be miles faster than a wood or steel counterpart.

Aluminum boats can be built in most any boatshop that has been used to building in wood, because the same hand tools will work it; you'll need a welder and some compressed air for chipping, but that is about all, unless you want to go in for boiled-egg shapes, in which case a hydraulic bumping press will give you that capacity.

The skilled wood boatbuilder learns to handle this stuff, aluminum, in one or two boats, developing the same amazing skill with it he now has in wood. The aluminum weld is its own fastening; a builder won't be draining the gold reserves at Fort Knox buying fastenings—weld fastening is inherent in the technique.

Once a skill is developed comparable to that which the builder possesses in wood, he will find himself closing in hulls in one third to one half the time needed to bring a wooden hull to the same condition. In this respect a boatbuilder overtakes the slightly higher raw material cost of the metal. This "cost" is a chimera, anyway, and amounts to only pennies: the quotations I have worked with in writing this chapter place steel in 1971 at 16 to 17 cents a pound. Aluminum cost, at the same time, was 55 cents a pound. Horrors? Not a bit of it! See here:

It takes three pounds of steel to cover as much area as one pound of aluminum, generally. Three pounds of steel at 17 cents equals a tab of 51 cents. The same area in aluminum is 55 cents. For four cents a square foot premium, you get practically indefinite hull life, miles more speed, quicker building time than in steel, and a much more amenable hull-shaping metal.

Where baulks in this proposition are offered, you will find them coming from a builder whose experience and skills are oriented to either steel, or wood, or plastic. I happen to have worked in all mediums. I know the stuff both from designing in all and from having my hands feed my head the knowledge of the materials. I think my statement about aluminum is fair and justified.

Any naval architect who has designed a lot of motor yachts, out of the nature of things, works with and for a good many very wealthy men. These fellows all have one trait in common: they know values and the meaning of money, and are hounds for detail in getting a buck's worth. This smart money has been going for aluminum for more than 15 years. The whipped cream on top of the wedding cake for these owners has been the simple umbrella of aluminum advantages: low maintenance problems, greater speed by miles, controllable electrolytic problems, great tankage capacity and hence much higher cruising range, and the highest resale value to be found in any material. This has been the history of ownership in the aluminum motor and sailing yacht field.

The Burger Boat Co., of Manitowoc, Wisconsin, is the leader in building aluminum motor yachts in the luxury field. In the early 1970s, it was turning out about eight or nine boats a year in the $200,000 to

$900,000 range and had a two-year backlog of owners waiting for their boats. Burger, as a company, since abandoning wood and steel in favor of aluminum, has built over one mile of these craft in overall length. Their joinerwork and finish in general are very high.

Another bunch of Wisconsin Dutchmen operate a crackerjack boat-building plant at Palmer Johnson Inc. in Sturgeon Bay, Wisconsin. This is the best tooled yard I know about, and the Sturgeon Bay skills in plating are never so evident as here. They use sawn-out frames, which hold their shape, and can plate a hull of complex shape to the smoothness of a boiled egg—but then, Sturgeon Bay is unique.

There are three shipbuilding and boatbuilding yards in this enchanting small town at the base of the Green Bay thumb on your map. Out of a population of about 7,000 people, nearly every kid who graduates from high school starts in one or the other of these yards. Nearly everybody knows how to toss plates at a hull. You may see a

A scene in the bustling erecting shed of Palmer Johnson, Inc., of Sturgeon Bay, Wisconsin, as Robert C. Burwell's *Misty* is nearing completion from plans by the author. Photo courtesy of Palmer Johnson, Inc., which specializes in aluminum luxury yachts and state-of-the-art sailing yachts.

man delivering your laundry one day and find him doing complicated loft work the next. Half the bartenders in town are ace joiner men. So it is little wonder that Palmer Johnson, or Peterson Builders, or the Sturgeon Bay plant of the Bay Shipbuilding Co. can do an eggshell plating job.

I have been in a number of other yards specializing in aluminum. From them I have walked away with one potent observation: it is a mistake for a boatbuilder to go at aluminum as though he were building in wood, substituting aluminum for the usual wood stringers, clamps, and all. He will use twice as much metal as needed. His first boat should be built to well-prepared plans for aluminum. In such cases, the resale value of the boat will be high, because most boats in aluminum have been designed by crack naval architects who know skin-stressed engineering and who have aesthetic sense.

But that isn't the sole reason for owner preference. Aluminum does not rust as does iron or steel, staining everything brown or red. Any corrosion that eventually can be spotted in scuffed, bright areas, usually will have a light powder, whitish, that can be dusted away with a whisk broom, or will develop the dark oxide coating aluminum takes on if left unpainted. This aluminum oxide, or "aluminum rust" if you will, has the same chemical composition as carborundum. It is therefore extremely hard and durable. Many commercial vessels do not bother to paint, relying on the blackish oxide to form. This same oxide is hard enough to form cutting edges on the extruded reel blades of some golf course greens mowers, and is induced by unplating in an electrolytic bath, termed "anodizing."

Usually, one paint job in four or five years is all that aluminum needs in yacht service. The method of preparing the aluminum skin for painting is simple. It is best, and usually cheapest, to close up all hull openings with tough plastic sheet, wheel the hull into the yard, and sand blast the bright mill finish off. Some welding "welts" or swellings always occur on the outboard face of the hull plate; these are easily scuffed flush with a disc sander using proper carborundum grit.

I have frequently heard builders of wooden boats (who lean to Alotabul's camp) scoff at this small investment of labor. Fudge and fantods! They do not stop to think of the countersinking and plugging needed in wood to bury a fastening. When closed in, the aluminum hull is one-weldment, stiff as a casting; a wooden boat is never any better than, nor any stronger than, the pins with which she is pegged together. 'Jevver think of that?

After the hull has been sand blasted, usually some sort of chemical anodizing is provided. There is a preparation called Alodine which does this chemically, leaving the hull looking a puky yellow-green. Then an

146

Graceful flam can be worked into bow flare by using diagonal plates. These are shown here in the bright lines ground smooth along the weld seam. The small bright spots are flush-ground weld welts. At this stage before sandblasting, this motor yacht is mirror bright. Sandblasting dulls and flattens plates and puts a paintable tooth on them.

epoxy paint is applied, with such minor amounts of smoothing grouting as may be needed (a well-plated hull needs only touch-ups) in an epoxy cement. The epoxy will stick to the aluminum like a mortgage fancier sticks to his interest rates. The epoxy will hold vinyl paints, which aluminum will not, and you proceed to finish off the hull as you would an ordinary boat, observing one simple rule: around aluminum do not use any paint with copper in it. The copper-aluminum electrolytic chain in salt water or salt air plates the copper at the expense of aluminum.

Aluminum manufacturers and processors discovered that what destroyed early aluminum products in salt environment was the copper in early alloys. As a result, all present-day marine aluminum is, instead, alloyed with magnesium and sometimes silicon to give aluminum its "at-homeness" with salt water. Copper does well by itself as a plating material, but in salt water, aluminum and copper quarrel.

This brings up the interesting information that aluminum is not only eminently weldable, but is alloyed in a number of systems, each of which will give the user emphasis on the qualities he desires: it can be heat treated, strain hardened, welded by impact, by sound, by pressure if need be, but usually by what is called MIG welding or TIG welding, of which more in a moment. If a man knows anything about wrought iron, aluminum pretty much has the same traits.

The classification of these alloys is interesting, and useful to know. The system of nomenclature adopted by all makers of aluminum starts out with 1, and three digits thereafter.

The 1 and 3 lowercase x's series denotes 99 percent aluminum purity. If there is copper in the alloy, the number will start 2xxx. The manganese series is 3xxx, the silicon series is 4xxx, the magnesium series (marine usage) is the 5xxx band. The 6xxx series (used in extrusions) is magnesium and silicon. Zinc starts at 7xxx, and there is a wildcat group of special-usage formulae that is denoted by 8xxx.

Thus, in 5052-H36 aluminum plate, the first digit identified the magnesium (copper free) alloy system, the last two digits 52 identify the alloy or proportions, the internal digit zero would indicate any modification of the original alloy's purity limits. The H denotes strain hardened metal, the 3 denotes the type of hardening and the 6 denotes the temper. Once he becomes familiar with the nomenclature, a shop man can know exactly what is in his hands as he works with it.

Any of the aluminum makers of this country will supply technical data about all of this. Reynolds Aluminum, Kaiser Aluminum, Harvey Aluminum, and Aluminum Corporation of America all gladly supply such information. One extremely excellent handbook on the subject was supplied me early in the game by Carl W. Leveau, an old confrere of mine, who was Kaiser's·field man and a naval architect himself.

A letter of inquiry to the Kaiser Aluminum and Sales Inc. at Kaiser Center, Oakland, Calif. 94604, will bring information on this book, a Kaiser "house publication" called *Welding.* It is a honey, and describes MIG and TIG welding in abundant detail.

MIG stands for Metal, Inert Gas. The term doesn't need to throw anybody. Any high school kid can learn the welding theory and skill needed to produce reliable 90 percent welds with a MIG welding outfit.

In the MIG method of welding, aluminum wire is fed through a tool, a gun, that looks a little like a Colt .45 pistol. To the butt of this "gun" is led a series of lines looking like a ganglia of hoses. One contains the aluminum welding wire, fed into the electric arc at a speed which is the operator's option; another set of "lines" is the cooling water for the gun. This is a small stream, re-circulated by the pump on the welding generator which, taking 110-volt or 220-volt mainline juice, converts it by regeneration into DC voltage and amperage.

The wire forms the contact for the arc, and is fed as it melts. This wire is of carefully controlled alloying, usually from 1/16 inch to 3/32 inch in diameter, calculated to have a melting point at the fuse point of the metal in the plate, and a recalescence or solidifying point slightly below, so that the puddling metal cools last, absorbing in its puddling the cooling contraction. (As an aside, a 72-foot aluminum yacht such as is shown in my plans here will use about 900 pounds of this wire.)

The inert gas, argon, used in the MIG system is fed from a tank through a hose around the flame of the arc through holes in the barrel of the welding gun at very low pressure, 2 to 3 pounds. Its function is important: it forms a jacket to exclude air, the oxygen in which, combining with the molten aluminum, would form aluminum oxide. Of the same chemical composition as carborundum, this stuff renders a weld brittle. With argon, and no formation of oxide, the weld is tough.

TIG welding signifies Tungsten and Inert Gas. This method is somewhat like oxy-acetylene procedure, except that a tungsten electrode provides the heat of arc. Extraneous metal, as with oxy-acetylene, is puddled into the weld. Inert gas is of course used. TIG welding is generally used on large blocks of metal. Most all aluminum boatshop welding is done by the MIG method.

Aluminum has about ten times the impact-absorbing capacity of steel. A collision with a sharp rock that would puncture a steel shell, or shatter so friable a material as reinforced concrete, will produce only a large dent in aluminum. I have had actual experience with this.

Once, when I was aboard an aluminum motor yacht running at moderate speed up a channel, the bottom toggled against a lodged, up-ended deadhead pile. The whole 40-ton vessel gave a mighty lurch to port, then proceeded along unruffled. But the skipper turned white; he checked down and headed for the canal bank. There was no need to.

Engine room inspection showed that between the 1/4-inch by 3-inch frames, spaced on 15-inch centers, at the turn of the bilge in an un-tanked portion of the engine room, there was a pillow in the 1/4-inch aluminum hull plate about the size of the upper crown on a Derby hat. This was subsequently cut out with a sabre saw at the next haul-out, and a new flat was welded in.

Had the vessel been of steel in comparable tensile strength—strength, mind you, not thickness—the plate would have fractured, probably capturing the deadhead and admitting worrisome water. The accident proved to me that aluminum has the property of absorbing the kind of shocks which the producers of aluminum claim it has.

Aluminum marine alloys do have strength, comparable in some sheet forms to mild steel. A loading figure I have used in skin-strength calculations is 29,000 psi tensile, which is generally the most highly stressed condition. This allows a factor of safety of about 4, using 1/4-inch hull topside plating in up to 80-foot hull length. This may sound like a tin-can skin to those used to thinking of planking in wood, but it is about equivalent in shock/impact capacity to 3 inches of fir planking thickness.

As to girder plate strength, this 1/4-inch plate size, held on 15- to

16-inch frame centers, is abundant. Jet airplanes, with many times the G loads, which build up with much more violent rapidity, use skin-stressed air frames with plating of a few thousandths of an inch.

Take a look at the framing plan here for a 72-foot aluminum motor yacht. This is the Palmer Johnson stock, standard 72-footer, powerable with up to 1,000 hp in twin V-12 Detroit Diesels for sustained cruising at 20 mph. This hull, bare as shown, with her tanks comprising a series of boxes in her bottom, is strong enough to be elevated by a hydraulic jack at her center of gravity and, balanced there, to show no deflection or strain. How do I know? She has the same 3 inches by 6 inches by .500 inch extruded aluminum keel, 5/16-inch plate from skeg to turn of bilge, and the same 1/4-inch topside as a 77-footer that once got this accidental treatment.

That unbelievable demonstration of the strength of an aluminum hull occurred as a result of a comedy of errors about ten years ago when I was working at Burger's yard in Manitowoc. The 77-footer, an aluminum hull I had been engineering, had been completely closed in—hull, decks, tanks, but no deckhouse—when the occasion arose to settle the matter of the weight, and more important, the center of gravity—CG—of this vessel. I'd been getting some static from a few descendants of the desert sheik, and wanted to know.

Mr. Eli Gunnell, one of the owners and the engineering brain in that yard, who is a great good guy and wonderful fellow to work with, had agreed that when this hull went to the joiner and fitting out shop, he'd hang the hull in the big yard crane to give me a fix on the CG.

In the event, communications broke down, and the yard rigger pulled the outfit right past the crane, around in back of the plating shed like an ant pulling a shoe box. He wheeled the hull shell into place with his truck and crew in the outfitting shop.

Too late for my test! I told Eli that if he didn't give a darn, I sure wasn't going to worry. She'd float where she floated, and that would be that!

Next morning I met Eli in the administration building. He had a wide grin on his face. He had come down early, had cut the wheeling dollies away from the hull to which they had been welded, and with a crew had chocked the hull in place. Then, thinking he was well forward of my calculated CG (which he was by about a foot), he placed a 45-ton hydraulic jack under the keel. This was an ordinary Big Truck jack with a palm about the size of a man's shoe heel.

Getting under the hull on his hands and knees, operating the jack and watching the bow rise a foot off the blocking, the better to get some timbers under the keel, he turned around, squatting, to see how the other end was resting on the aft chocks.

This framing plan for a stock 72-foot diesel yacht hull of the Palmer Johnson Co. is reproduced to give an idea of how the framework of a large vessel is put together. The bare hull of a boat this size is so strong that it can be supported by a single bearing under its keel at its center of gravity.

To Eli's stunned alarm the stern end was above the aft chocks the same height as the bow. The entire 28,000-odd pounds of aluminum yacht shell was resting placidly a foot in the air on a jack palm no larger than the palm of your hand. By sheer accident he had placed the jack at the real center of gravity.

"I got to hell outa dere! Fast," was Eli's chuckling comment, adding, "I'd like to see any wooden hull you could do that with!"

As he gingerly bled the jack, lowering the hull, both ends kissed the chocks at the same instant. This proved there had been no distortion, no evident deflection. I report this at some length because it actually happened, proving the strength in aluminum I would not have, until then, believed.

It may be of value to note here for other naval architects that the true, or real, CG of a metal hull always in practice is a shade forward of the drawn, or expanded, CG. I also found by weighing this vessel with a system of beams and scale readings Eli rigged up for me that she was 7 percent heavier than my calculation. Later I discovered on another boat that the plate thickness was running 7 percent heavier by caliper than the handbook thickness weight given.

Aluminum, like all metals, is sold by the pound, not by plate size as is plywood. Toward the end of any mill rolling run, the rolls allow thicker metal through. The stuff is sold by weight and the vendor makes out.

As to the well-known propensity of metal hulls to be a shade down in the bow, I discovered by this test that there is more actual metal in the flam and flare forward than plate expansion shows. If you expand girths, you absolutely should expand lengths, too, to get the proper weight and the CG of the skin. If you will add 7 percent to handbook plate weight, and move your calculated CG forward 1/60 of the waterline length, you'll come out about right. In fact, on the money, because you will also have corrected for the built-in 5 percent error in Simpson's rule, which is not dead accurate, because it favors the "fat" end of the displacement curve by 5 percent.

Little pounds here, added to little pounds there, loom large at the polls on launching day when a vote is taken on your sharpness by a peek at the draft marks.

I can hear some descendants of Alotabul saying, "We never have any trouble. We keep throwing in a factor to correct it." This is bul spelled with two L's. I say to these sheiks, you'd better not forget to multiply your expanded plating area by two either. There are two sides to a boat. Port and starboard.

On one boat, 40 years ago, I forgot this. The ensuing launching was a thing of beauty for anyone who had it in for me. The hull went down,

down, down. Half an hour later, in the town's railroad station, I was shopping for a ticket to nowhere. It proved beyond my meager means. With a kindly wave of his hand, the station agent extended me the travel facilities of the entire railroad, at the same time graciously warning me not to climb aboard any rolling stock. Multiply by two!

Aluminum boats are faster. There is on record the case, completely factual, of a stock steel cruiser the normal speed of which was nine knots. When built in aluminum, the same hull cruised at 17, and topped out at 20. There had been some modification of line, but aluminum was the main difference, because the hull, weighing only a third of steel, did not have to lug around the equivalent of two more hulls in weight.

Now this brings aluminum squarely into the framework of plain horse sense for commercial boats. Forget the dollar picture I've painted for luxury yachts. That includes luxurious furnishings. It does not apply to working boats. If you can go faster, you have more at-sea time, or faster delivery to market. To put it in other terms, you can carry a lot more load with lower power, eating less out of your purse—a whole lot less, in most cases.

An aluminum workboat may get banged around a lot, just as a wooden one will. But she won't get dozy, nor need annual spring nursing, or as much maintenance as a wooden boat.

This story started out to be a gab session in the wheelhouse. I'll have to cut it short; there is more, much more—the subject is dendritic, like the roots of a tree—tap roots, feeder roots, hair roots of information beyond number. I don't pose as knowing very much—I'm just reporting my experience with the metal. It has been good to excellent.

There are a few wet cigar butts on top of the wedding cake: electrolysis—some, but not much, just different. There is the question of electrics and what to watch for, and sewage and how to handle it, and the wonderful fuel tankage you can get with lowered weight and great metacentric placement.

And the tale of how barnacles just love that bright spot in aluminum, and how you can knock 'em off like popcorn with a jolt of 220 volts, tickling their little feet until Pa Barnacle calls to Ma, "Hey, Mabel, what's that sizzle underfoot? This whole neighborhood has gone to hell. I'm leaving!"

But that'll all have to wait for another wheelhouse watch, Mates. Just open the wheelhouse door to windward, there, and let a little breeze into this feisty atmosphere. Before I go, I'm telling you how to handle Alotabul XXXVI if he gets to knocking aluminum.

The short yarn has to do with old Tom Day, founding editor of *Rudder,* who suffered no fools gladly. Some contributor to *Rudder,* many years ago, had dumped a manuscript on the Old Man's desk concerning the then-building new Cup defender. This story claimed inside knowledge that the new boat would be a world-beater because, on her 75-foot waterline, she would spread 14,000 square feet of sail. Day calculated the main boom would have to extend 40 feet abaft the taffrail to spread this canvas. The thought gave him the flydaddlin' fantods.

Now Tom Day was used to accepting his devoirs of respect—not piquantly, as a maiden courted, nor stolidly as a horse accepts hay, but regally in concordance with Nature's own plan, as a rose ingests the dew fore-ordained for its refreshment. To be asked to swallow the "expert's" statement about 14,000 square feet of sail as being fact put him beyond jumping on his hat or sailing an inkwell out the window.

Did he sit down to his old Oliver sidewinder typewriter and start, "D%xs@J@HN-YuoyY"? He did not.

He calmed himself, wiped the froth from his mouth, and with admirably restrained rage wrote and published to all his readers the lines I will use to the fence watchers on Mount Ararat when Noah builds his next Ark. They will be criticizing Noah for building her in aluminum. My text for that Day will come from the Tom of his Day:

"If some of you people will go to a mirror you will see a long tubular object rising above your collar. On this will be a round object covered with hair on top; this is your head, and inside under the crown is what we call brains. These brains are given to you to use, and one of their principal uses is to think. Many of you don't think; perhaps you don't know how. If you did you would not ask some of the questions you do or believe the absurd and exaggerated statements you hear . . . Think, think, think!"

There's a lesson there. If you're not inclined to accept aluminum, don't knock it or listen to the descendants of Alotabul. Think!

Just ask why the smart money has been going to aluminum. And lean toward Noah's camp; in years to come, a lot of guys are going to be left behind on Mount Ararat because a lot of Noah's boys are gaining on 'em. With that, I leave you till the next chapter.

18

42-Foot Aluminum Cruiser

Golden are the days and silvery the nights on a course from Gulf shores down toward Yucatan. The clear coral waters, the balmy equatorial ocean climate, and the friendly natives return you to uncomplicated simple values. The scuba diving is beyond belief.

For the run to just such a coast, *Simbie* was designed in 1972 for Lawson Clary, Jr., retired Air Force officer of Mobile, Alabama. Mr. Clary made out a superb case for a small, long-range aluminum vessel for use in the service described, writing about it in the April 1972 issue of *National Fisherman*. The tale was interesting in itself, but at that time the design had not been fully completed.

Here, then, for historians of the future, appear the full plans of *Simbie*. As far as I am aware, these are the only complete plans to have been published for an all-aluminum cruiser. They are submitted for the edification and noodlement of students interested in the drafting of metal hulls. There are four sheets in this series, with specs being printed on the plans.

What follows is neither hard sell nor soft sell, nor any sell at all: merely a brief description of some of the things her designing taught me, and a few words about how to go about getting her built.

After a visit to Mobile to deliver the plans when they were finished, and carrying the flotational model along for an "in-tank" demonstration, even Freda, the lovely Mrs. Clary, agreed that *Simbie* delighted the Clarys.

My initial premise about building was that a high-burden, multiple-man yard would price any one-of-a-kind boat like this out of sight.

What was needed was to locate a good, one-man yard that was adequately tooled to handle aluminum in the first place, and in the second place did not have flags flying, plate glass doors to the office, gals in bikinis strolling the lawn, or seagulls sitting on flag poles turning in time cards.

Cal Johanson of Warrenton, Oregon 97146, was in the process of phasing out steel construction and tooling up Johanson's Little Shipyard for aluminum at his location three miles west of Astoria. Lawson sent plan sets to Cal and a number of builders, and so also did I. The feedback was absolutely nutty, ranging from $16,000 for the hull work (builder to be furnished metal) to $120,000 ready to sail away from a Midwest yard. (Remember, this was in the early 1970s.) One builder even snorted that the materials couldn't be bought for $25,000! My suggestion to him today would be to take a gander at his plant's productivity.

Cal was narrowed down as being a builder whose work could be considered, but in the meantime, while gathering the "numbers," Johanson contracted for another boat to my design, a 42-foot gillnetter for Clancy Henkins of Douglas, Alaska. Projections for building *Simbie* went by the board for the time being.

Several interesting facts emerged during the numbers-gathering interval. One was that *Simbie* could be delivered by rail from the Oregon Coast to Mobile in a gondola railroad car for $1,200, or about $1 per mile. Steamship on-deck freighting was considered, but it was found no line serves both Astoria and Mobile. Furthermore, such loading is messy and risky without big equipment. The $1-a-mile figure seems extremely reasonable.

Another thing that was developed was the metal cost: 7,500 pounds of aluminum required. Add 20 percent for waste and spiling, and you come up with 9,000 pounds. At 62 cents, you have $5,580.

The small diesel was under $4,000. Glass, joinery, and painting were not considered, because Lawson wanted to finish off this work at leisure over a couple of winters. As far as joinery went, this could be whatever a man wanted to spend for decor: birch, pine, mahogany, or teak. There is little of it in this boat, and no figures were surfaced on this.

As far as shop time was concerned, the looney figures arriving from various yards showed they were operating on guessometry. The $120,000 tab was dismissed as frivolous. The "$25,000 for materials" was, I know, just young-kid wisenheimering. But an eye was kept on Cal Johanson's man-hours going into Clancy Henkins's boat, all this while a-building.

In November of 1973, I met Henkins at Cal's shop. I hadn't seen Clancy's boat since keel-and-lofting days the previous May. On my trip west, I was accompanied by William K. Bartig, president of the Long Lake State Bank of Long Lake, Minnesota. Bill wanted to see the hull of Henkins's boat, because he likes *Simbie*.

Both Bill and I were stunned when, after dark one wet afternoon, we opened the door to Cal's shop and saw the Henkins boat. She stood finished and was as fine a piece of work as I've seen in any of the Great Lakes shops that produce luxury stuff. Welding and finish were tiptop.

The time needed to build? Just under 2,000 man-hours—one man working alone. Lofting, welding, and erecting. At $14 an hour, which includes tooling, shop overhead, and applied time, *Simbie* could be built in the same time or less for $28,000 in man-hours in the same state as shown in the photos of Henkins's gillnetter. This figure proves my case about doing your building in an efficient Ma-and-Pa yard. Johanson quoted $32,000 for a *Simbie* in the stage shown by the Henkins photos, with Johanson to furnish the metal in that price. You take it from there.

One thing that made it very easy to build Henkins's boat is the employment of a waterplane harpin to replace the usual bilge stringer, which is generally installed after a hull is plated. With the waterplane harpin, a shelf is provided by which to erect the frames. The keel is set up, the bulkheads are targeted in with piano wire through temporary bulkhead holes, and then the harpin is welded in. It rests on jacks and levelling is absurdly easy.

Next, intermediate frames between bulkheads are tacked in from keel to harpin. The boat is framed below the waterline before topside work is begun. Cal told me the boat went together like an Erector set and faired naturally without sweat. So much for design gimmicks.

As you peruse the plans, I would call several matters to your at-

Side of Cabin
Crown Line
Plate Line
Grab rail to suit
Tumble home batter
Develop Transom at Lofting
Plate Line Parallels Shear
Under Side of Sheer
To Vertical
Developed Transom
Knuckle
Bearding Line
Keel Bottom
Fairbody Line
Channel Keel
Baseline
Stem
Ten Stations spaced 3'-5¼" apart. Measure from 0 to avoid creep.
Shear
Intersection at Fairbody

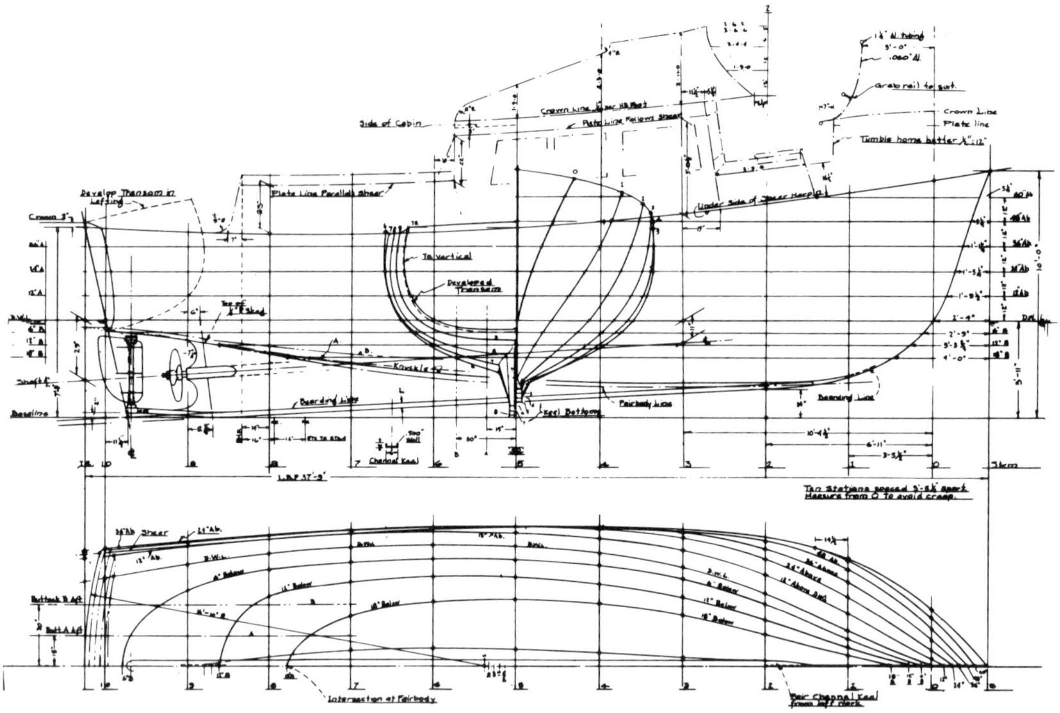

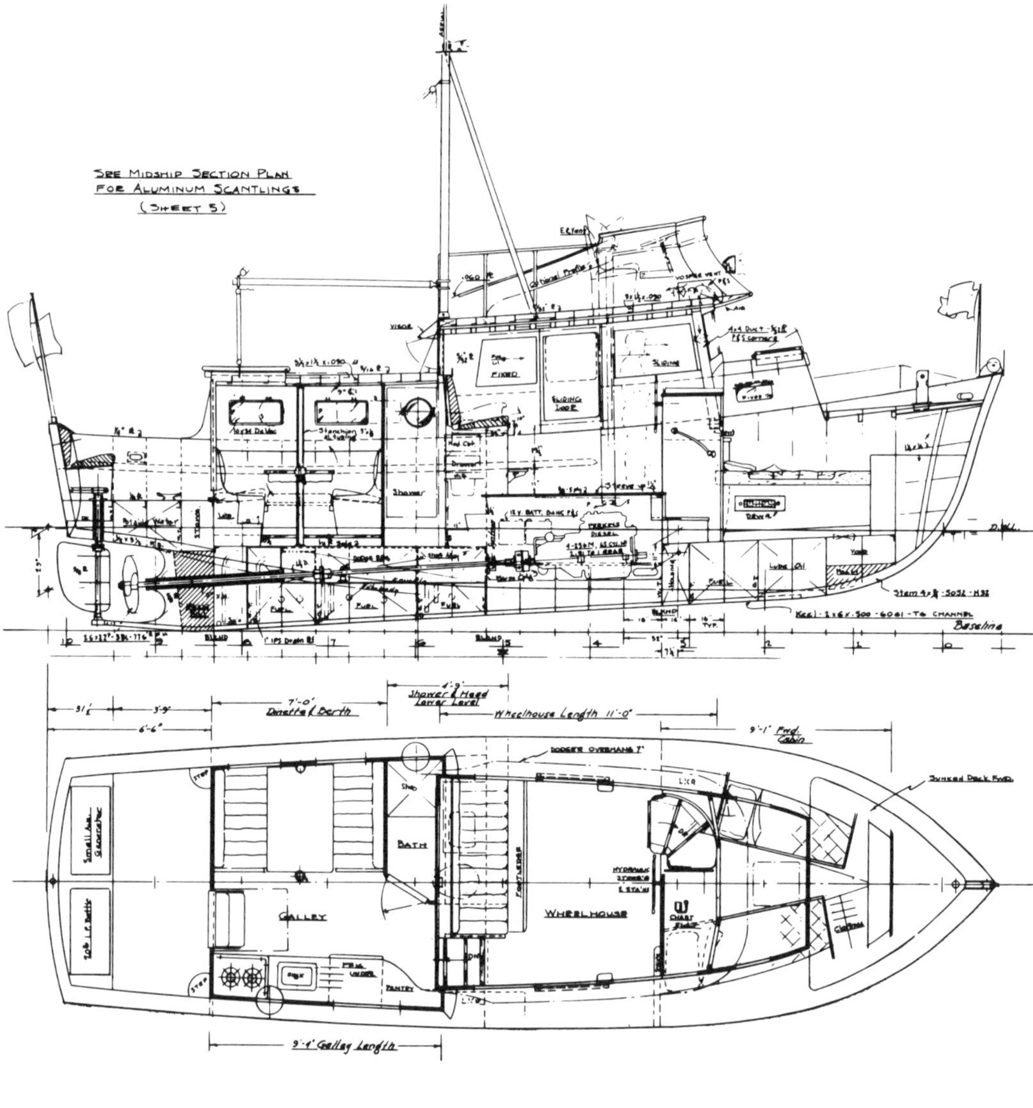

See Midship Section Plan
For Aluminum Scantlings
(Sheet 5)
Fixed
Sliding Door
Shower
Perkins Diesel
Fuel
Lube Oil
D.W.L.
Keel
Baseline
7'-0" Dinette & Berth
Shower & Head Lower Level
Wheelhouse Length 11'-0"
9'-1" Fwd. Cabin
Dodger Overhang 7"
Sunken Deck Fwd.
Bath
Galley
Wheelhouse
Pantry
9'-4" Galley Length

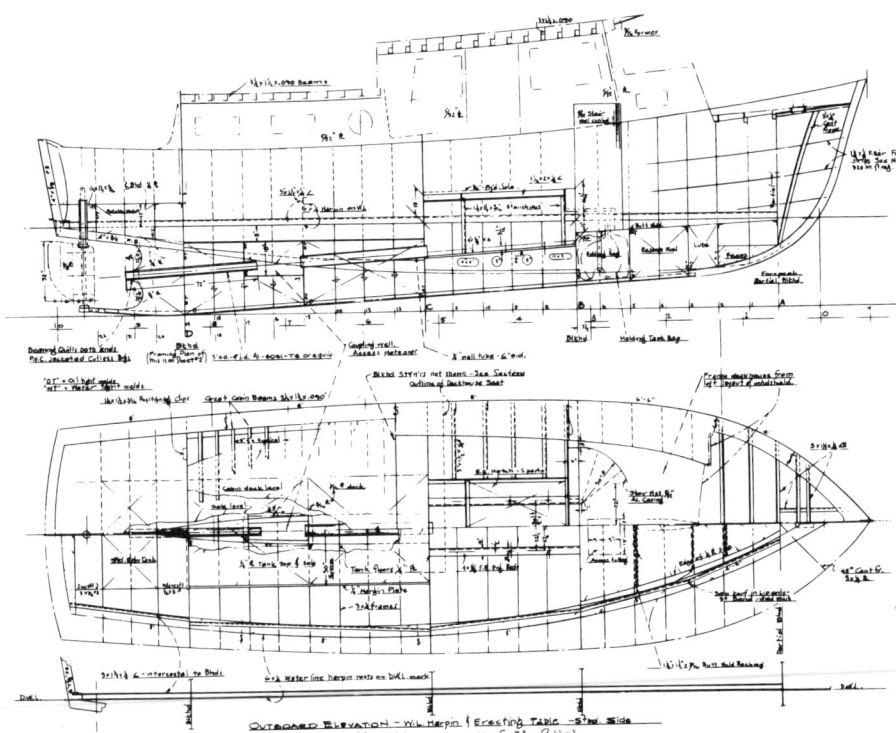

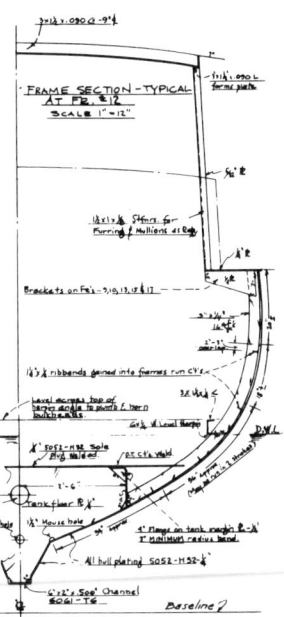

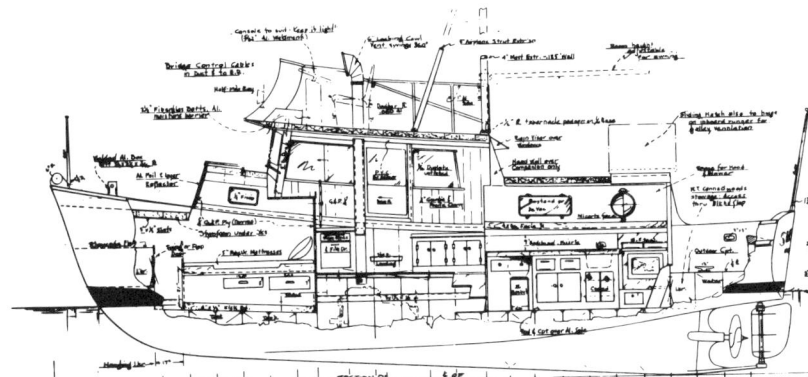

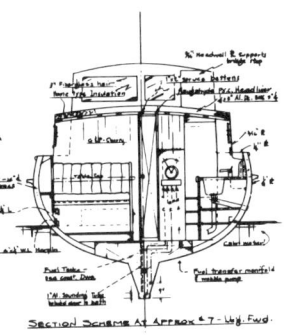

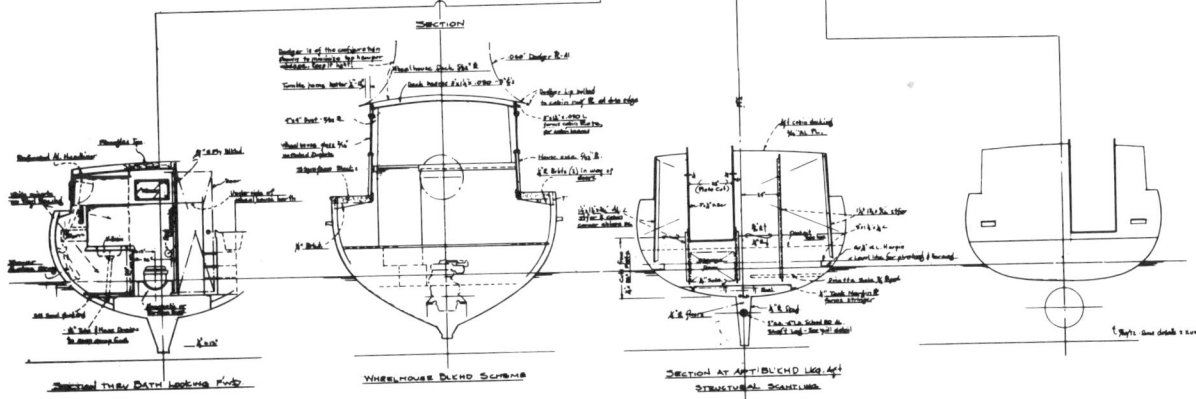

HALF BREADTHS from ₵ - Ft. Ins. & 8ths.

Station	Stem	O	1	2	3	4	5	6	7	8	9	10	TR.
Keel	0·0·3	0·0·3	0·0·3	0·3·0	0·3·0	→	St. Line →					0·3·0	.
Knuckle				0·3·0	0·4·4	0·6·5	0·8·1	0·8·5	0·7·4	0·4·5	Ends	⌐	
W.L.18"B			0·5·4	1·4·1	2·1·2	2·6·3	2·8·4	2·6·7	2·0·2	⌐	⌐	⌐	⌐
W.L.12"B			0·9·1	1·10·4	2·10·5	3·4·0	3·6·4	3·7·6	3·4·6	2·9·6	⌐		
W.L.6"B			1·1·1	2·6·1	3·6·2	4·0·6	4·3·6	4·4·2	4·2·4	3·11·0	⌐		
Datum W.L.			1·5·2	2·11·4	4·0·0	4·7·0	4·10·0	4·10·2	4·9·4	4·6·5	4·1·4	3·6·4	3·4·5
W.L.12"Ab.		0·3·6	2·1·7	3·8·4	4·8·6	5·2·4	5·4·4	5·4·2	5·4·0	5·1·6	4·9·6	4·5·0	4·4·4
W.L.24"Ab.		0·7·6	2·9·6	4·3·6	5·2·2	5·6·2	5·7·7	5·6·4	5·6·2	5·3·6	5·0·2	4·8·4	4·8·2
W.L.36"Ab.		1·0·4	3·5·0	4·8·6	5·5·1	5·7·4	5·8·0	5·6·5	5·5·6	5·2·6	5·0·0	4·8·2	4·8·0
W.L.48"Ab.		1·6·1	3·11·0	5·0·6	5·6·2	5·7·5	⌐						
W.L.60"Ab.		1·11·3	4·3·2	⌐	⌐	⌐							
Sheer	0·0·3	2·4·3	4·4·1	⌐	5·6·4	5·7·6	5·7·6-	5·6·2	5·4·2	5·1·4	4·10·4	4·6·6	4·6·2

HEIGHTS - Ft. Ins. & 8ths - Base 3'-11" Below D.W.L.

Station	Stem	O	1	2	3	4	5	6	7	8	9	10	TR.
Keel	10·0·0	3·11·0	1·7·5	1·2·0	St.	Line	to	→		0·1·2	Take	from	Loft ↑
Fairbody			1·5·2	1·3·3	1·2·7	1·3·0	1·5·2	1·6·2	1·11·7	2·6·2	3·1·3	3·6·0	3·6·7
Knuckle			1·4·0	1·4·7	1·5·0	1·6·6	1·9·4	2·1·6	2·6·4	Disappears	⌐		
Sheer		9·1·2	8·7·6	8·2·4	7·11·0	7·7·6	7·6·0	7·4·7	7·5·0	7·6·0	7·6·6	7·7·2	
Butt.A Aft								1·11·4	2·2·4	2·7·1	3·1·5	⌐	3·6·4
Butt.B Aft								2·4·3	2·6·6	2·10·0	3·3·3	⌐	3·7·6

tention. One is that her tankage is below the cabin floor, or sole, level. A small well, or cofferdam, is built into the tank to service the stuffing box. This puts the weight down low and permits a finer-lined hull than one would have to produce in a wooden vessel. *Simbie*'s body plan is drawn exactly as the weights require it to be—not in imitation of any wooden yacht. You'll just have to get used to looking at different sections in an aluminum boat, because the moments of inertia and the metacentric heights all must be different in aluminum work to get the correct time of roll.

You may also note that the turn of her bilges is above water, where they should be. Hard bilge turns, under water, do nothing to stabilize a roll because they are already loaded down, under water, and are in equilibrium there. It is the shoulder on the immersing side *above* the waterline and the pull-out on the emerging side that control stability. 'Jevver realize that?

Another thing: plans that seem to carry enough detail to build always look complicated or "over designed" to the accountants who twirl the estimating pencil. Actually, the more information you can get on a drawing, the easier a boat is to build. Ask the men in the shop!

That is why I bore down on the drawings, à la Elco. You can build *Simbie* from the drawings and offsets shown here. I commend her to you as being an easy steamer, with over 1,000-mile capacity, and the ability to take care of you when, on some dark night, you can't see through the black murk, you are a long way from home and Mother, and your boat has to sort it all out for herself.

Simbie will be able!

C[ompoun]d Curves in
L[...]el

[... builder]s are avid collectors of notes, tips, and pieces of
in[formation the]y can file away to be tapped later in problem-
so[lving. These usu]ally take the form of glimmers of truth gleaned
fr[om a source he]re, a published plan there—types of knowledge that
are [scattered an]d that must be gathered under the heading of
"lore."

Here, then, are some ramblements that concern metal boat construction; I commend them to you as genuine, heat-treated observations
that have been through the fire, normalized and annealed for long life
in your file of lore. First, a paragraph or two on orientation and basic
premise: you know that the Almighty Dollar is the ruler of all trends.
Trends in boat design and construction over the past seventy-five years
have followed cyclical patterns of from twenty down to five years,
leading from wooden construction to plywood building to fiberglass to
molded plywood to reinforced concrete.

What next? The Jell-O people have not yet perfected the heat-and-
serve package for a boat cast in a mold, but someone will do it eventually. Next we will have National Bakeoffs telling us how to get
boats out of an oven. As is always the case with any new method,
huckstering and ballyhoo will tell us that this boat is the biggest-bang-
for-a-buck.

In these changing fashions, the huckstering eclipses old skills. This is
tragic, because skills too long lost, not passed down from father to son,
or from journeyman to apprentice, are slowly, slowly forgotten. The
years of experience taken to develop the old art are wasted.

This premise points out that one skill that seems to have completely dropped from sight is the old art of plating metal boats, made possible by that understanding which produced wonderfully smooth, well-rounded Cup defenders in bronze or steel, or the beautiful little English steamers of the 1870s and '80s that once plied the waters of India and the rivers of England and Africa. These little vessels, built of charcoal iron of very light gauge, lasted 50 to 60 years. I have seen some that were that old. Rust was minimal. Their hulls were uncemented and as smooth as a baby's butt, one plate flowing into another all along the stream of the hull, so lofted and formed that the rivet holes all matched when laid home on the hull.

Where has this old art gone?

It has been lost a long time, because today only a few builders in this world know how to loft a plate for furnacing, and fettling (you do not recognize the term, do you?) is an art that few people have even heard of.

A hundred years ago on the Clyde, the fettler was the master mechanic who furnaced curvilinear plates, heating them on a large bed of coals, then rolling them to close perfection from lofted frame shapes. When cooled, they could be opened up slightly, punched for rivet holes in double rows. These would then fit, hole for hole, the next plate along the hull. I have seen work of this nature in final form. This was lofting! This was plating! I do not know where the art has gone.

In something like 50,000 hours at the board in design work, and in serving something like 25 yards, I have often puzzled about it. I have seen plates bent to shape, cold, on large brakes in an attempt to achieve curved form, but brake creases always show later. I have seen a few oxter plates retorted to red heat and shaped on steam hammers, but I have never seen any man perform the art of fettling on light metal. This loss is typical of an art lost to "progress."

There is a trend today back to the steel or aluminum boat. The arc welding of steel, or the welding of aluminum in MIG techniques, has knocked out the old, time-consuming riveting. Furnacing is so energy-intensive it would not be economic even if the old arts were known. Cold working of plates into multichine shapes, then welding plates butt-to-butt, is the order of the day.

About the only variation of the now-almost-universal slab-sider approach is in the construction of light aluminum boats and canoes, where skin stretching is a superior technique. By this method, large plates are thrown on a tool pit floor at each end of which hydraulic jaws clamp the plate at each end, then put such tension on the metal that, at its yield point when it becomes momentarily plastic, a number of knees of a form are next quickly brought up beneath the floor under the plate to give it its shape. At this point the tension is quickly released, and the metal instantly flashes into a work-hardened form. A pattern is laid over the curved plate and marked for sheer and stem, and the half hull is cut from this. It is a process similar to stretching a hot water bottle across your lap, and then jamming your knee up under it.

Mild carbon steel cannot be handled in this fashion at anything like economic tooling costs, and certainly not for hulls of multichine size. But there is a way to get smooth and nicely rounded "slab-siders" by understanding how to lay up plates on a welded steel hull. The trick lies in understanding what you are doing to the plate, and how the plate will respond to its geometric limitations. You can prove this to yourself very easily.

If you will cut a piece of fairly stiff mounting board, or cardboard, or sheet-metal flat about 3 inches by 18 inches, you will find that it can be twisted about a straight-line axis as at "d" in Figure 1, and that a straightedge held across the face of the plate will lie flat. If the axis wobbles, or is bent, the plate will cup.

If, as at "d," the plate is both twisted and bent longitudinally as it might be asked to do in going from the tumblehome at a transom to the flam in the flare of the bow, the plate will cup to quite a degree. This phenomenon occurs for a little-understood reason: steel is stronger in compression than it is in tension, as are nearly all materials. When twisted and turned inward, the inner face will not compact to the shortened radius. The outerface, being in tension and cranked about the inner face, yields. The interplay of forces between the inner face and the outer produces the cup.

Thus, if a plate be both axially twisted and bent around a hull shape along its axis fore and aft, you get a roundish surface. If the plate be merely twisted about a straight axis, it will lie flat, against straight frames.

If a twisted, axially bent plate is horsed home by welding against a series of flat frames as in "c," Figure 1, festooning and pillowing will result. This attempt to tie a plate down against the nature of the material is responsible for most of the wavy flats found in amateur welding.

By taking advantage of plate bellying, it is possible to reproduce many round-bilged wooden boats in steel, achieving nearly the exact immersed sectional areas so as to give the steel boat, properly ballasted, the same behavior as the parent boat. Take a look at the accommodation and framing plans shown on page 277.

A couple of years ago I had the inspiration to convert John G. Hanna's famed *Tahiti* into an updated version in steel by employing the curling, curving phenomenon as illustrated by "a" and "b" in Figure 1.

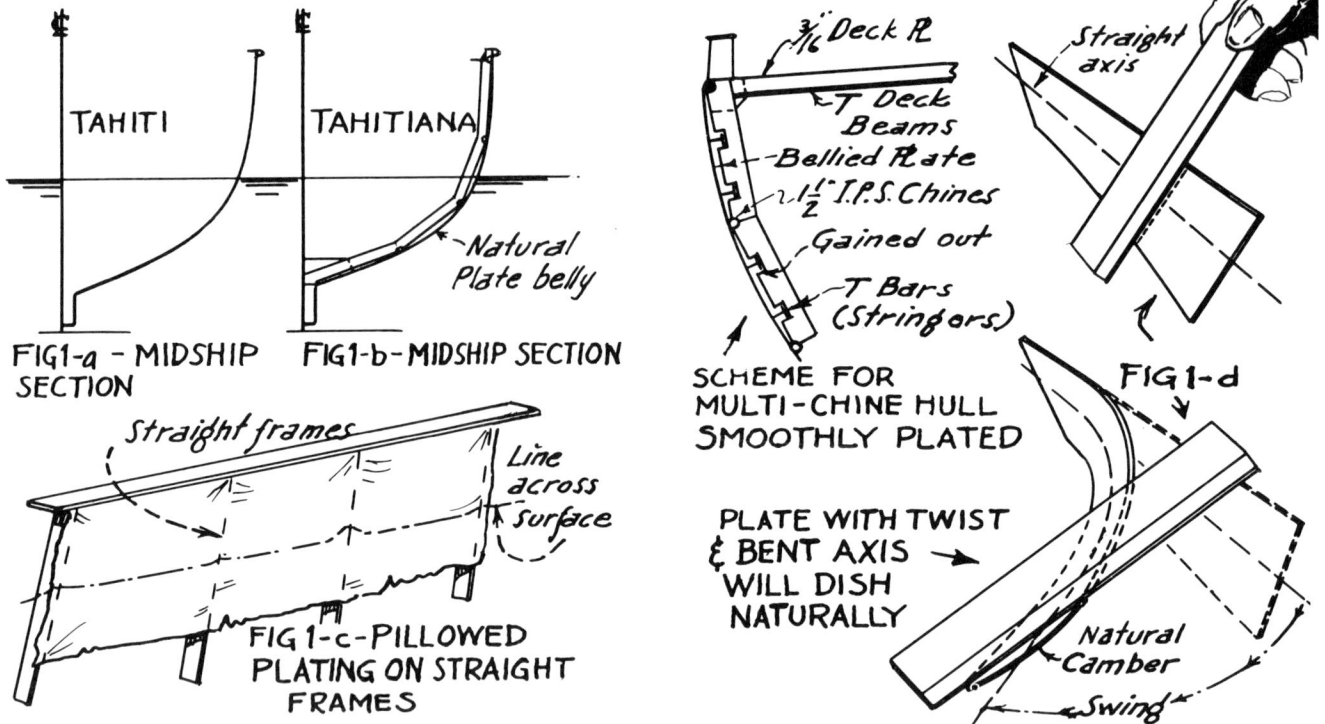

TAHITI   **TAHITIANA**

Natural
Plate belly

FIG1-a – MIDSHIP   **FIG1-b-MIDSHIP SECTION**
SECTION

Straight frames
Line
across
surface

FIG 1-c-PILLOWED
PLATING ON STRAIGHT
FRAMES

³/₁₆" Deck Pl.
T Deck
Beams
Bellied Plate
1½" I.P.S. Chines
Gained out
T Bars
(Stringers)

SCHEME FOR
MULTI-CHINE HULL
SMOOTHLY PLATED

PLATE WITH TWIST
& BENT AXIS →
WILL DISH
NATURALLY

Straight
axis

FIG 1-d

Natural
Camber
Swing

Figure 1.

The section at "a" shows the old round-bilged section of *Tahiti* as constructed in wood. The section at "b" shows how straight steel frames were employed with three chine rods, allowing the plates to curl, thus giving almost the same cross section in steel as the old wooden version had. She is also shown in the sail plan silhouette.

The scheme of the idea is clearly shown in the section in Figure 1 alongside the view of the ruler. The plates are allowed to belly to their natural lie. T-bar stringers are let into gains in the 1/4-inch steel bar frames. Before the plates are hung to the chines, and after the plate is tacked home, the T-bars are streamed out to the inner face of the plate, their heels at the T-head being tacked to the frame permanently, and thus the whole plate, constituting a gore in the outer shell, remains fair and smooth.

The resulting boat I termed *Tahitiana*. That the idea appealed to a great number of men is attested to by the fact that over 550 sets of plans were sold within 15 months. (Her plans appear in the Appendix of this book.)

If the plate axis has little warp from end to end, another satisfactory way to plate up a slab-sider is shown by viewing the 77 feet by 18 feet 6 inches by 4 feet steel passenger ferry designed for Gage Marine Inc. of Williams Bay, Wisconsin. Her body plan is shown in Figure 2. You will

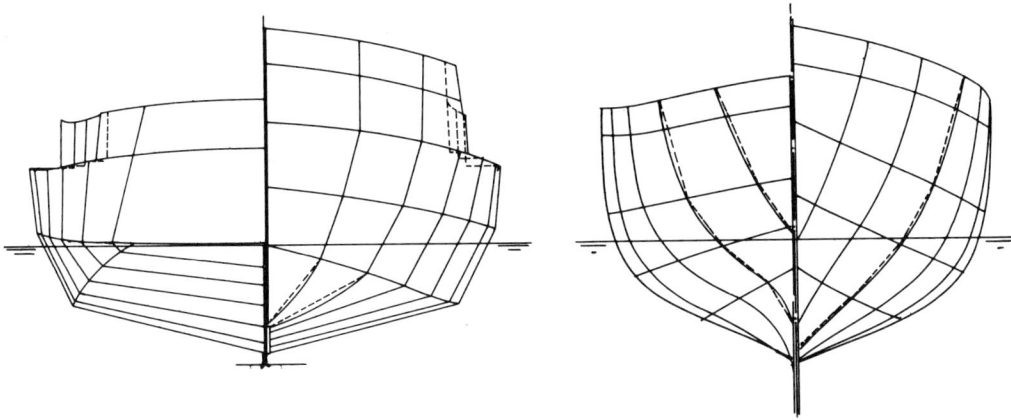

Figure 2 (right). Body plan of the steel 77-foot ferry *Walworth III*. The sections show minimal twist, and only gentle fore-and-aft bending of axis. Except near forefoot area, all plates will lie fair to straight frames. *Figure 3 (left).* Solid lines show body plan of *Tahiti* as built in wood. For steel construction, by use of chines on approximate diagonals, with frames shown as indicated by dotted lines, steel plates hung to chines will belly to near original hull form. Hence, *Tahitiana* is nearly the same boat.

note that the plates, while they bend in a fore-and-aft direction, do not have perceptible warp. Thus they can be made to lie against straight frames.

Some slight cupping is required at the ends, and in lieu of the inboard T-bars, flat strip stringers are let into the frames, which can back up the plate where it tends to lie off.

In these two illustrations of belly plating versus flat plating, the reasons for the behavior of the plates can be discerned from the axial twist exhibited in *Tahitiana*, Figure 3, and the lack of it in the Gage ferry, which is named *U.S. Mailboat Walworth III*, Figure 4.

An interesting boat she is, the *Walworth III*. Gage runs a heavily patronized Lake Geneva sightseeing service. The run around Lake Geneva takes a couple of hours. For this service three boats are in continuous operation: one a Mark Twain-type, stern wheel, river-type excursion boat, another a Great Lakes, old-time-type, shelter-deck, package-freight steamer. The clipper of the line is the *Walworth*. In this boat, Gage delivers the RFD mail by contract to lake homes in an acrobatic fashion.

The mail boat storms in toward the addressee's dock, seeing how close she can come to the dock on a wide turn without hitting it. From the wide guard, shown in the lower half of the boat's plan view, a beautiful blonde leaps to the dock, dashes to the mail box, deposits the mail, and hops on again at the next-to-aft stanchion at the sheer break. If she misses, she jumps in the lake, getting her neck washed. High

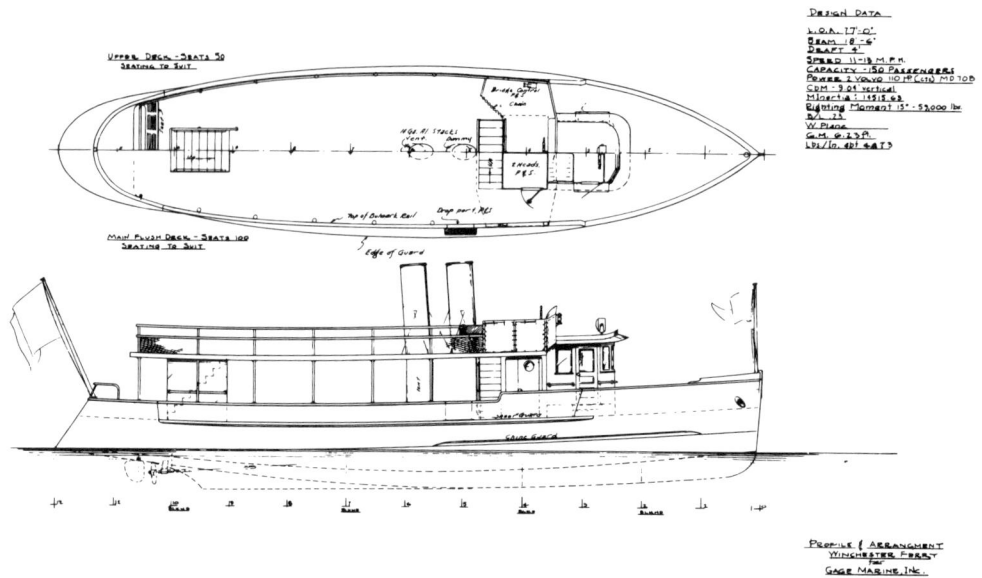

Figure 4.

school girls, with each of their 19-year-old charms showing, are clawing at each other for this starring role.

I found the designing of this boat most interesting. Gage wanted something that looked like the old steam yacht *Winchester*. Essentially a pair of raked stacks, long lean lines, and a beaver-tail stern were indicated. The latter, bringing the bottom up to the surface at the tail end, was, I knew, the secret of keeping her wake down. She was tank-tested for this feature. More lore! She moves with minimal wake and will not wash out docks or shoreline.

Not only was the plating kept in virtually untwisted planes, and only bent fore and aft so it would lie flat, but the rounded stern was kept in conical sections for easy fit after putting the cuff plates through rolls.

And if you think *Walworth III*, à la *Winchester*, won't be busy, please know I was stunned by Bill Gage's demand for Ma and Pa heads with a 1,000-gallon holding tank! So, in a way, this makes the new mail boat a head boat, at so much per head, heading for the heads. This is beer-and-offshore lore.

Pumping schedule, every 24 hours. Just where you will file this bit of information is entirely up to you.

I pass.

166

20

Power/Fuel

By the time this study appears in print, every man who depends upon a powered vessel for his livelihood or for his pleasure will have had to reassess his relationship to the energy crisis. No matter what government does or what the law of supply and demand decrees about the shortage of liquid hydrocarbon fossil fuels, it will all add up to one word: curtailment. In a nation of once free-wheeling energy hogs, there won't be enough fuel to go around unless economy and restraint are exercised by all.

If you hold back your throttle you are helping a fellow operator; by his holding back a bit, he is helping you. Fortunately, in the boating world, almost all boats are heavily over-powered and it will not affect operational speed much to cut back. I point out to you a simple fact: *There is no known form of locomotion that pays back such large fuel savings for cutting down speed as does a powered vessel.*

In most cases, if you cut down speed in a boat by a knot or two, you can usually *double* your cruising range. Twice as far on a gallon, or half the fuel—think of it either way. What is more, spectacular improvement in fuel economy frequently follows proper load balance. It is perfectly surprising to me how many boat owners haven't the slightest knowledge of why this is true. They'll operate a boat for years with little thought to what makes the craft behave the way she does.

It is in these two departments of vessel operation that the greatest economies can be found: checking down, and balancing the load to suit the hull. Let us see why.

Take a look at the brake horsepower graph shown in Figure 1. This is

Figure 1 chart description with axes: SHAFT HORSEPOWER (vertical, 0-100), ENGINE SPEED - RPM (horizontal, 1000-3000), FUEL GAL./HR (right vertical, 0-7). Labels include: RATED POWER OUTPUT GUARANTEED WITHIN 5% AT AIR TEMP 85°F. BAR (DRY) 29.00 IN HG, 92 SHP, RATED SHP, POWER-PROPELLER LOAD, FUEL CONSUMPTION, FUEL PROPELLER LOAD.

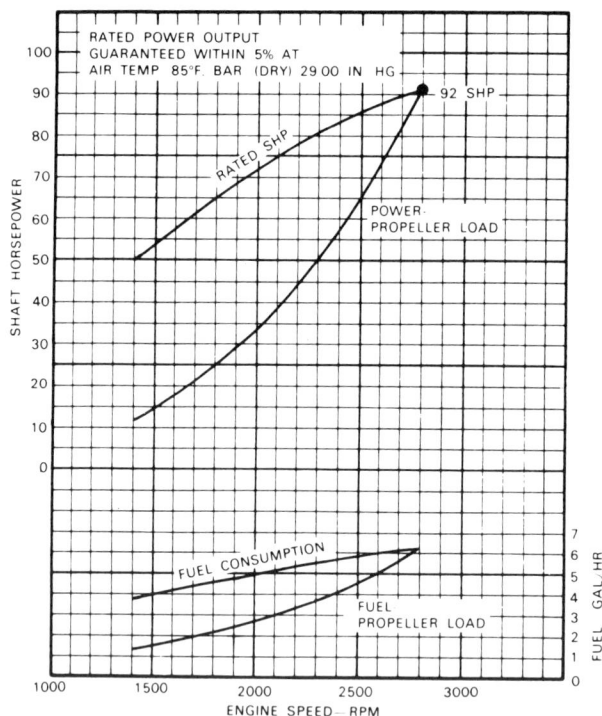

Figure 1. This set of power and fuel consumption curves for a small diesel graphically shows the savings in fuel that can be effected by lowered rpm. See text for directions for reading chart values.

for a GM series 5032-4000 engine developing 92 hp (rated "continuous") at 2,800 rpm.

The upper line is the curve for shaft horsepower. The propeller load curve below it shows the power demand of a typical hypothetical propeller for use with the engine in a boat of normal form. The relationship between shaft or rated horsepower and the propeller power required is typical of internal combustion applications.

You will note on this power graph that toward the 92-hp terminal dot, the power developed is all needed by the propeller when it operates at this speed. That's it—that's all, brother—the end of the line. Now drop your eye to the bottom of the chart. Here is a carefully accurate calibration showing fuel consumption in gallons per hour. At 2,800 rpm you get no more revs, and the fuel consumption is a shade above 6 gph. Thus, going gung-ho—all out—if your typical vessel makes 10 knots, you will be burning 6 gallons to get 10 knots. But wait a minute—let's take a second look at this curve, define its meaning.

In making such a curve, an engine-maker uses brake horsepower to get his total engine output. He then shades it back a bit to get continuously acceptable horsepower for decent engine life and a rating useful where a few auxiliary take-off features might be wanted. The result is the curve shown and is known as "Rated Shaft Horsepower."

Now the making of the brake horsepower curve means just what it says. The engine is stripped down of accessories, is fed all the fuel she can consume with throttle always at wide open, and is then *braked* down by dynamometer to see what torque is developed at given revolutions along the ascending curve. This torque, expressed in foot-pounds, is equated to horsepower, the points plotted, and you come up with *brake* horsepower.

This operation is blood-and-guts, feed-her-full, almost destruction testing. Figuratively, there is a nurse standing by with sutures, oxygen, needles, and Elmer's glue in the support of high-torque figures. Witness the clinical notes on ambient temperature and barometric pressure.

On full brake horsepower, the engine is aspirating (breathing) all the fuel that can be combusted. But in practical, or operational, use the engine is brought up by feeding the throttle whatever fuel is necessary to handle the load. Thus, though the engine is aspirating the same volume of intake air at any given number of revolutions, the difference between load demand and what would be consumed by brake demand means that on this system of acceleration, the amount of fuel aspirated is always much less.

There are interesting side observations to be made from this power graph. You will notice that the propeller load curve closely parallels hull resistance curves shown in Figure 2. What is being calibrated in both plots is the resistance that water has to being forced.

As the lines go into a vertical climb, further power input ceases to pay off. Fuel consumption soars, but speed does not improve. In fact, as the resistance curve goes into an asymptotic climb, input of excessive power results in the hull foundering. While I have not seen this phenomenon in actual use, I have observed it in tank testing. The curve breaks, wavers, and the vessel swamps in her own waves.

This is more true of round-bilge hulls than of Vee hulls. The round-bilger will drive far more easily than a Vee at low speeds. A Vee will, if lightly loaded, persist in making use of a planing facility through a wider range of speeds but can eventually be "killed" by overpowering. Heavily loaded round-bilged boats in normal speed ranges are much more economical than slab-siders. I mention these facts to keep your thinking in an applicable framework.

Let us read the power curve again. Take another look at Figure 1. Suppose you back off on the throttle and cease to be so demanding. Go from 2,800 rpm down to 2,400 rpm and the fuel consumption drops from about 6 gallons to just above 4 gallons on the propeller demand curve—about 33 percent saving. At 2,400 rpm your propeller needs

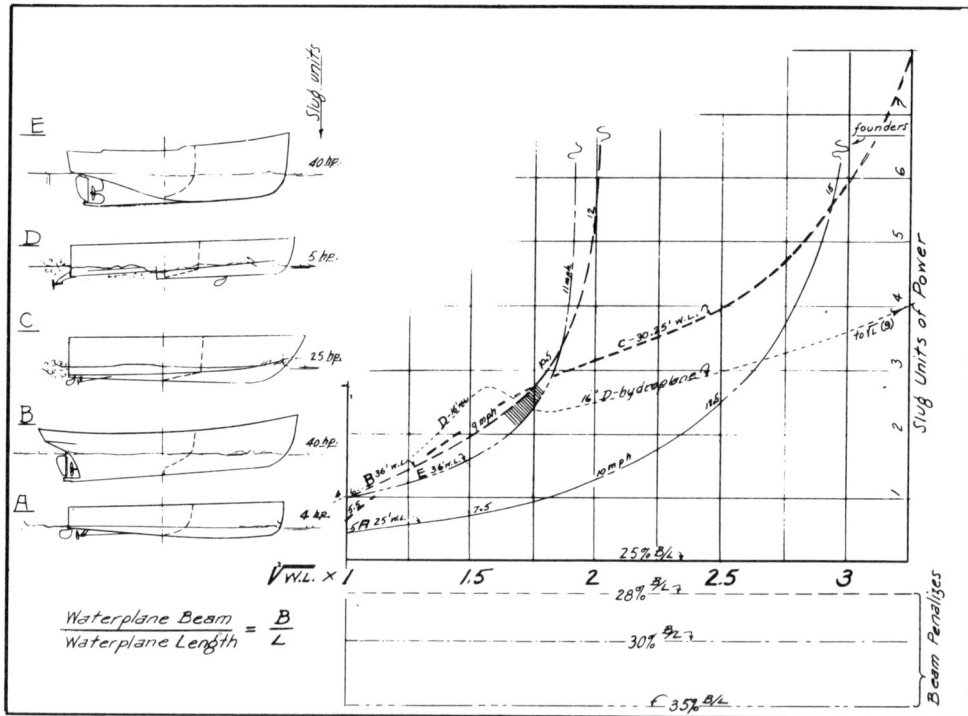

Figure 2. Comparative power demands plotted on the common denominator of speed/length ratios, showing where power is wasted. Lines of three of the hull types are shown on the following pages.

about 57 hp. The whole power train is operating under much less strain. You are not only saving in fuel, but you are adding thousands of hours to engine life.

There are some vessels in which pulling down to 2,100 rpm would not greatly affect the economics of cash income by slowing down rapid turn-around, and in such cases you'd be operating with a prop load demand of about 40 hp at a most economical speed consuming but 3 gph—half the normal fuel bill.

Every boatowner can make his own fuel consumption chart based on two or three runs over known distances. He can watch the tachometer, take a stopwatch time for a known distance, and by introducing a known quantity of fuel into the feed line by "Tee-ing in" a calibrated small tank, he can come up with a plot showing the actual results of economical running. The small tank is necessary. Dip-sticking a large tank isn't accurate enough. And with a diesel, you'll need an overflow tank as well to measure actual consumption, because all diesels over-pump and return the excess to the main tank. A difference must be established.

I should think that each vessel operator ought to get an accurate consumption curve for his boat. Use reduced, but satisfactory, speeds.

The point at which to operate will then become a definite quantity, not a guess. The point can be equated to operating dollars, and you will learn something that is apt to shock you: you'll be surprised to see how much "forced" speed costs you.

Now, let's say something about loadings. Sometimes spectacular gains in ease of driving, hence in reduction of power and cost of fuel, can be had by proper trimming. Here, you need to refresh your mind about a few basic principles of hull behavior. There are many types of boats, and each has its peculiarities.

In general, before examining the curves in Figure 2, let me say that most boats operating in a "soft"speed range, say, up to 8 knots, will run more cheaply if trimmed so that none of their length is submerged at the transom. In low-speed ranges, double-enders and fantail-stern types move with least power. Transom-sterned boats that have great areas of the transom under water, and cannot be made to plane, are energy hogs for fair.

There are, unfortunately, a lot of these boats around. Initially, the design thinking was good for high speed work, but at low speeds such boats (Type C in Figure 2) have a large burble following them, and are unmanageable as well as being drinkers of great gobs of power applied uselessly. Not all can be trimmed so that only an inch or two of the stern is immersed, but if this can be effected by load trimming without affecting steering too badly, you will find greater relative economy in getting places.

It seems a great waste of power to design a boat with a lobbed, flat transom that is good for planing speeds, and then build such a heavy, beamy boat that only partial planing results. I should say that this ridiculous and anomalous condition is the lot of 85 percent of this breed of boat. Few really plane—the fact that the transom clears at around 9 to 10 knots does not mean the hull is planing—it means merely that the propeller is pumping huge quantities of water out past the transom. This condition is the great power-wasting sector on any speed/length curve.

Let's take a look at Figure 2 to see how the average powerboat behaves, what her powered requirements are, and compare them with other members of the boat family. Fortunately, the quantities expressed are from actual tests made in a tank at one time or another, with the exception of hull E.

I have selected five boats, which pretty generally cover powerboat types, and have plotted them on one basic quantity, relative to size. This quantity is the speed in relation to the square root of waterline length. It has long been a tenet of naval architecture that the "natural" speed of any hull is the square root of her waterline length. This is the

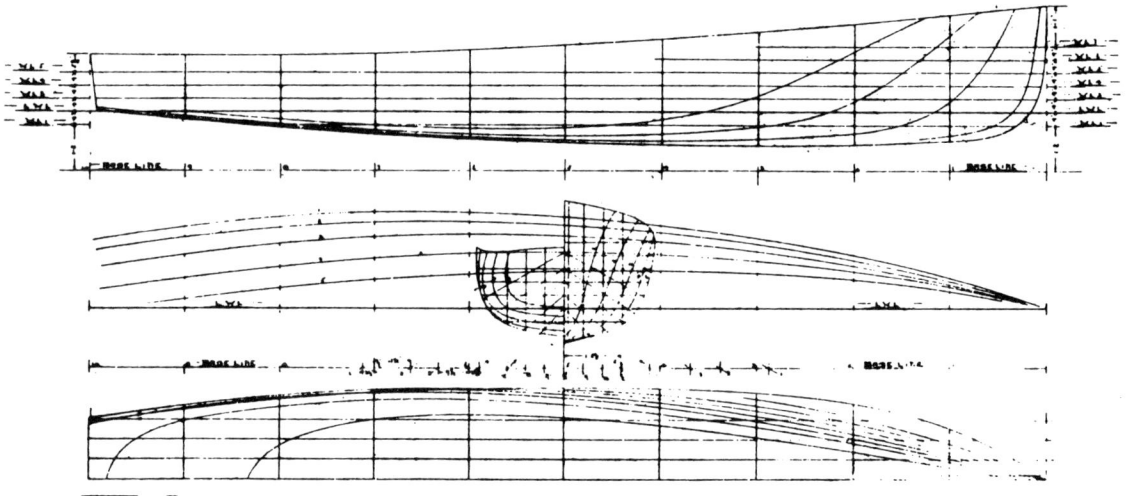

Type A hulls as charted in Figure 2, with sterns terminating at the surface of the LWL, move easily, showing little wake. The curve for this old-timer, designed by Edson B. Schock, shows that she traveled 12.5 mph with a mere 10 hp engine.

integer at which any boat is supposed to move at a speed in knots, most efficiently using the power required to drive her at that speed.

The curve in Figure 2 is adjusted to read not in knots, but in miles per hour. The values, with the exception of hull E, are tested tank values on boats I have known, and I have applied the 1.15 to 1 knots/ miles factor to make the graph easier to assimilate. Values are plotted in miles per hour. The units of power on this Figure 2 graph are in slug units, by which method of calibrating, a grid can be drawn relating boat characteristics in curve terms, showing the related merits of one hull against another when based on the common denominator, the S/L ratio.

Let's see what happens to hull A when we begin to power her. She is a lightly built, old-time launch of canoe construction that has going for her the advantages of a 25 percent B/L ratio, round-bilge hull, long waterline, and a transom that just kisses the water when at rest. She is so easily driven that it is hard to believe, yet boats once got their speed from these characteristics. The slug unit on the graph is a mere 4 hp.

At 5 mph she will need but 2 honest horses to push her at an S/L ratio of 1. At 7.5 mph and a speed/length ratio of 1.5, she will require just a shade over 3 hp, and at a speed/length ratio of 2.5, or 2.5 times her basic 5 miles, she will be doing 12.5 miles and will need 2-1/2 slugs of power, or 10 hp.

Now see what happens to power: she cannot be driven above a speed/length ratio of 3 without "freaking out." Just before 24 hp is installed, she'll founder in a high sheet of bow wave. Twelve times the power is required to increase the speed three times. I talked about this

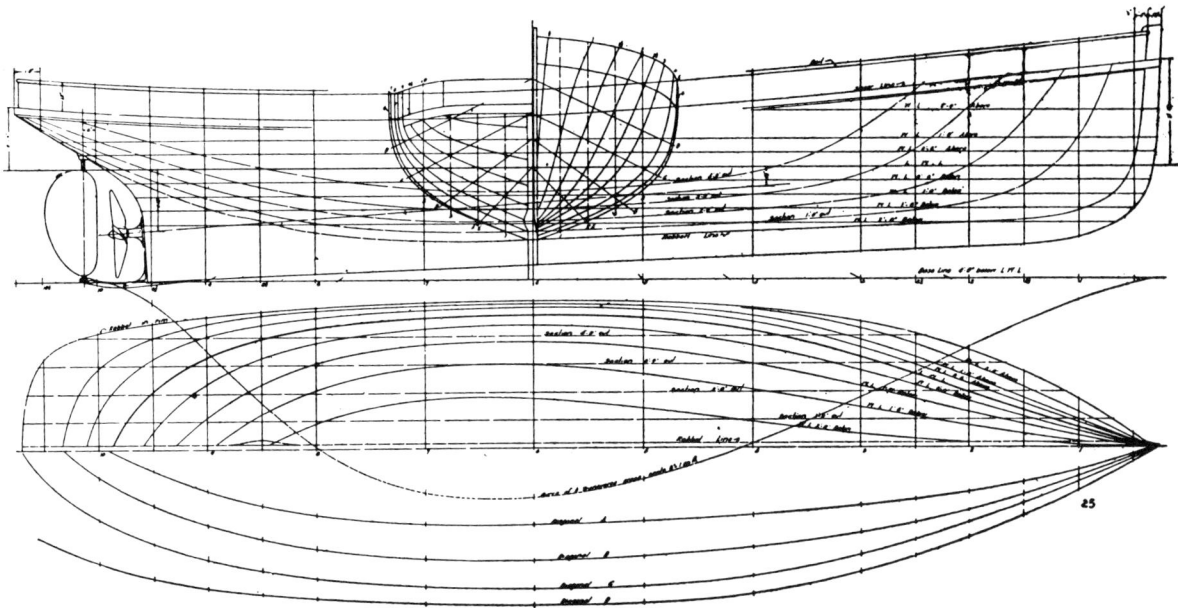

Type B hulls of the fantail stern variety want level trimming, in which condition they drive easily up to a square root of WL ratio of 1.5. Enormous power is wasted above that speed until foundering occurs by being overdriven. See Figure 2, curve B, on page 170.

boat, *Coyote,* with her designer, Edson B. Schock, the grand old man of early powerboat design, in his Los Angeles office nearly 40 years ago. Schock was an advocate of the unsubmerged transom.

Let's take a typical fantailer, as shown at B, Figure 2. This is a 36-foot-waterline vessel of a type illustrated by the lines of a similar vessel shown here. The boat calibrated is my design, but I have lost the lines, and borrow the work of P.H. Thearle, who once was the naval architect for the Skinner-Eddy Corp. of Seattle, to show the nature of the 36-footer. This boat has a speed/length base of 6, which is the square root of the waterline length. Thus the curve starts at 6, on unit slugs of 40 hp.

To bring the S/L ratio to 1.5, or 9 mph, the power must be doubled to 80 hp. It will need 100 hp to achieve an S/L ratio of 1.75, or 10.5 mph. Thereafter it will cost 240 hp to gain another mile and a half. Beyond this the speed curve breaks off and the vessel swamps. It is the nature of this type of hull to drive easily with low power at modest speeds, but tossing power into such a hull is folly at much above 1.5 S/L ratio.

A similar boat, Type E, perhaps more modern in deck area and position of weights up forward, has about the same characteristics, and probably because she does not squat so badly when driven, will appear

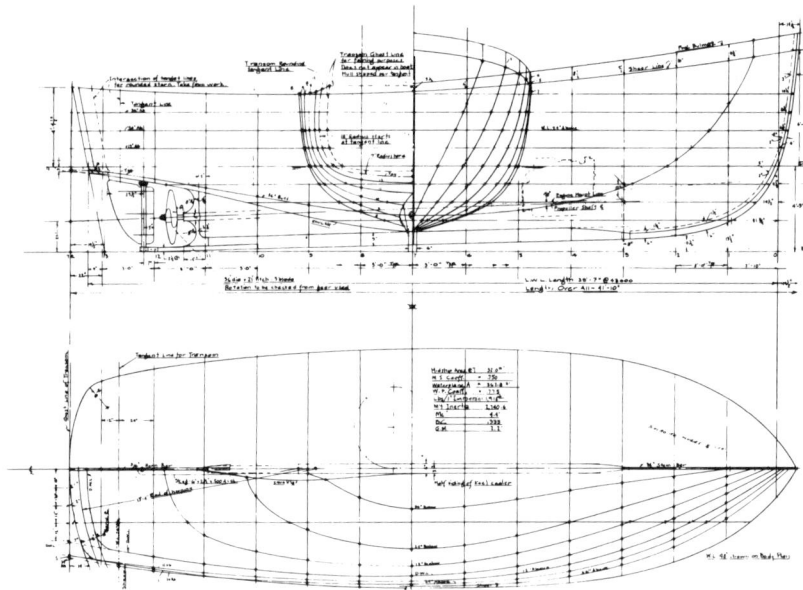

Type E hulls, full-bodied with rounded transom terminations at LWL surface, want the load forward, with center of lateral resistance at 52-55% WL. Such hulls have type B characteristics but move with slightly less resistance than B in lower speed ranges. Note shaded differences between curves B and E, Figure 2. Type E resists overpowering. These lines are of a fishing boat designed by the author and built in aluminum.

to advantage in the shaded area between curves B and E; thereafter, hull form due to bluntness penalizes performance, and the heavy bow wave prohibits reaching even the speed of the fantail-sterned hull. The low speed sector where the waterline at the transom is at natural level allows Type E a slight advantage.

As to Type C, let's give the type a gander: as any man knows who has owned one, these craft are unsteerable when checked down in a following sea. They have to be opened up to be controlled, and generally, then, overtake the seas, over-running and slamming. Obviously, these craft are not planned from seagoing knowledge. They do well as floating cottages in a marina, and, because they need wallops of power to move them, can often run from the weather. It is a good thing that they can, because when the wind blows hard enough to put white-caps in your coffee cup, these boxes are helpless at sea. The tiny propellers have to be wound up to be effective with the small rudders.

Take a look at a typical power curve for a Type C boat. The hull shown is 30.25 feet on the waterline, and the basic S is 5.5 mph. The slug unit of power is 25 hp. By the time this hull is doing 8.25 miles an hour, she'll need 50 hp. At about 10 miles per, the transom will clean off, and momentarily her power curve slacks off. Thereafter it goes up a-whooping. It will take about 100 horses to move her at an S/L of 2.5, or about 14 mph. At 16 honest miles an hour 150 horses will be required. After that, power investment becomes expensive! If you want to economize with this type of hull, get her rump up as close to the surface as you can and still steer her.

Tragically enough, this type of hull seems to be a product of the drawing room school of design; few of the gents who design them have ever been out on a dark night when the pistons are changing holes. All fogs in the drawing room are room temperature, and winds that have weight may be seen in paintings on the wall. These lads will argue that cubage is the cheapest dimension to construct. I won't argue that.

But since when has cubage had anything to do with adequate sea-keeping? The most expensive dimension in a boat, when it comes to driving her, is beam. Here again is the dry land sailor's bleat for "more beam for more stability."

If you look at boats that are indigenous to seafaring shores, you will find them to have been evolved through decades so that most of them are now between 25 and 28 percent B/L ratio when used with power alone.

An interesting curve for a type of boat we see little of today is for D, the step hydroplane. On a 16-foot waterline, her basic speed is supposed to be 4. Here is where I take issue with the square root theory. I cannot see that it applies because of excessive burble. However, plotting known speeds and powers, the curve shows a hump, and when this occurs, the steps are free and the boat scoots. Power can economically be applied to 36 mph, or an S/L of 9. Interesting, but don't chop a step into your hull to effect economy!

I have exaggerated an abscissa on Figure 2 to show how beam penalizes speed in the low-power, docile-speed ranges. The curves will shed engineering daylight as to the variables of power input, and point to the knowledgeable operator the probable economies obtainable as to types and hull loadings.

It is hoped that by paying attention to restraint on your engine's throttle, and by experimenting with hull loadings, you can see a way out of the fuel dilemma. It would insult a seaman's intelligence if I told him to keep the barnacles off his boat, or to grease his propeller blades to make it hydrophobic and cut down radio static as well as electrolysis, so I won't say anything about them.

But you can bet that Wilbur, the double-bifocalled gnome who inhabits library stacks with a slide rule, will rush out screaming, "You're wrong! It says on page 66 that a battleship uses only half a pound of coal per knot in summer in the Indian Ocean!" Then I'd have to kick him back to the hurricane deck of his boxcar, tell him I never have seen the Indian Ocean, and that I'd look silly defending irrational argument.

Let's let it rest at this.

21

Producer Gas, Part I

In the last few years, few are the men who have not felt physical pain at the financial stabbing they get in paying for fuel. The pleasure-boat man may be able to afford costs and shrug them off, or he can stop running and forget them. But a fisherman must keep running to sustain cash income; ditto for the commercial boat operator. Sometimes, the mere curtailment of running will throw an operation into the red. So, many's the man these days who has that rampaging Arab bull by its wild tail, forlornly hoping that somebody will come along and help him let go.

The options aren't simple. It's a case of hanging on until the bull kicks you to death, or letting go in the gamble you can streak over a fence before he gets you. I suggest that one way of letting go may be to go back to producer gas for fuel, burning anthracite pea coal in a gas produced right aboard ship. The resulting coal gas has about the same combustive and expansive properties in a spark-ignited engine as does carbureted gasoline. When you closely consider the engine you now operate, the carburetor produces a vapor, which is turned into a gas in the intake manifold. Even a diesel injection jet atomizes oil, which flashes to gas and ignites on adiabatic heat. In a sense, *all* internal combustion engines run on a gas.

Historically, all early internal combustion engines initially ran on "city gas" or "water gas" or "coal gas." It was all the same stuff. The first engines were called "gas" engines, and had run on coal gas for 15 years before petro-chemists finally evolved that stuff which at first was termed "gas-ol-ene."

The idea of producing gas aboard ship is not new. In the development of gasoline power plants for marine use, there was a period of six or seven years from 1910-11 to the end of 1917 when producer gas looked like the only way to beat rising gasoline costs. Nearly 1,000 gas producer plants were manufactured in this country and were sold and installed worldwide, giving reliable service with unheard-of economy. They could be run by any bush native anywhere who could light a fire, crank an engine, and aim a squirt oil can with passable accuracy.

The savings in operation ranged from 1/9 to 1/3 the cost of operating on gasoline. This is another way of saying that converted boats could run from three days up to nine days on the fuel money it formerly took to run one day.

The producer gas proposition was taking hold strongly when World War I erupted, turning economics topsy-turvy. When the smoke of war cleared, the diesel had become viable. Marine power then took off on the bandwagon of the then-surplus, unwanted, cheaper, and then-untaxed heavy fuel oils. Liquids were, and are, more convenient. Today they are prohibitive in cost, especially so when you add into capital investment the higher cost of the expensive diesel engine, which usually costs about two to three times the price of easier-to-build gasoline marine engines.

Hence the interest in coal and its gas. There is nothing mysterious about producer gas, except the public's general unfamiliarity with it.

The technology is voluminous. The literature on the subject is prodigious. I have much of it, saved from my college days in engineering school, when physics and chemistry and mathematics opened wonderful avenues to dreams of enterprise. One of my early interests was producer gas, on which I kept copious notes and design references. My design emporium is now awash in this producer gas technology, and there comes to the surface a most interesting early producer gas boat. Take a look at Figure 1.

The boat is a tunnel-sterned craft, 65 feet by 12 feet by 2 feet 3 inches, a fast mail and freight boat designed for a Guatemalan company by the late naval architect, J. Murray Watts, an old friend who gave the plans to me long ago. This shows how a producer plant was installed.

I see by the notation on the back of the prints that she was used in delta and upstream service on the San Pedro River, in South America. She is reported to have given years of service on a 200-mile run, operating on native-produced charcoal. She is equipped with a Galusha 65 hp producer gas plant mated to a 65 hp Wolverine engine of three cylinders with cranks set at 120 degrees, giving a power impulse every 2/3 revolution with steam-engine smoothness. The bore was 9-1/2 inches, stroke 12 inches; the rpm 300-350. The propeller is shown as a

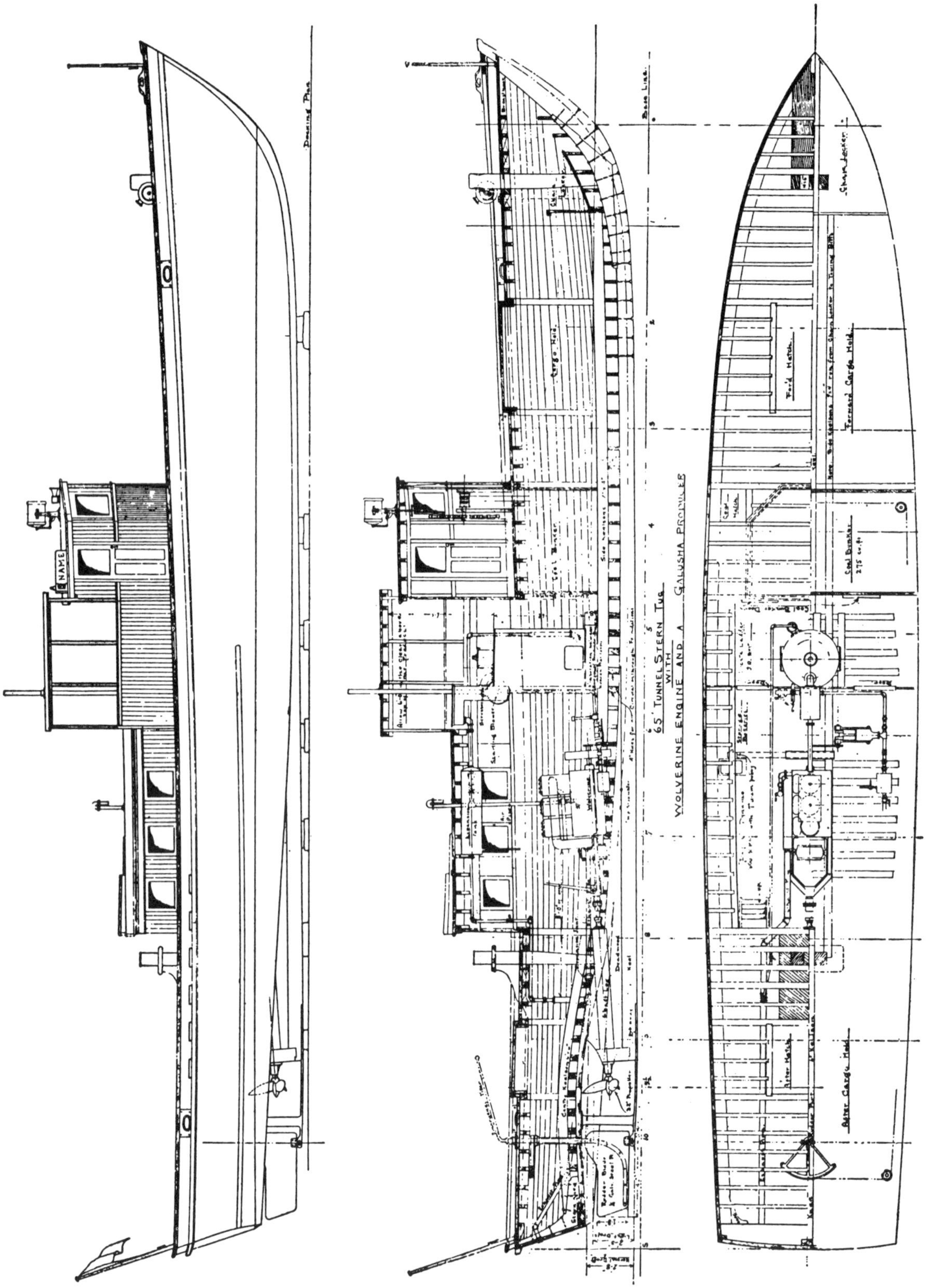

Figure 1. A producer gas, shallow-draft, freight and mailboat designed by J. Murray Watts for South American river service. Note the tunnel stern. (*Motor Boat*)

A Wolverine engine hooked up to a gas producer. "Only" 65 hp, the engine's three big cylinders and heavy flywheel give promise of mighty strong "animals" in her innards.

32-inch diameter by 48-inch pitch, Hyde 3-blade, delivering 11 mph, or 9.56 knots. The engine is a 4-cycle type, hence each cylinder aspirates only every second revolution, which works out at 177 to 200 cubic feet per minute of manifold intake. In a sense, the producer plant acts like a carburetor to the engine. Figure 1 is useful in acquainting you with the old-time thinking.

The boat herself would be good today, slim and fast for river-current work. The Galusha Producer was considered a marvel, having but one-quarter the weight of a steam plant, and requiring but one-third the space. On today's knowledge, we could beat this all hollow. Bear in mind that at the time this plant was installed, and considered a great engineering advance, it was in a day of the galvanic battery and telegraph key, the "Victor Talking Machine," chain-driven automobiles, and "city gas" on tap in every candelabra in a modern home—just in case the carbon filaments on those new-fangled electric lights gave out.

You will note that the Galusha plant in Murray Watts's boat apparently had no insulation against heat loss; the canopy roof is the tip-off. I can see where plenty of air might be needed around a furnace in the tropics, but the producer operates at the level of a banked fire, with temperature in the upper portion ideally at 183 degrees, and modern insulative materials could cut radiation losses way down. Might be a comforting source of heat in Alaskan waters. Almost any mechanic today who could weld up a furnace shell could come up with this producer.

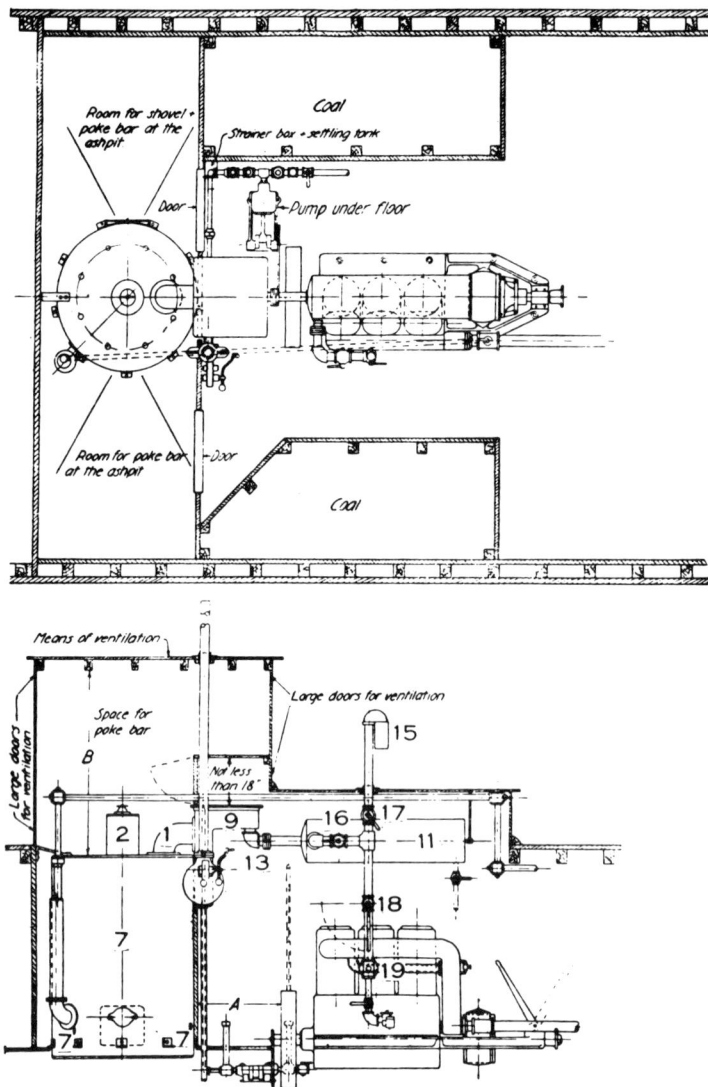

Figure 2. Layout of producer gas plant in Watts' design, showing piping plan and mechanical traverse of gas. (*The Rudder*)

It would work today. Physics principles have not changed. To understand how the outfit produces gas to run an engine, let's trace out the mechanical piping train with this typical outfit in Watts's boat. We'll take a look at the piping circuit first, and then go on to operating economies with documented dollar figures on coal gas versus gasoline costs, and then to combustive chemistry. Now, follow me through Figure 2.

In this drawing is diagrammed the installation shown in Watts's boat. The generator, or producer, is item 7. This is simply a cylindrical shell of steel, resting on end and held to a foundation bed by lugs as at 7', 7'. The shell is lined with refractory brick. In the bottom of the shell is an ash pit, above which is a shaking grate. As may be seen from a top view, there is an access door to the fire on the starboard side. This is dogged tight after the small generating fire is started. It can be used to remove ashes. Room is provided also on the port side for a poker or slice bar.

The smaller cylinder 2 on top of the generator is the coal hopper by means of which the generator is charged with coal or other solid fuel such as coke or charcoal. This hopper feeds down coal like a birdseed feeder operates. As the level of the charge settles in the burning, the hopper delivers more coal, maintaining a fairly constant level of coal.

Fuel consumption ran at 1 pound per 1 hp per 1 hr. Thus, a 65 hp engine would need 65 pounds of coal an hour, so the hopper would need 260 pounds per charge to last a 4-hour shift. There are 2,240 pounds of coal in a ton, which occupies 43 cubic feet approximately, in pea-coal size anthracite. This works out at 52 pounds per cubic foot, so a 260-pound charge would require but a 5-cubic-foot hopper.

What would be the smoke if this device were used for heating a house is, in this case, the gas. The gas generated leaves by the elbow 1, on top, and goes to the scrubber, 9. As the gas at this time is hot and dusty, it is treated with water in the scrubber, where it is cooled, washed clean of fly ash and "tars," and dried. The gas is then ready for use and goes through pipe 13 to chamber 11, and then through valve 16 and down to the engine. Air is drawn in through the rainproof gooseneck 15, the flow being controlled by the amount of opening in valve 17. The usual ratio is 1 part of gas to 1 part of air.

Thus, the suction demand of the 65 hp engine in Watts's boat, of 177 to 200 cfm is halved as to suction draft demand on the producer, so that the ash pit intake is only 88.5 to 100 cfm. The air intake, on a one-for-one basis, supplies the other half of the aspirating demand of the engine.

When the gas and air are mixed, there is then an explosive mixture in the pipe tee below 17. The throttle valve is 18, as can be seen by the swing quadrant. This controls engine speed in conjunction with advanced or retarded spark. The dotted line extending from the flywheel is the starting bar used to crank over the engine.

The manifold of the engine is 19. The starting blower, turned by hand to start the generating fire, is a blacksmith's forge type, and can be seen to the left of the number 13. The horizontal pipe running aft and overhead under the deckhouse and main deck beams is the air intake. This air intake goes to the ash pit under the producer and is led to a low point in the vessel aft and is covered with a miner's lamp screen. Here the coolest and dampest intake of air serves to scavenge the bilge as a ventilating updraft.

The fat pipe near the ash pit which covers the intake is a water jacket to prevent intake air from drying out as it passes the fire zone. On some models, a drip cock was needle-valved into the intake air at this point, because a balanced amount of water adds hydrogen to the beneficiation of the coal gas. The "burning of water" enriches the produced output 7 percent. When we get to the chemistry of combustion I will explain this.

The vertical vent pipe goes through the cabin canopy. In the tropics, this canopy is merely for cooling ventilation. It was a standard treatment on all Watts vessels designed for Indonesian and East Indian waters. It would not be necessary in colder climes. The vertical vent is opened to upper air while initially firing up, until the gas production gives a blue flame from a small side gas jet, showing the plant is producing and is on stream.

Just below A, under the sole, is a reciprocating pump to supply outboard water through the scrubber, and which water, with dissolved solutes, is run overboard again. These solutes are minimal with good anthracite, but are tarry with the use of bituminous coals or "carbonized trash." The latter two tend to be highly ammoniac in composition.

The anthracite gas is a *mix* of elements and separate heat-generated chemical compounds. Fed good carbonaceous fuel, it has the following composition.

CO	Carbon Monoxide	28%
H	Hydrogen	7%
CO_2	Carbon Dioxide	5%
CH_4	Methane	2%
N	Nitrogen	58%

The nitrogen is a diluent, inert and untroublesome if good, low-ash anthracite is used. Nitrogen comprises about 75 percent of air by volume, leaving only 24 percent to oxygen and less than 1 percent to rare gases like argon, xenon, etc. Nitrogen passes through this generating process innocuously with good anthracite, but grabs anything with amino acids in their composition and produces ammonia and nitric oxides, which are problems for the scrubber. In all producer gas installations in serious marine work, coal, coke, or charcoal always had to be used. Carbon of the highest quality, no matter its cost, would always sustain producer gas use as being most productive of energy per dollar. Anything else was "funny paper" stuff. It still is.

To illustrate what goes on chemically when the producer fire is lit, I have found a sectional view of a Dutch canal tug producer plant shown in Figure 3. The elements are essentially the same as in the Galusha plant shown in Figures 1 and 2, particularly parallel and identical as to the combustive end in the generator. The Dutch version of a scrubber is far more elaborate than the Galusha's efficient one, showing two large elements not needed or ever used by the Galusha. The large coke-filled container to the right of the furnace in Figure 3 is a spray water scrubber such as was needed if lignite or heavily bituminous coals were

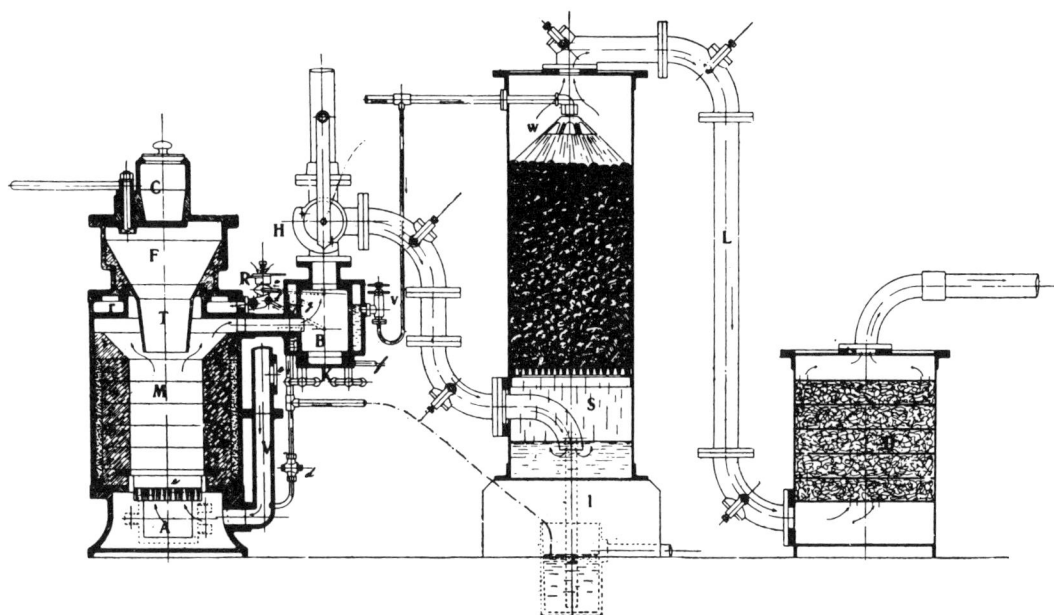

Figure 3. A sectional view of a Dutch canal tug gas producer. The elaborate scrubber and dryer are not needed with high-quality anthracite fuels.

burned. The small container O is filled with wood chips to arrest moisture and dry the gas. We will ignore these two appurtenances, using the furnace, which parallels the Galusha in form and section, to describe what happens in the combustive chemistry.

You may now consider that we are describing the operation of the Galusha plant, the train of which has been mechanically described as per Figure 2. In the main firebox M (Figure 3) above the grate A, a small fire of anthracite pea coal is started. Pea coal has a screen size of over 1/2 inch, passing through 3/4-inch mesh, and this size was chosen because it lies dense enough to give a nice balance in porosity to suction and combustion rate. The starting of this fire is assisted by a blower. When the small generating fire is glowing in a bed in the restricted fire pot, a large charge of coal is dumped in, filling through C, F, and T to the bottom of T. F and T are the supply hoppers, which correspond to the item 2 on the Galusha Figure 2 diagram, and C is a cofferdam with a swing bottom gate for the replenishment of F.

As the small fire glows, air is inducted in this producer across a water jacket atop the retort at r and R. This is drawn down the pipe V by engine suction. This air is saturated with water vapor. As the air burns the glowing coal, carbon dioxide is generated. The water vapor is dissociated into hydrogen, H, and oxygen, O. As this passes through the semi-ignited layer of coal lying just above the fire, the O from the water vapor and one molecule of O from the carbon dioxide are removed to support the oxidation (semi-combustion) of this layer. The resulting gas is CO, carbon monoxide, as already exhibited in the table of mixed gases. It is the carbon monoxide and the hydrogen on which the engine mainly runs.

The Dutch plant was complicated and excessively heavy because it was designed to burn carbonaceous junk—birch blocks and barnyard wastes. It seems complicated because the Galusha scrubber was so much more efficient. Galusha knew that the only sensible fuels were high-grade coal, coke, or charcoal. Coal was proven best; coke was more expensive; charcoal was prone to becoming wet, as it is highly hygroscopic. It will, unless used pronto, pick up 40 percent of its weight in water in marine use unless stored in dry bins. You can see there are problems with the pseudo-mechanical magazine ideas of using old mattresses, rotting manure, or old garbage. Too many ammoniac products and tar.

We are talking serious daily running in marine service, mile after mile, in which case, in a compatible boat in compatible service, producer gas *does work*. But if you've been reading science fiction and are planning to clean out the hen house and then to chug down through the Panama Canal on fried chicken droppings, forget it. You couldn't do more than get a strain on your dockline, or, used in your car, get more than a few ants killed in your driveway.

I am well aware that producer gas has been used for automobile use. The national hopes of Germany, Russia, England, Belgium, and France were pegged on the use of this gas prior to WW II, and I know that there must have been 200,000 vehicles so equipped. There may be a few still running. But fires do not respond to "stepping on her" in the same instantaneous fashion as do liquid fuels at a carburetor nozzle, and fires once burning at a 60-mph level do not die down on demand. The fact that plenty of photos have been shown of autos and truck installations does not document the viability of producer gas in jalopy service. I leave the automotive field as being alien to boat fanciers, consigning such dreams to the TV commentators and Sunday supplement editors who are perennially going to South America with a chicken in their tanks.

But we do have plenty of documentation about the viability of producer gas in marine installation. In this service, producer gas is eminently serviceable if the boat, the nature of her work, her size, and the speed needed are all *compatible*. For instance, I should think that in trolling, where long days are put in at a reduced set speed, needing only occasional acceleration, or in log booming and towing where the power plant is on full bore constantly, producer gas would make a bundle for the owner. The average, burdensome displacement boat, such as oyster tongers or shrimpers, tugs, or the Ma-and-Pa trollers of the Pacific Northwest, once did extremely well on producer gas.

Let us roll back our money ideas to 1914, a peak year before World War I diverted attention from this type of power. Here are actual, documented, financial records of producer gas economy:

One firm, the Clooney Construction Co. Ltd. of Westlake, La., fitted out a 50 hp gasoline towboat with a 50 hp Galusha Gas Producer, using the boat's same old engine. They had kept exact operating records while she had been running on gasoline. They found that the new producer plant burned the 50 pounds of pea anthracite coal per hour which Galusha had forecast—1 pound of coal per 1 hp per 1 hour. In the same operation and identical service, the boat had previously burned 15 gallons of gasoline an hour. The 15 gallons of gasoline at the 1914 price of 12 cents per gallon cost 15 times $.12, or $1.80 an hour. The 50 pounds of coal represented 1/40 of the 2,000-pound ton the Clooney accountants used, instead of the 2,240-pound long ton generally figured by most users. The cost of this coal was $8.25 per ton. Taking 1/40 the price of $8.25, the producer cost of operation was $.206 or 20.6 cents per hour. (Had the long ton been used, it would have been 1/45 of $8.25, or 18.3 cents per hour. The accountants were conservative.) A 9-hour day working on gasoline figured at 9 x $1.80, or $16.20. A 9-hour day on producer gas equalled 9 times $.206 or $1.85. The difference between $16.20 a day and $1.85 a day is a saving of $14.35.

I claim this is putting the brakes on outgo. But there it is, documented. Is the report believable?

When I dug out my old notes on this, I was inclined to think that the skipper had been carting home a 5-gallon can of gasoline each night. Then I came across this related record, which supported the first astonishment of the owners. The same boat, before conversion to producer gas, had delivered a tow from Westlake, La., to Port Arthur, Tex. The tow was a barge 130 feet by 30 feet by 9 feet, light. The distance from the point on the Calcasieu River where the barge was picked up to Port Arthur is 90 miles. It is an open sea run, subject to the vagaries of wind and sea conditions. The tow took 20 hours, and 300 gallons of gasoline were consumed, at 15 cents per gallon on this bunkering. Cost of the gasoline for the run: 300 times $.15, or $45.

The tug was converted to producer gas after returning from this trip. Three weeks after this, a duplicate of the first towing assignment was made by the same boat, with the same engine and propeller, over the same course, with a duplicate of the first barge. The running time for the 90 miles was 21 hours. The coal burned was 1,050 pounds of pea anthracite. At Clooney's cost of $8.25 per short ton, this equates to 1050/2000 times $8.25, or $4.33. Against 15-cent gasoline, producer cost was 1/10th!

The ratios of both reports are parallel, and confirming. I am glad to exonerate the skipper from the charge of swiping gasoline. Where would he put it on a 90-mile run? Swallow it?

Now, boats and engines and service conditions do vary. How did Galusha gas plants work out in other installations? In 1914, the Locke-Moore Co. Ltd. of Louisiana was engaged in towing logs along the Calcasieu. They owned a fleet of tugs, all about the same size. One of these vessels, 65 feet by 14 feet by 6 feet draft was converted from steam to a 100-hp gasoline engine—the heavy-duty type. Her service was a standard, repetitive run in lumbering operations 35 miles away, bringing along an average tow of 2,000 logs in 40 hours running time.

The 100-hp engine burned 20 gallons of gasoline per hour, or 800 gallons for the trip. At 12 cents a gallon, the fuel expense for the trip was $96. When a 100-hp producer plant was substituted for the gasoline tanks, but still retaining the original engine and propeller, the same trip consumed 4,000 pounds of coal. (There's that 1 pound to 1 hp per 1 hour yardstick again.) At $8.25 per ton on a "Louisiana ton," this equates to 4000/2000 times $8.25, which comes out at $16.50 per trip. The producer plant cost $.4125 per hour against $2.40 for gasoline. The saving on every run was $79.50.

This same tug was reported to have originally been operating on wood as a steamer. Wood in that area was plentiful and almost free, but proved excessively bulky, too messy, and slow in bringing up steam. As many who are familiar with the stuff know, wood has wide variations in quality, dryness, and heat value. Even with free wood, the report says that the tug cost $.75 per hour to run on that fuel. Steam, with everything connected with it free but the labor, still cost 169 percent of the per-hour cost of producer gas. A glimmer as to the reason for this is contained in the quaint comment, "An extra fireman is required at $2 per day."

Would 1975 ratios hold as to 1914 records? Pretty closely, I should say. If anything, coal has risen higher in proportion than gasoline has risen. A local wholesale coal dealer tells me, in April 1975, he is paying between $40 and $50 a ton at minehead for pea anthracite, and delivered, it runs up to about $65 per ton. Gasoline sells at my dock for 55.9 cents a gallon.

Tons are still tons, gallons are still gallons. The old 1 pound to 1 hp to 1 hour figure is sustainable as a fact of physics because nature laid down coal in pretty consistent quality with respect to carbon and ash content. If ash content is higher, the pounds per hp/hour might rise to 1-1/4 to 1-1/3 pound/hp. If you can subtract your road tax refund to get at your actual per-gallon cost, and use the $65 per ton delivered upset price for pea coal, which works out at 2.9 cents per pound, then multiply this by the continuous horsepower rating of your engine (which you should know if you keep records), you can find out what producer gas would cost you as a substitute fuel. Just multiply this hp rating by the 2.9 cents and you have the cost of producing gas, exclusive of the investment in plant.

High-speed engines of today that run on reduction gears have a pretty constant cubic foot/minute intake, even when throttled, because "on the gear" the rotative speed is high, and so these engines would work all right on producer gas. The thing to be avoided in the producer is wide fluctuations in draft. The expansion chamber takes care of ordinary backing and docking.

Gasoline weighs 6.17 pounds per gallon. With the usual accessories and power take-offs, a fuel consumption rate of .5 pound/hp/hour is the usual engineering rule-of-thumb figure for gasoline consumption. Thus, one gallon of gasoline should provide 12.34 hp for 1 hour.

An equivalent weight of coal will provide 6.17 hp for an hour. Coal is heavier, no doubt about it. But the pound of coal at 2.9 cents times 12.34 (hp) will be pocketbook drain of but 35 cents for the energy contained in 55-cent (or whatever) gasoline. These are conservative outside figures. I think the older ratios will come closer to the actual truth. These modern penny figures seem larger all of a sudden, because we have been comparing older money values. And in these last calculations, we have upped coal values 8 times, and gasoline values but 4 times. Your actual local values will establish applicable ratios.

I show in Figure 4 a 1922 tabulation of relative economies in all types of marine power for that time, showing producer gas far out ahead. This was furnished by the Nelson Blower and Furnace Company of Boston, Mass., who built the Galusha Gas Producer through the 1920s.

A number of exciting developments now seem in the offing in relation to producer economies. For one thing, the knocking off of the depletion allowance for major oil producers is going to send fuel up another 25 percent very soon. Another thing that is exciting to any engineer is that the production of producer gas aboard ship is an exothermic reaction. The cost of the material consumed in producing the gas is only a fraction of the value of the heat yield of the gas. Usually the yield is four times that of the material consumed. Another plus is that lube oil seldom needs changing. It stays bright and clear. The exhaust is colorless and practically odorless, smelling only of hot oily metal. Producer gas has no propensity to detonation and will stand high compression ratios.

I wouldn't be surprised if diesels could be used on producer gas if the injectors could be taken out and spark ignition threaded into the old

FUEL COSTS OF ALL KINDS OF POWER PLANTS
65-Horse Power

TYPE OF Plant	Fuel Used In 300 Ten-Hour Days or 3,000 Hours	Cost of Fuel at Price Named	
Steam	487.5 tons (2,000 lbs) of coal	$ 5/T $10/T	$ 2,437.50 4,875.00
Steam Oil Fired	30,643 gals. of oil	4¢/gal. 7¢/gal.	$ 1,225.90 2,145.00
Diesel Engine	13,000 gals. of oil	5¢/gal. 7¢/gal. 10¢/gal.	$ 650.00 910.00 1,300.00
Semi-Diesel Engine	19,500 gals. of oil	5¢/gal. 7¢/gal. 10¢/gal.	$ 975.00 1,365.00 1,950.00
Kerosene Engine or Gasoline Engine	24,375 gals. of oil	7¢/gal. 10¢/gal. 12¢/gal.	$ 1,686.25 2,437.50 2,925.00
Gasoline Engine or Kerosene Engine	24,375 gals. of oil	15¢/gal. 20¢/gal. 30¢/gal. 40¢/gal. 50¢/gal.	$ 3,656.25 4,875.00 7,312.50 9,750.00 12,187.00
GALUSHA Gas Producer with Gas or Gasoline Engine	97.5 tons of coal or charcoal 146 tons of Breeze coke	$ 5/T $10/T $20/T $ 1/T $ 2/T	$ 487.50 975.00 1,950.00 146.25 292.50

Figure 4.

injector seats. This is pure speculation on my part, as I have no schio-metric curves, nor do I know the kindling temperature of producer gas.

The disadvantages? Coal is dirty. It is heavy. It does require some attention. Liquid fuels provide at a carburetor or an injection jet a pre-manufactured hydrocarbon of standard quality. They are more convenient. They are more available in more places than is coal. And— Brother, here's the rub—they are going to be frightfully expensive in the immediate near future. I could gleefully shovel coal if I thought it would unseat some Bedouins on the Sinai desert from their Arabian horses as they rush about yelling "ki-yi-yi-yi-yi!" and waving their spears.

The thing that knocked producer gas sideways was World War I, as I see matters. There were three or four years, from about 1917 to 1921, when war economy gave way to "hang-the-cost" thinking. War surplus fuel, engines, and boats were dumped by the government. Cheap marine equipment was put into use, and the diesel came in with it. Cheap heavy oil prompted development of the higher-priced diesel engine. Today, I think the initial reasons for the diesel have been lost sight of.

If your boat is 40 to 45 feet long or better, and is of the displacement type, which is a good load carrier, the added weight of coal and producer equipment should not set her down in the drink much more than 2 to 4 inches. Boats of this size and above, operating at S/L ratios the hull likes, will return handsome savings. The coal can be packaged or sacked, and need not be too dirty—no more than the average home basement is on coal firing.

If the service is constant, modern high-rpm gasoline engines on reduction gears have about the same cubic foot/minute intake as the smooth, old, heavy-duty clunkers. They will work. The whole idea is *compatibility*. If your boat is a hog-nosed, ham-sterned speederino, forget producer gas. It is the attempt to apply gas to this type of hull that has resulted in sporadic failures. Producer gas will never fly your dory.

Don't knock producer gas—I was a typical scoffer, as are many naval architects and marine engineers, until I made a cruise in "prior art." What I have learned has surprised me, as I believe it will you.

22

Producer Gas, Part II

Come with me on a speculative venture. We are about to resurrect the lost art of coal-gas generator design. There'll be millions in it.

After we get some basic engineering savvy about this new-old fuel for running boats, we'll incorporate. You can be President and General Manager, and I'll be your Consulting Engineer. Then we'll issue stock in our Great Consolidated Fuel Cost Cheater and go into manufacturing.

Shortly, we'll sell the company at a profit of $14,000,000 and retire to the Sandwich Islands, where all the girls are beautiful and the sandwiches are free.

It is presumed you have read my yarn about producer gas in the last chapter. In that loose and rambling dissertation, I pointed out the enormous savings once possible in the heavy boat field in the use of a gas producer plant. These things burned anthracite pea coal to make a gas right aboard the boat—well, you've read the story, so I won't go into that.

But there was one area I left untouched. You'll remember that producer gas would never fly your dory; it was stated that there were limitations, but that if the boat was compatible with the limitations ·inherent in the weight of a producer gas plant, and in the kind of service where running all-out or trolling was your bag, and if you were an operator of the right temperament, producer gas would work. It could save you over half your fuel bill. I left that part of the pitch up in the air, stating I'd show you how to judge compatibility.

We have arrived at that point, and I, being your Consulting Engineer, will now issue a feasibility report.

One of the first essentials of a high-grade feasibility report is that it is wise to start with known facts that prove our Great Consolidated Fuel Cost Cheater is already feasible, and that it was in wide use 60 years ago.

To prove my point about prior feasibility, let me present the State of the Art as advanced in 1914 by the Wolverine Motor Works of Bridge-port, Conn. This company made a fine old internal-combustion engine that was ideal for working on producer gas. It was used in conjunction with the Galusha Marine Gas Producer, built in Boston by the Nelson Blower and Furnace Co. to designs drawn by A.L. Galusha, a marine engineer and naval architect of that city. Here, word for word, is the 1914 Wolverine statement about feasibility:

**Wolverine Marine Engines in combination with
Marine Gas Producers.
The most economical source
of power known.**

The marine gas producer is a well built, strong, substantial and carefully designed device that will withstand the hardest usage during the lifetime of any gas engine. In design, it is a radical departure from the usual land-producer which has been tried repeatedly for marine work, but which has been found too heavy and bulky for practical use.

Our marine producer plant consists of the *generator*, made of heavy steel plates lined with special high grade firebrick behind which is a special heat resisting and insulating material. The grate is of such design that it allows of cleaning easily.

The apparatus, other than the generator and the scrubber, consists of a plunger pump for supplying water to the scrubber and fire tools for cleaning the fire.

Fuel is supplied to the producer while the engine is in operation by means of a special form of coal hopper on top of the producer.

The *scrubber* is a device for cooling and drying the gas and removing from it ashes, tar or any other substances that should not pass through the engine valves. A series of glass tubes, acting as gauges, show at all times the exact condition of the scrubber device. Should any part need attention, the glasses will indicate it and give ample notice before the satisfactory working of the plant would be interfered with.

Reliability, Durability, Low Fuel Consumption, and Low Attendant Cost are the features of the marine producer in combination with the "Wolverine" engines.

The fire in the producer once lighted does not require being withdrawn for a considerable length of time. Plants have been run for six months and more without ever drawing the fire, and it then was still in as good condition as when first lighted.

Heat from the producer is in no way objectionable, even in tropical climates as the generator is air-tight and insulated with a heavy fire brick lining backed with a special heat resisting material, and further, moisture is introduced with the intake of air below the grate to prevent high temperatures in the fuel bed. This at the same time prevents the formation of clinkers and enriches the gas.

Method of operation—a fire is kindled in the generator and supplied with the fuel that is to be used—anthracite coal, coke or charcoal, and the gas is initially generated by means of an external hand blower or mechanically operated fan until such time as the gas can be lighted at a place provided on the generator or alongside the engine. After the engine is started on the gas and is in operation, the plant works automatically, the draft through the fuel bed being maintained by the suction of the engine pistons which draw the air through the fire, forming a gas and carrying it through the scrubber into the mixing valve alongside the engine at which place it is combined with the proper quantity of air, and exploded by means of the electric spark produced in connection with the "Wolverine" mechanical igniter.

The time required for building a new fire in a producer and getting gas of sufficient quantity for operation will not exceed one-half to one hour, after which the fire can be maintained for periods of as long as six months or more, in good condition. The time required for starting the plant, after a considerable layover, is from ten to thirty minutes.

In operation, the producer requires fresh fuel at intervals of one to three or four hours, depending upon the service in which the boat is engaged.

The producer can be filled and the fire allowed to remain for periods of as long as one week without attention if the boat is not in use.

There is no pressure on the gas anywhere outside of the engine as the apparatus works under slight vacuum. The danger from explosion, therefore, is absolutely eliminated.

The consumption of fuel in the producer when not in operation is practically nothing as it is only what is burned by natural draft through a small pipe with practically all air to the producer cut off.

Kind of Fuel Required—The Marine Gas Producer will operate equally well at sea or in river service, and practically any anthracite coal, pea size, lumps about 1/2 inch (13 mm), gas-coke or charcoal can be used as fuel.

Fuel Consumption—The fuel consumption of pea-size anthracite coal, working at full load, is only about one and one-quarter pounds (450 to 550 grams) per actual horsepower per hour, thus providing the *cheapest motive power in existence.*

Cost of Operation—Under actual working conditions, an operating cost equivalent to the cost of fuel oil at 3¢ (1-1/2 d.) (15 centimes) per gallon has been obtained, using anthracite costing $7.50 (£1-11-3) (Frs. 39.-) per ton of 2,000 pounds (910 kilos).

Economy—The saving in fuel cost is such that the difference in first cost is soon made up and the saving then becomes a large return on the investment.

Demonstrated Practicality—This device has been successfully operated, without the employment of skilled attendants, in commercial service in connection with the Wolverine engine since 1911 both in commercial fisheries at sea and in freight transportation at sea and on rivers, thus proving it to be entirely practical.

Flexibility of the Engine—The control of the engine in connection with the producer is very flexible and can be varied at the will of the operator. The engine, in fact, has all the niceties of control of a steam plant and the manoeuvering qualities are extraordinary.

Twin Screw Outfits—Installations can be furnished either for single or twin screw; in single units from 18 hp to 175 actual H.P., in twin screw units up to 350 actual H.P.

Where twin screw units are used, one producer only is necessary.

This is the end of the Wolverine feasibility report, stripped at the end of selling talk for their engines. These engines were of the old heavy-duty 300-400 rpm type and were nothing special for their time except they were heavy and long lived and reliable. Today's internal-combustion engines are lighter, have higher piston speeds, and slightly higher compression ratios (which does not matter with gas), and they aspirate on the intake just the same as did the older engines.

So there you have the mechanical feasibilities. What about the economic ratios of 60 years ago and today? If you will take a look at Figure 4 in the last chapter, you will see a compilation of costs prepared in 1922 by the Nelson Blower and Furnace Co. of Boston, who made the Galusha Producer. You can apply the ratios in this compilation to today's cost of liquid fuels, and the ratios will very nearly hold. Coal and liquid fuels have jumped in price. You now have something by which to assess feasibility, both mechanical and economic in nature.

This brings us to the matter of compatibility. If you take a look at the installation diagram in Figure 1, you will see the relative sizes of the Galusha gas producer in various horsepowers. From these figures you can measure the space needed in your vessel to accommodate the producer shell. As to the bunkering capacity needed, here are some measuring sticks: you'll need about 40 to 43 cubic feet per 2,000 pounds of pea anthracite. This quantity of coal will provide 1,600 to 2,000 horsepower hours. If, say, you have a 100 hp engine, rated 100 hp on continuous duty, divide the 1,600 hp hours by 100, and you get 16 hours of full-bore running, or 20 hours, as the case may be. The criterion is the application of 1-1/4 pound/hp/hour, or 1 pound/hp/hour. This figure gives the length of time the 2,000 pounds of coal will last. From the length of time you'll need to run your engine, you can gauge the number of tons of coal to be bunkered.

You will notice, from the table of weights, that a producer gas plant was heavy. Surprisingly, when the Galusha Producer was introduced, the fact that it weighed only one quarter the "gravitational component" of a steam plant and took but one third the space was considered an engineering marvel. By today's engineering standards, it should be obvious that a great deal of weight can be saved in the shell and piping, which might be of aluminum. Nothing could be done about the weight of coal, or, probably, about the weight of the refractory lining or iron firebox. You can see, by checking the weights, that your dory will not fly with producer gas, let alone a DC-10!

So this puts the usage proposition clearly down to compatibility, not to mere feasibility. Your boat must be large enough to be comfortable with the added weight.

If an aluminum shell and aluminum pipes could be used instead of steel, a producer shell weighing but 45 to 55 percent of the Galusha shell figures could be built. You'd need the cast iron firebox and grate. The refractory brick would protect an aluminum shell, I should think.

Now, if you subtract your tank weight and your fuel oil or gasoline weight, as in your present boat, and next add in the weight of the producer plant and coal, you'll come up with a moderate increase in total displacement. Can your boat handle this? Will she sink into the drink too much?

The secret lies in the size of your boat's waterplane as shown in Figure 2. The way to determine how much your vessel will sink with added weight is as follows: Get a close measurement on her actual

Figure 1. The dimensions, weights, and horsepower of Galusha Gas Producers are shown on this page from the Wolverine Motor Works catalog.

WEIGHTS

H. P.	18	27	40	50	65	75	100	150	200	250	300	350
Export Measurement (Cubic Feet)	75	110	130	175	200	224	290	405	540	675	840	995
Net Weight (Pounds)	1800	2500	3500	3900	5400	6000	7000	11250	15000	18750	22500	27000
Gross Weight (Pounds)	2400	4025	4200	4800	6150	7500	8500	14600	17000	21800	26500	32000
Weight of Coal Capacity (Pounds)	330	475	750	950	1400	1760	2300	4600	5550	8850	9300	9900

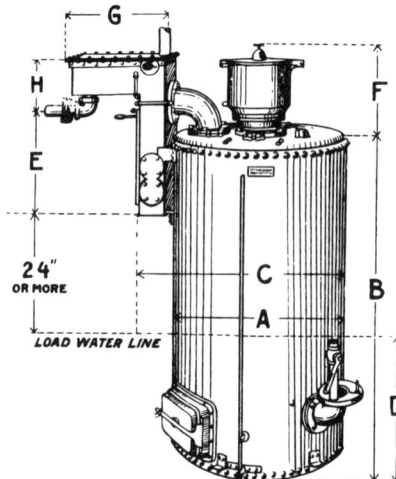

DIMENSIONS--MARINE GAS PRODUCERS (in inches)

H. P.	18	27	40	50	65	75	100	150	200	250	300	350
A	31	35	41	45	49	55	61	73	79	91	97	103
B	62	62	63	63	75	75	75	87	87	99	111	111
C	41	45	51	55	59	65	71	92	98	110	117	122
D	This varies and depends on the boat installation in each case											
E	36	36	36	36	48	48	48	50	50	55	55	55
F	18	18	18	18	18	18	18	18	24	24	24	24
G	28	28	28	28	30	30	30	40	40	42	42	42
H	12½	12½	13	13	13	13½	14	22½	7	7	8	8

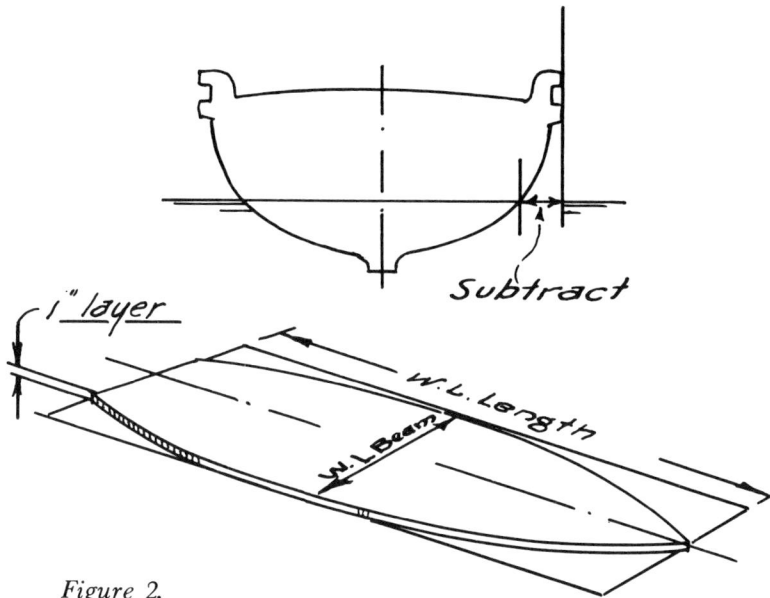

Figure 2.

waterline length. Then by dropping a plumb line over the guards at the point of greatest beam, measure back from the plumb line to the hull side. Multiply this by 2 for both sides, and subtract this from the overall beam. This will give you the actual waterplane beam. By multiplying this beam by the waterline length, you will come up with rectangular measurement in square feet.

Here, to get the estimated waterplane area, you have to apply a percentage. If your boat has a shoebox shape, pointed at one end and slab-sided the rest of the way, use a multiplier of .70, or 70 percent of the rectangular area. If you have a normal West Coast type of troller, say, of the guttsy-buttsy wide-sterned type, your hull will probably have sufficient trail toward the stern end to use a .65 to .68 factor with fairly accurate results. If she tends toward a double-ender, with sharp waterlines aft, use a factor of around .58 to .60. The resulting figure will be a close approximation of the waterplane area of your hull.

What you are trying to determine is the actual square feet of the waterplane slab that will be one inch thick. This can be turned into the number of pounds it will take to sink your boat one inch. You now have the number of square feet in a one-inch slab of water the size of your vessel. If you divide this figure by 12, it will give you the number of cubic feet contained in the area. One square foot of base area 12 inches high is a cubic foot.

When you get the number of cubic feet in the waterplane, multiply by 64 pounds for salt water, or 62.5 pounds for fresh water. This difference in calculation is frequently overlooked. To emphasize the difference, look at Figure 3, showing one cubic foot of fresh water.

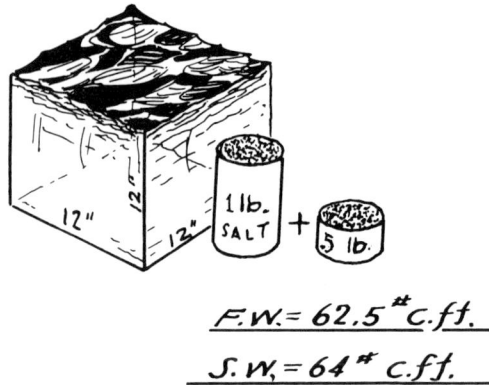

$$F.W. = 62.5^{\#}\ c.ft.$$

$$S.W. = 64^{\#}\ c.ft.$$

Figure 3.

Alongside it, in direct isometric proportion, is a 1-pound box of salt, along with another one-half pound of the same stuff. Sea water consists of fresh water with this amount of salt in every cubic foot of it. Odd, to think of the titanic amount of salt in the ocean. And all you ever see is just the surface!

Use either the 64 factor, or the 62.5 factor, depending on the water in which your vessel is used. You will come up with a "pounds per inch immersion" number. This shows the amount of weight it will take to sink your boat one inch. Next, take the weight you come up with for the coal and producer plant, over the bare weight with the tanks and liquid fuel load removed, and you will have the net weight to be added by using a producer plant.

Can your boat handle it? Will she be compatible, and lug the load? Or will she be set down in the water so far as to kill her?

Divide this added weight by the pounds per inch immersion and you have the amount of sinkage due to added load. Say, for illustration, your pounds per inch immersion is 1,000 pounds. The added producer gas increment will tot up to 1,500 pounds. By dividing the 1500 by 1000, the answer is 1.5, the number of inches of draft or sinkage added.

From Figure 1 and its tables you can get an idea of the proportions of various horsepower sizes required in the producer shell. If you are of a mind to experiment with building your own gas producer and want to calculate the pipe sizes and so on, and are puzzled by the function of the scrubber, take a look at the sectional schematic in Figure 4 and compare it with the isometric rendering in Figure 1. In Figure 4, as in the Figure 1 producer, air enters the ash pit enriched by an admixture of water trickling into the warm elbow. The ash pit is entered by a door dogged airtight for cleaning and grate shaking. The air goes up through the fire bed through the stages depicted and into the scrubber. Here the curtain of fine water spray cools the gas, which is baffled to go under water, and which traps most of the ash and all of the sulphurs emitted by the coal in gasification. Then the gas goes on through an adsorbing bed of charcoal sticks and twigs and pea-sized lumps that expose a lot of carbon surface to the gas. Note that the word is *ad*sorb—not *ab*sorb. The two actions are very different.

Sponges *absorb* by taking water into their structure. Carbon *adsorbs* by a surface chemical affinity for certain ammonic nitrous and some sulphuric traces that are undesirable. There will always be some of both nitric oxides and sulphurous compounds in coal. The function of the scrubber is very important.

The diagram is a reconstruction of the probable Galusha patented method, a copy of which is not at hand and which was issued sometime between 1910 and 1914 to A.L. Galusha of Boston, Mass. The diagram

Figure 4.

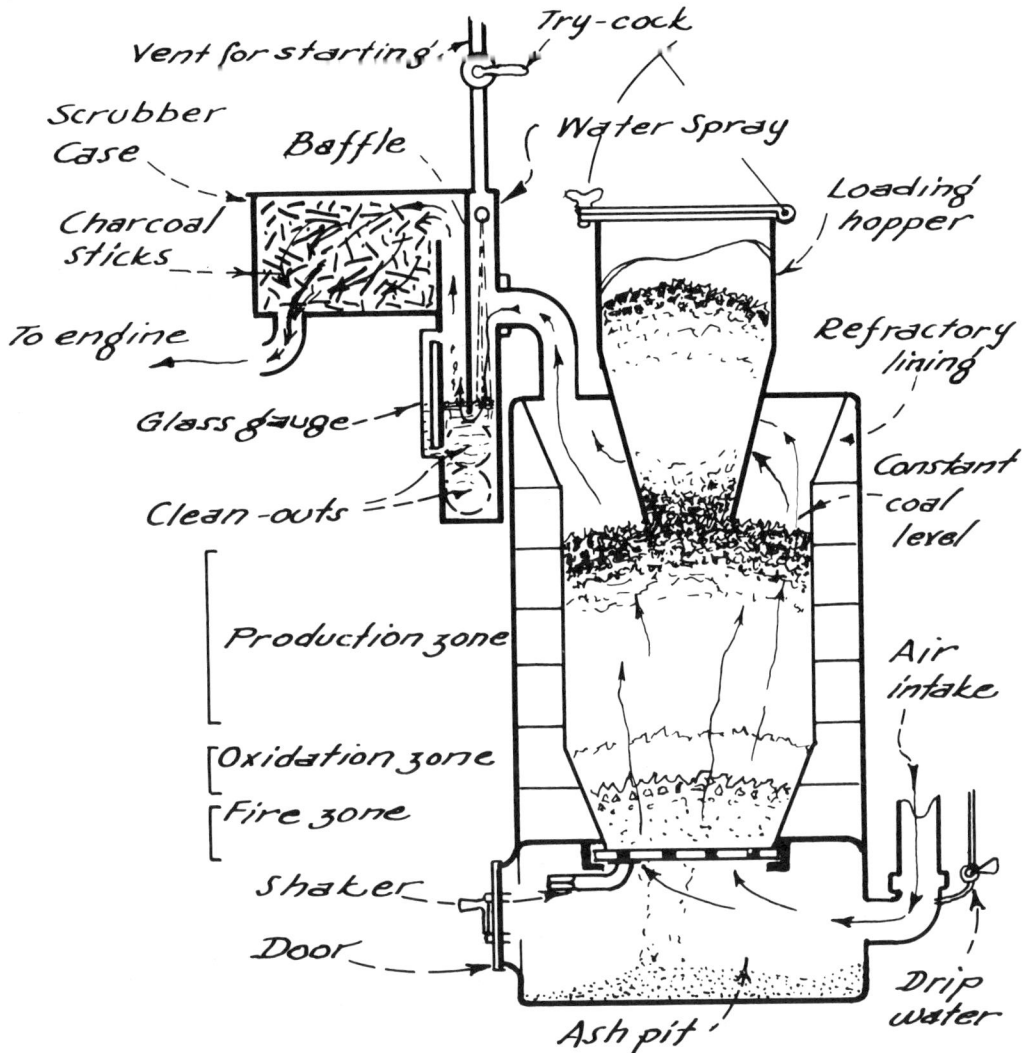

is schematic, applying the known scrubber cycle required in other plants. It may be that Galusha used a triplicate passage going athwartship rather than the unit passage diagrammed.

Although no mention is made in old technical references about the use of salt water versus fresh water in the scrubber, it is apparent that any R & D resurrection of this lost art would find that the scrubber case would have to be built of bronze sheet. Any seaman knows what ordinary sea water does to black iron. Under the heat of incoming gases, the corrosion might be most "corrodstipating," as I heard one sailor term it. It would seem prudent to build the scrubber out of cuprous metal—and hope for the best. Aluminum might do, too. It is at home in salt water.

From the charcoal end of the scrubber the gas is led by engine suction to the engine mixing valve. At the intake manifold of the engine, the coal gas is mixed in 1:1 proportion with air.

It should be obvious that with today's updated engineering knowledge we could beat weight by a considerable margin.

I like the suction gas idea better than some of the esoteric revolving grate notions that have been advanced, because the feasibility is already there, demonstrated, and proved generally workable in installations where boats of the peon variety find service—the luggers, the chuggers that do the hard work in the world, run by skippers who also are compatible to a little hard life in handling coal, and who don't mind what they look like so long as their bank accounts can buy out the Captains-Snooty-Off-The-Yachts.

You can see there are possibilities in reducing this proposition to practice again. We'll have to hurry and issue our stock and get our patents, though. Some kid with a wheelbarrow and a cold chisel and a couple of oil barrels who lives up on the malodorous waters of Clamtide Creek might beat us to it!

23

Where Have All the Old Marine Engines Gone?

Take an antique chair and sit in it. You'll find yourself exclaiming, "If this old thing could talk, what a story it could tell!" Sadly, it can't tell you a thing. But fire up an ancient marine engine, and she'll tell you plenty, in just the same voice she told the world of 60 or 70 years ago. "Klickety, klackety, binggety, banggety," she'll twitter, and then murmur it all over again with the unhurried deliberation of an octopus laying brick. Klickety klack.

You'll get the thrill of history talking to you, right out loud. If you are lucky enough to have been alive and aware of boats when every maker of trunk furniture or kitchenware or stove lids was making marine engines as a sideline, you'll get the old engine's message.

"I'm a motor, mister. Good to be alive again. Give me exactly eight parts of air to one of gasoline; give me a spark, and I'll run to eternity and one month more. I'm a motor that motes!"

She will be, too. She may be an old four-cycler, or a two-cycler with two- or three-port aspiration, but she'll turn a prop nearly the diameter of her flywheel. This will shove a boat along in unhurried but purposeful rush, bespeaking the authority of irresistible real horses tolerating no nonsense about the business. Clydesdale-type horsepower, or Belgian mares—not this hysterical Shetland pony stuff.

Probably this is why many of today's young men are so surprised when they can get a ride in a powerboat powered by the urge of a motor that was deliberately designed to push a boat at the speed the hull wants. The boat will nestle down in her element and slide along as she should. The newcomer to the feel will leap out enthused after the ride.

If one of these fellows happens to be a wise young man, not blinded by the juvenile doctrine that nothing in the world was worth a shuck until he was born, he'll exclaim, "Now that's comfort! And reliability. I'd like to have one. Where have all these old engines gone?"

There are plenty of fellows, alive and kicking and in good health today, who saw these old beauties in service and know that, historically, the marine engine was the parent of the automobile engine and has a fascinating story to unfold.

So there is more to the fad of collecting old engines than might be classified as a small-boy desire to collect Civil War cannons just to hear them bang. The marine engine romance is much richer.

The Mohawk model S-24, a 5-6-hp high-speed racing engine, turned over an earthshaking 1200 rpm at "normal speed." It was billed as "unexcelled for small boats where speed is desired."

What man who has been shipmates with an old, genuine marine gasoline engine doesn't remember their charm? Slow turning—so slow you could count the revolutions by eye when throttled down. They were designed by steam engine designers at the outset, and many had open bases with parts whirring in plain sight and cylinder walls a half-inch thick to handle the bang. The wall had to be "close-grained gray iron" to avoid being confused with Gruyere cheese, which is what most iron was then: malleable. The weights ranged from 50 to 85 pounds per horsepower, and revs ran from 450 to 800, 'wide open. A 1,000-rpm motor was considered dangerously fly-apart—raceboat stuff.

Who doesn't remember keeping the two-cycler's main bearings tight with Albany Grease, in brass grease cups, to avoid crankcase sneeze? Albany Grease was a yellow, soaplike gunk with an odor resembling a sweaty shoe full of hot applesauce. The smell wasn't what the barber sprinkled on Daddy—'twas more like elderly finnan haddie.

A crescent wrench, a pair of pliers, and a screwdriver made up a full tool kit. And they had glass oilers, with drip sight! All piping was standard gas pipe stuff. Half-inch, three-quarters, or one inch. Spark? Generally make and break, which was hot enough to light a cigarette.

Once in a while, of course, the best of them would balk. They were impervious to cussing, so you'd have to out-think them and get on a mental basis with their psyches. One good treatment was to pull 'em up on compression and walk away. They might get lonesome and start on the spark before you'd collected your presence of mind.

I remember one old one-lunger that exhibited definite feminine characteristics. When hot, she'd work with a right good will. I believe that motor would have run on greasy dishwater. But cold, she wouldn't start and had the enthusiasm of a freshly dredged clam.

I got tired of this nonsense and invented a cure. I made a quick-detachable, side base plate. Taking this off, I'd throw in a few fingersful of cotton waste dipped in gasoline and light it. As the fire burned down to ashes in her crankcase, I'd close the base and give her a twist. This worked better than all the perfumes of Nirvana. Yep, them were the days!

Let me explain to younger men why old marine engines are fascinating. I'll try to explain in terms that young men can grasp. For this exposition, we have to make a surprising statement: from the standpoint of good naval architecture, most of today's boats are floating garbage—chrome-plated. Classic dicta of naval architectural theory, and demonstrated best practice, go unrecognized in today's showroom

General installation plan of Standard marine engines.

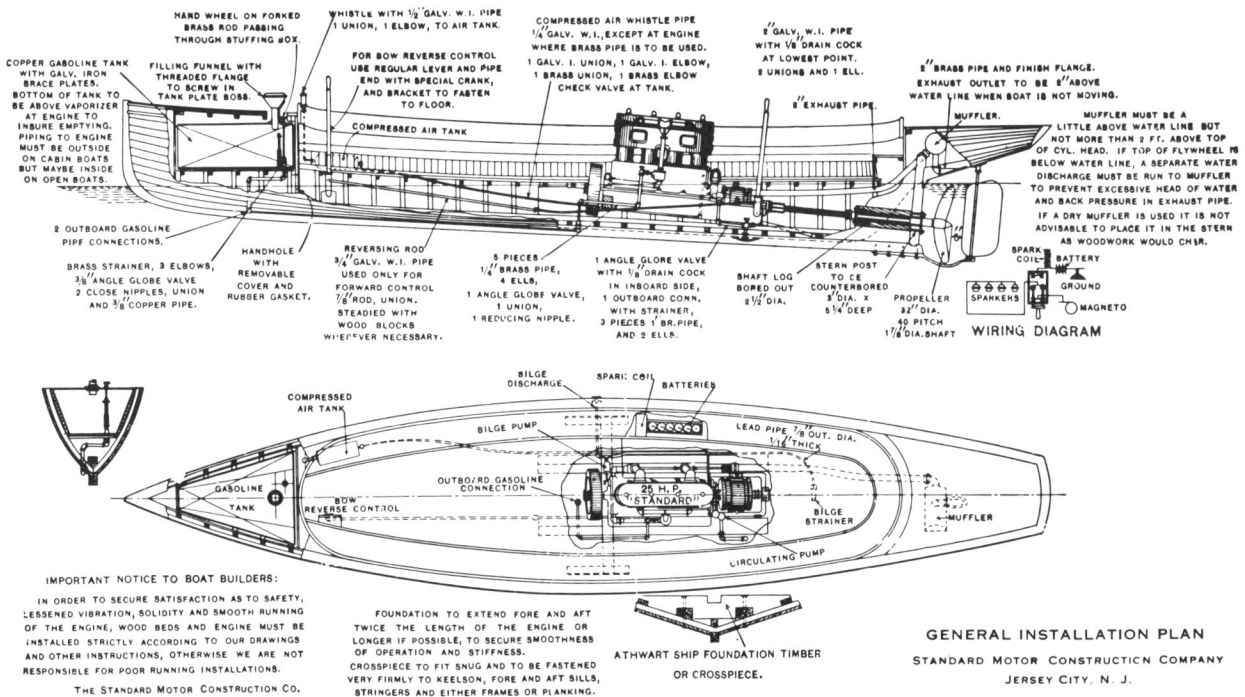

products (which is the kind I am talking about), and most of the "cruisers" are designed by—women!

The result of sales-oriented notebook eavesdropping at boat shows has developed boats that are broad-sterned, way overloaded for their lengths, and require horsepower that cheers the directors of oil companies. We are getting boats of planing, or hydroplane type, that won't plane because they are too heavy, too short, too wide. They may float on a morning dew, but they can't go much of anywhere without ducking in for weather, because unless they travel fast enough for the transom to clear, you can't steer them. At such speeds in following seas, they are hopeless. The design direction is both silly and tragic.

I know the reason for this, because I was there, Charlie. I have designed for, or served as naval architect in, 25 yacht-building plants. Some of these produced luxury cruisers. At shows, the management exhorted salesmen to eavesdrop and take notes. Later, planning new models, the notes thus taken, plus the bleats of dry-land salesmen, would be dumped into the hopper, and each succeeding year's models would depart further from the precepts of good naval architecture— victims to talk overheard on the showroom floor. The process, still going on, would go like this:

"I want more beam for greater stability." This is a perennial lulu, right from the mouth of some hay-tosser who has just harvested a bonanza bean crop.

"I gotta have more speed," comes from some fireman who has ridden the stern end of a hook-and-ladder and now, as newly elected mayor, is telling the boat what to do.

"My wife wants a bigger 'kitchen.' Our 'kitchens' have always been big ones, and we have six kids. We've gotta sleep eight people." So, this guy's wife sets the design trend. She gets a "kitchen" and room for an impending addition or two—all on a length of about 25 feet.

The results, from the standpoint of good naval architecture, are simply horrendous. What is produced is, foolishly, more beam; speed of a mile more with doubled horsepower and gas consumption; shorter lengths because dockage—instead of being based on cubage—is on a per-foot basis; a galley that is a kitchen; and extensively extendable extensions that masquerade as bunks. The resulting boat may be Gussie enough, but as a boat should be classed as a planked-up beer parlor.

Then next year's ads come out: "Only Whatsis could build more beam, more stability, more speed into the luxurious barracuda or hilton-de-gink or sardine, etc." Great-suffering-little-pink-fiddler-crabs! What childish crowing!

Now, any boat is better than no boat at all, and I am not quarreling with the bean-grower or the hook-and-ladder man, or the guy with the demanding wife. I am merely explaining why boats get this way. Back in Dad's day, it was different! Boats then were built, not manufactured. And when boatbuilders were in an honored trade, they were close to the water, knew what worked, and how to design to get it that way. Any customer who told an established boatbuilder how much he'd have to have in such and such a length, or how much speed, would be shown the door. The boat told the builder what was wanted, and the builder, with his name riding on the referral trade from a good boat, stayed within the dictates of good naval architecture. And the classic rules for good naval architecture were brought into the boatshop from the sea.

The rules had been evolved through centuries of experience, and were simple. Basically, a fat boat was anything over a beam-to-length ratio of one to four. Fat boats were stable, but the fatter, the slower. Slimmer boats, with beams one-fifth the length, moved through the water more easily. The narrower, within limits, the faster. This was admittedly rule-of-thumb, but it worked. From sail through steam, to the first naphtha and electric launches, these old rules worked and were found by experiments a hundred years ago in the then-new technology of the towing tank to depend on one fact: if you took the square root of the waterline length of a normal boat, that root was the natural speed of the boat. This means the speed at which she moved at optimum rate for the most economical power invested. It was also learned in this way that speed could climb with added power, but diminishing economy, up to the factor where speed equalled 1.4 to 1.5 times the square root of the waterline length. After that, the resistance curve shot up into the sky, at an asymptotic climb.

To make power pay off in the quest for speed, the V-bottom was introduced, notably by William H. Hand, Jr., the New Bedford genius who took the Chesapeake diamond bottom and developed the first true V types. The V was shaped to lift; the hope was to plane—get on top of the water. Up to a point, this worked, but no boat will fully plane unless shaped right, and unless it weighs under 40 pounds per hp. A figure of 36 pounds/hp is safer. Few early boats approached this, and as any experienced designer knows, the V-bottom boat and the round-bilged boat are two different breeds of cat, having only one thing in common—they float. To attest to this truth, remember that round-bottomed boats heel out on a turn, V-bottoms heel inward. This should be a sufficient convincer that design similarities between the two fall in two separate realms. The V-bottom becomes more efficient than the round at speeds only above two and one-half times the square root of the waterline length.

What we are getting in stock boats are planing types that won't plane. And this is not anything to take to sea. Such a shape has only

One way to make big engines out of small ones was to place cylinders in line—with most of the bits and pieces that would be used on a one-lunger included on all four cylinders. This is a 60-hp Fay and Bowen convertible kerosene-gasoline engine with reverse clutch. Spark and throttle control was made to operate from either end. The throttle operated the vaporizors on each cylinder, but the throttle on an individual cylinder could be cut out separately, if desired.

one advantage: as a shoe box; the showroom accommodations can be packed in.

Builders of the first motorboats understood the square-root law, so the first motorboats, being of normal form, were quite content with 4, 5, 6, or 8 mph. It didn't take much power to get this speed. That is why all early gasoline motorboat engines were of low power. Into this early thinking was carried a very good steamboat rule-of-thumb theory that a propeller, to command the boat, should have a disc area equal to one-fourth the area of the immersed midsection. This is still the rule that produces the most satisfactory propeller action, and I am using this rule on large yachts today. The early engines were deliberately designed to handle this torque requirement.

Thus you will see that early marine engines had a definite load factor to which they were designed: low speed with plenty of muscle to handle a sizable propeller. That is the reason, interpreted from today's viewpoint, for the old-fashioned slow-speed charm these old workhorses had. Dad knew what a good boat and a good boat ride was. Much in the good life has been killed by the shibboleth of Efficiency!

No story about antiques is complete without some of the flavor of history. Here, I borrow from Rudyard Kipling, who wrote he'd had six serving men who taught him all he knew. Their names were What and Why and When, and How and Where and Who. I've introduced four of these, now meet When and Who.

The first gasoline motors ever built were built for boats. In Tom

Built by the Union Engine Works of San Francisco in 1884, this first motorboat engine was tested on city illuminating gas and had ordinary Globe check valves converted to inlet and exhaust valves. This engine was later adapted to "gasoline vapor" intake and offered on the market. Carryover from steam is evident.

Edison's heyday, university laboratory experimenters had discovered that the power of explosive vapors climbed into the dynamite realm if compressed four or five or six times. A number of men started experimenting with the idea of superseding the steam engine by burning the fuel right inside the engine. A daring concept! In Germany, Dr. Rudolph Diesel hit on the idea of compressing fossil fuels in atomized form under high ratios, using the heat of compression to ignite the charge. His first engine, using powdered coal, blew to pieces.

Nikolaus August Otto, in Germany, conceived the four-stroke cycle and built an engine. Gottlieb Daimler, also in Germany, also built an engine. All of these were for marine use. In 1884, in San Francisco, steam engine designers at the Old Union Engine Works cobbled together the first marine engine built in this country. It was merely a cylinder with a crank attached to a large flywheel, on an adequate base, sparked by a make-and-break igniter, up which a piston traveled to compress city illuminating gas. No automobiles were then known, so this old Union was for a boat, and later, here and there, a few men started dreaming of building internal-combustion engines, looking to the marine field for their outlet.

During the Gay Nineties, the naphtha launch, and particularly Elco's electric launch, whetted demand to a pitch that could not be denied. Powered boats were "in." Termaat and Monahan of Oshkosh, Winconsin, started building cheap, two-cycle engines; so did Arthur Caille, a builder of one-arm-bandit slot machines in Detroit. In 1903, a young Ohio engineer named E.W. Roberts published in *Rudder* magazine, "How to Build a 3 h.p. Launch Engine." Soon, everybody was in the business. Within two years, the May 1905 issue of *Rudder* carried ads for, and illustrations of, 63 separate makes of marine engines.

In 1905, the Brooks Boat Company of Bay City, Michigan, sold 10,686 knocked-down launches, having sold over 6,000 the year before. The Medart Boat Company of St. Louis sold over 5,000 similar kits. At the same time, another outfit called the Michigan Steel Boat Co. was listed as larger than either of these other companies. Somebody had to supply motors for these boats.

Somebody did. And that is why there are some of them still around.

24

The First Gas-Powered Marine Engines

You can start an hour or two of absorbing speculation by pondering answers to the question: "Of all the inventions that have benefited mankind, which one would *you* choose to have invented?" By the word "invention," of course, one means a patentable artifact that you could spring on the world, then retire to a life of peace while growing comfortably rich.

If you pose the question to your crew in the dark of your wheelhouse some night as you sag back to port, you'll find that in each man among your companions there is a latent Willie Westinghouse Edison Marconi Bell. The answers to the question will range from the sublime to the ribald. Here are some that I've heard:

"The wheel!" No good—this was an evolution and did not upset an existing economy. Hence no patent, no royalties.

"The water closet!" The mantle of propriety must be lowered on that one.

"The steam engine!" You've got a good one there. Steam for more than a hundred years supplied the prime power supporting the entire Industrial Revolution. Steam amounted to little until James Watt improved its application with the condenser and double-acting piston. He became very wealthy.

"The electric light!" That's a dandy, and Edison's saga of devising glowing filaments of carbonized bamboo in an oxygen-starved bulb is known to almost everyone. So also is the struggle he experienced in wiring electricity to homes so that his flameless lamps could be used.

The list of enviable inventions is long: Bessemer's process for cheap steel production; Marconi and the wireless; the Wrights and the airplane; de Forest's vacuum tube. The responses of your friends will amaze you by their unsuspected variety.

Of all such great ideas, I would choose to have been the inventor of the internal-combustion engine. This device has supplanted steam, is responsible for the automotive rivers of metal choking our highways, and universally powers all of our modern fishing fleet and 99 percent of the world's pleasure craft. The wealth created by the telephone, the radio, and the electric light, in sum, is a weak whistle to the mighty blast of wealth founded on the internal-combustion engine. Consider it, then add to your obvious mental inventory also the roads it is responsible for, the cities, armies, navies, airlines, oilfields, and resulting power politics. No simple idea in the past one hundred years has so greatly altered the face of the earth as has the internal-combustion engine. All this has occurred within the lifetime of some men still living.

But who invented it? Do you know? Oh, sure—let's see, now—it was What's His Name? Back about 1872 or so—just over a hundred years. Let's see now, who the devil was he? Was it Sadi Carnot, the French engineer—not the politician? No, he schemed out the Carnot cycle showing the expansive characteristics of steam, and was earlier, 40 or 50 years or so, albeit he is known as the father of thermodynamic science. Was it Étienne Lenoir, the physicist? Around 1864? He had some sort of vapor engine using gunpowder for ignition, but he did not compress the gas, used no crank, and hence his "engine" was not efficient. Too feeble. Could it be Otto? The "Otto Four Stroke Cycle" was described in every post-1900 engineering and boating book, explaining the difference between a four-cycle and a two-cycle engine. Who, then, invented the two-cycle engine? Some one man had to be behind each of these ideas.

I had pondered this all my life in a vague way until just the other day the true inventor's name spilled at my feet. Cruising my chilly attic, which is lined knee high with engineering records and memorabilia on two sides of a 30-foot aisle, I knocked over a stack of old scientific papers. I had been trying to find out the first recorded advertisement showing the maker of an actual early gasoline motorboat engine. There, lying on the floor before me, was an 1876 supplement to the *Scientific American* magazine of that year containing a lay reporter's story of developments at the Paris Exhibition of 1876. His theme was a "Gun Pile Driver" type of internal-combustion engine, which he thought might interest his American readers for its novelty.

He little knew its importance! Facing me on the exposed page was a steeple-like engine pictured in an engraved cut. I would have ignored this had it not been evident that the flywheel and valve-chest signified

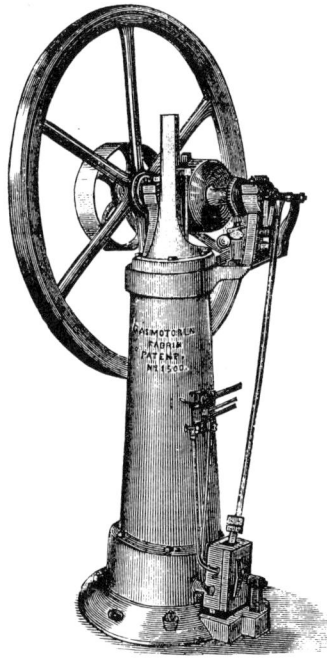

Figure 1. The first gas motor built by the N.A. Otto Co. in Dentz, Germany, was exhibited in 1876 at the Paris Exhibition.

"engine." The cut is reproduced here exactly as printed in 1876, just as I found it. (See Figure 1.) From this old paper, I learned a startling set of facts. Here was a description of the first workable, efficient, manufactured internal-combustion engine, telling how the first gas engine worked!

As a midwife to the marine design art for many years, I had never seen the true story. I doubt if many other engineers have, or that they ever concerned themselves with the engrossing human story behind the development. I read the text, which obviously was written by a man who was steam-engine oriented, then did some digging in various encyclopedias, of which research more a little later.

Here is the *Scientific American* yarn; it is word-for-word as printed. Some of the paragraphing is mine.

The Langen & Otto Gas Motor at the Exhibition

This is a Prussian exhibit, deserving of careful attention by all who desire to avail themselves of a good substitute for small steam engines.

An explosively acting gas-engine is in reality a gun, discharging shots whose force should be fully realized and converted into steady work. The "gun powder pile driver" is an instance in which explosive force is converted into work, and in which that explosive force would be fully utilized were it not that the bore of a gun is so short as to allow the gases to escape at very high pressure.

But in the gunpowder pile-driver the full recoil of the gun is at once realized and converted into work, and the force expended in driving the piston or shot to the top of the shears is all (less a trifle for friction) returned and used when that shot falls. The gunpowder pile-driver is, in fact, a single-acting explosive engine, with an "exhaust" of 500 lbs. pressure to the square inch.

If, now, it were possible (1) to exhaust at atmospheric pressure, (2) to prevent waste of force in a ruinous heating of the parts of the machine, and (3) to apply the explosive force to produce steady rotary motion, the gas-motor problem would be far towards a complete solution.

(1) To exhaust at a lower pressure, requires merely a lengthening of the gun. In the gunpowder engine the volume of the charge is increased by explosion from 1 to 2,000, hence the length of the stroke would have to be at least 2,000 times the depth of the charge.

The substitution for gunpowder of a gaseous explosive, in which the products of explosion are but eleven times the volume of the charge, would necessitate a length of stroke but little more than eleven times the depth of the charge.

(2) To prevent the heating of piston and cylinder, the action of the explosive force upon the piston must be unimpeded. The full amount of force is then expended in the increase of the volume of the gases, and the direct propulsion of the piston.

(3) To apply the great explosive force directly in actuating ordinary machinery, is impossible.

To utilize on the return stroke the force of the explosion stored up in the piston, is possible, but necessitates a special mechanical adaptation for its accomplishment.

In other words, the following features should, and it is claimed in this device do, find place in an economical engine: 1, a free piston; 2, great length of cylinder; 3, the entire abandonment of the crank (a device of itself, irregular in action and unsatisfactory in result, even in its use with a slow and steadily expanding motive agent, as steam).

The devices for aspiration, explosion and exhaust, may best be understood from the accompanying diagrams:

The engine is shown in elevation in Fig. 1. Fig. 2 is a vertical section of the lower portion through the slide valve. The piston f, being lifted about 1/11 the length of the stroke, gas and air are thereby drawn in through the channel x. The power to effect this movement is obtained from the momentum of the flywheel.

On the igniting of the charge, the piston flies freely up to the top. As it ascends, the plenum caused by the explosion changes to a partial vacuum, reaching 22" of mercury at the top of the stroke, and thus the motion of the piston is quickly reversed, and the down stroke is performed under a pressure of about 11 lbs. per square inch, derived from the atmosphere, this driving power being communicated to the rack and toothed wheel to the shaft.

When the piston has reached within a given distance of the bottom, the vacuum, which has gradually been decreasing, is again changed to a plenum, and the weight of the piston and rack expels the burnt gases during the last few inches of the stroke, thus completing the cycle of operations.

From this lucid, if involved description, the writer of 1876 then sails into the proposition of the clutch, which, as shown in Figure 3, is a wedge-and-roller rig, locking onto the shaft when the piston descends, and also containing a governor operated by pawl and cam. The description of this is prolix, and I'm inclined to hand the proposition a

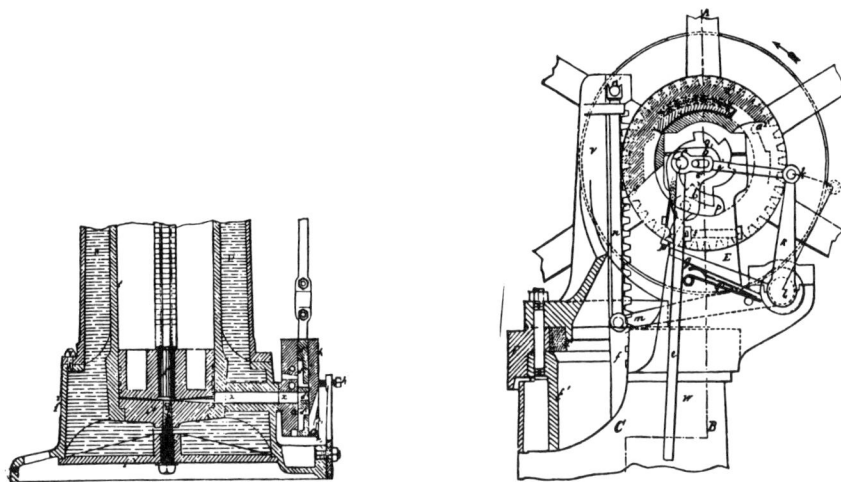

Figure 2 (left). A section through the Langen & Otto gas engine cylinder, showing slide valve porting and ignition system. *Figure 3 (right).* The rack-and-pinion clutching used to give single-direction rotation in the first workable gas engine.

high mark in verbal salad making—say, a B plus—and accept the fact that it worked because somebody drew it.

Immediately the thought occurs: how are you going to get a six-cylinder engine out of a stack of calliopes the pistons of which operate on load demand only, and are independent of each other? Aweel, this was the granddaddy of all gas engines, and granddads are notoriously unsophisticated and rustic.

One subsequent paragraph is worth quoting on the subject of ignition: "The igniting of gases is performed by the slide valve and two lighting jets, burning one before the other, in the valve itself, in the excavation d3. By the motion of the valve the space d3 first goes down and ignites its contents (gas and air) at the flame burning continually before the valve, then comes up to x where it ignites the charge."

Another paragraph gives an 1876 assessment of the engine from a steam man's point of view: "The Langen & Otto engine has the demerit of being noisy, and of requiring a very large cylinder. It has this great merit, that the governor may stop the motion of all parts except the flywheel and shaft. It starts with full power at a moment's notice; uses no fuel when not running, and but little when exerting only power enough to effect the regular rotation of the flywheel; requires but trifling attendance; gives no trouble with coal or ashes; requires very little water; is free from danger and does not affect insurances."

The power of this son of a gun was .86 hp! The atmospheric action provided 30 strokes per minute.

Now obviously this engine did not operate on the Otto 4-stroke cycle, which reads: induction of charge, compression of charge, power stroke, exhausting of burned charge—and repeat. This is the sublime principle that made Nikolaus August Otto's name famous, later earned him a doctorate, and is today, unchanged, the same principle on which your boat engine operates, and your automobile, too. Thereby hangs a fast bit of development.

The Langen-Otto engine of 1876 became the 4-stroke cycle Otto engine by 1878, and was licensed the world over. American patents were granted to Otto on August 14, 1877, and the first "Otto" engines were licensed to be built in the United States by the firm of Schleicher & Schumm & Co. of Philadelphia. Thus, in 1878 the Otto 4-stroke cycle gasoline or gas engine was being sold on this side of the Atlantic.

Most of the early gasoline engines were either horizontal types for farm use (a huge market) or were uprights usable either as stationary engines or boat engines. That was their immediate use, and since the automobile had not been invented, one market was in powerboats. By taking an upright off its flat-footed base, it could be installed in a motor launch, and the flat-footed base persisted in marine engine design for 15 years. You can type a pre-1900 engine by observing its base.

Aside from Otto's devising of the 4-stroke cycle, he also got away from an element of steam engine design that decreed that a connecting rod should go to a cross head to remove the side thrust of the connecting rod. Otto's patents show the piston performing that function, largely because his gas engine was single acting.

If you will look at Figure 4, you will see a stylish steam engine of 1875 that was highly thought of. The flywheel of such engines went

Figure 4. A high-quality 1875 steam engine for stationary work, showing the Stephenson reverse linkage and piston cross head. Engines were supposed to look this way then.

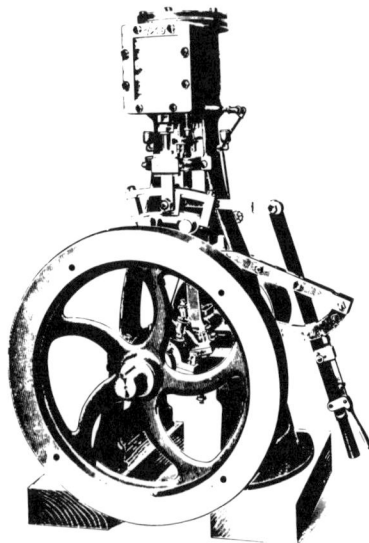

212

with them when they were employed in intermittent-load work, such as well-drilling and sawmill work. In a launch, the flywheel was not needed, because the great, heavy propellers provided much of the function. This type set the design style.

Who, then, built the first marine engine to operate on gasoline in this country? I do not know exactly. I believe the Union Engine Works of Oakland, California, with its 1884 trial horse was certainly one of the first. This is six years after the Philadelphia firm of Schleicher and Schumm got busy. That seems a long time. Whether this engine, alleged to have been built in 1884, beat the Schleicher & Schumm first effort is not known. But Union patented the first electric ignition system used to fire a gas engine. The patent was issued June 14, 1885, and covered fully the make-and-break type of ignition. Until that time, Otto's original flame-transfer ignition had been superseded by an idea of Gottlieb Daimler, who was employed by Otto. Daimler developed the hot-bulb ignition scheme as he continued to experiment, using the Otto 4-stroke cycle idea.

The records of the East Coast are not as clear as are those of the West Coast, where certainly there was a scramble to capitalize on the 4-cycle principle. The earliest mention of "boat" or "marine" I can find appears in an ad (Figure 5) dated 1890, inserted in the *Pacific Rural Press* of San Francisco by the Pacific Gas Engine Co., 230 Fremont Street, San Francisco. The upper half of this ad is reproduced here. Note the

Figure 5. Advertised in 1890 by the Pacific Gas Engine Co. of San Francisco, this "Pacific" clearly shows steam engine design thinking.

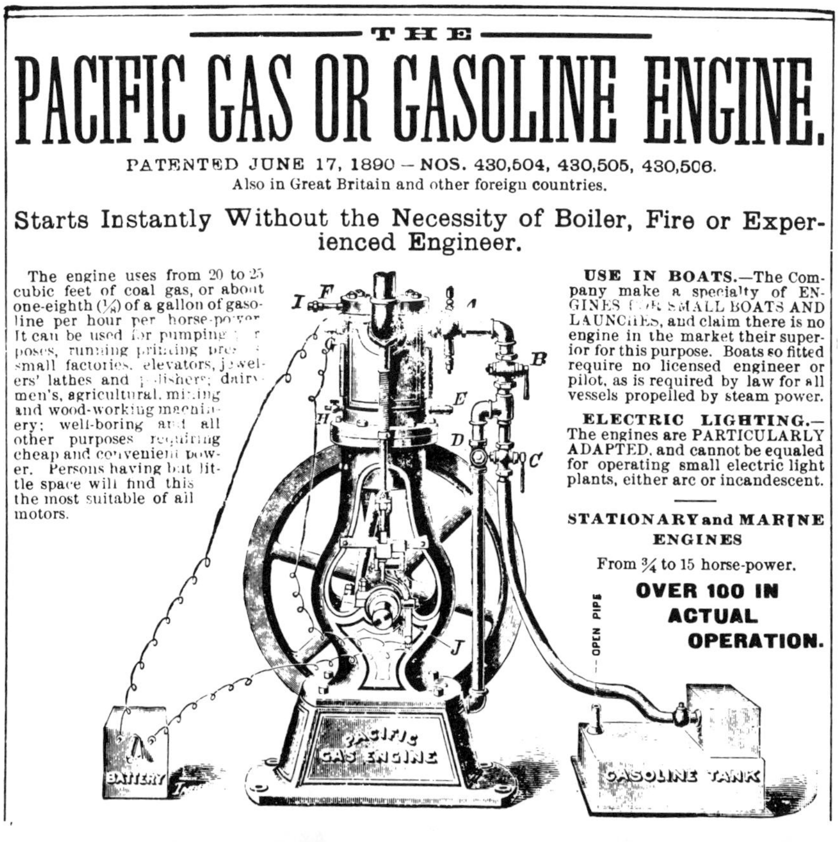

Figure 6 (left). The first gasoline engine to bear the Palmer name was sold in kit form by the Mianus Electric Co. in 1897. *Figure 7 (right).* An engine produced in Grand Rapids, Michigan, was one of a great number of marine products turned out in that city: Wilmarth & Morman propellers, Sintz-Wallin engines, Dake deck and steering engines.

little box in the upper right hand corner for which the lead is "Use in Boats."

The influence of steam engine design is apparent. The wiring is deluxe, and the carburetion unbelievable. The upper chamber of the gasoline tank was a multiple curtain of rags soaked like lamp wick in gasoline. The valve C apparently adjusted the gasoline feed in, and the pipe D was the air intake manifold, cunningly led from the base so that backfires would be contained. B seems to be the throttle, and A is the ordinary Globe valve adapted for atmospheric aspiration. J is obviously the timer, and E and F seem to be water intake and outlet. 'Tis a wonder the thing ran!

Another engine of the same period was termed the Regan, too poorly illustrated to reproduce here. Its two main claims to fame were that the "carburetor may be located from five to fifty feet away, reducing danger." Another catch line was, "You don't even need a match!" This, of course, had reference to lighting the fire under a boiler and waiting for steam.

On the East Coast the earliest engine I know of was an 1897 Palmer, then made by the Mianus Electric Company of Mianus, Connecticut, and sold in kit and casting form! See Figure 6. Another 1897 engine was made in Grand Rapids, Michigan. It is pictured in Figure 7, showing the copper water jacket popular with early engine makers.

The Palmer and the Grand Rapids, as you will note, are two-cycle engines, and by merely mentioning that the two-cycle engine was the

1878 invention of the Scotsman Dugald Clerk of Glasgow, I must brush that development aside for lack of space. It is a whole 'nother story. (In passing, let us salute Sir Dugald Clerk's two-cycle engine by tipping our hat to the fellow who first reversed one on the spark. William Harnden Foster's famous cartoon is a fitting historical memento.)

Encyclopedias are contradictory on the story of Nikolaus August Otto. They do not even agree on his name spelling. One is with a "k" and the other with a "c." I have gone back to the papers of the time for a thumbnail on this, thinking that source to have passed through fewer opinionated filters.

Otto was born in Holzhausen, Nassau, in Prussia in 1832. According to the translation, he was:

. . . occupied in purely commercial matters to his twenty-ninth year, though having a taste for natural sciences he acquired an extensive insight into natural questions . . . he left his secure position as soon as he had found the right way. In 1863 he got his first engine made by a machinist at Cologne, the result of which

Dr. Nikolaus August Otto, inventor of the Otto four-cycle gasoline engine and producer of the first commercially successful gas engine.

was little satisfactory, as Otto at that time had hardly any knowledge of machine construction. He got into difficulties and despondency, when he had the good fortune to meet with Mr. Eugen Langen, a member of one of the principal manufacturer's families at Cologne, and to inspire him with his own confidence in the future of the gas engine.

Mr. Langen was a thoroughly trained mechanical engineer and skillful designer of machinery, and putting Otto's ideas into good form they produced the atmospheric gas engine in 1864, which proved a success almost from the beginning.

By the time of the Paris Exhibition the engine was no experiment, and some 5,000 had been sold, necessitating a move from Langen's sugar refinery into new premises at Dentz. The Paris Exhibition engine, as we have seen, was *not* the 4-stroke cycle engine as some references blithely state. But within the year from the 1876 Paris Exhibition, the sublime 4-stroke cycle principle had apparently dawned on Otto, because he began licensing worldwide in 1878 on patents granted in 1877 that prescribed the 4-cycle idea. So, through confrontation with a problem and, as is so often the case, by groping in dim light toward revelation, Nikolaus August Otto isolated the famous and simple principle on which today most of the world rides.

Otto's death occurred at age 59 in 1891. In 1887 he was honored by the Society of German Engineers when the Wurzburg University conferred on him the honorary Doctor's degree, an honor rarely accorded to an engineer. The translator goes on: "Its conferment, in our opinion, on eminent engineers is much more deserved and warranted than on successful politicians. However, without any official acknowledgment, his name will survive as the author of one of the most important inventions of this century."

If Otto could only see his baby now! If nowhere else, he would have earned his PhD in the School of Experience, majoring in Hard Knocks, and graduating "summa cum laudanum." And very rich!

25

Two Beginners—
Waterman Outboard Engines

The older a waterman gets, the more his affections go back to beginnings—to the first boats he remembers building or owning, and the first exposure he had to the gasoline engine. I do not know why this is true, but in my own experience I have seen wealthy men who, as they advanced in years, shucked off their palatial yachts and went back to rowboats, or something simple they could enjoy. My earliest affections dealt with the first two gasoline engines I yearned to own.

One was the original Waterman outboard engine that my uncle, Earl Neutson (Kneutson), installed on our family rowboat on Snug Harbor at Isle Royale, Michigan. I can remember the commotion at dockside when this old lunker was clamped to the stern of our gig-sterned lapstraker. I remember vividly the red cylinder, the queer color of the bare metal crankcase that I was told was the new metal, aluminum. I remember the varnished tiller of wood, on which was strapped a neat red gasoline tank. It was 1907, and I was four years old. The novelty of seeing a boat "rowed" by an engine will stay with my wonderments until I die.

My friend Armand Hauser recently sent me the accompanying photo of one of these 1907 Waterman engines, from his files at Mercury Outboard Motors of Fond du Lac, Wisconsin. With the photo came some interesting information:

The Waterman was the first commercially successful outboard engine marketed. It had been developed by Cameron B. Waterman of Spruce Harbor, Michigan, on Lake Superior. Waterman was a Yale law student at the time, and in experimenting with a gas engine to drive his bike, he

The original Waterman
Porto of 1907.

had strapped a home-made engine to the bedstead in his college dormitory and was the center of a huge ruckus when he fired up the original motor in his bedroom at the fraternity house. The adaptation to a bike was successful.

Reasoning that if the engine could drive his bike, Waterman set about adapting it to propelling a rowboat by using a chain from the upright engine down to a propeller on an underwater jackshaft.

In 1905, winter tests on the Detroit River proved that a chain drive could easily be knocked off the lower sprocket. Then Waterman and his friend George Thrall, owner of a Detroit boiler factory (and the only fellow who didn't laugh at Waterman's idea), adopted a very satisfactory drive shaft and bevel gear arrangement. The engine flywheel was in the crankcase. In 1906 commercial production of the Waterman Porto Motor was started, and the unique engine was exhibited at the 1906 National Motorboat Show held in the old Madison Square Garden in New York. Photos of this first motorboat show depict boats actually afloat and on exhibit in a large pool at the center of the lowest floor!

The engine shown here was the first mass-produced outboard engine, and the beginning of an industry that has been the reason why, today, so many people enjoy boating as a popular family sport.

There had been previous engine-building attempts dating back to the late 1800s. William Steinway and Gottfried Daimler showed a gasoline model in the United States in 1892. The first gasoline outboard made in this country was introduced in 1896 by the American Motor Company of New York, but only 25 models of the four-cycle, air-cooled engine were produced.

Waterman produced 25 engines in 1906 and 3,000 in each of the next two years, 1907 and 1908. In 1909, Ole Evinrude, who built inboard two-cycle engines in his machine shop in Milwaukee, started to market his outboard for the first time. That year Waterman sold 6,000 engines. By that time, both builders had put the flywheel flat for easy cranking and had extended the crankshaft directly downward. Big development!

It was Waterman, in fact, who coined the term "outboard motor," but he was unable to copyright it because of its generic derivation. In his patent, No. 851,839, the Waterman Porto was described as a "self-contained motor and propeller." His first model was the 2-hp upright shown here. The first known public advertising of this mass-produced engine appeared in *Motor Boating* magazine for January 10, 1908.

Ole Evinrude sold out his outboard interests in 1914, the year World War I broke out. Waterman's career in the outboard industry ended in 1917 when the U.S. declared war on Kaiser Wilhelm's Germany. The stringencies of war manufacturing prompted Waterman to enlist in the U.S. Army Signal Corps, so it seemed prudent to sell out to the Arrow Motor and Marine Company of New York, having up to that date produced 30,000 Portos. The Waterman Porto continued to be marketed until 1924.

Few people realized that Waterman had founded the robust industry of the outboard motor. The "portable substitute for a pair of oars" was stepping up in power and weight, driving larger boats to higher speeds, and pulling more people into boating. Thus, in 1955 Waterman was given recognition for his pioneering invention and for his acumen when, at the New York Boat Show, on the 50th anniversary of his initial enterprise in founding the first outboard motor company, he was presented with a new runabout and a Mercury outboard motor.

Cameron B. Waterman died a year later, at the age of 79, a successful lawyer and devoted sportsman.

As recently as 1977 at Clayton, New York, at the 13th Annual Antique Boat Show, where I served as one of the judges, I saw a 1907 Waterman Porto still in running condition strapped to an angle iron stand. Its proud owner succeeded in firing her up, and when the old "beginner" started barking, I was mentally back on Snug Harbor in 1907, realizing that time had come full circle for me, and that I had lived it all. For me it was a powerful montage of memories.

Today, people who flip from coast to coast in a few hours do not

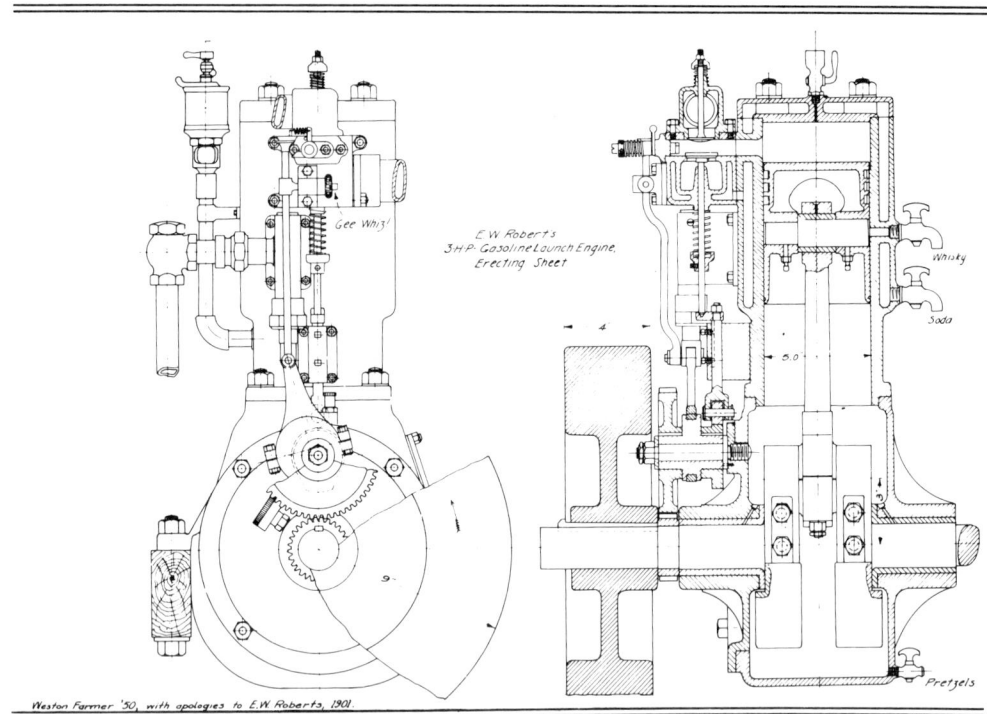

E.W. Roberts 3 H.P. Gasoline Launch Engine. Erecting Sheet

Weston Farmer '50, with apologies to E.W. Roberts, 1901.

realize that within the lifetime of many men now alive and active our country was regionally and railroad-oriented. And in the beginning of powerboating, many, many men built their own boats.

So limited was knowledge of the gasoline engine that plans were published for the construction of this new marine motive power. Down the block from where I lived as a child, a man named Louis Bartholomew, son of the cartoonist for our local newspaper, had built his own boat and then turned to building his own engine on a lathe in his basement. He was working from plans published in a 1903 *Rudder*.

Remembering the thrill of hearing the very first bang of Louie's engine on the test bed, I later secured a copy of *How to Build a 3 h.p. Gas Engine* at a time when, around 1925, *Rudder* was disposing of all early book remnants. It was from a plate by E.W. Roberts in this book that I drew the illustration shown here, the erecting sheet for assembling the parts of the very first gas engine plan aimed at the popular backyard market.

Mr. Roberts, a mechanical engineer from Sandusky, Ohio, designed many of the early marine engines, and at one time produced his own line of Roberts two-cycle motors. When I was making this drawing, I remembered standing near Louie Bartholomew when he was admonishing us kids to "Get out of the way," and I remembered his answer to me when I asked him what all those little faucets were for, sticking out all over the engine. "One's for whiskey and the other for soda," he said.

"And this"—he pointed to the igniter—"is, well, Gee Whiz! Don't you know *anything*?"

Looking back on this nostalgic old drawing, I have to ask myself the same question after a lifetime at the design game. The quest for answers in the great game of guessometry goes on and on. It is part of the American genius for things mechanical. Even whiskey, soda, and Gee Whiz do seem to have played their part.

26

The Old Elco

The historical year was 1914-1915 when Elco, under the managerial genius of Henry R. Sutphen, decided to produce motorboats on a standardized quantity basis. As anyone who had been in the boatbuilding business a hundred years or so could tell you, the idea in its day was as startling as putting a man on the moon is today. The idea worked, and it produced wonderful little motor yachts of a perfection rarely seen these days. Starting in 1914 with a 32-foot cruiser termed a "Cruisette" (trade mark!), the Elco line saw an increase in size through several series, to 34 feet in length, which was standard for years as the Elco 34. I consider this boat the best motorboat I ever had my hands on. Hundreds were built. There are still a few in existence, cherished as collector's items in the same sense as are Rolls-Royce automobiles of vintage dates.

There is a Port Elco Club of Elco owners numbering several hundred members who own an old Elco model still afloat. They are maintaining, or restoring these Tiffany examples of fine boatbuilding. Membership also includes a few of the old-time craftsmen and personnel of Elco, some of the whom-and-which of us are no longer spring chickens. But let me tell you—

Consider the American boating scene at the time of Elco's block-busting boatbuilding decision: Every watering place had its own local boatbuilding plant. It follows geographically that there were hundreds of these boatbuilders. The shop's clientele came to lake or harbor or island "for the season." Dad sent Mother and the kids to the cottage for the summer and came out for weekends on the 5:15 steam train commuter—that is, if the distance wasn't much over 30 miles.

When the family wanted a boat, Dad would go down to the boat works and have Old Bill, the boatbuilder, cobble up a model to embody Dad's ideas. Proper cash having exchanged hands—say, $300 to $500 as half payment on a 30-foot motor cruiser—Old Bill would select properly apprenticed boatbuilders and set to work for the winter. The method was universal.

The resulting boats bore the local stamp and generally were beautifully built. But no two were ever alike. They might work, and run well, or might not. Every owner made his own guess as to which engine he needed. There were several hundred makes of engines being manufactured. Then came the next question: what reverse gear? Paragon? Gies? Capitol? Joe's Gear? The permutation possibilities for mismatched trouble were endless. With all the unskilled guessometry involved, including propellers, it frequently took two or three engines and many sizes of props (some costing as much as $10) to reach a satisfactory mating of boat, powerplant, and propeller. Few owners felt they had j-u-ust the right wheel working for their boat.

It was considered a very tough contract that included a guaranteed speed. If Old Bill's boat made good on it, Dad passed out cigars, Mother fainted, the kids got an extra 10 cents a week allowance money, and Old Bill issued a strong ration of grog to all hands. Boatbuilders drank

Introduced in 1914, the Cruisette had become a 33-footer by 1922. This 1922 photo of the Elco plant at Bayonne, New Jersey, shows a series of 1921 Cruisette hulls being readied for customer delivery. (*Motor Boat*)

their whisky neat, for men were men and nothing could be done about it. They had no need to grow a face full of oakum-whiskered under-brush to prove it. The 10-mile speed was always claimed as 15, and boats of that era bore sizzling names like *Humdinger* or *Gunfire* or *Holy Smoke*. Such boats became regionally famous. But—duplicated? Never!

All of which outline tells why, in this loosey-goosey method of getting a new boat, the Elco notion of producing a standardized boat was a blockbuster. It seems old hat now. Henry Ford had done it with his Model-T car. Why should not Elco try it with a cruising boat?

The idea was to start out with a good, time-tested hull, work out any possible sea bugs, power her with a good reliable motor of economical horsepower—a mill with all the gears and pumps and auxiliary stuff built in—and then put this model through the shop in quantities of 20 to 50 at a clatter.

The first Elco.

Starting with a 32-foot double-cabin model in 1914, Elco found that the market soaked up these boats. As each succeeding year pointed to a small improvement here and a new idea there, the double-cabin model became a single-cabin model, of what was known as the "hunting cabin" type, as opposed to the raised deck type. This went into a number of series. The '21 series became a 33-footer. By '25 that series became a 34-footer, and that became the standard cognomen: the Elco 34 Cruisette.

No great change in the basic layout occurred for about 15 years, from 1921 until about 1934. I have several prints that show a growth in beam (very slight) aft of amidships, but the same basic boat continued popular for a very long time. This boat ran smoothly—3 to 4 mph faster than boats from other shops carrying comparable power, and made very little wake. Note the beautiful wave formation shown in the photo—one wave from bow to stern. Little tricks were evolved that added to sea-worthiness, balance, and speed, until, with characteristic Elco under-statement, the cataloged speed with 48 hp at 1,000 rpm became 13 to

The Elco Cruisette was a smooth-running boat. Probably the most desirable stock cruiser ever built, with hundreds marketed, she was the queen of Elco's line for 25 years. At a price of $7,000, she came with everything but bedding and silverware.

14 mph. Elco never made a statement that couldn't be backed up by closest scrutiny.

The engine that became standard in this marvelously balanced hull was termed, at the time, an Elco engine. Actually, the original of this engine was a JVB, so named for its designer, Joe Van Blerck, who at the time had the boating world by the tail for a downhill haul in the 100 to 200 hp "high" speed department. He was originally based in a small factory at Algonac, Michigan. When World War I came along with U.S. involvement, Joe was asked to come up with a simple, sturdy, high-torque engine for use in the unwieldy looking World War I tanks envisaged and demanded by Winston Churchill. The JVB tank engine was a four-cylinder affair of 4-3/4 inches bore by 6 inches stroke rated 48 hp at 1,000 rpm. This basic engine went on to become the first boat engine to have a sliding, or selective, gear shift as opposed to the planetary type. A revolutionary idea in Joe's engine design was to have as much motor as possible cast *en bloc*—French for "in one hunk."

Vicissitudes beset the Van Blerck motor building operation at Algonac after the war. Airplane engines such as Curtiss OX-5 90 hp V-8 were dumped by the War Department for $50 apiece, and went begging at that, packed in original crates, never used. Their conversion to use in fast boats killed Van Blerck's speedboat engines, which were in that power range. A firm named Wellman-Seaver-Morgan produced the JVB

The Joe Van Blerck WW I infantry tank engine powered almost all early Cruisettes. Later reworked as the WSM, then by Elco as their engine, this mill was notable for having auto-type reverse shift and for having almost the entire engine in one casting. (*The Rudder*)

for a while. Somehow, in a manner not known to me, this was eventually slightly re-worked and became an Elco engine. Thus, JVB, then WSM, then Elco—the same engine.

I can say from personal experience that the JVB, or Elco, was darned good, and, that having owned an Elco 34 myself at one time, I always felt her to be the best balanced, most highly developed motor craft I ever skippered. I say this from a classical standpoint based on a naval architect's point of view, and an understanding of the engineering music in her make-up.

Now just as the reading of music looks obscure to a duffer, but is part of an orchestra conductor's second nature, so to a naval architect is the engineering music in a balanced boat design. To a professional the art in a boat reads easily. Art exalts the soul of one who can see its presence, even as the lack of it disgusts. When I first watched an Elco 34 dash by, her aesthetics and noble engineering bombed my innards. I stood stupefied in appreciation of her beauty and silky rush. I hoped then to find out someday what made this boat tick. As fate ordained matters, I went to work for Elco about 1937 and was with them for quite a spell. I was "on staff" as a designer, eventually ending up working with Irwin Chase on a secret propeller matter. I can attest that getting wrapped up around the Skipper's technical axle was exciting for anyone who objected to getting dizzy! We were most compatible.

But I didn't know all this, and hadn't yet lived it, when the Elco 34 resolution hit me. I wanted some day to publish her lines. They're the heart and guts of the whole matter. Quite naturally, with all the development work behind the plans, the drawings for all Elco boats were carefully guarded. Constructional or hydrostatic or lines plans were never, ever published. In fact, the lines drawings from the Elco drafting room were kept in a separate vault, and the offsets for each design were kept somewhere in another place.

It is presumed that the great fire storm at Bayonne in 1948, which I am told consumed the plant, also charred these basic records. I do not know. But, by methods which will never show on any exhumed Elco

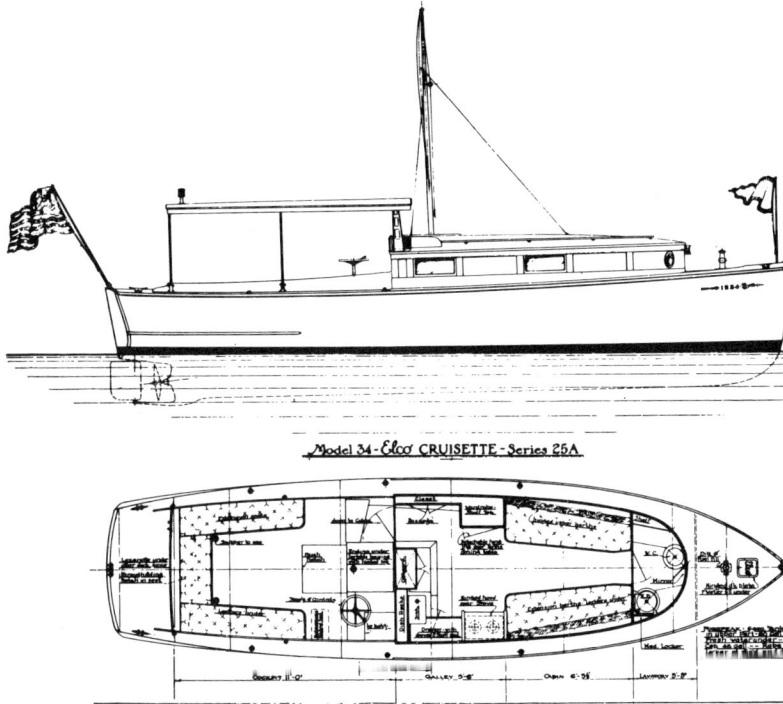

Model 34 - Elco CRUISETTE - Series 25A

By 1925 the Elco Cruisette advanced to the 34-foot length and became known as the Elco 34 Cruisette. This 1925A series plan and profile by Bill Fleming, Elco naval architect, became the final standard for 10 years.

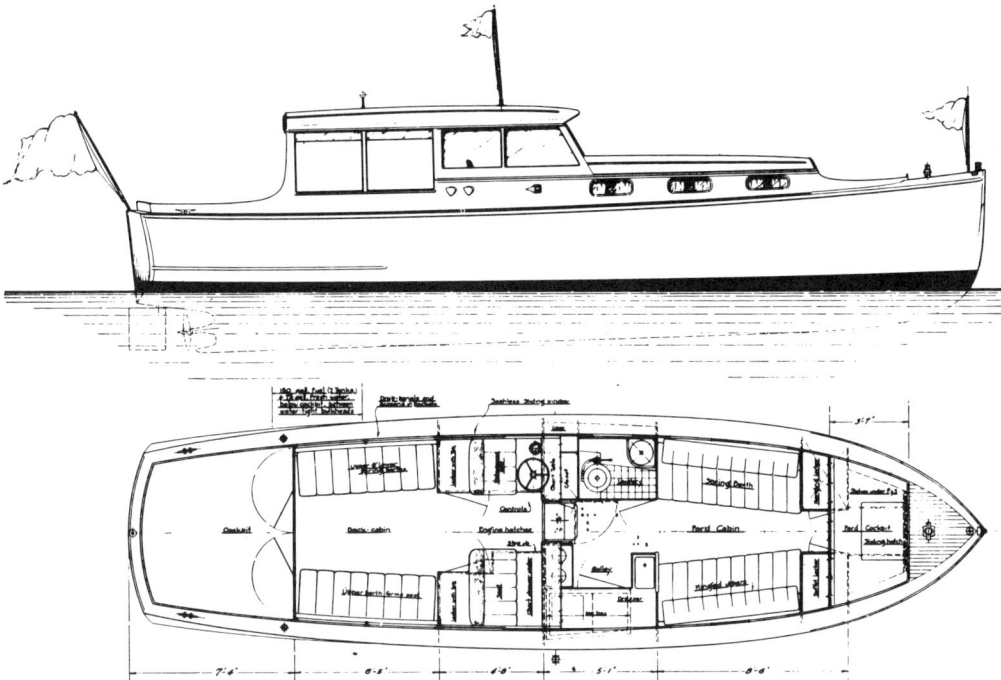

In the mid-1930s the Elco 34 was augmented by another 4 feet in length and the addition of a convertible Pullman-type aft cabin—all to take advantage of reduction-gear Chrysler Royals and Crowns, and affording single and twin screws. This boat, the Elco 38, was the last Elco round-bilger.

Spring Inventory, I managed to secure blueprints of the 34s from 1914 on up—that is, all but the lines of this one boat, the Elco 34 Cruisette. Neither the tracings nor offsets were to be found. But, I did find one constructional drawing for the '25 series, which was in effect until the '34 25A series and which is the boat pictured running here. This was the construction profile, the deck and keel plan, and had three sectional views transversely from which I can reconstruct the lines. These are enough points to work from, as the scale on the print remains very accurate.

I am under the impression that the first Elco Cruisette was the work of Irwin Chase. I know Glen Tremaine had a hand in later versions, but I believe that beloved Alfred (Bill) Fleming was the Michelangelo hand behind most of her. I do know it was Bill Fleming who put the pullman-type deckhouse cabin on the 34 eventually, which by 1938 had become the Elco 39, phasing out the old 34 Cruisette. The 39's were the last of the great, round-bilged, yachty Elco masterpieces. The profiles shown here, showing advancement from the original Elco 34, are all Bill Fleming's skilled work. You will never see lovelier or more delicately executed profiles and arrangement plans.

Alfred the Great, as I like to think of him, died October 2, 1971, in Bradenton, Florida—his retirement home.

I've a unique theory about the comfort and behavior of the Elco. Aside from the fact that she was a normal quarter-beam boat, I think her secret lay in one thing: the pounds-per-square-foot of waterplane loading. What is this? Well, we'll have to wait for publication of the lines to see the great engineering magic in this boat. Until I have it worked out,* I predict no droop in the inscrutable smile of the Sphinx.

*A follow-up figure from a rough set of lines indicated 64 pounds per square foot loading.—WF

27

The Lovely Fantail Launch

If you have never heard of Fred W. Martin, Yacht Designer, you have lots of company. Few men in this day and age have known of his work, which was prolific at the turn of the century. In looking at some of it, you are in for a great treat.

Fred W. Martin was a naval architect in the tradition of Charles L. Seabury, Edward Burgess, and Nathanael Herreshoff. Artistically, and possibly technically, he was easily the equal of any of these better-known greats. He was their contemporary, a product of mid-America. He was overlooked and unreported by the eastern seaboard yachting press of his time simply because of the state of the nation: the geographic isolation of steam-train times, the slow, two-week mails, and the fact that Big City editorial interest seldom extended beyond the end of the Flatbush subway lines.

Frederick Martin lived in Racine, Wisconsin, and was, in 1902, the naval architect for the once great Racine Boat Co. of that city. Racine Boat built in wood and in steel many of the elegant steam yachts owned by Chicago tycoons such as Armour, Swift, Montgomery Ward, and other members of the Chicago and Milwaukee yacht clubs. Martin was one of those designers serving the inland seashores of the Great Lakes, the coastline of which (it may surprise you) is greater than that of the entire Atlantic seaboard.

It is a forgotten fact now that there was much nautical development in this region. In Martin's contemporary group were such skilled and prolific naval architects as Carlton Wilby of Detroit, and Charles Desmond of Manitowoc. Little is now remembered of Wilby, but

229

Charles Desmond is best remembered by his book *Naval Architecture Simplified,* which is still the best amateur's instruction ever written on the subject. This work, serially published in *Rudder* during World War I, was taken by the then editor, Gerald Taylor White, and made the basis of the correspondence course run from White's home, Westlawn, in New Jersey, when White was dismissed from *Rudder.* Desmond was the founding father.

But Fred W. Martin? I had never been fully aware of this man and the extent of his work until Dave Robb of Milwaukee mailed to me an old 1902 catalog of Martin's designs. Robb had got it from Tom Owen of The Yacht Shop, Racine. Upon opening the well-preserved, half-inch-thick old paper album of Martin designs, I saw 72 of the sweetest drawings one could imagine.

The great mastery of Martin's work in the old tradition of designing can instantly be recognized by all who had the depth of experience to "read" it. I pass on to you here a few of Martin's fantail hulls, and thereby get to the nut of my story:

A year ago, at the prompting of my old friend William Garden of Victoria, B.C., Canada, whose brilliant work is known the world over, I got busy on the design of an old-time steam launch. It was Bill who suggested that I reach back in my experience and turn out a fantail-sterned launch for steamboat buffs. It was to provide an authentic launch in the old fashion of lovely grace that *Diana* was designed. Her profile, lines, and construction plan are shown here. In preparing these drawings, my research showed that there were between 1,200 and 1,500 known steam launch fans in this country and Canada.

Most of these men owned some steam equipment—an engine, or a boiler, and gauges, injectors, whistles, condensers, and the like, but—alas!—usually had to put their antique goodies into any old tub they could find. It was these men I wanted to reach. *Diana's* plans appeared in the December 1975 issue of *Rudder.* It is through the courtesy of Martin Luray, former editor of *Rudder,* that this boat appears here.

Diana was most popular. Within 60 days of publication, 91 sets of prints at $20 the set had been mailed to old launch aficionados in such far-off places as Australia, Honolulu, England, and Canada, as well as most of the United States. The interest surprised me and turned up some startling facts. I found that there were many men who can remember the sweet ride, the graceful glide, and the low-pressure comfort of this long-neglected hull form. Some wrote to me saying that they were turned off by the money-burning, mile-a-minute thunder mugs masquerading as boats under some catchy drugstore label. From all this, it would seem that the charm of a boat that will slip along at natural hull speed under low power is again being avidly sought.

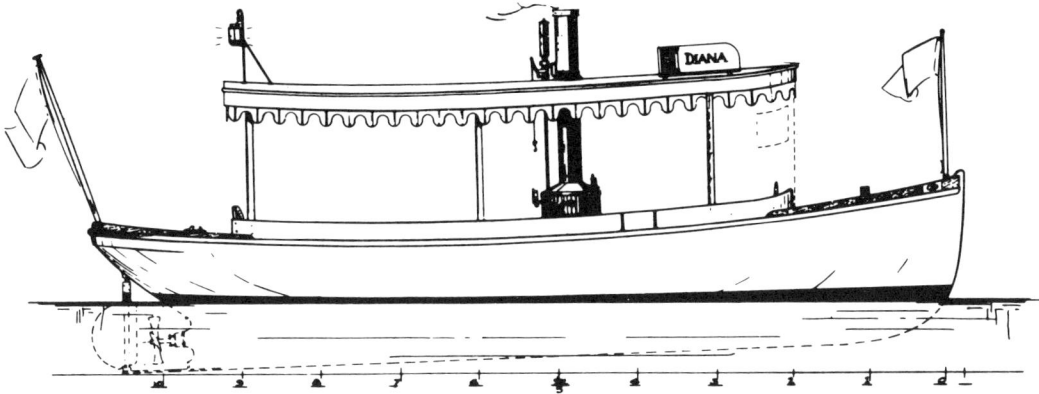

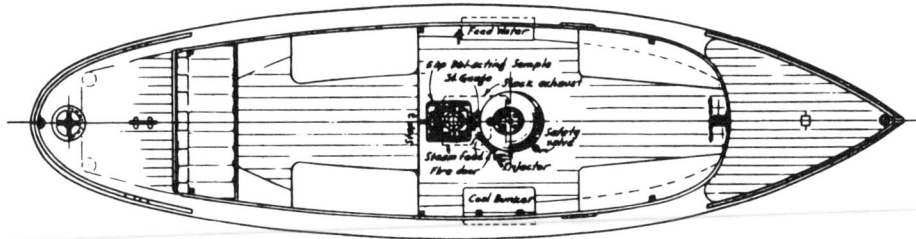

L.O.A. 25'-0"
BEAM 6'-6"
DRAFT 2'-0"
SCALE ¾"=1'0

THE "GAY NINETIES'
STEAMER
DIANA

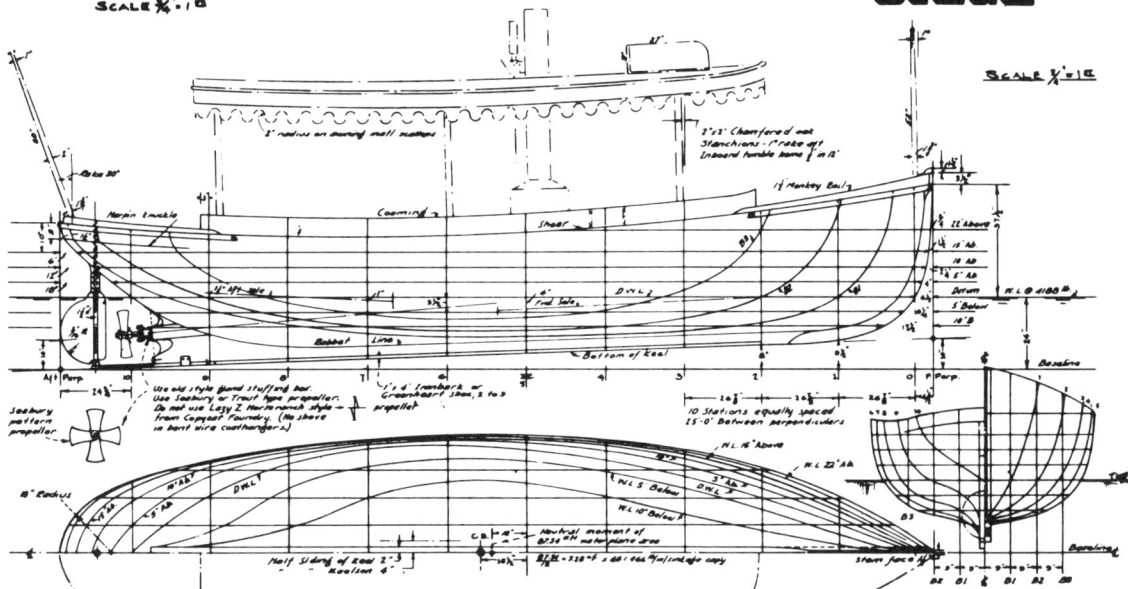

LINES OF DIANA

Designed for RUDDER

by Weston Farmer 1945

FROM MY OLD BOAT SHOP

For lazy rides of an evening along a harbor or the shores of a lake, or sagging off to town to get Daddy on the train, old-time launches of this kind are a delight. But they do have their peculiarities, whether driven by steam or an old-time gas engine. One of the fantail's strong points is that boats of this type are great "load luggers." They hunker down in the water, move sedately, and are excellent family boats, because even the smaller craft can accommodate a load range of from one to a dozen passengers without its affecting their behavior very much.

The first ones to become powerboats were cast-off naphtha launches with wall-sided bows, a carryover from fashionable plank-on-edge sailing cutters. In a brisk breeze, the older models became intimately wet—wetter than a mixed foursome in a Turkish bath. I contend this would be quite moist and disrespectfully intimate. The wall-sided bow of the very earliest boats can be discerned from Figure 1. This shows the first 18-foot naphtha launch built by the Gas Engine and Power Co. To the left in the gray fedora is Mr. Frank Ofeldt, inventor of the naphtha engine. Next in order are Irving Snodgrass, Hank Fleming, and Bert Fiedler of the Gas Engine shop.

Four people and 300 pounds of engine do not seem to burden the little craft. The date of this photo is circa 1895-96, courtesy of the late Rev. Malcolm MacDuffie of Bernard, Maine, a naval architect who forsook M.I.T. engineering and the feast-or-famine yacht designing game to

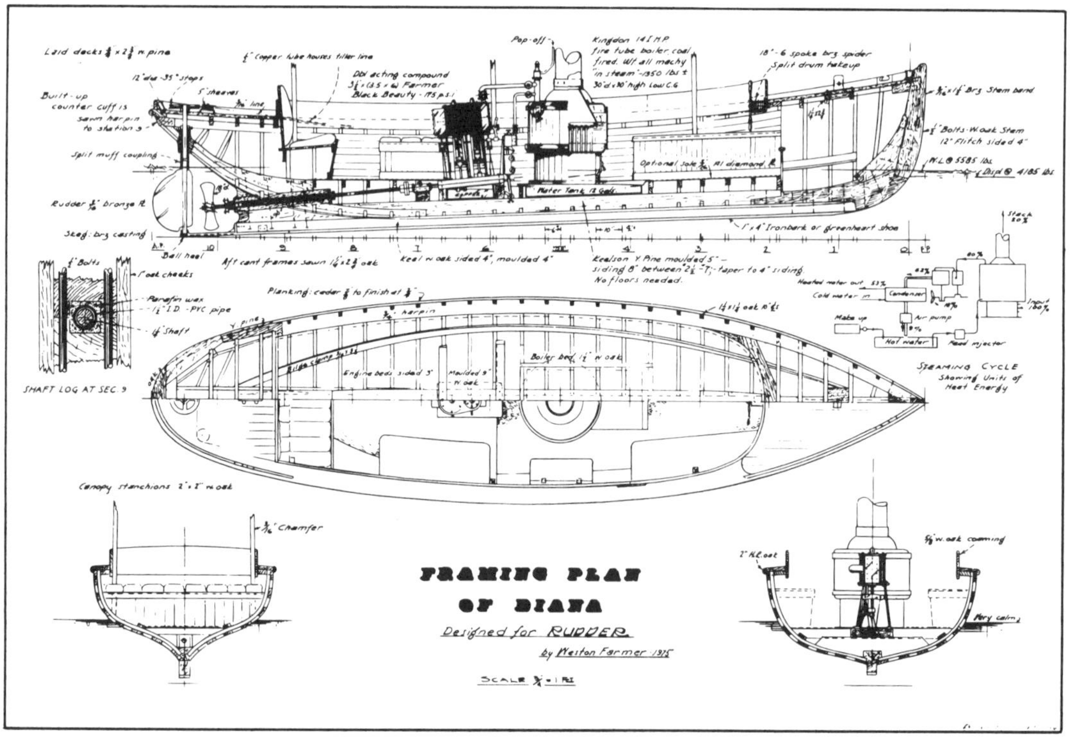

232

Figure 1. The first little 18-foot naphtha launch of the 1890s had a wall-sided bow and fantail stern. Frank Ofeldt, inventor of the naphtha engine, sits to the left in a grey hat.

teach religion and do his praying in church—a most competent, practical and large-hearted man. As shown in the photo, the 1-1/2 hp launch, ready to fire up and chug away, sold for $360. Today she would probably cost $4,000, which is a good argument for keeping legislators at home.

The cure for wetness in this type of hull was found by rounding the forward bow portions more, and keeping the turn of the bilges high. It is at the waterline, at the in-and-out wedge of the hull as she inclines, that stability and dryness are to be found. Hard bilge turns below water have almost nothing to do with it. They are already below water level, serving as displacement bulk. They've already done their work.

Another cure for wetness is to keep the ends of this type of boat light. The machinery should be installed amidship in a fore-and-aft direction and be "wung out" as far as possible toward the beam ends. This cures the overloaded pitching caused by the enormous bow tanks, which are discernible in the Martin drawings.

See Figure 2. This shows *Fanny,* an 18-foot gas-powered fantailer once owned by MacDuffie. Here you will see the machinery installed in the proper place in such a hull. In this picture, the stream of the bow wave forming again under the counter, or fantail, shows the condition of the phenomenon that has become fixed in the public mind as "hull speed." This is a condition generally peculiar to all double-ended vessels, differing as to S/L (speed-length) values with every boat. *It cannot be pegged by a precise ratio. Aside from length, the beam and draft will also affect this figure. Most notions of S/L values have been lifted from early texts, which were concerned with tank tests on steamship and battleship models long before transom sterns were thought of.*

Lines and layouts for boats of the fantail era are mighty scarce. The

Figure 2 (above). This 18-foot fantailer is the late Malcolm MacDuffie's old launch *Fanny.* Her engine is amidships. She is running at hull speed. *Figure 3 (below).* The counter stern is difficult to make graceful unless the framing is understood by the builder. This is a 20-foot fantail launch steamer built in Canada.

framing of the stern structures seems to be absolutely nonexistent in printed history. When I laid out *Diana,* I went back to apprentice days in boatbuilding and dredged out of memory the stern framed in West Coast fashion, using a built-up sawn harpin to form the cuff at the counter. This is one way to do it. See the framing plan of *Diana.*

If the stern end of a fantail frame is not understood by the builder, some awkward results show up. See Figure 3. Very often the stern looks to have been built by two men, each working aft on opposite sides of the hull, ending up on the principle that the last man to finish was a monkey's uncle.

Here is where Fred W. Martin's catalog illustrations and fantail designs became rare diamonds of reference. See Figure 4. At the top is shown Martin's design No. 54, which he termed a "Half Clipper Launch," 32 feet overall, by 23 feet 2 inches waterline, by 2 feet draft. Below the lines and body plan are Martin's drawings, which show with informative clarity how master launch builders of the old school framed

234

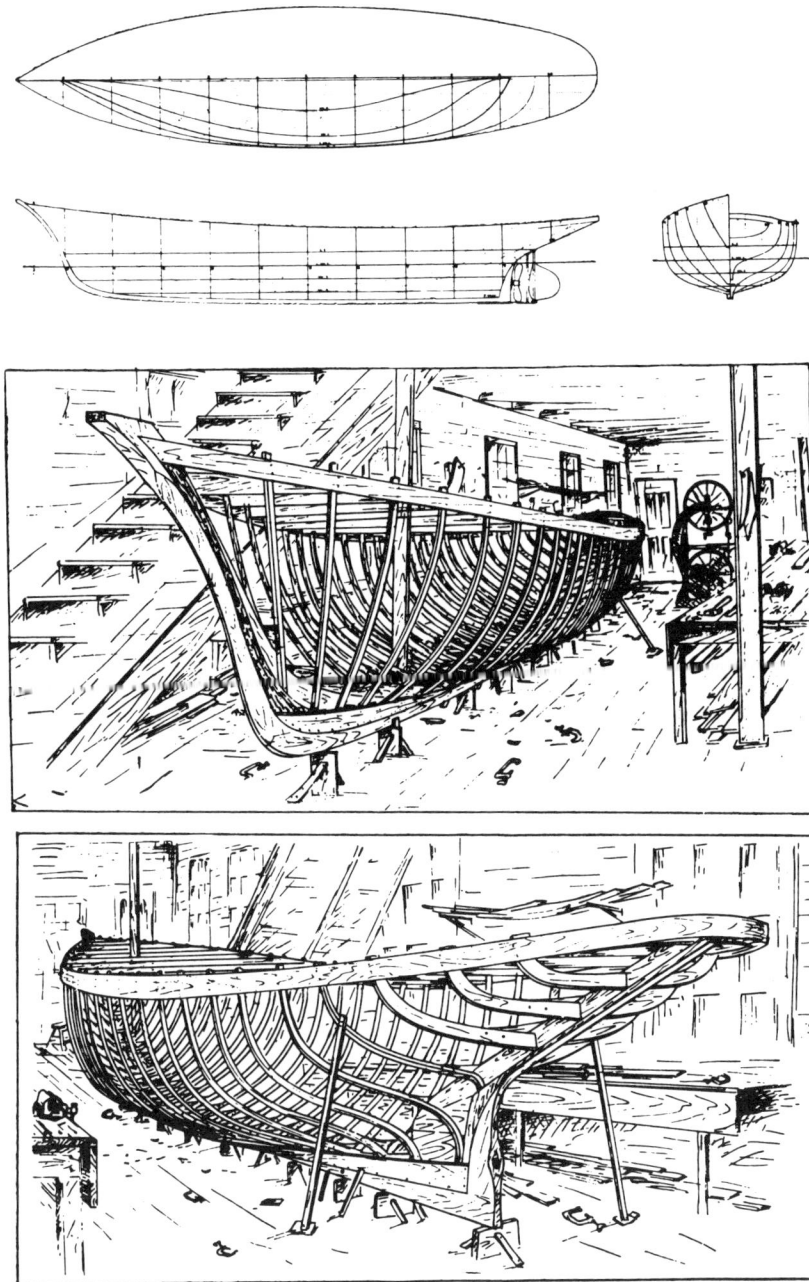

Figure 4. These superbly detailed Fred Martin drawings show the frame of Martin's 32-foot clipper model ready to knock down for shipment to another shop.

out a steam-bent stern piece with sawn frames—futtocks, they called them—between the elliptical fantail, down along the horn timber, until the hull shape allowed normal steam bending.

I notice a couple of things in these sketches that I believe students of boatbuilding should burn into their noggins to help them with their designing. First note that in the stern view, Figure 4, that the upswept turn of the bilge keeps rising toward the sheer very quickly and hardens to beat the band as it approaches the stern frame. The turn must be kept far outboard, becoming so acute that, along the horn timber, the turn of the bilge must resort to sawn frames. This is the secret of getting fair hull modelling and sweet plank layup in a fantail, to avoid the pinched, starved look apparent from some angles as in Figure 3. If you do not see this at first, rotate any of Martin's body plans 90 degrees, looking from the stern and treating the sheer line as the center-line of the boat, and the stern frame as a bent stem. The stern framing will appear as bow sections and you can then plainly see why the carrying of the bilge turn outboard is required for a fair stern.

Another thing that might give old-timers a jolt is that the hood end of the garboard plank, aft, where it rabbets into the skeg, is shown hard, squarish, and sharp. When I saw this, I thought of some of the "jumping fantods" a few of my old-time boatbuilder partners would have thrown at the sight. Bror Tamm of Lawley, Slim Stocking at Fellows & Stewart, Dick Dittmar at South Coast, and John Fruehauff at Elco would have put an ax through a man's wrist for suggesting such heresy. The main reason against the practice is that during the winter, with the hull lying out of water, bilgewater drips to the lowest point and rot sets in here, the first place for it to show up in any later survey. You will notice that in most of the later Martin designs he rounds the hood end and rabbet line at this point.

Another thing against the practice is that nearly 90 degrees of roll, twist, or sny—call it what you will—will require steam bending and cold pre-setting so that torsional forces will not split the plank at the fas-tenings. If the tuck in the rabbet is unswept and rounded at this point, not only is rot minimized, but also the hull is easier to plank.

If all of this seems a minor bit of art, treated like killing a gnat with a hammer blow, I grant that it is. But as long as the subject and the exact illustration for it are here visible, I bring down the hammer, because I have never seen the point treated before. You will probably never see it ever again.

Of course, there are plenty of vessels that have been built with hard hood ends on the aft garboard strake. Vertical stern posts almost re-quire it, but it is interesting to take a gander at the rest of Fred Martin's drawings, noting that almost all of them have the unswept aft rabbet line.

While the explicit perspective drawings in Figure 4 are before your eyes, look also at the frames in the bow view. Here is a piece of boat-building lore, the art of which should not be passed by. Note that the forward frames in a steam-bent hull frame must be canted. There are two simple, mechanical reasons for this. The first is the geometry of the matter. Given a certain number of frames to space out, the over-reach of the sheer is a greater distance from mold to stem than the fore-and-aft distance at the forefoot. The spaces at the top of the frame are greater than the spacing at the foot. Mechanically, when steam bending the frames in place, the frames must fay flat to the planking. In doing this, they will exhibit roll and twist in the elevation view of the framing plan. Their spacing and canting are both geometrically and mechanically required. Any time you see an inboard profile where the frames are drawn vertically and parallel right up to the stem, you have been told something about the "designer" who drew the plan: he doesn't know what he is doing, and likely enough never had his hand on a hot frame in his life. I have seen some of this stuff recently. The framing of a fantail hull is old-hat boatbuilding if the above minor, but very important, points are understood.

Because the lines drawings of good boats of this persuasion are so hard to find in extant literature, I am setting the table here with a feast of these grand examples from the hand of a master. By using proportional dividers, any good draftsman can enlarge any of the lines here to almost scale perfection. All that is necessary is the length, beam, and draft, and you can find the setting at which to enlarge. A pantograph, or photostatic blow-up to nearly full scale, finishing with dividers, would be two methods by which any marine draftsman could re-create Fred W. Martin's work. Let us look at some.

See Figure 5. The upper design, No. 50, is listed in Martin's catalog as "Thirty Foot Launch." No waterline length is given, but the beam over the body plan is 6 feet 8 inches, and the draft is given as 2 feet. This gives a dimensional fix for expansion of the lines, because the buttock lines are four to a side, or eight all told. In 6 feet 8 inches of beam, we have 80 inches to be divided into 8 parts, which sets the buttock spacing of No. 50 at exactly 10 inches. From this fix, the expansion is a cakewalk. Another check on No. 50 would be the 16 station spacings on a 30-foot length, or 30 times 12 equals 360 inches, which divides into 16 parts of 22.5 inches spacing.

I can see this graceful hull (which has a whopper bow fuel tank) powered with an old two-banger turning about 350 rpm and, to judge from the size of the propeller, going two feet per bang.

Martin's No. 55 is listed in the catalog as "Thirty Two Foot Regular Launch." Her length overall is 32 feet, beam 7 feet, draft 2 feet 6 inches. No waterline length is listed. The best fix for expanding to a workable scale may be taken from the 16 station spacings on the 32-foot length, or 2-foot station spacing. In this case the buttocks do not help, because Martin in this design did not adhere to this usual practice of putting in four buttock spacings per half-breadth of beam. His original drawings were listed as being in 3/4 inch to 1 foot scale.

Shown in Figure 6, Fred W. Martin's hull No. 56 was termed in his

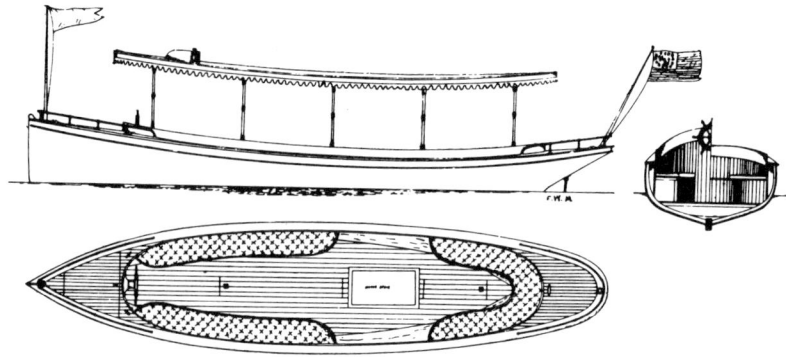

No. 50.

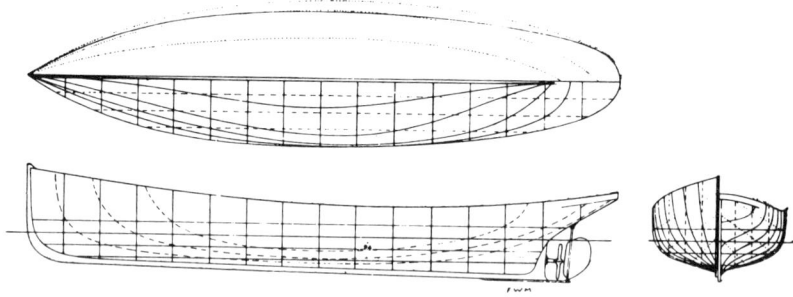

No. 55.

Figure 5.

catalog. "Thirty-five Foot Half Cabin Launch." Her listed dimensions are: length overall 36 feet 6 inches, beam 7 feet 6 inches, and draft 2 feet 6 inches. The best two-dimensional fixes for expanding the lines to scale (1/2 inch to 1 foot in the original) would be the buttock lines, four equal spaces to the half-breadth or 11 1/4-inch spacing. There are 18 sections shown, or a station spacing of 2 feet.

I like "Thirty-five Foot Half Cabin Launch" the best of all Martin's designs because his label for her is a footnote to the simple honesty of the man. If he lived today he'd probably have to call her *El Superbo* or *Fenestra de Gink* or *Sola Meeo* or some other Madison Avenue term. In 1902, praises be, Madison Avenue had not yet been hatched, so this boat stands as her own testament to art, not having to ride a jackass

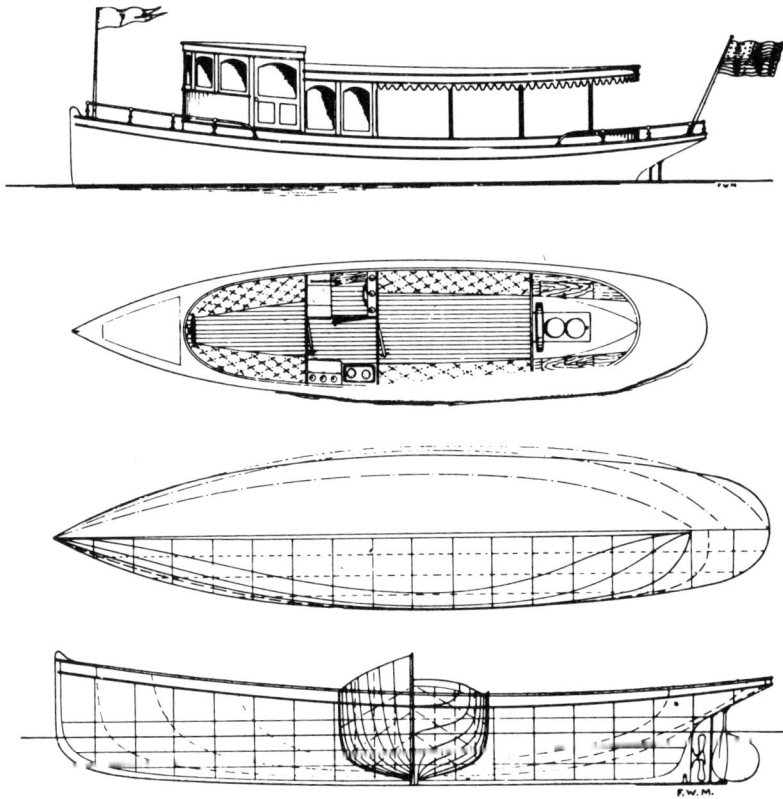

No. 56.

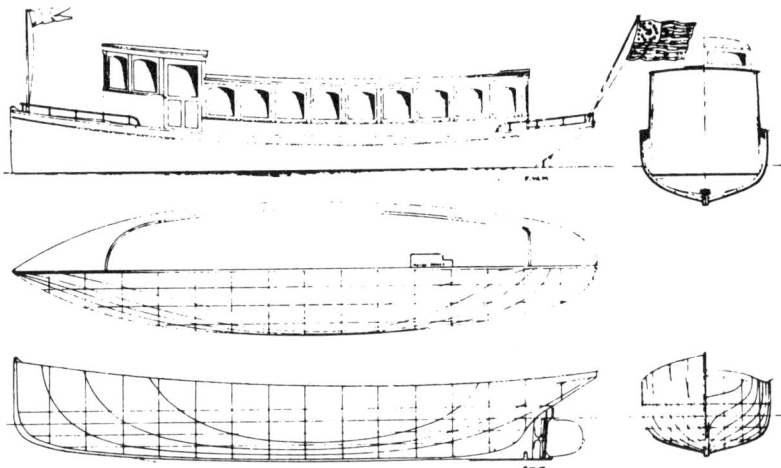

No. 57.

Figure 6.

label for some of the "corporate image" pop bottles now floating. Simply, "Thirty-five Foot Half Cabin Launch."

She is refreshing to look at. The glass wheelhouse resembling a greenhouse, her offside galley and head abaft this, and the "sequestered" machinery space way aft remind me of just such a boat owned by my family when I was a child. I can practically smell the soured grape jelly in the galley, and the awful odor of the airtight head, unventilated and sunny. Don't tell me history has no romance!

About 25 to 30 hp would be right for this craft. She'd be a dilly of a lakeside excursion boat.

No. 57 was chopped off for the market by Martin at 38 feet. Her beam is 8 feet 6 inches, draft 2 feet 8 inches. Her buttock spacing is 12-3/4 inches. Her station spacing is 28-1/2 inches. Note that her deckhouse topsides are tumbled home 1/2 inch to 12 inches—still standard for good deckhouse sides today in all knowledgeable designing that avoids the outhouse look of vertical fore-and-aft bulkheading.

And so, here we have had a fantail feast. I have been surprised beyond measure at the nostalgic hook these old craft have for the leisure sector of the boating public, but it is not only these graceful old boats that are being yearned for. The hunger seems to be for the older engines and means of soft, big-kick propulsion.

Today, looking at the equipment guides put out annually by the yachting press, a fellow is hard put to find any engine listed in the inboard sector that is from 4-6 hp to 18-24 hp. When you examine the overall dimensions of the engines offered, the catalog figures are there for horsepower, but the engine turns out to be an insect with a big 3,000 rpm buzz and no kick.

As a gas-engined launch, *Diana,* 25 feet overall, would want from 4 to 6 hp delivered at around 600-800 rpm on a big propeller. Martin's bigger boats would be happy with 25 to 30 hp tops, at not over 900 rpm shaft speed. The best place to get these old power values in an up-to-date, modernly efficient engine is to go foreign: to Norway for the Sabb, to Denmark for the Marstal, or to Great Britain for a goodly number of makes. For instance, the Sabb, built by Sabb Motor, A.S., Box 2626, Bergen, Norway, builds a full line of small diesels that are superbly marine all the way. See their HG model, 6-8 hp with chain rear starter, or the 18 hp model 2H, electric starting. These engines are today's answer to the need for 800-900 rpm prop-shaft speeds, as they have built-in reduction gears right along with their reverse gears.

What is wanted for launches of this type is something like the 1902 Borden & Selleck engine which was illustrated on the inside last cover in Martin's catalog. See Figure 7. Note that the ad says, "By one small lever the engine can be regulated to any speed, stopped, and reversed, or with the load you can make two or three revolutions in one direction, and then two or three in the other direction, or you can keep the engine swinging a half revolution one way, or half a revolution the other." Just like teaching a polar bear to waltz to Strauss music! I claim this is what we used to call "steamboating."

Steamboating, did I say? That brings me back to *Diana* and the steam buffs, who really know what it meant by soft kick and big power.

Yes, *Diana* is buildable today, and the engines and boilers are available. In the accommodation plan below the outboard profile of *Diana* is

GASOLINE MARINE ENGINES.

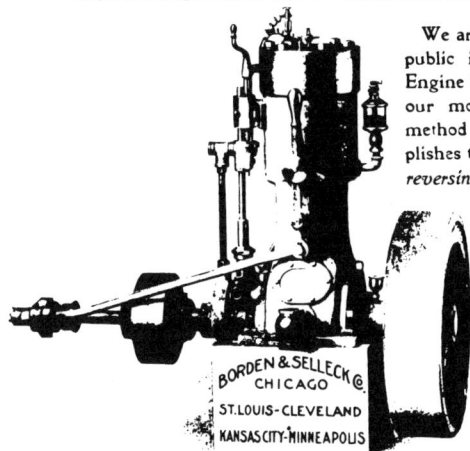

Figure 7. An advertisement in the back of the Fred W Martin catalog describes the load-lugging mill needed for a fantail launch.

The Sabb 2H is an 18-hp, two-cylinder engine with variable-pitch propeller. Like her small sister, the 2H has built-in 2:1 reduction, low fuel consumption, and comes with everything but a polishing rag.

The Norwegian-built Sabb diesel is a modern, heavy-duty, low-horsepower engine. This is the 6-8-hp HG, a single-cylinder thumper that hits its maximum rating at 2000 rpm and is designed for boats up to 23 feet.

shown a Semple 5-hp engine and a Semple fire-tube boiler. These engines and boilers are built by the Semple Engine Co. Inc., Box 6805, St. Louis, Missouri 63144. The Semple boiler seems to be the favorite among American owners today. The Semple literature is fulsome and descriptive, and the price of their powerplants is competitive with inboard heavy-duty gas or diesel engines.

If you are a classicist in steam, see Figure 8. This is the superb little

Figure 8. This steamboat buff's dream is now being built in Great Britain by the Beaumaris Instrument Co. Ltd. The engine is tandem compound, 2¼" x 4½" by 4" stroke. It is 25" high, 21" long, and 12" wide.

compound designed by Victor Mills, who died in 1974. This engine was designed for the Beaumaris Instrument Co. Ltd., Rosemary Lane, Beaumaris, Anglesey, Wales, Great Britain. They are in production, and H.A. Jones, head of the company, tells me he has just put through the shop a run of 11 of the hand-built beauties. These are expensive, of course, but a number have been sold and, being of exhibition quality, a few of them have graced some offices and baronial homes where, without pistons, they are moved by hidden electrical power. In a boat, these engines steam at 150 psi for about 6 hp. In initial tests, 4-3/4 hp was developed at 500 rpm on 100 pounds/square inch, and the phenomenally economical consumption of 36 pounds of steam per hour. (Doesn't take much fuel to heat about half a pail of water!)

The Mills compound is 25 inches high, 21 inches long, and 12 inches wide. The cylinders are 2-1/4 inches by 4-1/2 inches by 4 inch stroke.

Now, any such story as this has always evoked much correspondence for me, which is time-consuming and hence expensive. I cannot supply further data or copies of the Martin designs. But I must say that if you are serious, and a steam "nut," I will be glad to supply prints of *Diana* from my original tracings if you care to reimburse me for my time and trouble. I state this to discourage the merely curious.

For $30 I will supply large, clear drawings in 3/4-inch scale, 18 inches by 28 inches, on black Ozalid print paper, made from my originals. Address: Weston Farmer, N.A., 18970 Azure Road, Wayzata, Minnesota 55391. They will be sent return mail, first class prepaid.

28

The Hampton Launch
Whistler

There are so many ways to start the story of William Harnden Foster's self-designed, self-built Hampton boat *Whistler* that I hardly know where to begin.

Here is a barebones introduction:

Whistler, a 24-foot by 6 feet 9 inches by 2 feet 6 inches draft Hampton boat designed and built over 50 years ago by William Harnden Foster, nationally famed marine artist, and powered by a 25-hp Gray 4-cylinder VM marine engine, made 10 mph on trials. She is of strip construction with 1 inch by 7/8 inch white pine strips laid 1 inch to the hull thickness, and has an oak keel sided 3-1/2 inches with frames of oak 1 inch by 1-1/4 inches laid on 12-inch centers. She follows the type of boat used on Maine's Casco Bay between Cape Elizabeth and Small Point as developed by generations of fishermen.

So far, so good. Just bare bones; but bare bones carry no philosophical meat that gives nourishment to the judgment, to knowledge, or to dreams.

Then there is the poetic introduction, frequently used by men who Sit Down To Write and Who Take Pen In Hand. Like this:

Here is *Whistler,* designed and built by William Harnden Foster for his own use on Casco Bay. Although the design is over 50 years old, because *Whistler* is built of wood on time-tried proportions, and because the wind, the rain, and the pitch or scend of the ocean are timeless, she can be built today and will be as new as tomorrow morning's dew. Father Neptune can toss his trident fork at her, but *Whistler* will survive these dents with impunity.

This intro may fire up the dreamer, but really, isn't it just a poetic selling pitch? Neither approach has told why the design is so treasurable. Not much paper and ink have been chewed up.

What is needed is to combine the bare bones and the poetry with a dash of today's hard-nosed acerbic philosophy so that the men who were not here 50 years ago, or even 30 years ago, will know the excitement that is stirred by this Foster find. Men who know what a real motorboat looks like and smells like already sense the best way to introduce the vintage wine bottled up in *Whistler*. This is to compare the condition of boatbuilding art in her day against the state of the art today. An oblique introduction is needed.

Here is the introduction to *Whistler* that I have chosen in order to put some philosophical meat on the bare bones, It reads as follows:

Recently I went to a boat show. I was not at home with the floating rocket missiles and butter tubs that were on exhibit. These bore names intended to lead a fellow to believe that each was a super boat; was, in fact, the fullest flower of design genius since Neanderthal man first went to side wheeling on a log. I could see that most of the new boats would probably float and would probably go forward when the clutch was thrown in, but what boating had to do with an exhibition atmosphere of blasting-off-to-the-moon escaped me.

Then a profound truth struck with electric suddenness: the Golden Age of powerboat construction had reached its zenith just prior to World War II. I was glad to have lived and worked in that era of prideful, competent craftsmanship in the working of wood. It was the order of that day that the designers who turned out boats had to have a long apprenticeship in the shop, had to be schooled in the art of marine usage, and had to have an intimate knowledge of the sea—most especially an intimate knowledge of the sea. There really is no other way to competence.

At that time, if a man had tried to build a boat out of tissue paper and spit held together by stenographers' staples, and had managed to market her as being a Stella de Gink, he would have been jailed for swindling. Today, it seems, the only apprenticeship necessary for some fellows in marine design is a transcontinental voyage on the hurricane deck of a box car.

As I left the show, "them was my sediments." I reflected that we who lived in the day of great craftsmanship were not then aware that the boat and yacht building trade was at its ultimate height. The peak time came; it faded, vanishing in the turmoil of World War II reconstruction. A corollary thought belongs with this observation, which brings me to the nut of my praise for Foster's *Whistler*.

The nut of the matter is this: although there have been abundant

William Harnden Foster at the tiller of *Whistler*.

plans in the published record for the past 50 years as to sailing yachts, some of which have been resurrected and brought to light again, as Roger Taylor has done in past issues of *National Fisherman,* very few complete plans for unusually good small powerboats have been brought to light. The reason is that very few *complete* plans for *unusually good* small powerboats were ever published.

One of the best of these powerboat designs made such a profound impression on me over 50 years ago during my initial days as a ship draftsman that I have put in years of search for this boat. Yep, she was Foster's *Whistler,* published in the October 10, 1921, issue of *Motor Boat*—the Old Green Sheet. And so, by bare bones, by poetic introduction, and by comparative philosophies of yesterday's standards vs. today's Hard-Sell boating, you know that *Whistler* is something special, and you have some knowledge of her by the visual impact of her drawings.

Here is some meat for the hungry, further particulars of her construction condensed from the original story. *Whistler* was planked by the strip method as exposed in the detail nailing drawing on the next page. Foster explained that the original Hampton boat was invariably strip planked, but had a deep stern post and a tuck which was difficult to plank, so he eliminated it. Foster suggested using a mold at each station on his drawings, made of stout 7/8-inch pine well stayed. He said, "By using plenty of molds and fitting each strip carefully, one cannot go wrong. To be sure, it is a slower process than set work [carvel], but the fact that there is no caulking to be done evens the score. The difficulty of steaming ribs, which is the bane of most ama-

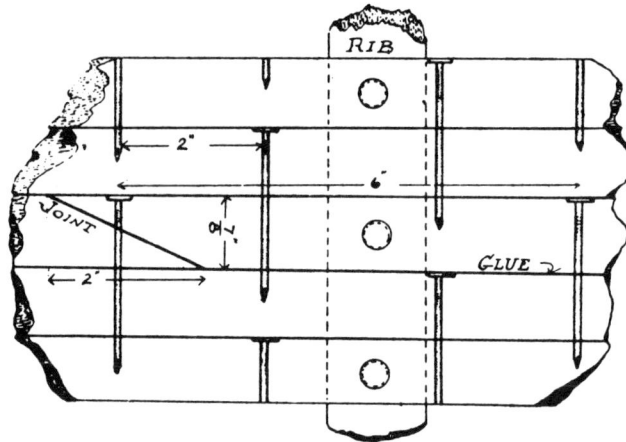

The strip method of construction

teurs, is reduced to a minimum. The planking is so rigid that a hot rib may be taken from the steam box and riveted in without danger of distorting the lines."

One thing seldom seen in the Hampton boats of today, which now center in indigenous population around Harpswell and Bailey and Orrs islands, is the yachtish, rounded transom. On *Whistler* the radius is 5 feet 6 inches, steam bent into oak transom planks of 1-1/2 inch oak. This is a large order for a backyard builder. I would set up such a transom on formed harpins, using double planking with vertical heavy strakes inboard, and lighter 1/2-inch by 6-inch steamed strakes, riveted, if the rounded transom was wanted. Pure practicality might dictate a usual flat transom, in which case it would be of 1-1/2 inch oak.

Whistler's girths are such that the spilings are nearly all equal, and call for only one or two stealers. It is this constancy, or near constancy, of girth that gives the Hampton the wide beam aft where the sheer is lower in freeboard, and results in the highly steeved bow usually seen in these hulls.

Foster's fine drawings show the disposition of most floor scantlings, and the small nailing plan, detailing the use of coated galvanized nails, also shows the making of a slash scarph in each strake where it may be needed. The planksheer, wale, and decking are drawn as he installed it. The decking is 1-1/4 inch white oak with laid, bunged fastenings. Otherwise the construction is old hat. The guts of the matter are illuminated in the offset table—the heart of all design.

Let me tell you something about Foster. William Harnden Foster was born in 1886 and was basically an artist by training, having studied at the Boston Museum of Fine Arts and later with the great magazine illustrator, Howard Pyle, at the latter's home in Wilmington, Delaware. During World War I, Bill Foster was a ship draftsman at a yard in South

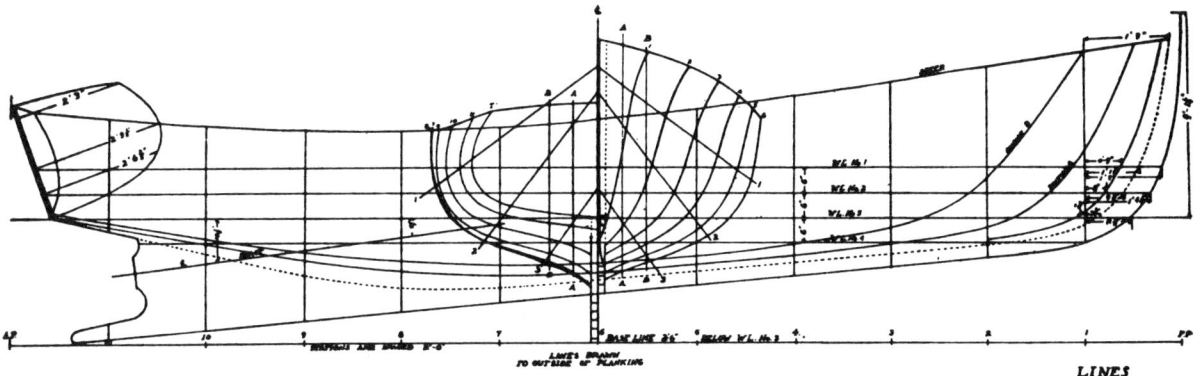

LINES
OF
"WHISTLER"
A 24 FOOT HAMPTON

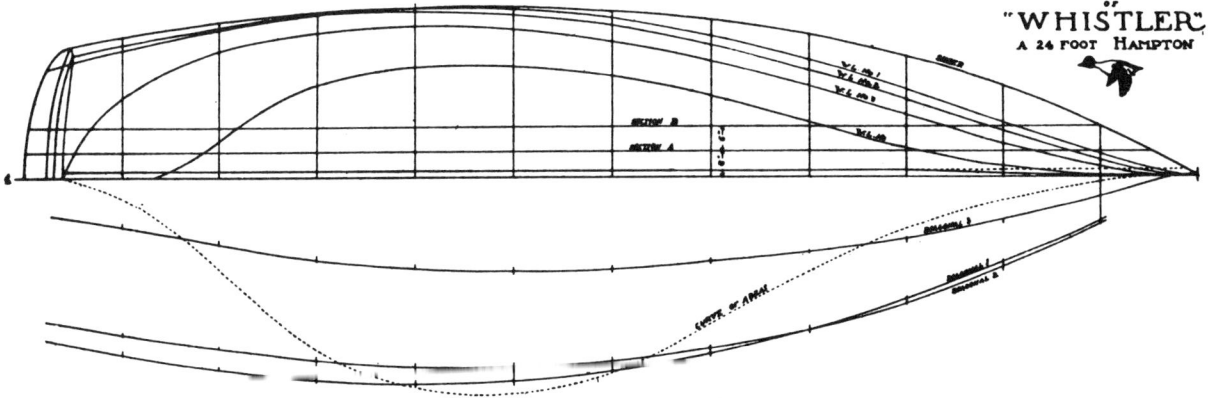

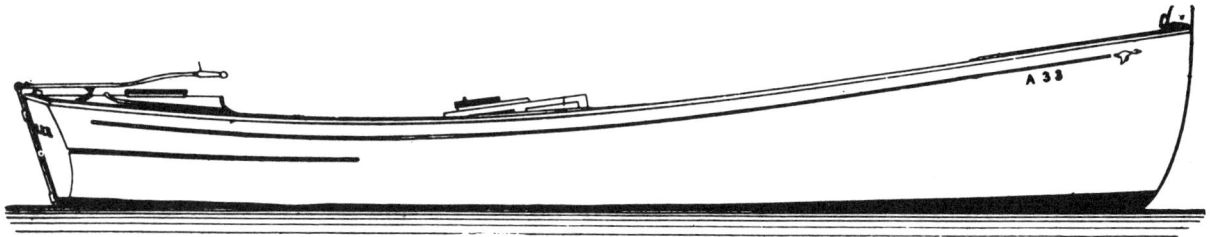

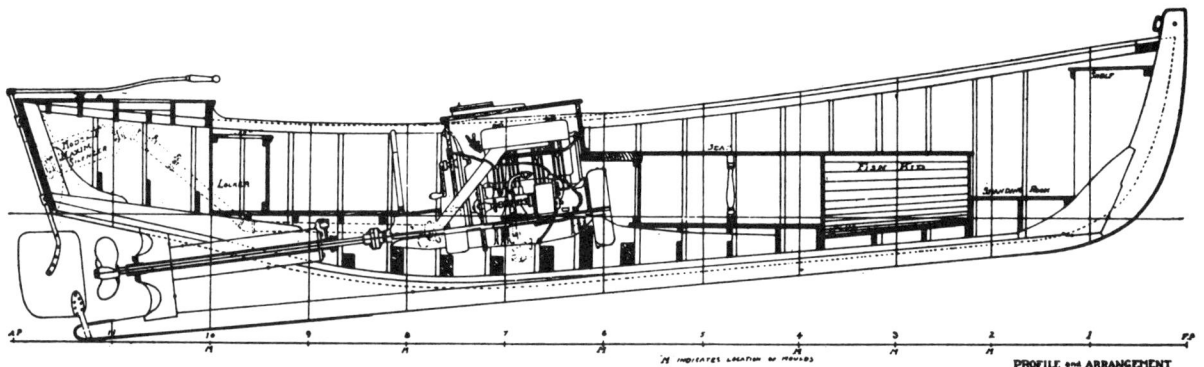

PROFILE and ARRANGEMENT
OF
"WHISTLER"
A 24 FOOT HAMPTON

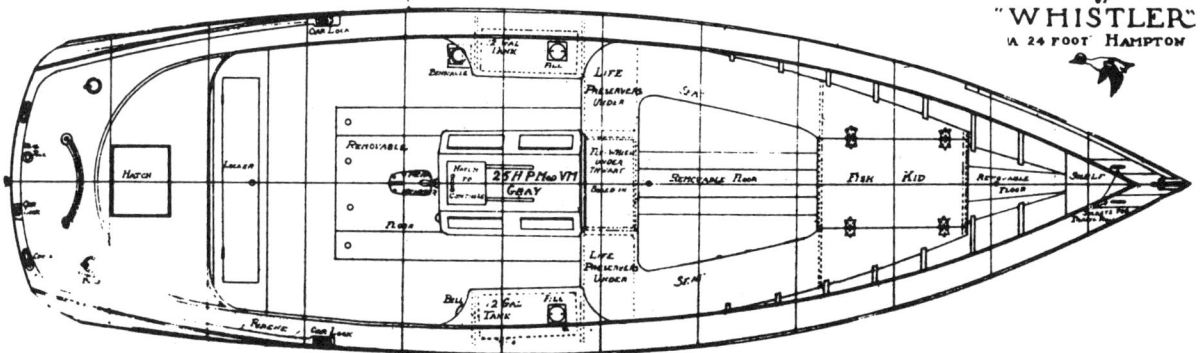

Freeport, Maine, that was building wooden cargo ships. His series of superb caricatures about the early scene in motorboat development were done in a period from 1919 to 1921, when he assumed the editorship of *Hunting and Fishing Magazine,* which was combined with the *National Sportsman.* He held this chair until 1936. Always in love with the sea and boats, he built a number of them near his summer home in Andover, Massachusetts.

Foster was a fine writer, specializing in outdoor subjects, and was a great expert with guns and dogs. In fact, he did many calendar oils for such companies as DuPont and Remington which depicted dogs in hunting scenes. Perhaps his best-known work of art was a picture of the New York Central's 20th Century Limited racing up the Hudson. This picture was in many railroad stations on railroad calendars for some time. He also painted pictures for the Missouri Pacific.

William Harnden Foster was the inventor of skeet shooting and was inducted into the Skeet Hall of Fame in 1970. Some of his thousands of illustrations are included in his book *New England Grouse Shooting,* which is a real classic and was recently reprinted after 30 years.

Bill died after the conclusion of field trials on October 31, 1941, at Scotland, Connecticut, of a heart attack at age 55. It is given to few men to be so gifted.

TABLE OF OFFSETS FOR "WHISTLER" — A 24 FOOT HAMPTON

Dimensions are given in feet, inches, and eights. Dimensions are to outside of planking.

STATIONS	F.P.	1	2	3	4	5	6	7	8	9	10	11	A.P.
HEIGHTS ABOVE BASE													
SHEER	6.0.6	5.9.6	5.6.2	5.2.6	4.11.3	4.8.2	4.5.6	4.3.6	4.2.7	4.3.1	4.4.2	4.6.1	4.8.0
RABBET		2.4.0	1.11.4	1.9.3	1.7.2	1.5.1	1.3.1	1.1.3	1.1.2	1.4.3	1.9.4	2.3.0	2.6.0
KEEL BOTTOM		2.0.0	1.8.4	STRAIGHT		LINE						0.1.1	
SECTION A		3.10.4	2.3.3	1.11.4	1.8.6	1.6.4	1.5.7	1.4.2	1.5.0	1.7.1	1.11.3	2.3.6	2.6.3
" B			3.2.6	2.3.4	1.11.4	1.8.6	1.7.1	1.6.5	1.7.4	1.9.3	2.0.6	2.4.4	2.6.7
HALF BREADTHS													
SHEER		1.0.0	1.10.1	2.5.2	2.10.3	3.1.6	3.4.0	3.5.0	3.4.5	3.3.0	2.11.5	2.6.6	2.2.0
RABBET	0.1.6	0.1.6	0.1.6	0.1.6	0.1.6	0.1.6	0.1.6	0.1.6	0.1.6	0.1.6	0.1.6	0.1.6	0.1.6
KEEL BOTTOM	0.0.2	0.0.2	0.0.7	0.1.6	0.1.6	0.1.6	0.1.6	0.1.6	0.1.6	0.1.6	0.1.6	0.1.6	
W.L. No.1		0.5.1	1.1.0	1.8.7	2.4.2	2.10.1	3.1.7	3.4.2	3.4.6	3.3.4	3.1.2	2.10.0	2.7.0
W.L. No.2		0.3.7	0.11.0	1.6.6	2.1.6	2.8.0	3.0.2	3.3.0	3.3.4	3.2.3	2.11.6	2.8.0	2.4.0
W.L. No.3		0.2.2	0.7.7	1.2.6	1.9.4	2.3.7	2.8.4	2.11.5	3.0.2	2.10.5	2.6.4	1.7.2	
W.L. No.4			0.2.5	0.6.7	1.1.0	1.1.4	2.0.3	2.2.4	2.2.3	1.10.2	0.8.7		
DIAGONAL 1		0.10.5	1.8.4	2.4.6	3.0.1	3.6.0	3.10.2	4.1.0	4.1.4	4.0.3	3.9.6	3.6.1	3.2.4
" 2		0.11.2	1.9.6	2.6.4	3.0.4	3.5.1	3.7.6	3.9.2	3.9.2	3.8.0	3.4.6	3.1.4	2.10.7
" 3		0.5.1	0.11.1	1.2.6	1.5.6	1.8.1	1.9.6	1.10.4	1.9.6	1.7.6	1.3.7	0.11.4	0.8.4

DIAGONAL No.1 INTERSECTS PERPENDICULAR 5.6.4 ABOVE BASE LINE and W.L. No.2 3.5.4 OUT

" No.2 " " 5.0.2 " " " W.L. No.4 2.3.7 "

" No.3 " " 3.1.0 " " " BASE LINE 2.3.6 "

In the October 10, 1921, *Motor Boat* story about the building of *Whistler,* which is much too long to reprint, Foster had this to say:

Before starting my design I measured some of the products of the best builders, and by comparing these figures I got a pretty good line on what the conservative dimensions should be. Next I made the model scaled 1 inch to the foot, using white pine in half-inch thicknesses.

As a naval architect I had not reached the stage where I felt that I could start the design of a boat with the flourish of a drawing pen and a T-square. I wanted to be able to look at the lines in a more material way, hence the model. When I got what seemed good to me, I took the model apart and by carefully measuring, developed a table of offsets from it, and from this table began my drawings. I do not imagine that this is the approved method of procedure, and yet it worked out quite well in my case.

As soon as I had carried my calculations as far as I could, I swallowed what pride I had in the matter and sought out William J. Deed, whom I knew to be an authority on small boat designing, and who had made a particular study of the type in which I was interested. Mr. Deed was kind enough to be interested in my efforts, and after going over the entire matter, I was greatly pleased when he handed down the decision that my plans were entirely practical as they stood.

I knew Billy Deed intimately in later years. And he was a good designer, any way you slice it. *Whistler* is doubly blessed.

There is an epilogue to this yarn:

I am something of an outdoorsman myself. Each winter I love to look outdoors at the snow piled 5 feet on the flat outside my study window. I perceive that the Groundhog has seen his shadow, and urged by the delicate art of the forest, aided by a thermometer at 20 below zero, the sap stirs in me for a new boat, which each spring jumps magically in ghost form from the snowdrifts. It is time for that old outdoorsman in me to dream up a new boat. Indoors.

Now it happens that I have an 18-24 hp Model A Red Wing unit powerplant with less than 10 hours of running time, but which is 57 years old. Her magneto is yet lively, she bars over freely, and she is itching to go again. Her particular charm is that she is equipped with what John G. Hanna's term for a rear starter was, "a second story backporch Armstrong twister." Her 24 horses are of the Clydesdale variety that will lug a 16 inch by 16 inch prop at 900 rpm, just ideal for a boat like *Whistler,* which would sag along with 9 knots in her teeth, nice going in this husky boat.

Whistler, I remembered, had had a 25 hp overhead valve Gray VM under a housing arrangement ideal for second story starters. *Whistler* would be the very thing! So I started a search for the Foster plans. She was a good boat, and this would be easier than working up a set of lines myself. Naval architects, like opera singers, sing their arias without loving it much, and at the end of a job, or performance, wash their hands and forget it. So I started searching for Foster's plans.

By the process of making new piles of magazines out of old piles of magazines, I found the October 10, 1921, true and fateful issue containing Foster. This was just before I was ready to unscrew my wig, peel my pants, throw my hat on the pile, and jump on it. Ah! Perseverance paid off. And so it has for you, dear reader. I am glad to share *Whistler* with you.

One or two closing notes: her offset table is not standard. The waterline is 2 feet 6 inches above base. The station spacing is 2 feet. Aside from these omissions, I think you have here enough so that any good boatbuilder could reproduce her.

29

William J. Deed's Hunting Cabin Launch

How many men have been around long enough to remember the term "hunting cabin launch"? Once considered the height of elegant indulgence in motorboats, the hunting cabin evaporated from national fashion along with detachable hard collars, high-buttoned shoes, and Rajo kerosene lamps. When the limitations of the superseding raised-deck cruiser again called for something better, the coach-roof hunting cabin was revived under the name "trunk cabin."

Here, right before your eyes, is an authentic hunting cabin launch designed by a great old master, William J. Deed. She stands out as a cameo of art, doubly appreciated by all old-timers who remember when boatbuilding was a trade that called for skilled artisans at the bench. She is not only put together as a good wooden boat should be, but she also has a hull form which was well understood before boatbuilding became a plasterer's picnic.

This hull is of just the right size to fill a neglected gap in today's boating market: 20 feet length overall by 7 foot 6 inch beam by 2 foot 6 inch draft. She is designed to give 6 to 8 mph with from 5 to 10 hp—an engine that can swing an 18-inch propeller is recommended by Deed as being the right prescription. Only with a slow-turning engine, able to handle a wheel of from 16 to 18 inches, will this little vessel deliver the kind of ride that is now almost a memory, and is, unfortunately, unknown to legions of today's younger people.

Let me make an illustrative comparision: a rowing shell with eight oars, each pulled slowly on the haft end of a big blade, will shoot a shell along with a powerful glide that is a delight to watch. It is a quiet speed. Theoretically, it is possible to crew the shell with 300 midgets, each dipping frantically with soda straws to produce the same muscular output and deliver the same shell speed. The output and uproar would be frantic. Today's 2,500 to 3,000 rpm engines are soda-straw stuff alongside the loafing old one-lung whompers of yesteryear. The new midget engine horses snarl and bite, but the old horses could kick.

The simple technical reason for the difference in characteristics is easily explained. Engine ratings today at high rpm show a steeply climbing torque curve. Cut off the revolutions by a slight load, and the torque falls off rapidly. Older engines, based on slowly swept piston volume, have flat torque curves, and an overload that reduces the rpm a few revs does not kill the engine's output much.

You will note that at the business end of William J. Deed's power train he shows a proper propeller, not a bent-Z wire coat hanger seemingly considered very "in" by young designers who copy each other. This proper propeller is a pump. A large-diameter pump is more effective when moving a large mass of water at relatively low velocity than is a small-diameter pump moving a small mass of water at high velocity. To put it another way, it is the nature of water to cooperate with large mass and low velocity better than with small mass at high velocity. This is the secret of the ride that a boat like *Cameo* here will give you.

While on the subject of propellers, let me add a few jig steps of lore about wheels. It is my practice to allow between the hull and blade tips at least the space of a doubled-up fist. As the propeller draws water to accelerate it aft, the slipstream becomes contracted. If the blade tip comes close to the hull, the suction effect of the blade drawing water will produce both a thumping noise and severe erosion in the hull paint, wood, or metal. This thump is not "throw off" as is popularly supposed. It is a starved, suction effect. Of course, if you use a Lazy Z, horseranch, bent-wire propeller, none of this applies, because a bent wire will not propel the boat. Deed's drawing shows a 20-inch wheel with 1-1/2 inch tip clearance, so there is plenty of room to feed water to an 18-inch wheel.

There are a number of other very interesting subtle points of art about the design of this Deed masterpiece. Note that the aft running lines come to the surface. There is no submerged transom. This is one of the secrets of an easily driven boat with low wake in the low-speed range. Another thing that will grab the eye of any old pro is the fact that the deck outline in plan fits the sheer sweep in profile. For lack of any better term, this is what is known as a "homogeneous curve"—that is, one curve belongs to another. They are related.

The young designer who tosses a swept sheer with one curve, and any

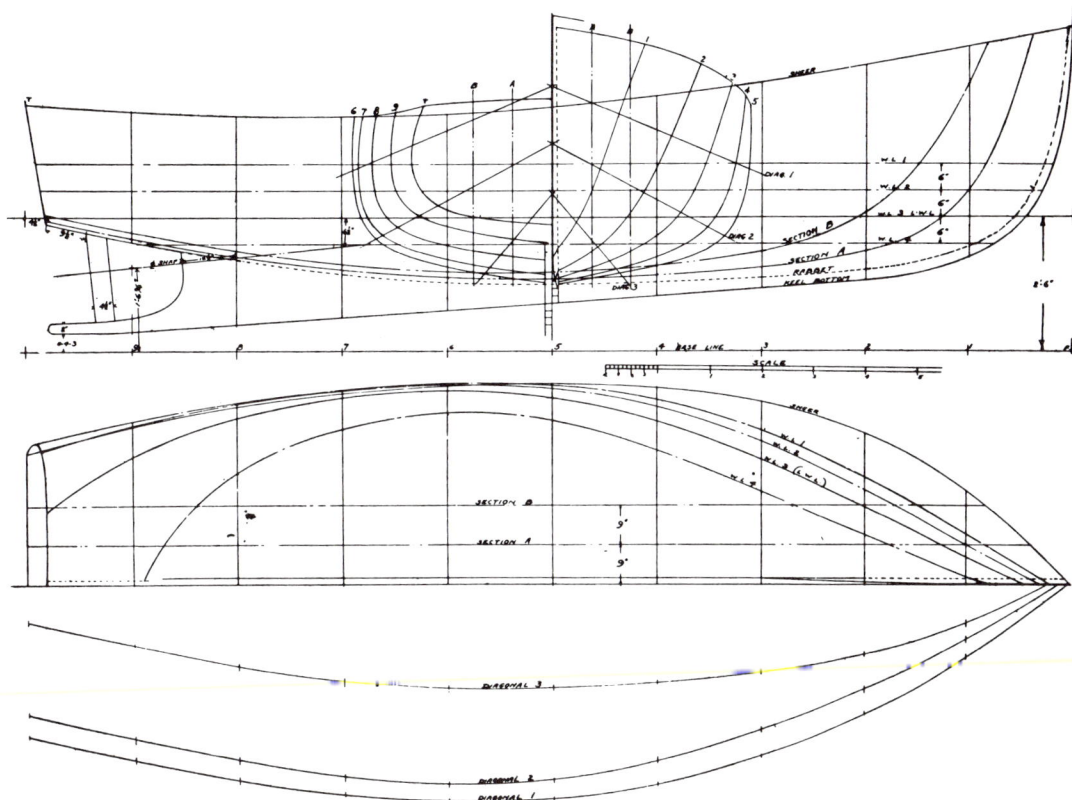

	STATIONS	F.P.	1	2	3	4	5	6	7	8	9	A.P.
HEIGHTS ABOVE BASE	SHEER	6-0-2	5-8-1	5-4-0	5-0-1	4-9-1	4-6-6	4-5-1	4-4-5	4-4-6	4-5-5	4-7-3
	RABBET	—	1-11-3	1-6-1	1-4-3	1-3-4	1-3-0	1-3-3	1-5-1	1-8-3	2-0-4	2-4-4
	KEEL BOTTOM	—	1-9-0	1-3-6	1-2-0	STRAIGHT				0-4-3		—
	SECTION A	—	3-0-0	1-10-3	1-6-6	1-5-0	1-4-3	1-4-2	1-6-0	1-9-1	2-1-2	2-5-0
	" B	—	5-0-0	2-7-0	1-10-3	1-7-1	1-5-7	1-5-5	1-7-3	1-10-4	2-2-5	2-6-2
HALF-BREADTHS	SHEER	—	1-9-2	2-10-1	3-5-3	3-8-4	3-9-4	3-9-0	3-7-1	3-4-0	2-11-5	2-5-2
	RABBET	0-1-4	0-1-4	0-1-4	0-1-4	0-1-4	0-1-4	0-1-4	0-1-4	0-1-4	0-1-4	0-1-0
	KEEL BOTTOM	0-0-2	0-0-2	0-0-5	0-1-4	0-1-4	0-1-4	0-1-4	0-1-4	0-1-4	0-1-4	—
	W.L. 1	—	0-11-3	2-0-3	2-11-0	3-6-0	3-9-1	3-9-4	3-8-1	3-5-0	3-0-5	2-8-0
	W.L. 2	—	0-9-0	1-9-2	2-8-3	3-4-2	3-8-2	3-9-0	3-7-6	3-4-3	2-11-4	2-5-5
	W.L. 3 L.W.L.	—	0-6-2	1-5-1	2-4-3	3-1-2	3-6-2	3-7-4	3-6-0	3-1-4	2-5-4	1-4-4
	W.L. 4	—	0-2-0	0-11-2	1-9-0	2-6-3	3-1-2	3-2-3	2-11-0	2-1-0	—	—
	DIAGONAL 1	—	1-4-5	2-5-4	3-3-0	3-9-4	4-0-6	4-1-2	3-11-7	3-8-4	3-3-6	2-10-4
	" 2	—	1-0-3	1-11-5	2-9-1	3-4-0	3-8-4	3-9-4	3-7-6	3-3-7	2-10-3	2-5-4
	" 3	—	0-8-3	1-3-6	1-8-0	1-10-3	1-11-4	1-11-6	1-9-7	1-6-1	1-1-3	0-8-5

OFFSET TABLE of **20 FT. CRUISER** DESIGNED FOR *"POWER BOATING"* William J. Deed NAVAL ARCHITECT - NYACK, N.Y.

DIMENSIONS ARE GIVEN IN FEET, INCHES AND EIGHTHS — 5-8-1 READS 5'-8⅛"

DIMENSIONS ARE GIVEN AND LINES ARE DRAWN TO OUTSIDE OF PLANKING.

DIAGONAL 1 INTERSECTS PERPENDICULAR 4-11-3 ABOVE BASE AND W.L. 2 - 4-8-4 OUT
" 2 " " 3-10-4 " " " W.L. 4 - 3-6-6 "
" 3 " " 2-11-2 " " " BASE LINE 2-6-4 "

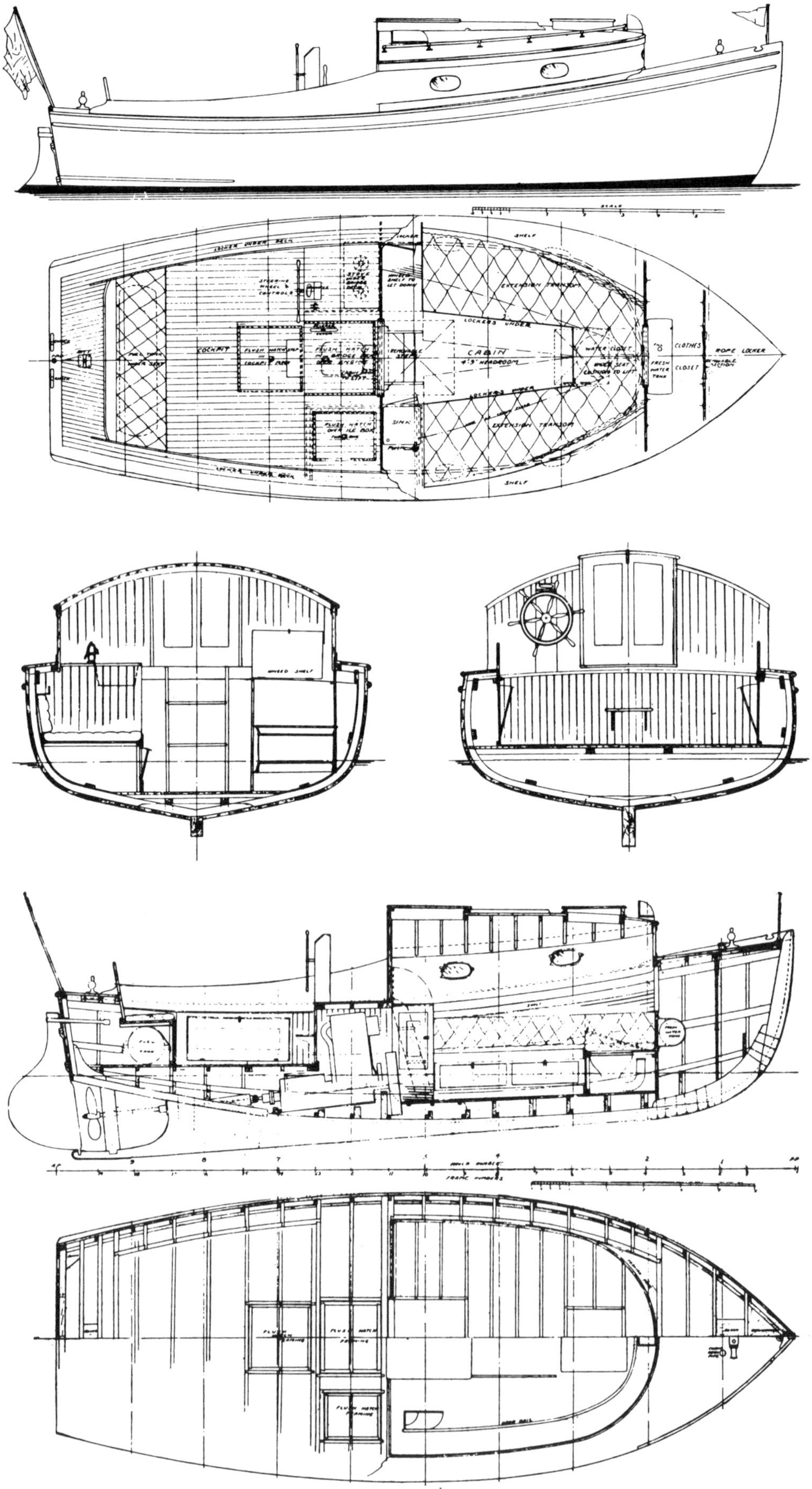

SCALE
SHELF
LOCKER UNDER DECK
COCKPIT
CABIN
4'-3" HEADROOM
LOCKERS UNDER
EXTENSION TRANSOM
WATER CLOSET
FRESH WATER TANK
CLOTHES CLOSET
ROPE LOCKER
SINK
HINGED SHELF
FLUSH HATCH OVER ICE BOX
FUEL TANK
FRAME NUMBERS

arbitrary plan curve with another tossed curve, will find the resulting hull to have a cowhorn or moose-shouldered sweep that is anything but sweet. An easy way to make the two curves homogeneous is to cut the plan curve in cardboard, and take the sheer heights from the desired sag of the cardboard when in a catenary condition. (No charge for the tip; it is a good one.)

You will note that Deed shows his floors abaft the frames from the midsection forward and aft as the hull narrows down. In the mid-portion of the hull where the hull shape changes little, floors can be fitted easily. Where the hull narrows down, they can only be snugly fitted from abaft the frame. Note, also, the sturdy deck construction. It is refreshing to see.

When I leap gracefully from the pier to the deck of my trusty yacht, I want my twinkling toes to land on something that will stay put. I don't hanker to flap on into the bilges with a load of busted lumber jamming my crotch. *Cameo*'s scantlings will not let this happen.

Her keel is of white oak or yellow pine, sided 3 inches and molded as shown. Her stem is of white oak, sided 3 inches. Planking is specified as white cedar, white pine, or cypress to finish 7/8 inch. Floor timbers are sided 1 inch, fitted to frames of white oak sided 1-1/8 inches and molded 1-3/4 inches on 12-inch centers. The clamp is to be of Douglas fir, or yellow pine in one length, 1 inch by 3 inches. These are the main specs.

It seems to me that this hull could be built as an open boat with only a spray hood forward, and, rigged out as a family picnic outfit, she would be of just the right size to be trailerable for this service. Her inboard volume would be copious enough to accommodate a variety of layouts of this nature. Yes, after great and lengthy deliberation, the right word is "copious."

William J. Deed designed this boat in 1923. Deed was, at that time, the chief naval architect for the International Shipbuilding Corp. at Nyack, New York. He later went to the design department of the Gas Engine and Power Co., and Charles L. Seabury Co., Consolidated. This mouthful of corporate image was later shortened to Consolidated, and as everybody knows who has been in the boat game for any time at all, Consolidated was the builder of fine yachts of Steinway quality. I first met Bill Deed when he was working at Consolidated.

In initial exposure, this boat was called *Flapper*. At that time, the term was a derisive label for young ladies who flouted convention and decorum by swishing about with their galoshes unbuckled and flapping. These gals are now grandmothers going "Tch! Tch!" at the didoes of young female rebels who wear about nothing at all, or pack it into men's Levis. I like the name *Cameo* better, and have applied it to Deed's timeless masterpiece.

30

The 18-Foot Runabout
Pollywog

Because of the national cackling and henhouse uproar over the United States eke-onomy, one outcome is as predictable as is tomorrow's sunrise. There will be a new trend in powerboating. Gone will be the boats demanding wads of petro-chemicals in their construction that burn enough gasoline in one day to run an automobile for weeks.

You can bet your bottom Swiss franc that men who seek true peace and serenity afloat will be demanding simpler boats. I do not mean the three-boards-and-a-shingle variety. I mean the small powerboats we used to know in the early decades of powerboat evolution. These were all of traditional wooden construction, considered smallish if under 22 feet in length. They were powered with one-cylinder or two-cylinder marine engines, either 2- or 4-cycle and usually under 10 hp swinging propellers with "big buckets." Speeds of 7 or 8 mph would give you a fine day's outing and would get you back home on time if you had sense enough to know when to turn around. Low-pressure craft like this had highly developed hull forms in their day, because their power was low. There was none of this butting an ankle-deep wave three times and then going around it, as is mostly the case with top-of-the-water shingles. The old launches were weighty enough to sit *in* the water instead of *on it*.

One of the best of this kind of little boat was *Pollywog,* designed by that prolific old master, William J. Deed, who was most knowledgeable in early motorboat designing. After much search, I have found the full plans Bill Deed drew for this boat. They appeared in the December 10, 1919, show issue of *Motor Boat*.

Pollywog is 18 feet long, 6-foot beam over the planking, and has a designed draft of 1 foot 10 inches. She is 15 feet 1 inch on the water-line and has a maximum waterline beam of 5 feet 6 inches. Her keel is to be of 2-inch by 12-inch oak, with the apron being yellow pine 1 inch by 5 inches. Stem, knees, and horn timber are from 2-1/2 inch by 8 inch white oak. Frames are to be spaced 6-inch centers of 7/8 inch by 7/8 inch white oak or elm. Decking to be 3/4 inch by 2 inch white pine. The coaming is to be of 5/8 inch by 7 inch white oak.

Such are the main scantlings. Deed published a bill of materials along with the design, but for the man who reads and runs, both the bill of materials and Deed's seven pages of leisurely text are too long to re-print.

Of her powerplant, I quote Bill Deed directly:

Now a word about the engine. There are so many suitable ones for such a boat that we shall not attempt to make a choice. We believe that either a two- or four-stroke cycle motor of from 5 to 10 hp developing this at between 500 and 800 rpm and swinging a propeller 14″ or 16″ in diameter is the proper outfit for this boat. With such a motor you can expect a speed of from 7 to 9 mph. If the motor you install requires an 18″ propeller, you can enlarge the propeller port and obtain clearance for an 18″ wheel by simply cutting into the rudder support and the skeg a trifle or dropping the latter an inch.

You can plainly see, from the foregoing amount of type, paper, and ink that Deed took to say "open up the propeller port," why his highly detailed story ran to seven pages. Also, he describes engines in plentiful supply as to type, available 56 years ago, and the like of which are getting rarer.

It will be of no use to build *Pollywog* and put in a 2,500 rpm mill of *any* horsepower that must use a wee wheel with teaspoon blades. The whole idea of the old-time low-powered motorboat was hung around the idea of *shove,* which can only be had with a large wheel of the diameter Deed recommended, turning at the shaft revs usual with the old one-lung two-cyclers.

Large disc area on the propeller in relation to the midsectional area of the hull was an old design secret in getting shove. Anything less than 25 percent of midsectional area in a wheel usually produces a prop that simply makes whipped cream out of sea water and gets the boat no place. I suppose that some such mill as a 6 hp air-cooled engine could be used and would possibly be amenable to gearing down from 2,500 rpm to a fourth of that number of shaft turns at the wheel, but it has been my experience that high-speed mills whirr so much they render passengers "nervous from the service."

Inasmuch as this engine problem today is a real one, let me give you a few engineering hints. I have run my planimeter over *Pollywog*'s

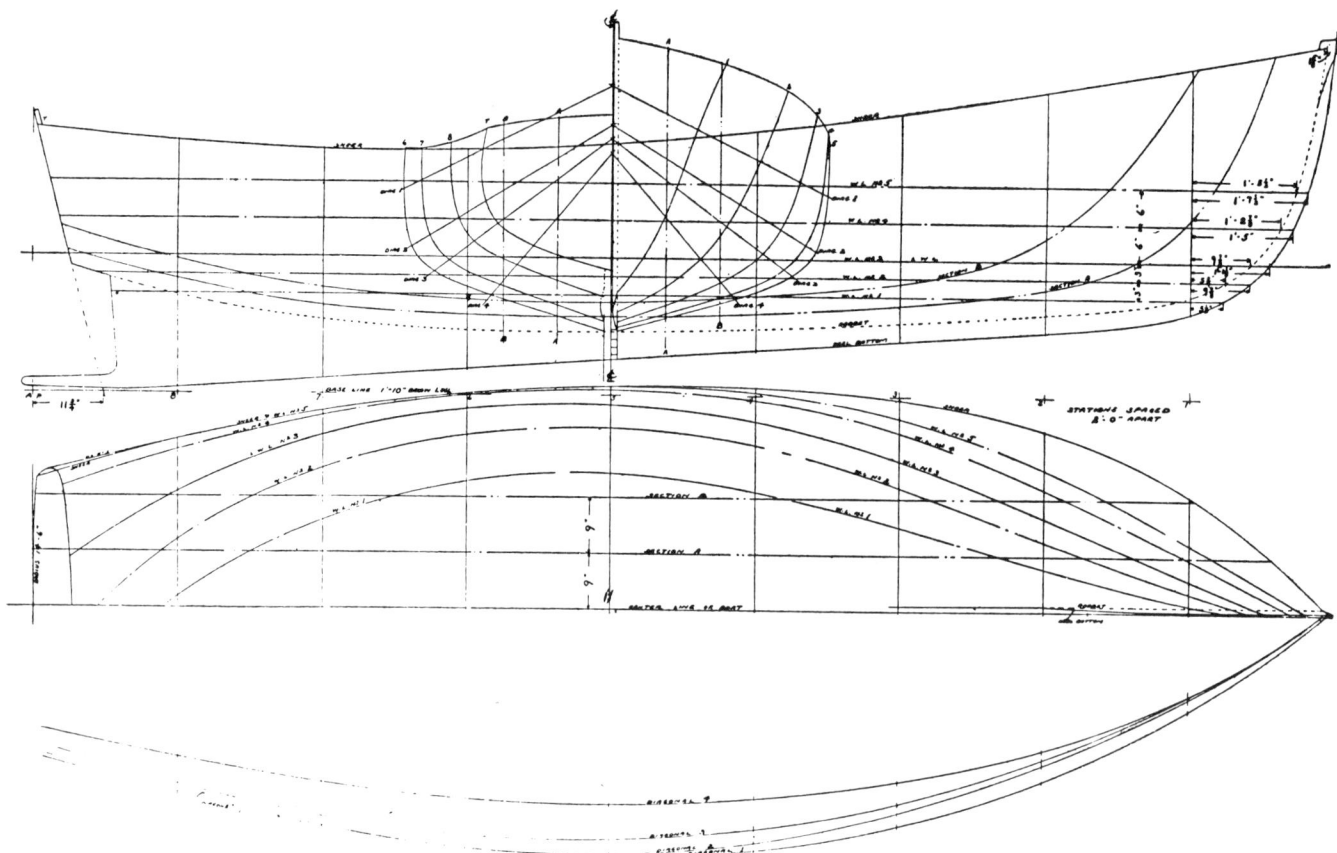

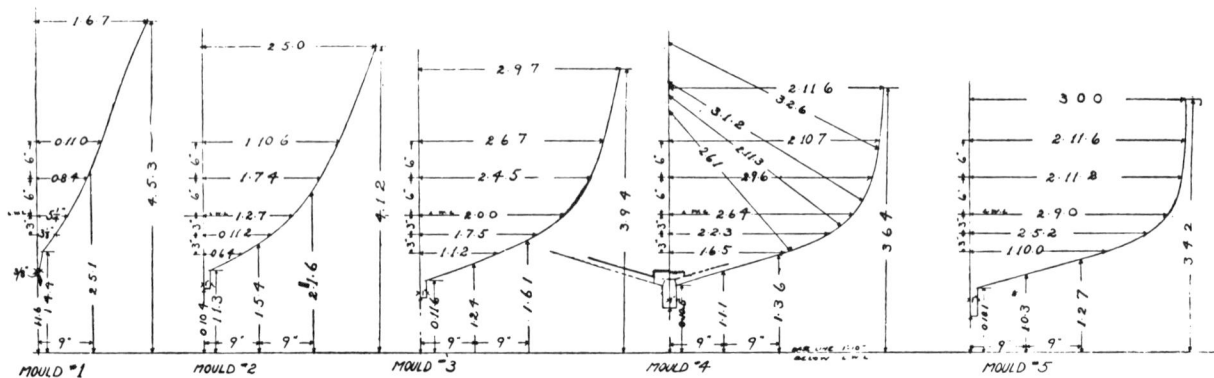

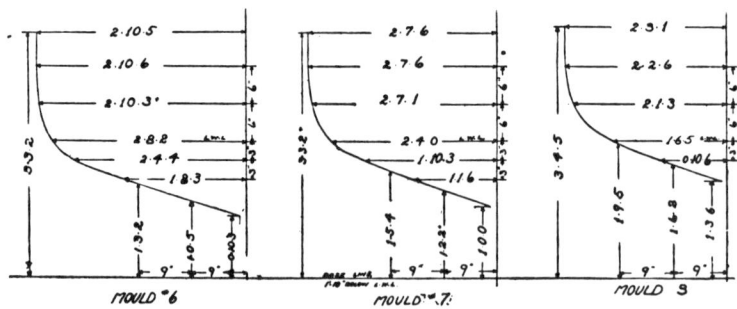

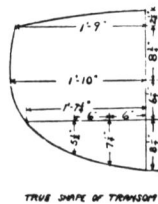

TRUE SHAPE OF TRANSOM

MOULD #1   MOULD #2   MOULD #3   MOULD #4   MOULD #5

MOULD #6   MOULD #7   MOULD #8

TABLE of OFFSETS
DIMENSIONS IN FEET, INCHES AND EIGHTHS

	STATIONS	FP	1	2	3	4	5	6	7	8	AP
HEIGHTS ABOVE BASE	SHEER	4.9.2	4.5.3	4.1.2	3.9.4	3.6.4	3.4.2	3.3.2	3.3.2	3.4.5	3.6.6
	RABBET		1.4.4	1.1.3	0.11.6	0.10.3	0.10.1	0.10.3	1.0.0	1.3.6	1.8.2
	KEEL BOTTOM		1.1.6	0.10.4	STRAIGHT		LINE			0.0.7	
	SECTION A		2.5.1	1.5.4	1.2.4	1.1.1	1.0.3	1.0.5	1.2.2	1.6.2	1.10.4
	" B		4.4.0	2.1.6	1.6.1	1.3.6	1.2.7	1.3.2	1.5.4	1.9.5	2.2.6
HALF-BREADTHS	SHEER		1.6.7	2.5.0	2.9.7	2.11.6	3.0.0	3.0.5	2.7.6	2.3.1	1.8.7
	RABBET	0.1.0	0.1.0	0.1.0	0.1.0	0.1.0	0.1.0	0.1.5	0.1.0	0.1.0	0.1.0
	KEEL BOTTOM		0.0.3	0.1.0	0.1.0	0.1.0	0.1.0	0.1.0	0.1.0	0.1.0	0.1.0
	WL No.5		0.1.0	1.0.6	2.6.7	3.0.7	3.1.6	3.0.6	2.7.6	2.2.6	0.9.6
	WL No.4		0.8.4	1.7.4	2.4.5	2.9.6	2.11.2	2.10.3	2.7.1	2.1.3	1.7.2
	WL No.3		0.5.2	1.2.7	2.0.0	2.6.4	2.9.0	2.8.2	2.4.0	1.6.5	0.8.0
	W.L No.2		0.3.1	0.11.2	1.7.5	2.2.3	2.5.2	2.4.4	1.10.3	1.0.6	
	W.L No.1			0.6.4	1.1.2	1.6.5	1.10.0	1.8.3	1.1.6	0.2.1	
	DIAGONAL 1		1.3.6	2.3.1	3.10.5	3.2.6	3.3.5	3.2.5	2.11.2	2.6.0	2.0.0
	" 2		1.6	2.0.4	2.8.4	3.1.2	3.3.4	3.2.5	2.11.1	2.5.4	2.0.2
	" 3		1.2	1.11.5	2.7.0	2.11.3	3.1.0	3.0.4	2.9.1	2.4.2	1.11.8
	" 4		1.3	1.10.4	2.3.5	2.6.1	2.7.1	2.6.3	2.4.1	2.0.0	1.7.6

DIAG "1" CROSSES ℄ 4.1.4 ABOVE BASE AND WL No5 2.8.2 OUT
DIAG "2" " " 3.7.2 " " WL No3 3.0.1 "
DIAG "3" " " 3.5.0 " " WL No2 2.6.4 "
DIAG "4" " " 3.2.6 " " BASE LINE 2.10.2 "

midsection as laid out in 1-inch scale on my board. I find her midsectional area to be 3.40 square feet. From her offsets of 5.5-foot beam by 15.08 feet waterline length, times .958 feet mean draft to rabbet, her water block is 79.45 cubic feet. About .33 to .38 will be found to be the usual block coefficient in boats of this character, so, using a water block coefficient of .35, and multiplying the block volume of 79.45 by .35, *Pollywog* displaces 27.80 cubic feet. Multiply this by 64 pounds (the weight of a cubic foot of sea water) and we have 1,779 pounds as *Pollywog*'s weight. You can see how some slowly applied blade area will be needed to get authority into moving her. A 16-inch wheel will have just under 40 percent of midsectional area swept by the wheel's disc. A 14-inch wheel will have 33 percent of the midsectional area. A 12-inch wheel is 25 percent of the midsectional area. Anything less is just "whiffin."

There are still a couple of engines, of the kind that are required, being made today. One is the Acadia, a brawny, well-made engine available in either make-and-break or jump-spark ignition. This is a Canadian engine, built in Bridgewater, Nova Scotia. The 4 hp Acadia would do well in *Pollywog,* because Canadian horses are of the beer-wagon variety, not little Shetland ponies that scream at what is happening to their innards if you try to get rated horsepower out of them. The 4 hp Acadia is easily equal to an American 6 hp mill. I have been told that the Atlantic motor is still being made in Lunenburg, Nova Scotia, at the Lunenburg Foundry there. These, too, are husky engines. And it is

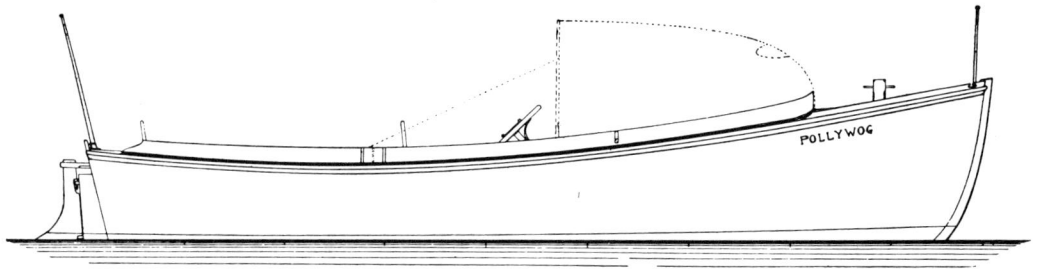

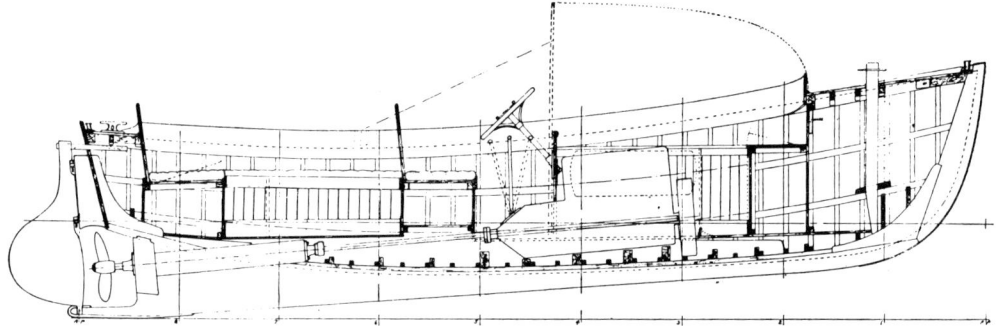

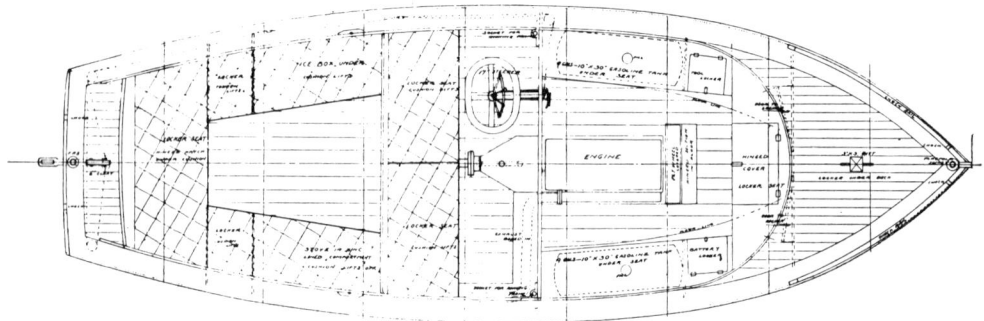

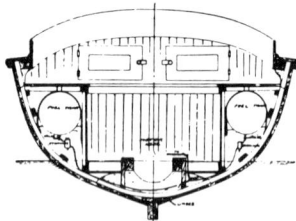

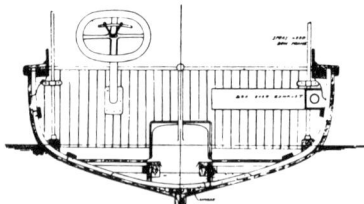

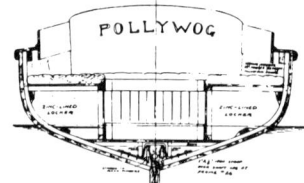

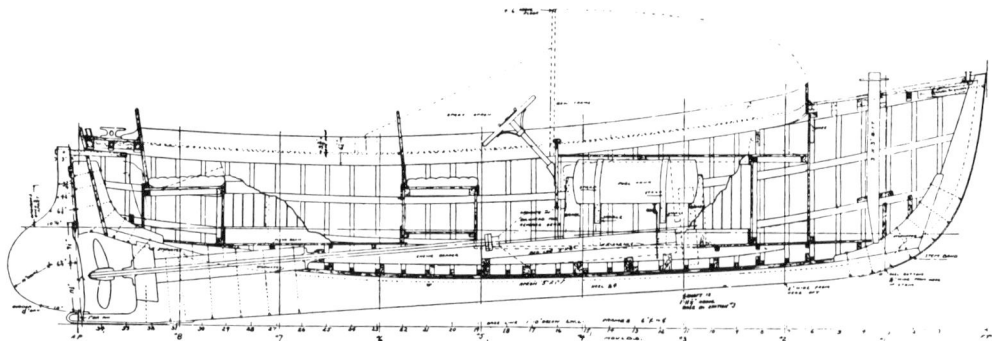

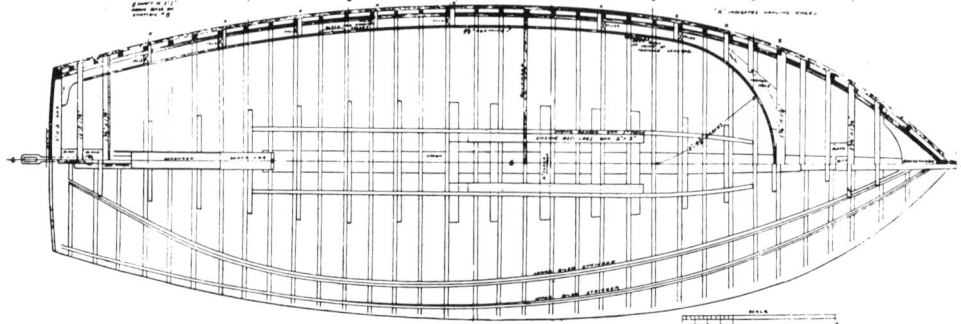

perfectly surprising how many old one-and two-barrel mills are still around.

I confess I have not followed the current small-engine field as it exists today. There may be some weighty small engines being produced in this country that will fill the bill.

Having dwelt on the power problem to some extent because it is important in getting from a boat of *Pollywog*'s nature the inherent qualities to be had in the ride she'll give you, let me dwell a bit on some of the old-time art in her design. Designers who worked out the correct proportions of motorboats in the era of low-powered craft had to get their mobility and comfort from hull form. Few men were better at this than William J. Deed. You will note that *Pollywog*'s turn of the bilge comes *above* the waterline. A small boat's transverse stability comes in the rapid shift from port to starboard, or on the other hand, in the rapid build-up of the "in wedge" and the rapid falling off of the "out wedge." The proper way to do this is to carry the turn of the bilge pretty well out of water.

Also, you will note there is considerable trip to the stem. This makes for dryness. Also, these old motorboats had what is known as "trail" to their deck lines in plan. Clean release of the wake requires that no very great amount of transom be submerged. This trail feature is always the earmark of these easily driven craft. In fact, so ingrained was this notion that when the American Power Boat Association set up gentlemen's runabout racing rules, no boat was allowed to race in competition if the immersed area of the transom was over half the area of the midsection area. This caused a lot of Leaping Lena boats as power increased.

So, William J. Deed knew what he was doing when he designed *Pollywog*. I knew Bill in later years, and his ending is a tragic one. Once the fair-haired naval architect up around Boston, he gravitated to Nyack, New York, where he produced the International 32-foot standardized cruisers produced by the International Shipbuilding Corp. of Nyack. These gave the Elco 34 Cruisettes a good run for the money. Bill later set up a design office in the old World Newspaper Building in New York City, facing City Hall square. I last saw him during these days, a sad but dignified little man whose cuffs were frayed and whose vest was liberally sprinkled with gravy stains.

Once, some years later, I found a book containing a lot of his designs and sent him a copy, with complimentary comments. From this I heard nothing at the moment. Shortly afterward, I was visiting Bill Crosby in his office when Crosby took over the editing job on *Motor Boat* after World War II service at Huckins. The office of that magazine was, at that time, in a dingy section around the lower Manhattan financial district. The name Beekman Street flashes to mind. Bill Crosby and I had been out behind the main office in a cavernous storage room when, returning, I spied a rickety little drafting board sitting all alone by a cob-webbed window that had an air space to the adjacent brick wall. I asked Crosby if he was setting up in the art business, thinking to pull his leg.

Crosby swept his arm toward the pitiful display, and said, "The end of Billy Deed."

Returning to Lake Superior and my home on Isle Royale, I received a letter from Mrs. Deed. The book I had sent Deed had reached her hands. "I want to keep this to show our boys in what high esteem some men held their father." That was all.

In about a week I got a note from Bill Deed himself. It stated he had walked out of his New York office one day and was now in New Jersey. He would never go back—and didn't know or care what had happened to the office. I later learned from a mutual friend that William J. Deed had died in an obscure town in New Jersey. At that time, in the 1950s, I should imagine Deed was about 65 years old.

This story has been kept short so that *Pollywog*'s art may be long. A few anomalies appear: Deed shows a four-cylinder powerplant, although in his quoted text he opted for the then-standard one-cylinder or two-cylinder inboards. The reason for the difference is that, at the time of *Pollywog*'s publication, there were a few four-cylinder small powerplants hitting the market. The "unit powerplant" idea was a new thing. Palmer's "Little Pal" of 15 hp, Red Wing's Baby Doll of 10-14 hp, and Universal's 9-12 hp motor were being introduced. Deed allowed for the space and weight on his drawings.

It may seem anomalous to suggest that the knock-down boat kit game may come back again as a result of high-cost gasoline, taxed to the prohibitive point on some sort of horsepower rating. Washington cannot penalize automobiles without taking a swipe at the boating scene. Boats such as *Pollywog* may again be offered. If, 50-odd years ago, there were over 15,000 backyard boats built every year—published statistics of that time support the figure—certainly today's boat bugs have equal skill and enterprise. Knock-down boats were once big business.

One thing is certain: smaller boats of lower pressure will again become the only sensible thing to own.

I am glad to share with you Bill Deed's taut drafting. It is the work of a man who worked in ink in the thorough fashion normal with early draftsmen in the design trade. The work shown here must have taken a month to six weeks of careful drafting to produce. I think of Billy Deed, and then think of some of the presumptuous drafting splashology done in whim-wham, thank-you-ma'am style by some of today's kids who think their work professional. (You will note that Bill Deed did not try to drive a boat with a Z-shaped coat hanger.)

Pollywog is pure gold, done by a master of his craft.

31

The Low-Powered Launch Coyote II

There's something about a small, old-time, low-pressure motorboat that grabs many a man. These boats are easy to read as boats, using the word "read" in the sense that one can look at them and instantly know how they will ride, what their feel for the water will be. The amount of glowing satisfaction they give in ownership comes forth from the printed page like a gentle sea breeze on a summer afternoon.

These truths, I am finding, are shared by the widening number of men who have written to me about such boats as *Whistler,* by William Harnden Foster, and Billy Deed's *Pollywog*, which have their own chapters in this book. I clearly discern a two-fold reason for this interest. One is that of late years the inboard small launch has been neglected. The attention has all swung to the Jazza Maru drugstore speederinos, of which the public is getting a bellyful. And the second reason is that small inboard power has a special charm that has been overlooked. At least half the fellows who like these old launches are "engine oriented" more than they are "boat oriented."

Because there have been no boats of modern derivation that could touch the work of the old masters who developed power boating in the 1895-1920 period, and because even in that day the published plans for unusually good small boats were few and far between, I have been digging backward in my lifetime files to share with you the thrills of finding some of the real daisies.

One of these old, easy-to-read boats, a type once referred to reverently as a "launch," was *Coyote,* designed about 1907 by Edson B. Schock, one of the early greats in yacht and motorboat design.

Coyote moving along, making little wake.

Coyote's lines appeared in the February 1974 issue of *National Fisherman* and are reprinted in this book in Chapter 20. A picture of her underway appears in this chapter as Figure 1. This entrancing launch was referred to as a type that was easily driven, for *Coyote* was credited by *The Rudder* as having a speed of 12.5 mph with a 10 hp, 2-cylinder engine.

Coyote in February of 1974 touched a live nerve of interest. I jumped for glee when Edson I. Schock, son of the original designer, wrote to me, stating that in 1946 he had taken the lines of *Coyote* and had produced *White Swan. White Swan,* pictured in Figure 2 shows the 1946 version to advantage.

Here is Edson I. Schock's letter:

Dear Mr. Farmer:

Naturally, I was interested in the discussion of *Coyote*, designed by my father in 1907, which you published in this issue of the *Fisherman.*

I thought you might be interested in knowing that a copy of this launch was built in 1946, and is still in use, as far as I know.

Mr. W.H. Nichols of Waltham, Mass., wanted a coaching launch for use on the Charles River. The Nichols Company owned several rowing shells, and rowing was a company recreational program.

Coyote was selected because she made almost no wake at the speed of a shell, so would not interfere with shells coming either way when she was following a rower. The original lines were used, but the scantlings were made to conform to the Herreshoff Rules for Yacht Construction, which made a few small changes in the

Figure 2. White Swan running cleanly at slightly above natural hull speed.

scantlings. Just for fun I figured the Herreshoff sizes and tabulated them alongside the original ones. They agree pretty well considering that the *Coyote* was built long before there were any rules of this kind.

For an engine we used a Gray Sea Scout, 25 hp (catalog hp) with an 11-inch by 11-inch Equipoise wheel.

At 600 rpm, speed was 5 mph

1100	8
1600	12
2100	15
2450	18

At 12 mph, about the speed of a shell, she kicked up no wake at all.

This boat was given to me some years later, and I used her on Point Judith Pond, and inside the Point Judith breakwater for a few years. In the August '54 hurricane she came ashore and was repaired. Very little damage was done. She was a lovely little boat to "go for a ride" in. The original *Coyote* was reputed to be a good seaboat, and probably was by 1907 standards, but by my standards she was pretty rolly . . .

Her next owners were colleges. She went to Rutgers University as a coaching launch in 1959. From then on what I know is hearsay.

I believe she was sold to M.I.T. to be used as a form for building some fiberglass coaching launches. M.I.T. was to use two or three of these, and sell some to other colleges. How this turned out I never heard; in fact, maybe it never happened.

This would have been a better boat if she had had a foot more beam. I do not think it would have slowed her down at all, and she would have been much more stable.

I am enclosing a picture, and the comparison of scantlings mentioned above. You referred to *Coyote* as of light construction, but as you can see she was pretty close to modern recognized weight of material. The strength of a boat is in her planking, and *Coyote* had thicker planking than Herreshoff's Rules recommend—a little bit.

Thanks for listening—

E.I. Schock

266

Thanks for listening? I lost no time in phoning Mr. Schock, and agreed to present eventually a re-worked version of *White Swan,* ex-*Coyote,* and after an interchange of letters, Mr. Schock supplied me with the lines of the 1946 version. It was most generous of him. He also supplied negatives from which the accompanying photos were made.

In going over the lines, I found that Mr. Schock had added a couple of inches more half-breadth beam at the transom. I also learned that his father had felt that a foot more beam was in order.

If you will take a look at Figure 3, you will see the outline of the transom section of *Coyote,* which scaled out at 34 inches total beam at the deck at this point—pretty skinny for a 25-foot boat, although it was the early design gambit for getting speed: use a narrow hull (and part your hair in the middle, for stability). In Figure 3 the dot-dash-dot line is the *White Swan* transom. To the right side of Figure 3, I have used a dashed line to indicate the original *Coyote* forebody.

It was suggested that I enlarge the lines by the use of proportional dividers on a lot of waterlines, leaving the molded depth and inboard heights the same, rather than to add a six-inch sliver or wedge from transom to stem. I have obeyed Mr. Schock, who is a retired professor of mechanical engineering, still issuing assignments with authority. Figure 3 shows the method.

Although strict interpretation of adding a foot more of beam would have called for a proportional divider setting of 1.21 to 1, my dividers lock on a 1.25 index, so, rather than risk a slip, I used the calibrated mark for fear of losing the proportion. The side sketch on Figure 3 shows how this is done. Once locked, the proportion remains constant, but the dividing points are free to swing and to caliper the distances offset.

As the hull half-breadths grow larger in working upward, the expansive proportions become larger toward the sheer. The resulting boat is a shade more bulky than the original and will ride a shade higher at launching, as per the waterline indication to the right of the drawing, Figure 3. This won't affect her sea behavior or speed in any substantive way, but it will erase the crankiness of the original *Coyote.*

I have used the name *Coyote II* as being obvious genealogy. I had thought of *Cygnet,* but all young ducks and swans are supposed to fall into the ugly duckling class. Who could offend such a beautiful hull as this?

I trust all parties involved will be happy, including posterity, who inherit the Research and Development of about 70 years. This should be an awfully good boat.

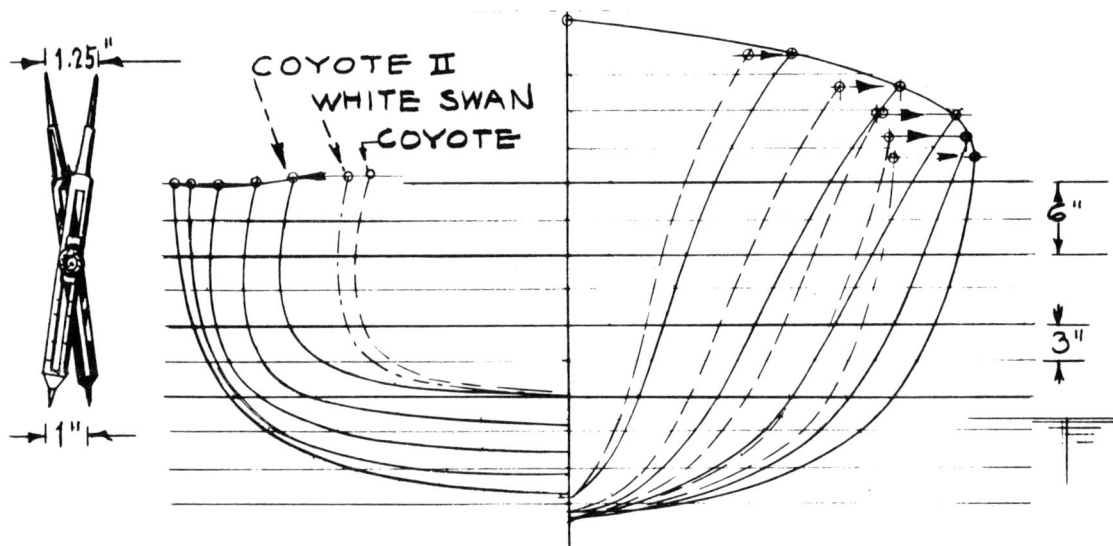

Figure 3. This shows how the body plan of the *Coyote II* was arrived at from dashed lines of original by expansion with proportional dividers set to give 1'2" more beam, as recommended by Schock. Molded depth and freeboard are unchanged.

Here is the scantling bill:

Deck—1/2-inch white pine

Beams—5/8-inch by 1-1/4-inch spruce

Clamp—3/4-inch by 1-1/2-inch spruce

Planking—1/2-inch white cedar

Frames—5/8-inch by 5/8-inch white oak, 6-inch centers

Bilge stringer—1-inch by 1-inch spruce

Floors—5/8-inch plank: under engine, 1-inch white oak

Keel—1-1/2-inch by 4-inch white oak

Engine beds—2-inch oak

Engine stringers—1-3/4-inch by 2-1/2-inch spruce

Cockpit floor—5/8-inch white pine

Transom—3/4-inch mahogany

Cockpit coaming—1/2-inch white oak

Deck beams at hatch headledges—1-1/4 inches square

Stem—white oak 2-1/2 inches, 2 inches at rabbet.

It is my belief that the drawings I have prepared will enable any professional boatbuilder to construct *Coyote II.*

No yarn based on the early 1907 *Coyote* should overlook the man who designed her. I knew Edson Schock, the elder, in my West Coast designing days and met him under peculiar circumstances, which seem worth remarking on. I had been working at yacht design for Walton Hubbard, Jr.'s company in Los Angeles. Hubbard had a design office and yacht brokerage on Wilshire Boulevard a block east of the Fox

Coyote II

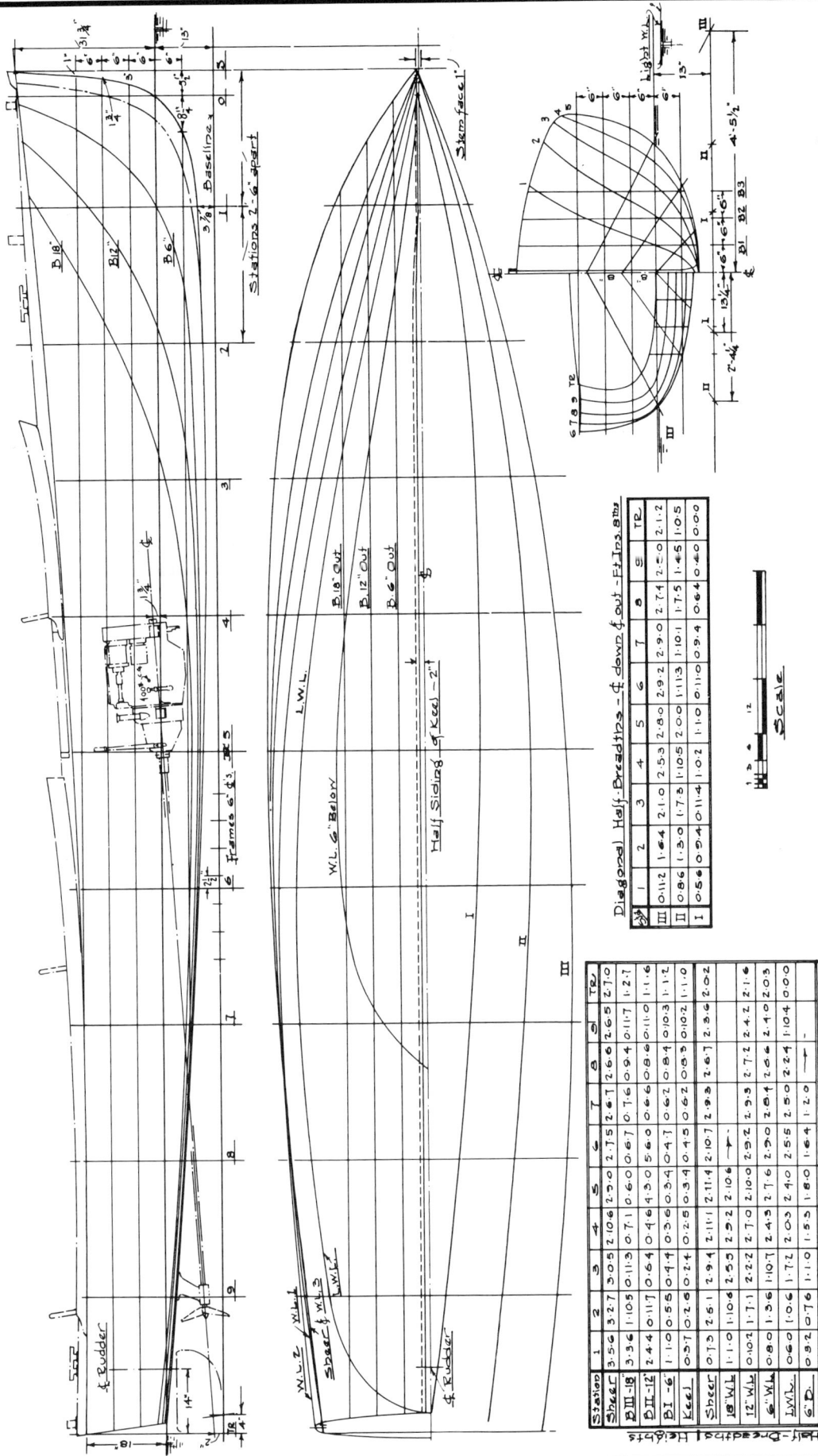

Stem face 1"

B 18"
B 12"
B 6"
Baseline
Stations 2'-6" apart

₵ Rudder
5OP
Frames 6"+3" #5

W.L. 2
W.L. 3
Sheer & W.L.3
L.W.L.
₵ Rudder

B 18" Out
B 12" Out
B 6" Out
L.W.L.
W.L. 6" Below
Half Siding of keel - 2"

Light W.L.
₵ B1, B2, B3

Weston Farmer -'75

Scale

Diagonal Half-Breadths - ₵ down ₵ out - Ft.In.8ths

	1	2	3	4	5	6	7	8	TR
III	0-11.2	1-6.4	2-1.0	2-5.3	2-8.0	2-9.2	2-9.0	2-7.4	2-3.0	2-1.2
II	0-8.6	1-3.0	1-7.5	1-10.5	2-0.0	1-11.3	1-10.1	1-7.5	1-4.5	1-0.5
I	0-5.6	0-9.4	0-11.4	1-0.2	1-1.0	0-11.0	0-9.4	0-6.4	0-4.0	0-0.0

Half-Breadth Heights

Station	1	2	3	4	5	6	7	8	TR
Sheer	3-5.6	3-2.7	3-0.5	2-10.6	2-9.0	2-7.5	2-6.6	2-6.5	2-7.0
B III-18"	3-3.6	1-10.5	0-11.3	0-7.1	0-6.0	0-6.7	0-7.6	0-9.4	0-11.7	1-2.7
B II-12"	2-4.4	0-11.7	0-6.4	0-4.6	0-3.0	0-3.6	0-4.0	0-6.0	0-8.0	0-11.0	1-1.6
B I-6"	1-0.0	0-5.5	0-4.9	0-3.6	0-3.4	0-4.7	0-6.2	0-8.4	0-10.3	1-1.2
Keel	0-5.7	0-2.6	0-2.4	0-2.5	0-3.4	0-4.5	0-6.2	0-8.3	0-10.2	1-1.0
18"WL	0-1.5	2-6.1	2-9.4	2-11.1	2-11.4	2-10.7	2-9.3	2-6.7	2-3.6	2-0.2
12"WL	1-0.1	1-10.6	2-5.5	2-9.2	2-10.6	2-10.0	2-9.2	2-7.2	2-4.2	2-1.6
6"WL	0-8.0	1-3.6	1-10.7	2-2.2	2-4.5	2-7.6	2-8.4	2-8.6	2-4.0	2-0.3
LWL	0-6.0	1-0.6	1-7.2	2-0.3	2-4.0	2-5.5	2-5.0	2-2.4	2-2.4	1-0.4	0.00
6"D	0-3.2	0-7.6	1-1.0	1-5.5	1-8.0	1-6.4	1-2.0

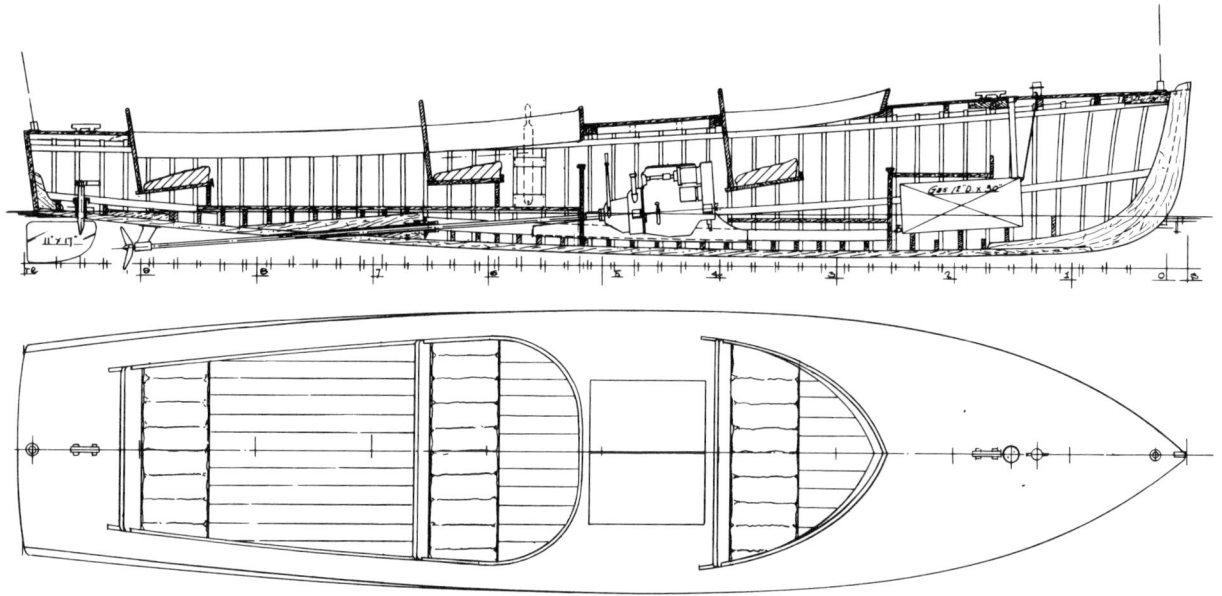

Construction plan of *Coyote II.*

Theater on Wilshire and Western. Westlake Park, with its lovely little lake and oasis of calm, was a short spin at noontime from Hubbard's office, and I frequently took my brown sandwich bag to the park for a park-bench rest to watch the kids sail their model yachts.

One Saturday noon I found myself sandwiched between two older fellows who were intently watching a model-yacht regatta. I had sat down between them as a public right to use the bench, not realizing that they had been talking. I listened in silence as they talked across me and was very tolerant of two old gafoozlers who were arguing the fine points of sailing model Star boats. The old boy on my right seemed to have the real inside dope about reaching, apparent wind, and so on. The darker, heavier man to my left seemed to have instant uptake on all the points being discussed. I was being very noble, keeping my mouth shut about what a hot-shot yacht designer I was.

The following Saturday afternoon I kept a date in the downtown L.A. office of Edson B. Schock, of whose work I had long been worshipful. The man who greeted me, Edson B. Schock himself, was the fellow who had sat to my right on the Westlake Park bench!

In a "Well, whaddaya know!" exchange of small talk, I asked Edson if he had known the man he was talking to—the dark, hearty man who had sat to my left.

"Yes. He is Lee De Forest, inventor of the vacuum tube."

I could scarcely have been found, even to be picked up with tweezers, after this news.

Edson B. Schock was one of the early greats in powerboat and yacht development, designer of the famous *Scaramouche,* and *Wiletie,* and other schooners that cleaned up on the West Coast 40 years ago.

270

Schock was a real pro, and could handle anything—tugs, large power yachts, sleek schooners, R boats, and masterpieces like *Coyote*. Early on, around 1905 or so, he was staff N.A. for Tom Day on *The Rudder*. Clearly, Edson B. Schock was one of the greats of early yacht design. I frequently encountered him down at the South Coast yard at Newport, also owned by Hubbard, when I went to Newport-Balboa to work on the board there. A fine old gentleman.

Before I leave you to your study of *Coyote II*'s lines, a few words about appropriate power: The light engine like the Gray Sea Scout is getting to be hard to find. Universal's Atomic Four, made now by Medalist, Inc., of Oshkosh, Wisconsin, which firm took over the Universal engine line, is still being made and is about the same package as the Gray. The Palmer Engine Co., of Cos Cob, Connecticut, once turned out a 22 hp outfit based on the International Harvester Cub engine. It was a dandy.

If you will write to Stokes Marine, at Coldwater, Michigan, they may have an engine of this type that would be serviceable. Stokes deals in used marine engines, and some of their trade-ins are jewels. You will need an engine of about 91 cubic inches up to 112 cubic inches, weighing 425 to 500 pounds. With such an outfit, you can duplicate the quoted rpm and speeds listed.

So, *Coyote II* comes to you from Edson B. Schock, courtesy of his son's generosity and your Old Uncle Westy's sweat.

I hope you like her.

Appendix: Some Classic Designs

In this day of hyper selling by boat "manufacturers," a perfectly normal rebellion has set in among younger people. Not willing to mortgage their futures for glamour boats at absurdly inflated prices, they seem to be turning in droves toward the old kind of boat that they themselves can build. They have begun using the term "classic boat" to identify the hand-crafted, locally indigenous craft of yore. Home boatbuilding seems to be very much "in" again.

Little wonder! It is a lot more fun to select a boat design, give her a romantic name of your own, and mog along at your own building pace in getting afloat. Besides, it's cheaper!

To this end, not many current designs are worth much. You have to go back to the day when boats were boats, smelled a mite mushroomy, and had an aura of their own that came from living with clams and crabs and tides and weeds.

I have dug back through tubes and plan baskets of my older boats to exhume a few of those that at one time were as popular as movie stars. These hand-crafted boats for woodworking artisans were built by a goodly number of yearning young craftsmen. Some are even in steel. What you see on the following pages are boats that have been proved.

I have resisted the impulse to parade a number of my Struttin' Boats—those that I'd hope would build up some Brownie Points in quarters where preening and status thrive. Matter of fact, most of that class of my work never saw a line of ink, having been drawn to inform professionals in the shop. I have discovered that old pencil tracings fade too much to let a repro camera grab them.

Perusing some of these old tracings, I see a couple of steam tugs

272

designed for the Lackawanna Railroad, a 100-foot wooden schooner built for cargoing lumber from Venezuela, a steel tuna clipper designed for John Rados, and a lot of cruisers I'd forgotten about. Sadly, I realize that the biggest body of work lies in the drawers of the many yards where I have worked as a temporary resident consultant.

Pondering past scenes, I realize I have the engineering knowledge and administrative experience—ahem—to design and build for you the Queen Mary, given time and money enough! I'd need your order, expecting you to be qualified by an irrevocable letter of credit on the First National Bank of Saudi Arabia, payable upon sight draft with bill of lading attached. Dissenters to this premise who cannot qualify will kindly keep yo' naughty bad moufs shut!

So what you see here is small boat work inked in a classic manner. And, once again, in style. I am bound to admit some of these are boats that a good number of men have held in mind for years. Within the past month I have heard from a few of these fellows. One man is a letter carrier in the Upper Peninsula of Michigan who tells me he has saved his small change for 40 years to build one of my early designs during his retirement. His time has come, and his little *Hoocares* now takes shape.

May the Good Lord bless such people, and such boats! The first deserve not to fail, and the second cannot—they are time-tried.

Because of the restrictions of a book's pages, I will be glad to provide the same plans in the original 3/4-inch-to-the-foot scale on black-line Ozalid prints. They are almost necessary for noodling and actual building or figuring materials. I'd like to give them away and play Santa Claus, but that old blueprint machine needs juice, and so does the car I drive to the post office to get the plans weighed and mailed. If you'll reimburse me for my time and costs and trouble, you can have copies to the original full scale of any of these designs, looking just as they did when I drew them. Generally, the price of a weekend bag of groceries will get them into your hands within 10 days. Each of the following descriptions states the conditions and price. Foreign orders will come folded, airmailed as printed matter, thus to escape customs; for instance, over 700 sets of prints of *Tahitiana* have been mailed this way with no snags. Domestic plans are shipped in mailing tubes, first class mail. I do not provide study plans nor engage in the come-on business. The reason is simple: it costs about three or four dollars' worth of time to answer even the simplest ol'-Buddy letter. You can't ask a lawyer the time of day without expecting a bill for consultation. Naval architects are professionals too, no less. I prefer low-cost evening phone calls if you have questions. I guarantee to be sweetly amenable: dogs love me, I pat little kids on the head at times, but if they are quarrelsome, I prefer them well cooked.

Happy noodling!

TAHITIANA

The action on *Tahitiana* started in the spring of 1976. By June of that year I finished an analysis of the ketch *Tahiti* and another on the new design of her steel counterpart, *Tahitiana.* These two stories were sent off to my friend Joe Gribbins, then on the editorial staff of *Motor Boating and Sailing,* and they appeared in that venerable and respected magazine's October and November issues for 1976.

Later, *Modern Boating* (Australia) and *Yachting Monthly* (England) published thumbnail treatments emphasizing steel as a building material. Next, mighty *Mechanix Illustrated,* with 1,600,000 worldwide circulation, folded this steel version of *Tahiti* into its bosom. *MI* was the original publisher of John G. Hanna's Depression-spawned escape machine, always having had a parental interest in her.

At the present writing, over 700 sets of plans of *Tahitiana* have been sold worldwide. A number of versions have been launched and are proved out. All builders report high satisfaction. *Tahitiana,* with a finer bow, halved angle of entrance, greater length, and much increased sail area, has proved to be a good engineering peg. She sails well, is close-winded, and is a couple of tons lighter than the original *Tahiti.* A cutter version has carried 700 square feet of sail, doing 6-1/2 knots (measured) in a Force 4 afternoon breeze. It takes a full two years for a designer to get this kind of view of what he has strived for.

Tahitiana's parent boat, *Tahiti,* was given that name when, so long ago, I commissioned John G. Hanna to re-design his *Neptune,* a double-ender that Hanna designed in 1923 for Dr. Anton Schneider of Lakeland, Florida. The plans for the new boat, which I named *Tahiti,* were first published in the November and December 1933 issues of *Modern Mechanix* magazine, now *Mechanix Illustrated.* It is now the general consensus, proved by thousands of *Tahitis,* that her hull makes one of the best small blue water cruisers ever. There are 13 known circumnavigations at the hands of different builders. Two *Tahitis* are known to have turned the global trick twice.

Tahitiana—pronounced with a hard "t"—saves most of the high cost of fastenings needed in wood by using multi-chine steel construction, where about 80 percent of the fastenings are eliminated by the arc weld. The increase in sail area from Hanna's original grudging 420 square feet (badly underrigged) to 550 square feet in a tall ketch rig still retains the highly desirable ability of the ketch rig to be self-steering. Sail area is horsepower, so I added what was needed. I also drew out the

Al. Airfoil taper Spreader
Luff 34'-9"
Reef Pts
Reef Pts
Extruded Al. Mast
Kenyon 5072 Section
7/8" Internal track
Foot 13'-0"
Foot 9'-3"

Tahitiana

Displacement 18,134 lbs
Waterplane Area 156.4 □'
W. Plane Loading 116.17 lbs □'

Scale 3/4" = 1 ft.

— Line, Body Plan of TAHITI
--- Line, Straight Frames of TAHITIANA

These are Chine Lines, NOT Diagonals

Designed by Weston Farmer

Dotted line shows discarded old Tahiti bow. Too blunt to plate.

Mainmast

Mizzen 4½" x 6" Al., .188 wall

4½" x 6" Al., .188 wall

Sheer
Deck
Top Chine
Mid Chine
Bottom Chine
Bearing Line
6" x 12" Keel (Bottom)
CLR

Deck
Bottom Chine
Mid Chine
Top Chine
Sheer
Bearing Line
Half siding of Keel 3"

Half-Breadths — Heights above Base

Station	0	1	2	3	4	5	6	7	8	9	10	11
Sheer	9.10.0	9.3.6	8.11.2	8.6.5	8.3.3	8.0.6	7.11.4	7.0.2	7.9.6	7.9.7	8.0.1	8.3.2
Deck	8.11.4	8.5.4	8.0.6	7.8.4	7.8.2	7.4.0	7.3.0	7.2.0	7.1.4	7.2.0	7.3.5	7.7.0
Top Chine	7.5.0	6.9.0	6.2.6	5.9.4	5.5.6	5.3.4	5.2.2	5.1.6	5.2.2	5.3.6	5.6.5	6.25.0.0
Mid Chine	5.10.6	5.3.0	4.9.1	4.3.6	3.11.4	3.8.2	3.6.4	3.6.6	3.8.2	4.2.6	4.8.0
Bottom Chine	4.3.1	3.7.0	5.3.6	3.0.0	2.8.6	2.6.4	2.5.4	3.7.0	2.9.6	3.3.2	3.11.2
Bearing Line	7.6.0	3.9.2	2.5.4	1.10.6	1.9.2	St. Line	1.4.6	1.4.2	2.3.0	4.6.0
Keel/Bottom	3.6.0	2.1.0	1.1.6	0.9.2	0.3.0	St. Line	0.3.0
Keel	0.02	0.0.2	0.0.2	0.3.0	0.3.0	0.3.0	0.3.0	0.0.2	0.0.2	0.0.2
Bottom Chine	0.7.4	1.3.5	1.10.0	2.3.4	2.6.0	2.6.2	2.3.3	1.9.4	0.10.6
Mid Chine	1.7.2	2.6.6	3.6.0	4.0.6	4.3.5	4.2.2	3.10.4	3.2.3	2.1.4	0.3.0
Top Chine	1.2.2	2.5.4	3.5.4	4.2.2	4.7.5	4.10.1	4.10.0	4.6.4	4.0.0	2.11.3	1.1.2
Deck	1.8.6	3.0.6	4.0.3	4.7.6	4.10.1	5.0.2	4.11.5	4.9.0	4.3.6	4.4.2	1.8.5
Sheer	2.0.2	3.3.6	4.2.6	4.9.7	5.0.2	5.1.2	5.0.3	4.5.7	3.6.3	1.11.6

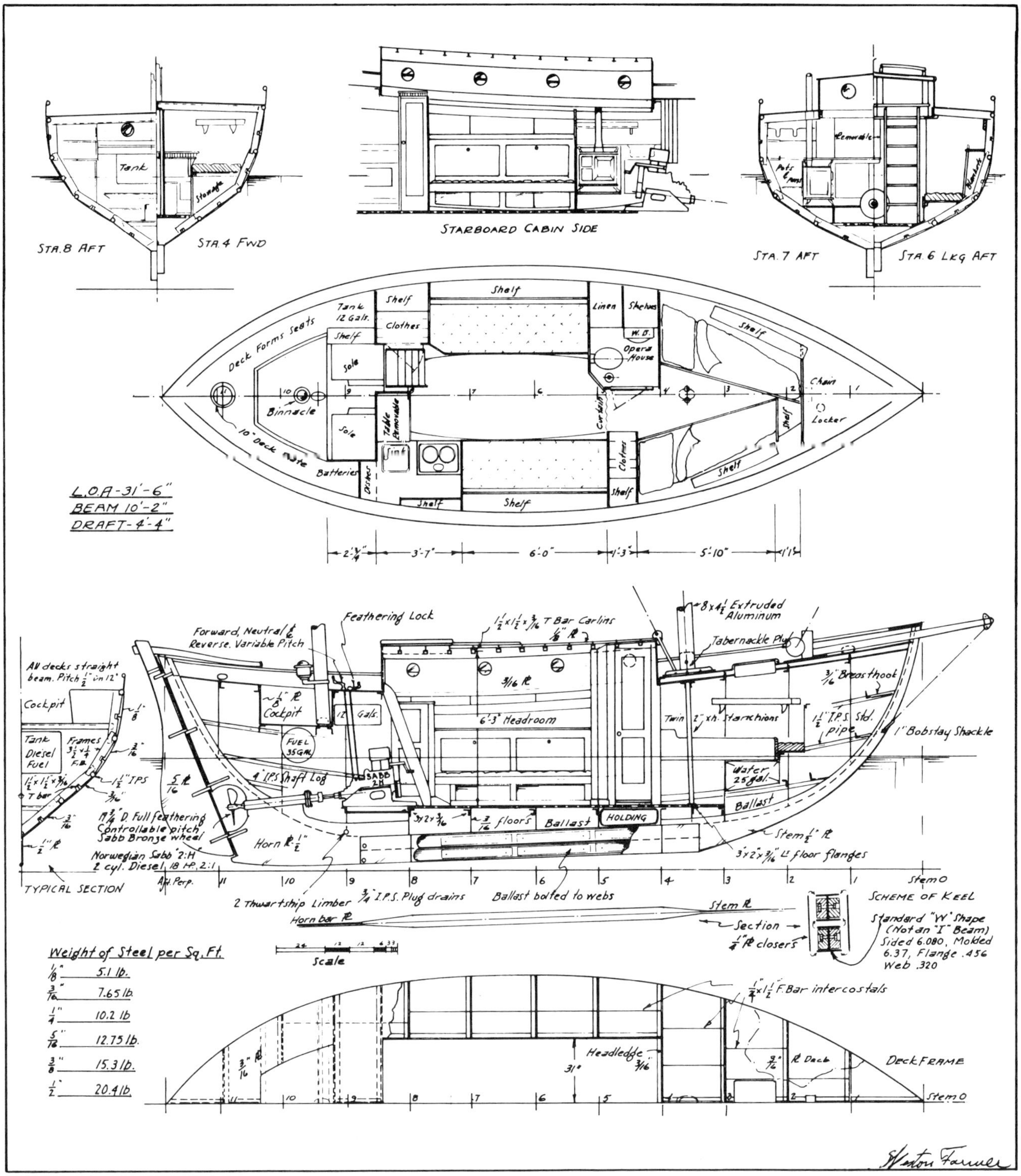
STA. 8 AFT
STA. 4 FWD
Tank
Storage
STARBOARD CABIN SIDE
STA. 7 AFT
STA. 6 LKG AFT
Removable
Shelf
Tank 12 Gals.
Clothes
Linen
Shelves
W.B.
Opera House
Deck Forms Seats
Sole
Binnacle
Table Removable
Curtain
Chain
Locker
Batteries
Shelf
L.O.A - 31'-6"
BEAM 10'-2"
DRAFT - 4'-4"
3'-7"
6'-0"
1'-3"
5'-10"
Feathering Lock
Forward, Neutral & Reverse, Variable Pitch
1 1/2" x 1 1/2" x 3/16" T Bar Carlins
8 x 4 1/2 Extruded Aluminum
Tabernackle Plt.
Breasthook
All decks straight beam. Pitch 1/2" in 12"
Cockpit
Tank Diesel Fuel
Frames
12 Gals.
FUEL 35 GAL
6'-3" Headroom
Twin 2" xh. Stanchions
1 1/2" I.P.S. Std. pipe
1" Bobstay Shackle
4" I.P.S. Shaft Log
SABB 2H
Water 25 gal.
Ballast
floors
HOLDING
Horn
Norwegian Sabb 2:H
2 cyl. Diesel, 18 HP, 2:1
TYPICAL SECTION
2 Thwartship Limber
3/4 I.P.S. Plug drains
Ballast bolted to webs
Stem 0
SCHEME OF KEEL
Standard "W" Shape (Not an "I" Beam) Sided 6.080, Molded 6.37, Flange .456 Web .320
Stem R
Horn bar R
Section
1/4" R closers
Scale
Weight of Steel per Sq. Ft.
1/8" 5.1 lb.
3/16" 7.65 lb.
1/4" 10.2 lb
5/16" 12.75 lb.
3/8" 15.3 lb.
1/2" 20.4 lb.
1/4 x 1 1/2 F. Bar intercostals
Headledge 3/16
31"
Deck Frame
Weston Farmer

bow of *Tahitiana* by a foot and a half, which halved the angle of entry of the older boat. With modern Dacron sails, aluminum spars, and consequently lowered tophamper weight, *Tahitiana*, I am told, foots out with the best of them, eliminating also the kelp-catching characteristics and poor grounding ability of the fin-keel Clorox bottles. The latter types are merely designed that way to give lateral plane to hulls that weigh about half of a normal boat, and must therefore have stern skegs and rudders weakly cantilevered down from the hull to prevent broaching. A long-keeled double-ender, with outboard rudder, will steer herself, sit on the hard when the tide is out, and will not wear out a helmsman who has to continually watch following seas.

The entire story of *Tahitiana* and her parent boat is contained in the reprints and plans I have furnished to hundreds of builders who know metal and can work it. Six sheets comprise the bundle. The cost, adjusted to the shenanigans of inflation, is $49. Upon receipt of a bank cheque for that amount, I'll mail foreign orders in a manila envelope as printed matter to avoid customs delays. Usually, these packets go through in about 10 days. Domestic orders go first class, rolled in a stout mailing tube. This is not the place to put on a high-pressure sales pitch, but there has been one gratifying quality about the hundreds of transactions on this boat: not one check has been returned NSF, nor has there been a single gripe from anyone.

But, I have been jumped on by members of my guild for being Santa Claus, selling too cheaply. These guild members do not understand mass marketing: there are a lot more 10-dollar bills in the world than there are hundred-dollar bills. Being a working stiff myself, I understand that fellows who build *Tahitiana* are closer to a time clock and wages than to stocks and bonds. The wage earner who works in steel is a square-shooter and deserves a fair price. This boat appeals to hundreds of mechanics who do know steel but who couldn't saw a board straight, or bore a hole straight in wood, or shave a fine curl.

I cleave to one philosophy about a blue water boat: keep her simple, keep her small, keep her strong. But go now!

Tahitiana's vital statistics fit the philosophy: length overall, 31 feet 6 inches; length on waterline, 25 feet 7-1/2 inches; beam, 10 feet 2 inches; draft, 4 feet 4 inches. Displacement is 14,000 to 18,000 pounds, depending upon desired ballasted stiffness. With engine but no joinery, she weighs seven short tons.

She fits the universal urge among sailors to put a thumb up above one's oral cavity and direct five-finger words toward landbound bipeds who are captives of taxation and politics.

Go now!

278

Assassin

One of the entrancing dreams of boyhood that time can never give again was the love affair I had for two small launches described in a 1911 catalog of the Brooks Boat Company.

Brooks was the original "Save two-thirds" supplier of backyard boatbuilding kits. From their factory at Saginaw, Michigan, the Brooks firm shipped upwards of 5,000 knocked-down boatbuilding kits each year for many years, peaking out just before we entered World War I in 1917. The Brooks catalog fired up in me so much fervor for two of their small launches that I can, even today, conjure up the yearning hunger I had for their small, double-ended, 16-foot launch (a fine sea boat, y'see) or an 18-foot power dory. (Kinda wet, thought the kid.)

I agonized for two years over which boat to buy. That decision had to be made before I'd start to save the $150 for the knocked-down hull, or the $29.50 for any one of eight or nine 2-hp, one-cylinder, two-cycle marine engines the market then offered. On 50-cent tips for hustling bags as a boy bellhop at Isle Royale's Rock Harbor Lodge, owned by the Farmer family, and on an occasional $1 wage for a morning of splitting firewood, I slowly realized that I'd be 179 years old before I could buy a cherished money order and stun the Brooks Boat Company with payment in full.

Payment in full. That was the route I'd have to take. I had finally decided on the 16-foot double-ended launch. Brooks offered to ship the boat with 25-percent down payment, with "balance on sight draft with bill of lading attached." I didn't want a boat with something called a bill of lading attached to it. To me, that idea smacked of a Wall Street shenanigan: I had overheard my father and grandfather mention the horrors of being caught short in the market. I was very short, and didn't want to get burned, so I settled the dilemma at the end of the second year by sending 79 cents to Monkey Ward for a shingling hatchet.

Boyhood dreams do not die—they just change size and relative importance. This proves that the difference between men and boys is the size of their toys.

By this devious chain of events we thus have *Assassin* —a growling boyhood word for the near-Brooks double-ender that I designed in mature years to allay that early hunger, and to finally document for myself the shape and size and spirit of a fine small launch. I had later realized her truly workable appeal, well above toy range. She is 16 feet 2 inches overall and 14 feet 7 inches on the waterline.

Table of Offsets ~ Ft.-Ins.& 8ᵗʰˢ

		Heights				Half-Breadths						
Sta	Sheer	Rabbet	Keel	Butt 9"	Butt 18	Keel	W.L.3B	L.W.L	3"Ab	6"Ab	9"Ab	Sheer
0	3.2.7									0.2.1		0.3.3
1	3.0.7	0.11.3	0.9.2	0.2.4		0.1.0	0.2.4	0.4.7	0.6.4	0.8.2	0.9.1	0.11.0
2	2.11.3	0.10.5		1.3.4		0.1.2	0.5.4	0.9.5	1.0.1	1.2.1	1.3.1	1.5.4
3	2.10.5	0.9.1		1.1.1	1.5.0	0.1.4	0.9.0	1.2.0	1.5.1	1.6.6	1.8.1	1.9.4
4	2.9.6	0.9.5		0.11.5	1.4.4		1.0.4	1.5.7	1.8.8	1.10.3	1.11.4	2.0.3
5	2.9.0	0.9.7		0.11.0	1.2.4		1.3.1	1.8.6	1.11.3	2.0.5	2.1.2	2.1.5
6	2.8.4	0.10.1		0.10.7	1.1.7		1.5.0	1.10.0	2.0.0	2.1.1	2.1.4	2.2.0
7	2.8.3	0.10.5		0.11.2	1.3.0		1.3.4	1.8.3	1.10.4	2.0.0	2.0.4	2.1.3
8	2.8.3	0.11.4	0.9.4	1.0.0	1.5.3	0.11.4	1.5.1	1.7.2	1.8.5	1.9.7		1.11.0
9	2.8.7	1.1.0		1.3.1			0.2.7	0.10.5	1.1.2	1.3.2	1.4.5	1.6.6
10	2.9.2	1.4.0				0.1.4		0.3.7	0.4.0	0.6.5	0.8.0	0.10.7

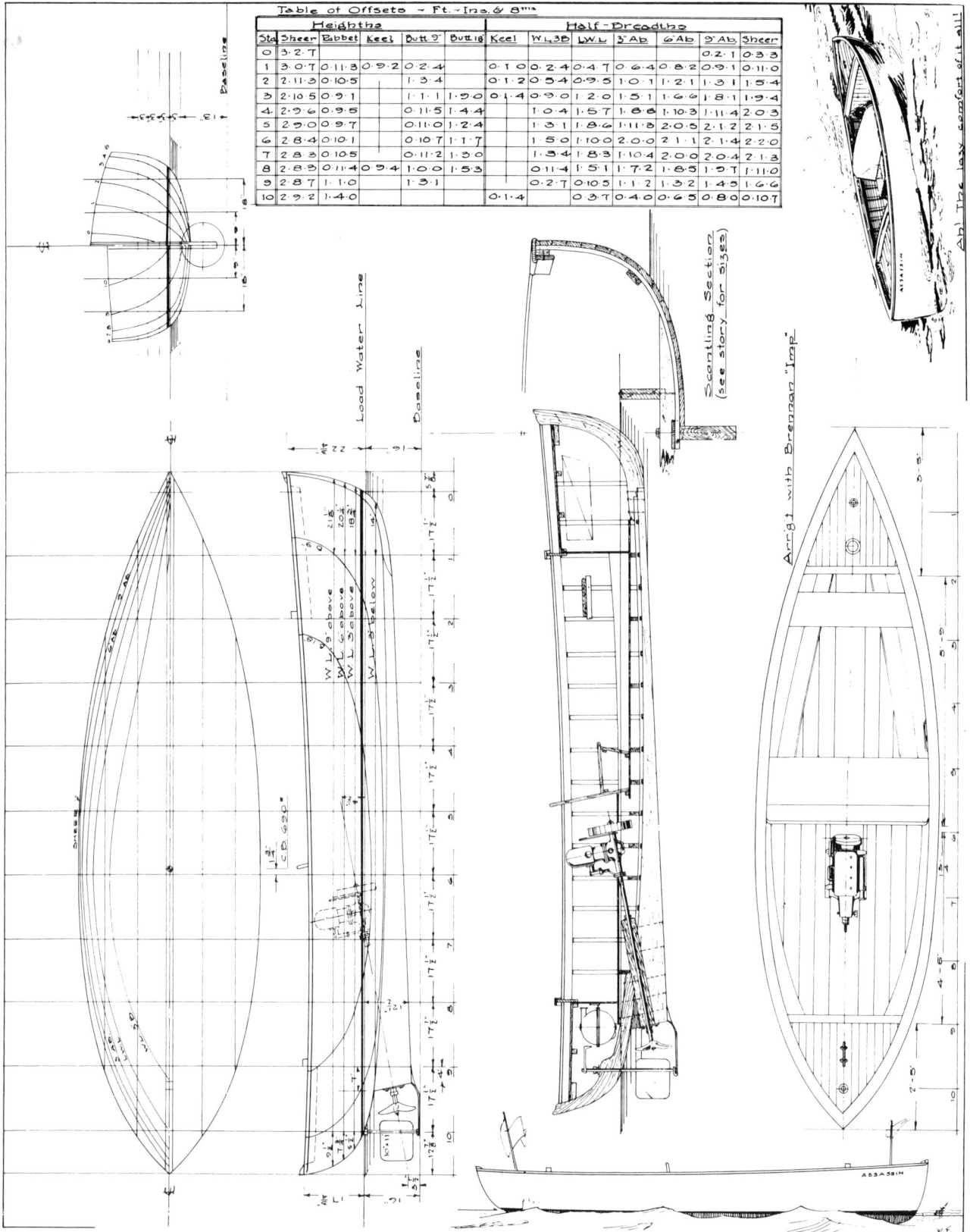

Ah! The Joy comfort of it all!

Scantling Section (see story for sizes)

Arr'gt with Brennan "Imp"

To this day, I'd love to have one of these hulls and power her with an old one-lung, two-cycle banger. I can't imagine a more satisfying boat ride, or a better little boat for snuggled-down Saturday afternoon ditch-crawling or harbor-browsing. But, strangely, it is as a toy that she has appealed to others. After making the drawing, I sent it to my old friend Boris Leonardi, of *The Rudder,* who fractured the *Rudder* treasury by giving me $75 for the design. Poor way to get rich.

Then her toy appeal became manifest: Stuart Babcock, a tycoon in the electrical industry, had the notion of building a real, live, grown-up little steamboat, so he had this boat built by professional builders in Costa Mesa, California. He equipped her with a British Stuart 5A steam engine and suitable boiler. Her new name was *Sparky.* She was launched, unbeknownst to me, at the yard of the South Coast Company at Newport Beach, California, where, unbeknownst to Babcock, I had been the yard designer years before.

The *Sparky* story added another fillip to the dual love affairs connected with this boat. As does the hull, her romance had two ends—mine and Stu Babcock's.

She could be built using strip construction and powered with an air-cooled mail-order engine today, making a fine grown-up toy for boys of any age.

Sparky's crew waiting for "steam up."

Piute

William H. Hand, Jr., was the inventor of the vee-bottom motorboat. He took the Chesapeake diamond bottom, or deadrise boat, that had constant deadrise throughout the length, and from it, by elevating the chine forward and experimenting with increased deadrise, evolved what came to be known as the Hand V-Bottom boat. This was a completely different boat in behavior from either a deadrise hull or the long, lean, round-bottom speedboats of his time.

Hand had begun in 1903 by designing some simple cross-planked little launches for home building. As powers of marine engines increased and engine weights came down from 40 to 10 pounds per horsepower, the advantages of the high forward chine and the increased amount of vee became startling. No longer did hulls lean outboard on turns as do round-bilge powerboats. Speeds unobtainable with pure displacement hulls increased dramatically. By 1914, Hand's cruiser *Flyaway*, powered with a 100-hp, 1200-pound Van Blerck engine, was loping easily through heavy chop and sustaining 20 miles per hour. *Flyaway* was one of those breakthrough boats that sent the Race Committees back to new rule-making.

Of course, it was not long before many designers were either imitating or producing their own versions of the chine boat. My entire lifespan covers the development of the motorboat, so of course I was (as were all early powerboat designers) a student of the work of William H. Hand, Jr., and envious of his success, without knowing how to cope with the forces he had perceived and knew so much about. John L. Hacker and George F. Crouch seemed to understand the critters, and they produced superb runabouts that, even today, are being restored and venerated for their beauty and performance.

Eventually I got a "handle" on the work of Hand, and secured a lot of his work. I learned that he never varied the amount of deadrise, that the slight hollows to the frames forward were a result of the way planking had to lie. The feature contributed to dryness. His early designs were slab-sided, and the design fraternity as well as boatbuilders demanded that he hide the vee-ness by rounding the topsides into tumblehome aft and flammed flare forward. As each new design came out, Hand built it in his own shop in New Bedford. He made excellent money supplying the home market with his plans.

Lindsay Lord eventually discovered that a constant deadrise, fully flat all the way to the transom, improved running. Lord called his style

of bottom a monohedron, the proper mathematical term for a prism of constant face. The next big development in the vee bottom came when Raymond Hunt asked Fenwick C. Williams, an old Alden drafting genius, to draw up a hull with a deep vee. In asking Fenwick Williams how he arrived at the 22-1/2-degree angle, I was amused when he told me it was snatched out of thin air, and had something to do with an angle to a star, or a fix on a lighthouse, or something of that nature. At any rate, it worked, and with the powers of the day, the deep vee as advocated 20 years earlier by Gordon B. Hooton became possible.

However, in the new developments, something Hand had was left out. Hand's boats were able to check down to accommodate seas bigger than the boat wanted to handle. They were steerable throughout their

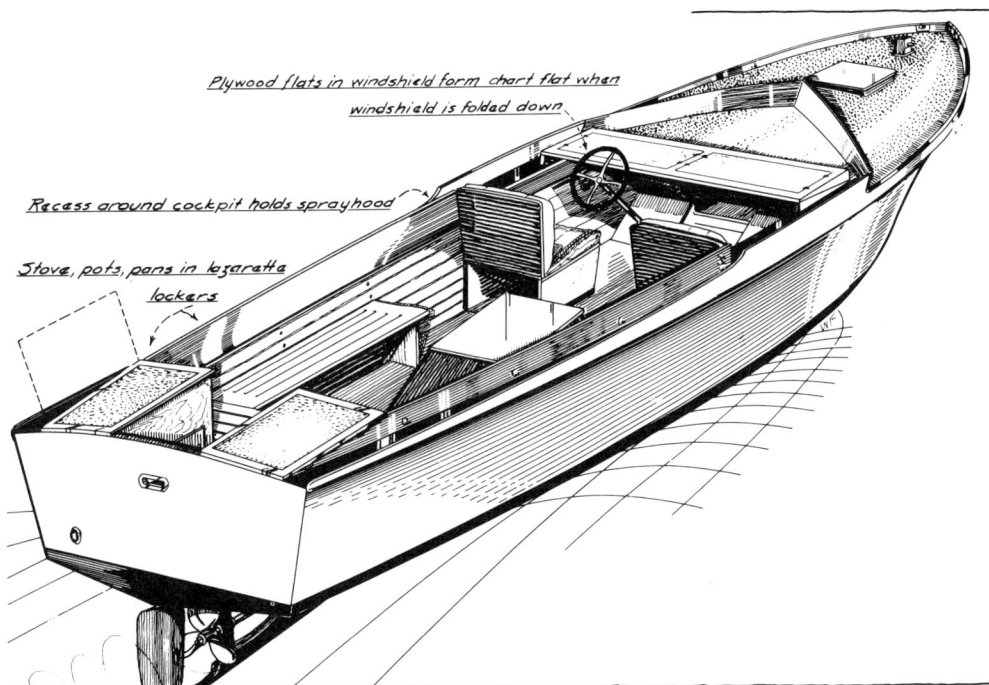

Plywood flats in windshield form chart flat when windshield is folded down

Recess around cockpit holds sprayhood

Stove, pots, pans in lazaretta lockers

LINES DRAWING - "PIUTE" - Measurements for shape of hull

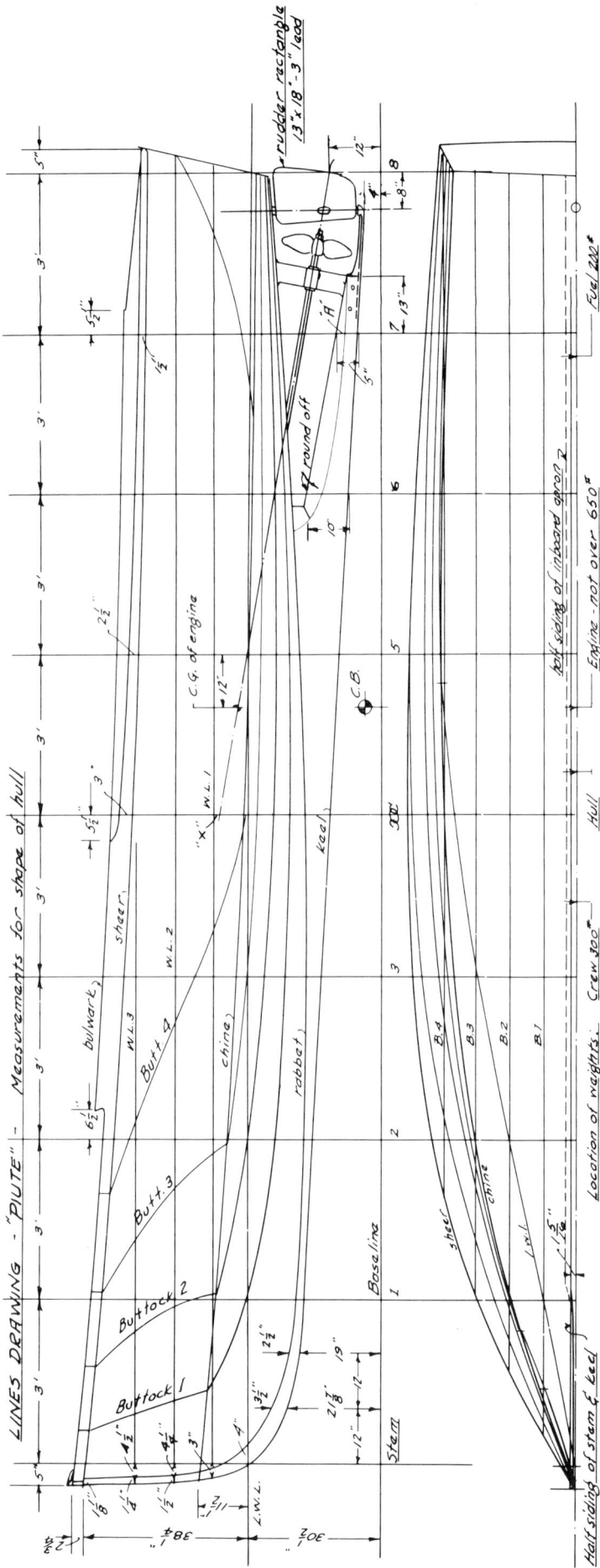

Scale - F+g inches

Buttock 1 · Buttock 2 · Butt. 3 · Butt 4

bulwark · sheer · WL3 · WL2 · china · rabbet · keel · L.W.L.

Baseline · Stem

Half siding of stem & keel

C.B. · C.G. of engine

rudder rectangle 13"×18"-3" lead

"x" round off

Location of weights. Crew 300#

Engine - not over 650#

Half siding of inboard apron

Fuel 200#

Hull

"x" Take this distance from motor actually used allowing pan clearance of frame 5. Make full sized plan and keep C.G. motor as shown.

"x" Point of reference for shear

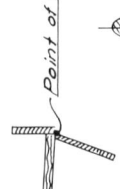

Point of reference

Section of skeg at "A"

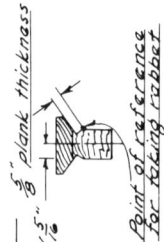

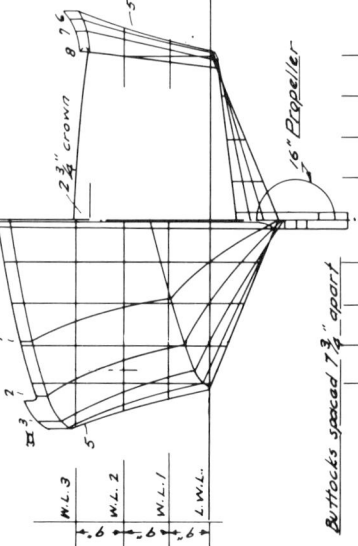

⅝" plank thickness

Point of reference for taking rabbet

Body plan drawn to outside of planking

Buttocks spaced 7¾" apart

2¾" crown · 16" Propeller

Frame #	Heights above Baseline									Half breadths from ℄						
Buttock	Shear	Butt 1	Butt 2	Butt 3	Butt 4	China	Rabbt	keel	Shear	WL3	WL2	WL1	China	LWL	Roof+
Stem	5.7.4	5.2.6														0.1.5
1	5.7.4	5.4.5	2.7.4	3.8.0			3.2.3	1.8.2	1.6.0	1.10.6	1.6.6	1.4.3	1.2.7	1.2.5	0.7.6	"
2	5.4.5	5.2.0	2.0.6	2.6.4	2.11.0	4.10.4	2.11.6	1.6.3	1.4.1	2.9.2	2.5.4	2.1.7	2.0.2	1.11.2	1.3.4	"
3	5.5.4	4.11.9	1.10.0	2.3.0	2.7.1	3.7.2	2.7.4	1.5.5		3.2.0	3.0.0	2.8.0	2.5.4	2.4.1	1.10.6	"
IV	5.1.0	4.10.0	1.9.4	2.1.0	2.5.0		2.8.0	1.6.0		3.3.1	3.2.0	2.8.2	2.6.4	2.3.7		"
5	4.10.6	4.8.6	1.9.4	2.0.5	2.3.5		2.6.7	1.7.2		3.2.6			2.9.2	2.7.4		"
6	4.9.2	4.7.4	1.10.6	2.0.6	2.3.4		2.6.0	1.9.0		3.1.2			2.9.0	2.7.0		"
7	4.8.3	4.6.6	2.0.4	2.1.6	2.3.6	2.9.0	2.5.4	1.11.3	0.5.4	2.10.7			2.5.7			"
8	4.7.4	4.6.1					2.5.0	2.1.6		2.4.0			2.7.7	2.4.0		"

Table of offsets in Ft. Inches & 8ths to outside of ⅝" planking. Waterlines spaced 9" - Buttocks spaced 7¾". All frames to be diminished by planking thickness after fairing.

Decking $\frac{3}{8}$" x 3" w.pine

1" Jackstaff socket

W.oak Bsth'k

Stemband $\frac{3}{8}$" R.

Stem bolts $\frac{3}{8}$" x 5" galv.

Stem & gripe $2\frac{5}{8}$" w.oak

Cockpit sole 1" above chine at 3 and XX, 1" above W.L. abaft XX

Stem

3" bitt

$\frac{5}{8}$" hatch cove'

$\frac{3}{4}$" x $2\frac{1}{2}$" clamp

$\frac{3}{4}$" x3" ceiling, mahog.

$\frac{3}{4}$" x $2\frac{1}{4}$" beams

$\frac{1}{4}$" w.oak floors

$1\frac{3}{4}$" x 3" frames

$2\frac{5}{8}$" w.oak keel

Windshield hinges down

($\frac{1}{2}$" visor)

$\frac{3}{4}$" mahog covering board

$\frac{3}{4}$" mahogany

$\frac{5}{8}$" mahog. coaming

$1\frac{1}{2}$"riser

Ceiling

20-30 h.p. @
1,000 r.p.m. 640#

motor bed 2"

Apron $\frac{1}{4}$" x 5" Ga. pine

Aft cockpit seats $\frac{5}{8}$" x 3" mahogany, $\frac{5}{8}$" sp

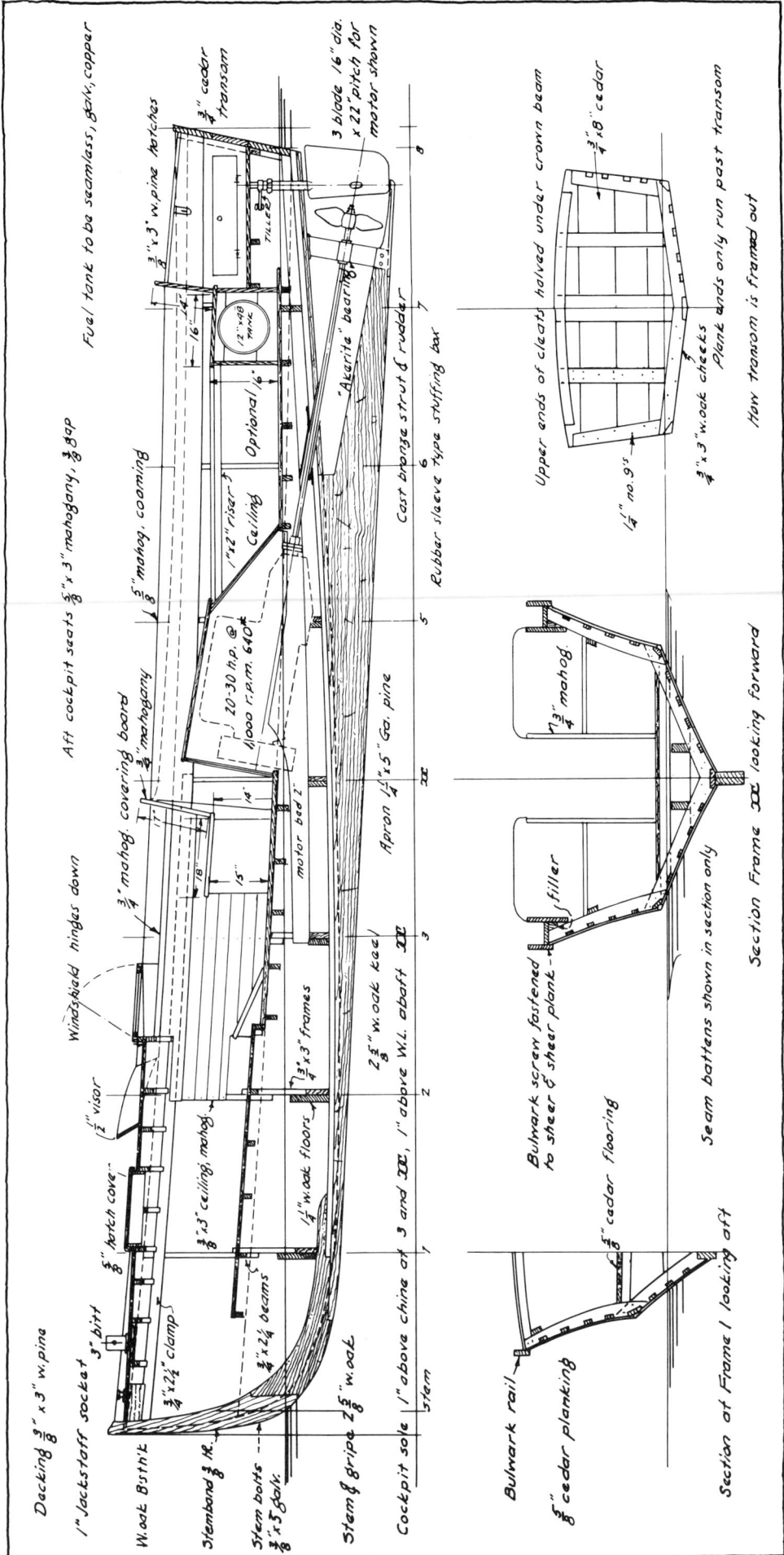

Fuel tank to be seamless, galv, copper

$\frac{3}{4}$" x 3" w.pine hatches

$\frac{3}{4}$" cedar transom

3 blade 16" dia.
x 22 pitch for
motor shown

$1\frac{1}{2}$"riser

Optional $\frac{1}{16}$"

"Akarite" bearing

Cast bronze strut & rudder

Rubber sleeve type stuffing box

8

7

6

5

XX

3

2

1

Upper ends of cleats halved under crown beam

$\frac{3}{4}$" x 8" cedar

Plank ends only run past transom

How transom is framed out

$\frac{3}{4}$" x 3" w.oak cheeks

$\frac{1}{4}$" no.9's

Section Frame XX looking forward

Bulwark screw fastened
to sheer & sheer plank

$1\frac{3}{4}$" mahog.

filler

$\frac{1}{2}$" cedar flooring

Seam battens shown in section only

Bulwark rail

$\frac{5}{8}$" cedar planking

Section at Frame 1 looking aft

entire range of speed in following seas. The full-planing boat is a dog in this department. Unless they are banging along full bore, you cannot steer them. And full bore, in some seaways with this type of boat, demands Polident for the helmsman's teeth and metal brassieres for the ladies.

All of these truths bore in on me one October afternoon 40 miles offshore when the mahogany basket of slats I was ferrying across 60 miles of open water just about drowned me. She couldn't take it. I got to longing for the sweet, soft, loping ride of one of Bill Hand's boats. I resolved to nitpick my files of Hand's work and produce one, because I knew that all of Hand's work had been blown to limbo or washed away in the devastating tides and seas of the 1938 hurricane.

So, to you old-timers who want a Hand replica, here is *Piute,* named after one of Bill Hand's first famous small boats. The drafting and inboard arrangement are mine; the proportions, lines, and general idea are pure Hand. She is 24 feet 10 inches overall, with a beam of 6 feet 4 inches and a draft of 2 feet 4 inches. She is easy to build, will accommodate a wide range of power plants, and will make a grand boat for family picnics and afternoon gadding to places on the horizon.

Within a few years after I first exposed this boat, I had heard from several men who had built her. One was a man in Chile, another boat was built in California, some in other places, but I was intrigued when I got a photo of this hull expanded to 46 feet, powered with a Kermath 400-hp Sea Raider of 12 cylinders. She had been built at Guaymas, Mexico, and was used by the seagoing gendarmes of Sonora to exact tithes from tuna clippers who fished the Gulf of California for sardines without first paying at the turnstiles.

I'll be glad to supply reproductions of my original drawings in 3/4-inch-to-the-foot scale for 49 bucks. All of the specifications are lettered on the plans, and I can also supply a reprint of the original story when it was initially exposed. These will build this boat.

Tintillee

Steel as a material for building small boats is staging a strong comeback. Time-tried and once well known as a separate and particular sector of the boatbuilding art, steel has been rediscovered in the massive revolution that has been going on in the search for a hull building material that will supplant chemical mixtures, staples, and glued slats, or calcined mud solidified around a chicken wire armature. Whatever the virtues of these substitutes for traditional wood boatbuilding may be, they all add up to about the same cost when labor and supply logistics are tossed into the budget.

The boat shown here, *Tintillee*, was designed some time ago to take advantage of the economy to be found in arc-welded steel construction. Her design represents steel scantlings formulated in 1973 by the American Bureau of Shipping, unchanged today.

The economy of steel is found in the fact that the arc-welding technique supplies 80 percent of the fastenings otherwise needed in wood. No falsework is required. No housing is required, because steel can be built outdoors. Tooling required is just a cut above a pair of pliers and an office chair in an alder bush. Any man intelligent enough to supply the missing letter in Chi-ago can become a skilled welder in reasonably short order. Let's look at this boat:

Tintillee is an open utility runabout small enough to be a beginner's boat. She is 18 feet overall, by 6 feet 6 inches beam, drawing 23 inches of water. She is built entirely of arc-welded mild steel, commercial common grade. She would make an ideal boat for beginners who want to get into the boatbuilding business.

There are strong economic pluses for going this route. Steel has advanced in price less than all other building materials. The one place that building costs can be reduced in getting afloat is in a boat's hull. All equipment purchased outside a boat shop will cost the same for any boat: engines, sails, shafting, and propellers will be the same for one boat as for another. But the strongest economic argument for a welded steel boat lies in the fact that a boat like *Tintillee* can be built, as to hull, in about one-third the time it takes to build a wooden, plastic, or concrete hull. This is a ponderable competitive edge.

A study of my drawings will show how her frames, keel, and hull are put together. The shell plating is 12-gauge, which means it is 7/64 inch thick, just a shade under 1/8 inch. This is abundantly heavy; in fact, if commercial production was contemplated and the welding skill of such

TINTILLEE

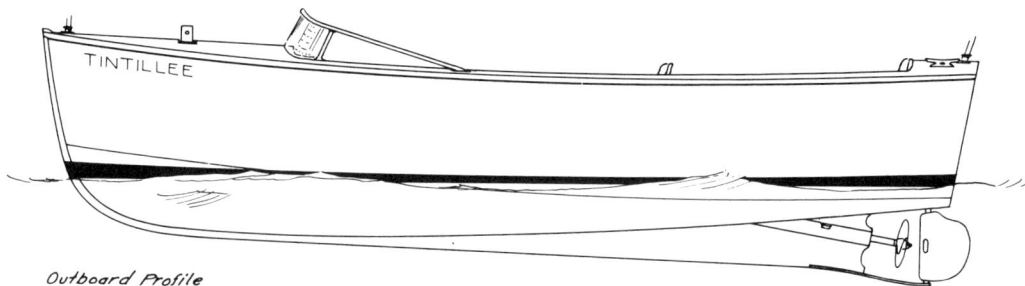

Outboard Profile

Scale of Drawing

2 FT.   1 FT.   6"   3" 1"

Section #1 Looking F'w'd.

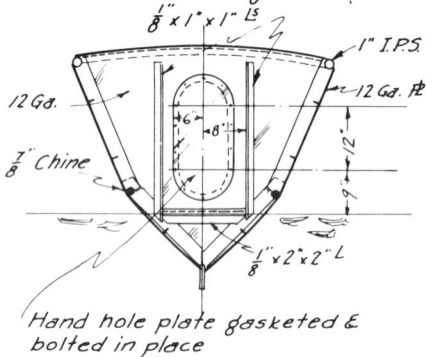

$\frac{1}{8}" \times 1" \times 1"$ L.S.

1" I.P.S.

12 Ga.

12 Ga. Pl.

$\frac{1}{8}"$ Chine

6"   8"

9 $\frac{1}{2}"$

$\frac{1}{8}" \times 2" \times 2"$ L

Hand hole plate gasketed &
bolted in place

Section Abaft #2 Looking F'w'd.

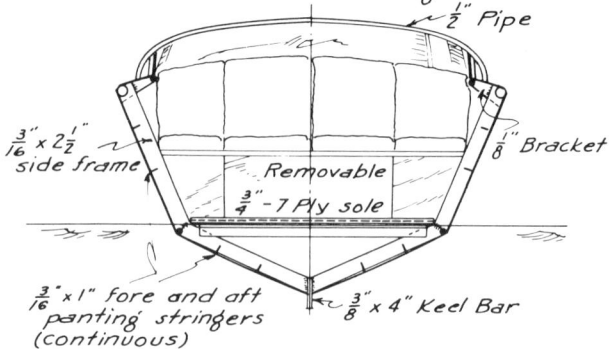

$\frac{1}{2}"$ Pipe

$\frac{3}{16}" \times 2\frac{1}{2}"$
side frame

Removable
$\frac{3}{4}"$ - 7 Ply sole

$\frac{1}{8}"$ Bracket

$\frac{3}{16}" \times 1"$ fore and aft
panting stringers
(continuous)

$\frac{3}{8}" \times 4"$ Keel Bar

Section Thru #3 at Motor Box

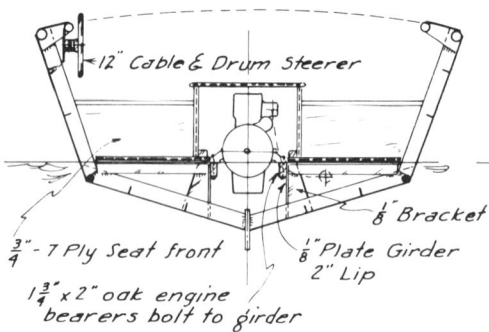

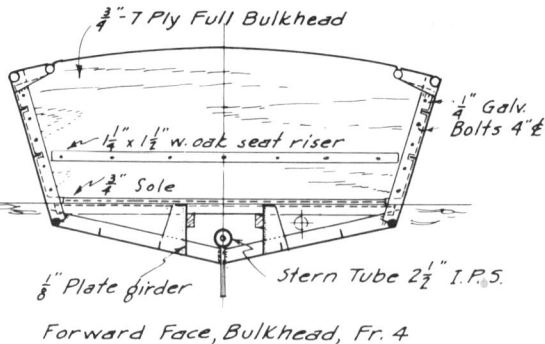

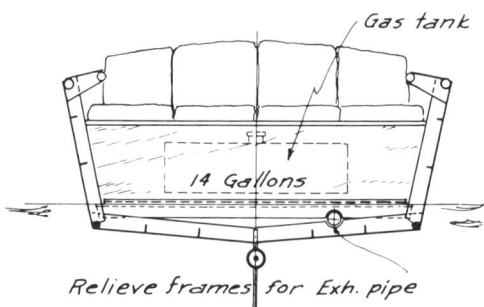

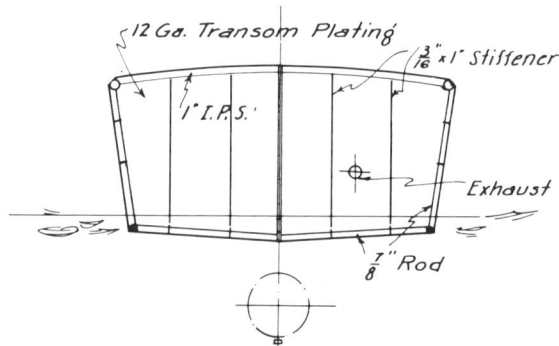

12" Cable & Drum Steerer

$\frac{1}{8}"$ Bracket

$\frac{3}{4}"$ - 7 Ply Seat front

$\frac{1}{8}"$ Plate Girder
2" Lip

$1\frac{3}{4}" \times 2"$ oak engine
bearers bolt to girder

$\frac{3}{4}"$ - 7 Ply Full Bulkhead

$\frac{1}{4}"$ Galv.
Bolts 4" ₵

$1\frac{1}{4}" \times 1\frac{1}{2}"$ w. oak seat riser

$\frac{3}{4}"$ Sole

$\frac{1}{8}"$ Plate girder

Stern Tube $2\frac{1}{2}"$ I.P.S.

Forward Face, Bulkhead, Fr. 4

Gas tank

14 Gallons

Relieve frames for Exh. pipe

Section #5 Looking Aft

12 Ga. Transom Plating

$\frac{3}{16}" \times 1"$ Stiffener

1" I.P.S.

Exhaust

$\frac{1}{8}"$ Rod

Transom Framing

288

caliber that 14-gauge (.078 inch thick) could be used, it would be strong enough. The 12-gauge stuff is about the thinnest that an average welder can weld without burning holes through the plate. The frames are of 3/16-inch bars, the stringers of 1 inch by 1/8-inch material, and the stem and keel members are of 3/8-inch plate—all pretty much standard for this type of boat.

Because a number of the plans sold for this hull have gone into the hands of young fellows who have built the boats as sturdy boatyard tugs, or who have started businesses by building one, perhaps a description of the tooling required is in order. The list is minimal.

A transformer-type AC welding outfit can be purchased from Sears or Montgomery Ward for around $250 at the present writing. A 1/2-hp disc sander will be needed, and an acetylene outfit for flame cutting of plates from templates. Some clamps and a chipping hammer will also be needed. The hammer can be electric, but compressed air is more useful, because the compressor can double as a source of air for sand-blasting.

I know of one first-class steel hull builder who totes all of this equipment comfortably in a two-wheeled trailer behind his car, ready to set up work and build a boat on any piece of firm ground offered. He has never been idle when he wanted to work. He charges the going hourly rate as a self-employed man, gets a huge tax break because his expenses for living away from home are deductible—meals, motel, mileage are legitimate deductibles—has no payroll overhead, no strikes or labor problems.

The procedure in building a welded steel hull follows this line: The boat must be lofted and faired out. Then templates are transferred from the stem and keel and horn bar to plywood, which is then sawed out for templates. The templates are laid on the steel and marked out with a slate or grease pencil. A scrieve board of the body plan serves as a welding jig for the transverse frames. These are erected on a suitable base, and the stem and keel pieces are welded in. Next, the chine bars are streamed and tacked. The stringers can be streamed then or can be put inboard separately in intercostal fashion between frames. Next, the side plates are patterned out. This includes the transom plate. The sides are hung on the upside-down frame skeleton as the perspective shows in conjunction with the inboard framing plan here. Masonite or thin cheap plywood can be used to template the shell plates for side and bottom. The side will be tacked to the stem, and streamed aft. To help in the bending, it's useful to have a Spanish windlass—rope loops tightened with a wooden bar, looped across the outer aft ends of the side plates. Tack as you go until the plates lie fair, and stream smoothly.

When the hull is closed in, it should be immediately sand-blasted outboard and zinc sprayed, or painted with zinc chromate, or coated

Measurements for Shape of Hull - 18 FT. Steel Bangabout "TINTILLEE"

	Stem	Keel	₵Line	Chine	Sheer	Fr. #
Distance from Floor, given in Ft, ins, & 8ths	0.4.0				2.5.1	0
		4.1.6	4.0.0	2.9.5	0.8.0	1
		4.1.4	3.1.2		0.10.7	2
		4.1.1	3.3.3		1.0.7	3
		4.6.0	3.11.2	3.4.2	1.1.2	4
		4.7.5	3.8.0	3.4.4	1.0.2	5
		3.4.6	3.4.6	3.3.4	0.11.2	TR
Distance from ₵ in Ft, ins, & 8ths	0.0.1½	0.0.1½			0.0.1½	0
				1.2.3	2.0.2	1
				2.1.4	3.1.4	2
				2.7.1	3.5.5	3
				2.8.7	3.4.7	4
				2.7.4	3.1.6	5
	0.0.1½	0.0.1½		2.4.5	2.9.6	TR

Fore — Body — see text

Aft — Body — 2½" crown — swing, 12" dia.

Sheer

Floor Line

Load W.L.

4"
32½"
34¼"
32⅝"
29½"
12⅜" 9" 9½"
9" 9"

Plate Line

Chine Line

Keel

-10°

Length O.A. - 18 FT.

25"
14½" 3"
23"

Half Breadths

Sheer

Chine

Stations spaced 36"

Frame Plan, Hull

Half siding keel bar ⁹⁄₁₆"

Engine bed

1" pipe

⅞" rod

1" x ¾" stringers spaced on 3 rds.

¾" x 2½" Frames

2½" I.P.S. stern tube

¾" I.P.S. rudder tube

Layout for Keel

Stem furnaced to template

¾" x 2½" bar

Weld

Mark plating line

Continuous weld

2½" I.P.S. stern tube

⅜" Plate

⅜" x 4" Keel Bar

Transom piece 3" x 2½" and horn bar ⅞" x 2½"

Fill ⅜" Pt.

Rudder stock

2½" 12" 31½"

0 — 36" — 1 — 36" — 2 — 36" — 3 — 36" — 4 — 36" — 5 — 36" — TR

76¼"

with zinc-rich epoxy paints. Sprayed hot zinc is best, but zinc-rich paints have become acceptable. The hull is then turned and sand-blasted. *Use silicon sand or sharp sand;* beach sand is rounded and will not abrade the mill scale and rust. Immediate coating inboard after all sand has been removed is necessary to avoid overnight rusting when the uncoated steel is eaten by moist oxidizing air. Rust scratches, however, need not be alarming.

At the start of this yarn I promised a few words on welding advice. For the 3/8-inch keel plates and bars, the proper welding potential would be about 250 amps at 45 volts. For the 3/16-inch stuff, use about 200 amps at 35 volts. The 12-gauge (7/64 inch) shell skin will weld up properly at lower currents, avoiding excessive heat and the consequent tendency to warp if too hot. I'd try 120 to 130 amps and around 25 to 30 volts. (You'll recall that amps are the quantity of current, volts the pressure.)

All of this was dealt with in the original story about *Tintillee*, a reprint of which is furnished with each set of prints in 3/4-inch scale from my original drawings. These prints I will mail postpaid, for $49, to any part of the world. The drawings include six hull sections of the framing, the lines and the offsets for laying down, the deck framing plan, a sheet of perspectives and the outboard profile, and the inboard arrangement, together with a diagram for setting up. Fourteen separate views in all: a complete bundle.

There you are, Shipmate (if I may borrow the friendly term from William Atkin), and as I close this dissertation on steel in particular and free enterprise in general, let me arm you with a truism that can help all young men: it is a fact of life that The Law of Averages will take care of any man who will *work*.

Not all men will want the drawings for going into the steel boat game. In this morning's mail as I write this, I have word from a customer who wants to build *Tahitiana* and is using *Tintillee* as a pilot project to learn welding before he tackles The Big Dream. I have told this canny man to send a cheque for $15.00 to International Marine Publishing Co., 21 Elm St., Camden, Maine 04843, for a copy of *Boatbuilding with Steel,* by Gilbert Klingel. Mr. Klingel is a retired steel boatbuilder who has had years in the art and who is a superb writer. Klingel's instructive book is the best one for the studious amateur or budding professional.

Galatea

Here we have *Galatea*, a sensible girl whose name must be pronounced softly according to the tenets of Greek mythology—not *Gala Tea* as in primitive English. No slim, ascetic girl is she, wearing hardware jewelry to pain your eye. There is no air about her that says Daddy Must Pay. She is not a graduate of a boat show course in barbershop glitter and plumbing. She is, rather, just what she is: a wholesome 19-year-old girl with enough of wieners and potato salad in her makeup to be serenely competent in "go" and "blow"—not in cosmetic "show." But let us attend to statistics, then to philosophy.

Galatea is 22 feet 11 inches overall, by 8 feet 3 inches beam. She draws 3 feet 10 inches when down to her marks, with displacement at 5,052 pounds. Her sail area is 285 square feet, moderately loaded at 17.5 pounds per square foot, which means she has plenty of sail per pound. This has been proved by boats that have been built to this design. She also has enough cutaway to her forefoot to let her come about handily, letting the bow pay off on a tack, which is the purpose of a cutaway forefoot. There is enough rake to the keel so that she can sail through kelp beds in a fashion no vertical fin-keel boat can. Her 1500 to 1700-pound iron keel runs full shoe length, protecting the rudder pintle so that if you are hung up on rocky shoals at an ebbing tide, you escape the terror of having a vertical keel under you that will pinion your hull into uncontrollable grinding gyrations as seas hit you. Despite the fashion now prevalent for rudder bottoms extended in line with the keel, I have held to a standard rudder cam contour that will not snag rocks on a return bounce. Here is where the experience of an Old Salt departs from the school exercises that say the lowest part of the rudder is the most efficient. It may be, a bit, but I'll take a rudder that won't snag the bottom, strain the pintle or gudgeon pins, or add to repair bills. Hence the upswept trailing edge, according to the gospel of those who sail more and read less.

Galatea is just a shade larger than the toy tabloids that will be studied by any man stricken with a yearning for a small family sloop. The standards are *Picaroon* by Sam Rabl; *Poco Dinero* by John G. Hanna, and one or two others—check any public library. *Picaroon* will require an oil squirt can for your joints as you grease your hide to get into her cabin. *Poco* is too heavy and slow, being underrigged. By adding about 18 inches to either end of these volumetric charm boats, I have designed something that a young husband can build for about the

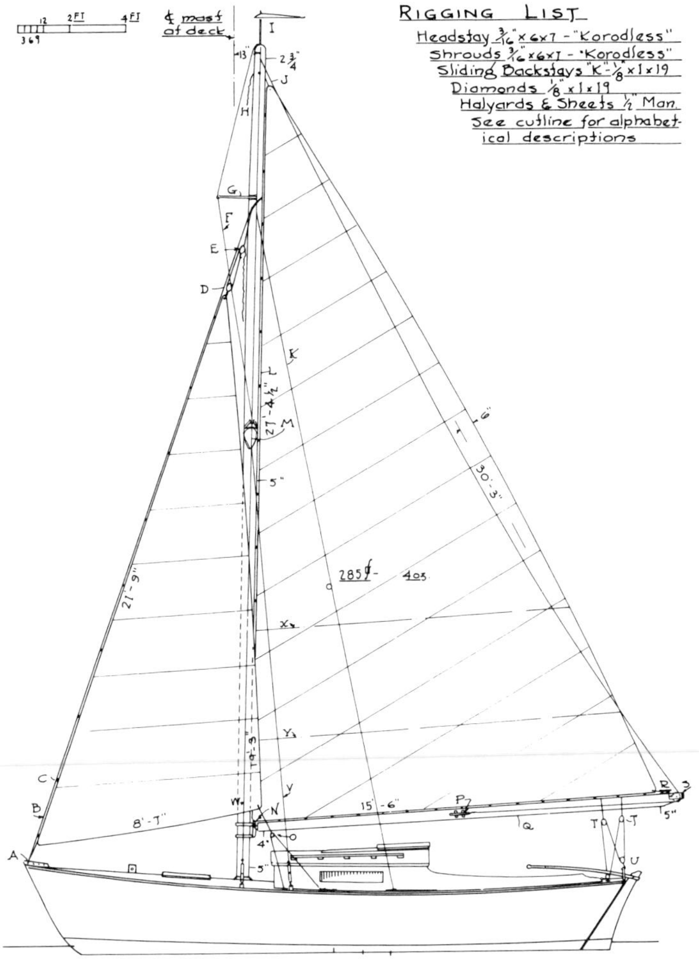

RIGGING LIST

Headstay ³/₁₆" × 6×7 - "Korodless"
Shrouds ³/₁₆" × 6×7 - "Korodless"
Sliding Backstays "K" - ¹/₈" × 1×19
Diamonds ¹/₈" × 1×19
Halyards & Sheets ½" Man.
See cutline for alphabet-
ical descriptions

¢ mast
at deck

2 FT   4 FT

2850# - 403

21'-9"

30'-3"

27'-4½"

15'-6"

8'-7"

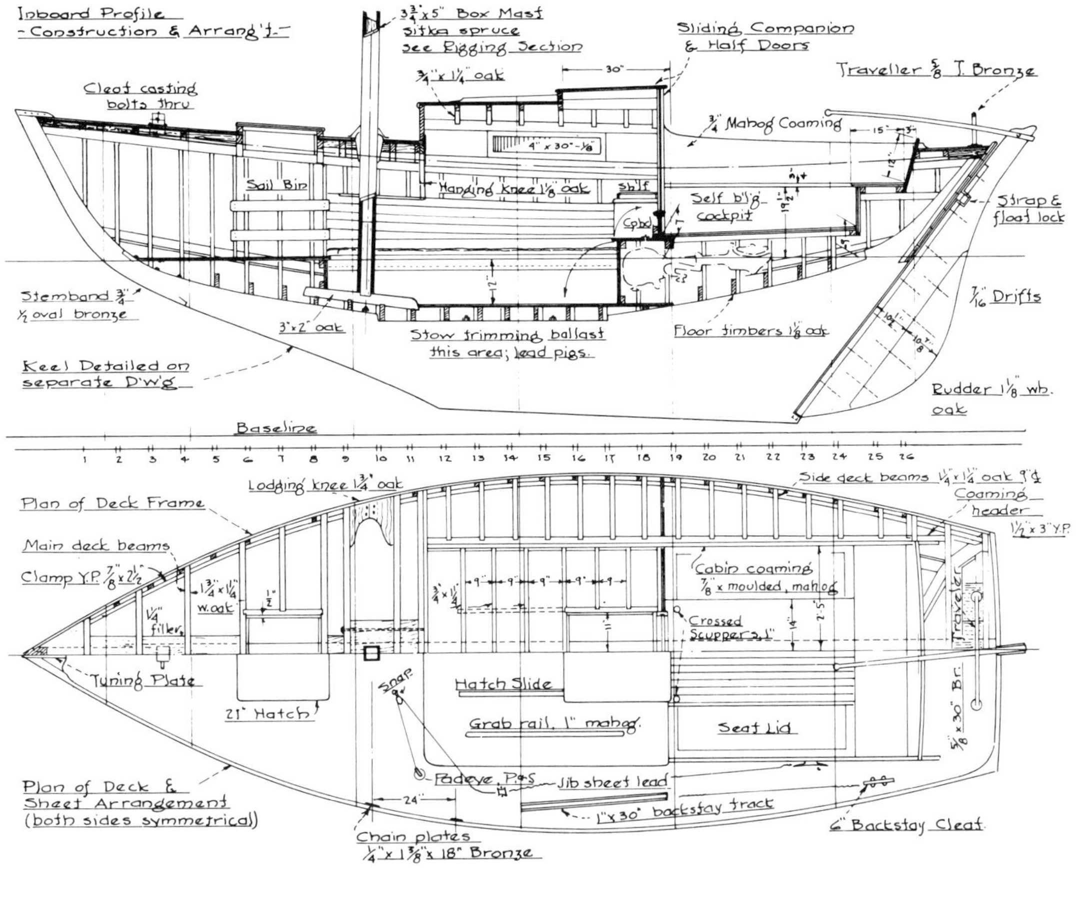

Inboard Profile
- Construction & Arrang't -

3¾" × 5" Box Mast
Sitka spruce
See Rigging Section

Sliding Companion
& Half Doors

Traveller ⅝" T. Bronze

Cleat casting
bolts thru

¾" × 1¼" oak

30"

¾" Mahog Coaming

4" × 30" - ¹/₈

Sail Bin

Handing Knee 1⅛ oak

Shelf

Self b'l'g
cockpit

Strap &
float lock

Stemband ¾"
× ½ oval bronze

3" × 2" oak

Stow trimming ballast
this area; lead pigs

Floor timbers 1⅛ oak

¹/₁₆ Drifts

Keel Detailed on
separate D'w'g

Rudder 1⅛ wb.
oak

Baseline

1 2 3 4 5 6 7 8 9 10 11 12 13 14 15 16 17 18 19 20 21 22 23 24 25 26

Plan of Deck Frame

Lodging knee 1¼ oak

Side deck beams 1¼"×1¼" oak 9¼
Coaming
header
½" × 3" Y.P.

Main deck beams

Clamp Y.P. ⅞" × 2½"

1¾" × 1¼"
w. oak

¼"
filler

Cabin coaming
⅞" × moulded, mahog

Crossed
Scupper 3/1"

Turning Plate

Traveller

4" × 30" Br.

21" Hatch

Hatch Slide

Grab rail, 1" mahog.

Seat Lid

Snap

Plan of Deck &
Sheet Arrangement
(both sides symmetrical)

Padeye P & S

Jib sheet lead

1" × 30" backstay track

6" Backstay Cleat

Chain plates
¼" × 1⅛" × 18" Bronze

Note: Boat must be lofted full size and faired from these scaled dimensions.

Shop floor

Mold 5   Mold 4   Mold 3   Mold 2   Mold 1

37"   23"   46"   46"   46"

24¾"

9'-5"
8'-3"
7'-0"

Sheer—Top of Planking
Top of Deck Edge
Chine
Rabbet
C.B. 5052#
Area Lateral Plane without Rudder 48.9#
Note "A"

22'-11" L.O.A.
19'-0" L.W.L.

LINES PROFILE

For laying down use 1" sq. w. pine batten

₵ Mast at deck

Base

LINES PLAN

Sheer
Chine

Frames ⅞" x 1⅛", 9 ₵

Note A—"Fair keel fwd & aft broken line
(Half siding thru A-A shown)

Decking to sand & plane to ¾"

KEEL TIMBERING LAYOUT

Keel, iron—15-1700 lbs
Inboard ballast 2-300 lbs

(Centerline of 1⅛" Rudder stock)
½" drifts
1" dia. Keel Bolts
½" bolts (3)
csik & plug
Stopwaters

BODY PLAN

Note B
Expanded Crown
Transom = 4"
(Projected, 3")

Note B— Diminish fully faired body plan by 1⅛" plant thickness when extending molds.

TYPICAL MOLD

Showing how 1"x2" ribbands are left in to hold frames while steaming in.

Gain out for chine after which is streamed after frames are bent

Gain mold to receive keel

handclasp Scarph

1"x2" ribband
¾" x 4"
clamp
⅞" x 1⅛" frame
¾" x 6" cross spall

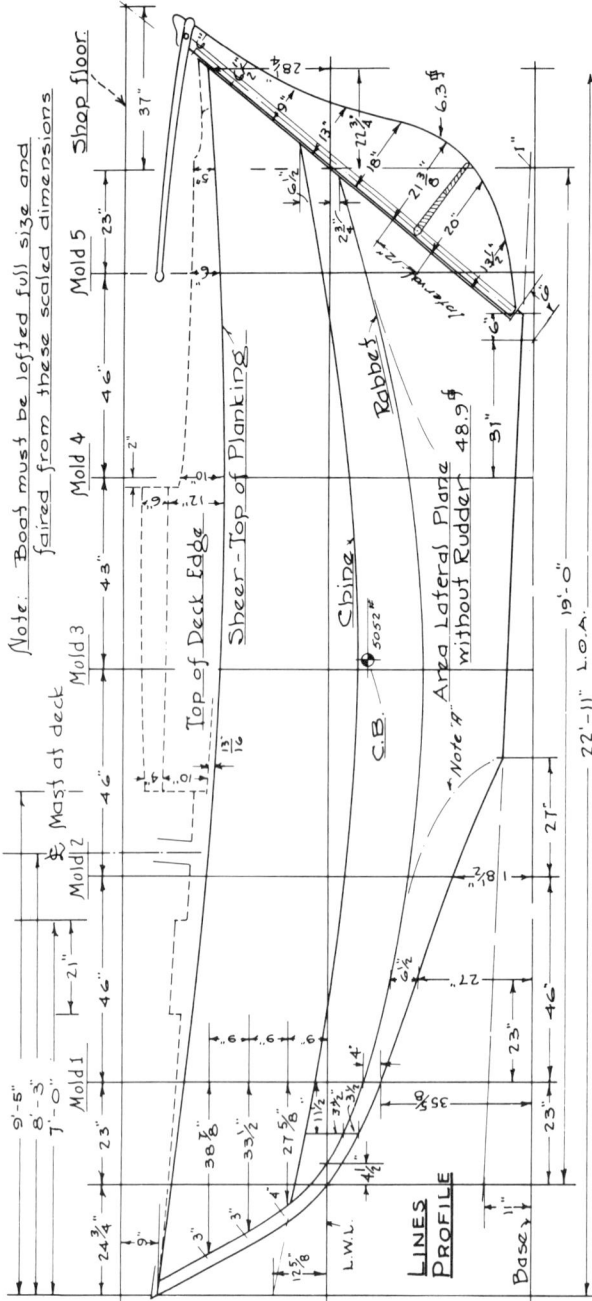

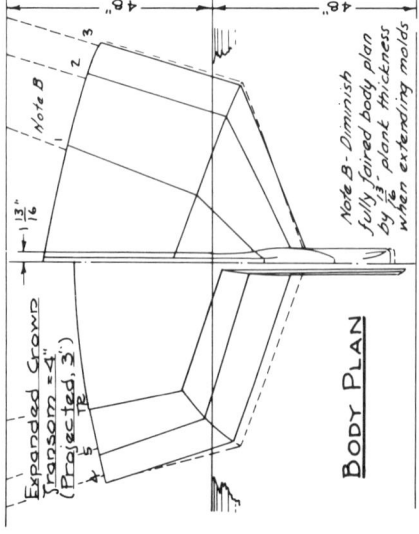

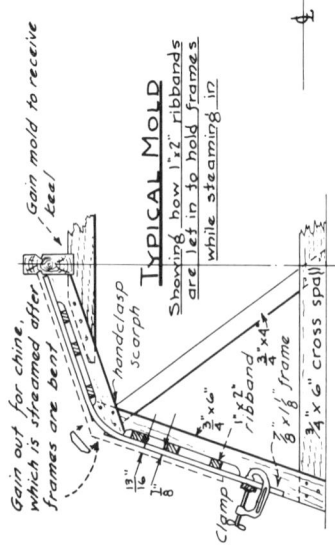

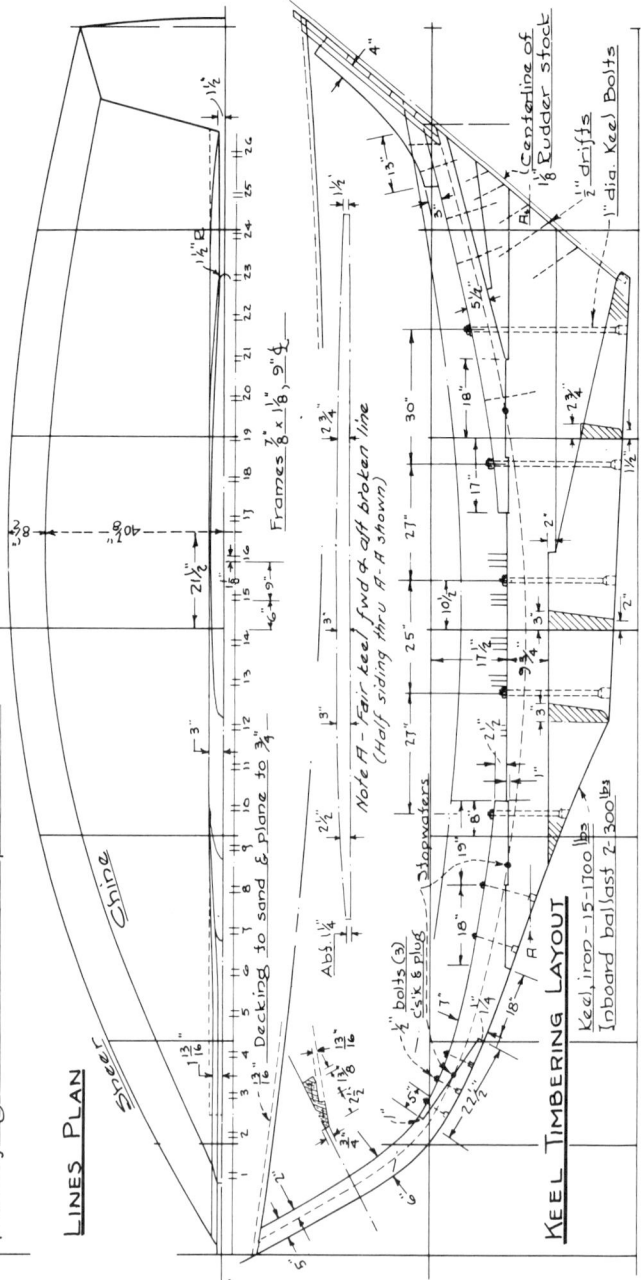

TABLE OF OFFSETS for HULL LINES
All dimensions given in Ft., Ins. & 8ths

Mold No.	Heights above Base			Half Br'dths from ₵		
	Sheer	Chine	Rabbet	Sheer	Chine	Rabbet
Stem	7.3.0	0.9.1	4.3.6	0.0.4	0.0.4	1 13/16
1	6.9.1	4.8.6	3.3.5	2.2.0	1.2.7	0.2.0
2	6.4.2	3.8.1	2.5.2	3.6.0	2.8.7	0.3.0
3	6.1.2	3.5.0	2.1.7	4.1.1	3.4.1	0.3.0
4	6.0.5	3.6.6	2.5.3	4.1.0	3.3.7	0.3.0
5	6.1.3	3.1.2	3.3.6	3.7.2	2.10.3	0.3.0
TR	6.4.2	4.6.4	3.9.2	2.9.3	2.4.4	0.1.4

Lbs. to Immerse 1" at W.L. 532.43

price of an average automobile (sail, hardware, and outboard included) if he persists in the application of accumulation, building with determined planning. She will even be large enough to take along a couple of children later, and you can sell her as a usable proposition on any used boat market when you want to move up in size. *Galatea* will not be looked upon as a toy, a freak. So much for statistics and general design scoop.

Because I have asked the editor of this family compendium of lore to run the drawings up and down the backbone of the book, the better to enchant you with what one of my Bronx customers calls "clear drorings," I have a chance to extend the relevant text. What better place than this to become Captain Hornblower, stomping the quarter-deck in verbal fury, pulling the guns to the wale ports, repelling challenges? I have some gunpowder to touch off; let us attend to philosophies.

The current crop of factory-built sailboats in general do not appeal to me. I have sailed many of them. They are woefully deficient as sea boats. Their fine bows make them root when running off. I have come to the conclusion that the true reason they will sail through a fleet of safe, traditional boats is that the factory boats are extremely light. If you compare displacement figures, you will at once note that these craft weigh about *half* as much as standard boats. Skinned out of frames, skin stressed, skimped on materials, relying on bulkheads to maintain shape, the "racer/cruiser" naturally weighs up shy when stacked against what experienced men require when taking cruising seriously. Racing-cum-cruising is cum neither.

It does not take outright genius to blow a thistle across the face of the water. Minimal wetted surface calls for a cylinder; high ballast-to-displacement ratio is easy to get, and any reference to Deafandumb angles of entrance is merely applying the simple physics principle of the wedge to what is essentially a water machine comprised of wedges: a boat. At some place the wedge theory that produces fine snoots, along with hog-fat rumps, becomes a by-product of rating rules that are being cheated.

To a point, hull shape can cut 10 seconds off a nautical mile, but weight is the key; sail area is horsepower and light weight means a more easily driven boat. But all good things can be overdone—like yodeling in a vaudeville act. It is from the engineering criterion of weight per horsepower that the lightweight factory-to-distributor-to-customer sailboats get their celerity, if any—not from form, in my opinion. The point of payoff in hull shapes that depart from those of a normal boat can be shown at "stop" by calculus: a problem in mechanical advantage against drag. All compromise choices go up against the law of diminishing returns for results against input—so does a diet of prunes.

The form of our trendy current boats of the finny type is due to the lightness of construction. Most of them are skin stressed and carry almost no framing. With the engineering choices left for stabilizing a fiberglass eggshell, fin keels are the logical method of extending keel weight downward. In the compromise of balancing sail area to lateral plane with the low wetted surface of an ovoid flat hull, a designer *has* to come up with an old-time fin-keel boat. Then, to be able to steer her, and to avoid the broaching ardency of the type, he has to put a trailing skeg aft, with or without a separate rudder, all cantilevered downward from the hull.

In whirling seaways, all of the rudder stress is carried by this appendage. If the rudder serves wholly for directional stabilization, every ounce of stress concentrates on the rudder stock at the point where it leaves the hull. This is bad engineering. Time after time I have seen these rudders break off right there where the topmost rudder plate bolt pierces the rudder stock. This always happens when the chance is hard, the water wild, and you are a long way from home and mother.

One other peculiarity of eggshell-hulled sailboats that carry low ballast in low appendages is the reverse pendulum effect possessed by this type in a fore-and-aft direction. If the swells are the right length, they pitch up and down in waning winds like mating gooney birds. With fin pendulum weight low, and inertial forces damped by a medium 800 times as dense as the air in which the rigging thrashes, water and gravitational inertia limit the motion of the keel. Result: the boat and mast do the swinging, like an inverted clock. You become the cuckoo. Keel weight carried full length fore-and-aft gyrates much more slowly.

There now, Mates! Captain Hornblower has fired his first fusillade, not to denigrate a particular boat, but a type thought to be the One and Only among young designers today. Designers are known to be great copycats; they are like sheep, following some Head Ram who is considered to be the pure Merino, shedding bankable golden fleece. What I have said is to educate. There is still great virtue in a potato-salad-and-wiener boat like *Galatea.* She is not the glamour girl you'd chase in the conquistadorial hope she'd soak her socks in your coffee. She is the full-breasted traditional peasant whose services are invaluable in washing your dishes.

I have earned my living at hull design for most of my life, and analyzing boat behavior provides points of departure for making decisions. Observed fact, not opinion, becomes the basis for engineering skill. It is time—and this is the right place—to petition for traditional wooden boats if it is known they will be more satisfactory. *Galatea* fills the bill.

Are your dreams becalmed?

If your dreams are stirred, I can send a full set of *Galatea*'s drawings, in original 3/4-inch-to-the-foot scale, first class or airmail to any part of the world for $49.00. Plans include drawings for a light wooden box mast, whisker-stayed, that you can build. Today a light aluminum mast might be the thing. So much for mundane commercials. The first step in energizing dreams is to send for plans.

Whence the name *Galatea*? At the start of this yarn I mentioned Greek mythology. Galatea was the name of a statue, carved in ivory, of a young girl so pretty that she took the fancy of mythological old Greek king Pygmalion. Gazing at the statue, Pygmalion fell in love with Galatea, so he prayed to Aphrodite, and the statue was given life by that Goddess of Love. Much of Greek mythology seems to have been fueled by high-octane praying.

To the above proposition, and those preceding it, I commend your study. It will pass your polygraph test and a reading on your own Beaume scale.

Robinson Crusoe

Most boatmen know that the sea skiff is a popular type of boat. Originally thought of as a boat developed along the New Jersey seacoast from Sandy Hook to Cape May, where it was generally termed the Seabright skiff or Jersey sea skiff, today in the motorboat world the public's mind has turned the term generic, so that "sea skiff" is thought of as classifying all clinker-built runabouts or cruisers. Thus, alas, does the terminology of J.Q. Public water down marine specifics.

Here is a design for what the term sea skiff has come to mean. This is for a smallish cruiser, or largish runabout, depending upon how you look at it. She was designed long enough ago to have been built successfully by amateur builders, as she incorporates knowledge gained in my long experience with the type.

Feminine boats should not have masculine names, I grant, but the clinker-planked Jersey fishing boats from which today's types evolved were so tough-gutted that they did man's work, were hard-life outfits, and in deference to this quality, I labeled this one *Robinson Crusoe*. I couldn't think of any human who had survived a harder life than that old buzzard.

Robinson Crusoe was a real man named Alexander Selkirk. Having been a survivor of a wreck off the shore of an uncharted, unknown island in the southeast Pacific off Chile, he eked out a living for over 30 years. He was rescued by fortunate accident and returned to England, where his story was fictionalized by Daniel Defoe in a book that became a world classic: *Robinson Crusoe*. He was gutsy, a romantic roughneck. The name fits this design.

The Jersey skiffs evolved out of hard-life work. They got knocked around in being launched daily across a shallow tidal beach shingle when leaving for the day's commercial fishing. They had to beach again at night.

As power crept into the fishing fleet, boats became heavy. The launchings were done by wagon-wheeled cradles marched into the surf by teams of horses. At the end of a day's work these boats had to run the surf and be floated back onto the tongued pair of wheels, load and all, for a two-horse team pullout. I have watched this event at times, and am here to say a lot for horse sense, because some of these teams of horses were innate seamen (sea horses?) that jockeyed the cradles intuitively and with no fear of being surf-swept. Some of these teams, it seemed, were at communal beck and call and keep.

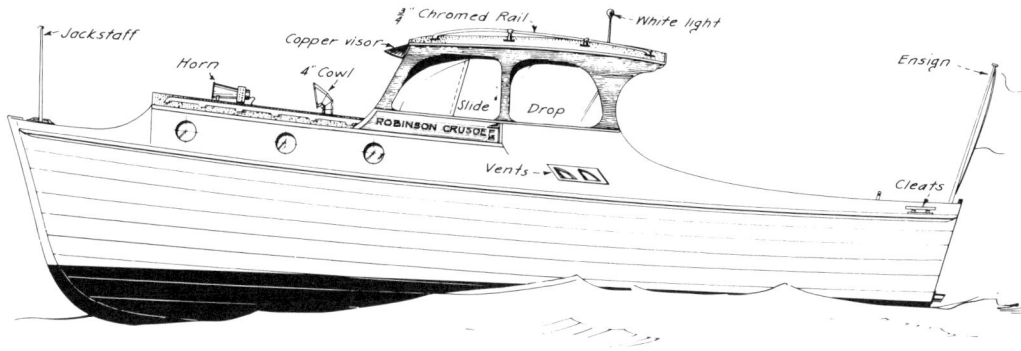

This kind of work naturally produced a construction that would survive on the hard sand shingle. The bottoms were dory-like flats of heavy stuff. Clinker construction was used in token acknowledgment of the rule of survival of the fittest for intermittent launching and drying out, because there is no type of wooden construction that has the quality of taking up tightness faster than the lap seam. All ship's lifeboats on ocean liners, and dinghies used by yachtsmen in the heyday of wooden building, were always clinker-built because they would leak less and tighten sooner in emergency launching. Correct bevels on the laps are easier to cut than the seamed edge required in finicky fits with carvel planking. Clinker planking is a forgiving method. Unpainted seam faces are always used, because wood has a gleet that, when first wet, seals the seam.

When drawing the sections of this boat, I used carvel planking to the turn of the bilge because (1) bottom resistance is lower, and (2) it is easier to rabbet planking into the turn of the forefoot on the stem with carvel than with clinker—only in this spot on a boat does carvel have an advantage. There is no law that says you couldn't clinker-plank her all the way. Today, I would do that for low power.

In the Seabright hull evolution, it became necessary to have power to compete in the fishery. In the development to power, the bottom was kept heavy and flat, and a tuck was worked up around a boxed skeg so that the upsweep of buttocks would let water into the propeller. The props were two-bladed so that they could be turned flat athwartships to avoid scragging the sand when grounding on the beach. Thus specialized, the right term is Seabright skiff.

The designer who was most responsible for developing the type into a workable high-speed powerboat was E. Lockwood Haggas of Atlantic City. Haggas, who had been an understudy and draftsman for J. Murray Watts, the prolific and versatile Philadelphia naval architect, straightened out the Seabright's lines, eliminated the flattened bottom, and used a vertical plank keel for high-speed offshore work when 100-, 200-, and 400-horsepower motors were demanded for speed work in

MEASUREMENTS FOR HULL SHAPE

L.O.A. 25 Ft. 7¼"

Floor line if ROBINSON CRUSOE is built upside down

Shear, upper edge of strake

Top edge, planksheer

Outline of maximum engine
Gray Lugger 6-72

Lap line

Apron face

Round off

Circumscribed
Rudder rectangle
15" x 21 - 3" lead

Load W.L.

Baseline

Tran.

28¼"

10¾"

15"

1" dia.

Shaft ₵

Frame line

Rabbet Line

Keel, St. Line

Stem

28 Frames – ¾" x 1⅛" – 9" ₵'s

Half Siding of Apron 2¼"

Keel & Rabbet Line

C.B.

Note "A" – Lap line: clinker planking
above – smooth seam (carvel) below

2¾" Crown TR 98765

Note "A" – Lap line

15" d x 12 p for motor shown

Area of W.L. Plane
137·70 sq. ft.

Lbs. per inch
Immersion
734·72 lbs.

Stem face ⅝
½ Siding Stem 1⅜

Scale

Baseline

12" B.

6" B.

L.W.L.

9" AB.

18" AB.

27 AB.

OFFSETS in Feet Inches & 8ths to outside of ⅝ planking

	Station	Stem	1	2	3	St.	4	II	6	7	8	9	Tr.
Heights above Base	Keel	3·0·0	1·6·4	1·4·2		Line to —						0·3·0	
	Rabbet	3·7·4	1·9·5	1·8·7	1·8·7	1·9·3	1·9·6	1·9·7	1·10·3	1·11·2	2·0·4	2·2·0	2·3·4
	Butt.1	5·11·5	2·0·4	2·0·0	1·9·6	1·9·6	1·9·7	1·10·7	1·11·7	2·0·7	2·2·3	2·3·3
	Butt 2	4·4·3	2·6·2	2·0·4	1·11·0	1·11·0	1·10·5	1·11·4	2·0·5	2·1·4	2·3·0	2·4·1
	Butt 3	6·1·4	4·3·6	2·7·7	2·2·4	2·0·4	2·1·5	2·3·0	2·3·6	2·51	2·6·4
	Shear	6·6·0	6·3·2	6·0·4	5·10·7	5·8·2	5·6·5	5·5·3	5·5·3	5·4·3	5·4·1	5·4·2	5·4·4
Half-breadths from ₵	Rabbet	0·1·3	0·1·3	0·1·3	0·1·3	0·1·3	0·1·3	0·1·3	0·1·3	0·1·3	0·1·3	0·1·3	0·1·3
	12" B.		0·3·4	0·10·3	1·7·2	2·2·3	2·5·7	2·7·2	2·2·0	1·31
	C.B.		0·10·4	1·9·3	2·6·3	3·0·5	3·4·9	3·4·7	3·3·5·5	3·1·0	2·10·0	2·7·0
	L.W.L.		1·2·2	2·1·6	2·10·5	3·5·3	3·8·4	3·9·1	3·8·0	3·6·3	3·4·0	3·1·0
	9" Ab.	0·2·4	1·6·4	2·5·4	3·1·6	3·7·6	3·11·2	3·11·5	3·11·5	3·9·0	3·7·0	3·3·3+
	18" Ab.	0·4·2	1·10·1	2·8·6	3·3·0	3·9·4	3·11·6	4·0·3	3·11·4	3·9·6	3·7·5	3·3·5
	2T Ab.	0·7·0	2·1·3	3·1·0	3·7·4	3·11·1	4·0·4	4·0·3	4·0·6	3·10·6	3·94	3·6·3·6
	Sheer	1·2·3	2·9·4	3·6·6	3·11·3	4·0·6	4·0·6	3·11·5	3·10·6	3·92	3·6·6	3·2·5

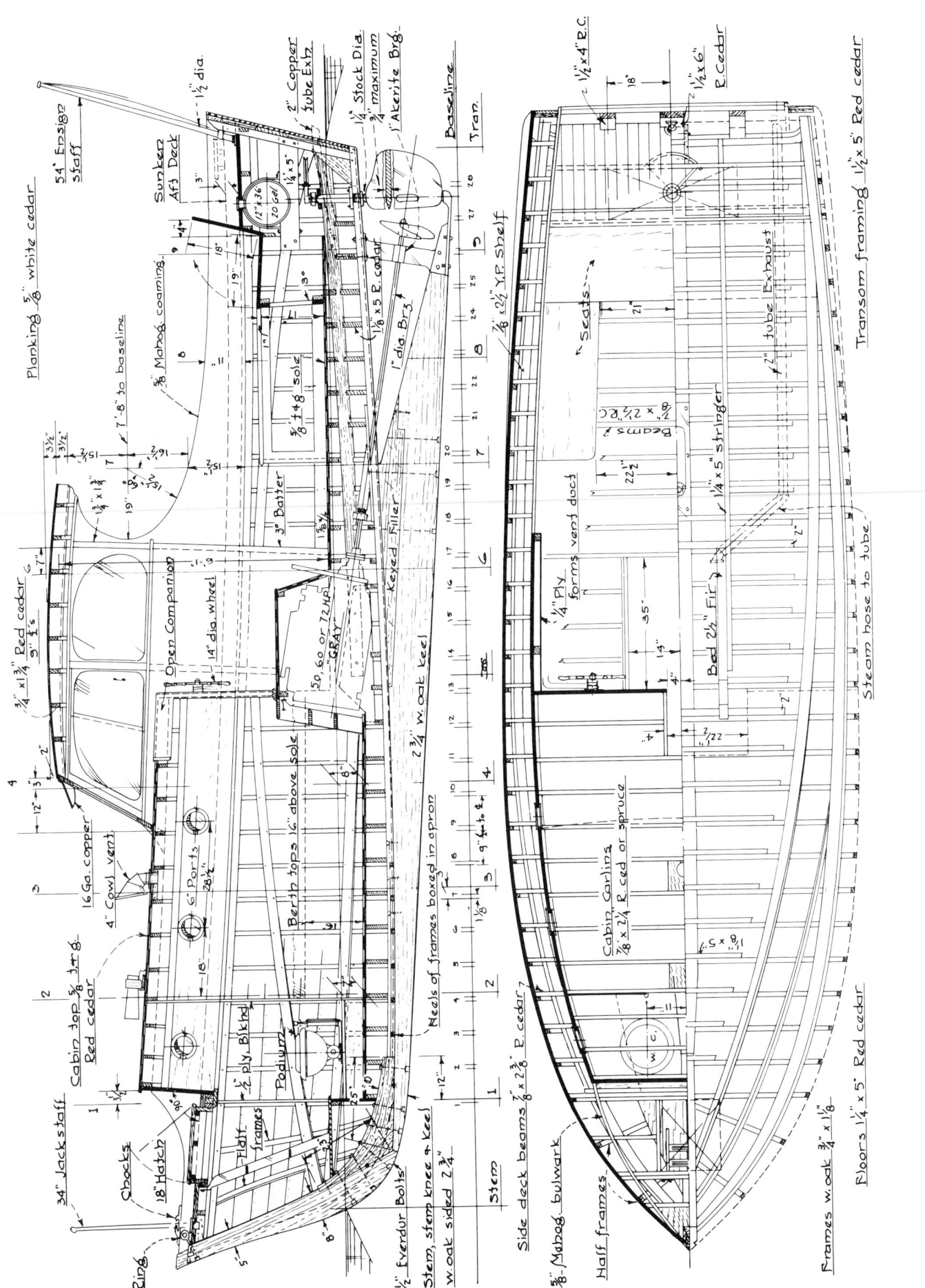

Planking ⅝" white cedar

54' Ensign Staff

Sunken Aft Deck

2" Copper tube Ext.

¼" Stock Dia.
¾" maximum

1" Akerite Brg.

Baseline

Tran.

1½ dia.

Mahog coaming

¾" x 2½" Y.P. Shelf

1⅛ x 5 P. cedar

1" dia. Br3

3" Batten

Keyed Filler

Open Companion

50, 60 or 72 H.P.
"GRAY"

14" dia. wheel

2¾" oak keel

Reals of frames boxed in apron

¾ x 1¾" Red cedar
5" ½'s

Cabin top ⅝" 3 + 8
Red cedar

16 Ga. copper

4" Cowl vent

6" Ports

28½"

Berth tops 16" above sole

Flat frames

½ Everdur Bolts

Stem, stem knee + keel
w. oak sided 2¾"

¾" Jackstaff

Chocks

18" Hatch

½ Ply Blkhd

Podium

Stem

Side deck beams ⅞" x 2⅜" R. cedar

⅝" Mahog. bulwark

Half frames

Cabin Carlins
⅞" x 2¼" R. ced or spruce

Frames w. oak ¾" x 1⅛"

Floors ¼" x 5" Red cedar

Ring

1½ x 4" R.C.

1½ x 6"
R.Cedar

18"

R.Cedar

Seats

Beams 2
⅞" x 2½" R.C.

7" tube Exhaust

¼" Ply
forms vent duct

1¼ x 5 stringer

Bad 2½" Fir

22¼"

35"

4"

Steam hose to tube

W.C.

Transom framing 1½ x 5" Red cedar

12" x 36"
20 Gal.

rum running, a service in which cheap, tough boats earned great virtue—as outlaws!

The demand was spawned by Prohibition, during and after World War I. Rum-running outlaws had need for a cheap, rugged, high-speed boat in their continuous tilts with Revenue agents and the Coast Guard patrols. These patrols guarded the three-mile band of water that separated the coastal United States waters from the high seas, a band of jurisdiction beyond which hove-to vessels with cargoes of "The Real McCoy" were waiting for gangster cash.

Both E. Lockwood Haggas and Walter McInnis, of Boston, highly regarded designers, brought the sea skiff to high development, powering some of these boats with twin 400-hp Liberty airplane engines. Boatbuilders who built these boats then sold them to little old ladies who used the boats to go clam digging, I don't think. *Robinson Crusoe* stems from this lineage.

Many fine boatbuilders later discovered the manufacturing economy of the clinker hull. Wheeler, Thompson, Lyman, Morton, Century, Chris-Craft, and other builders entered the field. In the PR wars that followed in selling, fine definitions were dropped, and all boats of the type became sea skiffs.

The boat shown here has been built from Santiago, Chile, to British Columbia, and from Maine to the Chesapeake, all satisfying the need for an inexpensive, easily driven man-size boat for fishing, weekending, and the like.

Today, the lines and construction are standard. The profile of the deckhouse may be dated by the watermelon contours once thought fashionable. By straightening these out to suit yourself, you could bring her into the current scene. Remember the adage, "Once a good boat, always a good boat."

The drawings of *Robinson Crusoe* are in black line Ozalids in 3/4-inch-to-the-foot scale, indispensable for shop use in laying down, fairing out, and building. The tab is $49. With the bundle comes the original building article containing specs and procedures.

The boat is 25 feet 7-1/4 inches overall, by slightly more than 8-foot beam (roadable), drawing about 30 inches of water. She will travel 13-15 mph with from 50 to 72 hp. A nice compromise between economy and speed, with a layout you can alter to suit your needs.

Kingfisher

Have you noticed that names identify a boat better than a number does? If George Pullman, inventor of the railroad hotel-on-wheels known as the Pullman Car, could best keep track of his rolling empire by naming each car, the idea has merit for boatbuilders and boat designers. Rather than calling this boat the GT 26-7B or Fatso 56, I named her *Kingfisher*. There were several reasons for this.

First, Kingfisher is the name of a feisty seagoing bluejay that swoops from one tree branch to another along our waterways. He feeds with a spearing, fearless dive into any water, scissoring his minnow lunches with a joyous call. He is thoroughly at home around water. The association between that bird and this boat is calculated and obvious. But that is not all.

Second, the ends of the storage tubes in which my tracings of designs are kept can be much better identified if a name is taped across the upright end. Put a numerical moniker on the tape, and any vanity you have about being an operative guarding the secrecy of your great industry will go up in a smoke of cuss words.

Third, small chance any of us delineators will turn out boats at the rate George Pullman turned out rolling hotels! His was a respectable industry, and any young man going the GT 26-7B route need never fear that some junior designer will interfere with The Master's treasures. No design office ever becomes the overfat, unincorporated, unlimited asylum for the wised-up wayward dollars of fellow boat lovers.

Hence *Kingfisher*, not *GD%#!QWt3½/a!!* it.

Want to know about her? I hasten to oblige: *Kingfisher* is a clinker-built small inboard motorboat of a perennially popular type known variously as a picnic boat, a deep-water runabout, a sea skiff, or just plain family putz-about.

The arrangement is one I used in the design of *Kidette* in 1931, which appeared in the Show Issue of *Motor Boating* for that year. That design became a product that put a number of boat companies into business.

The activities of small boat companies were severely curtailed a few years later by World War II. Clarence Ackerman, later of *Newporter* fame, had built *Kidette* as a standard and had asked for an easier boat to build than the vee-bottom *Kidette*. I myself was caught up in war work, riding herd on the Americanization of the Vosper PT boats that were being built by Annapolis Yacht, Harbor Boat, Robert Jacob, and

Herreshoff. Knowing that "after de wah" there would be a rush of capital into the boat business—all patriotic ads were bragging about it—and that possibly some firms might pick up the utility runabout idea first invented in *Kidette*, I whiled away a few rare leisure hours with drawing a clinker-built round-bilge hull that would fill in at the place where pre-war utility inboards had been arrested. *Kingfisher*'s lines, hull framing, arrangement had all been drawn up by the time the war was over. Then. . . .

Bingo! Half a dozen boat companies hit the market with utilities using the by-now-popular *Kidette* cockpit layout. Just two thwarts and a box over the motor. Chris-Craft, Gar Wood, Dodge, Dee Wite—any number of builders built "utility" or "fisherman" models. Lyman of Sandusky came out with their Islander—and right there before my eyes was a boat almost the same as my *Kingfisher*. Lyman employed the *Kidette* layout, I "employed" Lyman's windshield—fair is fair. What you see in *Kingfisher* is a boat like a Lyman Islander, about the same size, preconceived without any interconsultation whatever. Just an idea that was in the air.

Any old-timer in the boat business will tell you that time is circular—popular boats seem to fade in the crush of new ideas, then the new stuff fades, and the old ideas that have better values return. Witness the resurgence today of the rowboat fad. Colloquially called "pullin' boats" down New England way, rowboats of clinker persuasion were once the staple product of all watering places and all nearby boat shops. I cut my apprentice teeth building these craft, and there was a time when clinker rowboats were beached almost beam end to beam end on lakeshore and oceanside. Circular time has brought them back again. Exercise fashions in jogging, the kick toward cardiovascular fitness, have now found the rowboat to be fine for the biceps and the seat of the pants. Circular time returns the good things.

Circular time has also returned the *Kingfisher* type of boat. What you see on these pages is a phenomenon: these are the only plans I know of that have ever been published for this type of boat! Plenty have been built, but . . . no plans published. Here we have the second exposure for this particular design. Again in fashionable demand, she first appeared in the 1955 issue of *Boat Building Annual*, here exposed by permission of the original publishers. No prints were ever available.

The original Bristol board drawings have now been photo-processed into mylar tracings which I cannot distinguish from my original ink work. But whoa, there, old kid—don't be so crazy for customers! Let's get the wheels on the track and deliver the vital statistics with a proper sales pitch. The previous pedigree is not enough.

I call to attention her size: *Kingfisher* is just a shade smaller than a Lyman Islander. She is 17 feet overall. She has 6 feet 6 inches of beam, draws about 20 inches of water, and will weigh as drawn about 1,300 pounds. She is therefore eminently trailerable. She is a high-sided little mite, having 34-1/2 inches of freeboard at the stemhead, and 27-1/2 inches of freeboard at the transom. She has good long legs in her lateral plane and crosswinds do not knock her about. Her deep entering forefoot helps in that regard. A slight hollow to the deeper waterlines results, which purls the bow wave down dryly.

Any garage that houses the average 20-foot automobile will be large enough in which to build her. She does best with a 60-hp 133-cubic-inch, four-cylinder, 4-cycle engine, but even the Universal Atomic Four, still being built, will deliver 13-mile speed. Sixty will get you 22 miles. Perhaps it was fortuitous thinking that prompted me to indicate an outboard version treatment that will accommodate up to 50 hp. A number of home builders have built her under garage conditions.

Here I can pass along some lore for young designers who may be studying yacht design via the correspondence route. This is a very good way to begin, but unfortunately schools cleave too much to the academic and the gimcrack coefficient side of their teachings, not being able to convey via the paper lesson route any of the inside thinking that goes on among hard-knuckled boatbuilders who are called upon to estimate the cost of a boat to be built to inadequate, slapdash plans. Schools promote foibles, sometimes.

One is the notion that all boats must be shown facing bow to the right. This is utter steaming Crockpot hogwash. I draw sometimes to the right, sometimes to the left. If the schools are correct, then William H. Hand was wrong, John Hacker was wrong, Edward Burgess was wrong, and sometimes C.P. Kunhardt, Dixon Kemp, Howard Chapelle, and others, including this old dog, have been wrong. It's a matter of being comfortable with what you see. Some men are left-eyed, some are right-eyed. There is no inside, in-loft shop standard. No more sense to righthandedness than that all ball pitchers must be righthanded.

Another amateurish practice is the triangular zip-zap, wire hanger

Fore Body

Aft Body

Transom Crown 1¾"

Scale — 1 ft 6" 3" INS

Buttock A   Buttock B

Propeller 10"d x 10"P. 3 Blade R.H. "Federal"
Shaft bronze -⅞"d.; 60' coupling to thrust
Strut: "casting, 1"x 3" section "Aerite" bearing
Rudder: "cast Rectangle 9¼ x 13½; 2" lead; 1" stock
Skeg B, "cast & Tee Section

¼" copper rivets

2" copper clouts, 1½"

tapered gar

How lap is made at hood ends of planking

Shop floor level

Sheer line

Buttock B

Buttock A

Universal "Atomic Four" 25 H.P.

Apron

Keel

Baseline

Stem

L.W.L.

Half siding Stem ¾

Half siding stem, ⁷⁄₁₆

Stem face ½

29 frames on 6" ctrs. — ¾"

Half siding Apron ⅜

Half siding Keel 1½

C.G. @ 1300#

Buttock B

Buttock A

Sheer

L.W.L.

W.L's 24", 18" not shown aft of 'G

OFFSETS — In Ft., Ins. & 8ths to outside

Station	Half Breadths from Centerline									Heights Above Baseline				
	Keel	6"Below	3"Below	L.W.L	6"Above	11"Above	18"Above	24"Above	Sheer	Sheer	Butt.B	Butt.A	Rabbet	Keel
1	0:1.6/16	0:1.5	0:3.7	0:6.4	0:10.5	1:2.4	1:5.3	1:7.6	1:10.2	4:7.5	—	3:2.2	1:5.2	1:2.4
2	0:1.5/16	0:3.6	0:8.0	1:0.4	1:6.3	1:11.3	2:2.6	2:5.3	2:7.3	4:5.7	4:10.2	3:3.0	1:3.7	1:0.4
3	0:1.4	0:6.1	1:1.2	1:7.2	2:1.1	2:5.5	2:8.5	2:10.5	2:11.7	4:4.4	2:7.3	3:0.1	1:7.4	1:3.7
4	0:1.4	0:10.4	1:6.6	2:0.2	2:6.1	2:10.2	3:0.2	3:1.5	3:2.1	4:3.2	3:2.1	2:2.6	1:4.2	1:3.7
5	0:1.4	1:0.2	1:10.0	2:4.0	2:9.5	3:0.6	3:1.5	3:2.3	3:2.7	4:2.3	2:2.6	1:6.7	1:4.2	
6	0:1.4	1:0.4	2:0.2	2:6.5	2:11.5	3:2.0	3:2.5	3:2.7	3:3.0	4:1.6	2:0.6	1:6.2	1:4.7	
7	0:1.4	—	2:0.6	2:7.4	3:0.6	3:2.0	3:1.5		3:0.7	4:1.6	to sweep	2:0.7	1:5.6	
8	0:1.4	—	1:10.7	2:6.5	2:11.6	3:1.3	3:1.1	3:1.1	3:0.7	4:1.7	2:0.4	1:7.3	1:6.4	
9	0:1.4	—	1:4.6	2:4.5	2:11.4	2:10.3	3:0.1	2:11.4	2:11.3	4:2.6	2:2.2	1:8.6	6:0.4	
Trans.	0:1.4	—	0:1.4	2:2.4	2:8.4	2:10.3	2:10.2	2:9.7	2:9.2	4:3.4	2:9.2	1:9.4	1:8.5	

straight line

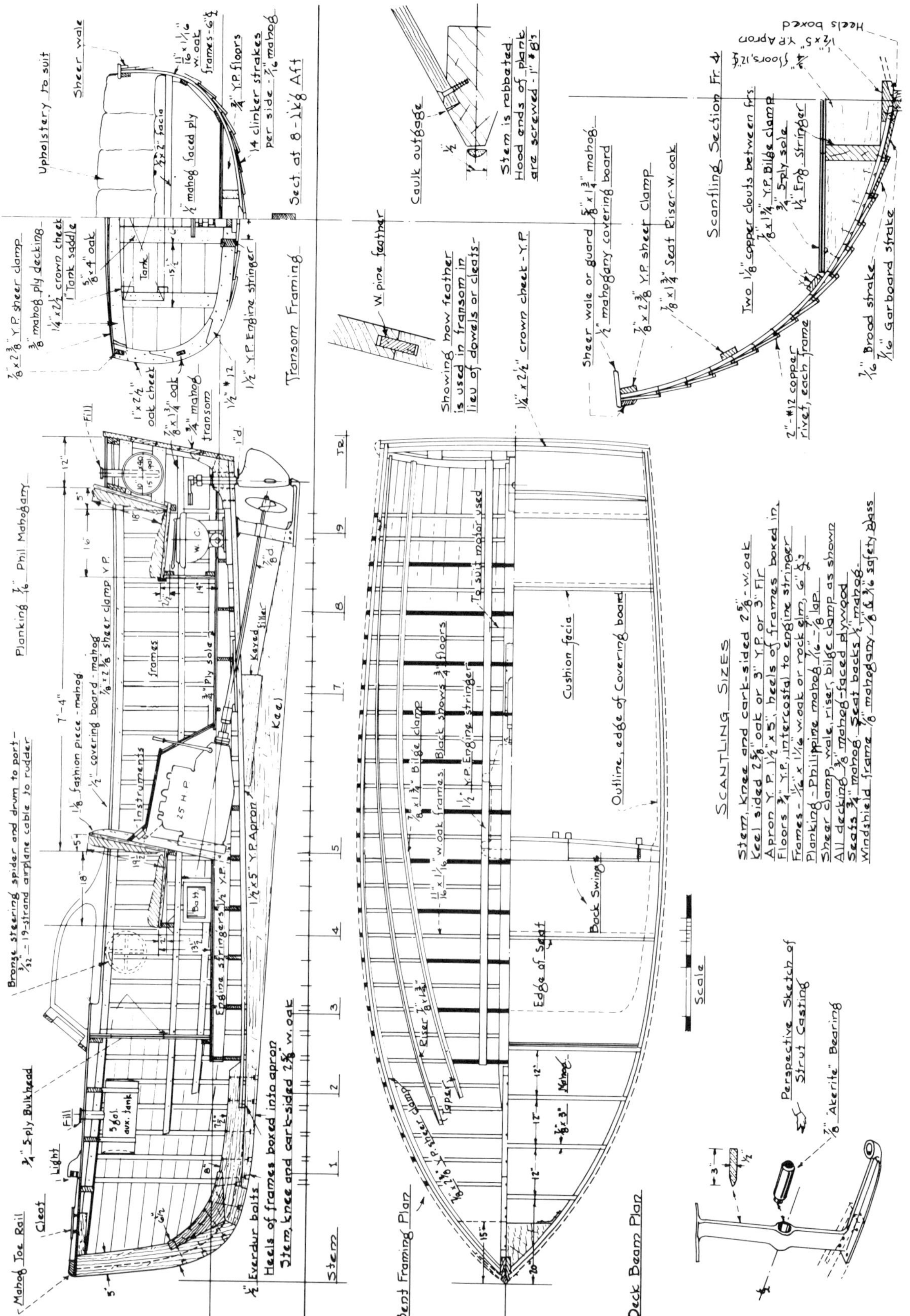

Sheer wale

Upholstery to suit

$1\frac{1}{8}$ x $1\frac{1}{2}$" w.oak Frames - 6"¢

$\frac{3}{4}$" Y.P. floors

14 clinker strakes per side - $\frac{5}{16}$" mahog

$\frac{3}{4}$" mahog faced ply

Sect at 8 - 1x8 Aft

2 x 2 facia

$\frac{7}{8}$ x $2\frac{3}{8}$" Y.P. sheer clamp

$\frac{3}{8}$" mahog ply decking

$1\frac{1}{4}$ x $2\frac{1}{2}$" crown cheek

Tank saddle

5 x 4" oak

Tank

1 x $2\frac{1}{2}$" oak cheek

$1\frac{1}{2}$" Y.P. Engine stringer

$\frac{3}{4}$" x $1\frac{3}{4}$" oak

$\frac{3}{4}$" mahog transom

$\frac{1}{2}$" x #12

Transom Framing

Caulk outgage

Stem is rabbated Hood ends of plank are screwed - 1" #8's

W.pine feather

Showing how feather is used in transom in lieu of dowels or cleats.

$1\frac{1}{4}$ x $2\frac{1}{2}$" crown cheek - Y.P.

Sheer wale or guard $\frac{5}{8}$ x $1\frac{3}{4}$" mahog

$\frac{7}{8}$ mahogany covering board

$\frac{7}{8}$ x $2\frac{3}{8}$" Y.P. sheer clamp

$\frac{7}{8}$ x $3\frac{1}{4}$" Seat Riser-w.oak

Heels boxed

$1\frac{1}{2}$ x 5" Y.P. Apron

$\frac{3}{4}$ floors, $12\frac{1}{2}$"

Scantling Section Fr. 4

Two $1\frac{1}{8}$" copper clouts between frs.

$\frac{7}{8}$ x $1\frac{1}{4}$" Y.P. Bilge clamp

$\frac{1}{2}$" Eply sole

$\frac{3}{4}$" Eng stringer

2" #12 copper rivet each frame

$\frac{5}{16}$" Broad strake

$\frac{5}{16}$" Garboard strake

Planking $\frac{5}{16}$" Phil Mahogany

Bronze steering spider and drum to port.
$\frac{3}{32}$ - 19-strand airplane cable to rudder.

$\frac{3}{4}$" 2-ply Bulkhead

Fill

Light

Cleat

Mahog Toe Rail

$\frac{1}{4}$" Everdur bolts

Heels of frames boxed into apron

Stem, knee and cark-sided $2\frac{5}{8}$ w.oat

$1\frac{1}{2}$ x 5" Y.P. Apron

Engine stringers $1\frac{1}{2}$" Y.P.

$1\frac{1}{8}$ covering board - mahog

$\frac{1}{2}$" x $2\frac{3}{8}$ sheer clamp Y.P.

$1\frac{1}{8}$ fashion piece - mahog

Frames

Instruments

25 H.P.

Keel

$\frac{3}{4}$ Ply sole

Keyed tiller

Bent Framing Plan

Scale

To suit motor used

Bilge clamp

$\frac{7}{8}$ x $1\frac{1}{4}$" Y.P. intercostal or rock elm, 6"¢

Black shows 3 floors

$1\frac{1}{2}$" Y.P. Engine stringer

$1\frac{1}{8}$ x $1\frac{1}{2}$" w.oak frames

Cushion facia

Outline edge of covering board

Edge of Seat

Riser $\frac{7}{8}$ x $3\frac{1}{4}$"

Dock Swings

Deck Beam Plan

Perspective Sketch of Strut Casting

$\frac{7}{8}$ "Akerite" Bearing

Scantling Sizes

Stem, knee, and cark-sided $2\frac{5}{8}$ w.oak
Keel sided $2\frac{5}{8}$ oak or 3" Y.P. or 3" Fir
Apron Y.P. $1\frac{1}{2}$ x 5", heels of frames boxed in
Floors $\frac{3}{4}$" Y.P. intercostal or rock elm, 6"¢
Frames - $\frac{1}{8}$" x $1\frac{1}{2}$ w.oak or white oak, 6"¢
Planking - Philippine mahog $\frac{5}{16}$" - $\frac{1}{8}$ lap
Sheer clamp, wale, riser, bilge clamp as shown
All decking $\frac{3}{8}$ mahog-faced plywood
Seats $\frac{3}{4}$" mahog. Seat backs $\frac{1}{4}$ mahog
Windshield frame $\frac{7}{8}$ mahogany $\frac{1}{8}$ & $\frac{3}{16}$ safety glass

propeller. I know one fine old boatbuilder who automatically adds 15 percent to an estimate when he sees a copycat propeller on a set of plans. "Danged fools!" he once exploded, "Any guy who draws a boat and then doesn't know that the propeller is where the machinery all ends up is telling on himself! None of 'em can draw 'em, that's why!" Thus the whole work becomes suspect, and on goes 15 percent to cover probable boo-boos to be unearthed in the loft. Slapdash work always costs somebody down the line a lot of work. Draw the propeller.

Fred Goeller used to draw both sides of a boat's lines. I did it on *Kingfisher* for the fun of seeing what Goeller's idea produced. To an intuitive designer, the twin lines fine down an elegance. Elegance cannot be described. It must be felt.

As to the rudder: the underside cam contour prevents damage on rock bumping. The cut-down upper edge knocks down the rooster tail on turns. Plate rudders right up under a hull, in fast boats where the transom runs clear, will throw a tail envied by any Chanticleer who crows 'ere break o' day.

Ozalid prints from these tracings come at $49. With them is a reprint of construction details, as well as a perspective of setting up the molds. Prints as complete as this set will almost build the boat if you will supply the muscle. There's many a small shop whose owners have found that small clinker-built boats are merely wages —IF you can sell the boat.

But build a clinker hull like *Kingfisher* at very little more expenditure for materials and time, then *power* her, and you not only can get wages, but your selling price is both much higher and more respected, your sale is quicker, and the dollars march in double file to the bank instead of straggling singly. Get out a pencil, compare competition, and you'll make this amazing discovery. It is a better employment of shop time by far.

The Elco 30

Captain Joe Scudder, skipper of Benson Ford's *Onika*, became a friend of mine when I was engineering the Ford boat at Burger in Wisconsin. During some of the gab sessions we had in the drafting room, Joe at one time remarked, "The best small cruiser I ever knew was the Elco 30. I had one at my home up on Barnegat Bay."

Comparative notes were exchanged, and it developed that I had been the man from Elco who had been given the plum of delivering Joe's boat. I remembered leaving the works at Bayonne after work one evening, glad to be anticipating a cool outside run through Kill Van Kull, over to Sandy Hook, and outside down the Jersey shore to Manasquan Inlet in the penumbral light of a summer evening. Offshore, a low, lazy swell was running, and I sensed that I had an unusual boat under me. This Elco 30 was light-footed, clipped off an easy 13 knots with only 90 horses from her Chrysler Ace, and was romping when I pulled into the Manasquan Yacht Club docks as shore lights began to twinkle in the evening afterglow.

Joe had asked me to get him a profile of this boat, and I later saw it framed in an honored place in Joe's home in West Palm Beach.

I have worked up this famous boat just as she was built by Elco 15 or 20 at a time, during the late 1930s. She is such a fine combination of afternoon picnic boat and overnight cruiser, and has so fine a relation of weight to waterplane size, that she also makes a lovely boat for fishing, because her motion, while idling or trolling, is so easy on your internal workin's.

From lines and a construction plan I had fortunately saved before Elco was destroyed by fire, I have drawn up this boat. She was exposed in several publications about 1950-52, a good generation ago. The "locomotive" treatment of her cockpit canopy and windshield may seem archaic, but the feature makes the best of sense: easy side access to lines, and overhang to protect from rain. She is replete with many little subtleties that were added here and there by her original designer, Bill Fleming, in the inevitable small twists, wrinkles, and dodges that, as every designer knows, vastly grades up the performance of a boat—just little things.

The boat you see here has been built by numerous amateurs. Today, I cannot see why she could not be built by the strip-planked method, although the first person I heard from with photos built her in Baltimore just as designed, with straked, spiled planking.

Note: Hull as drawn shows LWL in light condition. With full fuel and water load hull will trim 1¼" by the stern. Point w.L. as per dotted line at "X-X".

Transom drawn projected. Must be expanded full size from loft layout.

See inboard profile for coaming heights.

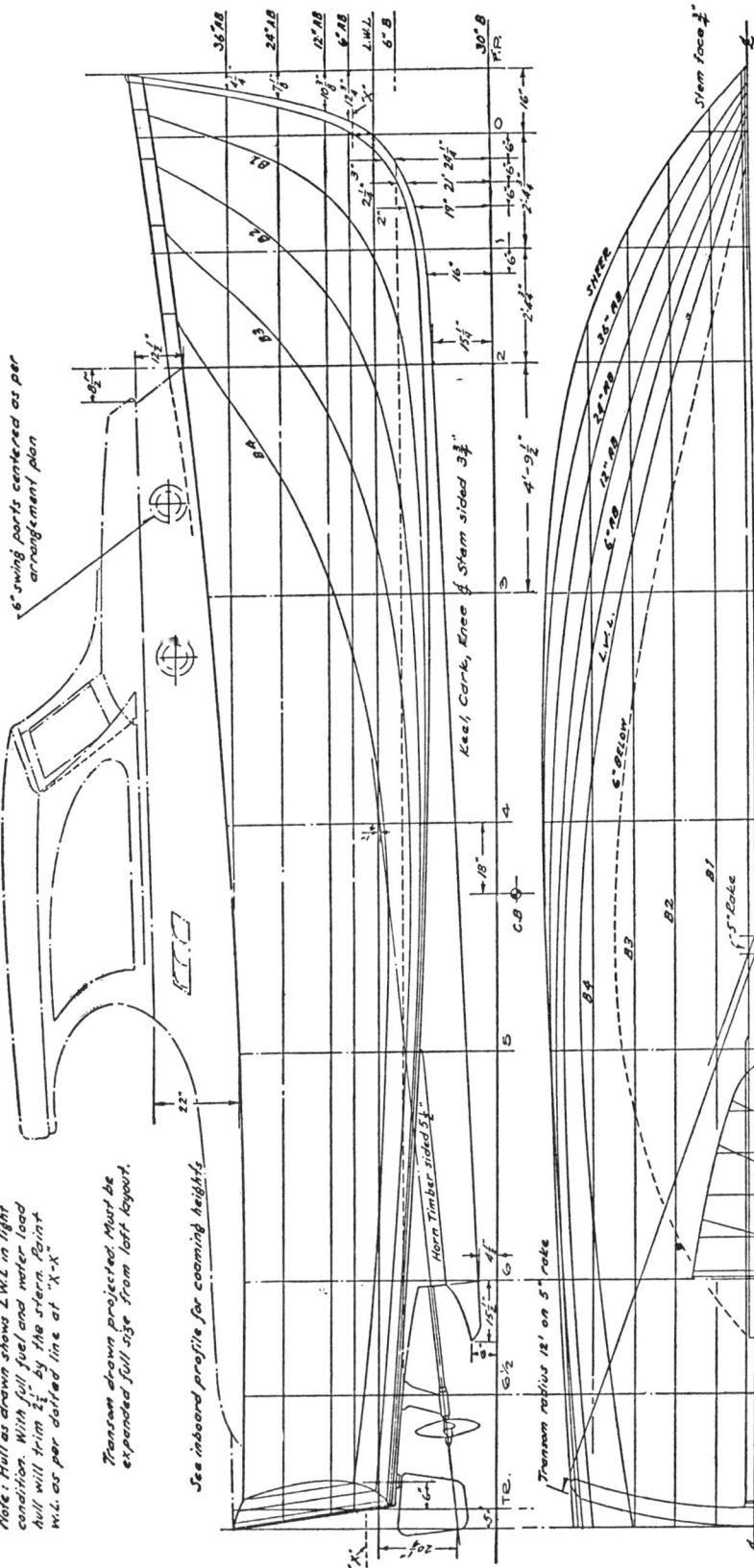

6' swing ports centered as per arrangement plan

Keel, Cork, Knee & Stem sided 3¾"

Stem face ½"

Horn Timber sided 5½"

Transom radius 12' on 5" rake

1'-5" Rake

18"p. x 18"d. Propeller

Dimensions in Offset Table given in feet, inches and 8ths

SECTION	Heights above Baseline							Half-breadths from Centerline							
	SHEER	BUT. 4	B.3	B.2	B.1	RABBET	KEEL	SHEER	36" AB.	24" AB.	12" AB.	6" AB.	L.W.L.	6" B	RABBET
Stem															0.1.7
0	7.3.5							1.3.0	0.9.3	0.6.2	0.2.4		0.0.3		0.1.7
1	7.1.5		6.5.1	5.10.4	5.10.4	2.0.5		2.9.7	2.2.7	1.9.7	1.4.4	1.1.4	0.9.6	0.5.7	
2	6.9.5	6.0.5	4.1.1	4.3.5	2.7.0	1.7.1	1.3.2	3.9.1	4.3.5	2.9.7	2.4.0	1.11.7	1.7.2	1.0.7	
3	6.6.3	3.4.7	1.3.2	2.7.7	1.10.1	1.5.5	1.46	4.5.4	4.6.1	3.10.3	3.7.0	3.2.7	2.10.3	2.2.6	
4	6.0.6	2.4.4	1.10.0	1.9.2	1.6.2	1.5.3		4.6.6	4.5.4	4.6.1	3.11.3	3.7.0	2.10.3	2.10.1	
5	5.5.2	2.4.3	1.10.0	1.9.0	1.5.7	1.7.4		4.5.0	4.5.0	4.1.5	3.11.4	3.7.3	3.8.4	2.11.1	
6	5.4.1	2.7.1	2.2.4	2.0.2	1.8.2	1.10.6	0.8.4	4.1.4	4.2.4	4.3.3	4.1.2	3.10.4	3.12	2.6.2	
6½	5.4.0	2.9.9	2.4.1	2.2.0	1.11.4	2.0.5		3.11.1	4.1.0	4.1.6	3.11.7	3.10.4	3.8.5	1.0.6	0.2.4
TR	5.1.2	3.0.3	2.6.1	2.3.6	2.3.0	2.2.6		3.8.7	3.0.2	3.9.2	3.5.3	3.5.3	2.7.2	3.0.5	0.2.4

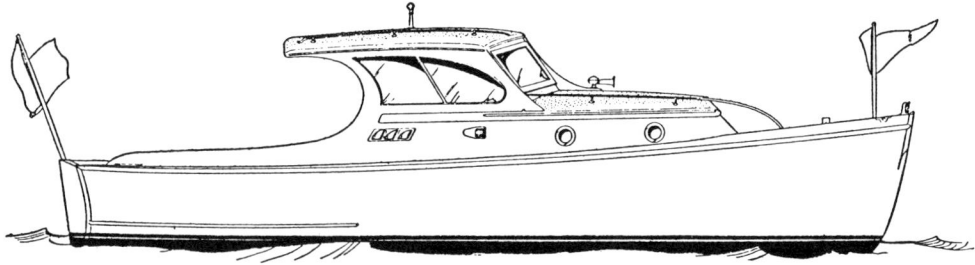

The dimensions of this boat are: length overall, 30 feet 6 inches; beam, 9 feet 4 inches over the guards; draft, 25 inches. Speed, a shade over 13 knots for an honest 15 mph.

Inevitably, I'll be asked to provide these plans to the original 3/4-inch-to-the-foot scale for shop or noodling use. From the original inked drawings I can supply working plans for less than two dollars per foot of overall length. Say, $39.95. She's a honey.

Strip Boat Construction

Throughout history the Ides of March have seemed to heighten dramatic intensity for all men. For one thing, this was the day that Caesar was stabbed in the Roman Senate, giving rise to Bill Shakespeare's immortal words, "Et tu, Brute!" For another, this same date, March 15, used to be D-day for American taxpayers until President Eisenhower let out a little slack in the noose. The latest dramatic impact for me was the discovery of the drawings you see here on Deadline Day for the closing of this book. Let me tell you . . . .

For years I had been collecting photographs of boats I'd designed—some good photos, some not—but all stuffed into a generous manila envelope for safekeeping. To round out the shipment of visual convincers to the publisher as this book's deadline drew close, I went to the place of safekeeping and the entire envelope was missing. A complete, tornadic upheaval of all records and papers failed to produce any photos save those sent earlier to International Marine. Deadlines are deadlines. I've exhausted all recourse. And here are the Ides of March! Stark drama, fitting the date. But there was one plus that developed in a complete inventory: I discovered 41 sheets of drawings and plans I'd forgotten about. Among them were the drawings for the boat shown here—*Scamper*—a fine strip-planked cedar rowboat adapted to carrying an outboard motor. A great many have been successfully built. The very thing to convey building lore and information *From My Old Boat Shop.*

The strip method of planking a boat has much to recommend it to the home builder of boats. It is very economical of lumber; 7d (seven penny) galvanized finishing nails are low in price, and the strips can be applied one or two an evening until, lo!, a boat grows into being. Materials can be purchased in almost any town that has a lumberyard; if they do not have cedar or oak, they can get it for you. It is to be presumed that the builder will have a decent circular saw, maybe a bandsaw, a jointer of four-inch size or up. A planer would be ideal, and almost the most indispensable item would be a shaper—the upright whirling spindle that holds knives cut to contour for the shaping of strips and frames.

I have shown the way professional shops are set up to turn out hull after hull in the many small shops that dot the lakes of Mid-America, where so much small boat development has taken place. They are fewer in number now, but I recall boat works at Shell Lake, Eau Claire,

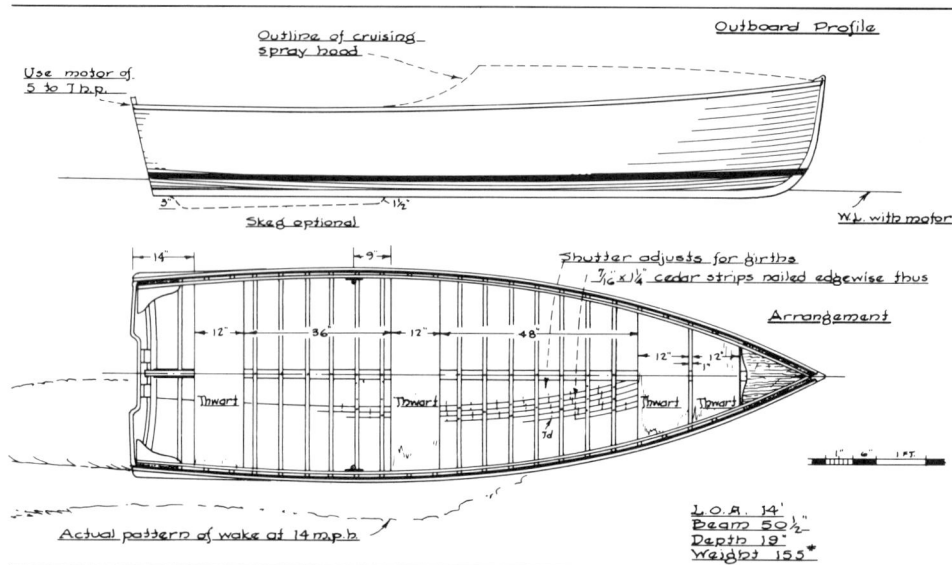

Alexandria, Little Falls, Detroit Lakes, Minnetonka, Duluth, Madison, Bayfield, Houghton, and numerous other watering places that used to build this type. Lately, my mail has shown much interest from men new to the game who want to know about strip planking.

The outboard profile and arrangement drawings show a boat 14 feet overall, 50-1/2-inch beam, 19 inches deep, weighing 155 pounds, and suitable for engines from 2-hp fisherman-type outboards to 5 to 7-hp whiz mills. Anything above that is too much.

The theory of the commercially produced small strip boat is based on a shutter plank, or stealer plank, rabbeted in upside down from the normal boatbuilding practice. This plank is shaped so that, after it is installed, all the strips will end up at the proper point at the sheer. The shutter is the only plank spiled. The rest go on one at a time until the sheer is reached. The method of setting up the molds is graphically shown in the perspective that also depicts the nailing sequences.

To get the shape of the shutter, set up the molds and run a strip around the molds at the sheer height. Measure down the molds to figure out the number of strips you plan to use. Mark the mold underside at this point. Then transfer the distances from each mold to the keel rabbet, and that is the set of points you use to stream a line for the shutter pattern. The so-called shutter then is the garboard. Strips are applied in the fashion shown in the nailing diagram and the sketch in the upper right-hand corner of the drawing. If you want to join strips, butt them end to end and drill a hole for a dowel. This is a stopwater.

The lines drawing showing the mold dimensions for this boat seems clear and descriptive enough. It is in the method of shaping the strips and the frames that a few words will steer you.

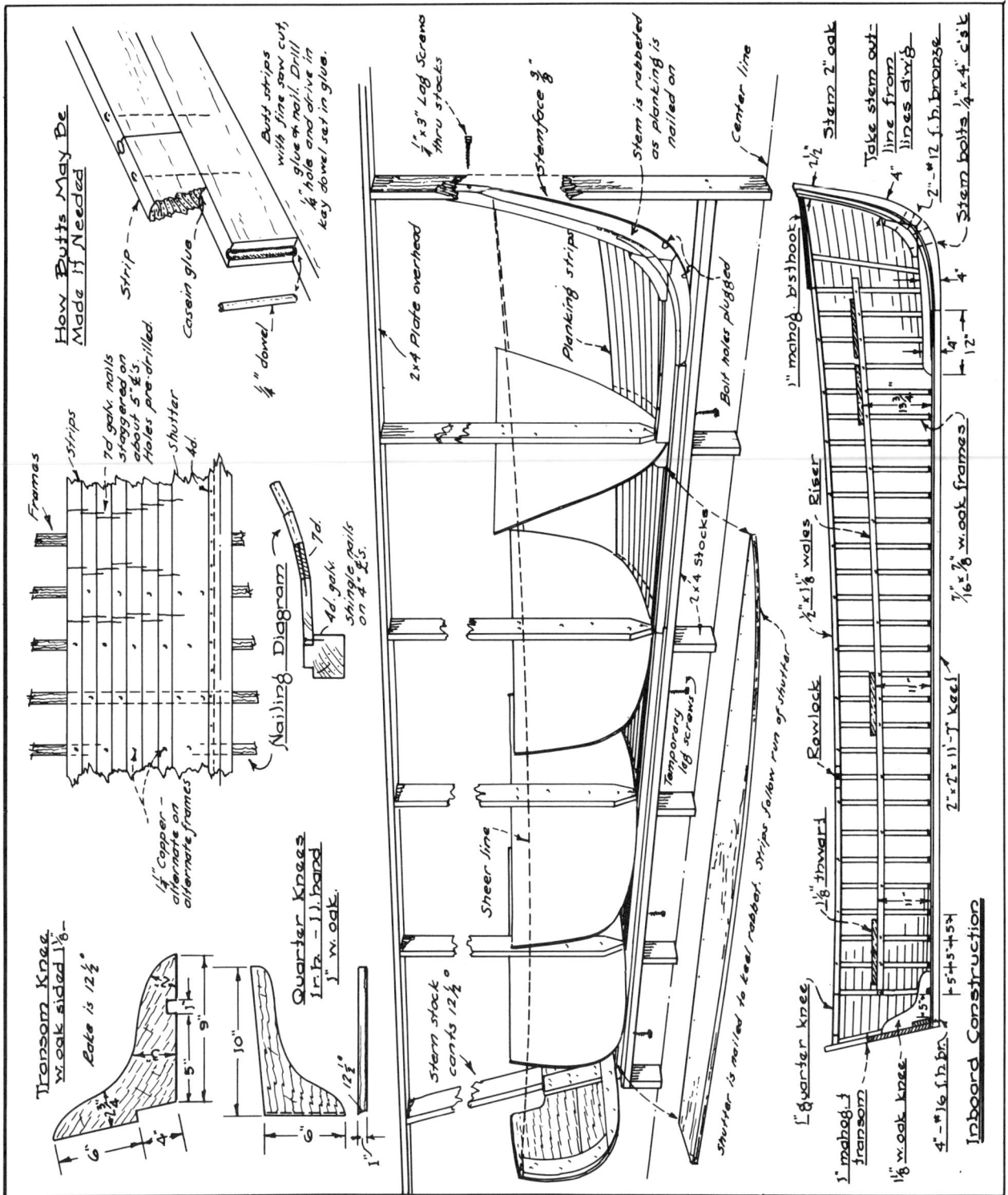

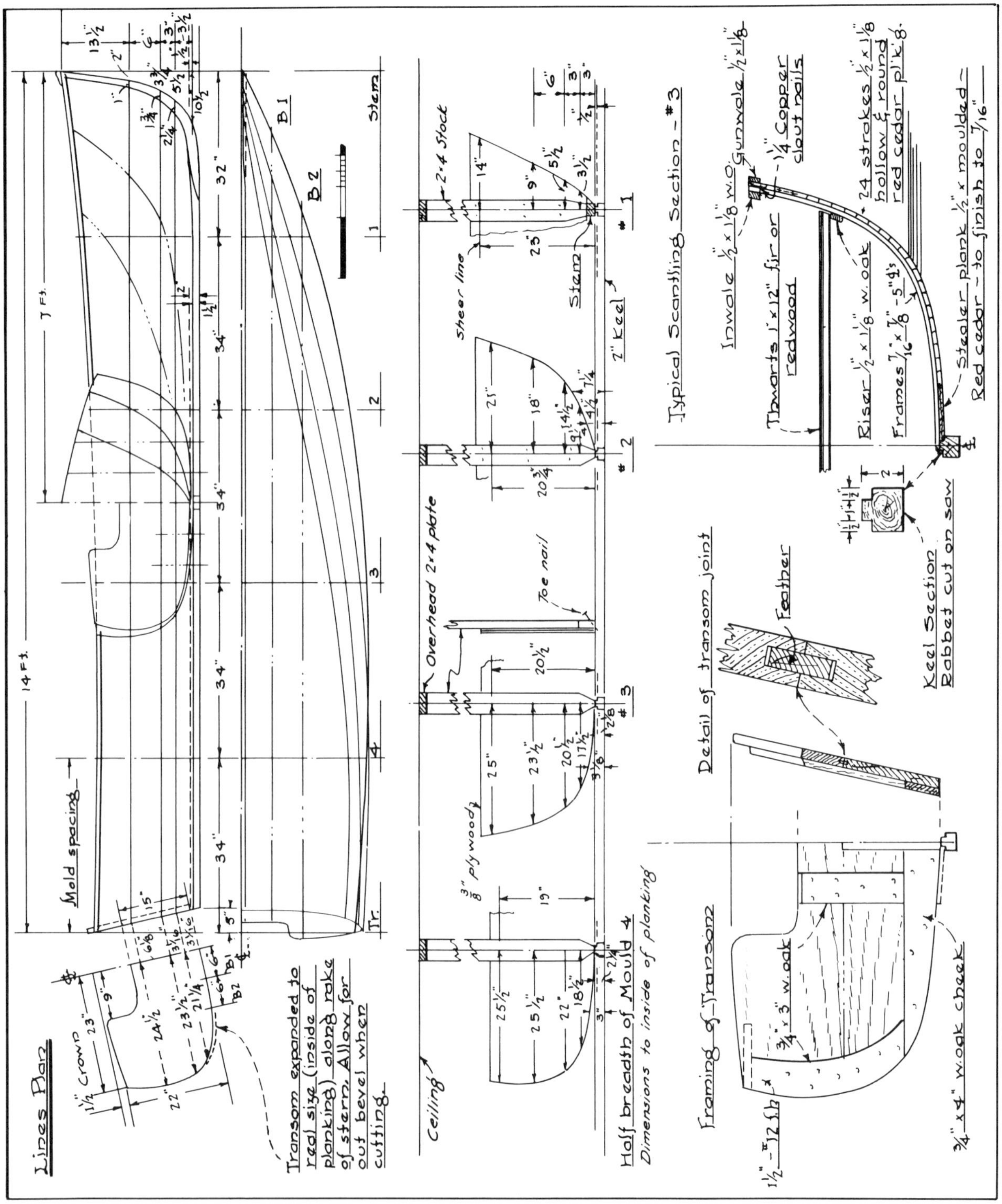
Lines Plan
14 Ft.
7 Ft.
Mold spacing
Stem
B 1
B 2
Tr.
Transom expanded to real size (inside of planking) along rake of stern. Allow for out bevel when cutting.
1½" crown
Ceiling
2×4 Stock
Sheer line
Stem
2" Keel
Overhead 2×4 plate
Toe nail
3/8" plywood
Half breadth of Mould 4
Dimensions to inside of planking
Typical Scantling Section - #3
Inwale ½" x 1⅛" w.o.
Gunwale ½" x 1⅛"
1¼" Copper clout nails
Thwarts 1" x 12" fir or redwood
Riser ½" x 1⅛" w. oak
Frames 7/16" x 7/8" - 5" c's
24 strokes ½" x 1⅛" hollow & round red cedar pl'k'g.
Stealer plank ½" x moulded - Red cedar - to finish to 7/16"
Keel Section
Rabbet cut on saw
Detail of transom joint
Feather
Framing of Transom
¾" x 3" w. oak
¾" x 4" w. oak cheek
1½" - 12 f.h.

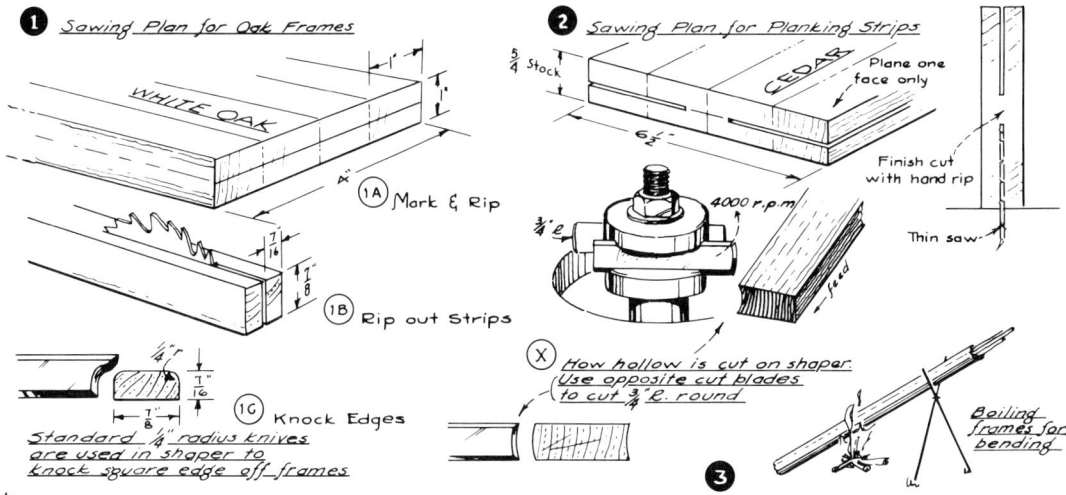

① *Sawing Plan for Oak Frames*
② *Sawing Plan for Planking Strips*

(1A) Mark & Rip
(1B) Rip out Strips
(1C) Knock Edges

Standard ¼" radius knives are used in shaper to knock square edge off frames

(X) *How hollow is cut on shaper. Use opposite cut blades to cut ¾ R. round*

Boiling frames for bending

③

Look at Figure 1. This shows a white oak board about two feet longer than the full girth of the boat. It can be planed to 1 inch by 4-3/8 inches with the grain as shown. Then this changes from the fix shown in (1a), to ripped-out strips as at (1b). This will provide 7/16 inch by 7/8 inch strips for the frames. Shown in (1c), grind some contour knives for rounding the edges that will be inboard after bending. I have found that the advice to use frames with flat grain is no good for small frames, because the grain, which bends easily in flat grain, will in small sizes have the grain running tangential to the curve of the bilge, and will split. Quarter-sawing is better, because a boiled frame (Figure 3) is very easy to bend and will not split; also, it holds fastenings better and is much less wasteful.

The planking, of rift-sawn white or Port Orford cedar, is prepared as outlined in Figure 2. Two sets of shaper knives will be required for rounding and hollowing the strips. My set cost $7 for my Delta shaper, which was worth its weight in gold when it came to centering the strips as they streamed along. Without the hollow-round—very slight, about 1/16 inch of arc—you will find that the strip nails will make the strips wobbly, which complicates finish planing. Don't use too much arc—the inboard edges show a seam that cannot be planed. Usually, as in most commercially built hulls like this, no gunks were allowed in the seams between planks. The upper rounded piece was rolled down under pressure from a wheel when it was ready to contour. Then when the seam became wet, the rolled bead swelled tight.

I do not favor gunks or glues on a strip boat, but some do. It has been my experience that wood has a natural gleet that will seal up every year for years, even if the hull dries to open the strips, whereas gunks and paint perish and become encrusted—and then the wood cannot close again.

317

I turned out three boats like this in my shop, and they were great little boats. Small boats like this must be tailored to the man who wears them—critical measurements are seat heights, oar haft lengths affecting the dip, and placement of seats from the rowlocks so that the oars and oarlocks may move freely. And—nope, sorry! I do not have prints of this available. What you see here is the whole story.

Simplex

In drawing *Simplex* I was moved by a wish and a frustration. The wish was to give outboard motorists who want to make weekend trips a boat that could be easily built and easily trailed, and that would be inexpensively adequate. The frustration was caused by having to realize that many people who would like a boat of this kind could not read the ordinary boat shop drawings. Something like a presentation as seen in the comics might be in order.

I combined the two approaches. *Simplex* is accompanied by standard lines, profile, accommodation plan, and inboard construction sections. These are all that a boatbuilder—a professional—would need. In fact, these are generally more than they will look at or follow. Next, to supply understanding of the names and relationships in the *Simplex* structure, I drew the exploded perspectives. These have great visual value in instruction and elevate the text of the usual how-to-build story up above the level of two parrots discussing the weather.

There is no doubt in my mind that that is what we are coming to: boat designs presented in comic book fashion, with balloons extending from mouths of men and women. Their content will be determined by TV commercial writers who believe the public cannot possibly grasp the fact that one nail is stronger than another. So when hubby tells his wife this startling fact, the dumb woman who watches over finances, raises the kids, gets the meals, and knows enough to come in out of the rain will sweetly respond, "One nail *stronger* than another?" Heaven help the art of design when comic book artists and TV writers discover the boating game!

The frustration mirrored in the above thumbnail essay, and which exasperation prompted the drawing of the perspectives, is based on solid statistics. To wit:

My mail shows that half the people who ask questions did not read what had been written. They read *at* a story, not *into* it. And they form half-baked notions from eyeballing drawings without studying them. Last May I ran out of letterheads, ordered 500 more, and they were gone in a few months. At half an hour per answer apiece, that is 250 hours, or 6-1/4 solid weeks of 40 hours each, answering—gratuitously— queries to which the answers had already been given. To avoid that repetitive moonshine, I do think some new method of plan presentation must be invented. So I have suggested comic book pictures, which by the year 2,000 may be required by John Q. Public.

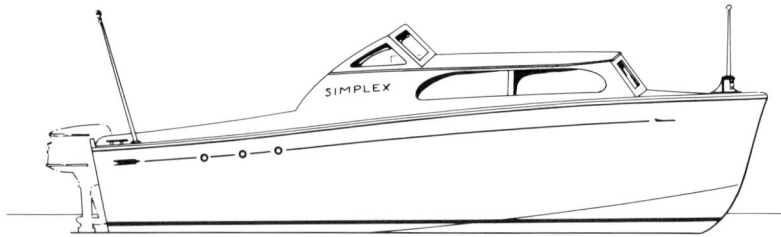

Outboard Profile

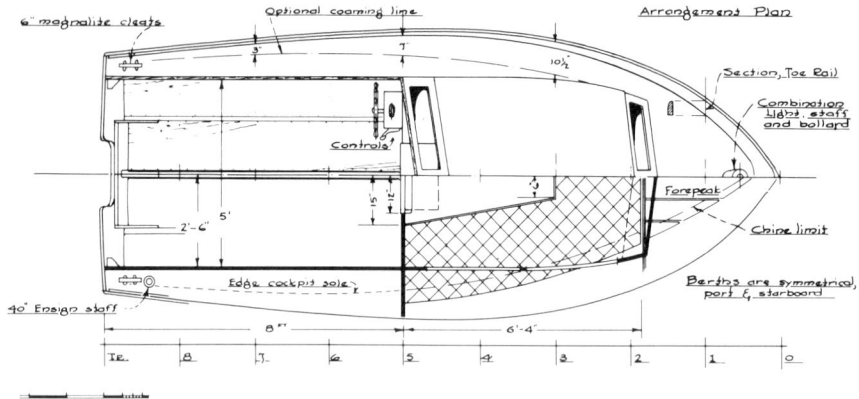

Arrangement Plan

As to the boat, *Simplex*: she is an easily built plywood outboard cruiser that has been built by many men who live near, but not on, watering holes, rivers, lakes, and oceansides that cannot be reached except by automobile and trailer. She is 18 feet long, has 7 feet 5 inches beam and a hull draft of 13-1/2 inches. She is capable of handling up to 50 hp in a standard outboard of any make and will deliver about 25 mph when light. She is completely trailerable and launchable from an ordinary two-wheeled boat trailer. Her planking is of plywood, marine grade, and her framing is generally of oak or fir.

One builder widened the transom box, beefed it up, and installed two 35-hp outboards, "for twin-engine reliability," as he put it.

One builder, James Parrot (pronounced Parow) did not build a low transom but used an outboard bracket to hold his 35-hp Evinrude. He stated he couldn't read a drawing, but by buying a board here and there, he built his *Buckaboard* version of *Simplex*. Not a bad choice!

I will mail the drawings, building specs, and info for $49.00, postpaid domestically in tubes, or airmailed abroad in a manila envelope as printed matter, which is customs-free most places except in some Spanish-speaking countries, where *Muestra Commercial* (duty-free) means, "Oh, boy, Zapato, looka thees new wallpaper!" as they open a line of chatter along with the envelope, trilling from the mellifluous Iberian or Castilian down into Gatling-gun r's that sound like a string of Chinese firecrackers. I report a once-witnessed event.

If these drawings look labored and complete, they were and are. It took me a month to do them. It took me years to learn how.

I commend *Simplex* to you as a fine boat.

320

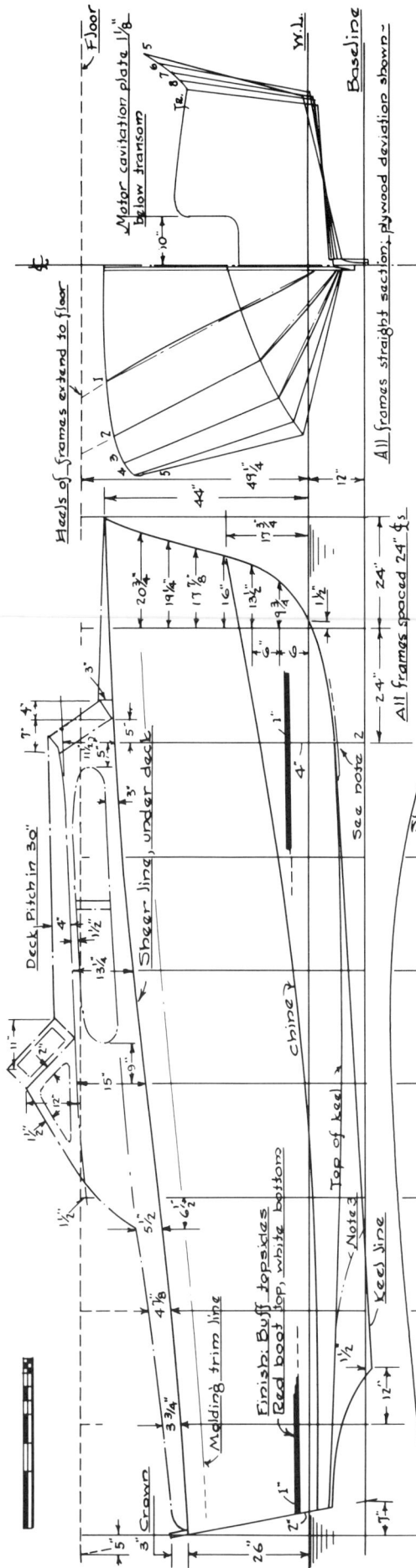

Lines, Body Plan & Offsets
of
SIMPLEX

Notes:

1. Motors vary. Cut transom height from motor as per cavitation note on body plan.
2. Stem nosing $\frac{3}{4}$" oak or $\frac{1}{2}$" oval bronze
3. Fair from full width at this point to $\frac{1}{2}$" aft.
4. Frames placed forward of Sta. 5 to bevel. Aft of #5 frames are abaft of frame line because of bevel.

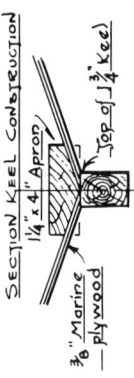

Heads of frames extend to floor

All frames straight section, plywood deviation shown

All frames spaced 24" ℄s

Motor cavitation plate 1/8" below transom

Floor

W.L.

Baseline

SECTION KEEL CONSTRUCTION

$\frac{1}{4}$ x 4" Apron
Top of 1 $\frac{3}{4}$" keel
$\frac{3}{8}$" Marine plywood

Deck Pitch 1 in 30"

Sheer line, under deck

Chine

See note 2

Top of keel

Keel line

Crown

Molding trim line

Finish: Buff topsides
Red boot top, white bottom

Extended sweep of batten so sheer will fair 0 to 2

Sheer

Chine

Half siding keel apron 2"

Half siding keel 1/8"

Offsets in Ft. Ins. & 8ths

Stations	0	1	2	3	4	5	6	T	8	Te.
Heights above Baseline										
Keel						St line				
Top of keel	2.5.6	2.3.1	1.10.5	1.6.6	1.3.3	1.1.0	0.11.2	0.10.4	0.10.3	0.10.2
Chine	4.6.4	4.6.1	4.4.3	4.2.1	3.11.3	3.8.6	3.6.0	3.4.0	3.2.0	
Sheer		0.1.0	0.0.7	0.0.7	0.0.7	0.0.7	0.0.7	-0.0.6		0.7.7
Half Breadths										
Keel	0.1.0	0.1.0	0.0.7	0.0.7	0.0.7	0.0.7	0.0.7	Tapers to ½	bottom	
Chine	0.9.4	1.8.2	2.4.2	2.9.1	3.0.0	3.1.0	3.0.3-	2.11.0	2.10.0	
Sheer	2.0.6	3.0.2	3.6.0	3.8.5	3.8.3	3.7.0	3.5.0	3.3.0	3.0.4	

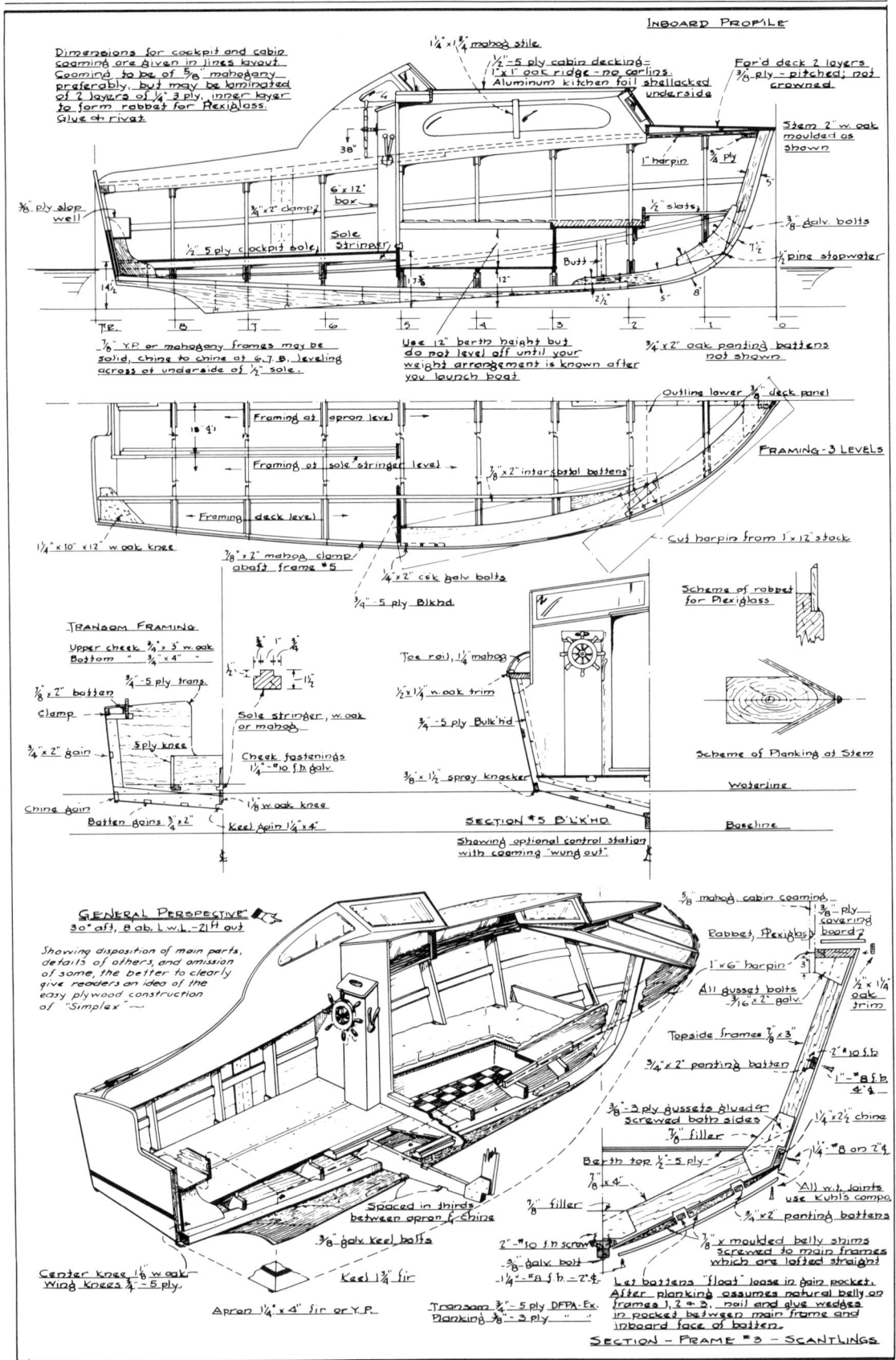

Trumpet

The boat shown here, *Trumpet*, was long in the cooking, or gestational period, and highly successful in execution. She is the keystone piece in my ganglia of narrative design hooks, which I dangle overside in our voyage through this book, trolling in the usual voyaging pastime of fishing for nourishment for the fun of it.

What I wanted (on my way to the drawing board) was a soft-riding, full-hydroplaning runabout that wouldn't change trim from zero speed to full-bore work. The design problem had puzzled all early designers of high-speed motorboats—men like George and Ab Crouch, William H. Hand, Jr., John Hacker, and others who were feeling their way into high-speed, high-powered boats. The early boats of these designers all stood on their tails, running with their bows to the sky and their sterns depressed and nearly awash. At Ramaley Boat Company, where I apprenticed, we built boats from plans of all these early designers. They all behaved alike: the bows planed, the sterns did not. But step hydroplanes, with one step in their hulls, would jump out of water, level down, and go like blazes.

The first mile-a-minute motorboat was *Miss Minneapolis*, designed and built by Chris Smith of Algonac, Michigan, in 1916. She ran on home waters near Ramaley's plant, and from that day onward there was sparked a 10-year fervor for speed over the water. As an apprentice squatting on the conical sawdust teepees outside the boat shop, I listened with flapping ears for some inkling of engineering rationale that would unravel the mysteries of planing boat behavior that came from the journeyman boatbuilders who had worked at Herreshoff, at Hacker's early shop in Albany, and for the Smith Boat Works near Detroit.

All of this chin music was pure chatter, based on hunch, and did not come from engineers. It became an obsession with me to learn why narrow monoplane hulls would not flatten down and run level. My initial designing experience would be with this type of boat; that was where boat demand was at that time by a factor of 10 to one over sail, cruisers, or any other type of hull. One goes with the money. The buying power of the time dictated that I concentrate on high-speed planing boats.

I designed, lofted, and participated in the building of about 20 runabouts aimed at the cure of planing angle, of improving the breed.

Then a dramatic fluke loomed on the engineering horizon from the

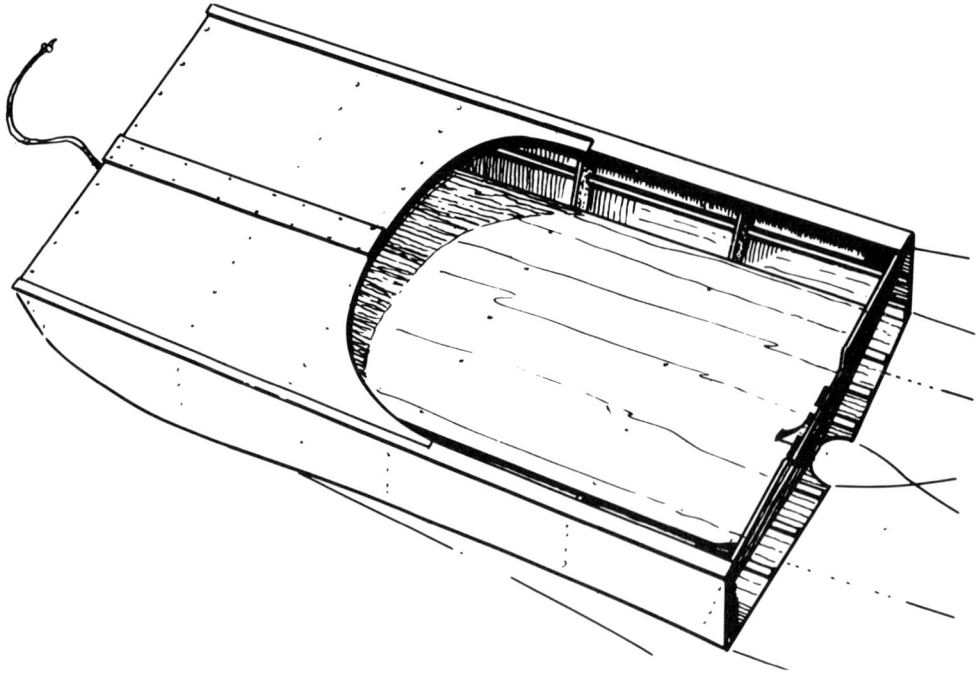

Nize Baby, Bruno Beckhard's sled-type hydroplane with decalage chines. The decalage principle is found today in Boston Whalers and other high-speed planing boats, such as *Trumpet*.

unlikely source of the outboard motor. An old and long-respected builder of cast-iron launch engines, the Lockwood-Ash Company, over in Jackson, Michigan, produced a 4-hp lightweight outboard motor that had enough zap to plane a tiny eight-foot monoplane! Bruno Beckhard, an experimenter on Long Island, had startled a Mississippi Valley hydroplane regatta by running right alongside some of the Valley Champions boasting from six to 40 times the power. Bruno's boat was a four-foot-by-eight-foot mortar tub of 3/8-inch mahogany he called *Nize Baby*, driven by a 4-hp Lockwood Ash outboard motor. I doubt that Bruno's boat cost $150, all up, including the motor.

Suddenly the secret was out: mahogany runabouts had followed the old narrow-hulled, round-bilge configuration. More beam was the answer; also, fewer pounds per horsepower. *Nize Baby* also had an interesting innovation: she was a sled type of hull, the chines of which, forward, were at a lower angle of attack than the chine as it streamed aft. Suddenly, every man who could nail up a box became a speed nut. The Lockwood-Ash power breakthrough let into the boat game men who could not afford the $2,500 mahogany runabouts. And, because I had puzzled over the planing problem from sawdust days, I saw at once that enough beam was the same problem for boats as aspect ratio had been for airplane designers. Because men like Starling Burgess and John Hanna had been airplane designers before switching to naval architec-

324

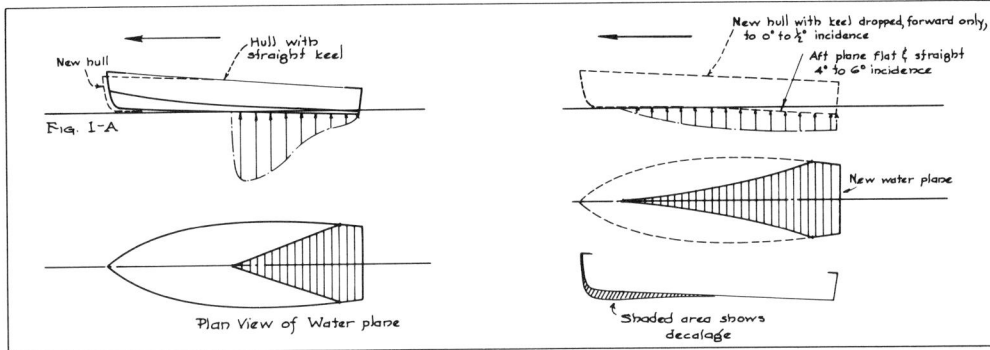

Fig. 1-A

A comparison between a regular planing-type hull (*left*) and one based on the decalage idea (*right*). Because of its deepened forefoot, the latter gains lifting surface forward, softening the way for the planing surface aft.

ture, I had read some of their writings. Burgess was involved with flying boats with the Burgess-Dunne Airplane Company, and Hanna had worked for Glenn Curtiss. I felt at home with the early evolving airplane design problems, romancing the design of a small flying boat. Thus, when *Nize Baby* came along, I started designing and building runabouts for Ramaley that ran high and flat, planed fully, went like blazes, won regattas, but would still jar your teeth out. The secret was proper beam, putting power far aft, limiting deadrise to five degrees. *Nize Baby* was the key that unlocked the way to diagram the forces, turning all previous thought upside down.

Still, the soft ride eluded me. A chap over in Grand Rapids, Michigan, named Gordon B. Hooton, who built light hulls, claimed he had got a soft ride by going up to 10 degrees in deadrise from the then-standard five degrees promulgated by William Hand in his early runabouts. Hooton built some 10-degree boats, but the power wasted by steep deadrise always left his boats in the slower categories. He wrote many pseudo-scientific articles in the old *Power Boating* magazine, now long defunct. Pseudo stuff is baloney, yet if Hooton had had motors of high enough power, he could have found the soft ride.

One day it all came together for me. Why not meld a hull running at normal attitude into the profile of a boat with level running forefoot? The hull aimed at the usual four-to-six-degree running angle would be hidden in the profile where the keel, like Bruno Beckhard's chines, monitored the running angle with just enough lift and deep vee forward to prevent rooting, and to soften the way for the planing surface.

I built a model, and the idea worked perfectly. Then came some sketches. What I had come up with was about parallel to the thinking, unbeknownst to me, of Ray Hunt, who went to Fenwick C. Williams, an old Alden hand, and got Williams to draw up a deep-vee hull with

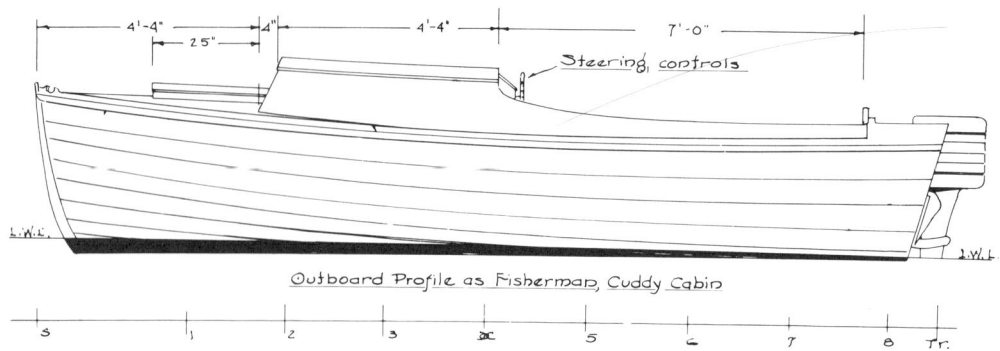

Outboard Profile as Fisherman, Cuddy Cabin

22-1/2 degrees of deadrise, a ski nose, and lots of power. The performance of the Williams-Hunt hull and mine were about the same, except that the *Trumpet* idea would use less power, as I later found. Who would build my *Trumpet*? I sought a customer, and ran into some of the oddball dealsmiths you sometimes find in the boat business who want to work both ends against the middle.

One of these gents was a fellow who shifted gears on a big cigar and who always was talking about a big stock deal he was about to swing. I'd met him before, calling him Hot Air Lane. Mr. Lane, it turned out, was a graduate in bankruptcy from a scheme to set up a company for the sharpening of pre-1910 lightning rods, and was now touting opportunities in drilling offshore for oil in Mexican waters, a concession he had won in a game of five-card-draw from the mayor of Nogales. It was for drilling in the middle of the Rio Grande—offshore, of course. Things get pretty tough when you have to listen to stuff like that, and

Trumpet as built by George Stevens for John W. Rollinson of St. Simons Island, Georgia.

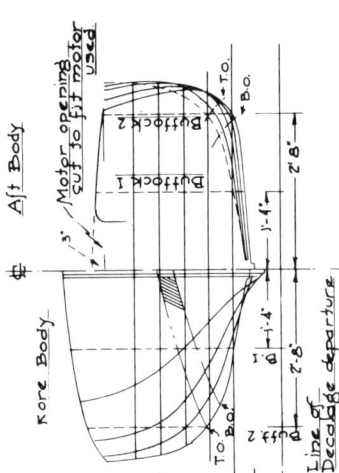

LINES DRAWN TO OUTSIDE OF
SMOOTH-SKIN. Subtract one thickness
of planking ($\frac{5}{8}$) for clinker planked frame
Body plan laid out for 12 strakes per side
Transom to be expanded along face of rake

OFFSETS IN FEET, INCHES & 8ths

HEIGHTS above Baseline

	Stem	1	2	3	4	5	6	7	8	Tr.
Sheer	3.10.3	3.6.0	3.3.6	3.2.0	3.0.6	3.0.0	2.11.6	3.0.0	3.0.6	3.1.2
Buttock 2			2.3.6	1.8.1	1.3.6	1.1.4	0.11.5	0.10.6		0.10.0
Buttock 1			1.8.5	1.1.5	0.8.7	0.9.6	0.5.2	0.8.7	0.8.3	0.7.3.4
Rabbet			0.5.0	0.6.0	0.7.0	0.7.4	0.6.5	0.7.2	0.6.3	
Bottom K'l			0.4.4	0.5.4	0.6.4	0.7.0	0.6.1	0.6.6	0.5.7	
T.Outlap	2.1.7	1.9.3	1.7.0	1.5.2	1.3.5	1.2.5	1.1.5	1.0.7		1.0.4
B.Outlap	1.10.2	1.6.5	1.4.0	1.2.2	1.0.5	0.11.5	0.10.5	0.11.1		0.3.4

Note: Take mold shape for #8 from lofted lines

NALF BREADTHS from ℄

	Stem	1	2	3	4	5	6	7	8	Tr.
W.L.1	0.1.1	0.5.2	0.9.1	1.1.0	1.4.7	1.8.6	2.0.4	2.3.7		2.7.7
5" Ab	0.1.1	0.10.3	1.6.5	2.1.4	2.7.2	2.10.1	3.0.5	3.1.2		3.10
10" Ab	0.1.1	1.3.4	2.2.2	2.8.0	3.0.0	3.1.5	3.2.3	3.2.2		3.11
15" Ab	0.1.1	1.7.6	2.6.3	2.11.4	3.2.3	3.3.1	3.3.1	3.2.5		2.11.3
20" Ab	0.1.1	1.11.2	2.8.5	3.1.1	3.2.3	3.2.6	3.2.4	3.1.1		2.11.4
Sheer	0.1.1	2.5.2	3.0.4	3.1.7	3.2.6	3.2.4	3.1.4	3.0.1		2.5.4
Keel	0.1.1	0.1.3	0.1.3	0.1.3	0.1.3	0.1.3	0.1.3	0.1.3	0.1.3	
Top O'lap	0.1.1	1.5.0	2.0.7	2.5.1	2.6.7	To sweep				2.10
B. Outlap	0.1.1	2.0.1	1.8.4	2.0.3	2.3.3	2.4.5				2.7

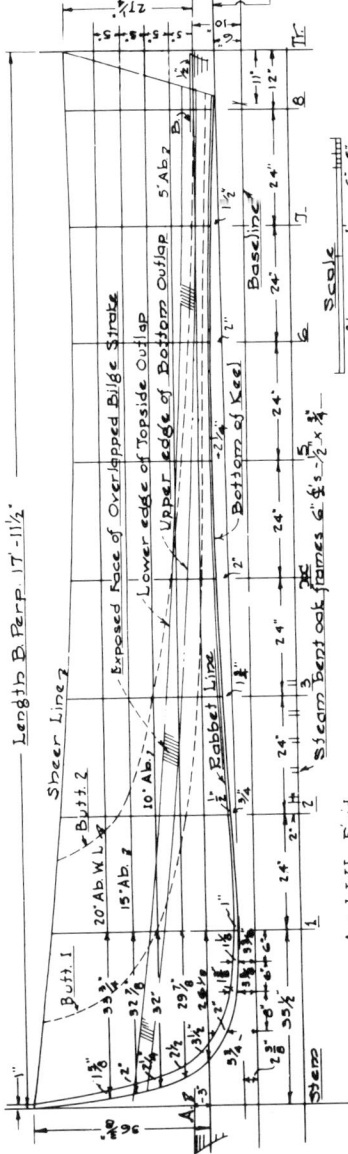

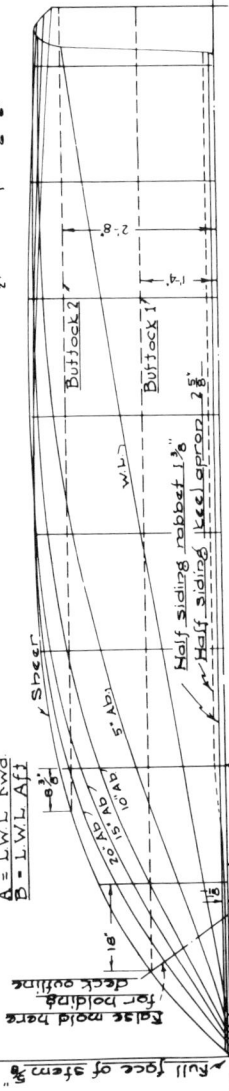

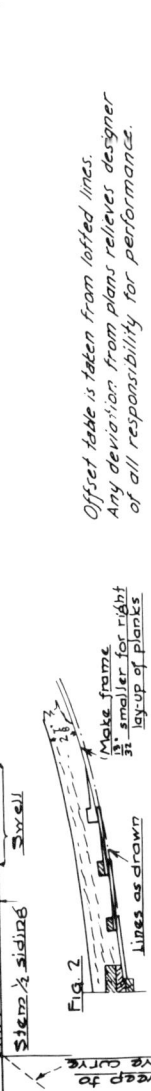

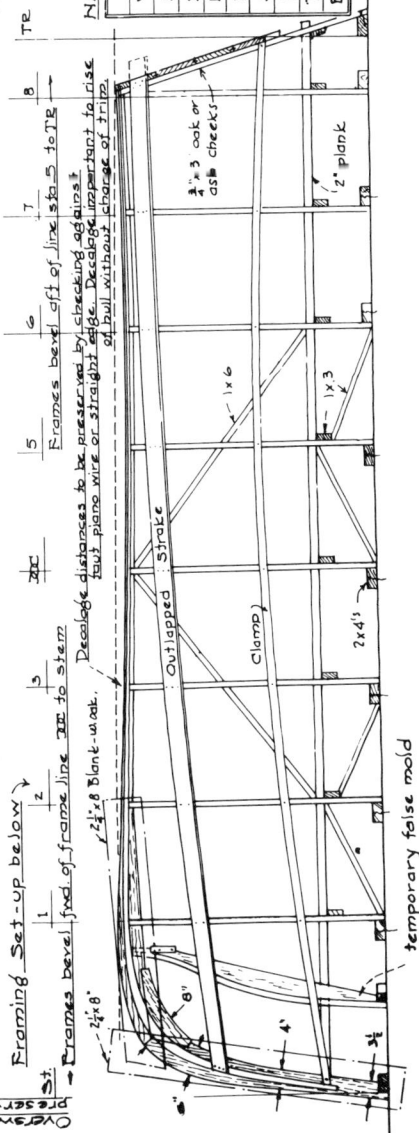

Offset table is taken from lofted lines.
Any deviation from plans relieves designer
of all responsibility for performance.

Length B. Perp 17'-11½"

Sheer Line 2

Exposed Face of Overlapped Bilge Strake

Lower edge of Topside Outlap

Upper edge of Bottom Outlap

Rabbet Line

Steam bent oak frames 6"s–½"×¾"

Baseline

Scale

A = LWL Fwd
B = L.W.L. Aft

Sheer

Bottom of Keel

Half siding of Keel

Half siding rabbet 1⅜"

Buttock 2

Buttock 1

W.L.

Swell

False mold here
for holding
deck outline

Lines as drawn

Make frame
1⅜" smaller for right
3½" lay-up of planks

Fig. 2

Stem ½ siding

Full face of stem ⅞"

Oversweep to
preserve curve

Framing Set-up below

Frames bevel fwd of frame line III to stem

Frames bevel aft of line sta 5 to TR

Decalage distances to be preserved by checking against a raise
taut piano wire or straight edge. Decalage unimportant to raise
of hull without change of trim.

⅞"×3 oak or
ash cheeks

1'' plank

Outlapped Strake

Clamp

1×6

1×3

2×4's

temporary false mold

Aft Body

Fore Body

Motor opening
cut to fit motor
used

Line of
Decalage departure

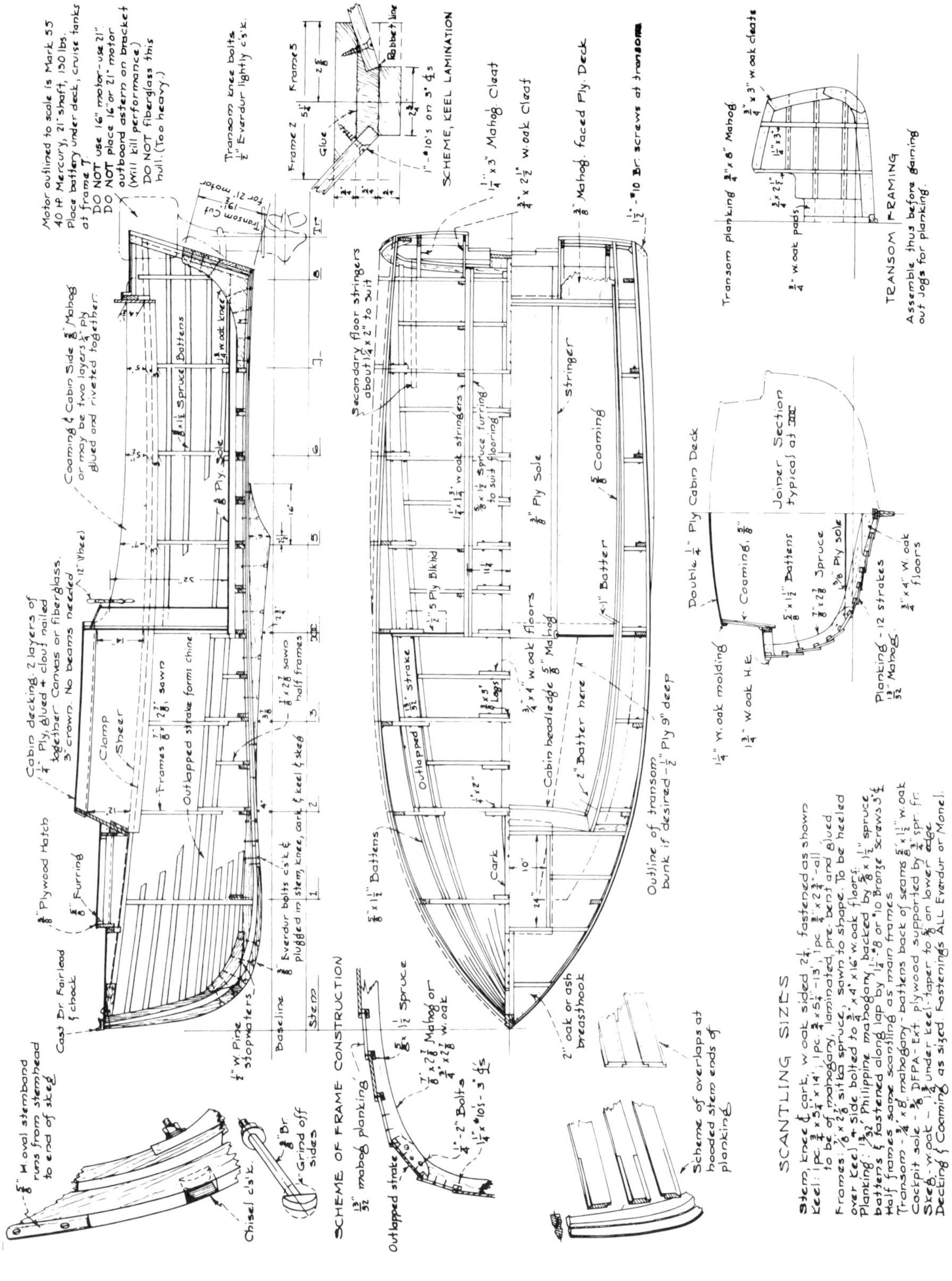
5/8" H. oval stemband runs from stemhead to end of skeg
Chisel c's'k.
5/8" Br.
Grind off sides
Cast Br. Fairlead & chock
3/8" Plywood Hatch
5/8" Furring
Cabin decking: 2 layers of 1/4" Ply, glued + clout nailed together. Canvas or fiberglass. 3" crown. No beams needed
12" Wheel
Clamp
Sheer
Frames 7/8" x 2 7/8", sawn
Outlapped strake forms chine
1/2" W. Pine stopwaters
Baseline
3/8" Everdur bolts c's'k & plugged in stem, knee, cark & keel & skeg
7/8" x 2 7/8" sawn half frames
Stem
Coaming & Cabin Side 5/8" Mahog or may be two layers 1/4" ply glued and riveted together
5/8" x 1 1/2" Spruce Battens
3/8" Ply. Sole
1 1/4" w. oak knee
Motor outlined to scale is Mark 55 40 HP Mercury, 21" shaft, 130 lbs. Place battery under deck, cruise tanks at frame 7.
DO NOT use 16" motor - use 21"
DO NOT place 16" or 21" motor outboard astern on bracket (Will kill performance)
DO NOT fiberglass this hull. (Too heavy.)
Transom Cut 19 1/2" for 21" motor
Transom knee bolts 1/2" Everdur lightly c's'k.
Frame 2
Frame 5
Glue
Rabbet line
1" - #10's on 3" c/s
SCHEME, KEEL LAMINATION
SCHEME OF FRAME CONSTRUCTION
13/32" mahog planking
Outlapped strake
5/8" x 1 1/2" Spruce
7/8" x 2 7/8" Mahog or 3/4" x 2 7/8" w. oak
1/4" - 2" Bolts
1 1/4" x #10's - 3" c/s
5/8" x 1 1/4" Battens
Outlapped 13/32" strake
1/2" 5 Ply Blk'hd
1 1/4" x 1 3/4" w. oak stringers
5/8" x 1 1/2" Spruce furring to suit flooring
Secondary floor stringers about 1 1/4" x 2" to suit
1 1/4" x 3" Mahog. Cleat
3/4" x 2 1/2" w. oak Cleat
Cark
1 1/4" x 2"
3/4" x 3" Logs
3/4" x 4" w. oak floors
3/8" Ply Sole
Cabin headledge 5/8" Mahog
Stringer
3/8" Mahog. faced Ply. Deck
2" oak or ash breasthook
2" Batter here
1" Batter
5/8" Coaming
1 1/2" - #10 Br. screws at transom
Outline of transom bunk if desired - 1/2" Ply 9" deep
Scheme of overlaps at hooded stem ends of planking
Double 1/4" Ply Cabin Deck
1 1/4" W. oak molding
1 3/4" W. oak H.E.
Coaming, 5/8"
5/8" x 1 1/2" Battens
7/8" x 2 7/8" Spruce
3/8" Ply sole
Joiner Section typical at III
Planking - 12 strakes 13/32" Mahog.
3/4" x 4" W. oak floors
Transom planking 3/4" x 8" Mahog.
3/4" x 3" w. oak cleats
3/4" x 2 1/2"
1 1/4" x 3"
3/4" w. oak pads
TRANSOM FRAMING
Assemble thus before gaining out Jogs for planking.
SCANTLING SIZES
Stem, knee & cark, w. oak sided 2 1/4, fastened as shown
Keel: 1 pc. 3/4 x 5 1/4" x 14'; 1 pc. 3/4 x 5 1/4" - 13'; 1 pc. 3/4" x 2 3/4" - all to be of mahogany, laminated, pre-bent and glued.
Frames: 7/8" x 2 7/8" sitka spruce, sawn to shape. To be heeled over keel + side bolted to 3/4" x 4" x 16" w. oak floors.
Planking: 13/32" Philippine mahogany, backed by 5/8" x 1 1/2" spruce battens & fastened along lap by 1 1/4" #8 or #10 Bronze screws 3" c/s
Half frames same scantling as main frames
Transom - 3/4" x 8" mahogany - battens back of seams 5/8" x 1 1/2" w. oak
Cockpit sole - 3/8" DFPA - Ext. plywood supported by 3/4" spr. fr.
Skeg - w. oak - 1 3/4" under keel - taper to 5/8" on lower edge
Decking & Coaming as sized. Fastenings ALL Everdur or Monel.

just at that time I got a letter from John W. Rollinson, Jr., of St. Simon's Island, Georgia, asking for a high-speed, clinker-built, round-bilged, soft-riding outboard boat he could use to bang out to sea for a day's fishing, and then scoot home in at the end of a day. I had found a customer for *Trumpet*!

Mr. Rollinson, a retired executive of the telephone company, had used a somewhat conventional small inboard runabout for the service, but she was wet, and pounded. In any event, Mr. Rollinson liked *Trumpet*, had her built, and thereby proved that my idea of bent keel—*decalage*, per French aviation terminology—would work beautifully. His boat, powered with a 40-hp Mark 55 Mercury motor, is pictured in this chapter. The photo shows a slick hull of excellent seakeeping qualities that has proved a delight to the eye, a treasure to own, and is envied by all who have seen her. Here are the vital statistics of this keystone piece: length overall, 17 feet 11-1/2 inches; beam, 6 feet 5-1/2 inches; hull draft, 10 inches; displacement, 1635 pounds with motor; Wt/Hp ratio, 40.8 pounds/hp; B/L ratio, 36 percent. Her transom clears at 10 mph. The hull rises bodily throughout the entire speed range. Note that the bottom up to the turn of bilge is *outlapped* clinker. This is the same as providing peeler strips to out-flying water, and making it thus self-reefing. This was no great invention of mine; George Crouch was using the idea 20 years earlier, providing longitudinal steps, or ventilators, along the bottom long before either Hunt or I thought of it. I had used it for 10 years prior to *Trumpet* and knew it worked to free a bottom of atmospheric pressure.

Trumpet steers like a dream, handles well in a tide inlet, and, today, would make a grand hull in which to install an inboard/outboard combination plant. A number were built, here and there, by other men than John W. Rollinson, and an ancillary reprint of *Trumpet*'s original exposure is furnished with the full 3/4-inch scale Ozalid black-line prints that I can supply for the minuscule sum of $35.

Some wrap-up reflections: the 40.8 pounds-per-horsepower figure is a loading at about the top of weight per horsepower that can provide full planing. The old hydroplane rule discovered during the flourishing Mississippi Valley One-Design days of the M.V.P.B.A. races dictated that 40 pounds per horsepower was about top loading, and that most of the hydroplanes were under 36 pounds per horsepower for full planing. Also, too much beam is much worse than not enough. The 36 percent figure applies to *waterplane*. Anything over that will cost power through the nose. Between 30 and 33 percent became the range I used for aspect ratio of the planing surface. Young designers today haven't learned that beam, especially in displacement or semiplaning boats, is instant poison to speed if it goes much over 33 or 34 percent, in *any* hull.

You may have noticed a variation in the lettering on my plans. Some are in classical lower-case engineering lettering, other plates are done in a vertical style that seems to me now to fall between some of Fred Goeller's old chirography and that of Charles D. Mower's (pronounced Moore) or Ab Crouch's style. Sometimes an unsteady hand called for the flowery stuff, because it has an inbuilt shakiness that disguises occasional nervousness. Hmmm!

And whence the name *Trumpet*? British practice bestows the feminine gender on boats. German practice says they're masculine, hence the "-ia" or Latin vowel ending for many British ships and ocean greyhounds of yore, and the *Kronprinz* or *Bismarck* style for Germanic vessels. I called this boat *Trumpet* in the neuter gender, waiting to see what her sex really was, and motivated by some of the few bars of music that Alfred Fleming of Elco used to grace his lovely work when he was proud of it. Tapped out on the piano, I learned they were musical footnotes—bars such as "How dry I am," or "Sweet Adeline." On one botched lettering job, the notes produced a Woody Woodpecker cackle, "Can't get me!" Now, *Trumpet* implies "Ta-na-a!" A fitting name, and better than that of my undesigned Blue Ribband ocean greyhound, which I have mentally named *Fat Chance*.

Luxury in Aluminum

Over the past 10 years it has been my good fortune to have designed six large luxury yachts in aluminum. The first was Benson Ford's *Onika*, which Tony Lefky of the Burger design staff had typed as to profile and arrangement when Burger Boat Company's designer Ray Franz died suddenly. I was asked to furnish the lines, hull structure, and the marine engineering aspects of power plant, tankage, and the like. Mr. Ford kindly sent me a set of photos via Captain Joe Scudder. *Onika* was a success all around.

Shown here is *Patrician*, designed for Jon Bowman, of Seattle, Washington. She is a 63-footer embodying Mr. Bowman's own long-thought-out ideas. Note the seagoing piano in the main saloon. Pat Bowman, Jon's lovely and talented wife, is a pianist of concert *virtuosa* grade, so musically skilled that when Pat Bowman plays, the room becomes quiet, eyes close, and the euphoria of music soaring forth from her fingers transports one's soul to Aeolian heavens.

A fluke of preservation in black line enables publication of the entire set of lines, arrangement, and framing plan for this boat. Jon Bowman has kindly assented to let me run them.

The third boat of this class was *All-Ten-B*, 57 feet long, built in aluminum by Palmer Johnson, Inc., of Sturgeon Bay, Wisconsin, for Mr. and Mrs. Allan L. McKay, of Fond du Lac. After a number of years on Lake Michigan, Mr. McKay sold *All-Ten-B* to Charles Guy, of Tampa, Florida, and she made it on her own bottom to the Yacht Club basin there via the Mississippi on one filling. The drawings for the *All-Ten-B* were in heavily detailed pencil, too faint to reproduce.

A much larger boat, *Misty*, was designed and built for R. C. Borwell, Sr., of Chicago. She was 85 feet overall and became quite a complicated boat, with freshwater maker, two radars, a telephone system, and Vosper stabilizers. A photo is shown, but the drawings I made of everything from profile, arrangement, lines, framing, and sections—some 80 drawings in all—are also in pencil, unreproducible. A generous patron, Mr. Borwell has cruised *Misty* through all the Great Lakes, down the St. Lawrence, and throughout the Caribbean.

A much smaller version of the cruising long-distance boat was *Simbie*, shown elsewhere in this book.

A 94-foot palace awaits business arrangements by the owner before being tendered for bids. One version of this hull may see government service as a fast ferry for Lake Superior daily round trips of 150 miles. At this writing it is too early to tell whether she will be built.

Onika (*top*) and *Misty* (*bottom*) underway.

But the plans of *Patrician* shown here will show the young designer the kind of naval architecture and marine engineering that will be expected: the naval architecture of hull lines, hydrostatics, stability calculations for metacentric height, and the volumetrics of weight calculation. The marine engineering aspects of powering, propulsion, tankage, cruising range and speeds, as well as the plumbing, piping, and electrics, all fall within the design work of the marine engineer.

Two classes of boats are difficult to design: large metal power yachts such as *Patrician*, where weights must be *on the money* and where the right size for everything must cater to human comfort, and, next, the very small one- or two-man rowing or powerboat. In-between lengths seem to be easier. Few things are as tricky as a small boat that you *wear*, such as a rowboat, or shell, or wee sailboat. The intermediate boats, and sailboats in particular, are much easier. Ballast is added as needed, and the weights can usually be pegged by coefficients. In sail, this usually is expected. Not so with power. Your credibility as an engineer rides with the launching celebration. If she is on her marks, your boat says you are good. You had better be, with a fee of ten to thirty thousand dollars riding on the outcome!

All-Ten-B can cruise at 10 knots.

As I dim the lights on this chapter, memory supplies the fact that I have another design, a 72-footer, all ready to build for Palmer Johnson when they tell me what they want in the way of deckhouse accommodations. The memory bank also says that flotational models were made for these boats, so you can see that yer Old Uncle Westy "practices as preaches." And, oh, yes: the volumetric weight calculations for a yacht like *Onika*, line by line on yellow legal paper, when pasted together, came to 18 feet in length. These boats are not exactly "Look Ma, no hands!" propositions.

JOINER PROFILE - PORT SIDE

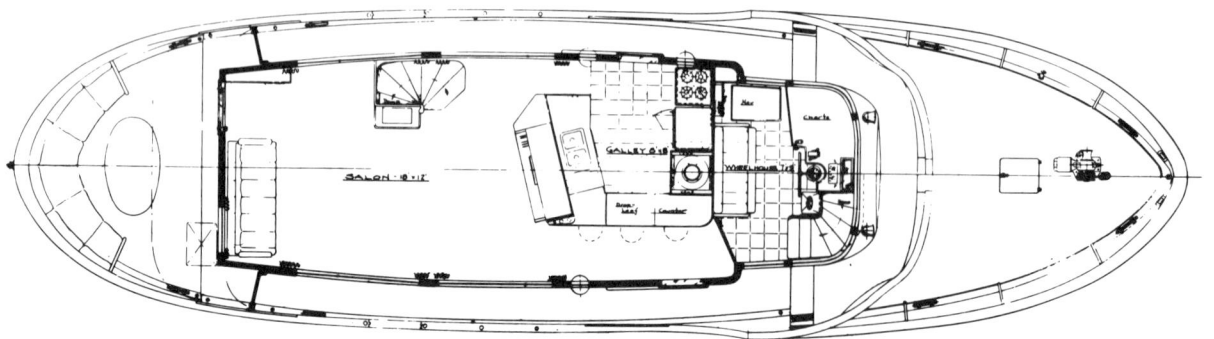

MAIN DECK ARRANGEMENT

334

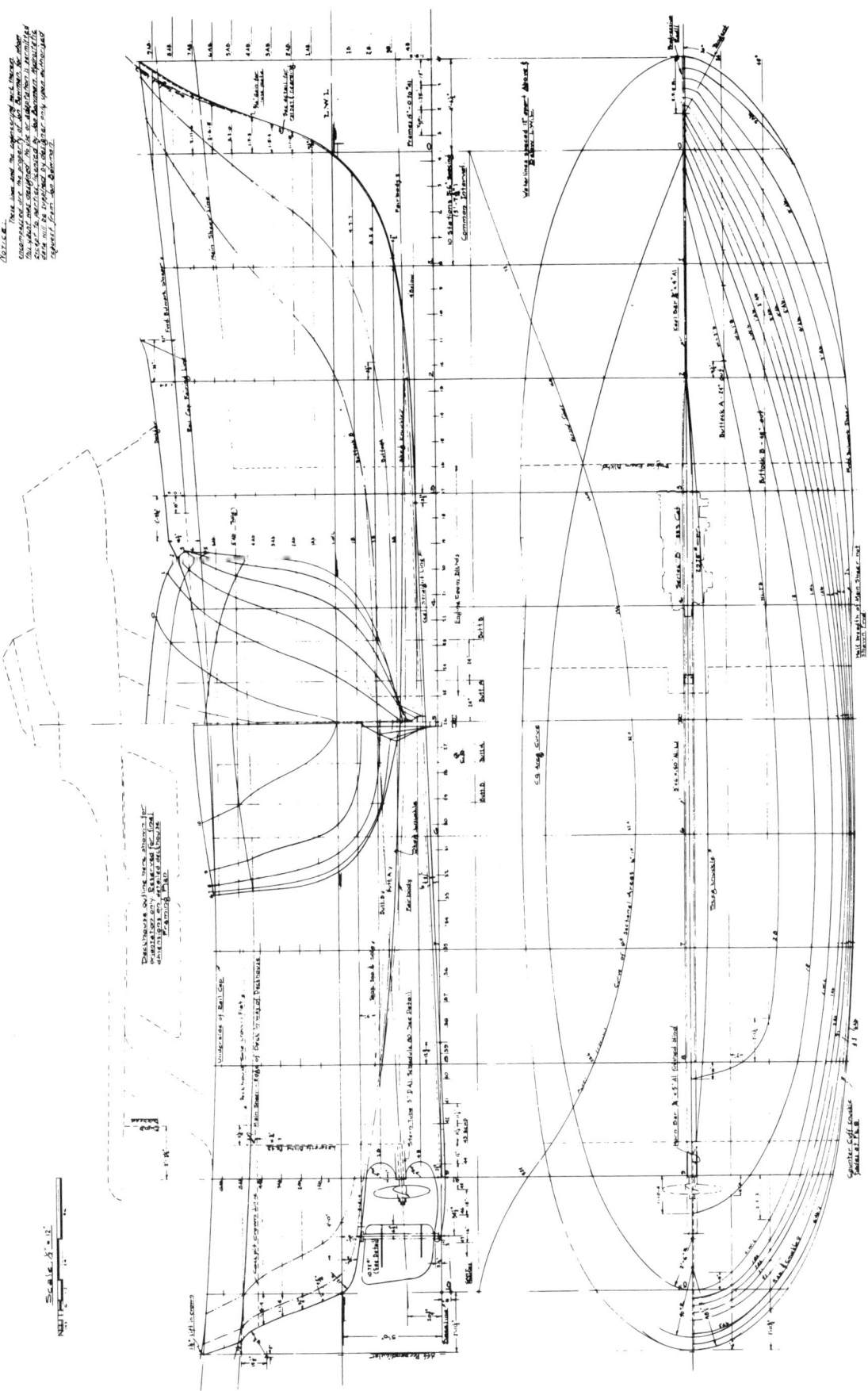

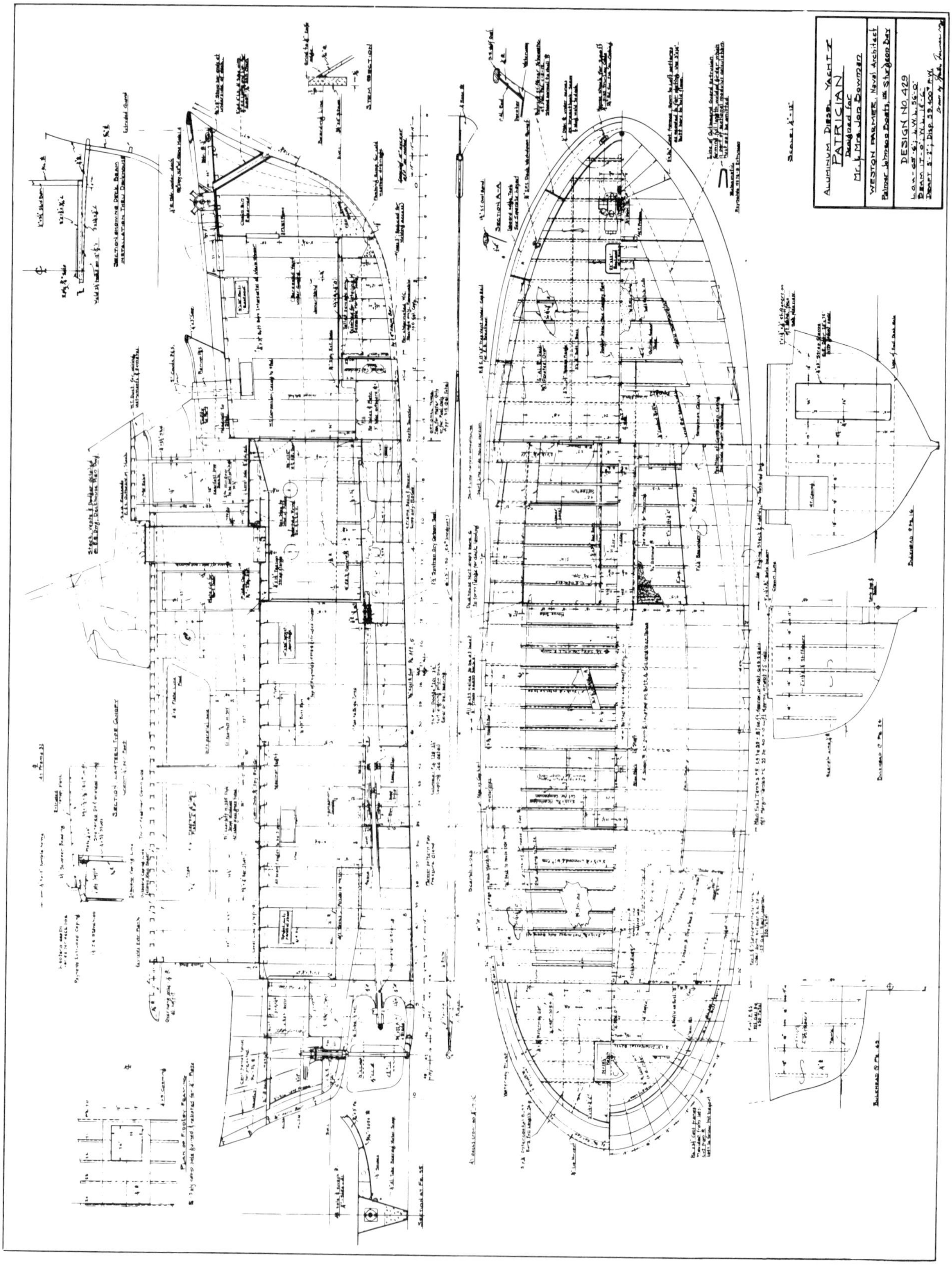
ALUMINUM DIESEL YACHT
PATRICIAN
Designed for
WESTON FARMER, Naval Architect
DESIGN NO. 429

Red Herring

Your eye has been caught by the seductive lines of this boat or you would not now be reading that her name was originally *Whistler*, or now be learning that she has been renamed *Red Herring* for screening her abdication from my list of active plans. I have put her into protective custody.

She abdicates the ornithological title in deference to a better *Whistler* discussed in this book, a boat designed by William Harnden Foster. *Red Herring* is a better *nom de guerre*, or name of war, under which to cloak why she was a near-miss and did not work. She was underpowered and was wet.

But the drawings are of classical quality; students of boat drafting see here a full set of drawings in the time-honored old method of full presentation. Wherefore, I let my hair down:

There was nothing the matter with *Red Herring* as a boat. The problem lay in the powering. I think it refreshing to admit it, and tell you that every designer has had one or two near-misses that seem to occur when he takes everything for granted. In this case, it was the rated power of the tiny power plant that gave only 12 of its supposed 32 horses. I had misinterpreted the torque curve and the manufacturer's rating. Had I followed the usual design-office procedure of asking for a certified installation diagram and power curve, I would have caught the error. One should always follow through on this—manufacturers are always glad to comply. It is standard practice on all new designs.

The little engine had been cobbled into marine use from the cylinder block of a British mini-car, and had an *en bloc* 4-cylinder casting the size of a storage battery. With this engine, there was not enough poop to scoot her along. The passenger weight forward, therefore, prevented lifting of the bow. There was just enough forward motion in the boat to run up a lulu of a bow wave because the breast presented to the water had too steep an angle of attack: roundish surfaces moving over or through water tend to suck downward when speeded up or overpressed.

You can prove this by dangling the fat side of a tablespoon into a down-running stream of water from a tap. Does the spoon kick away from the running water? It would if general supposition were true. Try it and be educated. All of design work has these hidden reversals of supposed hypotheses. Traps like this are the red herring of engineering and conform in parallel to the political tradition of smelling up the scene with something fishy.

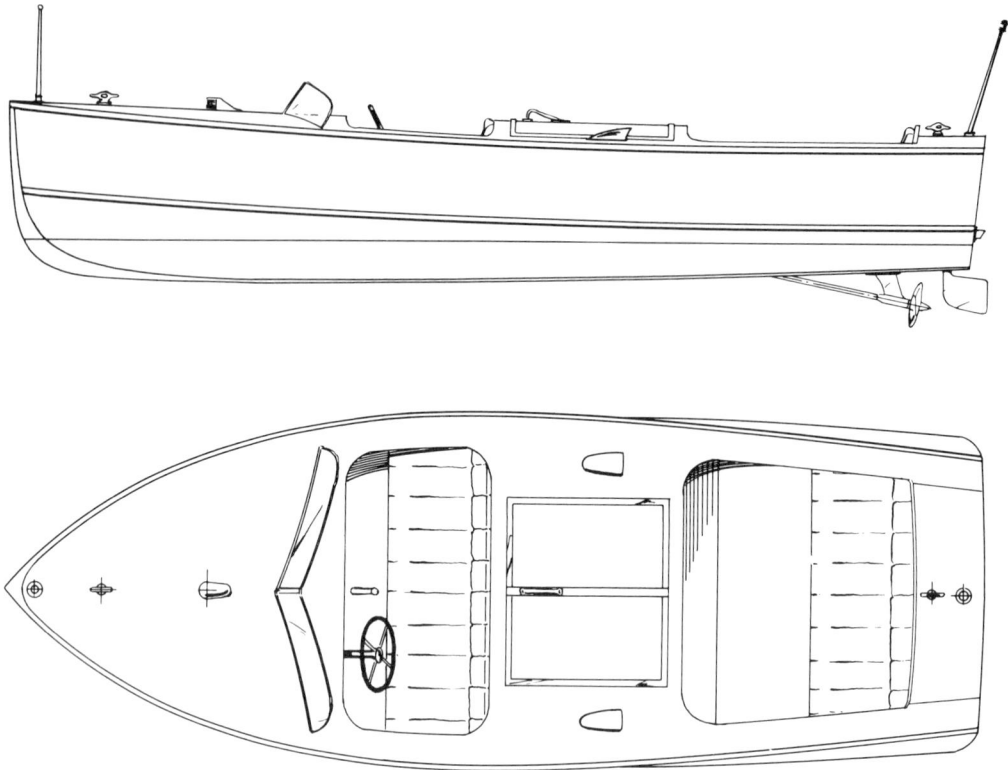

Until you know where some of these fish are hiding, you will be shocked to learn how hard they can hit you when they bite. Some of the red herring that have bitten boat designers and naval architects and marine engineers have been terrific stinkers.

I know of one 63-footer in aluminum that was launched with fanfare and ta-da that settled 14 inches heavy by the stern and listed so far to port that eight men had to be put on her starboard rail to bring her level. "I just didn't believe my own figures," said the beleaguered young ennay. Mmm Hmm.

Even the big boys get "herring-bit." Vladimir Yourkevitch, the young Russian engineer who resided in France as designer for the Compagnie Generale Transatlantique and designed the *Normandie*, turned out an eye-filling masterpiece as to hull elegance and general lovely French beauty, but missed a monumental marine engineering peg with her four turbine-driven, nineteen-foot-diameter, three-bladed propellers. Throughout the life of the otherwise lovely running ship, vibration at the stern was untenable. After this young Russian employee of the French Transat had badgered the management into building a 28-foot model for extensive hull-form tests, everything was serene until the turbines turned over. Then it was discovered that the four huge wheels produced such enormous vibration that dishes jumped over the

pin rails on the aft mess tables, and could not be held even by wetting the tablecloths.

At some time after the *Normandie*'s first crossing, and after much beefing-up of the shaft tubes and frames aft, a dynamics expert was called in to try to damp the destructive gyrational imbalance.

No problem! Four-bladed wheels were introduced, and on trials with these propellers it was noticed, after a trial crash reverse test, that the grand new ship became docile. A diver was sent under and came up with a startling report: the portside inboard propeller was missing—dropped off totally in the crash reverse maneuver. I will draw down the mantle of charity on such pervasive bad luck.

Every professional I have known has had one or two near-misses. My contribution toward bringing the herring industry to its knees is found in this tiny boat. Can I interest a wallpaper firm in turning out rolls of her drawings for use as graphics for a saloon decor, or for kitchens, rumpus rooms, or restaurants? No fee, and no regrets. But study of the drafting will show the acceptable way of presenting fully detailed inboard profiles, construction sections, lines and offsets. I was watched over by masters in my apprenticeship days, learning everything but humility and wariness about being cocky until the trial runs were over. It is a recommended course but hard to teach.

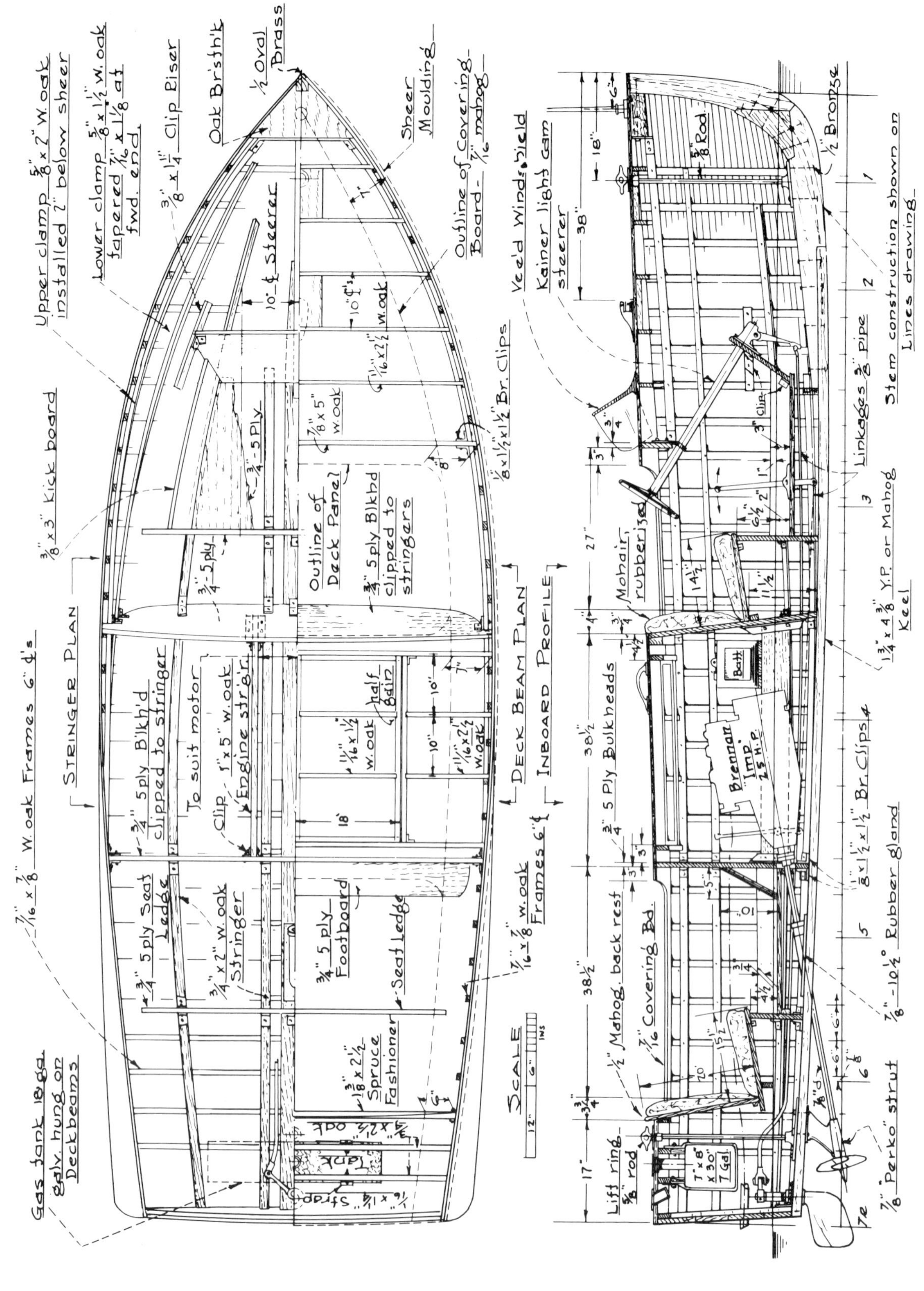
Upper clamp 5/8" x 2" W.oak installed 2" below sheer
Lower clamp 5/8" x 1 1/2" W.oak tapered 7/16" x 1 1/8" at fwd. end
3/8" x 1 1/4" Clip Riser
Oak Br'st'h'k
1/2 Oval Brass
Sheer Moulding
Outline of Covering Board - 7/16" mahog
Vee'd Winds'hield
Kainer light cam steerer
1/2 Bronze
5/8 Rod
Stem construction shown on Lines drawing
Linkages 3/8" pipe
1 3/4" x 4 3/8" Y.P. or Mahog Keel
Br. Clips
Rubber gland
"Perko" strut
Lift ring 5/8" rod
Gas tank 18 gal. galv. hung on Deckbeams
7/16" x 7/8" W.oak Frames 6" ¢'s
STRINGER PLAN
3/8" x 3" Kick board
3/4" 5 ply Seat Ledge
3/4" x 2" W.oak Stringer
3/4" 5 ply Footboard
Seat Ledge
Spruce Fashioner
3/4" 5 ply B'lkh'd clipped to stringer
To suit motor
1" x 5" W.oak Engine str'gr
Clip
Outline of Deck Panel
3/4" 5 ply Blkhd clipped to stringers
DECK BEAM PLAN
INBOARD PROFILE
3/4" 5 Ply Bulkheads
Mohair, rubberized
1/2" Mahog. back rest
7/16 Covering Bd.
SCALE
Batt
Brennan Imp. 25 H.P.
7" x 8" x 30" 7 Gal.
Tank

LINES DRAWING – "WHISTLER" – Measurements for Hull Shape

RUDDER

Rudder stock ⅞″ dia. Tobin Bronze
Blade cast Bronze

Pin

Engine, "Brennan "Imp" – 186 lbs.
25 h.p. Install with c.g. engine on line shown.

C.B. 1261 lbs.

Floor Line

Deck edge
Sheer, top of planking
Under edge of wale
⅞″ bronze prop shaft
Wale

Buttock 4
Buttock 3
Buttock 2
Buttock 1

Waterlines 3,5,7,6 not shown. Take from offset table for mold shape.

Mould

Sheet
L.W.L.
1B

½″ Mahogany transom planking
⅝″ x 2″ w.oak seam cleats
Transom cheeks ⅝″ x 2½″ w.oak
¾6″ x 4″ Bronze transom clip
⅞″ Rudder stock in 1¼″ Br. pipe secured by flange & lock nuts

Shaft hole 1″

Full depth 1⅜″
Apron depth ¾″
Rabbet depth ½″
Outboard face ½″

Stem Plan
Stem Profile
Back rabbet sided 2″
Face sided ⅝″
Rabbet Sided 1½″
Stem bolts ⅜″ Tobin bronze c's'k & plugged

Nib for frame end
Half Section of Keel
Point of Reference for Rabbet

Crown 1½″

Baseline

Table of OFFSETS in feet, inches and eighths to outside of ½″ planking

Sta.	Heights Above Baseline								Half Breadths from Center Line										
	Sheer	Keel	Rabbd	Butt.1	Butt.2	Butt.3	Butt.4	Sheer	Sheer	WL.7	WL.6	WL.5	WL.4	WL.3	WL.2	WL.1	LWL	WL.1B	Rabbet
Stem	3-2-0	0-4-5							0-1-1½	0-1-1½	0-1-1½	0-1-1½	0-1-1½	0-1-1½	0-1-1½	0-1-1½	0-1-1½	0-1-1½	0-0-6
1	3-0-5	0-3-6	0-6-6	1-1-6	2-7-0			1-9-3	1-3-2	1-1-0	0-9-3	0-8-2	0-6-0	0-3-1	0-0-6				
2	2-11-0	0-3-2	0-5-0	0-8-2	1-1-3	10-5		2-0-6	2-0-7	2-0-4	1-10-0	1-9-5	1-7-6	1-4-6	1-1-2	0-8-4	0-1-1½		
3	2-7-3	0-3-7	0-4-3	0-5-6	0-7-7	0-10-7	1-5-3	2-9-2	2-9-1	2-8-5	2-6-3	2-3-6	2-0-0	1-6-0					
4	2-6-7	0-4-0	0-4-4	0-5-2	0-7-0	0-8-5	0-10-2	2-10-3	2-10-4	2-10-6	2-10-6	1-9-7	1-9-7	2-5-6	1-11-0			
5	2-6-3	0-5-1	0-5-5	0-6-2	0-6-5	0-7-2	0-10-3	2-8-0	2-8-0	2-8-7	2-9-5	1-10-0	2-9-2	2-7-4	2-3-0			
6	2-6-3	0-6-0	0-6-4	0-6-7	0-6-5	0-7-5	0-11-1	2-5-2	2-5-3	2-6-5	2-7-7	1-8-5	2-8-6	2-8-2	2-6-5	2-2-1		
Tr.	2-6-6	0-6-2	0-7-6	0-6-7	0-7-2	0-8-2	1-0-5	2-2-3	2-2-3	2-4-2	2-5-6	1-6-5	2-6-7	2-6-5	2-5-2	2-0-4	0-1-1½	

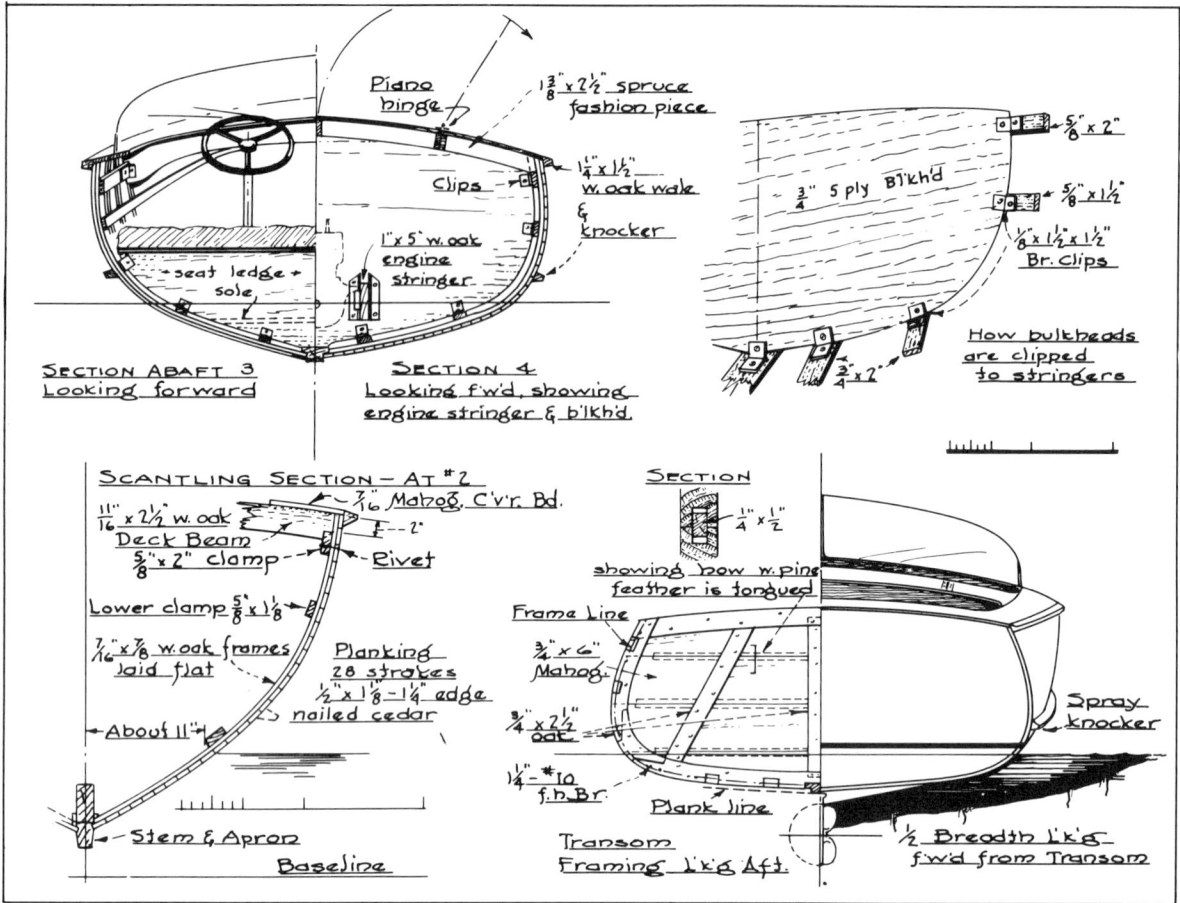

Piano hinge

$1\frac{3}{8}" \times 2\frac{1}{2}"$ spruce fashion piece

Clips

$1\frac{1}{4}" \times 1\frac{1}{2}"$ w. oak wale & knocker

$1" \times 5"$ w. oak engine stringer

seat ledge + sole

SECTION ABAFT 3
Looking forward

SECTION 4
Looking f'w'd, showing engine stringer & b'lkh'd.

$\frac{3}{4}"$ 5 ply B'lkh'd

$\frac{5}{8}" \times 2"$

$\frac{5}{8}" \times 1\frac{1}{2}"$

$\frac{1}{8}" \times 1\frac{1}{2}" \times 1\frac{1}{2}"$ Br. Clips

$\frac{3}{4}" \times 2"$

How bulkheads are clipped to stringers

SCANTLING SECTION – AT #2

$\frac{3}{16}$ Mahog, C'v'r. Bd.

$\frac{11}{16}" \times 2\frac{1}{2}"$ w. oak **Deck Beam**

$\frac{5}{8}" \times 2"$ clamp

$2"$

Rivet

Lower clamp $\frac{5}{8}" \times 1\frac{1}{8}"$

$\frac{7}{16}" \times \frac{7}{8}"$ w. oak frames laid flat

Planking
28 strokes
$\frac{1}{2}" \times 1\frac{1}{8} - 1\frac{1}{4}"$ edge
nailed cedar

About 11"

Stem & Apron

Baseline

SECTION

$\frac{1}{4}" \times \frac{1}{2}"$

showing how w. pine feather is tongued

Frame Line

$\frac{3}{4}" \times 6"$ Mahog.

$\frac{3}{4}" \times 2\frac{1}{2}"$ oak

$\frac{1}{4}" - \#10$ f.h. Br.

Plank line

Transom Framing L'k'g Aft.

Spray knocker

$\frac{1}{2}$ Breadth L'k'g f'w'd from Transom

342

Urges and Yearnings of Messing with Boats

Because the volume you now hold in your hands became a book before I knew it had been written or had become one, in closing I deem it fitting to volunteer some steering advice to those whose course of life may be urging them toward earning a living in the callings connected with boats. The fantasies of youth, the yearnings for ownership and adventure, the hard realities of dollars-and-cents rewards, the foibles of human comedy endemic to the sea-related callings—these have all been experienced in my own three-score and 15 years' romances. Below is how the course seems to me.

The formative years generally involve dreams of derring-do, or becoming a nationally acknowledged boat or yacht designer—even a designer of big ships. As some skill is picked up at the bench in building a boat, this insight into processes will encourage study of the mathematics or the physics of puzzling problems: how to determine in advance what your dream ship will be? This leads a fellow into design; i.e., the engineering aspects—not industrial "design," which is mere cosmetic or interior decorator stuff. (*Styling* is not designing, in the true engineering sense.)

The urge to identify oneself with designers—called, correctly, naval architects if they are true engineers—is an early urge for young men with mechanical skills and love of boats. Young men always have the urge to become somebody, and the drawing of plan-pretty profiles, then getting them published, is a laudable and natural urge. If you have a gift for what old-time draftsmen term "the elegant eye," you will be recognized. Your initial yearnings will put you on the road.

But before you get into the whys and wherefores and techniques of design, either by reading or by studying a good home-correspondence course, or becoming a fully qualified professional naval architect and/or a qualified marine engineer, you ought to—nay, MUST—have shop experience. In no other way can you understand materials, their limitations, and what to do with them. The hand feeds the brain. Knowing *how* a boat or ship is put together is the only safe foundation for full professionalism. The correspondence course will equip you as a boat and yacht designer, but it is a misdemeanor in most states to call yourself a naval architect or marine engineer unless you are a professional engineer, graduated from an engineering college. This is the real road into the business. It is a long road, and on the way you might ponder the economics of what you are getting into.

You may love the water, may love boats, love to sail them, but if you follow that route you should know that if you decide to earn your living this way, you will be earning your living with your fun. Few men who pursue a life of fun ever die rich. Here let me insert words of wisdom I have frequently quoted from John G. Hanna, designer of *Tahiti, Gulfweed, Foam,* and other famous boats, who was the most popular engineer-philosopher of 50 years ago. In his column, "Heaving the Lead," Hanna remarked: "There are a million kinds of work in the world, each and all returning some money, but only one kind for any certain man that pays the richer gold of fulfilled desire, of captivated interest, of contentment that obliterates weariness. Why shouldn't he choose that one kind?"

The study of why boats "get that way," or what philosophies of choice are behind the presentation of any design, is a hobby for you who are loners, because your inquisitive fun cannot be shared as you work up your drawings. You pursue competence in the art entirely on your own. There is personal satisfaction in this hobby, and it is a lot cheaper and safer than whiskey, wild women, and stud poker.

Most of the gifted men who emerge from the straw pile of humanity into the limelight of design prominence are, I have discovered, heavily introverted men. Some are antisocial, scoffing at the work of anyone else on the scene who may be scoring. I can go along with a few kindly jeers at the phonies in the game, but it does no man any service to himself by trying to diminish the stature of another. Those who succeed seem to have an extra dimension to their awareness. This awareness is a sense of the economics of life: what to charge for your work, whom to deal with, how to sell.

It would seem to me that awareness of other values than mere design techniques should be just as essential to a naval architect's knowledge as is his depth in the mechanics of design. Unfortunately, economic awareness is a black hole in most loners' kits. Look about you. . . .

Have you ever walked down a prosperous residential street without wondering, "How in the dickens do people earn the money to build and run such lovely homes?" Behind every one of these homes, of whatever size, is a story of the head of some family who has been a producer, a worker, a thrifty man. In simplest boildown, he has behind him a record: he has been selling something. He may have sold his services, or he may have been a manufacturer who bottled red water and called it a product, or he may have produced toys, or sold fish, books, or groceries. The theory of economics has slots that label all these efforts, such as that for the grocery man who relates a "time and place convenience" to the supply of food.

Everybody of productive age, self-supportive in a capitalistic society, provides a service for his fellow man. The naval architect provides a specialized service for men who want to build new boats. He has spent years accumulating the skills of building and design that will enable him to get his customer's ideas first into drawings, then into building and launching. The naval architect must be paid for this service. How much? Usually a percentage fee is applied—say, 12 percent for designing, or 15 percent of the boat's cost for supervision, too. In very posh boats, the cost of a percentage is out of line with the work, and then the designer may quote a fixed fee for the drafting, and write a separate contract for supervision. It's a deal-and-dicker relationship.

One thing not generally known to young designers is that the customer does not own the design, even if he commissions it. The courts have repeatedly held that the plans are a record of an engineer's thinking, and that the title to that work resides with the designer. This should be understood very early in the designer-customer relationship. An informative small book could be written about the rewards, relationships, pitfalls, and human comedy of this trade. The subject is too long for anything but a broad-brush swipe here at the canvas of life in this calling.

In the old tradition, competence in design usually led a man into the business of boatbuilding. The ownership of a prestigious yard was a dream sometimes brought to fruition by competent designers. N.G. Herreshoff's competence as an engineer enabled him to establish the Herreshoff Manufacturing Company in Bristol, Rhode Island, over a hundred years ago. John G. Alden found the rewards of design so slim that he built his own schooners in liaison with good Down East yards. Then he had a product he could sell, and on which he could turn a better profit than he could get designing. Fifty-two years ago John Alden told me, "Young man, there isn't the price of a turkey sandwich in the design game. It's a feast-or-famine business. Put your work into a product. Men buy boats, not paper plans."

It was such economic thinking that caused Alfred E. Luders to leave

Elco and establish the Luders yard in Stamford, Connecticut. F.W. Ofeldt invented the naphtha launch, and was set up in business by a wealthy patron, Jabez A. Bostwick, in the Gas Engine and Power Co. There, three thousand naphtha launches were built in the plant on the Harlem River in New York City. Charles L. Seabury, draftsman for the Herreshoff yard, later set up in business at Nyack, New York, to turn out steam yachts. Still later, Gas Engine and Seabury joined forces as the Gas Engine and Power Co. and Charles L. Seabury Co., Consolidated. This became Consolidated, a yachtbuilding name to conjure with.

These vignettes are mentioned merely to illustrate that the product of a designer used to be a better way to collect on his work than from the sale of design skill. And though it may have been true in the last quarter of the 19th Century and in the first quarter of this 20th Century, it may be doubtful if the same tenet holds good in the present society made mobile by the automobile and the airplane.

Today, a young man who demonstrates great skill will find people coming to him, and I believe it is now possible to earn a living at pure, outright design. But the road is rocky, and still feast or famine; a man becomes a product of his times. I still think he must work alone; if he hires help, he then must make good for them, and he will also have a new kind of partner never suffered by the older companies: he will have bureaucratic government in his hair, in his soup, and into his pocket at every turn. He is better off working alone, picking and choosing.

The other side of the coin, building, is now one of the chanciest businesses in the world. Before his death, Charles Chapman, then editor of *Motor Boating*, told me he was willing to bet that more outside invested capital had been lost in the boatbuilding business than had been made in profits. He cited the usual cycle: great expectations, then funded advertising, then glutted inventories. Today, with the advent of plastics providing manufacturing opportunities for untrained labor and resulting cost economies, the boat business has ridden a wave of escapism that has brought the public into boating in droves.

The two big hazards in this segment of boating, as I see it shaping up, are these: (1) All plastics are re-worked petrochemicals. Started on oil foundations of $4 a barrel at the refinery, plastic boat companies are now at the mercy of $20-a-barrel oil. The cost of plastics will eventually kill off outfits that are marginally capitalized, because their product will have to sell at a price that can be beaten all hollow by Ma-and-Pa yards working in more traditional materials, such as metal and wood. (2) Men in the boat business know little of the economics of capital turnover and cash flow: they produce so many models that they become like a shoe store. Many models, much capital tied up in stock, slows capital turnover and leads eventually to bankruptcy. Thus Chapman's cycle can become operative again. A product of the times.

With the boating explosion of the past 15 years has come another phenomenon of the times: the proliferation of periodical magazines jumping into the boating scene. Last year I subscribed to each one as it was presented—in all, I believe, 16 periodicals, all with the name "boat" or words related to boating in their titles. Here again is something that affects the young man looking at marine-related matters for his future.

The old-line magazines of yesterday are not today the informative sources of deep knowledge about design matters that they once were. Formerly, boating magazines received a circulation profit from the per-copy sale of their monthlies. Advertising was welcomed to help out on production costs, but the editor was the star of the show: if his magazine sold well and prospered, he could print matters as they were. You could read his magazine and believe what you read.

Today, a great proportion of the numerous periodicals are *supported* by advertising, and the competition for ad space has made sheep out of publishers and editors alike. In staffing their editing departments, many publishers have hired mere *enthusiasts*, who then determine the editorial content. Once ensconced in an editor's chair, these young people soon exhaust their enthusiasms, and the entire output seems to be conned from the ads of boat brokers who formerly were used-car salesmen. The respected terminology of marine usage has become a tin-eared cacophony; respected old marine terms like flying bridge show up in print as "fly bridge," and the deckhouse type of yacht stemming from the Pacific Northwest troller becomes a "trawler." All of which puts a warning finger on omnivorous reading: think it out, young man! Don't buy it if it isn't true! Go back to books—the classics—written by old-timers. Their prose may be pedantic and hard to wade through, but style is not their forte; solid information is their contribution.

This self-discipline will be difficult; we are taught from childhood to believe the printed word. Recently I saw the report of a school teacher who had fielded a theme from an eighth-grader that said, "The Mississippi River, if it was straightened out, would go a lot farther out into the ocean. I can show you where it says."

Much of my knowledge about boats has been picked up from magazines. They are a wonderful carrier of nourishment to any hobbyist. But I have seen too many shaggy, unkempt, puffed-up egos hammering away at typewriters in some editorial sanctums to believe that what they say, when printed, amounts to anything more in depth than exists in the minds that put the work into print. "Where it says" is now too often mere half-hatched opinion. Textbooks, edited by men who have been over the road of experience, are the way to travel on today's reading route. In hard-covered media, you have the best chance of picking up authoritative reading.

One more aspect of the choices for a young man is the service business—hauling, repairing, storing boats. This business might be classified as a boat janitor's job and always has great seasonal fluctuations, but at today's $12-an-hour rate for claw-hammer carpenters, a good wage is always there for a man who will work. It is the best place for a young man to start on the long road to picking up the art leading to his heart's desire.

This one thing I do know: the law of averages will always feed a man who is willing to work. Depth in the marine arts, as in any other calling, eventually demands the respect and rewards that will provide an adequate, and sometimes abundant, living. This makes the American Dream work.

In reviewing the past years, I wonder, sometimes, what the motivating force has been. I have never known a day from earliest childhood when I didn't want to become a designer of fine yachts and ships. What was the prod? The interest? Why develop creativity in this direction? The answer with me lies in one word: *water.*

If there be magic in this world it will be found in water—all of it, not just the mystery of how a hull acts in a seaway. A sketching artist sees the ocean as scenery, but he looks only at the surface. An engineer sees it differently.

To him, the ocean is a liquid hide covering three-fourths of the earth's surface. It is composed of two gases, hydrogen and oxygen, in tight chemical embrace but with room enough between the molecules to dissolve a pound and a half of sodium chloride per cubic foot. This soup is the cradle of all developed life on this planet, yet it can be lifted by sunlight, purified in its ascent into absorbing air, rolled into clouds, and transported by wind. Every drop of fresh water on earth has at one time been part of a cloud. Every lake, every river is a gift from the sky. That such enormous weight can be lifted into thin air and become such a devastating force, or useful force, has been an entrancing mystery to me. That it *weighs* enough to float big ships, or little chips, is a mystery. Why it should be a universal solvent, part of everything that lives or breathes, the transporter of life, an immense storage house for heat, has gripped my curiosity all my life.

Alongside two minor mysteries, such as the way of a man with a maid, or the way of a hull in a seaway—both predictable in outcome—the magic in water has been the unseen moving force piquing creative curiosity throughout my lifetime.

Is it not water's magic ambience that powers our urges and yearnings when we dream of boats? I believe it is.

Index

Brown, James. "Weston Farmer's Cherub,"
  Small Boat Journal No. 37 p.11 (June/July 1984).
  23'3" Steel Sloop; design comments, plans

Farmer, E. Weston. "A little Inland Laker,"
  Fore 'N Aft (July 1927). p.12

Farmer, Weston. "A Hanna Masterpiece,"
  Small Boat Journal No.1 p.56 (August 1979).

Farmer, Weston. "ANDALUSIA,"
  Sports Afield Boatbuilding Annual (1955). p.60
  34' power cruiser; plans

Farmer, Weston. "BABY KILLDEER,"
  Sports Afield Boatbuilding Annual (1957). p.30
  12' outboard skiff; plans

Farmer, Weston. "BADGER,"
  Sports Afield Boatbuilding Annual (1956). p.62
  15'1" modified dory skiff design; plans

Farmer, Weston. "BINKY - An All-Around Tender,"
  Sports Afield Boatbuilding Annual (1954). p.82
  12'6" skiff; plans

Farmer, Weston. "Boatbuilding Principles,"
  Sports Afield Boatbuilding Annual (1954). p.4

Farmer, Weston. "CHIPPEWA - Plywood Canoe,"
  Sports Afield Boatbuilding Annual (1955). p.48
  15' plywood canoe design; plans

Farmer, Weston. "Charles G. Davis Artist, Author, Pioneer,"
  Nautical Quarterly No.2 p.54 (January 1978).

Farmer, Weston. "Dock Yacht,"
  Sports Afield Boatbuilding Annual (1957). p.60
  20' x 8'6" steel cruising houseboat; plans

Farmer, Weston. *From My Old Boatshop.*
  Camden, ME: International Marine Publishing, 1979.
  not completely indexed; Autobiography; design theory, plans

Farmer, Weston. "Halcyon Days,"
  Nautical Quarterly No. 30 p. 120 (1985).

Farmer, Weston. "How Prams Are Built: Plans for JENNIE,
  an 8-ft. Pram,"
  Sports Afield Boatbuilding Annual (1954). p.66.
  8' plywood pram; plans

Farmer, Weston. "How to Understand a Boat Plan,"
  Sports Afield Boatbuilding Annual (1954). p.59

Farmer, Weston. "KINGFISHER,"
  Sports Afield Boatbuilding Annual (1955). p.22
  17' inboard/outboard runabout design; plans

Farmer, Weston. "LITTLE ROUGE."
  Sports Afield Boatbuilding Annual (1955). p.42
  19' tabloid sloop design; plans

Farmer, Weston. "Model Your Own Dreamboat."
  Sports Afield Boatbuilding Annual (1954). p.91
  how to build a cardboard & balsa model

Farmer, Weston. "PIUTE,"
  Sports Afield Boatbuilding Annual (1954). p.10
  24'10" runabout design; plans

Farmer, Weston. "POOR RICHARD,"
  Woodenboat No. 20 p.76 (Jan./Feb. 1978).

Farmer, Weston. "POOR RICHARD,"
  Sports Afield Boatbuilding Annual (1953). p.65
  20' 7" power launch design; plans

Farmer, Weston. "Power Tools for the Home Boat Shop,"
  Sports Afield Boatbuilding Annual (1955). p.9

Farmer, Weston. "QUICKSILVER,"
  Sports Afield Boatbuilding Annual (1955). p.14
  11'6" outboard hydroplane design; plans

Farmer, Weston. "ROB ROY - A Combination Canoe-Kayak,"
  Sports Afield Boatbuilding Annual (1954). p.16
  15' canoe/kayak design; plans

Farmer, Weston. "ROBINSON CRUSOE,"
  Sports Afield Boatbuilding Annual (1956). p.78
  26' inboard cruiser design; plans

Farmer, Weston. "SCAMPER - How to Build a Strip Boat,"
  Sports Afield Boatbuilding Annual (1954). p.33
  14' outboard boat design; plans

Farmer, Weston. "SEA BISCUIT"
  Sports Afield Boatbuilding Annual (1955). p.68
  8' outboard speed box; plans

Farmer, Weston. "SHOREBIRD,"
  Sports Afield Boatbuilding Annual (1956). p.49
  14'4" flat-bottom skiff design; plans

Farmer, Weston. "SIMPLEX - A Military Type
  Outboard Cruiser,"
  Sports Afield Boatbuilding Annual (1954). p.86
  18' outboard cruiser; plans

Farmer, Weston. "SUN DANCE - an Outboard Cruiser,"
  Sports Afield Boatbuilding Annual (1953). p.58
  17' 3" outboard cruiser; plans

Farmer, Weston. "SUN DOG,"
  Sports Afield Boatbuilding Annual (1954). p.22
  30'6" power cruiser design; comments, plans

Farmer, Weston. "SURE MIKE II,"
  Sports Afield Boatbuilding Annual (1956). p.25
  21' outboard cruiser design, plans

Farmer, Weston. "Strip Planking,"
  Fore 'N Aft (1927). p.12

Farmer, Weston. "THE WANIGAN,"
  Sports Afield Boatbuilding Annual (1958). p.47
  15' outboard garvey design; plans

Farmer, Weston. "TINTILLE,"
  Sports Afield Boatbuilding Annual (1956). p.89
  18' steel inboard runabout design, plans

Farmer, Weston. "TRUMPET,"
  Sports Afield Boatbuilding Annual (1958). p.70
  18' outboard boat with cuddy cabin; plans

Farmer, Weston. "Tips on Transporting Your Boat,"
  Sports Afield Boatbuilding Annual (1955). p.82

Farmer, Weston. "Understanding a Boat Plan,"
  WoodenBoat No.21 p.30 (Mar/April 1978).

Farmer, Weston. "WHISTLER,"
  Sports Afield Boatbuilding Annual (1956). p.13
  15'9" inboard runabout design; plans

Farmer, Weston. "Woods for Boatbuilding,"
  Sports Afield Boatbuilding Annual (1956). p.4

Farmer, Weston. "YO HO!-Plywood Cartopper,"
  Sports Afield Boatbuilding Annual (1954). p.51
  12' skiff/outboard boat; plans

Fawcett Library,. *How to Build 20 Boats. NO. 1.*
  Minneapolis, MI Fawcett Publications, Inc.,1933 p.38
  Mayfay power cruiser; Scram runabout, Katusha cabin
  launch, Sez You runabout, All Sorts sailing skiff; Whizzer
  hydroplane; Sea Skeeter pram; Wink runabout;
  Bouncer catboat

Fawcett Library,. *How To Build 20 Boats. No. 11.*
  Greenwich, CT: Fawcett Publications, Inc., 1943.
  p.135 Portable duck boat

Getchell, David R.. "Remembering Westy,"
  Nautical Quarterly No. 30 p.107 (1985).